THE
DEAN & DELUCA
COOKBOOK

David Rosengarten
with
Joel Dean and Giorgio DeLuca

Lori Longbotham, Contributing Editor

Ebury Press
London

Also by David Rosengarten

Red Wine with Fish: The New Art of Matching Wine with Food
Hugh Johnson's Wine Cellar
A Dictionary of American Wines

1 3 5 7 9 10 8 6 4 2

First published in the United States of America in 1996 by
Random House, Inc., New York and simultaneously in Canada by
Random House of Canada Limited, Toronto.

First published in the United Kingdom in 1997 by Ebury Press

This paperback edition first published in the United Kingdom in 2000 by
Ebury Press, an imprint of Random House,
20 Vauxhall Bridge Road, London SW1V 2SA.

Random House Australia (Pty) Limited
20 Alfred Street, Milsons Point, Sydney, New South Wales 2061, Australia

Random House New Zealand Limited
18 Poland Road, Glenfield, Auckland 10, New Zealand

Random House South Africa (Pty) Limited
Endulini, 5A Jubilee Road, Parktown 2193, South Africa

The Random House Group Limited Reg. No. 954009

A CIP catalogue record for this book is available from the British Library

ISBN 0 09 186956 0

Papers used by Ebury Press are natural, recyclable products
made from wood grown in sustainable forests.

Printed and bound in Great Britain by
Butler & Tanner Ltd, Frome, Somerset

CONTENTS

Four: Pizza and Pasta   101

Five: Vegetables   157

Six: Rice, Beans and Grains   219

Seven: Fish and Shellfish   273

Eight: Meats 363

Nine: Condiments and Sauces 477

THE AMERICAN GASTRONOMIC REVOLUTION… AND A SHOP IN NEW YORK'S SOHO

For the last 20 years, Americans have been on an incredible culinary odyssey. Once accustomed chiefly to meat-and-potatoes cookery, with only a few tentative forays into dubious versions of ethnic dining, Americans now have before them the most staggering array of ethnically authentic foods and restaurants anywhere in the world—as well as, arguably, the largest workforce of creative chefs.

Principally through visits to restaurants, as well as foreign travel, Americans have fallen in love with whole categories of cuisine that they'd never considered before. Once upon a time, clichés (of the veal parmigiana ilk) reigned at ethnic restaurants in America; today, many of us have become enamoured of 'new' ethnic classics (like risotto) from cuisines we once thought we knew. We've also discovered many cuisines we really didn't know at all before, and—from the pad thai of Thailand to the couscous of Morocco—have embraced a host of ethnic classics.

Furthermore, American chefs have rediscovered and revitalised old favourites, once-loved classics (like Caesar salad and meatloaf), from foods we grew up with and dishes we'd forgotten about for several decades. We've gone on to discover classic dishes (like gumbo and posole) of our own American regions, dishes that were once rarely seen on a national scale. And, as if all this weren't enough, at thousands of restaurants across the country we have witnessed the birth of new classics (like aubergine and goat cheese terrine), as the most creative generation of American chefs ever writes a new national menu.

For 20 years, many of us have built a relationship with these dishes, happily consuming them at restaurants. But dishes are never truly assimilated into a nation's cuisine if only the restaurant chefs are making them—and many Americans, in recent years, have developed the desire to bring these delights home, to cook them, and cook them well, in their own kitchens.

Given the vast diversity of the movement, however, it's not an easy thing to do. How does one master 20 years of rapid culinary change? Where should Americans go for guidance?

Well, for a Thai hot-and-sour shrimp soup, they could start buying Thai cookery books, hoping that at least one of them will provide the right taste. For a frisée salad with lardoons and maybe a goat cheese croûte on top, they could scour the shelves for bistro cookery books, California cookery books or New American cookery books. Quesadillas will lead them to Mexican cookery books, biryani will lead them to Indian cookery books, tempura will lead them to Japanese cookery books—and most of the new 'classics' devised by creative American chefs will lead them nowhere, because many of these dishes have yet to be anthologised. And that's just scratching the surface.

For there are a lot of books, a lot of new authors to become familiar with, and a lot of missing information to complicate the search.

We've got a better idea.

This Dean & DeLuca cookery book puts it all together for you in one volume. Think about the logic of it. Has anyone had more contact with more corners of the American gastronomic revolution than we have? Is anyone in a better position to document the food that Americans have come to love over the last 20 years?

Since the start of the American food surge, Dean & DeLuca, a purveyor of high-quality foodstuffs, has been in the forefront of the movement, importing and selling the ingredients that chefs need for these new favourite dishes. Moreover, Dean & DeLuca has often been the first to import ingredients into the United States which have become key elements in our gastronomic turnaround. In many ways, Dean & DeLuca has exerted a powerful influence on the burgeoning American food scene all through these years.

Things started humbly enough, in 1977, when Joel Dean, a former publishing executive, and Giorgio DeLuca, an ex-history teacher and son of a food importer, opened a shop in New York's SoHo district. It was not a glamorous neighbourhood at the time. Printing businesses and small factories provided most of SoHo's economic life, and the area had a worn-out, run-down feel to it. But Dean and DeLuca had a feeling that a renaissance was at hand—that SoHo was about to become a major magnet for artists, designers and other innovators—and our decision to place a 2,600-sq. ft/935 sq. m. food shop in the midst of it all helped set the tone for the emerging conflation in this country of food and art.

Soon enough, many of the marketing and merchandising ideas that Dean and DeLuca hatched, including designer Jack Ceglic's sleek, minimalist look, had major impact on the way Americans think about food.

For one thing, we rejected the sterile, pre-wrapped environment that had characterised the sale of food in the United States and had come to symbolise our national indifference to freshness. We substituted the traditions of the European marketplace. We were the first to use steel-and-wire display cases, open on all sides, so that customers could come into closer contact with the food they were viewing. The same goal was achieved by a shocking move for its time: some cheeses and meats were placed on top of display cabinets, out of refrigeration, so that the look and smell of a vibrant European marketplace could be created here. These subtle changes helped give professionals the notion that food in America could be like food in Europe, and opened the eyes of amateurs to the European food sensibility.

Moreover, Dean & DeLuca literally brought Europe to the United States. Through his extensive travel through Europe in the early years of the shop, Giorgio DeLuca was able to discover and import a raft of ingredients of which Americans knew nothing. Where would our gastronomic revolution be today without balsamic vinegar? Sun-dried tomatoes? Pesto in jars? Dean & DeLuca was the first to bring high-quality versions of these products into the United States, and to bring them in on a large scale.

The list of other ingredients that Dean & DeLuca has championed is long. It's also surprising to many people. Because after all the attention we paid to classic Mediterranean ingredients—like olive oil, our great assortment of fine olive pastes, and great, hand-made pasta—Dean & DeLuca turned to other areas of Europe, and then to other areas of the world, for inspiration. Dean & DeLuca has been in the forefront of the great American movement towards beans and grains; scores of bean and grain varieties, many of them imported by Dean & DeLuca, appeared on the shop's shelves long before they became widely popular. Spices have been another specialty; the mind-boggling array of home-packed little tins in our spice section represents our acquisition of the finest, freshest spices from all around the globe. Even Asian bottled products, from Thai fish sauce to Japanese sesame oil, are subjected to the same rigorous standards of quality and are presented with our characteristically dizzying variety.

One of the most exciting sources of all for food had nothing to do with 'the rest of the world'. As the American gastronomic movement grew, along with the shop, so did the quality of ingredients that were available from American producers. Dean & DeLuca is one of the finest sources in the United States for the chillies of the American south-west, for example, as well as American and Caribbean hot sauces, to say nothing of American barbecue sauces. Our fresh food departments hold the best of American fish and meats, with many speciality items that are difficult to find elsewhere. One of the most important features of our American food acquisition has been our work with American producers, encouraging them to reach ever higher in their quality standards. We work with an array of American cheese-makers, ham manufacturers, cooked meat producers, bread bakers, and pastry chefs to get the very best that America has to offer into our shop.

One of our first efforts to encourage American production of high-quality foodstuffs was one of our most important, in the larger picture. In 1980, in our efforts to upgrade the variety and quality of salad greens available to the American public, we began flying in lamb's lettuce (mâche) from France and radicchio (red chicory) from Italy. But we realised early on that a much more efficient system would be to grow European-style lettuces in the United States. We sent our produce manager to Europe in the early eighties to smuggle back seeds we could use in planting these lettuces. Early efforts failed—the radicchio we tried to grow in Pennsylvania in the early eighties kept coming up green—but we persisted, and now have a web of producers around the country who supply us, and others, with fabulous greens. West Coast restaurateurs like Alice Waters were busy at the same time encouraging the growth of greens in California; together, we've helped to put leafy possibilities on the American table that were once unimaginable.

It was pure luck that our early efforts attracted the attention they did, thereby enabling us to spread our philosophy of food so widely; we've always wanted to play an educational role in the American food world, and several factors allowed us to do so.

Most important was our fortuitous hiring of Felipe Rojas-Lombardi, in 1977, as our first executive chef. He worked with us until 1981—before he opened The Ballroom in New York City, America's first widely recognised tapas bar—and he supplied our take-away counter with extraordinarily good food. This, of course, helped to put us on the map. But Felipe's connections advanced the cause immeasurably. For one thing, Felipe was the executive chef of *New York* magazine when he came to work for us, and his downtown exploits were regularly covered by his old employers. Moreover, Felipe was great friends with James Beard—and Beard, of course, was the don of the food mafia. Through that Beard connection, writers for *The New York Times,* such as Mimi Sheraton and Craig Claiborne, became intimately familiar with our operation and wrote about it frequently. Mimi would call to ask 'Do you have quail eggs?' We'd say 'yes', she'd mention it in the *Times,* and we'd go from selling a dozen a week to thousands. Moreover, lots of people would become educated about quail eggs. This pattern was repeated with countless products, and we were mentioned in the paper every week for years. At one point, Mimi said to us, 'I really can't put you in the *Times* anymore—they'll think I'm on your payroll'. Lots of shops get support from their local paper, but when your local paper is *The New York Times,* you have the fantastic opportunity to reach millions with what you're doing and disseminate your philosophy widely.

Twenty years later, our philosophy and goals remain the same. Our new main shop—opened in SoHo in 1988, and four times larger than our old SoHo shop—still eschews fancy design elements so that all attention can be focused on the ingredients themselves, an echo of the way modern chefs go about their cooking. We still emphasise primary ingredients, rather than bottled convenience foods, so that customers get the message that the thrill of cuisine is making it yourself, no matter how simple it is. We continue to believe in the importance of a food purveyor doing its own selection and importation of goods, and encouraging food producers. And our love of cooking with the ingredients we offer has led us to maintain our enormous selections of cookery books and cooking equipment.

Over time, we've added such features as catering, personal shopping, gifts and mail order, as well as delivery and national shipping departments. In 1990, we began opening Dean & DeLuca Espresso Bar and Cafés across the country, and plan to open many more. Additionally, our two main shops in New York and Washington, D.C., will soon be joined by other full-scale shops in many American cities. Our latest moves are being planned in coordination with our new partner, Leslie Rudd Investments, a dynamic private investment company based in Aspen, Colorado. The firm's vast experience in consumer products, beverage production and distribution, multi-unit retailing, publishing and broadcasting meshes perfectly with the assets and talents that we've developed over the years.

So, as you can see, we've been there. We helped bring this revolution about. We've supplied, worked with, and in some cases helped to inspire, the top chefs in the movement. Is there a more logical candidate to take *your* hand, lead you through the marketplace, help you find the best ingredients, then escort you into the kitchen to give you the very best information on putting it all together and creating great meals for your family and friends?

You have developed fantastic new tastes over the last 20 years. Simply stated, we want you to learn to cook what you've learned to eat. With this cookery book, the adventure continues.

S A L A D S

TALK ABOUT AN EXPANDED DEFINITION— THIS ONE HAS PRACTICALLY EXPLODED!

TWENTY YEARS AGO, TO MOST AMERICANS 'SALAD' MEANT WEDGES OF ICEBERG LETTUCE WITH SOMETHING GLOPPY FROM A BOTTLE POURED ON THEM. AND THE SALAD'S MOMENT IN THE SUN WAS ALMOST ALWAYS THE SAME—AS A SATELLITE DISH TO THE MAIN COURSE.

TODAY, SAVVY AMERICAN DINERS HAVE MOVED AWAY FROM THE OLD STANDARD SALAD IN TWO DIRECTIONS: FIRST, TOWARDS LIGHTER, SIMPLER GREEN SALADS (BASED ON THE CLASSIC FRENCH GREEN SALAD, OR *SALADE VERTE*); AND SECOND, TOWARDS EVER MORE COMPLICATED *SALADES COMPOSÉES*, OR COMPOSITE SALADS, OR SALADS WITH LOTS OF STUFF IN THEM (MANY INSPIRED BY A RANGE OF INTERNATIONAL IDEAS AND ALSO BY SALADMAKERS IN THE SALAD STATE, CALIFORNIA). FURTHERMORE, WE NOW CONSUME ALL TYPES OF SALADS EITHER AFTER THE MAIN COURSE, OR *AS* THE MAIN COURSE, OR, MOST COMMONLY, AS A *FIRST* COURSE. THE OLD SALAD-*WITH*-THE-MAIN-COURSE PRACTICE IN AMERICA HAS DECLINED—AND WE'RE HAPPY ABOUT THAT, BECAUSE A GREAT SALAD DESERVES TO HAVE THE SPOTLIGHT ALL TO ITSELF.

MASTERING THE SIMPLE GREEN SALAD

Nothing could be simpler than the simple green salad. To make a great one, all you need are great ingredients, a few basic techniques and intelligent fingertips.

SELECTING GREENS

This is where the salad gets made or broken. Buy a head of dried-out iceberg at the market, or a head of browning romaine, and you won't have much of a salad. But select the freshest, tenderest, brightest, healthiest, most interesting lettuces available and you're well on your way to a master salad.

There are scores of lettuces and greens in our markets today. Our advice: for a great green salad, buy at least four different types, selected for their variety and compatibility. If you can find them, 6, 8—even 10 or 12!—make things ever more interesting. Consider variations in colour (dark green, light green, whitish, red); shape (round leaves, long leaves, pointy leaves, thick leaves, thin leaves); texture (crunchy, soft, velvety, frilly); and flavour (bitter, sweet, acidic, grassy, spicy).

These days, you will often see a premixed pile of salad greens in the marketplace called *mesclun*. This idea comes from southern France, where mesclun mixture (from the Niçoise word for mixture, *mesclumo*) is a staple at every local market (it's also a tradition in Piedmont, where the mix is called *misticanza*). There are often a dozen different lettuces mixed together, and mesclun has the additional advantage of being washed and salad-ready. The down side? It costs an arm and a leg ($12/£7.50 per lb is not uncommon), and many mesclun mixes we're seeing in the United States include leaves at something less-than-peak condition. So, unless you're shopping at a top-flight gourmet shop, it's wisest to buy your own lettuces and make your own combination.

Make sure, of course, that the greens you buy are crisp, moist and fresh. Heads of lettuce should be tight and firm. Avoid anything that's droopy or browning.

Make sure the base has been freshly cut (not too brown).

Here are some of the many wonderful greens that you're likely to find in the markets today.

Amaranth This is also known as tampala, Chinese spinach and Joseph's-coat. It is available in many sizes and in different varieties. Most leaves are a beautiful green with rich purple centres. Larger leaves have an earthy, primitive quality; smaller leaves are more tender and have a milder flavour, something like spinach. Wild amaranth, or pigweed, is often used in Mexican cooking; in Mexico it is called *quelite*. It is hard to find in the United Kingdom, but that is the sort of situation that can change at any time.

Chicory The terminology is very confusing, because there are lots of lettuces called chicory or endive that are frilly, curly, leafy (see endive, escarole, frisée). But what the Americans call Belgian endive, and the Belgians call *witloof* (white leaf), and the French call *endive,* and the English call chicory is actually one variety of the root of the chicory plant. It is a small, elongated, compact bundle of white, green and yellow leaves, not at all frilly or curly. The whole head (referred to as a *chicon* in France) is usually just 10 to 15 cm (4 to 6 in) in length. It is grown in the dark, to keep the leaves as white as possible and less bitter; when you're shopping for chicory, choose whiter heads if you want less bitterness. All chicory, however, will have some bitterness—which you can make a virtue by slicing the plant into thin rounds and tossing the very crunchy rounds with 'sweeter' greens. Chicory on its own has traditionally been a winter salad, often tossed with strips of sweet red pepper (from Holland) to offset the bitterness.

Chrysanthemum Also called chop suey greens because of its common use in stir-fries and other cooked dishes, chrysanthemum is the fragrant, pine-flavoured edible version of the plant. Used sparingly, the thin, spiky leaves are great additions to cold oriental salads or to small, delicate salads of field greens. The petals are also edible if you can find them.

Cos A long, full head of lettuce, also known as romaine, with crisp, crunchy leaves. Cos lettuce has a very green, springlike taste when it's fresh. If you're particularly lucky, you'll find a virtual sweetness in it. With the introduction of more upscale greens—mesclun and the like—the ever-faithful romaine has become the iceberg lettuce of the nineties. Nevertheless, it is one of the most readily available, all-purpose lettuces in the market, and is perfect for dressing with heavier flavours like bacon, garlic and blue cheese. It is, of course, absolutely essential to a Caesar salad. As with many head lettuces, the smaller, light-green inner leaves are milder, more tender, and often more attractive than the outer, darker, larger leaves. A thick rib runs down the centre of the larger leaves; some chefs like to remove this entirely before tossing the rest of the leaf into the salad bowl.

Dandelion Greens These greens, like beetroot or turnip greens, are a rather recent addition to the salad roster. They are sold in large, forest-green bunches. When dandelion is fresh, the long, spiked greens have a pleasant, chewy texture and a slightly bitter flavour—a bit like curly endive or kale—which, in moderation, supplies a delicious counterpoint to a salad largely composed of more delicate greens.

Endive This plant (originally, wild chicory) is the botanically correct name for a large, confusing category of plants that we'll call the chicory-endive group. There are so many in this family because the original wild chicory gave rise to a myriad of cultivated greens that resemble it. Don't panic! All of these lettuces can be used more or less interchangeably. Endive, curly endive, frisée, escarole, and batavia are all names you're likely to see for the related greens of this group. Even radicchio (red chicory) is part of the group. Chicory itself is a name we're seeing less frequently these days in British

markets; if you see it, it may refer to curly endive or to any green, frilly member of the endive family. By the way, the roots of a chicory variety *not* eaten as a vegetable are toasted and ground to use in the chicory coffee of New Orleans.

Escarole Also called batavia or Batavian endive, escarole is another member of the chicory-endive group. Its cachet is in its chew: it's denser than many other members of this clan. Be careful, though: this means that older plants can be tough, even leathery. And the pleasing bitterness it shares with other chicory-endive lettuces can also become unpleasant in older specimens. We usually use escarole in salads very sparingly, just when we're looking for a bit of firm texture for contrast. In Italy, escarole is a favourite cooking green and is often tossed with lemon, garlic, and good olive oil, or made into a soup.

Frisée The darling of our new generation of American salad-makers—so much so that lots of frilly greens from the chicory-endive group are now labelled *frisée* in our markets, because the name is commercial magic. Let's start untangling the confusion by looking at the French terminology. In France, when they say *frisée,* they mean chicorée frisée—or what we would call curly endive. Chicorée frisée is the dark-green tangle of curly, wiry leaves—rather bitter—that is the basis of the great French bistro *salade frisée aux lardons*, or curly endive tossed with bacon and a warm vinaigrette.

For a while, people who said *frisée* in America (there were very few of them at first) also meant curly endive. However, in recent years, other members of the same lettuce family have come into our markets, and *frisée* in America today usually denotes a frilly lettuce that is lighter both in colour and texture than the classic curly endive. What you see most at greengrocers, in fact, is a striking tangle of delicate white and yellowish-green leaves, connected at a core, which is usually identified as 'Italian frisée'. The centre is nearly white, because producers cover the interior of the heads as they're growing to protect them from the sun, to whiten their colour, and to make them less bitter.

All forms of frisée are wiry and crisp, perfect for dramatic, mile-high salads. Just make sure your dressing isn't heavy, or it will clump the leaves together. Though frisée is hearty, it goes bad fairly quickly—and separating good leaves from spoiled ones can be a chore. Buy it fresh and use it immediately. Look carefully for browning leaves, and edit them out if you want restaurant-quality salads. We have to admit that we go with fashion on this particular green; a salad that's 75 per cent Italian frisée, along with one other green for flavour contrast—a tasty one, like rocket —is fine by us.

Green-Leaf Lettuce This is a soft, bulky, floppy, crinkled, fairly flavourless lettuce that is used a great deal in restaurant salads today—presumably because it's not too expensive and its bulk really increases the size of the salad. Gardeners put it in the group of lettuces known as loose-leaf, or cutting or bunching lettuces; this means that the leaves are loosely joined at the base, rather than forming a compact head. Green-leaf lettuce is very delicate, and sometimes wilted heads remain on supermarket shelves days past their prime. Indications of freshness are a garden-fresh smell and full, beautiful, bright green leaves. We like green-leaf lettuce as a backdrop for firmer and more assertive lettuces. (We especially like it as a soft bed on a good sandwich; nothing beats it on a BLT.)

Iceberg This compact, much maligned, admittedly pedestrian head of light green leaves can be—despite its reputation—terrific in salads if you use the hearts torn into chunks. They're not super-flavourful, but they do have a wonderful, crunchy texture and a delightful, moist, refreshing quality. Sometimes we use irregularly shaped chunks from the heart as the crunchy contrast in a salad of serious greens; no guest has ever complained.

Lamb's Lettuce (mâche) Also known as corn salad, this green has reached its current gourmet status, and its stratospheric market price on the basis of texture alone. There is nothing quite like the soft, fuzzy feel of lamb's lettuce in the mouth, which, after a few chews, turns into something like velvet. Flavour-wise, it's altogether quiet, certainly less than remarkable. To get the most out of it, unfortunately you have to use a lot of it in a salad (unfortunate, because it is rather expensive, despite the fact that it is classed as a weed in wheatfields!). When lamb's lettuce is mixed with other greens, both its unique texture and its subtle flavour tend to get lost. Make sure the leaves you buy are not limp.

Little Gem This lettuce looks like a miniature Cos lettuce, though it's in the family of lettuces that gardeners call cabbage lettuce. It occupies a unique position, because its sweet leaves (usually 10 to 15 cm (4 to 6 in) long) are softer and less watery than Cos leaves, but firmer and crunchier than the leaves of fellow-cabbage lettuce. We like to include the smallest whole leaves we can find as the 'crunch factor' in an otherwise soft salad, but at a pinch Little Gem lettuce has enough flavour and body to stand alone as a single-lettuce salad.

Lollo Rosso A curly head lettuce that has tufts of green leaves with beautiful, wine-coloured edges. It is similar in flavour and texture to both green-leaf and red-leaf lettuces, but is firmer, crisper, tangier, tastier. Lollo rosso is now being grown as baby lettuce, and these small, firm leaves make a stunning presentation when combined with small frisée leaves and other small green lettuces. Lollo rosso is very expensive—but, if you can afford it, it's great as the base lettuce of substantial, main-course salads.

Loose-Leaved Lettuce This is the ultimate in soft lettuce, if that's what you're looking for. It has a round, compact head, but you won't see that compact core in the store—because it's hidden by lots of fragile, slippery outer leaves. We're rather fond of the core, which can have a slight bitterness and crunch, but we find the outer leaves boring. We like to combine Webb's Wonder lettuce, even the more flavourful core, with spicier greens that have a firmer bite.

Mizuna A Japanese green traditionally used in stir-fries and vegetarian dishes, mizuna has flat, individual leaves that are long and spiky, and feature an intense mustard-radish flavour. Mizuna, like watercress and rocket, is generally too spicy to use by itself, but is a wonderful flavour-picker-upper alongside Cos, Iceberg or other mild lettuces.

New Zealand Spinach An entirely different plant from the familiar spinach, this green looks and tastes much like fresh pea shoots with a slightly bitter aftertaste. We find it works well with baby lettuces, where unusual flavour and appearance give an exotic twist to more traditional greens.

Purslane Essential in the Middle Eastern bread salad called *fattoush,* purslane is a fleshy, water-filled leaf that has the sourness of sorrel. Some say it tastes like lemon; the French detect a nuttiness in it. The wild, deep-green leaves are tiny, tear-shaped, hard and thick; the stems are red. In addition to using purslane in Middle Eastern salads, we really like to include it in salads with a Mexican accent. Golden purslane is a cultivated version of the plant and has larger, fleshier, more tender leaves.

Radicchio Starting in the late seventies, Americans went from being a country totally ignorant of the Italian red chicory to a country obsessed with it. However, few Americans know that there are many types of radicchio. The most common by far in the United States is the Verona radicchio—a small, compact, round head of deep purple-red lettuce, candy-striped with white. Its condition in most markets is appalling; though it does lend a pretty colour to salads, most round radicchio sold

in America has leathery, bitter leaves with little flavour.

Increasingly, you can find another type of radicchio, the elongated Treviso radicchio, which, depending on its size, can resemble a little gem or cos lettuce. The Treviso is usually in much better shape than the Verona: fresher, crisper, lighter, more flavourful but no less red. Buy it if you can find it.

Both types of radicchio are varieties of chicory, and both have the slightly bitter flavour associated with the chicory-endive family. Small, torn pieces of radicchio supply lovely flavour and texture to a salad composed largely of other, softer greens. By the way, we love to grill whole heads of Treviso radicchio, anoint them with fine-quality olive oil and balsamic vinegar and scatter shards of Parmigiano-Reggiano over the top.

Red-Leaf Lettuce This lettuce very much resembles green-leaf lettuce, except for the scarlet tinge of the ruffled leaves at the edge of the plant farthest from the base. See green-leaf lettuce for a description of general qualities. Actually, we more often choose red-leaf lettuce than green-leaf lettuce to use in salads, because the red colour adds a most attractive visual counterpoint to otherwise-green salads.

Red Oak Lettuce By and large, we prefer red oak lettuce to red-leaf lettuce. For starters, its look is quite different—smaller heads, smaller leaves, each leaf with a lovely indentation pattern and each leaf more fully coloured with red (actually, a kind of red-brown). Then there's the crucial issue of texture. Red oak doesn't have the soft, sloppy, spreading quality that red leaf has; it's a little tighter, a little firmer, a little more interesting to chew. If you're looking for a splash of non-bitter red in your salad, you'll want to sample this variety.

Rocket Rocket is also called rocket plant, the Americans call it rocket, the Italian name. It has bright green, long and tender leaves with spicy flavours—most people think of pepper and radish, but if you taste rocket with your eyes closed you'll find something like peanut.

You can make a full-flavoured salad from rocket exclusively, or you can use it as an accent for other, less boldly flavoured greens. Rocket tends to be 'hotter' in summer months than in winter months—something to think about if you prefer milder greens. Also, old rocket is more bitter than young rocket. Rocket doesn't add much to a salad texturally, though its stems can be a little crunchy. Rocket can be among the droopiest lettuces in the market; buy a good fresh bunch, with lots of dirt clinging to the roots. Then make sure to wash it carefully.

Sorrel This is the sour lettuce (the acidity comes from its high oxalic acid content). Popular for the delicious soup it makes, sorrel has dark, rich-green leaves that vary in size. If you eat uncooked sorrel, you might feel as if you have bitten into a lemon—the sorrel has a sweet-sour burst with a tartness not far from fresh rhubarb. If you are going to prepare it in raw salads, you should tear the leaves and remove the stems (they have even more pungency than the leaves) before adding bite-size pieces to milder lettuce leaves.

Tatsoi Chinese greens traditionally used, like mizuna, in stir-fried dishes, tatsoi greens consist of long stems and flat green leaves. The thick and generally bitter leaves provide the perfect target for light, Asian, nut-oil-based vinaigrettes.

Watercress A spicy green from the mustard family, watercress has a sharp, peppery, fresh-picked flavour. With bright, petal-like leaves and thin, crunchy stems that need not be discarded, watercress is a welcome flavour accent in any salad chiefly composed of less-vivid greens. You can also make a salad from watercress alone—but make sure that the dressing is full-flavoured and that any accompanying dishes are as well.

Note: Though they are not considered lettuces, things like mange-tout, sprouts of all kinds, purple and green

basil tips and varieties of mint are seen more and more in innovative salads. Try them, by all means. Edible flowers are also getting tossed in the salad bowl with regularity; you'll sometimes see them in mesclun mixtures. We find most of the flowers odd, but are mad about the radishy flavour of nasturtiums—a great salad accent.

An ideal blend

There are literally millions of possible salad permutations, and we urge you to start experimenting tonight. In case you're a little timid about choosing greens, get started with this mixture that we heartily recommend. It will make enough salad for 6 people:

- 1 large head of cos lettuce, pale-green inner leaves only, the larger ones torn in half and the smallest left whole
- 1 medium head of curly endives, thin spikes torn away from the base
- a few small heads of lollo rosso (for colour)
- 1 bunch of rocket, stems removed (for spiciness)

WASHING AND PREPARATION

It's very simple: to make a transcendent salad, you have to enjoy standing at the sink, tearing away and discarding unacceptable bits of lettuce, and washing the precious gems that have passed your lettuce censor. We do. Here's how we recommend going about it.

If you have a double sink, fill up one sink with cold water, and plunge your lettuces into the bath. If you have a single sink, fill up a very large bowl with cold water, plunge your lettuces into the bowl, and place the bowl next to the sink. If you notice that your lettuces are especially sandy or gritty, drain the water from the sink or bowl, and fill it up a second time.

Tear a few lettuce leaves away. Hold them over an empty sink, under running water, washing off any dirt or sand. Tear them by hand into pieces that you think will be appropriate for your salad (we usually go for uniformity, most pieces about 3 cm (an inch or so) wide, a few cm in length). Some salad-makers like to discard the thick ribs in some types of lettuce, such as cos (we discard, especially if we're after a delicate salad). Discard anything that you won't be proud of in your salad bowl. Please note: this may mean you'll be 'wasting' a lot of the lettuce you bought, but it's the only way to achieve a restaurant-quality salad! You want gems in that finished product.

As to quantity: about 125 g (4½ oz) of torn lettuce is sufficient for a single serving of simple green salad. Remember, though, if you're weighing, don't tamp the greens down on the scales. They must be loosely packed for this measurement to be accurate.

After you've washed, torn, and weighed the lettuce pieces, place them in a salad spinner (yes, this piece of equipment is very handy). Don't fill the spinner up too full. Spin until dry. Remove lettuce. Repeat, until all of your lettuce pieces are dried.

When the lettuce is dry, it is ready to dress and serve as salad. But if you're not ready to dress and serve your salad—or if you wish to wash and dry your lettuce in advance—you may carefully roll it up in paper towels (making sure not to bruise the lettuce), then place the towels in polythene bags. Place the bags in the refrigerator. This will keep the lettuce perfectly well for a good 8 hours.

ASSEMBLING AND DRESSING THE SALAD

Simple green salads should be assembled, dressed and seasoned immediately before serving.

Place your washed and torn greens in a very large bowl (the bigger it is, the easier it is to dress the salad). You may now either prepare a dressing in a separate bowl and toss it with the lettuce or pour the dressing ingredients (oil and vinegar) directly over the lettuce.

The first way, preparing a separate vinaigrette, is very French. If you wish to do it in this way, you can choose from two major types of vinaigrettes: fairly thin or rich and mustardy.

Whichever one you choose, you'll need about 1 teaspoon of vinaigrette per person (that's for each 125 g (4½ oz) of loosely packed greens) if you wish to dress your greens lightly. You'll need 2 teaspoons of vinaigrette per person if you wish to coat the greens more heavily. Any more dressing than this and you won't taste the greens.

When the dressing is made, simply toss it with the lettuce pieces in the large bowl. We like to use our hands for tossing; large wooden spoons are also acceptable. Season the salad with salt and pepper immediately before arranging on plates, taste for seasoning and serve it immediately.

ARRANGING THE SALAD

If you really want to make your salad look like something from a great restaurant, don't just plunk your big old wooden salad bowl on the table. Instead, you might want to consider dividing the salad among individual plates. We recommend dinner-sized plates. If you really want to impress, chill the plates as well as the forks.

Most important: stack the salad on each plate with care. Modern restaurant practice is to build the salad, give it some height on the plate. Don't spread the greens out to the edge of each plate. Put a small quantity of greens at the centre of each plate, then stack the rest of the greens on top of those. It will add immeasurably to the elegance of your presentation.

Another thing you could do, of course, is take your simple green salad and convert it into a complex one by adding all manner of things: grilled chicken, olives, or pieces of goat cheese, for example. Your imagination is your guide, and your good taste will help you determine how to arrange your salad on the plate with the other ingredients.

Or, you can continue and consider any of the more complicated salads that begin on page 11.

Basic Italian oil and vinegar dressing

Here's our standard version of a toss-it-on-the-greens dressing. We love the way the garlic blends with the other flavours in this simple dressing, but you may omit it if you wish a quieter effect. In any event, make sure you use a high-quality balsamic vinegar; the cheap stuff that's industrially made, though adequate in sauces, tastes harsh and unforgiving in salads.

ENOUGH FOR 12 LIGHTLY DRESSED GREEN SALADS OR 6 HEAVILY DRESSED GREEN SALADS

1 large garlic clove
1.25 g (¼ tsp) salt
5 ml (1 tsp) good-quality balsamic vinegar
25 ml (5 tsp) red-wine vinegar
30 ml (2 tbsp) extra-virgin olive oil

1. Peel the garlic clove, and smash it with the side of a heavy knife. Add the salt and chop garlic until mixture forms a paste. Place in a small bowl, and add the two vinegars. Mix lightly.

2. Add the olive oil to salad greens in a large bowl. Mix thoroughly with your hands. Add the vinegar-garlic mixture. Mix again. Taste for seasoning.

For more complicated dressings and vinaigrettes, see Chapter Nine.

BASIC MUSTARD VINAIGRETTE

And here's a good version of the richer, mustardy vinaigrette. Ever wonder why the vinaigrette in classic French restaurants is so thick and yellow? Usually, mustard is the answer. If you beat vinegar and oil slowly into mustard, the texture of the dressing will remain about the same as the mustard you started with. You may, in fact, find this a little too thick; we do, and add a little water at the end to thin it out. The water also seems to focus the flavours of the vinaigrette.

ENOUGH FOR 12 LIGHTLY DRESSED GREEN SALADS OR 6 HEAVILY DRESSED GREEN SALADS

10 ml (2 tsp) Dijon mustard
10 ml (2 tsp) red-wine vinegar
30 ml (2 tbsp) plus 10 ml (2 tsp) extra-virgin olive oil
10 ml (½ tsp) cold water (optional)
salt and pepper

1. Place the mustard in a small bowl. Slowly whisk in the vinegar so that the mustard remains creamy and smooth. Slowly whisk in the olive oil; once again, the dressing should remain creamy and smooth. (If the dressing 'breaks', or separates into oil and vinegar, you can revive it by adding more mustard to another bowl, then beating the 'broken' dressing slowly into the mustard.)

2. If desired, thin the vinaigrette with the cold water. Season well with salt and pepper.

Now, if you prefer to dress your salad directly—that is, by pouring the oil and vinegar right onto the greens in the salad bowl—you're drawing on the Italian tradition. It's less formal but equally delicious.

The most important thing to keep in mind is that oil must precede vinegar as you dress the lettuce. If you add the vinegar first, it soaks the lettuce and makes it limp; if you add the oil first, it protects the lettuce from this change.

You may be expecting us to recommend balsamic vinegar for this Italian-inspired salad treatment, because we were instrumental in popularising balsamic vinegar in America. But the truth of the matter is this that we're tired of seeing it on every salad in almost every Italian restaurant in America. The Italians themselves, in Emilia-Romagna, where it's made, don't use it this way. It's too sweet, too intense for delicate greens.

We say: use a little, but mix it with red-wine vinegar (this is a classic Italian practice). We say: sometimes substitute sherry vinegar, which is more subtle. And we say: use more bitter greens (such as chicory, radicchio and endive) in a salad that has a balsamic-based dressing.

BASIC VINAIGRETTE WITH WALNUT OIL AND WHITE-WINE VINEGAR

Here's a good version of the fairly thin French vinaigrette. The combination of walnut oil and white-wine vinegar, with its echoes of southwest France, is hauntingly delicious—and the two liquids blend together seamlessly in a light, creamy emulsion. Make sure you buy high-quality, fresh-tasting walnut oil. We use this dressing as our basic vinaigrette. You may, of course, substitute any other oil or vinegar.

ENOUGH FOR 12 LIGHTLY DRESSED GREEN SALADS OR 6 HEAVILY DRESSED GREEN SALADS

15 ml (1 tbsp) white-wine vinegar
45 ml (3 tbsp) walnut oil
salt and pepper

Place the vinegar in a small bowl. Slowly whisk in the walnut oil until a light, creamy emulsion is formed (about a minute). Season well with salt and pepper.

Choosing oils and vinegars for your salad dressing

Your choice of oil and vinegar is a crucial factor in the success of any salad. We like to vary our choice, depending on the greens, the season, the menu—and our mood! Here are some of our favourites for salad dressing.

Oils

Olive Oil For salad dressings, we like to use a good, but not great, extra-virgin olive oil. Lesser olive oils have no flavour. The most expensive oils have exquisite but subtle flavour, which will be drowned out by vinegar and greens. Therefore, a robustly flavoured extra-virgin oil, costing no more than £7.50 a litre, is the perfect compromise choice. Very fresh Greek olive oil is great for salads.

Nut Oils We are crazy about these oils in salads, since their pronounced, nutty flavours stand up well to vinegars and greens. In fact, we particularly like them with strongly flavoured greens, like watercress, and with strongly flavoured vinegars, like sherry vinegar. Both walnut oil and hazelnut oil from France are among our favourites, with a slight edge given to the latter due to its greater delicacy. Often, we cut these oils in a dressing with neutral vegetable oils. These oils are very unstable and lose their freshness quickly, so buy small quantities and use soon after purchase.

Japanese or Chinese Sesame Oil These dark oils—unlike the light, unroasted sesame oils found in health food shops—are the strongest flavoured oils of all. A mere drop in a salad will make its presence known. We eschew them in Western-style salads, but when we're creating fanciful salads with an Asian spin, these oils come in handy.

Neutral Vegetable Oils If you're looking for a light flavour in your dressing—perhaps you really want the flavour of the greens to come through—you might consider using safflower oil, sunflower oil or our favourite neutral oil, rapeseed oil (an oil that is low in saturated fats and high in monounsaturates). There's nothing to be ashamed of! We even like these neutral oils when making mayonnaise.

Vinegars

A key factor in your vinegar choice should be the relative sourness of the vinegar; this will be expressed on the label by a number that tells you the percentage of acetic acid. Vinegar can normally be as low as 2.5 per cent acetic acid, as high as 7 per cent acetic acid. It's up to you whether you want merely a mildly piquant dressing or a sharp one with lots of acid bite.

Distilled White Vinegar This is the supermarket classic, sometimes simply called acetic acid. It is made from grain and is colourless. It tastes merely acidic. Use it only if you want no flavour to compromise the flavour of your greens. It is usually from 6 per cent to 6.5 per cent acetic acid.

Apple Cider Vinegar A big step up. Made from apples, with an onion-skin colour and a subtle apple taste. We love it in coleslaw. It can be cloudy or filtered, and usually weighs in at 6 per cent to 6.5 per cent acetic acid.

Wine Vinegars These can vary quite a bit in sharpness and intensity. Usually the mildest-flavoured of the group is **white-wine vinegar** (often 6 per cent to 6.5 per cent acetic acid), which works nicely in delicate salads. **Red-wine vinegar,** often at the same level of acetic acid, somehow seems coarser, rougher; it also tastes more strongly of wine. We love it with more assertive greens, but it's also our all-around top choice for salad dressings. **Sherry vinegar** has the most character of the bunch (the nutty, oxidised flavour of sherry), and often zooms up to 7 per cent acetic acid; we like to use it on strong greens, but cut with a milder vinegar. One wine vinegar we don't use much is **champagne vinegar**—which is often quite delicate, but includes none of the bubbles you pay so dearly for in a bottle of champagne (and the vinegar ain't cheap either!)

Balsamic Vinegar Real balsamic vinegar, usually referred to as *tradizionale,* takes a long time to make. It may wander through a series of barrels (made from different woods) for as long as one hundred years before it reaches its dark-brown, sweet, syrupy state. *Industriale* is what you'll find in most stores, stuff made quickly and sold cheaply, stuff that only approximates the grandeur of the real thing. We're not crazy about either for salads. Sometimes, however, we will mix a good (not super-great) *tradizionale* with some red-wine vinegar for an interesting variation. Balsamic vinegar is usually high in sugar and low in acid.

Fruit Vinegars The shops are loaded these days with raspberry vinegar, blueberry vinegar, cranberry vinegar and others. These vinegars are usually made by adding the fruit, or syrup made from the fruit, to fairly neutral white vinegar. Sometimes they are sweetened. Despite its dated nouvelle cuisine connotations, raspberry vinegar can be especially lively in a delicate salad. Pineapple vinegar is another interesting one, and is often used in Mexico. Fruit vinegars are made in both high-acid and low-acid styles; check your label.

Herbal Vinegars By steeping herbs in vinegar, producers come up with these gourmet grocery items, which can cost a pretty penny. We keep a little in the cupboard in case an herbal burst is needed on a snowy winter's day; normally, we prefer snipping fresh herbs into the dressing. Tarragon vinegar is the most widely known. Acidity varies.

Asian Rice Vinegars These vinegars are great in Asian-style salads, but great in Western salads too if you're looking for a mellower flavour. Rice vinegars, which can vary from clear to black, usually have under 5 per cent acetic acid and a subtle sweetness to boot.

SALADE COMPOSÉE: CLASSICS AND VARIATIONS

Popular as the simple salade verte is, the salade composée—lettuces and/or other vegetables with even more stuff added to them—is the real darling of the day. Some of the salades composées Americans eat a lot of today are standards of international cuisine. Here we present great versions of the hottest ones in homes and restaurants plus some creative twists on them that we find equally delicious.

Classic

MOZZARELLA, TOMATO AND BASIL SALAD

In Italy, it's often called *insalata caprese* (Capri salad). Now, every Italian restaurant in America is serving this dish, which spread like wildfire in the eighties. There's only one problem: unless it's made with absolutely fresh, stunningly high-quality mozzarella, it can be a leaden disappointment. Mozzarella tastes best within hours of its manufacture, when the cheese is still soft, resilient and oozing milk. After 24 hours, it loses those properties altogether. Another potential stumbling block in this recipe is the tomatoes: unless they're rich and ripe, the dish, once again, turns pallid. If fresh mozzarella and ripe tomatoes are not available to you, skip ahead to the next recipe.

SERVES 12 AS A FIRST COURSE

about 12 large basil leaves
6 medium tomatoes
900 g (2 lb) fresh mozzarella at room temperature,
  cut into 5mm (¼in) slices
125 ml (4 fl oz) extra-virgin olive oil
salt and freshly ground pepper

1. Remove basil leaves from stems, rinse and pat dry. Rinse, core and slice tomatoes lengthways into 5 mm (¼-inch) slices.

2. On a large round dish, alternate the tomatoes, basil and mozzarella in a circular pattern, starting from the middle and working outwards.

3. Drizzle the olive oil evenly over the salad and season generously with salt and pepper. Allow the salad to sit at

room temperature for 15 to 30 minutes before serving. Serve with crusty fresh bread.

Variation

WARMED MOZZARELLA WITH TOMATO AND ROCKET

We have the secret for resuscitating too-old mozzarella: warm it briefly in the oven. You'll be amazed at the difference it makes. And if your tomatoes are less than perfect, you can take the focus away from their imperfection by chopping them and dressing them. This is a great mozzarella and tomato salad when you don't have great mozzarella and tomato.

SERVES 4 AS A FIRST COURSE

450 g (1 lb) fresh mozzarella at room temperature
1 fresh tomato (about 115 g (4 oz))
1 tsp extra-virgin olive oil
1 tsp red-wine vinegar
salt and pepper to taste
12 fresh rocket leaves, torn into large pieces
coarse salt to taste

1. Preheat oven to 130°C (275°F)

2. Cut the mozzarella into 16 slices, each approximately 5mm (¼ in) thick. Arrange 4 slices at the centre of an ovenproof dinner plate, overlapping them slightly. Repeat with 3 more plates. Place the plates in the oven for about 5 minutes, or until the mozzarella looks soft and moist. (Do not allow it to melt.)

3. While the mozzarella is warming, stem the tomato and chop it into small dice. Mix with the oil and vinegar and season with salt and pepper.

4. When the mozzarella is softened, immediately top the cheese with the rocket leaves, scattering them evenly. Sprinkle with coarse salt. Place one quarter of the tomato mixture at the centre of each plate. Serve immediately.

Variation

SMOKED MOZZARELLA SALAD WITH GRILLED RED PEPPERS

We'll never forget watching mozzarella being smoked in the parking lot of a mozzarella factory near Naples; the result, when tasted on the spot, was absolutely delicious. Smoke your own, if you can—or buy a freshly smoked one from an Italian grocer that smokes its own.

SERVES 4 AS A FIRST COURSE

2 sweet red peppers about 115g (4 oz)
225g (8oz) smoked mozzarella at room temperature
10 g (2 tsp) finely ground fresh parsley
10 ml (2 tsp) extra-virgin olive oil
5 g (1 tsp) garlic chopped to a paste
salt and pepper to taste
225 g (8 oz) lightly dressed, frilly salad greens

1. Place the red peppers over the burners of a gas range (if you don't have a gas range, you can place them under a grill, or over an outdoor barbecue). Cook, turning with tongs, until the peppers are blackened. Place them in a paper bag, and let them rest for 20 minutes. Remove from bag, and peel off the blackened skin (do not run the peppers under water). Remove the stem, seeds and ribs. Cut into little cubes.

2. Cut the mozzarella into small dice, and mix with the red pepper. Add the parsley, the oil and the garlic. Season with salt and pepper.

3. Divide the salad greens among 4 plates, and top with the smoked mozzarella mixture. Serve immediately.

Smoking your own

Unless you can buy mozzarella that has been smoked within the last few hours, there is no substitute for smoking your own mozzarella. And it's actually very easy, especially if you own the Max Burton Stove Top Smoker (made in Tacoma, Washington, tel: [206] 627–2665), which will allow you to smoke mozzarella in your kitchen, on top of your range, in just a few minutes.

Follow the manufacturer's instructions for setting up the smoker and preparing the wood chips. When ready to smoke, place a very fresh ball of mozzarella on the rack; you may need to cut it in half to make it fit inside the cover. Smoke for about 5 minutes. It should become light brown on the outside. Make sure that you remove the smoked mozzarella before it starts to melt.

Let it sit on the counter for a few minutes, then proceed with the recipe.

Classic

SALADE NIÇOISE

What *is* the classic salade niçoise? There are three main flash points of controversy.

Controversy 1: Everyone agrees that there must be canned tuna in the classic version—but what kind of vegetables surround the tuna? One faction insists that only *raw* vegetables, like tomato or radish, belong in the salad. Another faction wouldn't think of a salade niçoise without *cooked* vegetables, such as potatoes and French beans.

Controversy 2: What's a salad without lettuce? *Everything,* to a certain group of niçoisistes. No leafy greens for them to interfere with the pure chunky pleasure of their salade niçoise.

Controversy 3: Once you've chosen your ingredients, do you toss them all together with the dressing, or do you arrange them carefully on a plate and drizzle the dressing over them?

As to the ingredient controversy: we feel that cooked vegetables add fabulous depth and interest to this salad. Purists be damned! And we think lettuce makes an attractive base. As to the controversy over arrangement: our version of the classic has it both ways. Most of the elements in our salade niçoise are casually tossed together, but there is a decorative arrangement on the plate of eggs and tomatoes.

Additionally, we discovered something new and remarkable about salade niçoise. If you toss the ingredients with olives and let the mixture sit in the refrigerator for a few hours, the other ingredients take on the unmistakable flavour of olives—a wonderful addition to this dish, which happens to taste very authentically niçoise. If you're in a hurry, of course, you could skip this extra step—but we hope you don't.

SERVES 6

225 g (8 oz) thin French beans, blanched, refreshed, and halved

450 g (1 lb) red new potatoes, peeled, cooked, and cut into 3-mm (⅛-in) slices

1 small red onion, cut into thin rings and soaked in cold water for 5 minutes

2 x 175-g (6-oz) cans tuna (packed in olive oil) flaked into large chunks

115 g (¼ lb) black olives, stoned and halved

10 g (2 tsp) finely chopped garlic

10 g (2 tsp) finely chopped shallot

12 anchovies, soaked in water for 5 minutes and finely chopped

45 ml (3 tbsp) fresh lemon juice

50 ml (2 fl oz) red-wine vinegar

225 ml (8 fl oz) olive oil

10 ml (2 tsp) salt

2.5 ml (½ tsp) black pepper

1 head red-leaf lettuce, leaves torn roughly

6 hard-boiled eggs, quartered lengthways

4 small tomatoes, quartered

1. Combine beans, potatoes, red onion, tuna and olives in large bowl and toss gently to combine, so as not to break up the tuna chunks. Cover and refrigerate for 4 hours.

2. Place garlic, shallot, anchovies, lemon juice and vinegar in a small bowl and whisk in olive oil. Season with salt and pepper.

3. Lightly dress lettuce with vinaigrette and divide among 6 plates. Decoratively arrange hard-boiled egg slices and tomatoes on lettuce, and drizzle with a little vinaigrette.

4. Dress vegetable and tuna mixture with remaining vinaigrette, tossing gently. Divide evenly among the plates.

Variation

STACKED SALADE NIÇOISE WITH SEARED FRESH TUNA AND CREAMY VINAIGRETTE

And now for the most controversial variation of all! Many restaurateurs today, both in the United States and France, have abandoned the classic canned tuna altogether and are making a fresher-tasting salade niçoise with very trendy pieces of sashimi-quality fresh tuna, typically seared on the outside, and raw or rare on the inside. We've made the following version even more of a departure from the original. There's no lettuce in this very chunky salad, and the ingredients are stacked (New American–restaurant style) on dinner plates; it's a beautiful presentation. Furthermore, the dressing contains such un-niçoise elements as Dijon mustard and sherry vinegar—both of which contribute to a new taste that is utterly delightful with the tuna.

SERVES 8

30 ml (2 tbsp) Dijon mustard

50 ml (2 fl oz) sherry vinegar

225 ml (8 fl oz) extra-virgin olive oil

1 garlic clove, very finely chopped

salt and pepper to taste

8 anchovy fillets

900 g (2 lb) fresh tuna steaks
coarsely cracked black peppercorns to taste
450 g (1 lb) thin French beans
8 plum tomatoes
coarse salt to taste
1 green pepper, cut into thin strips
1 red pepper, cut into thin strips
8 small red new potatoes, peeled and cooked
6 hard-boiled eggs, shelled
50 g (2 oz) fresh parsley, finely chopped
32 black olives, stoned

1. *Prepare dressing:* In a medium-sized bowl, add mustard, then vinegar. Whisk until smooth. Whisk in olive oil a little at a time (the dressing should have a creamy consistency). Add garlic and season with salt and pepper.

2. In a small bowl of cold water, soak anchovy fillets for 5 minutes to remove excess salt and oil. Cut each fillet into 4 pieces.

3. Brush tuna with a little olive oil, then press cracked peppercorns into the tuna. Grill over an open fire until seared outside and still raw inside (you may cook it further, but not more than rare), or grill under the oven grill. Brush tuna with a little of the dressing and cut into 1-cm (½-in) cubes.

4. Bring a large pot of water to a boil. Add a large handful of salt. Cut stems off beans and cook until just tender, about 4 minutes. Refresh in ice water. Strain, cut each bean into 3 pieces and reserve.

5. Cut tomatoes into large dice. Sprinkle with coarse salt and set aside.

6. When ready to assemble the salad, cut the strips of green and red pepper into 3 pieces each. Cut the potatoes into 5-mm (¼-in) thick slices, and then cut each slice into 4 chunks. Cut the eggs into 5-mm

(¼-in) thick slices, and then cut each slice into 4 chunks. In a large bowl, mix together the anchovies, tuna, beans, tomatoes, green pepper, red pepper, potatoes, eggs, parsley and olives. Mix with dressing. Taste for seasoning. Divide among 8 plates, stacking the salad in as high and narrow a tower as possible on each plate. Serve immediately.

Note: For an even trendier presentation, drizzle a little extra vinaigrette around the tower, and scatter finely chopped parsley leaves around the plate and its rim.

Classic

CURLY ENDIVE AUX LARDONS WITH WARM VINAIGRETTE
A new generation of adventurous diners has discovered this old bistro classic: frizzy, slightly bitter lettuce tossed with croutons and crusty bits of cured pork (lardons), and dressed with a warm vinaigrette made from the oil in which the pork was cooked. We've tweaked it a bit, adding fresh herbs and thinly sliced shallots to ratchet up the flavour level even higher. If you're looking for additional thrills, toss in some diced, sautéed potatoes and top with a poached egg.

SERVES 6

10 x 2.5-cm (1-in) thick slices of French or Italian
    bread (7.5 cm (3 in) in diameter)
50 ml (2 fl oz) extra-virgin olive oil
salt and pepper to taste
225 g (8 oz) skinned lean and meaty salt pork, cut
    into 2-cm (¾-in) dice
4 shallots, sliced thin crosswise
45 ml (3 tbsp) red-wine vinegar
15 ml (1 tbsp) chopped fresh parsley
5 g (1 tsp) fresh thyme leaves
3 g (½ tsp) chopped fresh rosemary leaves
2 garlic cloves, finely chopped
450 g (1 lb) curly endive (frisée), torn into pieces,

washed thoroughly, and spun dry (about 2 large heads)

1. *Make the croutons:* Preheat oven to 180°C (350°F). Brush both sides of bread slices with 3 tablespoons of olive oil and season with salt and pepper. Cut into 2.5-cm (1-in) cubes and bake croutons in oven on a baking sheet, shaking tin occasionally, until golden brown, 12 to 15 minutes.

2. Boil the salt pork in cold water to cover in a saucepan for 2 minutes and drain in a colander. Rinse salt pork under cold water and pat very dry with paper towels.

3. Heat remaining 15 ml (1 tbsp) olive oil in a large frying pan over moderate heat, and cook salt pork, stirring frequently, until golden brown, about 10 minutes. Remove salt pork with a slotted spoon and drain on paper towels.

4. Pour off all but 125 ml (4 fl oz) of fat from the frying pan, and add the shallots, red-wine vinegar, herbs and garlic. Cook the dressing, stirring, for 4 minutes, or until shallots are wilted. Season with salt and pepper.

5. In a large bowl toss the curly endive, salt pork, croutons and warm dressing. If salad seems dry, add a little more fat and vinegar. Divide salad among 6 plates and serve immediately.

Variation

CURLY ENDIVE WITH CRISPED SALMON SKIN AND WARM SHERRY VINAIGRETTE

In case you shy away from the pork-fat dressing of the classic frisée, you can always turn to this lighter, but equally delicious version, which substitutes crackling salmon skin for the lardons. Grilled salmon skin is a sushi bar staple, and the ginger in this dish echoes that

connection. And further interest is provided by a very sympathetic dose of sherry vinegar. A multi-cultural triumph!

SERVES 6

10 x 2.5-cm (1-in)-thick slices of French or Italian bread (7.5 cm (3 in) in diameter)
45 ml (3 tbsp) olive oil
salt and pepper to taste
skin from a 900-g (2-lb) salmon fillet*
130 ml (9 tbsp) hazelnut oil
5 shallots, sliced thin crossways
10 ml (2 tsp) lemon juice
45 ml (3 tbsp) sherry vinegar
30 g (2 tbsp) grated fresh ginger
2 garlic cloves
450 g (1 lb) curly endive (frisée), torn into pieces, washed thoroughly and spun dry

1. *Make the croutons:* Preheat oven to 180°C (350°F). Brush both sides of bread slices with 3 tablespoons of olive oil and season with salt and pepper. Cut into 2.5-cm (1-in) cubes and bake croutons in oven on a baking sheet, shaking them occasionally, until golden brown, 12 to 15 minutes.

2. Remove salmon skin from fillet and reserve fillet for another use. Lightly brush ½ tablespoon hazelnut oil on both sides of salmon skin and place on preheated griddle or under a preheated grill until crispy, about 2 minutes per side. Pat salmon skin dry with paper towels, cut it into 2-cm (¾-in) dice and set aside.

3. Combine shallots, lemon juice, sherry vinegar, ginger, garlic, 125 ml (4 fl oz) of hazelnut oil, salt and pepper in a small saucepan and cook the dressing over moderate heat until shallots are wilted, about 3 to 4 minutes.

4. In a large bowl toss the curly endive, salmon skin and

*We would advise making this dish only if you have plans for the rest of the salmon fillet!

croutons with warm sherry vinegar dressing. Divide among 6 plates and serve immediately.

Classic

———

CAESAR SALAD

Caesar salad, that ever present item on 'Continental' restaurant menus of decades past, doesn't come from the continent at all—it's from Tijuana, Mexico, where Caesar Cardini, an Italian restaurateur, created it on Fourth of July weekend in 1924. This version follows his classic recipe—except that it's much, much lighter, more refreshing, and more lemony than any version you've tried before. By the way, Cardini did not include anchovies in his original. He did include Worcestershire sauce, which is made, in part, from anchovies. Later salad revisionists added the small fillets themselves.

SERVES 6

For the croutons
50 ml (2 f l oz) olive oil
2 garlic cloves, halved lengthways
350 g (12 oz) 2-cm (¾-in) cubes of French or
    Italian bread
salt and pepper to taste
For the dressing
4 garlic cloves, peeled
1 egg, boiled for 30 seconds
20 ml (4 tsp) fresh lemon juice
3 ml (¾ tsp) Worcestershire sauce
125 ml (4 fl oz) extra-virgin olive oil
4 heads cos or romaine lettuce, the pale green inner
    leaves washed, spun dry, and torn into bite-size
    pieces
Parmigiano-Reggiano curls formed with a vegetable
    peeler

1. *Make the croutons:* Preheat the oven to 180°C (350°F). Warm the olive oil with the garlic in a small

saucepan over moderate heat. Remove from heat and let stand for 10 minutes. Discard the garlic. Toss the bread cubes with the oil, spread them on a baking sheet and season them with salt and pepper. Bake the croutons for 12 to 15 minutes, or until golden brown.

2. *Make the dressing:* Finely chop the garlic to a fine paste. Whisk together the garlic paste, egg, lemon juice and Worcestershire sauce in a small bowl. Add the olive oil in a stream, whisking, and whisk the dressing until it is has emulsified.

3. In a large bowl toss the lettuce with the croutons and the dressing until the salad is combined well. Top the salad with the Parmigiano-Reggiano curls.

Variation

———

CAESAR SALAD WITH ROQUEFORT DRESSING AND CRISPY WALNUTS

You want a rich and creamy Caesar salad? Try this startling variation, in which all of the elements merge seamlessly. The walnuts, substituted here for the croutons, are a special treat; their sweetness is a perfect foil to the salty Roquefort. This version, by the way, contains no undercooked egg, in case you worry about that sort of thing.

SERVES 6

4 flat anchovy fillets, or to taste, rinsed and drained
4 garlic cloves, peeled
10 ml (2 tsp) sherry vinegar
10 ml (2 tsp) fresh lemon juice
5 ml (1 tsp) Worcestershire sauce
3 ml (½ tsp) dry mustard
125 ml (4 fl oz) extra-virgin olive oil
4 heads romaine or cos lettuce, the pale green inner
    leaves washed, spun dry, and torn into bite-size
    pieces
125 g (4 oz) Roquefort cheese, crumbled

crispy walnuts (recipe follows)

1. *Make the dressing:* Mince and mash the anchovies with the garlic to form a paste. Whisk together the anchovy paste, vinegar, lemon juice, Worcestershire sauce and the mustard in a small bowl. Add the olive oil in a stream, whisking, and whisk the dressing until it is emulsified.

2. In a large bowl, toss the lettuce with the dressing. Add the Roquefort cheese, and sprinkle the salad with the crispy walnuts.

CRISPY WALNUTS

    225 g (8 oz) walnut halves
    85 g (3 oz) icing sugar
    vegetable oil for frying
    5 g (½ tsp) salt
    2 g (⅛ tsp) cayenne pepper

1. In a saucepan, simmer the walnut halves in water to cover for 5 minutes, or until they are slightly softened. Drain the walnuts and transfer to paper towels to dry completely.

2. In a bowl, stir together the walnuts and icing sugar. In a heavy pot, heat 7.5 cm (3 in) of vegetable oil to 180°C (350°F). Fry the walnuts in batches for 1 to 2 minutes, or until they are brown and crisp. Transfer the walnuts as they are fried with a slotted spoon to a baking sheet and season with salt and cayenne pepper. Cool.

Classic

TABOULEH

This is a bright, lemony, perfectly balanced version of the classic Middle Eastern bulgur wheat and parsley salad. Serve it immediately if you prefer more texture in the bulgur wheat. But we prefer to cover it and refrigerate it for two hours . . . yielding the advantage of flavours that have mingled deliciously.

SERVES 4

    125 g (4 oz) dry bulgur wheat
    5 bunches of fresh parsley, finely chopped (about 175 g (6 oz))
    10 g (2 tsp) finely chopped mint
    1 medium tomato, seeded and diced
    1 small red onion, finely chopped
    5 g (1 tsp) finely chopped garlic
    45 ml (3 tbsp) fresh lemon juice
    45 ml (3 tbsp) olive oil
    2.5 g (½ tsp) salt
    1.25 g (¼ tsp) black pepper

1. Wash the bulgur in several changes of cold water, pouring it back and forth between a large bowl and a very fine sieve, until the water runs clear. Drain the bulgur in the fine sieve. Return bulgur to the bowl, cover it with 2.5 cm (1 in) cold water, and let it soak for 1 hour.

2. Place bulgur, parsley, mint, tomato and red onion together in medium bowl and stir well to mix.

3. Whisk together garlic, lemon juice, olive oil, salt and pepper, and pour this over other ingredients. Stir well.

Variation

SPICY CORIANDER TABOULEH

We think this variation is even better than the original. We've added lots of fresh coriander to the usual parsley and mint, as well as toasted coriander seed and other spices to give the salad more flavour and interest. Letting the spices cool completely before grinding them retains more of their volatile oils and taste.

SERVES 6

175 g (6 oz) fine bulgur
5 g (1 tsp) whole coriander seeds
2.5 g (½ tsp) each whole cumin and fennel seeds
10 whole allspice berries
175 g (6 oz) finely chopped red onion
5 g (1 tsp), or more to taste
175 g (6 oz) finely diced seedless cucumber
175 g (6 oz) finely diced seeded tomato
85 g (3 oz) each minced fresh coriander and fresh
   flat-leaf parsley
55 g (2 oz) fresh mint leaves
55 g (2 oz) finely chopped spring onions
55 ml (2 fl oz) fresh lemon juice
55 ml (2 fl oz) extra-virgin olive oil
cayenne pepper to taste

1. Wash the bulgur in several changes of cold water, pouring it back and forth between a large bowl and a very fine sieve, until the water is clear. Drain the bulgur in the fine sieve. Return bulgur to the bowl, cover it with 2.5 cm (1 in) cold water, and let it soak for 1 hour.

2. While the bulgur is soaking, toast the coriander seeds, cumin seeds and fennel seeds in a small frying pan over moderate heat until very fragrant, 1 to 2 minutes. Let the seeds cool completely and then grind them fine with the allspice berries in a spice grinder or pound to a powder in a mortar and pestle.

3. Stir together the red onion, ground spices and salt in a large bowl and let stand while the bulgur is soaking, at least 30 minutes.

4. Drain the bulgur in the sieve, pressing hard to extract as much water as possible. Add the bulgur to the onion mixture with the cucumber, tomato, herbs, spring onion, lemon juice, olive oil and cayenne pepper; toss the salad well. Taste and adjust seasonings, adding more salt if necessary. This salad is best if served immediately.

Variation

COUSCOUS TABOULEH WITH RAISINS

This unusual tabouleh-style salad—made with couscous not bulgur wheat!—is the lightest, fluffiest 'tabouleh' we've ever tasted. There are other highlights as well. The couscous takes on a beautiful orange colour from its bath in tomato juice. The raisins add sweetness as a foil to the lemon juice and the inclusion of sweet peppers gives the salad an almost gazpacho-like taste.

SERVES 8

225 ml (8 fl oz) tomato juice
juice of 3 lemons
125 ml (4 fl oz) olive oil
350 g (12 oz) couscous
3 large, ripe tomatoes
1 green pepper, seeds and ribs removed
1 red pepper, seeds and ribs removed
1 large cucumber, peeled
115 g (4 oz) dark raisins
1 small garlic clove, finely chopped
55 g (2 oz) finely chopped fresh mint leaves
225 g (8 oz) finely chopped parsley leaves

1. Pour the tomato juice, lemon juice and olive oil into a medium-size bowl. Whisk together. Add couscous and stir until just combined. Cover and let it stand overnight.

2. Bring a medium-size pot of water to a boil. Plunge tomatoes in for one minute and peel. Cut them in half lengthways and remove seeds. Then cut into small dice. Cut green and red pepper into small dice. Cut cucumber in half lengthways and remove seeds. Dice finely. Place all vegetables in a medium-size bowl.

3. Cover the raisins with warm water and soak for about 10 minutes, or until they plump up. Add raisins and garlic to bowl of vegetables. Cover bowl and refrigerate overnight.

4. The next day, add the bowl of vegetables to the couscous, along with the mint and parsley. Taste for seasoning. Let rest for at least 4 hours, covered, in the refrigerator.

Note: When ready to eat, check the texture of the couscous. Since it's uncooked, it may be too firm. If so, add warm water until it reaches the desired consistency.

SUBSTANTIAL VEGETABLE SALADS

Over the last 20 years, Americans have increasingly wanted to eat salad as a first course. But the appetite isn't always tempted, or appeased, by a mere plate of greens. The solution that has emerged is a rich variety of 'vegetable' salads, much heartier than the classic salade verte. Here are 5 great ones, some classic, some creative, all in the spirit of the day.

WARM ARTICHOKE SALAD WITH BACON AND MUSTARD VINAIGRETTE

Once you master the knack of extracting the heart of an artichoke—it's really easy—this impressive salad is a snap to make.

SERVES 8 AS A FIRST COURSE

55g (2 oz) plain flour
50 ml (2 fl oz) fresh lemon juice
5 ml (1 tsp) salt
15 large artichokes
10 rashers bacon
20 ml (5 tsp) Dijon mustard
30 ml (2 tbsp) red-wine vinegar
125 ml (4 fl oz)olive oil
1.25 g (¼ tsp) finely chopped garlic
salt and pepper to taste
30 g (2 tbsp) finely chopped parsley

1. *Prepare a blanc:* Place the flour in a large pot, and beat in just enough cold water to make a smooth, medium-thick paste. Then beat in 2 litres (3½ pints) of cold water, the lemon juice and the salt. Bring to a boil, lower heat and simmer for 5 minutes.

2. Remove hearts from artichokes (see box).

3. Add the artichoke hearts to the water, bring to a boil, then simmer gently until the hearts are just tender when pierced with a knife, about 25 to 30 minutes. Remove pot from heat and allow the hearts to come to room temperature in the liquid.

4. Gently fry the bacon rashers. (Do not cook until crisp). Remove and reserve on paper towels.

5. Place the mustard in a mixing bowl. Using a whisk, beat in the vinegar. Drop by drop at first, then in a thin stream, beat in the olive oil; the mixture should be medium-thick. Add the garlic and season vinaigrette to taste with salt and pepper.

6. Remove warm artichoke hearts from liquid. Using a combination of spoon and sharp knife, remove the fuzzy choke from the centre of each one. Discard. Cut the remaining hearts into sixths. Place in large mixing bowl, and season with salt and pepper. Cut each bacon rasher into 6 pieces, and add to bowl. Toss with vinaigrette. Serve on 8 individual plates, sprinkled with chopped parsley.

Extracting an artichoke heart
You only need three things to extract an artichoke heart: a sharp little knife, a cut lemon and your hands. Putting all three to use, make sure to rub all cut artichoke surfaces immediately with the lemon.

First, remove the artichoke stem by bending it back until it snaps off. Place the artichoke on a flat surface; if it doesn't sit evenly, cut away any remaining pieces of stem until the artichoke has a smooth bottom. Don't forget to rub with lemon.

Pick up the artichoke in your hands, and start pulling leaves away from it. These leaves can be reserved for another use, like making an artichoke soup. Keep pulling until you have torn most of the leaves off, and you're left with something that looks like the old Apollo space capsule about to land in the water. You'll see immediately where the artichoke bottom is (it comes about a third of the way up the capsule), and you'll also see the cone of inner leaves rising out of the bottom. Cut off the cone of leaves, and use for soup. You are now holding an untrimmed artichoke heart. Your job is to trim it.

Make sure that the heart has no more leaves attached to it. Take your sharp knife, and cut around the heart to remove all bits of green; a whitish colour will emerge. For some dishes, you may want to make the heart look even, perfectly sculpted. For the warm artichoke salad with bacon and mustard vinaigrette, imperfection is just fine (because the heart's getting cut up later anyway). If you're not cooking the hearts immediately, keep them in a bowl of water to which you've added the juice of a lemon.

GRILLED AUBERGINE WITH FRESH MINT AND BALSAMIC VINEGAR

This delicious dish is great on its own, or over grilled slices of bread, as an appetiser. Or serve it as an accompaniment to any main-course grill.

SERVES 6 AS A FIRST COURSE

3 aubergines (about 450 g (1 lb) each)
30 ml (2 tbsp) extra-virgin olive oil plus a little additional for brushing aubergine
3 medium onions, thinly sliced
800-g (28-oz) can of tomatoes
115 g (4 oz) firmly packed, torn fresh mint leaves
30 ml (2 tbsp) balsamic vinegar
8 flat fillets of anchovies, finely chopped

1. Prepare a very hot charcoal fire.

2. Cut the top third off of each aubergine; reserve tops for another use. Cut a thin slice off of the other end. Stand each aubergine on a cut end. Peel one side of each aubergine (peeling away about one quarter of the skin), and then peel the opposite side (another one quarter of the skin). With each aubergine still standing on its cut end, and the unpeeled flesh of each one facing left and right, cut each into 8 vertical slices, approximately 8 mm (⅓ in) thick. The 24 slices should be rectangular, with a thin border of peel on two sides. Plunge them into salted, simmering water for 2 minutes. Remove and brush them lightly with olive oil.

3. When the fire is ready, place the aubergine slices over it in a single layer. Cover, but turn frequently, checking every 2 minutes or so to make sure the aubergines are not burning. (Alternatively, you can cook the aubergines under a grill on an oiled baking sheet.) The slices are done when they're brown on the outside, just tender within. Lay them out on one or more large dishes, in a single layer, and season both sides with salt and pepper. Transfer to a large mixing bowl.

4. *Prepare the tomato mixture:* Heat the olive oil in a large, heavy pan over moderately high heat. Add the sliced onions, and fry until they just start to turn yellow and soften (about 3 minutes). Squeeze the juice out of each canned tomato in your hand (reserving juice for another use), and add the tomatoes to the onions. Sauté for 1 minute. Season to taste.

5. In the large mixing bowl, cover the aubergine slices with the tomato-onion mixture. Add the mint leaves and sprinkle with the balsamic vinegar. Very gently, toss the salad together, trying to keep the aubergine slices as whole as possible. Let cool for 15 minutes, and serve at room temperature within a few hours. Just before serving, top with the chopped anchovies.

TUSCAN BREAD SALAD (PANZANELLA)

Now that the peasant dish panzanella has achieved near-cult status among American aficionados of authentic Tuscan cuisine, we are seeing all kinds of mixtures. If you want to taste the salad Tuscans love to eat in the summertime, you have to use the right bread, wet it properly and, most important, understand the kinds of versions. Consider what bread texture you're looking for in the finished salad. The bread in traditional panzanella is not like croutons. It is not chewy. It is not crusty. To the surprise of many Americans tasting the dish for the first time in Tuscany, the bread is light, a bit wet, airy, just short of mushy—something, believe it or not, like light, feathery matzo balls that have been broken up with a spoon.

SERVES 8

450 g (1 lb) coarse Italian bread (see box)
450 g (1 lb) long cucumbers
450 g (1 lb) sweet onions
10 g (2 tsp) salt plus additional to taste
700 g (1½ lb) ripe tomatoes, quartered
55 g (2 oz) torn fresh basil leaves
90 ml (6 tbsp) fruity extra-virgin olive oil
45 ml (3 tbsp) red-wine vinegar
pepper to taste

1. Cut the crusts off of the bread, tear the bread into large chunks and let stale for a week (see box).

2. When ready to make panzanella, peel the cucumbers, leaving alternating bands of peeled and unpeeled areas. Slice into rounds as thinly as possible. Peel the onions, cut in half, and slice as thinly as possible. Toss the cucumber and the onion in a colander with the salt. Place a weight over all, and let drain for 20 minutes.

3. While the cucumber and onion are draining, cut the tomatoes into thin slices, and measure out the basil leaves.

4. When ready to serve the salad, soak in cold water, then squeeze out the water (see box). Place the soaked bread in a large bowl. Mix in the cucumbers and onions, the tomatoes and the basil. Toss with the olive oil and the vinegar. Season to taste with salt and pepper and serve immediately.

Staling and soaking the bread

It's hard to give exact instructions for a perfect panzanella, because so many bread variables are involved: the type of bread you're using, how stale it is, whether your house is dry or humid, exactly how you soak and squeeze the bread.

For traditional panzanella, we like to use bread that is about a week old. When it's fresh, cut off the crusts, then tear the bread into large chunks. Leave out, uncovered, for a week. When ready to prepare panzanella, soak the staled bread in a bowl of cold water for about one minute, or just until it loses its firmness and becomes spongy. Squeeze the water out with your hand, but be careful to squeeze gently; squeezing too hard compacts the bread and destroys the airiness. Tear the bread into pieces about the size of wide, fat chips. Now you're ready for tossing.

If your bread is less stale—say, four days old— soak the staled bread in a bowl of cold water for half a minute or so, then proceed.

If your bread is less stale still—say, two days old—you probably won't need to soak it at all. Just run it briefly under cold water, then start squeezing. The finished product won't have as much texture as the week-old bread.

If your bread is only one day old, you won't need any water at all. Just toss it with the other ingredients, let sit for 30 minutes, and serve.

If you have no stale bread, don't despair. Place torn chunks of fresh bread in a 250°C (500°F) oven for 15 minutes. When they're crisp and golden, toss them with the tomatoes. Let sit for 30 minutes. Then toss with the rest of the ingredients.

Best Bread for Panzanella

The Tuscans use their wonderful, coarse, crunchy-crusted, unsalted loaves for panzanella. They are difficult to find elsewhere. So look for loaves of coarse, rustic, country-style bread from a good bakery. But make sure that the bread is not too dense. Though you want texture and structure in the bread, it should be shot through with airy holes that will make the finished product light. Ciabatta or foccacia from the supermarket will do in a pinch. Do not use soft bread such as white bread.

Crust or No Crust?

Traditional panzanella features crustless bread. But if you include the crust you may sacrifice the light and airy texture of the soaked bread although you will get more nutty flavour. If you're using bread with crust for our panzanella recipe, use only 350 g (12 oz) of bread.

Variations

Another surprise to Americans confronting real panzanella for the first time is the simplicity of ingredients: usually, only tomatoes, cucumbers, onions and basil are tossed with the bread. But you can supply all kinds of add-ons that will blend beautifully with panzanella's basic flavours, including chopped anchovies, stoned olives, diced celery, capers, chopped parsley, roasted red peppers and marinated artichoke hearts.

SALADE VERTE WITH HERBS AND WARM GOAT CHEESE CROÛTES

This simple French bistro idea has become wildly popular in many forms at everything from cross-cultural 'bistros' to informal California-style restaurants, to hoity-toity New American places. The reason? Goat cheese is great with greens. The standard version features goat cheese that's spread on round toast and grilled.

SERVES 6

1 shallot, finely chopped
30 ml (2 tbsp) fresh lemon juice
1 garlic clove, finely chopped
10 g (2 tsp) fresh thyme leaves
5 ml (1 tsp) Dijon mustard
50 ml (2 fl oz) walnut oil plus additional for
   drizzling on bread
salt and pepper to taste
six 2-cm (¾-in)-thick slices of Italian bread
   (7.5 cm (3 in) in diameter)
225 g (8 oz) log of soft mild goat cheese such as
   Montrachet, cut crossways into 6 rounds
450 g (1 lb) mesclun or other mixed greens, washed
   well and spun dry
45 g (3 tbsp) fresh parsley leaves

1. Whisk together the shallot, lemon juice, garlic, thyme and mustard in a small bowl. Add the walnut oil in a stream, whisking, and whisk the vinaigrette until it is emulsified. Season with salt and pepper. Reserve.

2. Preheat the grill and grill bread slices until lightly toasted. Drizzle with walnut oil and sprinkle with salt and pepper. Place goat cheese round on each slice and place back under grill until goat cheese is slightly melted, about 2 minutes.

3. While the goat cheese croûtes are grilling, toss the greens with the parsley, then with the reserved vinaigrette. Season with salt and pepper.

4. Divide the salad greens among 6 plates, arrange 1 goat cheese croûte on each plate, and serve salads immediately.

Variation: crusted goat cheese rounds

Instead of the goat cheese croûtes, you will also quite frequently see a round of goat cheese coated with crumbs and/or nuts placed on a green salad. This round has no bread base, as the croûtes do.

To make 6 crusted goat cheese rounds, preheat the oven to 200°C (400°F). Stir together 85 g (3 oz) breadcrumbs and 55 g (2 oz) ground walnuts on a plate. Whisk together 1 egg and 15 ml (1 tbsp) water in a shallow bowl. Dip 6 goat cheese rounds into the egg wash, dredge them in the crumb mixture and transfer to a lightly oiled baking sheet. Bake the goat cheese for 6 minutes. While the goat cheese is baking, toss the greens with the vinaigrette (see step 3). Divide the salad greens among 6 plates, arrange 1 goat cheese round on each plate, and serve salads immediately.

FRESH PORCINI SALAD WITH FENNEL, ROCKET AND SHAVED PARMIGIANO-REGGIANO

We're not generally enthusiastic about raw mushrooms. But if they're shaved paper-thin to make this classic Italian first course, they really are delicious. Porcini, of course—the wild mushrooms called cèpes in France— are by far the best mushrooms to use for this dish, by dint of their soft texture and deep, bosky flavour. If they're not available, however, you may substitute other mushrooms (see Note).

SERVES 4 AS A FIRST COURSE

55-g (2-oz) piece of Parmigiano-Reggiano
175 g (6 oz) thinly sliced fresh fennel
225 g (8 oz) fresh porcini mushrooms, stems
  removed and the mushrooms thinly sliced
50 ml (2 fl oz)extra-virgin olive oil
15 ml (1 tbsp) fresh lemon juice, or more to taste
salt and pepper to taste
bunch of rocket, stems discarded, leaves washed
  and spun dry
a few drops white truffle oil (optional)

1. Shave the Parmigiano-Reggiano into paper-thin slices with a vegetable peeler and set aside.

2. Combine the fennel and mushrooms in a bowl. Whisk together the olive oil and lemon juice in a small bowl. Season with salt and pepper. Pour the oil mixture over the mushroom mixture and combine well. Mix in the rocket leaves.

3. Arrange the mushroom mixture on 4 plates and top with the shaved cheese. Drizzle with truffle oil if desired.

Note: Here are the qualities that other raw mushrooms bring to this dish (mushrooms are listed in order of preference):

- Oyster mushrooms: spongy and chewy, like a bowl of rustic pasta—a surprising amount of flavour.
- Hedgehog mushrooms: soft like porcini, but little flavour.
- Regular cultivated (or button) mushrooms: a good crunchy chew, but devoid of flavour.
- Fresh shiitake: watery and tasteless.

For the mushrooms lacking flavour, a drizzle of white truffle oil supplies all the flavour you could ever want. We like to leave it off the salad, however, when the mushrooms (like porcini) already have their own flavour.

MAIN-COURSE SALADS

Twenty years ago, you'd have found virtually no one in America eating salad as a main course, either at dinner or lunch (except for the occasional chef's salad). During the gastronomic boom, however—which coincided with the health boom—Americans wanting lighter, more flavourful meals came up with all kinds of ways to have salad for lunch or dinner. Many of these salads include meat or fish, but protein's not at the centre of the plate. Here are some new, creative ideas for such salads.

SMOKED SALMON AND LENTIL SALAD WITH WALNUT OIL VINAIGRETTE

This winning combination is based on a dish we tried at a deluxe restaurant in Germany. Many chefs around the world today are bringing salmon and lentils together, in all kinds of dishes, but we've not tasted a union that beats this one. Follow with a hearty soup for a great wintertime dinner.

SERVES 4 AS A FIRST COURSE

115 g (4 oz) dried lentils (preferably French puy), washed
½ bottle dry white wine
salt to taste
10 ml (2 tsp) Dijon mustard
30 ml (2 tbsp) white-wine vinegar
125 ml (4 fl oz) walnut oil
pepper to taste
2 rashers bacon, fried and broken into small, crispy shreds
40 g (4 tsp) finely chopped shallots
225 g (8 oz) smoky smoked salmon, sliced thin
30 g (2 tbsp) fresh dill, finely chopped, plus additional dill for garnish
225 g (8 oz) salad greens
50 ml (2 fl oz) sour cream

1. *Prepare the lentils:* Place them in a small saucepan with the white wine, and add an equal amount of water. Salt to taste. Bring to a boil, then simmer until the lentils are just past tough (about 20 minutes). You must be very careful to taste constantly, for in 2 minutes the lentils can go from al dente to mush. When the lentils are done, drain them in a sieve and reserve. You will have about 225 ml (8 fl oz).

2. *Prepare the vinaigrette:* Place the mustard in a small mixing bowl. With a whisk, slowly beat in the vinegar until a yellow cream is formed. Drop by drop at first, then in a thin stream, beat in the walnut oil. You may have to beat vigorously to achieve a creamy-smooth dressing. Season to taste with salt and pepper.

3. Mix the reserved lentils with the bacon crisps, the shallots and one third of the walnut-oil vinaigrette.

4. Cut the salmon into 16 pieces; ideally, each one would be about 10 cm (4 in) long and 5 cm (2 in) wide. In a bowl, toss the slices with the lentils. Add 30 g (2 tbsp) dill. Wash and dry the salad greens and, in another bowl, toss them with half of the remaining vinaigrette.

5. *Assemble the dish:* Divide the salmon-lentil mixture among 4 plates, filling one side of each plate with it. Place the greens on the other side of each plate. Pour the remaining vinaigrette over the salmon, and decoratively spread some sour cream between salmon and salad. Garnish with dill.

SALAD OF BITTER GREENS WITH POACHED EGGS AND PROSCIUTTO FETTUNTA

One of our favourite dishes in French bistros is salad that has warm, runny eggs in it. This version, no less delicious, has an Italian accent: a slice of fettunta (the Tuscan name for bruschetta) with a piece of prosciutto sits under a poached egg. The bitter, Italianate lettuces are perfectly mellowed by the yellow yolk. This lightly dressed salad is a great brunch dish; you could make it more substantial by doubling the amount of eggs (serving two poached eggs per person).

SERVES 4

For the salad
50 g (2 oz) finely chopped shallots
(1 tbsp) balsamic vinegar
1 garlic clove, finely chopped
1 tsp Dijon mustard
50 ml (2 fl oz) extra-virgin olive oil
salt and pepper to taste
450 g (1 lb) coarsely shredded batavia
50 g (2 oz) very finely shredded radicchio
For the fettunta
4 x 1-2 cm (½-¾-in) slices of Tuscan or other crusty peasant bread
2 garlic cloves, halved

30 ml (2 tbsp) extra-virgin olive oil

2.5 g (½ tsp) chopped fresh herbs (such as flat-leaf parsley and/or rosemary)

salt and pepper to taste

115 g (4 oz) prosciutto

For the eggs

10 ml (2 tsp) white-wine vinegar

4 large eggs

1. *Make the salad:* Whisk together the shallots, balsamic vinegar, garlic and mustard in a large bowl. Add the olive oil in a stream, whisking, and whisk the vinaigrette until it is emulsified. Season to taste with salt and pepper. Wash and dry the escarole and radicchio and set aside.

2. *Make the fettunta:* Grill the bread on a rack set about 10 cm (4 in) over glowing coals, turning it once, until it is golden. (Alternatively, the bread may be toasted on a rack under a preheated grill about 10 cm (4 in) from the heat, turning it once or on a ridged grill pan over moderate heat.) Rub one side of each toast slice with the cut side of one of the garlic cloves, drizzle with the olive oil and sprinkle with herbs. Season the fettunta with salt and pepper and arrange it over each slice.

3. *Make the eggs:* Fill a wide frying pan with 5 cm (2 in) water and add vinegar. Bring to a rolling boil over high heat and reduce heat to a bare simmer. Poach eggs by breaking one into a saucer and sliding it into the water. As each egg goes in, immediately push white back towards the yolk with a large slotted spoon, moving egg gently, and simmer 3 minutes. Drain eggs separately in a slotted spoon, blot them carefully with paper towels, trim ragged edges of whites and sprinkle with salt and pepper.

4. Toss the batavia and radicchio with the vinaigrette until combined well. Season to taste. Divide the salad among 4 plates, arrange poached egg on the fettunta in centre of each plate and serve immediately.

GRILLED PRAWN SALAD WITH SUN-DRIED TOMATOES, CAPERS, FRESH BASIL AND TOASTED PINE NUTS

If you're in the proximity of a barbecue, a patio, a dozen friends—and if you're in the mood to reduce your guests' conversation to unintelligible semi-orgasmic murmurs—look no further than this outrageously delicious summertime salad. Is it Provençal? Ligurian? Californian? Who knows? Geography just doesn't count when food is this good.

SERVES 24 AS A BUFFET COURSE

1.8 kg (4 lb) medium prawns (about 120 to the pound), shelled and butterflied

10 g (2 tsp) salt

30 g (2 tbsp) finely chopped garlic

45 ml (3 tbsp) olive oil plus an additional 125 ml (4 fl oz) olive oil for dressing

freshly ground pepper to taste

2 tins flat fillets of anchovies

50 ml (2 fl oz) freshly squeezed lemon juice

55 g (2 oz) pine nuts

coarse salt to taste

225 g (8 oz) marinated sun-dried tomatoes, cut into large shreds

125 g (4 oz) capers

125 g (4 oz) torn fresh basil leaves

1. Toss the prawns with the salt, all but 5 g (1 tsp) of the garlic, and 45 ml (3 tbsp) olive oil. Season with freshly ground pepper. Let it sit for one hour, refrigerated.

2. *Prepare the dressing:* In the work bowl of a food processor, place the anchovies (including the oil from the tins), and the lemon juice. Purée. With the motor running, slowly drip 125 ml (4 fl oz) olive oil into the food processor, then thin with 30 ml (2 tbsp) of cold water. You should have a smooth, medium-thin dressing but if it's too thick, add a little more water. Reserve.

3. *Toast the pine nuts:* Place them on a roasting tin in a single layer, and cook them in a 200°C (400°F) oven until they turn golden-brown, about 6 minutes. Sprinkle with coarse salt and reserve.

4. Prepare a very hot charcoal fire. When the shrimp are ready to cook, place them on a fine-mesh grill over the coals. Turn them once for even cooking. Remove them as soon as they turn opaque (over a very hot fire, this may take as little as 2 minutes). (Alternatively, you can grill them under a grill, turning once.) Keep the prawns at room temperature until ready to assemble salad (up to 1 hour).

5. *To assemble:* Place the prawns in a large bowl. Mix well with the rest of the chopped garlic, the reserved pine nuts, and the reserved anchovy dressing. Toss the mixture with the sun-dried tomatoes, the capers and the basil. Serve immediately on a large platter or on individual plates.

Note: To serve this dish as a first course, simply correlate your guests' appetites and the number of prawns. The recipe can be divided in half, thirds, quarters, etc. If you wish to serve first-course portions to 6 guests, and if you wish those portions to have 5 prawns each (an adequate amount for a light starter), make only a quarter of this recipe. You could serve the salad on a bed of greens.

PASTA SALADS

Public confession and apology: Felipe Rojas-Lombardi, the first chef in our kitchen, was the chef who put pasta salad on the map. Since he more or less invented the modern genre, we have sold countless amounts of it. Today, the monster is out of control; bad pasta salad is everywhere, turning tons of good dried pasta into trays of gluey, soggy starch with very little flavour. Most Italians won't even go near the stuff, even if it's well made, claiming that pasta loses its attractive texture

once it loses its warm temperature.

We're not wild about pasta salad either, but we don't go as far as the Italians in denouncing it. If you choose the right pasta, the texture can remain interesting.

Generally, we like little shapes (though you'll see some exceptions below). We don't like fresh pasta or stuffed pasta in pasta salads. Don't overcook the pasta; in fact, undercooking it slightly is a good idea. Run the pasta under cold water when you remove it from the hot pan; this is heresy for regular hot pasta, but it makes a better texture in a pasta salad. Don't sauce the pasta until it's cool. And don't sauce it in advance, or it will soak up the sauce and the dish will seem dry.

LINGUINE WITH RAW TOMATOES AND BASIL

This is our favourite kind of pasta salad, a hot pasta dish that is served at room temperature. We know— we're cheating. But it's a delicious dish, anyway, especially in the summer: hot linguine tossed with fresh, uncooked tomatoes. This is an exception to the pasta salad rule we gave you before: for this dish, do not drain the pasta under cold water before using it.

SERVES 4 TO 6

1.3 kg (3 lb) very ripe tomatoes
45 ml (3 tbsp) red-wine vinegar
50 ml (2 fl oz) extra-virgin olive oil
15 ml (1 tbsp) pure olive oil
55 g (2 oz) coarsely chopped fresh basil leaves
30 g (2 tbsp) finely chopped garlic
salt and pepper to taste
450 g (1 lb) linguine
55 g (2 oz) freshly grated Parmigiano-Reggiano

1. *Prepare the sauce:* coarsely chop the tomatoes, making sure to reserve juice. Place tomatoes and juice in large bowl. Add the vinegar, 45 ml (3 tbsp) extra-virgin olive oil, and the basil.

2. Add the pure olive oil to a small frying pan over medium heat. Sauté the garlic for 3 minutes, stirring. (Do not allow it to brown.) Add to tomato mixture. Season to taste with salt and pepper. Let mixture sit at room temperature for at least 4 hours.

3. When ready to serve, cook linguine in a large pot of boiling, salted water. When pasta is al dente, drain in a large colander, then transfer to a large bowl. Toss the linguine with the rest of the extra-virgin olive oil and then with the Parmigiano-Reggiano.

4. Divide linguine among 4 to 6 bowls. Top each bowl with about 225 g (8 oz) tomato chunks, retrieved from the tomato mixture with a slotted spoon. Ladle the remaining liquid around the linguine in each bowl.

ORZO SALAD WITH LEMON, MINT AND RICOTTA SALATA

Orzo is a tiny form of pasta that resembles rice. Traditionally used in soups and as a Greek side dish, orzo is light and delicious in pasta salads. Ricotta salata is a firm, salted cheese made from sheep's milk with a texture similar to feta (which you could substitute); it's available at Dean & DeLuca and most Italian specialty food shops. This is one of the lightest pasta salads you'll ever taste; it's especially good in the summer alongside grilled fish.

SERVES 4 TO 6

50 ml (2 fl oz) extra-virgin olive oil
70 g (2½ oz) finely chopped shallots
30 ml (2 tbsp) fresh lemon juice
1 garlic clove, finely chopped
2.5 ml (½ tsp) finely grated lemon zest, or more to taste
salt and pepper to taste
225 g (8 oz) uncooked orzo
55 g (2 oz) very finely diced yellow pepper
125 g (4 oz) very finely diced seedless cucumber

75 g (3 oz) crumbled ricotta salata cheese
45 g (3 tbsp) finely chopped fresh mint leaves

1. Stir together the olive oil, shallots, lemon juice, garlic and lemon zest in a small bowl. Season to taste with salt and pepper.

2. Cook the orzo in a large pot of boiling salted water until al dente. Drain pasta completely in a colander, running under cold water. Transfer orzo to a bowl, stir in the olive oil mixture and let cool. Stir in the pepper, cucumber, ricotta salata and mint until well mixed. You could serve the salad immediately, but we think it tastes best if it stands at room temperature for 2 to 3 hours.

RADIATORE SALAD WITH OLIVES

Though we find that thick, short shapes of pasta often make a starchy chew in pasta salad, the convoluted radiatore (they look like little heaters) create a very complicated chew—which adds lots of fun to any pasta salad. This one tastes like a salad version of a good southern Italian pasta dish.

SERVES 12

900 g (2 lb) radiatore
salt and pepper to taste
25 g (1 oz) sun-dried tomatoes
900 g (2 lb) plum tomatoes
125 ml (4 fl oz) olive oil plus additional for brushing tomatoes
2 garlic cloves, peeled and crushed
2 tablespoons fresh basil leaves, chopped
30 ml (2 tbsp) balsamic vinegar
225 g (8 oz) full-flavoured black olives, stoned and sliced
225 g (8 oz) full-flavoured green olives, stoned and sliced
115 g (4 oz) very finely chopped parsley

1. Cook pasta in a large kettle of boiling salted water

until al dente. Run under cold water, drain, and place in a large bowl. Season pasta with salt and pepper.

2. Place sun-dried tomatoes in a small saucepan with enough water to just cover them. Bring to a boil, turn off heat, and let sit for a few minutes.

3. Preheat oven to 230°C (450°F). Remove the stems from the plum tomatoes, cut each tomato in half lengthways, and place on a roasting tin. Brush tomatoes with a little olive oil and bake for 10 minutes, or until tomatoes are light brown on both sides. Remove and let cool.

4. In a food processor purée garlic, basil, sun-dried tomatoes and the balsamic vinegar. Add olive oil in a thin stream.

5. Add the roasted tomatoes and the olives to the bowl of pasta. Add the dressing. Season with salt and pepper. Garnish with parsley. Serve at room temperature.

PERCIATELLI WITH A VEGETABLE JULIENNE
This light, fresh, summery pasta salad features the crunch of julienne vegetables. It's a bit like pasta primavera at room temperature, minus the cream.

SERVES 12

900 g (2 lb) cooked perciatelli or spaghetti
12 spring onions
4 large carrots, peeled
2 large courgettes
2 large yellow marrows (squash)
4 large garlic cloves
90 ml (6 tbsp) olive oil
salt and pepper to taste
225 g (8 oz) fresh basil leaves
30 ml (2 tbsp) Dijon mustard
125 ml (4 fl oz) red-wine vinegar

1. Cook perciatelli in a large pot of boiling salted water

until just al dente. Run under cold water, drain and place in a large bowl.

2. Remove roots from spring onions and slice into rings. Slice carrots, courgettes and yellow marrow in half at the middle. Cut again into thin strips lengthways, the thickness of the pasta.

3. Preheat oven to 180°C (350°F). In a medium bowl mix together all cut vegetables, garlic cloves, 30 ml (2 tbsp) olive oil and salt and pepper to taste. Place vegetable mixture on roasting tin and cook for 4 minutes, or until just softened. (Be careful not to overcook.)

4. Remove garlic from roasting tin, and place it in a food processor. Add the mustard and vinegar. While the machine is running, add the rest of the of olive oil. Season with salt and pepper.

5. Add vegetables and dressing to the pasta and mix well. Chop the basil, reserving a few whole ones for garnish, and add it. Serve at room temperature, garnished with the whole leaves.

PENNE WITH ROASTED TOMATOES AND FENNEL
Here's another pasta salad that has the best possible recommendation: it tastes like a pasta dish, not a pasta salad.

SERVES 18

1.3 kg (3 lb) penne
2 kg (4½ lb) plum tomatoes
200 ml (7 fl oz) olive oil
salt and pepper to taste
3 large fennel bulbs, thinly sliced
3 medium onions, thinly sliced
3 garlic cloves, crushed
350 g (12 oz) chopped mixed stoned olives
75 ml (5 tbsp) balsamic vinegar
75 g (3 oz) fresh dill, coarsely chopped

1. Bring 4 l (7 pints) water to a boil. Add a handful of salt. Cook the penne for about 8 minutes, or until al dente. Drain and refresh under cold water. (If pasta sticks together, add a few tablespoons of olive oil and gently toss.) Set aside in a large bowl.

2. Preheat oven to 200°C (400°F). Remove stems of tomatoes and cut the tomatoes in sixths lengthways. Put on a roasting tin, brush with 3 tablespoons olive oil and sprinkle with salt and pepper. Roast in oven for about 15 minutes, or until tomatoes are very soft. Remove pan from oven. Set tomatoes aside on a plate to cool.

3. Slice fennel and onions thinly. Spread evenly on roasting tin. Brush with 45 ml (3 tbsp) olive oil and sprinkle with salt and pepper. Roast, stirring occasionally, for about 15 minutes, or until softened but not mushy. When done, remove from oven and set aside.

4. Add 175 ml (6 fl oz) olive oil and the garlic to a small pan and heat slowly. Once hot, remove from heat and add olives.

5. Add the olive oil, olives, balsamic vinegar, cooled tomatoes, fennel, onions and dill to the bowl of pasta. Mix well. Season to taste with salt and pepper.

POTATO SALADS

Potato salad once meant only the mayonnaise-based stuff at the deli counter—and it still means that to many Americans! Well, it can be delicious when it's done right. The last two decades have brought a greater latitude in potato salad, with new ideas streaming in from several directions.

GERMAN POTATO SALAD

Out of fashion for some years, a mayonnaise-less potato salad cooked with bacon, dressed with vinegar and served warm is being rediscovered today by a new generation of Americans. It was originally associated with German immigrants and was usually called 'German potato salad'. This one has been modernised with an intriguing twist: the addition of a little cornflour, which gives the salad a sophisticated, velvety texture.

SERVES 4

1.8 kg (4 lb) red potatoes
140 g (5 oz) bacon, in 5-mm (¼-in) dice
2 finely chopped medium onions
125 ml (4 fl oz) white-wine vinegar plus a little
   additional to taste
7 g (1½ tsp) sugar
10 g (2 tsp) cornflour
175 ml (6 fl oz) water
salt and pepper to taste
1 egg, beaten
10 g (1 tbsp) chopped fresh chives for garnish

1. Fill a large pot two-thirds full with water, add salt, and bring to a boil. Cook potatoes with skins on until just past crunchy, about 7 or 8 minutes. Drain and set aside.

2. Cook bacon and onions in a large heavy frying pan over moderate heat until the onion softens but does not brown, about 6 minutes.

3. Add the vinegar and sugar to the pan and bring to a boil over high heat.

4. Mix the cornflour with a few teaspoons of the water and make a smooth paste. Add the paste to the frying pan and mix well, scraping the bottom of the pan with a wooden spoon. Add the remaining water and return to a boil. Reduce the heat to low and continue to cook for 10 minutes, or until the mixture has a velvety texture.

5. When the potatoes are cool enough to handle, peel them, cut them into 5-mm (¼-in) slices and place them in a large mixing bowl. Sprinkle with salt and pepper to taste. Pour the bacon and onion mixture, along with the beaten egg, over the potatoes. Gently mix all ingredients well; do not break the potato slices. Mix in a little additional vinegar to taste. Sprinkle salad with chives and serve warm.

WARM POTATO SALAD WITH SWISS CHEESE AND GARLIC SAUSAGE

When you turn to French-style potato salad, there's still no mayonnaise! The key to a great, French-style potato salad is mixing the potatoes *while they're still warm* with stock or wine, giving the potatoes an extra measure of flavour. There's no dearth of flavour in the following variation—the potatoes are joined by thin slices of garlicky sausage, great herbs and little flecks of Swiss cheese (which bring everything meltingly together).

SERVES 4 AS A FIRST COURSE

4 x 175-g (6-oz) potatoes, peeled
225 ml (8 fl oz) chicken stock
75 ml (3 fl oz) white wine
10 ml (2 tsp) Dijon mustard
60 ml (4 tsp) white-wine vinegar
75 ml (2½ fl oz) olive oil
coarse salt to taste
freshly ground pepper to taste
115 g (4 oz) French garlic sausage
  (saucisson à l'ail)
60 g (4 tsp) finely chopped fresh tarragon leaves
10 g (2 tsp) finely chopped fresh chives
10 g (2 tsp) finely chopped fresh parsley
60 g (4 tsp) tiny, tiny bits of Gruyère cheese (the
  size of sesame seeds)
leaves of soft lettuce

1. Steam the potatoes in salted water until just tender (about 30 minutes); they should still be ever so slightly crunchy at the centre. While the potatoes are cooking, boil the chicken stock and the white wine in a heavy saucepan until reduced to a scant 125 ml (4 fl oz).

2. Meanwhile, prepare the vinaigrette. Place the mustard in a small bowl, whisk in the vinegar, then, drop by drop at first and later in a thin stream, whisk in the olive oil. Blend until smooth. Set aside.

3. When the potatoes are cooked, cut them in 3-mm (⅛-in) slices, and place on large plate or in roasting tin. Drizzle the reduced chicken stock over the potato slices. Season on both sides with coarse salt and freshly ground pepper. Let the potatoes absorb the stock for 5 minutes, then pour off any extra stock. Meanwhile, simmer the garlic sausage in the water used to steam the potatoes. Remove when just warm, and slice into thin rounds, about 2.5 cm (1 inch) in diameter. If the diameter of the sausage is larger, cut each round into smaller pieces. Intersperse sausage slices with the potato slices. Sprinkle the tarragon, chives, parsley and Swiss cheese bits over all. Whisk the vinaigrette a moment, and spread evenly over the potatoes and sausages. Toss very gently. Place soft lettuce leaves on each of 4 plates, and top with potato salad. Serve while salad is still warm.

GARLIC-ROASTED NEW POTATO SALAD

Finally, the mayonnaise you've been waiting for— though this spectacular New American version is different from any standard potato-and-mayonnaise salad you've ever tasted. It is for garlic lovers only. We like it best when it's warm or at room temperature.

SERVES 4 AS A SIDE DISH

650 g (1 lb 8 oz) small new potatoes, quartered
30 g (2 tbsp) olive oil
5 g (1 tsp) dried rosemary
8 cloves garlic, finely chopped
10 g (2 tsp) salt
5 ml (1 tsp) coarsely ground black pepper
125 ml (4 fl oz) mayonnaise
45 ml (3 tbsp) finely chopped parsley
1 lemon, halved

1. In a large gratin dish, toss the potatoes, olive oil, rosemary, two thirds of the garlic and the salt and pepper until the garlic and oil are well distributed. Spread the potatoes in a single layer with the skin sides facing down. Preheat the oven to 230°C (450°F). Place gratin dish in the oven and cook for about 45 minutes, or until potatoes begin to brown; shake pan after the first 20 minutes and again after 15 more minutes. Take potatoes out of the oven and let cool for 15 minutes. Remove potatoes from the pan with a metal spatula to avoid breaking the potatoes and place them in a large bowl.

2. In a small bowl, mix the mayonnaise with the remaining garlic and the parsley. Squeeze the juice of the lemon halves, making sure to remove seeds, into the mayonnaise. Stir until it is smooth.

3. Combine mayonnaise with the potatoes and serve.

ASIAN SALADS

Our modern national passion for salads has been abetted by our growing familiarity with Asian cuisines; we are plucking the classic salads of Thailand, Japan, Vietnam, China and India and putting them on tables across America. We are also deliriously creating new variations on ancient oriental themes.

CHINESE CHICKEN SALAD WITH CARROTS AND STAR ANISE

This creative, light, room-temperature salad features a subtle whiff of anise. If you want more anise flavour (not everyone likes it), include the optional 5-spice powder listed below, which includes anise. By the way, the unusual technique for cooking the chicken breasts ensures moist, tender slices of chicken.

SERVES 4 AS A FIRST COURSE

175 ml (6 fl oz) thin soy sauce
35 ml (7 tsp) sugar

2.5 g (½ tsp) 5-spice powder (optional)
175 ml (6 fl oz) light rice-wine vinegar
3 g (¾ tsp) Chinese sesame oil
50 g (2 oz) crumbled star anise
50 g (2 oz) broad, thin slices of peeled fresh ginger root
450 g (1 lb) skinless boneless chicken breasts
500 ml (18 fl oz) chicken stock
8 medium spring onions
115 g (4 oz) carrots
45 ml (3 tbsp) groundnut oil
salt and pepper to taste

1. In a bowl blend the soy sauce, 40 g (4 tsp) of the sugar, the five-spice powder (if used), 50 ml (2 fl oz) of the rice-wine vinegar, and 1.25ml (¼ tsp) of the sesame oil. Blend in the star anise and the ginger. Place the chicken breasts in the mixture, making sure that they're covered by the marinade. Cover, and refrigerate for at least 8 hours and no more than 24 hours.

2. When ready to serve, remove the chicken breasts from the marinade, and place the marinade, including the ginger and star anise, into a small saucepan. Add the chicken stock and bring to a boil. Turn off the heat, and place the chicken breasts into the saucepan. Leave until the chicken breasts are just barely past pink at the centre, about 10 minutes. Remove. Slice as thinly as you can into broad, horizontal slices,and place the slices in a bowl. Chop 2 spring onions very finely (white and light green parts only), and mix with chicken slices. Reserve.

3. Peel the carrots, and make long, thin diagonal slices. You should have approximately the same number of carrot slices as chicken slices. To the pan in which you cooked the chicken, add the rest of the rice-wine vinegar, the rest of the sugar, and 4 finely chopped spring onions (white and green parts). Bring mixture to a boil, then add the carrot slices. Boil until the carrots have just lost their crunch, about 7 minutes. Remove carrots, and reserve. Continue boiling the mixture until it is reduced to a scant 125 ml (4 fl oz). Strain the mixture into a small bowl. Slowly beat in the rest of the sesame oil and the peanut oil, and beat until the oils are well incorporated.

4. Toss the chicken slices and carrot slices together with the dressing. Bring to room temperature (about 15 minutes), season well with salt and pepper, and serve. Garnish with the remaining 2 spring onions, very finely chopped.

Note: If you want a more striking, more elegant presentation, arrange the carrots and chicken slices on four small plates. They look best if arranged on each plate in a circular pattern, with alternating chicken and carrot slices. Pour the sauce over the salads, distributing evenly. Wait 5 minutes and serve, garnished with chopped spring onions.

THAI SQUID SALAD

SERVES 4 AS A FIRST COURSE

450g (1 lb) squid, on the small side, including
  tentacles
30 ml (2 tbsp) vegetable oil
2.5 g (½ tsp) Thai chilli powder, or more to taste
2.5 g (½ tsp) salt
10 g (2 tsp) very finely chopped hearts of
  lemongrass
4 cloves garlic, ground to a paste
2 inner celery stalks, cut into julienne strips
3 slices purple onion (about 5-mm (¼-in) each),
  broken into rings
50 ml (2 fl oz) fresh lime juice
30 ml (2 tbsp) Thai fish sauce
15 ml (1 tbsp) sugar
10 fresh mint leaves, chopped
75 g (3 oz) coarsely chopped coriander leaves
leafy green lettuce as a base

1. Clean the squid (see page 373), or get the fishmonger to do it for you. Cut the tentacles into several serving pieces. Cut the main part of the squid into two long halves. Score each half with a sharp knife, making a diamond pattern. Then cut the halves into strips that are approximately 5 x 1 cm (2 x ½ in).

2. Add the oil to a large, hot omelette pan over high heat. When the oil is sizzling, add the squid. Sauté for about 5 minutes, or until the squid has rendered some liquid and the liquid has evaporated. Remove squid and toss with chilli powder, salt, lemongrass and garlic. Let cool.

3. Just before serving, toss squid with celery and purple onion. Mix together the lime juice, fish sauce, and sugar and add to squid mixture. Toss with mint leaves and coriander. Lay salad on a bed of leafy green lettuce (either on a dish or on individual plates), and serve immediately.

THAI CUCUMBER SALAD
This is an extremely refreshing accompaniment to an authentic Thai dinner, or to any meal that could stand a bit of sweet-sour excitement on the side. The salad is best when made just before serving; when it's held, the flavours get more profound but the cucumbers get more watery.

SERVES 4 AS A SIDE DISH

2 large cucumbers (about 350 g (12 oz) each)
1 large purple onion (about 280 g (10 oz))
10 g (2 tsp) very finely minced lime zest (green part
  only)
30 g (2 tbsp) finely slivered green or red hot chillies
  (optional)
30 g (2 tbsp) sugar
50 ml (2 fl oz) fresh lime juice
30 ml (2 tbsp) Thai fish sauce
fresh coriander leaves for garnish

1. Wash the cucumbers, and, with a vegetable peeler, cut 8 evenly spaced strips of peel off each one. Cut the cucumbers into extremely thin diagonal slices, and place in a large mixing bowl.

2. Peel the onion, cut into the thinnest possible slices, and place them in the bowl with the cucumbers, breaking the onion slices into individual rings. Add the lime zest and the chilli slivers (if using), and toss together well.

3. In a separate mixing bowl, place the sugar. Whisk in the lime juice until the sugar is well blended. Whisk in the fish sauce. Pour mixture over the cucumbers, and blend well. Garnish with coriander leaves, and serve immediately.

Thai salads

Nothing in Thai cuisine excites us more than salads. The Thai salad concept differs from the traditional Western one; Thai salads are often made with fish, or poultry or meat; always dressed with a thin sauce that contains no oil; traditionally served at the same time as all the other courses in a Thai meal; and invariably garnished to the nines.

The Thai squid salad is authentic, but you could substitute for the squid 450 g (1 lb) of any fish, poultry or red meat that you desire. The dressing in this salad— 50 ml (2 fl oz) fresh lime juice, 30 ml (2 tbsp) Thai fish sauce, and 15 ml (1 tbsp) sugar—is a good basic dressing for any Thai salad.

As to garnishes, the Thais employ elaborately carved fruits and vegetables to garnish their salads, which are usually presented on platters to make the greatest visual impression. Feel free to take your knife to cucumbers, chillies, spring onions, lemons, limes and other fruit and vegetables to create garnishes for these salads.

JAPANESE SPINACH SALAD (OSHITASHI)

There's a wonderful method in traditional Japanese cooking: quickly boil leafy vegetables, then mix them with a cooled, flavoured stock and let them sit for 3 to 6 hours. The result, served cold or at room temperature, might be construed by Westerners as a light and lovely salad. You could serve it either as a first course (for which you might pack the prepared spinach into small round or rectangular moulds, and then unmould them on hors d'œuvre plates), or as a side dish.

SERVES 4 AS A SIDE DISH

> 900 g (2 lb) fresh, tender spinach, untrimmed (or 650 g (1 lb 8 oz) trimmed and washed fresh spinach)
> 450 ml (18 fl oz) strong dashi, cooled (see instructions for homemade or powdered dashi on page 64)
> 20 ml (4 tsps) thin soy sauce
> 10 ml (2 tsps) Japanese rice vinegar
> a few drops dark sesame oil (about 1 ml/ ⅛ teaspoon)

1. Bring a large pot of salted water to a boil.

2. Trim the roots (about 2.5 cm (1 in)) off the spinach leaves. If your leaves have no roots, only stems, leave the stems. Wash the spinach in a large bowl, changing the water several times. Plunge the leaves into the boiling water and cook for one minute. Remove, and refresh with cold water. Wring out the spinach gently in your hands. Don't squeeze too hard; don't bruise; spread the leaves out after squeezing so they don't compact.

3. Mix together the dashi, soy sauce, rice vinegar, and sesame oil. Place the spinach in a bowl, and pour the dashi mixture over it (it should just cover the spinach). Refrigerate for 3 to 6 hours, then serve spinach, with a little of the stock sprinkled over it. At 3 hours the dish is light and clean; at 6 hours it has maximum flavour from the stock.

Serving options

One of the virtues of *oshitashi* is its simplicity and cleanness. But if you'd like a bit more drama—particularly if you're serving it as an appetizer—you could add one or more of the following:

- Sesame oil—just drizzle on a bit before serving
- Toasted sesame seeds—sprinkle on top
- Lemon juice—squeeze a little on top, and garnish with a thin slice of lemon
- Shaved bonito—sprinkle on top
- Shredded nori (Japanese seaweed sheets)—toast, cut and sprinkle on top

A great, ultra-convenient way to get shredded seaweed is to buy nori komi furikake—dried seaweed shreds with sesame seeds in a jar, available in Japanese groceries. All you have to do is open the jar and sprinkle. They make a great garnish for vegetables, or any Japanese-inspired salad.

INDIAN RAITA WITH CUCUMBER, TOMATO AND ONION

The thin, watery side-dish served in many Indian restaurants does not even suggest the sumptuousness of a proper Indian raita, or yogurt salad. For starters, Indian yogurt is quite rich, and so in this recipe we recommend draining the yogurt in cheesecloth. An Indian raita can have a variety of ingredients, from raw vegetables to cooked vegetables to fruit and nuts. We love the following recipe—crunchy with raw vegetables, fragrant with fresh herbs—which serves as an ideal accompaniment to any Indian main course.

SERVES 4 TO 6 AS A SIDE DISH

2 long cucumbers (about 350 g (12 oz) each)
15 g (1 tbsp) salt
500 ml (18 fl oz) plain yogurt
1 large tomato, seeded and diced
1 medium red onion, finely chopped
45 ml (3 tbsp) fresh lemon juice

45 ml (3 tbsp) chopped fresh mint
50 g (2 oz) roughly chopped coriander plus
    additional leaves for garnish
½ teaspoon ground cumin

1. Slice cucumbers thinly, and place in a colander set over a bowl. Add 10 g (2 tsp) of the salt and stir. Allow to drain for 2 hours.

2. Place yogurt in a colander lined with a layer of cheesecloth (muslin) and allow to drain for 2 hours. (Yield after draining should be 225 ml (8 fl oz).)

3. Combine cucumbers and yogurt in a medium bowl and stir well. Add tomato, onion, lemon juice, mint, coriander, cumin and the rest of the salt (or to taste). Mix well. Refrigerate for 2 to 3 hours to allow flavours to mingle.

S O U P S

SOUP WAS ONCE THE LEAST INTERESTING PART OF AN AMERICAN MEAL. MUCH
OF IT CAME OUT OF CANS, AND EVEN THOSE SOUPS THAT DIDN'T WERE
NUMBINGLY DULL IN THEIR PREDICTABILITY. SOUP WAS ALWAYS SERVED BEFORE
THE MAIN COURSE AND RARELY SET HEARTS AFLUTTER.

HAPPILY, THE CATEGORY HAS BOOMED IN AMERICA IN SEVERAL WAYS OVER
THE LAST 20 YEARS. OUR NATIONAL QUEST FOR LIGHTER DINING HAS CREATED
A GENERATION OF AMERICANS HAPPY TO MAKE A MEAL OUT OF SOUP—AND
THIS HAS NECESSARILY LED TO MORE INTERESTING SOUPS, AND MORE VARIETY
IN SOUPS. AT THE SAME TIME, WE HAVE BECOME INCREASINGLY FAMILIAR WITH
OUR OWN REGIONAL TRADITIONS, WITH EUROPEAN REGIONAL TRADITIONS AND
WITH THE CUISINES OF ASIA—ALL OF WHICH HAVE SUPPLIED RICH
POSSIBILITIES FOR SOUP-MAKERS.

AMERICAN CLASSICS AND VARIATIONS

Classic

NEW ENGLAND CLAM CHOWDER

There have long been two main styles of the white-coloured New England clam chowder, both of which we find unattractive. Under the name of this great soup, mediocre restaurants throughout New England serve a thick sludge that can be used as book paste. Many home chefs, however, serve a thin version, unthickened with flour, that has the consistency of boiled milk (which is what their chowder is made from); we find this too thin to be truly interesting. The following version is neither too thin nor too thick; to our taste, it is what New England clam chowder oughta be.

SERVES 8

48 cherrystone clams (or cockles)
a little bottled clam juice (if necessary)
500 ml (18 fl oz) milk
500 ml (18 fl oz) double cream
3 large potatoes, peeled and cut into 1-cm (½-in)
  cubes
115 g (4 oz) bacon, cut into
5-mm (¼-in) dice
2 medium onions, finely chopped
3 stalks celery, cut into 5-mm (¼-in) dice
30 g (2 tbsp) flour
1.25 g (¼ tsp) cayenne pepper
salt to taste
white pepper to taste
50 g (2 oz) butter

1. Wash the clams (cockles) well under cold running water in a colander. Place them in a large pot, and add water to cover by 5 cm (2 in). Cover the pan and place over high heat.

2. When the water comes to a boil, give the pan a good shake. Turn the heat to low, and cook another 30 seconds or so. Remove from the heat, and remove all the clams that have opened, using a slotted spoon. If any clams remain closed, put back on the heat, with the lid on the pan, and cook another 1 to 2 minutes. Remove remaining clams, reserve, and discard any that have not opened.

3. Pour the cooking liquid through a fine strainer and set aside. You will need 1.3 litres (2¼ pints) of liquid. If you have more than enough, reduce it to 1.3 litres (2¼ pints). If you have too little, add some bottled clam juice or water to make 1.3 litres (2¼ pints) total.

4. Pour the milk and cream in a saucepan and bring to a boil. Bring the heat down to a low simmer, and reduce the mixture for 30 minutes.

5. Fill a large pan with water and bring the potatoes to a boil. Cook until the potatoes are just cooked through, about 8 minutes. Drain potatoes and set aside.

6. Put the bacon in a large, heavy saucepan and cook over moderate heat, stirring, until the bacon just begins to brown. Remove the bacon from the pan and pour off excess fat, leaving behind about 3 tablespoons of fat in the pan.

7. Cook onions and celery in bacon fat over moderate heat until soft, about 4 minutes. Add cooked bacon, lower heat and stir in flour. Cook for another 2 minutes, stirring to prevent mixture from sticking to pan.

8. Add reserved clam cooking liquid to onions, celery and bacon. Bring to a boil and stir well. Add potatoes, reduce heat and simmer for 5 minutes.

9. Add the cream mixture to the chowder, and simmer over low heat. While chowder is simmering, remove the clams from their shells and cut in quarters. Add the clams and cayenne pepper to the chowder, and season further with salt and white pepper. Simmer for 5 minutes more. Serve the chowder in warm bowls with a knob of butter in the centre of each serving.

Classic

___

MANHATTAN CLAM CHOWDER

New Englanders find the very idea of tomatoes in clam chowder to be abhorrent; of course, by referring to the aberration as 'Manhattan clam chowder' they're overlooking the fact that their own Rhode Islanders also add tomatoes to clam chowder. And let's not forget about the hundreds of ethnic cuisines around the world that combine tomatoes with shellfish in soups and stews. Unlike the New England purists, we just don't find an intrinsic problem with clams and tomatoes. We do find, however, that most Manhattan clam chowder served in restaurants is positively awful: thin, unclammy, often tasting like vegetable soup out of a can with a few canned clams thrown in. Try the following recipe, and you'll see how good this soup can be.

SERVES 6

48 cherrystone clams (cockles)
a little bottled clam juice (if necessary)
115 g (4 oz) bacon, cut into 5-mm (¼-in) dice
1 large onion, peeled and cut into 5-mm (¼-in) dice
1 celery stalk, cut into 5-mm (¼-in) dice
1 carrot, cut into 5-mm (¼-in) dice
2 medium russet potatoes, peeled and cut into 1-cm (½-in) cubes
800 g (1 lb 12 oz) canned plum tomatoes, drained and coarsely chopped
2 teaspoons fresh thyme leaves

1. Wash the clams well under cold running water in colander. Place in a large pot and add enough water to cover clams by 5 cm (2 in). Cover the pan and place over high heat.

2. When the water comes to a boil, give the pan a good shake. Turn the heat to low, and cook clams another 30 seconds or so. Remove from the heat, and remove any clams that have opened, using a slotted spoon. If any remain closed, cover and cook another 1 to 2 minutes. Remove remaining clams, and discard any that have not opened.

3. Strain the clam juice through a fine strainer and set aside. You will need 1.3 litres (2¼ pints) of liquid. If you have more than enough, reduce it to 1.3 litres (2¼ pints). If you have too little, add some bottled clam juice or water to make 1.3 litres (2¼ pints) total.

4. Put the bacon into a large, heavy saucepan and cook over moderate heat, stirring, until the bacon begins to brown. Pour off excess fat, leaving bacon and about 3 tablespoons of fat in the pan.

5. Add the onion, celery and carrot to the pan and cook until soft, about 10 minutes. Add potatoes, and cook mixture for 10 minutes more. Add tomatoes and reserved clam juice to the pan. Bring chowder to a boil over high heat.

6. While chowder is cooking, remove clams from their shells and chop coarsely. Add to chowder and reduce heat to low. Add thyme leaves. Cook over low heat for another 5 minutes; check to make sure potatoes are soft and chowder is well seasoned. Remove and allow to sit for 5 minutes. Serve in warm bowls.

Variation

___

THE COMPROMISE CLAM CHOWDER

If you can't decide which chowder to make—New England or Manhattan—pick this one. Yes, it has a few tomatoes in it (the result is pinkish, not red), but it also has a New England kind of creaminess. Most important, the incredible technique of puréeing clams and adding them to the chowder creates the clammiest, deepest version of clam chowder you've ever tasted. For avowed clamheads only.

SERVES 6

36 very large cherrystone clams (cockles) (or 450 g (1 lb) fresh shelled clams)
450 ml (16 fl oz) fresh liquid from the clams (or bottled clam juice)
450 ml (16 fl oz) non-salty fish or chicken stock
50 g (2 oz) unsalted butter
3 medium leeks, white parts only, cut into thin rounds
2 celery stalks, finely chopped
½ medium green pepper, finely chopped
30 g (2 tbsp) plain flour
2 medium potatoes, peeled and diced
800 g (1 lb 12 oz) can tomatoes
25 g (1 oz) fresh thyme leaves (or 5 g (1 tsp) dried) plus fresh thyme sprigs for garnish

1. Shell the clams (cockles), if using fresh ones, reserving 450 ml (16 fl oz) of liquid. Place the liquid (or the bottled clam juice) in a small saucepan with the fish or chicken stock, and bring to a boil.

2. Melt the butter over moderately high heat in a large, heavy pot. Add the leeks, celery and green pepper. Cook, stirring, for 10 minutes (do not allow to brown). Reduce heat to moderate and add the flour. Blend well, and cook for 2 minutes, stirring. Add the boiling clam juice and stock, and stir well. Add the potatoes. Mash each tomato in your hand over the soup pot, and drop the tomatoes into the soup (Reserve tomato liquid in can for another use). Add the thyme leaves. Simmer for 20 minutes.

3. While the soup is simmering, place 175 g (6 oz) of shelled clams in the work bowl of a food processor and purée. Coarsely chop the rest.

4. When ready to serve, reduce heat and bring the soup down to a bare simmer. Vigorously stir in the clam purée. Place the coarsely chopped clams in a small saucepan with a ladleful of chowder, and heat for 20 seconds over low heat. Divide the chowder among 6 warm bowls. Top each bowl with some of the coarsely chopped clams and garnish with a sprig of thyme.

Classic

MILD OKRA-THICKENED GREEN GUMBO WITH CHICKEN, PRAWNS AND FRESH HERBS

Owing to the immense popularity of Cajun food, no American soup has received as much attention in the American Soup Renaissance as gumbo. There are, of course, as many gumbos as there are Cajuns. This is a particularly lovely, bright-green, fresh-tasting version, without a spicy-hot payload.

SERVES 6

75 ml (3 fl oz) vegetable oil
12 rashers bacon
8 boneless chicken thighs
75 g (3 oz) flour
450 g (1 lb) chopped onion
225 g (8 oz) chopped green pepper
175 g (6 oz) chopped celery
450 g (1 lb) fresh or thawed frozen okra
60 g (2 tbsp) finely chopped fresh thyme leaves plus branches of fresh thyme for garnish
15 g (1 tbsp) finely chopped fresh rosemary
15 g (1 tbsp) finely chopped fresh sage
2 bay leaves
5 g (1 tsp) freshly ground black pepper plus additional to taste
big pinch of nutmeg
2 litres (3½ pints) chicken stock plus additional for thinning the gumbo if necessary
1½ pounds medium prawns

1. Place the vegetable oil in a heavy frying pan over high heat. Add the bacon. Dry the chicken thighs with a towel, and add them to the pan, skin side down. Sauté the chicken, on the skin side only, until the skins are golden brown, about 7 minutes. Remove the chicken and bacon and reserve.

2. Pour the oil from the frying pan into a measuring cup. Return 175 ml (6 fl oz) oil to the frying pan (discard the rest). Reduce heat to moderately high. Gradually add the flour, stirring continually. Cook the roux until it's a dark-tan or light-caramel colour, about 5 minutes. Immediately add the onion, green pepper and celery. Cook for 3 minutes, stirring.

3. Wash the okra, then cut off the stem ends, leaving a tiny bit of the stem at the top. Cut diagonally into 8 mm (³⁄₈-in) slices. Then add three-quarters of the okra to the pan. Add the thyme, rosemary, sage, bay leaves 5 g (1 tsp) black pepper and nutmeg.

4. Bring the chicken stock to a boil in a large pot. Add the roux with okra to the boiling stock in ladlefuls, stirring well after each addition. Bring to a boil, then reduce heat to a simmer. Chop the reserved bacon into coarse chunks, and add to the pot. Season the reserved chicken thighs with salt and pepper, cut each one in 4 to 6 pieces, and add to the pot. Simmer for 15 minutes. Add the reserved sliced okra, and simmer for another 10 minutes.

5. While the gumbo is simmering, peel and devein the prawns. Add to the simmering gumbo, and cook until the prawns are just pink, about 3 minutes. If the gumbo is too thick, thin out with a little chicken stock. Taste for seasoning. Serve over rice, New Orleans–style (see box, page 43). Sprinkle with fresh thyme leaves and garnish with branches of fresh thyme.

Note: For even more layers of flavour and texture, you may add two dozen raw, shucked oysters to the gumbo

just before serving. If the gumbo is a little too thick, be sure to add the oyster liquor.

Classic

SPICY RED FILÉ–THICKENED GUMBO WITH CAJUN CRAWFISH AND ANDOUILLE

If you're looking for Cajun fire, this one has it. Feel free to crank up the Scoville units by adding more cayenne. Cajun crawfish are crayfish.

SERVES 8

For the crawfish and crawfish seasoning mixture
7.5 g (1½ tsp) paprika
7.5 g (1½ tsp) garlic powder
5 g (1 tsp) salt
2.5 g (½ tsp) freshly ground black pepper
2.5 g (½ tsp) onion powder
2.5 g (½ tsp) dried basil leaves
2.5 g (½ tsp) dried thyme leaves
2.5 g (½ tsp) cayenne pepper
900 g (2 lb) shelled crawfish tails (or 900 g
  (2 lb) large shelled prawns)
For the gumbo
200 ml (⅓ pint) vegetable oil
100 g (3½ oz) plain flour
50 g (1¾ oz) finely chopped garlic
450 g (1 lb) finely chopped onions
450 g (1 lb) finely chopped celery
225g (8 oz) finely chopped green pepper
225g (8 oz) finely chopped red pepper
225g (8 oz) finely chopped spring onions
1.2 litres (2 pints) crawfish stock, prawn stock or
  bottled clam juice
2 x 800 g (1 lb 12 oz) cans of tomatoes
2 bay leaves
10 g (2 tsp) dried thyme leaves
5 g (1 tsp) dried oregano leaves
5 g (1 tsp) ground allspice

2.5 g (½ tsp) cayenne pepper, or to taste
2 cloves
2.5 ml (½ tsp) Louisiana hot sauce or to taste
60 ml (4 tsp) lemon juice
450 g (1 lb) andouille sausage, cut in 5-mm
  (¼-in) slices
15-30 g (1-2 tbsp) filé powder
cooked rice as an accompaniment
whole, boiled crawfish for garnish

1. In a bowl, blend together the crawfish seasoning mixture. Add the crawfish tails, and reserve in the refrigerator for 1 to 2 hours.

2. *Make the gumbo:* Place the vegetable oil in a heavy frying pan over high heat. When it's smoking, add the flour, about one third at a time, whisking in well after each addition. Cook over fairly high heat, whisking constantly, until the roux reaches a dark, reddish brown, about 10 minutes. If the roux seems about to burn (you'll start to notice a burning smell), move the pan off the heat for a few minutes, continuing to whisk.

3. When the roux is ready, add the garlic, onions, celery, peppers and spring onions. Place the pan over low heat, and cook the vegetables in the roux for 5 minutes.

4. Bring the stock to a boil in a large soup pot. When the vegetables have cooked in the roux, add the roux-vegetable mixture to the boiling stock by ladlefuls, blending well. Crush the tomatoes in your hands, and add them, along with the liquid in the cans, to the soup pot. Add the bay leaves, thyme, oregano, allspice, cayenne, cloves, hot sauce and lemon juice. Bring to the boil, then reduce heat to a simmer, and cook for 20 minutes, partially covered. Add the andouille, and simmer the gumbo for another 20 minutes, partially covered.

5. Add the seasoned crawfish tails, and simmer for 5 minutes. Off the heat, blend in the filé powder, blending until the desired thickness is reached. Taste for seasoning. Serve immediately over rice. Garnish with the whole, boiled crawfish.

Finding crawfish

Most American crawfish (crayfish), which look like miniature lobsters, usually 7.5-10 cm (3-4 in) long, come from Louisiana. May is the height of the live Louisiana crawfish season, though there's a pretty steady supply of live Louisiana crawfish from November to the following summer. But making gumbo from live crawfish takes a lot of work.

We prefer to make this gumbo at the height of the season, when 450-g (1-lb) bags of fresh crawfish tails, partially cooked and smothered in the delectable crawfish fat that collects near the head of the crawfish, are available by mail order from seafood companies in New Orleans. Of course, this means we sacrifice making our own crawfish stock, but a homemade prawn stock works equally well. This gumbo can be made at other times also, because these 450-g (1-lb) bags of crawfish tails freeze well and are available year-round.

The tails are also perfect for Cajun popcorn (see page 295).

The thickening question

It is the thickening, to a great extent, that really gives Louisiana gumbo its cachet.

First of all, there's roux—which differs greatly from the roux in classic French cuisine. The latter is a quickly cooked mixture of butter and flour used to thicken sauces and soups; its colour is yellow. Louisiana roux is a mixture of flour and some kind of fat (usually not butter), which is cooked much longer than French roux; its colour, depending on how long it's cooked, is anywhere from blond to tan to caramel to brownish-red to black. The longer it's cooked and the darker it looks, the nuttier it tastes. Intriguingly, as the darkness increases, the ability of the roux to thicken decreases. So the darkest roux has the most flavour and makes the thinnest gumbo. Seafood gumbos are usually made with dark roux.

After roux, further thickening of the gumbo usually occurs in one of two ways. 'Gumbo' comes from an African word for okra and, indeed, this delicious pod often appears in gumbo; when it does, its mucilaginous texture helps to thicken the soup. Or, Louisiana chefs might at the last minute add filé powder, first made by the Choctaw Indians from the bark of sassafras. It, too, thickens gumbo—and, if you make a mistake and let it cook just a little, it will form strings, or threads, from which it derives its name (same French root word as filament).

Normally, gumbo is thickened by roux and okra or roux and filé; okra and filé rarely appear together.

How to serve gumbo

The traditional New Orleans way to serve gumbo is over rice. For each serving, fill a teacup with fluffy steamed rice, then invert the cup into a wide soup bowl. Remove the cup, leaving a neat mound of rice. Ladle the gumbo all around the rice and serve immediately.

Classic

POSOLE VERDE

What makes a dish a classic? More often than not, it's the magical but logical marriage of flavours—a set of tastes just waiting to be brought together. If you've not had this classic of the American Southwest—a dish little-known outside its region—you will be amazed at the way the sweet, long-cooked flavours of pork dance with the flavour of posole, or dried, lime-slaked corn. We love it as a main course; serve lots of warm, soft, flour tortillas on the side, along with guacamole.

SERVES 6 AS A MAIN COURSE

30 ml (2 tbsp) vegetable oil
1 large white onion, very thinly sliced

2 garlic cloves, finely chopped
175 g (6 oz) green chillies (New Mexican, Anaheim, or poblano, roasted, peeled, seeded, and coarsely chopped
450 g (1 lb) boneless pork shoulder, cut into 2.5-cm (1-in) cubes
4 chicken thighs, boned, skins removed, cut into 4 pieces
175 g (6 oz) dried posole, soaked in water for at least 3 hours and drained
salt and pepper to taste
50 g (2 oz) finely chopped coriander
50 ml (2 fl oz) fresh lime juice

1. Place the vegetable oil in a large, heavy soup pot over moderate heat. Add the onion and garlic, and cook until the onion is soft, about 10 minutes.

2. Add the chillies, pork and chicken, and cook, stirring occasionally, until the meat browns, about 10 minutes. Add the soaked posole and hot water to cover by 2.5 cm (1 in). Simmer the mixture, adding hot water as necessary to keep meat just covered, for 2 hours, or until posole is soft and meat is fork tender. Add salt and pepper to taste. Serve the posole in deep, warmed bowls, and sprinkle each serving with some of the coriander and lime juice.

Variation

POSOLE WITH SHELLFISH

Here's an utterly unclassic variation—but a damned delicious bowl of soup, rich with the sweet flavour of crabs.

SERVES 4

225 g (8 oz) posole
1.125 kg (2½ lb) poblano chillies*
30 ml (2 tbsp) vegetable oil
12 garlic cloves, thinly sliced

45 ml (3 tbsp) masa harina
12 live hard-shell crabs
5 g (1 tsp) ground cumin
5 g (1 tsp) dried oregano
450 g (1 lb) small prawns, shelled
5 g (1 tsp) coarse salt
15 ml (1 tbsp) lime juice
225 g (8 oz) tomato, cut in large dice
25 g (1 oz) coriander leaves plus additional
  coriander for garnish
225 g (8 oz) cooked rice

1. The night before making the soup, cover the posole with water in a bowl. Soak overnight.

2. Hold the chillies over an open flame and cook until charred on all sides. Place chillies in a paper bag, and let rest for 15 minutes. Peel the charred skin away and cut away the seeds and membranes. Finely chop the remaining flesh of the chillies.

3. Pour the vegetable oil into a large, heavy pot over moderate heat. Add the garlic and cook, stirring, until it starts to brown. Stir in the masa harina and cook the mixture for 2 minutes. Whisk in 1.3 litres (2¼ pints) hot water, making sure the masa harina is incorporated. Bring to a boil, add the crabs and cover the pot. As soon as the crabs turn pink, add the cumin, oregano and half the chopped green chillies (reserve the other half). Reduce heat to low, and simmer for 3 hours.

4. Drain the posole, and add to the pot. Simmer for 2 hours more.

5. One hour before serving, toss the prawns in the coarse salt.

*You may substitute other green chillies for problano chillies, or make a mix of various green chillies. Just make sure your chillies are not too hot. If you have trouble finding green chillies, you can use sweet green peppers—or make a mix of mostly sweet peppers and a little hot green chilli (like jalapeño).

6. When ready to serve, remove the crabs from the soup pot. Cut them in half and squeeze the crab juice into the soup. Discard the crabs, reserving a few claws for garnish. Place a heavy pan over very high heat. After several minutes, toss the prawns in the pan and cook until just pink. Add the reserved chopped chillies, the lime juice, tomato and coriander leaves to the soup pot. Taste for seasoning. Place 55 g (2 oz) cooked rice in each of 4 soup bowls, fill with soup and garnish with shrimp and coriander. Serve immediately.

EUROPEAN CLASSICS AND VARIATIONS

Classic

MINESTRONE

The Ligurians claim minestrone as their own, but most regions of Italy make a thick, hearty vegetable soup called minestrone. Usually, it contains some kind of bean (borlotti are popular in Liguria, cannellini in other regions), some kind of dried pasta, and greens of some kind or multiple kinds. This minestrone trio is also the basic structure of Italian-American minestrone, which almost always includes cabbage as part of the greens. The following recipe is a marvellous, densely flavoured version, with no particular regional affiliation. It's even better if you cook it one day, refrigerate it overnight, then serve it the next day. The Ligurians, of course, would top it with pesto. By the way, it's not uncommon in Italy, particularly in summer, to serve minestrone at room temperature.

SERVES 8

50 ml (2 fl oz) olive oil
2 large yellow onions, cut into slivers
5 g (1 tsp) sugar

2 medium carrots, peeled and diced

2 stalks celery, diced

2 large red-skinned potatoes, peeled and diced

175 g (6 oz) French beans, trimmed and diced

2 small courgettes, diced

225 g (8 oz) finely shredded green cabbage

450 g (1 lb) canned, crushed tomatoes

500 ml (18 fl oz) beef broth

500 ml (18 fl oz) water

10 g (2 tsp) chopped fresh rosemary

5 g (1 tsp) chopped fresh thyme

5 g (1 tsp) chopped fresh basil

15 g (1 tbsp) coarse salt, or to taste

5 g (1 tsp) ground black pepper

225 g (8 oz) dried beans, such as cannellini, soaked
and cooked according to package directions

115 g (4 oz) short, dried pasta, such as ditalini or
elbow macaroni

115 g (4 oz) coarsely grated Parmigiano-Reggiano
for garnish

45 g (3 tbsp) finely shredded basil leaves for
garnish

1. Heat olive oil over moderate heat in large saucepan. Add onions and sugar, stir well and cover. Cook, stirring occasionally, for about 20 minutes, or until onions are wilted and light golden. Uncover and cook for another 20 to 25 minutes, or until onions are brown and well caramelised. (Watch carefully, so the onions don't burn.)

2. Add carrots, celery, potatoes and green beans, and cook for 10 minutes, or until vegetables soften slightly. Add courgettes and cabbage, and cook for 10 minutes. Add crushed tomatoes, beef stock, water, herbs, salt and pepper. Stir well and bring to a boil. Turn down heat to low, cover, and simmer gently for 2 hours. Add cannellini beans and cook mixture for another 30 minutes.

3. When ready to serve, cook the pasta in at least 2 litres (3½ pints) boiling, salted water until al dente. Drain. Add pasta to pan. Adjust seasoning. Ladle into

warmed soup bowls, and garnish each serving with about 15 g (1 tbsp) of Parmigiano-Reggiano and some shredded basil leaves.

Variation

RIBOLLITA

Ribollita means reboiled, and the soup is traditionally reboiled Tuscan minestrone. The minestrone is often made in very large quantities so there will be enough left for ribollita—most Tuscans prefer the ribollita to the minestrone. Cabbage is added, usually the black cabbage of Tuscany, cavolo nero. We use red cabbage as a substitute. Then comes the bread, which turns the soup into a thick mush—in fact, some places in Florence serve it with a fork. Ours is a bit lighter than the traditional one, but you should, by all means, drizzle great Tuscan extra-virgin olive oil over the finished product. The following recipe doesn't require you to make a minestrone first; in essence, you can make a bollita that tastes just as good as ribollita.

SERVES 8 TO 10

225 g (8 oz) cannellini or Jacob's Cattle beans

salt and pepper to taste

45 ml (3 tbsp) extra-virgin olive oil

115 g (4 oz) thickly sliced pancetta, finely chopped

2 large parsnips, peeled and finely chopped

1 large potato, peeled and finely chopped

2 small red onions, finely chopped

2 carrots, peeled and finely chopped

2 turnips, peeled and finely chopped

3 garlic cloves, smashed with a heavy knife

10 sprigs of flat-leaf parsley

5-cm (2-in) sprig of fresh rosemary

550 g (1 lb 4 oz) red cabbage, cored and thinly
sliced

400-g (14-oz) can peeled tomatoes, drained and
pushed through a food mill to remove seeds

small loaf of Italian bread, cut into 1-cm (½-in)
cubes
Parmigiano-Reggiano for grating
Tuscan extra-virgin olive oil for drizzling

1. Soak the beans in cold water to cover by 5 cm (2 in)
in a large pot overnight. (Alternatively, you can quick-
soak by bringing the beans and enough cold water to
cover by 5 cm (2 in) to a boil over moderately high heat
in a large pot. Boil the beans for 2 minutes and remove
the pot from heat. Cover and let stand for 1 hour.)
Discard bean-soaking water. Place beans in a large
saucepan with 3 litres (5¼ pints) cold water. Bring the
water just to a boil, reduce heat and simmer beans for
40 minutes, or until tender but still firm to the bite,
skimming off any scum that rises to the surface.
Remove half of the beans, purée in a food mill, and
return the purée to the whole beans and water in the
pan. Stir well, season with salt and pepper and reserve.

2. Heat the olive oil in a large casserole over moderately
low heat. Add the pancetta, and cook, stirring, for 5
minutes or until pancetta is beginning to crisp. Add the
parsnips, potato, onions, carrots, turnips, garlic and
herb sprigs, increase the heat to moderate, and cook,
stirring, for 6 minutes. Stir in the cabbage, and cook,
stirring, for 10 minutes. Add tomatoes, season with salt
and pepper, and cook, stirring, for 3 minutes.

3. Add the reserved bean–bean purée–water mixture to
the vegetable mixture in the casserole and simmer the
mixture for 15 to 20 minutes. (The cabbage should be
tender, and the soup should be medium-thick.)

4. Weigh out 900 g (2 lb) bread cubes. Lay them out on
a baking sheet, and place them in a preheated 200°C
(400°F) oven for 10 minutes, or until lightly toasted.

5. Stir bread cubes into soup, cover and let stand at
room temperature for at least 4 hours, or refrigerate,
stirring occasionally, for up to 2 days.

6. When ready to serve, remove herb sprigs and garlic
cloves. Stir vigorously to break up bread. The soup may
be served cold or at room temperature or heated. Serve
with freshly grated Parmigiano-Reggiano and a drizzle
of great Tuscan olive oil.

Variation

FENNEL MINESTRONE WITH WHITE BEANS AND SAUSAGE (MINESTRONE FINOCCHIO)
This creative take on the classic minestrone, though it
contains meat, is lighter than the standard dish.

SERVES 8

10 ml (2 tsp) fruity olive oil
450 g (1 lb) Italian sweet sausage, skinned and
crumbled
450 g (1 lb) coarsely chopped fennel bulb
225 g (8 oz) sliced leeks (white and green parts)
2 garlic cloves, finely chopped
7.5 g (1½ tsp) fennel seeds, crushed
1 litre (1¾ pints) chicken stock
800-g (28-oz) can tomatoes in tomato purée
225 g (8 oz) dried beans, such as cannellini, soaked
and cooked according to package directions
225 g (8 oz) cooked elbow macaroni
55 g (2 oz) firmly packed, shredded fresh basil
salt and pepper to taste
16 rounds of French or Italian bread, about 1 cm
(⅓ in) thick, well toasted and rubbed with split
garlic cloves
Parmigiano-Reggiano for garnish
fresh fennel leaves for garnish

1. Heat the olive oil in a large, heavy pan. Sauté the
sausage over high heat until well browned, about 5
minutes. Drain the fat from the pan, leaving a teaspoon
behind. Place pan over low heat, and add the fennel
bulb, leeks, garlic and crushed fennel seeds. Cook,
stirring occasionally, for 5 minutes. Add the chicken

stock and the tomatoes with purée, breaking up the tomatoes with a spoon. Bring to a boil and simmer gently for 30 minutes.

2. When ready to serve, add the beans, the macaroni and the basil. Season the soup to taste with salt and pepper. Place 2 rounds of toast in the centre of each of 8 wide, shallow soup bowls. Spoon the soup over the toasts. Grate the Parmigianio-Reggiano over the toasts to taste, and sprinkle the frilly fennel leaves in a circle around the toasts (use at least 15 g (1 tbsp) of leaves per bowl).

Classic

SOUPE AU PISTOU

You might call this soup the French version of minestrone, served with the French version of pesto. It is popular around Nice, in the south-east corner of France, and certainly feels the influence of Italy. As with many peasant dishes, there are almost infinite variations. We're crazy about this version, which features a deep, burnished soup that stands up beautifully to the basil-and-garlic paste called *pistou* in France. Let people stir in their own pistou at the table—it's a personal thing. Give people control over their own garlic intake! (But we think you'll need at least 5 g (1 tsp) per bowl.) Soup au pistou is often served as a meal in itself. In making the soup, by the way, use unseasoned stock so that salt doesn't stop the beans from cooking properly.

SERVES 8 AS A FIRST COURSE

200 g (7 oz) dried flageolet beans, picked over and rinsed
6 leeks (white and pale green parts only), quartered lengthways, sliced thin crossways, washed thoroughly and drained
55 g (2 oz) unsalted butter
50 ml (2 fl oz) extra-virgin olive oil

3 bay leaves
3 large garlic cloves, minced
5 g (1 tsp) herbes de Provence, crumbled
2.5 g (½ tsp) fennel seeds, crushed
2.5 g (½ tsp) freshly ground black pepper
2 litres (3½ pints) unseasoned chicken or vegetable stock
5 carrots, trimmed, peeled, and cut in 5-mm (¼-inch) dice
225 g (8 oz) potatoes, peeled and cut in 5-mm (¼-in) dice
1 medium fennel bulb, trimmed, cored, and cut in 5-mm (¼-in) dice
one 7.5-cm (3-in) strip of orange zest removed with a vegetable peeler
400-g (14-oz) can Italian peeled tomatoes, chopped
freshly grated Parmigiano-Reggiano for the table
225 ml (8 fl oz) pistou (recipe follows)

1. Soak the beans in cold water to cover by 5 cm (2 in) in a large pot overnight. (Alternatively, you can quick-soak by bringing the beans and enough cold water to cover by 5 cm (2 in) to a boil over moderately high heat in a large pot. Boil the beans for 2 minutes, and remove the pot from heat. Cover and let stand for 1 hour.)

2. Cook the leeks in 25 g (1 oz) of the butter and 30 ml (2 tbsp) of the olive oil in a large, heavy casserole over moderate heat, stirring frequently, for 30 minutes, or until dark golden brown. Add bay leaves, garlic, herbes de Provence, fennel seeds and pepper, and cook the mixture, stirring, for 1 minute.

3. Drain the beans and add to leek mixture. Add the stock and bring to a boil. Quickly reduce the heat, and simmer the mixture, partially covered, for 1 hour and 15 minutes, or until beans are tender. (Watch carefully so that the mixture does not boil but stays at a consistent bare simmer.)

4. While the bean mixture is simmering, cook carrots,

potato, fennel bulb and orange zest in the rest of the butter and olive oil in a large, deep frying pan over moderately high heat, stirring frequently, until the vegetables begin to brown, about 15 minutes.

5. When beans are tender (test by tasting or cutting a bean), stir diced vegetables and tomatoes into soup. Taste for seasoning. Cook soup over moderate heat for 5 minutes. Discard the bay leaves.

6. Ladle soup into bowls and serve with Parmigiano-Reggiano and pistou.

PISTOU

There is some disagreement about how *pistou* is translated, but, as is the case of the word *pesto*, the etymology certainly involves *pestle*, as in mortar and.... It does take some elbow grease, but there's no doubt that using a mortar and pestle, rather than a food processor, yields a version slightly superior in both texture and taste. If you're using a mortar and pestle, look for the large south-east Asian ones—which enable you to do a whole batch at once (the French ones are rather small). Then serve it right from the mortar, which looks great at the table. Pistou isn't always made with Parmigiano-Reggiano; sometimes Gruyère, Roquefort or goat cheese are used. Whichever cheese you choose, don't cook the pistou because the cheese can become stringy. Remember that pistou can be added to soups other than this one or to stews. It can also be used as a sauce for pasta.

MAKES ABOUT 225 ML (8 FL OZ)

5 large garlic cloves (or less, if you're garlic-shy)
pinch of coarse salt
225 g (8 oz) packed fresh basil leaves (preferably
    small-leaf basil), washed thoroughly and spun dry
115 g (4 oz) freshly shredded Parmigiano-Reggiano
75 ml (3 fl oz) Provençal extra-virgin olive oil

Place the garlic and coarse salt in a large mortar and pound vigorously to a paste with the pestle. Add the basil gradually and pound to a dark green paste. Add the cheese in 4 batches, and pound to the consistency of soft butter. Gradually beat in the oil until sauce has the consistency of coarse mayonnaise. (Alternatively, this can be made in a blender or food processor.) Hand round the pistou at the table as an accompaniment to soupe au pistou.

Classic

GAZPACHO

We'll never forget our first encounter with real gazpacho in Seville. Sitting on the counter behind a tapas bar were glass pitchers filled with a rich, creamy, orange liquid, looking for all the world like jugs of melon smoothies. But when we tasted a glass—as everyone around us was frantically doing—there was nary a fruit in this drink. It was stand-at-the-bar, drinkin' gazpacho, a pure taste of the Moorish south with no fancy garnishes. Follow this recipe to reproduce that sublime, simple treat—but do go ahead and add the garnishes if you're serving the soup in bowls at a sit-down dinner.

SERVES 6

115 g (¼ lb) crustless French or Italian bread
    (weigh after removing crust), torn into coarse
    chunks
350 g (12 oz) ripe, red tomatoes, cut in coarse
    chunks
140 g (5 oz) chopped onions
1 large garlic clove
175 g (6 oz) cucumber, peeled, seeded and cut in
    coarse chunks
175 g (6 oz) sweet red peppers, seeded and cut in
    coarse chunks
30 ml (2 tbsp) Spanish olive oil
125 ml (4 fl oz) sherry vinegar

salt and pepper to taste
For garnish (optional)
finely chopped green pepper
finely chopped red pepper
finely chopped onion
finely chopped cucumber
finely chopped hard-boiled egg
finely chopped olives
croutons

1. Pour water over bread to cover, then squeeze out the water and place bread in the work bowl of a food processor. (If bread is fresh, squeeze immediately. If bread is stale, wait a few moments.)

2. Place the rest of the ingredients, except garnishes, in the food processor. Purée until very smooth (2 minutes or more). Season to taste with salt and pepper and refrigerate for several hours.

3. Strain through a fine sieve. Just before serving, if desired, thin with a little ice water. Serve either in tall glasses, ungarnished, or divide gazpacho among soup bowls, offering as many of the garnishes as you wish.

Gazpacho Wars

Gazpacho is one of those classic regional dishes that not only feeds happy diners but feeds a lot of controversy as well. Here are the main issues and our stand on them:

Bread or no bread? Lots of modern gazpacho recipes—in the interest of 'lightness'—leave the bread out of the gazpacho. For God's sake, the word gazpacho itself comes from the Arabic word for bread. It's the soul of the dish. We think that without the bread puréed into the soup, gazpacho is just V-8.

Oil or no oil? Again, lots of modern recipes try to cut back calories by leaving out the olive oil. But a few tablespoons of a fabulous, typically herbal Andalusian extra-virgin olive oil give the dish very authentic flavour and a richness that's well worth the few extra calories.

Strained or not strained? We're not against a thick and hearty texture, but if you strain the gazpacho—making it thinner and smoother—you'll have something texturally close to what they serve in southern Spain.

Ice water or not? We leave this up to you. After straining—especially if you're serving the gazpacho in glasses, as a drink—you might want to thin the soup out a bit.

Peeled tomatoes or unpeeled tomatoes? This is a big gazpacho controversy, but we find that if you use the food processor and if you strain the soup, taking the trouble to peel the tomatoes first doesn't yield improved results.

Variation

WHITE GAZPACHO, MALAGA-STYLE

This white, silky-smooth gazpacho is a traditional variation from Malaga in southern Spain. We've added a little sugar to create a wonderful sweet-and-sour backdrop for the classic grape garnish.

SERVES 4

85 g (3½ oz) almonds, blanched in boiling water for 1 minute
4 large garlic cloves
50 g (2 oz) crustless French or Italian bread (weigh after removing crust)
1 egg
50 ml (2 fl oz) sherry vinegar
45 ml (3 tbsp) Spanish olive oil
225 ml (8 fl oz) ice water plus additional if desired
10 g (2 tsp) sugar
salt to taste
16 green, seedless grapes

1. While almonds are still hot, slip off their skins. Place the skinned almonds in the work bowl of a food processor, along with the garlic and bread. Process until you have a smooth paste. Then add the egg, vinegar, olive oil, water and sugar. You should have a medium-thick soup. Add additional ice water if a thinner consistency is desired.

2. Strain, season to taste with salt and refrigerate for several hours.

3. When ready to serve, divide the soup among 4 soup bowls. Cut the grapes in half, and garnish each bowl with 8 grape halves.

Gazpacho Variations

Gazpacho is hot these days among creative chefs all around the world. Here are a few ideas we've seen lately. *Gazpacho as a fancy drink:* You can add all kinds of things to the basic brew. How about a bloody gazpacho?—gazpacho with a bit of vodka and Tabasco. *Gazpacho as a salad:* Forget the purée part of gazpacho, but layer the usual chopped vegetables in a wide-mouthed jar, include a few creative extra bites (anchovies and olives, for example), pour a vinaigrette (made with sherry vinegar) over the layers and marinate for several days. Serve at table from the striated jar. *Gazpacho as a sauce:* Lots of chefs are pouring a thick, strained gazpacho on to a plate around a central player. How about ovals made of fresh crabmeat, held together with mayonnaise, surrounded by a gazpacho 'sauce' and topped with gazpacho garnishes?

Classic

FRENCH ONION SOUP

If you like it deep and rich, and with a gooey mantle, look no further. When accompanied by a wintry salad and a glass of Beaujolais, there is no better simple

supper.

SERVES 4

50 g (2 oz) butter
900 g (2 lb) yellow onions, cut into slivers
10 g (2 tsp) sugar
20 g (4 tsp) plain flour
850 ml (1¾ pints) beef stock, boiling
450 ml (16 fl oz) water
50 ml (2 fl oz) cognac
7.5 g (1½ tsp) salt
2.5 g (½ tsp) ground black pepper
12 slices stale French bread (each about 2 cm
   (¾ in) thick)
675 g (1½ lb) Gruyère or Emmenthaler cheese,
   coarsely grated

1. Melt butter over moderate heat in large saucepan. Add onions and sugar, stir well, and cover. Cook, stirring occasionally, for about 20 minutes or until onions are wilted and light golden. Uncover and continue to cook for another 20 to 25 minutes, or until onions are brown and well caramelised. (Watch carefully, so the onions don't burn.)

2. Add flour to pan, stir well to incorporate flour into onion mixture, and slowly stir in boiling stock, water, 3 tablespoons of cognac, salt and pepper. Boil for 5 minutes, then reduce heat to low, and simmer gently, partially covered, for 45 minutes. Uncover and simmer for another 10 minutes. Adjust seasoning and add the rest of the cognac.

3. While the soup is simmering, in a preheated 200°C (400°F) oven, toast the bread slices for 10 minutes, turning them once after 5 minutes (the croutons should be well toasted on each side).

4. Divide the soup among 4 ovenproof onion soup bowls (or any ovenproof soup bowls), each with a capacity of approximately 350 ml (12 fl oz). Arrange the croutons on top of soup (try to make an even layer of croutons that tops each bowl). Sprinkle croutons generously with grated cheese, allowing some cheese to spill over on to the rim. Put bowls on a baking sheet and place under a preheated grill until cheese melts and forms a crust over the tops of the bowls. Serve immediately.

Note: Instead of grating all the cheese, you can cut some of it into wide, thin slices and drape the slices over the sides of the bowls. This helps to prevent the cheese from slipping off the rims of the bowls.

Variation

MANY-ONION SOUP WITH GINGER AND GOAT CHEESE CROÛTES

Perhaps you want an onion soup without the traditional richness, heartiness, cheesiness—but one still deep in flavour. This is your solution. It's a much lighter soup, greenish-yellow in colour, with perfect balance and an intriguing whiff of something extra (which turns out to be ginger). Think of the onions, leeks, shallots, spring onions, garlic and chives in this soup as the 'lilies of the kitchen'; they are all from the lily family.

SERVES 8

85 g (3 oz) unsalted butter
1 large onion, peeled, halved through root, and
   sliced thin
5 medium leeks (white and pale green parts only),
   washed thoroughly and sliced thin crossways
115 g (4 oz) spring onions (white parts only), finely
   chopped
55 g (2 oz) shallots, finely chopped
10 g (2 tsp) garlic, finely chopped
10 g (2 tsp) grated peeled fresh ginger
10 g (2 tsp) plain flour
1.5 litres (2¾ pints) chicken or vegetable stock (or
   a combination of both)
125 ml (4 fl oz) dry vermouth

125 ml (4 fl oz) apple cider
30 ml (2 tbsp) Calvados or apple brandy
15 ml (1 tbsp) fresh lemon juice
225 g (8 oz) soft mild goat cheese, such as
   Montrachet, at room temperature
55 g (2 oz) snipped fresh chives or finely sliced
   spring onion greens
freshly ground pepper to taste
8 slices French bread, each about 2 cm (¾ inch)
   thick

1. Melt butter in a large, heavy casserole over moderately high heat. Add onion and cook, stirring, for 3 minutes. Stir in leeks, spring onions, shallots, garlic, and 1 teaspoon of the ginger. Cook, stirring, for 3 minutes. Stir in flour, and cook, stirring, for 2 minutes.

2. Stir in stock (or stocks) and heat to boiling. Reduce heat, and cook at a bare simmer, covered, for 30 minutes. Stir in vermouth, cider, Calvados (or apple brandy), lemon juice and rest of the ginger. Simmer for 10 minutes. Taste for seasoning.

3. Preheat the grill. Stir together the goat cheese and half the chives in a small bowl. Season with freshly ground black pepper. Toast the bread on both sides under the grill about 10 cm (4 in) from the heat until golden brown. Spread one side of each slice of bread with the goat cheese mixture, and toast again until cheese is lightly browned. Ladle soup into 8 bowls, and place a goat cheese croûte in the centre of each bowl. Sprinkle soup and croûtes with remaining chives and serve immediately.

Classic

LOBSTER BISQUE

In eighteenth-century France, a bisque was a game soup, thickened with a shellfish purée. As time passed, the word became increasingly associated with the shellfish purée, not with the game soup. Thus was lobster bisque born. It was one of the first ideas from classical French cuisine incorporated into the American tradition, and in the earlier part of this century 'lobster bisque' was such a mainstay at country clubs and fancy restaurants that many came to think of it as American. To make a good one takes time and trouble; all of the precious lobster flavour must be extracted from the shells and meat. The following version is exquisite: intense with lobster essence, creamy and light at the same time.

SERVES 6

175 g (6 oz) unsalted butter
115 g (4 oz) diced carrots
115 g (4 oz) diced celery
140 g (5 oz) finely chopped onions
2 x 550-g (1 lb 4 oz) uncooked lobsters
75 ml (5 tbsp) cognac
450 ml (16 fl oz) white wine
450 ml (16 fl oz) water
2 garlic cloves, peeled and crushed
30 g (2 tbsp) roughly chopped tarragon
1 bay leaf
800-g (28-oz) can whole plum tomatoes, drained
10 g (2 tsp) coarse salt
pinch of ground white pepper
140 g (5 oz) long-grain white rice
225 ml (8 fl oz) single cream
225 ml (8 fl oz) milk
chervil leaves or finely chopped tarragon leaves for garnish

1. Melt 50 g (2 oz) butter over moderate heat in a large saucepan, and add carrots, celery and onions. Cook for about 10 minutes, or until vegetables are soft. (Do not allow them to colour.)

2. Cut lobsters in half lengthways, and remove the sand sack, located behind the mouth. Separate into tail pieces, claws and chest pieces. Add lobster sections to vegetables, and sauté over moderately high heat until shells turn red. Remove lobster pieces from the pan, and, when cool enough to handle, remove the meat from the tails and claws. Reserve meat.

3. Chop all the shells into smaller pieces and return to the pan. Add 50 ml (2 fl oz) cognac and ignite, gently tilting pan to flame all the shells. When flames subside, add wine, water, garlic, tarragon and bay leaf. Stir to combine. Crush tomatoes with your hands and add to the pot along with the coarse salt and white pepper. Stir well and simmer over low heat for 45 minutes. (Do not allow the liquid to boil.)

4. Pull out as many pieces of shell as possible and reserve. Put the rest of the soup through a food mill, or into a sieve, pushing down on the solids to extract as much liquid as possible. Return milled broth to pan, and add reserved lobster meat and the rice. Simmer over low heat for another 45 minutes, or until reduced to 450 ml (16 fl oz).

5. Take reserved shells and place in the bowl of a food processor. Pulse processor for about 30 seconds, or until shells are finely chopped. Melt the rest of the butter in a medium saucepan and add chopped shells. Cook over moderate heat, stirring often, for about 20 minutes. Transfer to a fine sieve placed over a bowl. Push down on shells hard, forcing as much butter and liquid through the sieve as possible. Reserve butter and discard solids.

6. Remove reduced broth from heat. Purée in small batches in a blender and put through a fine sieve set over a mixing bowl. Use a ladle to push on solid matter, extracting as much liquid as possible. Return to pot, add lobster butter and stir together well.

7. Add the rest of the cognac to bisque, and heat gently for 5 to 7 minutes, or until alcohol is burned off. Add cream and milk and heat through. (Do not boil.) Serve immediately, garnished with chervil or tarragon.

Variation

THAI LOBSTER BISQUE

This creamy wonder is not a classic Thai soup, but it should be. The trick is preserving the lobster flavour alongside the riot of other flavours drawn from the Thai spectrum. Lots of lobster, and charring the lobster, both help to accomplish the goal.

SERVES 6 AS A FIRST COURSE

- 2 x 550-g (1 lb 4 oz) lobsters, cut up
- 1.3 litres (2¼ pints) water
- 55 g (2 oz) coarsely chopped fresh ginger
- 55 g (2 oz) coarsely chopped coriander stems and roots plus 175 g (6 oz) coriander leaves
- 2 jalapeño chillies chopped
- 2 garlic cloves, smashed
- 2 stalks lemongrass, sliced
- 4 thick slices dried galingale root
- 150 ml (¼ pint) nam pla (bottled Thai fish sauce) plus additional for sprinkling the lobster
- 150 ml (¼ pint) lime juice plus additional for sprinkling the lobster
- 20 g (4 tsp) sugar
- 10 small dried Chinese mushrooms
- 225 ml (8 fl oz) medium-thick coconut milk (canned or freshly made; see box, page 60)
- 115 g (4 oz) fresh bamboo shoots, cut in medium dice

1. Place a large, heavy soup pot (preferably cast-iron) over high heat. Add the cut-up lobster pieces, and sauté, stirring occasionally, for 10 minutes, or until the pieces are browned on the outside. Add the water, ginger, coriander stems and roots, jalapeño chillies, garlic, lemongrass, galingale, 50 ml (2 fl oz) nam pla, lime juice and sugar. Bring to simmer.

2. Simmer for 30 minutes, but check the lobster meat after just a few minutes. As soon as the meat is cooked, remove it from the shells. Return the shells to the pot to finish simmering. As soon as the lobster meat is cool enough to handle, slice it into bite-size pieces, sprinkling the pieces with a little Thai fish sauce and a little lime juice. Reserve.

3. While the soup is simmering, skim off any foam that rises to the top.

4. Place the Chinese mushrooms in a small bowl, and just cover with warm water. Let soak for 1 hour.

5. When the soup has simmered, strain it into a clean bowl. Pour the coconut milk through a sieve into a clean saucepan. Heat gently over low heat. Slowly add the lobster stock to the coconut milk. Heat, but do not allow to boil. Just before serving, add the rest of the nam pla and the rest of the lime juice. Cut the soaked mushrooms into small chunks, and add to the soup. Add the reserved lobster pieces, the bamboo shoots, and the coriander leaves. Stir well and serve immediately in soup bowls.

Classic

BERGEN FISH SOUP WITH FISH DUMPLINGS

This is one of the great dishes of Norway, though it's barely known outside of Scandinavia. In the beautiful city of Bergen, gateway to the western fjords, restaurant owners and home cooks select coalfish every morning at the open-air fish market to prepare this velvety soup. In classic Norwegian style, it is thickened with eggs and cream, but with no flour. If coalfish is not available, cod—also a Norwegian favourite—makes a good substitute.

SERVES 8

1.8 kg (4 lb) bones, heads, and trimmings of cod or
   other white fish
3 litres (5¼ pints) water
450 g (1 lb) leeks, washed and chopped
225 g (8 oz) parsnips, peeled and coarsely chopped,
   plus 115 g (4 oz) parsnips, peeled and diced
3 stalks celery with leaves, coarsely chopped
115 g (4 oz) fresh parsley sprigs with stems
5 g (1 tsp) black peppercorns
225 g (8 oz) potatoes, diced
55 g (2 oz) carrots, peeled and sliced into rounds
finely chopped parsley for garnish
For the fish dumplings
450 g (1 lb) skinned and boned cod
2 egg whites
5 g (1 tsp) salt plus additional to taste
450 ml (16 fl oz) double cream
1.25 g (¼ tsp) white pepper
a large pinch of freshly grated nutmeg
2 egg yolks
30 ml (2 tbsp) crème fraîche

1. Place the fish bones, heads and trimmings in a large
stockpot. Add the water, leeks, the 225 g (8 oz) of
chopped parsnips, celery, the 115 g (4 oz) parsley and
black peppercorns. Bring to a boil, skim off foam, then
simmer until reduced to 1.7 litres (3 pints) of liquid.
Keep removing foam as it develops on the surface.

2. When stock is reduced, strain through a fine sieve
into a clean pot. Add the potatoes, the carrots and the
rest of the parsnips. Simmer until the vegetables are
just cooked.

3. While the vegetables are simmering, make the fish
dumplings. Place the cod, egg whites and salt in the
work bowl of a food processor. Purée well. With the motor
running, add the single cream in a thin stream. Remove
purée and push it through a fine sieve. Add the white
pepper, nutmeg and additional salt if necessary. Pick up
a heaped tablespoon or so with a spoon, and drop into a

wide pot of salted, simmering water. Repeat, until all
the mixture is used up. You should have about 32
dumplings. Cook them for two minutes on each side.
Remove from heat.

4. When ready to serve soup, beat the egg yolks and
crème fraîche in a large bowl. Beat the fish soup into
the egg-and-cream mixture, slowly at first so as not to
curdle the eggs. When it's entirely beaten in, return the
soup to the pot and cook over low heat for 1 to 2
minutes. (Make sure that it does not come near a boil.)

5. To serve, divide the soup among 8 wide soup bowls,
float 4 dumplings in each one, and sprinkle all with the
finely chopped parsley.

Variation
———

NORWEGIAN CREAM OF SALMON SOUP
This unusual Norwegian fish soup is even richer than
the preceding one. Something like it was served to us by
a creative chef, one wintry day, in a ski chalet high
above the Oslofjord, when the soup's creaminess and
salmony intensity seemed very appropriate. At American
tables, it might be an idea to serve it in very small
portions, perhaps between courses, perhaps in little
intermezzo cups.

SERVES 16 AS A BETWEEN-COURSE TREAT

675 g (1½ lb) salmon bones, heads, and trimmings
1 litre (1¾ pints) water
225 ml (8 fl oz) dry white wine
675 g (1½ lb) leeks, cleaned and chopped
175 g (6 oz) parsley leaves and stems
175 g (6 oz) fresh dill leaves and stems plus 15 g
   (1 tbsp) chopped dill and, for garnish, dill sprigs
2.5 g (½ tsp) whole black peppercorns
1 litre (1¾ pints) double cream
115 g (4 oz) smoked salmon, cut into thin strips

1. Place the salmon trimmings, water, wine, 450 g (1 lb) of the leeks, parsley, the 175 g (6 oz) dill and the peppercorns in a stockpot. Bring to boil and skim off foam. Reduce heat and simmer until the liquid is reduced to about 350 ml (12 fl oz) (about 1 hour). Strain through a sieve and reserve the broth.

2. Place the cream in a heavy saucepan with the rest of the leeks. Reduce rapidly over high heat to 450 ml (16 fl oz). Strain out the leeks and return reduced cream to the pan. Over moderate heat, slowly blend in the reduced salmon stock. When soup is just below the boil, add the chopped dill and half the smoked salmon strips, cooking them until just past translucent, about 1 minute. Divide the remaining smoked salmon strips among serving cups, then pour the warm soup over them. Top each bowl with a sprig of dill.

Note: You could turn this soup into a hearty stew by adding potatoes and large chunks of salmon.

Classic

PAPPA AL POMODORO

This humble bread-and-tomato soup is from Livorno, Tuscany. It is fiercely Tuscan in its simplicity and therefore requires the ingredients to be perfect: the tomatoes must be very ripe, the basil must be very fresh and the bread must be very stale. *Pomodoro* means tomato and *pap* means something soft—and this 'soup' seems more like what we might call a porridge. You might find this dish odd at first, but it's rather easy to get used to. You can serve the soup at just about any temperature, but we're partial to room temperature. If you want to eat it the Tuscan way, drizzle obscene amounts of fabulous olive oil over it; to the Tuscans, in fact, the pappa is little more than an excuse for eating olive oil.

SERVES 4

50 ml (2 fl oz) extra-virgin olive oil
2 garlic cloves, halved
100 g (3½ oz) shallots, finely chopped
10 g (2 tsp) fresh sage leaves, finely chopped
55 g (2 oz) packed fresh basil leaves
4 x 2.5-cm (1-in) slices of stale Italian bread (about 7.5 cm (3 in) in diameter), cut into 2-cm (¾-in) cubes
1.6 kg (3½ lb) fresh ripe tomatoes (about 9 tomatoes), peeled, seeded and chopped
225 ml (8 fl oz) chicken stock
salt and pepper to taste
top-quality Tuscan extra-virgin olive oil for drizzling

1. Heat the extra-virgin olive oil in a large saucepan over moderately low heat. Stir in garlic halves, shallots, sage and basil leaves. Cook, stirring, for 3 minutes. Stir in bread cubes and stir constantly for 2 minutes.

2. Add the tomatoes and stock and cook, stirring occasionally, for 15 minutes. Remove from heat and season to taste with salt and pepper. Cover and let stand for 1 hour. Stir vigorously until bread and tomatoes are fairly smooth. Serve at room temperature. Divide among 4 soup bowls and pass Tuscan extra-virgin olive oil for drizzling.

Variation

BRUSCHETTA AL POMODORO

Here's something completely new under the sun— inspired by the American aversion to mushy textures. If you love the taste of pappa al pomodoro, but don't love its porridge-like consistency, try this variation, which mixes cubes of grilled bread with the tomatoes. It's loaded with texture and just as delicious as the original—maybe more, because the bruschetta adds a great grilled flavour.

SERVES 4

eight slices of Italian bread, 2.5 cm (1 in) thick and
 about 7.5 cm (3 in) in diameter
2 garlic cloves, halved
75 ml (5 tbsp) extra-virgin olive oil
100 g (3½ oz) finely chopped shallots
55 g (2 oz) packed fresh basil leaves
1.6 kg (3½ lb) fresh ripe tomatoes (about 9
 tomatoes), peeled, seeded and chopped
225 ml (8 fl oz) chicken stock
salt and pepper to taste
top-quality Tuscan extra-virgin olive oil for
 drizzling

1. Toast the bread slices and while they are still hot, rub
them with garlic halves and brush with 15 ml (1 tbsp) of
the olive oil. Set aside at room temperature.

2. Heat the rest of the olive oil in large saucepan over
moderately low heat. Stir in garlic halves from rubbing
bread, shallots and basil leaves. Cook, stirring, for 3
minutes. Add the tomatoes and stock and cook, stirring
occasionally, for 15 minutes. Remove from heat and
season to taste with salt and pepper. Let the mixture
rest until it comes to room temperature.

3. Cut or rip each slice of grilled bread into 6 chunks.
Add bread to soup, mix, then immediately divide among
4 soup bowls. Serve. Pass Tuscan extra-virgin olive oil
for drizzling.

Classic
———

CALDO VERDE

This classic Portuguese soup, which originated in the
northern Minho region but is today served all over
Portugal (and Brazil), is simplicity itself. The hardest
parts are finding Portuguese chouriço (you can
substitute chorizo, the similar Spanish sausage) and

finding couvé, the type of cabbage used in Portugal
(curly kale is a decent substitute). The key to
preparation is the cutting of the cabbage, or kale, into
very thin strips, which gives the soup its grassy, 'green'
look. You'll be amazed at the amount of flavour you get
for so little trouble. Serve the soup with its classic
companion, Portuguese vinho verde, a crisp, crackling
white wine.

SERVES 4

1.5 l (2¾ pints) water
450 g (1 lb) potatoes, peeled
175 g (6 oz) chouriço
4 garlic cloves, finely chopped
175 g (6 oz) curly kale without thick stems
Portuguese olive oil for drizzling

1. Bring the water to boil in a large, heavy saucepan.
Add the potatoes, chouriço and garlic. Simmer gently for
30 minutes or until the potatoes are soft.

2. Remove the chouriço and, when it's cool enough, slice
diagonally into very thin slices.

3. With a potato masher, mash the potatoes right in the
pan. (They will end up in little chunks.) Boil for 5
minutes.

4. While the potatoes are boiling, shred the kale. Gather
some leaves together, roll them up the long way and
then cut the rolls into fine shreds.

5. Bring the soup to a rolling boil. Add the kale and cook
for 5 minutes, or until it is just tender. Add the chouriço
slices and taste the soup for seasoning. Let simmer very
gently over low heat for 5 minutes before serving in soup
bowls. Drizzle each bowl with a little Portuguese olive
oil.

Note: We think this soup tastes best when it's held for a
few hours at room temperature, then gently re-heated.

Water or stock?

It is traditional to make caldo verde with water. This creates an extremely light broth—just a background, really—for the cabbage and sausage flavours. The effect is quite startling: wintry and light at the same time. Some chefs, however, prefer to make the soup richer by using chicken stock instead of water. This, too, though quite different, is good. Your call.

Variation

CALDO VERDE WITH SALT COD

The Portuguese are masters of salted cod; the dried fish, in fact, is called *fiel amigo* in Portugal (faithful friend). Therefore, it seems entirely appropriate to make the following creative leap: a seafood version of caldo verde, the national dish, made with the national fish. This variation can use a little more depth than the chouriço one, because the salt cod leaves a less marked taste than the sausage does. That's why chicken stock is recommended here, along with water. But use water alone, or fish stock, if you're looking for a light, non-meat version.

SERVES 4

450 g (1 lb) salt cod
30 ml (2 tbsp) olive oil
6 large garlic cloves, finely chopped
675 g (1½ lb) potatoes, peeled
1 litre (1¾ pints) non-salty chicken stock
450 ml (16 fl oz) water
175 g (6 oz) kale without thick stems
Portuguese olive oil for drizzling

1. Soak the salt cod in a bowl of water in the refrigerator for 2 to 3 days. Change the water several times a day.

2. When ready to make soup, drain and dry off the salt cod. Place the 2 tablespoons of olive oil in a large, heavy saucepan over moderately high heat. Add the garlic and half of the salt cod. Sauté until the garlic starts to brown, about 5 minutes. Immediately add the potatoes, chicken stock and water. Simmer gently for 30 minutes, or until the potatoes are soft.

3. With a potato masher, mash the potatoes and the cooked salt cod right in the pan. (They will end up in little chunks.) Boil for 5 minutes.

4. While the potatoes and cod are boiling, shred the kale. Gather some leaves together, roll them up the long way and then cut the rolls into fine shreds.

5. Add the kale to the soup, along with the remaining salt cod cut into 1-cm (½-in) pieces. Simmer for 5 minutes, or until the kale is just tender. Taste the soup for seasoning before serving in soup bowls. Drizzle each bowl with a little Portuguese olive oil.

ASIAN CLASSICS AND VARIATIONS

No region of the world has enriched our National Soup Kitchen as much in the last 20 years as Asia has. Most Americans, for example, have gone beyond won ton soup to find an authentic variety of fabulous Chinese possibilities; many a visitor to the Chinatowns of America today makes a meal from a steaming bowl of broth, noodles, vegetables and meat. We have discovered the fabulous soups of south-east Asia at Thai, Vietnamese and Burmese restaurants. The ubiquitous bowl of miso soup at sushi bars has led us into the startling range of austere, subtle Japanese soups. And, where once a few Americans knew only mulligatawny, a much wider group of Americans is now familiar with the staggering diversity of Indian soups. The quest for authenticity has fuelled the movement, to be sure—but creative American chefs have also played their own riffs on classic Asian themes.

Classic

THAI HOT AND SOUR PRAWN SOUP (TOM YUM KUNG)

Soups are tremendously popular in Thailand and this soup is one of the favourites there. It's little wonder that it has also become a Thai restaurant staple in the United States: it's easy to make, it's light and it packs a wallop of flavour from the shellfish-scented broth to the tingle of hot chillies. This version of the classic has even more punch, because the prawns are marinated with Thai flavourings.

SERVES 4

450 g (1 lb) medium prawns
50 ml (2 fl oz) lime juice
20 ml (4 tsp) nam pla (bottled Thai fish sauce)
55 g (2 oz) green chillies, finely chopped (more or
    less to taste)
30 g (2 tbsp) thin slices of fresh lemongrass plus
    10 g (2 tsp) very finely chopped lemongrass from
    the tenderest part of the stalk (chopped almost to
    a paste)
10 ml (2 tsp) vegetable oil
1 litre (1¾ pints) chicken stock
30 g (2 tbsp) dried kafflr lime leaves, crumbled
30 g (2 tbsp) finely chopped fresh coriander roots
    and stems, plus 45 g (3 tbsp) fresh coriander
    leaves
2 thick slices dried galingale root
2 medium shallots, coarsely chopped
10 g (2 tsp) dried tamarind pulp
125 g (4 oz) straw mushrooms
10 g (2 tsp) chopped spring onion
15 ml (1 tbsp) nam prik pao
    (optional, see box)

1. Shell the prawns, reserving the shells. Devein and butterfly each prawn. Place the prawns in a bowl and mix with 30 ml (2 tbsp) of the lime juice, 10 ml (2 tsp) of the nam pla, 5 g (1 tbsp) of the finely chopped green chillies and 5 g (1 tsp) of the lemongrass chopped almost to a paste. Set aside.

2. Add the vegetable oil to a soup pot over high heat. Add the prawn shells and cook, stirring occasionally, for 5 minutes, or until the shells have started to brown. Immediately add the chicken stock, 30 g (2 tbsp) of the ground chillies, the sliced lemongrass, the kafflr lime leaves, the coriander roots and stems, the galingale root, the shallots and the tamarind pulp. Bring to a boil, then simmer for 30 minutes.

3. Strain the soup into a clean pot over moderately high heat, pressing liquid out of the solids in the strainer. Discard the solids. Add the rest of the lime juice, the rest of the nam pla, the remaining 15 g (1 tbsp) of finely chopped chilli, the rest of the lemongrass paste, the straw mushrooms, the fresh coriander leaves and the finely chopped spring onion. Stir well. Just before serving, add the prawns along with the prawn marinade. Warm until the prawns are just cooked (about 30 seconds) and serve immediately. If desired, top the soup with *nam prik pao.*

Nam prik pao

Thai hot-and-sour prawn soup is already plenty hot—but the Thais like to send it over the top by floating a small quantity of 'chilli jam' on top of the soup. Here's how to make a scant cup of nam prik pao (it will keep for several months in the refrigerator, tightly sealed). The recipe is adapted from one by a famous Thai cooking teacher, Somi Anuntra Miller:

Char 8 large unpeeled cloves of garlic, and 2 unpeeled medium onions in a heavy omelette pan set over high heat. When skins are blackened, remove garlic and onions and let them cool. Peel and discard skins. Place 15 g (1 tbsp) of dried shrimp paste (available in

Thai groceries) in a little packet of aluminium foil. Place in same pan, over high heat and cook for 3 minutes on each side. Remove, cool, unwrap and place shrimp paste in a food processor. Add garlic and onions, as well as 6 dried red chillies, 30 g (2 tbsp) ground dried shrimp, 45 g (3 tbsp) palm sugar (or brown sugar) and 10 g (2 tsp) of tamarind concentrate that have been softened in 30 ml (2 tbsp) of hot water. Make a smooth paste in the processor, adding a little oil if necessary. Add a few tablespoons vegetable oil to the original pan and fry chilli jam over moderately high heat, stirring, for 2 minutes. Cool and use.

Variation

THAI HOT AND SOUR PRAWN SOUP WITH LIME AND LEMON RIND

In case you can't find kafflr lime leaves, lemongrass, galingale and tamarind, this version of the classic soup calls for more readily available ingredients—without sacrificing authentic flavour!

SERVES 4

450 g (1 lb) medium prawns
75 ml (5 tbsp) lime juice
20 ml (4 tsp) nam pla (bottled Thai fish sauce)
25 g (1 oz) finely chopped green chillies (more or less to taste)
10 g (2 tsp) grated lemon zest
10 ml (2 tsp) vegetable oil
1 litre (1¾ pints) chicken stock
30 g (2 tbsp) chopped lemon zest
30 g (2 tbsp) chopped lime zest
30 g (2 tbsp) finely finely chopped fresh coriander roots and stems plus 45 g (3 tbsp) fresh coriander leaves
2 medium shallots, coarsely chopped
140 g (5 oz) paddy straw mushrooms

10 g (2 tsp) finely chopped spring onion
15 ml (1 tbsp) nam prik pao (optional, see page 58)

1. Shell the prawns, reserving the shells. Devein and butterfly each prawn. Place the prawns in a bowl and mix with 2 tablespoons of the lime juice, 2 teaspoons of the fish sauce, 1 tablespoon of the finely chopped green chillies and 1 teaspoon of the grated lemon zest. Set aside.

2. Add the vegetable oil to a soup pot over high heat. Add the prawn shells and cook, stirring occasionally, for 5 minutes, or until the shells have started to brown. Immediately add the chicken stock, 2 tablespoons of the finely chopped chillies, the chopped lemon zest, the chopped lime zest, the coriander roots and stems and the shallots. Bring to a boil, then simmer for 30 minutes.

3. Strain the soup into a clean pot over moderately high heat, pressing liquid out of the solids in the strainer. Discard the solids. Add the rest of the lime juice, the rest of the fish sauce, the rest of the finely chopped chilli peppers, the rest of the grated lemon zest, the paddy straw mushrooms, the fresh coriander leaves and the finely chopped spring onion. Stir well. Just before serving, add the prawns along with the prawn marinade. Warm until the prawns are just cooked (about 30 seconds) and serve immediately. If desired, top the soup with nam prik pao.

Classic

THAI CHICKEN AND COCONUT MILK SOUP (TOM KHA KAI)

This Thai classic is a staple on Thai restaurant menus and one of the easiest dishes to prepare in the whole Thai repertoire. The only trick is finding the lemongrass, kaffir lime leaves and galingale that normally go into it.

SERVES 6 AS A FIRST COURSE

1½ litres (2¾ pints) chicken stock

25 g (1 oz) dried kafflr lime leaves

2 stalks lemongrass, chopped

3 thick slices dried galingale root

75 g (3 oz) coarsely chopped root ginger

3 hot green chillies, halved and seeded (preferably jalapeño)

75 g (3 oz) chopped coriander stems and roots, washed carefully

350 g (12 oz) skinless, boneless chicken breast, half-frozen (see pages 61-62)

salt to taste

600 ml (1 pint) medium-thick coconut milk (see box)

45 ml (3 tbsp) lime juice

15 g (1 tbsp) sugar

15 ml (1 tbsp) nam pla (bottled Thai fish sauce)

finely chopped spring onion and coriander leaves for garnish

1. Place the chicken stock in a heavy-bottomed pot over high heat. Add the kafflr lime leaves, lemongrass, galingale root, ginger, green chillies and coriander stems and roots. Bring to a boil, reduce heat and simmer until reduced to about 750 ml (1⅓ pints). Press occasionally on the solids with a wooden spoon to release flavour.

2. Working with a sharp knife, cut the chicken breasts into broad slices, as thin as possible. Salt lightly and reserve in refrigerator.

3. When broth is reduced, strain into a measuring cup. Press on the solids in the strainer with a wooden spoon. Place the coconut milk in the soup pot over moderate heat. Slowly stir in the reduced broth. Cook over moderately high heat, but do not allow to boil (otherwise the coconut milk will separate). When the soup is just below the boiling point, add the chicken slices. Remove from heat after 30 seconds (or when the chicken is just cooked through).

4. Just before serving, mix together the lime juice and sugar in a small bowl. Blend in the fish sauce. Pour mixture into hot soup, season to taste and garnish soup with a little bit of chopped spring onion and coriander leaves.

5. Optional step: If your soup has curdled a bit (which the Thais don't mind) or if you'd like a fluffier texture in the soup, place the soup in a blender on high speed for 30 seconds before you add the chicken. Then return to pot, add chicken (step 3, above) and proceed as recipe directs.

Variation: You can convert this soul-satisfying soup into a main course by doubling the amount of chicken and keeping the same amount of liquid. Simply place a mound of about 115 g (4 oz) of steamed white rice, pressed into a teacup, to one side in each of 6 wide, shallow bowls, then divide the soup/stew among the bowls. On the side serve a tomato salad that has been dressed with lime juice, sugar and fish sauce and topped with chopped peanuts and finely chopped coriander.

Coconut milk

Coconut milk, one of the staples of Thai cuisine, is not the liquid that is found in the centre of coconuts; that is coconut water, which is not very strongly flavoured. Coconut milk is obtained by soaking grated or dessicated coconut in hot liquid. It's easy to find unsweetened canned coconut milk at Asian groceries and in many supermarkets. You can also make your own coconut milk in several ways. You can make it from unsweetened dessicated coconut. To make 700 ml (1¼ pints) medium-thick coconut milk, bring 450 ml (16 fl oz) milk to a boil in a saucepan. Add 450 ml (16 fl oz) of the dessicated coconut to the milk, stir, turn off the heat and let the mixture come to room temperature. Press through a sieve to obtain coconut milk.

Or, you can make coconut milk from fresh coconuts.

Split open a large coconut and grate the flesh; you'll obtain approximately 800 g (1 lb 12 oz) grated coconut. Mix this with 125 ml (4 fl oz) hot water, let come to room temperature and press through a sieve; this will yield about 125 ml (4 fl oz) of thick coconut milk (if you need that). To make medium coconut milk, add another 450 ml (16 fl oz) hot water to the already-pressed grated coconut. Let come to room temperature and press through a sieve; combine this thinner milk with the already-made thick milk to obtain a little over 450 ml (16 fl oz) of medium-thick milk.

Variation

THAI CHICKEN AND COCONUT MILK SOUP WITH LIME AND LEMON RIND

Good news: you can make the classic Thai chicken and coconut milk soup even if you can't find kaffir lime leaves, lemongrass and galingale root. This ingenious variation—which substitutes lime and lemon rind for the other ingredients—is also very delicious and very authentic-tasting.

SERVES 6 AS A FIRST COURSE

1.5 litres (2¾ pints) chicken stock
zest of 3 large limes
zest of 3 large lemons
75 g (3 oz) coarsely chopped fresh ginger
3 hot green chillies, halved and seeded (preferably jalapeño)
75 g (3 oz) chopped coriander stems and roots, washed carefully
350 g (12 oz) skinless, boneless chicken breast, half-frozen (see box, opposite)
600 ml (1 pint) medium-thick coconut milk (see box, page 60)
45 ml (3 tbsp) lime juice
15 ml (1 tbsp) sugar
15 ml (1 tbsp) nam pla (bottled Thai fish sauce)

finely chopped spring onion and coriander leaves for garnish

1. Place the chicken stock in a heavy-bottomed pot over high heat. Add the lime zest, lemon zest, ginger, green chillies and the coriander stems and roots. Bring to a boil, reduce heat and simmer until reduced to about 750 ml (1⅓ pints). Press occasionally on the solids with a wooden spoon to release flavour.

2. Working with a sharp knife, cut the chicken breasts into broad slices, as thin as possible. Salt lightly and reserve in refrigerator.

3. When broth is reduced, strain into a measuring cup. Press on the solids in the strainer with a wooden spoon. Place the coconut milk in the soup pot over moderate heat. Slowly stir in the reduced liquid. Cook over moderately high heat, but do not allow to boil (or the coconut milk will separate). When the soup is just below the boiling point, add the chicken slices. Remove from heat after 30 seconds (or when the chicken is just cooked through).

4. Just before serving, mix together the lime juice and sugar in a small bowl. Blend in the fish sauce. Pour mixture into hot soup, season to taste and garnish soup with a little bit of chopped spring onion and coriander leaves.

5. Optional step: If your soup has curdled a bit (which the Thais don't mind) or if you'd like a fluffier texture in the soup, place the soup in a blender at high speed for 30 seconds before you add the chicken. Then return to pot, add chicken (step 3, above) and proceed as recipe directs.

Slicing meat thinly
The extremely thin slices of chicken breast needed for

this soup can be made by semi-freezing your boneless chicken breasts. Place the meat in the freezer for 20 to 30 minutes, or until it's almost frozen. Then remove the breasts and shave them as thinly as possible with a very sharp knife. The technique can be used for any meat that needs to be thinly sliced (such as pork for stir-fries).

Classic

MISO SOUP WITH BEAN CURD

Miso soups are always served for breakfast in traditional Japanese homes and they're often served for lunch and dinner as well. They may be served at the beginning or at the end of a meal. The solids in miso soup are eaten with chopsticks and the remaining liquid is drunk from the bowl; spoons are traditionally not served with Japanese soups. Miso soups (called *miso shiru* in Japan) are high in protein and contain several digestive enzymes. Many different flavourings and garnishes may be added to miso shiru: try using tiny blanched cubes of aburage (fried bean curd), thinly sliced fresh shiitake mushrooms, very thin diagonal slices of slender spring onion, carrots grated or cut into shapes of leaves or blossoms, slivers of lemon, or whatever sounds good to you. The following recipe is the austere classic that is served today as part of the 'dinner' at thousands of Japanese restaurants and sushi bars in America.

SERVES 6

1.5 litres (2¾ pints) dashi (see box, page 64)
45-60 ml (3-4 tbsp) red miso (depending on its strength)
5 ml (1 tsp) soy sauce
115 g (4 oz) very firm tofu, cut into 5-mm (¼-in) cubes
18 mitsuba (trefoil) leaves or fresh coriander leaves for garnish

1. Bring dashi to a bare simmer and add miso, whisking until smooth. Add soy sauce and simmer gently (never boil a miso soup because it will lose its delicate flavour and aroma) for 1 minute. Taste for seasoning; add salt if necessary.

2. Place the tofu in 6 soup bowls and ladle the soup into the bowls. Garnish with mitsuba leaves and serve immediately.

Note: If you wish, you might want to add to the soup pieces of kombu (kelp) that you simmered to make the dashi. If so, cut up 115 g (4 oz) kombu into chunks and add them to the soup just before ladling into bowls.

Variation

WHITE MISO SOUP WITH STEAMED CLAMS

This light, delicious soup is not as intense as the classic miso soup, which is made from red miso. This one calls for white or yellow miso and its motif is delicacy. By all means, use tiny clams (cockles) for this dish, such as cockles from the Gower Peninsula in Wales. Yuzu, one of the many Japanese citrus fruits that's unlike any of ours, is used extensively in Japanese cooking for its fabulous aromatic rind and its acidic juice. It is available in Japanese groceries in the form of bottled yuzu juice.

SERVES 6

36 small clams (cockles) in the shell
18-20 cm (7-8-in) piece dashi kombu (kelp)
45 ml (3 tbsp) white or yellow miso
10 ml (2 tsp) Japanese soy sauce
10 ml (2 tsp) mirin
few drops of yuzu juice (optional)
snipped fresh chives for garnish
very thin julienne of lemon zest for garnish

1. Your little clams probably won't be sandy inside, but if they are, scrub them and soak them in lightly salted cool water (about 1.35 ml (¼ tsp) salt for each 225 ml (8 fl oz) water) to cover for 30 minutes, or until the shells have opened slightly. Pour off the sandy water and repeat the process twice. Drain the clams and rinse them well.

2. Place the clams in a large pot with 1 litre (1¾ pints) fresh cold water, add the kombu and bring to a boil, uncovered, over high heat. The clams will open and the kombu will expand. Discard the kombu just as the water comes to a boil, reduce the heat and simmer for 3 minutes. Strain the liquid into a large bowl through a very fine sieve lined with damp muslin or a coffee filter.

3. Discard any unopened clams. Divide the clams, in their shells, among 6 bowls.

4. Stir together the miso, soy sauce and mirin in a small bowl, add 225 ml (8 fl oz) of the warm broth and stir until smooth. Add the miso mixture to the remaining broth in the large bowl and ladle the broth over the clams in the bowls. Add a few drops of yuzu juice, if available, to each bowl. Garnish soups with the chives and lemon zest and serve immediately.

About miso

Miso is a fermented and aged soybean paste used extensively in Japanese cooking—for soups, sauces, marinades, dressings and many other things. You might say it's analogous to butter in French cooking or olive oil in Italian cooking.

You can find miso at Japanese groceries and at health food shops. Once you start looking, you'll be amazed by the staggering variety that is available, ranging from pale white miso (usually the least intense, least salty and sweetest), through yellow and tan, all the way up to deep red, dark brown and almost black miso (the longest aged, the saltiest, the most intense in flavour). It's great fun to buy an assortment—and then to taste them to see which kinds you like best.

Classic

CHINESE HOT AND SOUR SOUP
This soup took America by storm as Szechuan restaurants spread like weeds in the seventies; its combination of spiky vinegar, peppery heat, rich broth and lots of exotic bits floating on top is an out-and-out winner. Ironically, it is not a Szechuan dish—it's one of the spicier and more downscale representatives of the normally opulent Peking cuisine.

SERVES 4

30 g (2 tbsp) dried cloud-ear mushrooms
5 dried, medium Chinese mushrooms
25 g (1 oz) dried tiger lily shreds
2 garlic cloves, finely chopped
30 ml (2 tbsp) peanut oil
115 g (4 oz) lean raw pork, shredded
1 litre (1¾ pints) pork stock (or you may substitute chicken stock)
3 spring onions, cut in 2.5-cm (1-in) lengths, plus 2 finely chopped spring onions for garnish
50 g (2 oz) bamboo shoots, sliced
15 g (1 tbsp) pickled mustard greens, thinly sliced
90 ml (6 tbsp) Chinese black vinegar
10 g (2 tsp) sugar
2.5 g (½ tsp) monosodium glutamate (optional)
45 ml (3 tbsp) light soy sauce
freshly ground white pepper to taste
50 g (2 oz) cornflour
1 egg, beaten with a little cornflour
115 g (4 oz) firm bean curd, diced
15 ml (1 tbsp) dark sesame oil

1. Place the cloud-ears and dried Chinese mushrooms in a small bowl and cover with boiling water. Soak for 20 minutes. Soak the tiger lily shreds in warm water to cover for 20 minutes. Drain, slice the mushrooms and set aside.

2. Sauté the finely chopped garlic in the peanut oil over moderate heat in a soup pot for 2 minutes. Add the shredded pork and cook for 2 minutes. Add the pork stock, soaked cloud-ears, soaked mushroom slices, soaked tiger lily shreds, spring onions, bamboo shoots, pickled mustard greens, vinegar, sugar, monosodium glutamate (if using), soy sauce and white pepper. Mix the cornflour with a few tablespoons of water, making a creamy liquid. Bring soup to boil and add cornflour mixture. Simmer for 30 minutes.

3. Before serving, bring soup to boil and add the beaten egg. Reduce heat, bring soup to a simmer and add the bean curd. Remove from heat and add the sesame oil. Divide among 4 soup bowls and top with finely chopped spring onion.

Dashi from scratch and from a package

Dashi is the ever-present ingredient that gives Japanese food its distinctive flavour. It's an amber coloured, sea-flavored, all-purpose Japanese stock. Unlike European stocks, dashi is not long simmering; it cooks for just a few minutes and still packs a lot of flavour. When made properly, dashi is subtle, crystal-clear and both sweet and smoky. It smells like the perfect sea breeze. Prepared with seaweed (kombu) and dried bonito, it is very easy to make from scratch—but it does require close attention and careful timing. If the seaweed is left in until the water boils, the stock will be bitter and if the bonito is steeped too long, the stock will taste fishy.

Here's a simple and authentic recipe:
1.5 litres (2¾ pints) fresh cold water
two 15-cm (6-in) pieces dashi kombu (giant kelp)
175 g (6 oz) large shavings of katsuobushi (dried bonito)

1. Place the water in a large saucepan and add the kombu. Bring the mixture to just before a boil over high heat and remove the kombu immediately (the kombu will expand and become soft). Reserve kombu, if desired, for miso soup.

2. Remove the pan from the heat and add the katsuobushi. Let it settle to the bottom of the pan; it should take about 7 minutes. Strain the stock through a very fine sieve lined with a finely woven cloth or several layers of damp paper towels, pressing gently on the solids to remove all liquid.Discard the bonito. Makes about 1.3 litres (2¼ pints).

Now here's some very good news: though powdered stocks and bouillons are usually poor substitutes for the real thing, the ingenious Japanese food industry has come up with a powdered product that, when mixed with hot water, instantly gives you a very credible version of dashi. One brand we like very much is called Hon-Dashi and is available at Japanese grocers. To make 1.3 litres (2¼ pints) of strong dashi for miso soup with bean curd, mix together 1.3 litres (2¼ pints) warm water in a saucepan with 45 g (3 tbsp) of dashi powder. Heat for 2 minutes, stirring well. Cool.

Variation

CHINESE HOT AND SOUR FISH SOUP
This delicious new variation is more subtle and more delicate than ordinary hot-and-sour soup. As you'll note, it's a light soup with no cornflour thickening.

SERVES 4

10 ml (2 tsp) peanut oil
1.3 kg (3 lb) fish heads, bones and/or trimmings
2 large garlic cloves, chopped
6 spring onions, 4 coarsely chopped, 2 very finely chopped
8 slices of fresh ginger (each the size of a 10-p piece)

1.3 litres (2¼ pints) water

50 ml (2 fl oz) Thai or Vietnamese fermented fish
   sauce

50 ml (2 fl oz) Chinese oyster sauce

50 ml (2 fl oz) light rice vinegar (or more to taste)

5 g (1 tsp) freshly grated white pepper (or more to
   taste)

2.5 g (½ tsp) monosodium glutamate (optional)

24 small clams (cockles), in the shell

24 small mussels, bearded and washed

8 dried, medium Chinese mushrooms, soaked for 30
   minutes in hot water to cover, then sliced

50 g (2 oz) fresh bamboo shoots, sliced

50 g (2 oz) firm bean curd, diced

a few drops sesame oil

1. Place the peanut oil in a large, heavy pot over high heat. Add the fish heads, bones and/or trimmings, the garlic, the coarsely chopped spring onions and the ginger. Sauté until the fish and flavourings begin to brown, about 10 minutes. Add the water, the fish sauce and the oyster sauce. Stir well. Bring to a boil and skim off the foam. Reduce heat and simmer for 45 minutes.

2. Strain broth into a clean pot, pressing hard on the solids in the strainer. To the strained broth, add the vinegar, the white pepper and the monosodium glutamate (if using). Bring to a boil. Add the clams and mussels and cover the pot. As soon as the shells open (about 1 minute), add the 2 finely chopped spring onions, the sliced Chinese mushrooms and the bamboo shoots. Stir well. Gently top with the bean curd. Divide among 4 soup bowls and add a drop of sesame oil to each one.

COLD SUMMERTIME SOUPS

COLD CREAM OF WATERCRESS

This pale-green soup is extremely light in texture,

unusually rich in watercress flavour and exceptionally refreshing.

SERVES 6 TO 8

4 bunches of watercress

1 litre (1¾ pints) chicken stock

75 g (3 oz) butter

1 Spanish onion, thinly sliced

40 g (1½ oz) flour

1 litre (1¾ pints) milk

salt and white pepper to taste

225 ml (8 fl oz) double cream, chilled

1. Remove the leaves from the stems of the watercress, reserving 16 leaves for garnish. Bring the chicken stock to a boil in a saucepan and add the stems. Reduce the stock by about half and strain the stock into a bowl.

2. Melt the butter in a large saucepan over moderate heat and add the onion. Cook the onion until transparent, about 5 minutes, and add the flour. Stir well and cook for 2 minutes. Gradually add the milk and bring to a boil. Add the watercress leaves and cook for 2 minutes. (Do not let the watercress darken.)

3. Pour the mixture into a food processor and purée, adding the strained chicken stock. Strain the soup through a fine strainer into a bowl that is sitting over a bowl of ice. Season with the salt and white pepper. Chill in refrigerator until ready to serve.

4. Divide among 6 to 8 soup bowls. Whip the cream and add a dollop to the centre of each soup serving. Garnish with reserved watercress leaves.

SPICY RAW CLAM SOUP WITH CORIANDER

This offbeat, sea-bright summer soup—it's almost a clam cocktail—offers a real chilli kick. Adjust the amount of chillies called for in the recipe according to your chilli threshold and to the heat of the chillies you're using. You can also adjust the amount of clams if you're serving clam fanatics. Simply double the amount of clams (only) and each diner will get a dozen.

SERVES 6 AS A FIRST COURSE

36 clams (American littlenecks, if possible)
75 g (3 oz) very finely diced sweet red pepper
45 g (3 tbsp) very finely diced green pepper
15g (1 tbsp) very finely diced hot green chilli pepper
  (preferably jalapeño)
75 g (3 oz) very finely finely chopped fresh coriander
  leaves
2.75 g (¾ tsp) garlic, finely chopped to a paste with
  a little salt
90 ml (6 tbsp) fresh lime juice
125 ml (4 fl oz) fruity olive oil
freshly ground black pepper to taste

1. Shell the clams over a large bowl very carefully, reserving the clam juice. Set aside the juice (you should have about 450 ml (16 fl oz)) and the raw clams.

2. In a large mixing bowl combine the diced peppers, the diced chilli peppers, the coriander and the garlic. Stir well. Add the lime juice, stir and, while stirring, add the olive oil in a stream. Finally, while stirring, slowly pour in the reserved clam juice. Season to taste with freshly ground black pepper.

3. Divide the soup among 6 wide, shallow soup bowls. Place 6 clams in each bowl and serve.

VICHYSSOISE

This granddaddy of cold summer soups, despite its French title, was actually created in New York City by Louis Diat at the Ritz-Carlton Hotel in 1910. But its ancestry is French; it's a cold version of the great hot French soup potage parmentier, or leek-and-potato soup. The following cold version is simply extraordinary, the

best we've ever tasted; though it's extremely light and refreshing, the depth of potato flavour is remarkably intense. This occurs because the potatoes are actually cooked twice—once in stock, once in milk.

SERVES 6 TO 8

6 large leeks (white parts only)
50 g (2 oz) butter
1 large onion, coarsely chopped
5 russet potatoes
1 litre (1¾ pints) chicken stock
350 ml (12 fl oz) milk
225 ml (8 fl oz) double cream
pinch of nutmeg
pinch of cayenne
30 ml (2 tbsp) vermouth
salt and pepper to taste
1 bunch of fresh chives, finely snipped

1. Split the leeks in half, clean out the grit and cut into thin slices. Melt the butter in a deep pot over very low heat and add the leeks and onions. Cook for 45 minutes, stirring occasionally. (Be careful not to brown the vegetables.)

2. While the vegetables are cooking, peel potatoes, chop coarsely and reserve in cold water.

3. When the leeks and onions have cooked, add the reserved potatoes and chicken stock to the pot and simmer very gently until the potatoes are falling apart. (Do not bring the soup to a boil. Gradually add water to simmering vegetables if vegetables dry out.)

4. Purée by passing the vegetables through a food mill, or mash thoroughly with a potato masher. Pour the puréed mixture into a fine strainer, such as a chinois, making sure all the liquid is passed into a large bowl. Reserve the puréed mixture and the liquid.

5. Bring the milk to a boil in a large saucepan and scoop the reserved puréed mixture into the hot milk. Simmer for 3 minutes. Pour the mixture into the strainer once more, making sure all the liquid is passed into the large bowl that contains the first straining. Discard the puréed mixture.

6. Completely cool the soup in the refrigerator or over ice. When it's cool, stir in the double cream and add the nutmeg, cayenne and vermouth. Season to taste with salt and pepper. Chill the soup overnight. When ready to serve, adjust the thickness with cream or water as desired.

7. Pour into chilled bowls and garnish with chives.

WINTER HOT POTS

WHEAT BEER SOUP WITH CHEESE CROUTONS

Beer soups are popular in Germany and eastern France. This great one has an impossible depth of flavour for such a short cooking time.

SERVES 4

For the croutons
225 g (8 oz) 2-cm (¾-in) bread cubes (see Note)
40 g (1½ oz) unsalted butter, melted
50 g (2 oz) freshly grated Parmigiano-Reggiano
For the soup
1 litre (1¾ pints) chicken stock
4 cloves
225 g (8 oz) parsnip rounds, very thinly sliced
225 g (8 oz) carrot rounds, very thinly sliced
5 g (1 tsp) finely chopped fresh thyme leaves
50 g (2 oz) smoked slab bacon, cut into fat
  matchsticks
40 g (1½ oz) shallots
25 g (1 oz) plain flour
50 ml (2 fl oz) wheat beer (a light beer may be
  substituted)
finely chopped fresh parsley for garnish

1. *Make the croutons:* Preheat the oven to 120°C (250°F). Toss the bread cubes in a bowl with the melted butter. Add the grated cheese, pressing with your hands to make the cheese adhere to the bread cubes. Spread cubes out on a baking sheet, place in oven and cook, turning once, for 45 to 60 minutes, or until the cubes are golden brown and completely crisp. Spread out and let cool, uncovered, at room temperature.

2. *Make the soup:* Place the chicken stock in a saucepan over high heat. Add the cloves, parsnips, carrots and thyme leaves. Cook for 10 to 15 minutes, or until the vegetables are soft and the stock is reduced.

3. While the vegetables are boiling, place the matchsticks of bacon in a large, heavy saucepan over moderate heat. Cook for 2 minutes. Add the shallots, stir well and cook for 3 minutes. Add the flour and cook, stirring, for 2 minutes. Add the boiling stock all at once, stir well with a whisk and bring to a boil.

4. Just before serving, whisk in the beer, preserving the foam that forms on top. Taste for seasoning. Divide the soup among 4 bowls, top each bowl with a quarter of the croutons and sprinkle all with the finely chopped parsley. Serve immediately.

Note: The best bread to use for these croutons is a crusty loaf or a baguette, but one that's light and airy on the inside. Dense breads will make the croutons too heavy. An airy, freshly cooked white bread is a decent substitute.

Wheat beer

Classic beer is brewed from malted barley. But an intriguing style of beer—variously called *weizenbier*, or *weisse bier*, or just wheat beer—is brewed from a mixture of barley and wheat (usually 30 per cent to 40 per cent wheat). Wheat beer is lighter in body than regular beer, more acidic and with an amazing range of flavours from bananas to cloves. It goes spectacularly well with most foods and even goes well in food, as this scrumptious beer soup attests. Wheat beer today is brewed in Germany, Belgium (*witbier* or *bierre blanche*) and the United States.

GALICIAN SAUSAGE AND KALE SOUP (CALDO GALLEGO)

The damp, cool, foggy weather of Galicia, Spain's verdant north-west corner, has inspired a wonderfully hearty cuisine. Oddly enough—despite the fact that many Spanish restaurants in the United States are owned by expatriate Gallegos—the great caldo gallego, one of the world's most satisfying soups, has not become a restaurant staple in the United States. This is starting to change. One taste of this amazing soup and you'll see why.

SERVES 6 AS A FIRST COURSE OR 4 AS A MAIN COURSE

45 ml (3 tbsp) olive oil
450 g (1 lb) chorizo, sliced 5 mm (¼ in) thick
1 medium onion, chopped
6 garlic cloves, finely chopped
280 g (10 oz) dried haricot or other white beans
2 bay leaves
5 g (1 tsp) dried thyme
5 g (1 tsp) dried rosemary
8 black peppercorns
2 cloves
175 g (6 oz) salt pork (cut in 6-mm (⅓-in) cubes) or a ham bone
2 litres (3½ pints) hot water
450 g (1 lb) potatoes, cut into 1-cm (½-in) dice
450 g (1 lb) kale or spring greens, chopped salt and pepper to taste

1. Place olive oil in a large, heavy soup pot over moderate heat. Add the chorizo and cook for 2 minutes. Remove chorizo with a slotted spoon and reserve.

2. Add the onion and garlic to the pot. Cook until onion begins to brown, about 7 minutes. Add the beans, herbs and spices, salt pork (or ham bone) and water. Increase heat, bring to a boil, then reduce heat and simmer, covered, for 1½ hours. Check the pot occasionally to stir and skim off any foam that may float on the surface.

3. Add the potatoes and the reserved chorizo. Cook for another hour, partially covered. Add kale and cook for another hour, uncovered, stirring thoroughly every 15 minutes. (By now, the soup should should be quite thick.) Season with salt and pepper to taste.

CABBAGE SOUP WITH PAPRIKA, POLISH SAUSAGE AND SULTANAS

There's a wonderful paradox in this soup (Waiter! There's a paradox in my soup!): it's filled with hearty ingredients and hearty flavours—and yet, the overall feel of the soup is light and delicate. A guaranteed crowd-pleaser in winter.

SERVES 8 AS A MAIN COURSE

6 slices bacon, diced
1 medium onion, halved and thinly sliced
4 medium garlic cloves, finely chopped
1.3 kg (3 lb) cabbage, cored and cut and separated into strips 2.5 cm (1in) wide
2.5 g (½ tsp) sweet paprika
2 litres (3½ pints) chicken stock
800 g (28 oz) canned tomatoes
225 g (8 oz) sultanas
675 g (1½ lb) Polish sausage (kielbasa), cut in 6-mm (⅓-in) slices
finely chopped fresh parsley for garnish

1. Place the bacon in a heavy-bottomed soup pot over moderate heat. Cook for 5 minutes or so, or until a good deal of fat is rendered. Immediately add the onion and garlic. Stir and cook for 5 minutes.

2. Add the cabbage and paprika, stirring well to blend. Cook for 5 minutes. Add the stock. In your hand, squeeze most of the juice out of the tomatoes, then cut them into coarse chunks. Add the tomatoes to the pot. Simmer for 15 minutes.

3. Add the sultanas and simmer for 10 minutes more. Add the sausage and simmer about 3 minutes, or just until the sausage slices are warmed. Divide among 8 soup bowls and sprinkle with parsley.

BEAN AND LENTIL SOUPS

Long popular around the world as an inexpensive and delicious way of filling up lots of bellies—but once lacking cachet in America—bean and lentil soups are now viewed almost reverently by American foodies.

PASTA E FAGIOLI WITH RIND OF PARMIGIANO-REGGIANO

Pasta Fazool, with its bizarre Brooklyn pronunciation, sounds like the ultimate Italian-American dish. And it was a staple for years of Little Italy's gingham-tablecloth restaurants—until the 'upscaling' of the eighties did away with such dishes. Today, of course, a new wave of rustic Italian restaurants in the United States is showing Americans that 'pasta fazool' was based on something authentic, *pasta e fagioli*, or a steaming, satisfying soup of beans and pasta.

The following version may be the best one you've ever tasted, because it calls for a rind of Parmigiano-Reggiano to be cooked right in the soup, which gives the dish amazing depth—and it certainly gives you something to do with your rind after you've grated the cheese away. By the way, Italians also make a pasta dish with beans, not a soup, which is called *pasta e fagioli asciutta* (*asciutta* refers to pasta served with a sauce, as opposed to pasta in a soup).

SERVES 4 AS A MAIN COURSE

15 ml (1 tbsp) olive oil
1 stalk celery, chopped coarsely
1 medium onion, coarsely chopped
2 garlic cloves, finely chopped
115 g (4 oz) dried cannellini beans
1 bay leaf
5 g (1 tsp) dried basil
2.5 g (½ tsp) dried thyme
2.5 g (½ tsp) dried rosemary
450 ml (16 fl oz) chicken stock
350 ml (12 fl oz) water
400 g (14 oz) canned tomatoes, drained
1 rind (about 115 g (4 oz)) Parmigiano-Reggiano
50 g (2 oz) very small cut tubular pasta, such as ditali
salt and pepper to taste
extra-virgin olive oil, grated Parmigiano-Reggiano and chopped fresh basil for garnish

1. Place the olive oil in a large, heavy saucepan over moderate heat. Add the celery, onion and garlic and cook until they're soft, about 5 minutes. Add the beans, dried herbs, stock, water, tomatoes and cheese rind. Bring to a boil, cover and reduce heat to low. Cook, covered, stirring occasionally, until the beans are soft, about 1 to 2 hours (depending on the age of your beans).

2. When beans are soft, remove cheese rind from the pot and add the pasta. Cook for another 10 to 15 minutes, or until pasta is done. Add salt and pepper to taste.

3. Serve in wide bowls, garnishing each serving with a drizzle of extra-virgin olive oil, about 15 g (1 tbsp) cheese and about 5 ml (1 tsp) fresh basil.

CUBAN BLACK BEAN SOUP WITH SHERRIED ONIONS

Lucky residents of Miami, Florida and Union City, New Jersey—the home towns of the two largest Cuban communities in the United States—know that even the humblest Cuban lunch counter harbours a gold mine of bold, vivid flavours just waiting to be tapped by adventurous diners. Black bean soup, of course, has left the *barrio* and is now on the menus of some of America's most upscale eateries. Our version of this delicious Cuban mainstay is humble at heart, but it does feature an upscale twist: paper-thin slices of red onion marinated in sherry vinegar. Note that no stock is used in making this soup, but the whole piece of bacon gives it a deep, meaty flavour.

SERVES 8

225 g (8 oz) smoked slab bacon

2 garlic cloves, smashed

350 g (12 oz) dried black beans

30 g (2 tbsp) ground cumin

2 small green chillies, seeds and stems removed, finely chopped

2 litres (3½ pints) water

salt and pepper to taste

1 small red onion, very thinly sliced and separated into rings

125 ml (4 fl oz) sherry vinegar

225 g (8 oz) diced fresh tomatoes

1. Put bacon, garlic, beans, cumin, chillies and water in soup pot. Bring to a boil, reduce heat, partially cover and simmer for about 2 hours, skimming foam if necessary. Add salt and pepper to taste.

2. While soup is simmering, place the red onion in a bowl to marinate with the sherry vinegar. When soup is ready, ladle into 8 bowls and top each serving with some marinated onion and a tablespoon of the diced tomatoes.

INDIAN SPLIT PEA SOUP WITH SEARED PRAWNS AND FRESH TOMATO RELISH

In most Indian restaurants, dal is a thin, unspectacular broth, made from lentils or split peas, that plays a distant supporting role to the main course. But the flavours of dal are so bright and wonderful, why not dress it up with a fresh relish and a trio of spicy seared prawns and let the spectacular result take centre stage by itself? You may never think of Indian food in the same way again. Serve as a main course with naan bread and a cucumber raita (see page 34).

SERVES 4 AS A MAIN COURSE

For the spicy prawns

12 large prawns, shelled

2.5 g (½ tsp) ground cumin seed

2.5 g (½ tsp) ground cardamom seed

1.25 g (¼ tsp) finely chopped garlic

1.25 g (¼ tsp) ground coriander seed

1.25 g (¼ tsp) ground cinnamon

pinch of ground clove

pinch of salt

pinch of cayenne pepper

30 ml (2 tbsp) light vegetable oil, such as safflower

For the soup

15 g (½ oz) unsalted butter

2 medium onions, finely chopped

20 g (4 tsp) garlic, finely chopped

20 g (4 tsp) fresh ginger, finely chopped

5 g (1 tsp) jalapeño, finely chopped (adjust to desired heat)

450 g (1 lb) yellow split peas, washed

5 g (1 tsp) ground coriander seed

5 g (1 tsp) ground cumin seed

5 g (1 tsp) celery seed

½ teaspoon ground cinnamon

1.25 g (¼ tsp) ground clove

2 litres (3½ pints) chicken stock plus additional if necessary

For the relish

225 g (8 oz) finely diced fresh tomato

115 g (4 oz) finely chopped onion

50 g (2 oz) finely chopped coriander leaves plus additional for garnish

2.5 g (½ tsp) finely chopped small green chillies

10 g (2 tsp) fresh lemon juice

2.5 g (½ tsp) grated lemon rind

1. *Make the spicy prawns:* In a bowl toss the prawns with the cumin, cardamom, garlic, coriander, cinnamon, clove, salt and cayenne pepper. Marinate, refrigerated, for 1 hour.

2. *Make the soup:* In a heavy-bottomed pot, melt the butter over moderate heat. Add the onion, garlic, ginger and chillies. Cook, stirring, for 2 minutes. Add the split peas, coriander, cumin, celery seed, cinnamon and clove. Stir to mix well. Add the chicken stock, stir again and bring to a boil. Reduce heat to low and simmer slowly, partially covered, for about 1 hour, or until split peas are just soft. (You may need to add additional chicken stock if peas become too thick and dry.)

3. While soup is simmering, make the relish: Toss all ingredients together in a bowl. Season to taste.

4. When soup is ready, butterfly the marinated prawns, removing the veins. Place a heavy sauté pan over moderately high heat. Add the vegetable oil, swirling around the pan. Add the prawns, cut side down, and sauté for 2 to 3 minutes, or until just cooked. Turn the prawns over and cook for 1 minute. Remove prawns from pan.

5. With a wooden spoon, crush a few of the soft peas in the soup against the side of the pot. Stir well. (If the soup is too thick, add a little chicken stock.) Season to taste. Ladle the hot soup into 4 wide soup bowls. Mix in most of the tomato relish, reserving about 50 ml (2 fl oz). Place 3 prawns in the centre of each bowl. Divide the reserved tomato relish among the bowls, placing it in the centre of the prawns. Top that with a few fresh coriander leaves. Serve immediately.

SPANISH CHICKPEA SOUP (POTAJE DE GARBANZOS)

Many of the hallmarks of Spanish cuisine (and its offspring cuisines in the New World) are relics of the Muslim occupation of the Iberian peninsula between the 8th and the 15th centuries. Dishes containing almonds, apricots, saffron, rice and chick-peas (all among the many ingredients brought to Spain by the Moors) fall into this category. Okay, so Spaniards today throw a little bacon into this great soup—it's still an irresistible whiff of the Middle East in the Middle Ages. You could make this soup with chick-peas out of a can, but you'll get much better texture and flavour if you start with dried chick-peas.

SERVES 8 AS A FIRST COURSE

225 g (8 oz) dried chick-peas

115 g (4 oz) slab bacon, cut into 6 pieces

5 garlic cloves, unpeeled

1 large onion, peeled and halved, studded with 4 cloves

10 g (2 tsp) ground coriander

salt and pepper to taste

225 g (8 oz) fresh spinach, washed carefully and chopped

extra-virgin olive oil for garnish

1. Place chick-peas in a medium bowl. Cover them with cold water and let soak at room temperature overnight.

2. When ready to cook, drain and discard soaking water. In a soup pot, cook the bacon over moderate heat until brown. Add the drained chick-peas and cook for 3 minutes. Add the garlic, clove-studded onion and coriander and cover with boiling water by 2.5 cm (1 inch). Bring to a boil. Reduce heat and cook, partially covered, for at least 2 hours, adding additional water as necessary to keep the chick-peas covered with liquid. When the chick-peas are no longer crunchy, remove the onion halves. Add salt and pepper to taste.

3. Remove about one half of the soup and purée it in a blender or food processor, or mash them in a bowl. Return it to the pot. Add the spinach and cook for another 2 minutes, or until spinach is bright green. Serve hot. Garnish each serving with a drizzle of olive oil.

ITALIAN LENTIL AND WILD MUSHROOM SOUP (PASTA E LENTICCHIE AI PORCINI)

Some call lentil soup, the pan-Italian classic, 'comfort food at its best'. We're tempted to agree. In Italy, lentil freaks prefer the tiny, extremely flavourful lentils from Castelluccio, an isolated village high in the mountains of south-eastern Umbria.

SERVES 6 AS A FIRST COURSE

20 g (¾ oz) dried porcini mushrooms
225 ml (8 fl oz) hot water
1 medium onion, finely chopped
1 carrot, finely chopped
1 garlic clove, finely chopped
5 g (1 tsp) dried thyme
1 bay leaf
30 ml (2 tbsp) olive oil
225 ml (8 fl oz) red wine
280 g (10 oz) lentils
1.5 litres (2¾ pints) water
125 g (4 oz) vermicelli or spaghettini, broken into
   5-cm (2-in) pieces
30 g (2 tbsp) finely chopped fresh parsley
salt and pepper to taste
extra-virgin olive oil for drizzling on individual
   servings

1. Place porcini in a bowl, cover with the hot water and let soak for 20 minutes, making sure to submerge the mushrooms. When mushrooms are soft, remove them from the water, squeezing the liquid back into the bowl. Reserve this liquid. Chop the mushrooms coarsely.

2. In a large saucepan, cook the onion, carrot, garlic,

thyme, bay leaf and chopped mushrooms over moderate heat in the olive oil. When onion is golden and translucent, about 5 minutes, strain the reserved mushroom soaking liquid into the pot. Add the wine, lentils and water. Simmer until the lentils are soft, about 20 minutes. Add the pasta and cook until the pasta is done, about 10 minutes. Add salt and pepper to taste. Serve in wide bowls, sprinkling parsley and drizzling a little extra-virgin olive oil onto each serving.

Note: In Umbria, lentil soups such as this one are sometimes served over a thick slice of toasted bread that has been rubbed with garlic and drizzled with olive oil. Just put the bread in the bottom of the soup bowl and ladle away.

CREAMY LENTIL AND ANCHO CHILLI SOUP

The technique of frying a chilli-and-spice purée in oil is central to Mexican cuisine. By changing the mix of chillies and spices, you can provide the seasoning foundation for a limitless number of sophisticated Mexican sauces, stews and soups. This one boasts a number of fabulous soup adjectives: creamy, hearty, complex, full-flavored. It employs the chocolatey ancho chilli, one of our favourite dried chillies.

SERVES 8 AS A FIRST COURSE

4 ancho chillies
225 ml (8 fl oz) hot water
2.5 g (½ tsp) ground allspice
pinch of ground cloves
15 g (3 tsp) ground cumin
2.5 g (½ tsp) dried rosemary
2.5 g (½ tsp) black pepper
15 ml (1 tbsp) tomato purée
1 white onion, finely chopped
2 garlic cloves, finely chopped
15 ml (1 tbsp) vegetable oil
225 g (8 oz) dried green lentils
1.5 litres (2¾ pints) water

grated zest of one orange
1 bay leaf
225 ml (8 fl oz) sour cream
salt to taste
90 ml (6 tbsp) fresh coriander, finely chopped

1. Toast the chillies in a 100°C (200°F) oven for 5 minutes. Remove and discard seeds and stems. Place in a small bowl and cover with the hot water. Cover bowl and let sit for 15 minutes.

2. Remove chillies from water, reserving the soaking water. Combine the chillies with the allspice, cloves, cumin, rosemary, pepper and tomato paste in a food processor or blender. Process until smooth.

3. Cook onion and garlic in the vegetable oil over moderately low heat until onion is soft, about 10 minutes. Add the chilli mixture and fry, stirring, for 2 minutes. Add the lentils, water, orange zest and bay leaf. Increase the heat, bring to a boil, reduce the heat and cook, partially covered, stirring occasionally, for 1 hour.

4. Remove from heat. Let soup cool, stirring every few minutes to speed up the cooling, for 15 to 30 minutes. (Ideal serving temperature is lukewarm). Stir in the sour cream and add salt to taste.

5. Serve with a sprinkling of finely chopped fresh coriander on each bowl.

MIDDLE EASTERN RED LENTIL SOUP WITH YOGURT AND LEMON

Most people think of soup as a dish requiring hours of advance preparation. However, by using the sumptuous, nutty-tasting, split red lentil from Turkey, you can enjoy a delicious, made-from-scratch soup just 30 minutes after you come home from work. We like this soup best when it has cooled off a little bit.

SERVES 8 AS A FIRST COURSE

15 ml (1 tbsp) olive oil
1 medium onion, finely chopped
7.5 g (1½ tsp) ground coriander
5 g (1 tsp) ground cumin
2.5 g (½ tsp) ground ginger
2.5 g (½ tsp) mustard powder
250 g (9 oz) split red lentils
1 medium lemon
1.25 litres (2 pints) water
salt and pepper to taste
225 ml (8 fl oz) plain yogurt
25 g (1 oz) finely chopped fresh coriander
Aleppo pepper for garnish (see box)

1. Place oil in a large, heavy saucepan over moderate heat. Add onion and spices and cook, stirring, until onion begins to brown, about 7 minutes.

2. Add lentils, 8 strips of lemon zest cut from the lemon, and water. Bring to a boil, then cover, reduce heat and simmer for 15 minutes, or until consistency is smooth. Add salt and pepper to taste.

3. Stir yogurt and coriander together. Add the juice of the lemon. Stir well until consistency is smooth and silken.

4. Pour the soup into wide bowls and let it cool for 15 minutes. Top each serving with a swirl of the yogurt mixture and sprinkle of Aleppo pepper.

Aleppo pepper

You'll find a coarse powder made from Aleppo peppers throughout the Middle East; in a sea of red pepper powders, it stands out for its earthier, more full-flavoured character. Sometimes it's labelled 'Near East Pepper', but you won't be sure it's Aleppo. We sell Aleppo pepper at Dean & DeLuca, but you may have trouble finding it elsewhere. Sweet Hungarian paprika mixed with any hot red pepper powder (like cayenne)makes a reasonable substitute.

JEWISH CHICKEN SOUP

Aside from its now scientifically documented salubrious properties, Jewish chicken soup is medicine for the soul as well—and delicious, too. So who knew that two guys named Dean and DeLuca—whose name on a soup would seem to indicate a country-club version of minestrone—also make the best chicken soup this side of a shtetl? You don't sell piece goods in New York for 20 years without learning something....

Chicken soup additions

Traditional possibilities for add-ins to your chicken soup range from the positively austere to the wildly baroque. Every Jewish mama has her own preference.

On the austere side: you may float a lonely matzo ball or a lonely kreplach in your soup. Great recipes for both follow. Or, you may serve 2 to 3 mandlen, or 'soup almonds' in each bowl; there are no almonds in these crisp little pastries (which you can buy in boxes), but they do resemble almonds.

For more farinaceous fun, you may want to consider rice in your chicken soup or the more popular noodle option. Many a Jewish mama has served Goodman's thin egg noodles in her chicken soup.

Next: the chicken and vegetable question. Do you add the pieces of cooked chicken that helped make the soup back to the soup bowl at the end? Or do you save them for chicken salad? Do you add back any of the flavouring vegetables? Some chicken soups are loaded with these things, some are free of them.

To make an austere soup, you might add one of any of the options mentioned above. But some people like to go for baroque. You could, for example, add matzo balls (and several of them), plus kreplach, plus thin egg noodles, plus pieces of chicken, plus pieces of parsnip, carrot and onion. If you add whole chicken pieces (breasts, legs, thighs), then you have a Jewish pot-au-feu called Chicken in the Pot, a wonderful one-course winter dinner. Serve with rye bread containing caraway seeds.

MATZO BALLS

The debate rages: heavy matzo balls or feather-light ones? The following matzo balls satisfy both camps; though they lean toward the light school, there's enough density and chew to please all palates. The key to texture is a brief sojourn in the refrigerator and the key to taste is good schmaltz, rendered chicken fat, which you can render yourself or buy at a Jewish grocery.

MAKES 8 MATZO BALLS

2 large eggs, well beaten with a fork
45 ml (3 tbsp) plain soda water
30 ml (2 tbsp) rendered chicken fat, melted (you could substitute vegetable oil)
1.25 g (¼ tsp) coarse salt
1.25 g (¼ tsp) freshly ground black pepper
50 g (2 oz) matzo meal

1. Mix the eggs, soda water, chicken fat, salt and pepper in a bowl. Gradually stir in the matzo meal, stirring until everything is well combined. Chill, covered, in the refrigerator for at least 4 hours and up to 8 hours.

2. Bring a pot of salted water to a boil. Using cool, wet hands shape the matzo mixture into 8 balls, each about 4 cm (1½ in) in diameter. Reduce the heat to simmering and gently add the matzo balls. Cover the pot and poach the matzo balls in the barely simmering water for 25 minutes.

KREPLACH

Kreplach are like Jewish won tons—and they actually may have been learned by Eastern European Jews who were trading in China. The Jewish version, of course, has no pork; leftover beef is substituted. If you have leftover flanken (boiled short ribs), this will be the best version of kreplach you've ever tasted.

MAKES 24 KREPLACH

225 g (8 oz) unbleached plain white flour

2 eggs, beaten

1 teaspoon salt

2 tablespoons rendered chicken fat

2 medium onions, chopped

450 g (1 lb) boiled beef cut into slices (cooked flank is best, but any leftover boiled or potted beef will do)

1.25 g (¼ tsp) allspice

salt and pepper to taste

1. Mix together the flour, eggs and salt, as if making pasta. You will probably need to add about 5 to 6 tablespoons of water to reach the desired elasticity in the dough. Work it on a floured board, kneading for about 10 minutes. When it's smooth and elastic, pull it into something resembling a square. Cover with clingfilm and let sit at room temperature for about 20 minutes.

2. Place the chicken fat in a heavy frying pan over high heat. Add the onions and sauté until the onions are medium-brown, about 10 minutes. Place the onions in the work bowl of a food processor and add the sliced beef and allspice. Purée until smooth. Taste and season well with salt and pepper.

3. Roll out the kreplach dough into a large square, about 5 mm (¼ in) thick. Cut into smaller squares, about 5 cm (2 in) each. You should have about 24 squares. Divide the beef mixture among them, placing 15 g (1 tbsp) or so of the beef mixture in the centre of each square. Triangular kreplach are traditional; fold each square once to form a triangle, then pinch the edges with your fingers. You could also make square or rectangular kreplach, depending on how you fold and pinch.

4. To cook the kreplach, drop them in a pot of boiling

chicken soup. Traditionally, they are cooked for half an hour or so, until the noodle is very soft. An alternative, giving the noodle a more 'Italian' bite, is to cook them for 15 minutes.

5. Serve the kreplach in soup, 3 to 4 to each bowl.

Note: Though it is traditional to serve these kreplach in chicken soup (3 to 4 per bowl), they can also make a terrific Jewish 'pasta' dish. For authenticity's sake, you can't use dairy products in the sauce—but a thickened sauté of mushrooms (in vegetable oil, of course) would be a great topping.

MAMA'S CHICKEN SOUP

SERVES 8

1 x 1.6-1.8 kg (3½-4-lb) chicken, quartered

2.5 litres (4½ pints) cold water

6 large carrots, thinly sliced

3 celery stalks with leaves, sliced

3 parsnips, sliced

1 large onion, chopped

1 medium turnip, chopped

2 garlic cloves, peeled

10 sprigs of fresh parsley

4 sprigs of fresh dill

7.5 g (1½ tsp) salt

freshly ground black pepper

15 g (1 tbsp) each chopped fresh parsley, dill and chives for garnish

1. In a stockpot heat the chicken and the water to boiling, skimming off foam. Reserve 2 cups carrots; add remaining carrots to chicken mixture with celery, parsnips, onion, turnip, garlic, parsley, dill, salt and a little freshly ground black pepper. Simmer, partially covered, until the chicken is cooked, about 1 hour.

2. Remove chicken to a plate and when cool enough to

handle remove meat and shred into bite-sized pieces. Reserve for another use, or for serving in soup. Add bones and skin to soup and continue to simmer for one hour more.

3. When soup is done, strain through a sieve into a large saucepan, pressing on solids to extract as much liquid as possible. You may refrigerate the soup overnight, then skim off the congealed layer of fat that forms on top.

4. When ready to serve, add the reserved carrots. Simmer soup, covered, for 15 minutes, or until carrots are tender. Serve in bowls with choice of soup additions (see box, page 74), topped with finely chopped fresh herbs.

BOUILLABAISSE

We couldn't conclude a chapter on soup without a show-stopping version of the world's greatest fish soup. Though bouillabaisse has utterly downscale roots—it was a simple supper for Marseilles fishermen who threw their unsold, least desirable fish in a pot—today it has taken on the aura of shabby-chic. This is abetted by the kind of prices they get for it in the Mediterranean and the kind of upscale restaurants that serve it.

BOUILLABAISSE IN THREE COURSES

At the Restaurant du Bacon in Cap d'Antibes, a Michelin two-star, the soup is divided into multiple courses and it will cost you upwards of £75.00 per person. Based on the Bacon bouillabaisse, the following recipe is a splendid way to throw an elegant and unusual dinner party. Your guests are treated to a simple first course of fish fillets in a light broth, a richer second course of shellfish in a more concentrated broth and a relatively austere but climactic third course of the heavily reduced, now-super-flavourful soup supporting a trio of rouille-

mounted basil toasts. The following recipes will make a complete dinner for 6 people.

BOUILLABAISSE BROTH

> 45 ml (3 tbsp) olive oil
> 675 g (1½ lb) leeks
> 6 large garlic cloves, chopped
> 1 sweet red pepper, chopped
> 25 g (1 oz) firmly packed fresh basil leaves
> 2.5 g (½ tsp) saffron threads
> 8 pieces dried orange peel (each about 5 x 2.5 cm (2 x 1 in))
> 15 g (1 tbsp) fennel seeds, crushed
> 2.25 kg (5 lb) very fresh fish, fish heads, fish bones (a mixture of things works best; avoid fish that are fishy or oily)
> 225 ml (8 fl oz) dry white wine
> 2.25 litres (4 pints) water
> salt and pepper to taste

1. Heat the olive oil in a large, heavy-bottomed stew pot. Split the leeks, wash away grit and chop the leeks into coarse pieces. Add the leeks, garlic and pepper to the olive oil. Stir. Cook over moderate heat for about 10 minutes, or until the vegetables have begun to soften.

2. Add the basil, saffron, orange peel and fennel seeds. Mix well with the leeks. Then increase the heat to high, add the fish pieces and fry for 5 minutes. Add the white wine and deglaze pot. Boil for 1 minute. Add the water, stir well and simmer for 1 hour, stirring occasionally and skimming foam off the top of the pot.

3. When done, select a clean pot that is large and wide. Strain the broth into the pot through a sieve, pressing on the solids in the sieve. Add salt and pepper to taste.

First Course
———————

FISH WITH POTATOES

SERVES 6

bouillabaisse broth
8 peeled small potatoes (about 450 g (1 lb))
2.7 kg (6 lb) of whole fish (A variety is preferable:
    whole red snapper, whole flounder, whole sea
    bass. You may include some chunks of larger fish,
    such as monkfish and haddock. Try to find an
    assortment of flavours and textures.)
30 ml (2 tbsp) extra-virgin olive oil
salt and freshly ground pepper to taste
90 ml (6 tbsp) finely chopped fresh parsley

1. In the large, wide pot, bring the bouillabaisse broth to
a simmer. Add potatoes to the broth. Simmer for 10
minutes. Then add the fish, adding the thickest and
firmest ones first. (You must use your judgment here;
the cooked fish should be firm, just cooked. Most fish
will not take longer than 5 to 7 minutes in the
simmering broth.)

2. When the fish are done, remove them to a platter.
Working quickly on a slotted board, fillet the whole fish
and divide the fillets evenly among 6 dinner plates.
Reserve the fish bones and heads. Cut up the chunks of
fish (such as monkfish and haddock) and divide among
the plates.

3. Remove potatoes from bouillabaisse pot and place a
cooked potato half in the centre of each dinner plate.
Ladle a few tablespoons of broth around the fish on
each plate. Drizzle a teaspoon of extra-virgin olive oil
over the fish on each plate and season well with salt
and freshly ground black pepper. Strew the chopped
parsley over the fish and serve immediately.

4. Return the fish bones and heads and all juices from
the slotted board to the bouillabaisse pot.

Second Course
———————

SHELLFISH WITH SAFFRON–OLIVE OIL BROTH

SERVES 6

the remaining bouillabaisse broth
3 x 550-g (1¼-lb) uncooked lobsters
1.25 g (¼ tsp) saffron
50 ml (2 fl oz) very rich extra-virgin olive oil
450 g (1 lb) large prawns (about 24 in all; shelled,
    with shells reserved)
450 g (1 lb) scallops
18 mussels

1. While your guests are eating the first course, bring
the pot of broth to a boil. Plunge the lobsters into the
broth, cover and cook for 12 minutes.

2. While lobsters are cooking, prepare the sauce: remove
225 ml (8 fl oz) of broth and place in a small saucepan.
Add the saffron and reduce the broth by about one third
over high heat. Reduce heat to low and slowly whisk in
the extra-virgin olive oil until well incorporated (the
sauce will be thickened). Keep warm.

3. Remove lobsters from broth when done and, working
on a slotted board, cut into 6 half-tail portions, 6 claws
and 6 first joints (the first joint is the part that connects
the claw to the body). Remove meat from shells,
reserving shells. Reserve chest and legs.

4. While working, slip the shelled prawns, the scallops
and the mussels into the simmering broth for about 1
minute, or until just cooked. Remove when done.

5. Now divide the shelled lobster pieces, the cooked
prawns, the cooked scallops and the cooked mussels

among 6 plates. Pour a bit of the warmed sauce over the shellfish and serve immediately.

6. Put the remaining pieces of lobster (including chest and legs), the juices from the slotted board and the prawn shells into the bouillabaisse pot. Cover the pot and turn the heat to moderately high. Boil the broth furiously for at least 20 minutes and up to 40 minutes (after 30 to 40 minutes the broth will pick up even more flavour, but it may be difflcult to wait that long).

Third Course

THE SOUP WITH BASIL TOASTS AND ROUILLE

SERVES 6

the remaining bouillabaisse broth
arrowroot for thickening soup (optional)
18 basil-rubbed toasts (recipe follows)
¾ cup rouille (recipe follows)
⅓ cup fresh basil leaves, shredded, plus 6 small
   basil leaves

1. You may want to thicken the bouillabaisse broth for the final course. If so, put a few teaspoons of arrowroot in a small cup and mix with cold water until a milky liquid is formed. While the soup is boiling, add arrowroot mixture in a thin stream until desired thickness is reached.

2. When ready to serve, season the soup to taste. Select 6 wide, shallow soup bowls and place three toasts in the centre of each. Ladle the bouillabaisse broth around the toasts and top the toasts with a dollop of rouille. Place a small basil leaf where the three toasts intersect and scatter the shredded basil over the rest of the soup. Serve immediately with additional rouille on the side.

BASIL-RUBBED TOASTS

MAKES 18 TOASTS

18 round slices of French bread, each about ½ inch
   thick
2 large garlic cloves, cut
handful of fresh basil leaves

Heat oven to 120°C (250°F). Place the bread slices on a baking sheet and bake, turning occasionally, for 45 minutes. When done, rub each slice with a cut side of garlic and rub with torn basil leaves. (Work carefully, because the toasts will be brittle. The toasts will pick up a rich green colour.)

ROUILLE

MAKES ABOUT 225 ML (8 FL OZ)

5 garlic cloves
salt to taste
5 g (1 tsp) tomato paste
5 g (1 tsp) Dijon mustard
30 g (2 tbsp) pimientos
15 g (1 tbsp) lemon juice
2 egg yolks
½ cup extra-virgin olive oil
cayenne pepper to taste

1. Using a mortar and pestle, crush the garlic along with 2 pinches of salt. Work it until you get a creamy thick paste. (If you don't have a mortar and pestle, crush the garlic and 2 pinches of salt with the back of a knife on a cutting board.) Add creamed garlic to the bowl of a food processor.

2. Add the tomato paste, mustard, pimientos and lemon juice to the garlic in the processor. Process until incorporated. Add the yolks and process until incorporated. With the motor running, add the olive oil slowly in a thin continuous stream through the feed tube. (The mixture will be thick but not stiff.)

3. Add the cayenne and salt to taste.

S A N D W I C H E S

THE HUMBLE SANDWICH HAS LONG BEEN ONE OF AMERICA'S MOST POPULAR FOODS, ESPECIALLY AT LUNCHTIME. WE DARE SAY THAT FOR DECADES HALF OF ALL AMERICANS HAVE HAD SOME FORM OF SANDWICH FOR LUNCH, BUT THERE HAS ALWAYS BEEN AN AIR OF SERVICEABILITY AND PREDICTABILITY ABOUT THESE SANDWICHES, YOU DIDN'T HAVE TO THINK TOO HARD TO SELECT ONE. WHADYA WANT? HAM SANDWICH? HAM-AND-CHEESE? BOLOGNA SANDWICH? TUNA SALAD? TURKEY WITH MAYO? BLT? THE LIST NEVER EXTENDED MUCH BEYOND THAT. AND CERTAINLY, NO ONE EVER GAVE TOO MUCH THOUGHT TO THE BREAD THAT WOULD SURROUND THE FILLING (THE WHITE LOAF KNOWN AS 'SANDWICH BREAD' WAS ALMOST ALWAYS USED), OR TO THE CONDIMENTS ON THE SANDWICH (LETTUCE AND TOMATO WERE THE OPTIONS FOR SOLIDS; KETCHUP, MUSTARD AND MAYONNAISE WERE THE POSSIBLE SPREADS). OH, YES, EVERY ONCE IN A WHILE, SOMEONE TOOK A SLICE OF CHEESE (AMERICAN YELLOW CHEESE OR SWISS-STYLE?).

THEN CAME THE REVOLUTION. AMERICANS DISCOVERED THAT YOU COULD PUT CENTRAL PLAYERS OTHER THAN HAM AND TURKEY ON SANDWICHES. YOU COULD TOP THOSE PLAYERS WITH ALL KINDS OF INTERESTING LETTUCES, VEGETABLES, CHEESES AND SPREADS. MOREOVER, THEY FOUND THAT SELECTING AN INTERESTING BREAD FROM THE NEW BAKERIES SPRINGING UP

AROUND THE COUNTRY BOOSTED THE EXCITEMENT LEVEL IMMEASURABLY.
SANDWICHES WENT FROM SERVICEABLE TO CHIC. THOUSANDS OF FANCY FOOD
SHOPS BEGAN MAKING 'CREATIVE' SANDWICHES TO SELL AT LUNCHTIME; NOT-
SO-FANCY FOOD SHOPS SOON FOLLOWED IN THEIR WAKE WITH IMITATIONS.
RESTAURANTS—LED BY UPSCALE EATERIES IN CALIFORNIA—BEGAN ORDERING
THEM FOR DINNER AS WELL AS FOR LUNCH.

SOMETIMES, TODAY, WE MUST CONFESS, IT'S AWFULLY NICE TO GO BACK TO A
HAM SANDWICH—BUT WE FEEL GASTRONOMICALLY ENRICHED BY THE
DIZZYING HEIGHTS TO WHICH AMERICAN SANDWICHERY HAS RISEN AND
WOULDN'T WANT TO LOSE THE PROGRESS WE'VE MADE.

DEAN & DELUCA LUNCH COUNTER

Our shop played a large role in driving the sandwich towards ever more interesting variations. Dean & DeLuca has been jammed every day for years with lunchtime customers lining up for our array of unusual sandwiches on delectable breads. Here are some of our largest sellers.

BRIE AND SMOKED HAM ON SOURDOUGH FICELLE

Whatever happened to ham and Swiss? In the eighties and nineties it became ham and Brie (and we like it!).

MAKES TWO 25-CM (10-INCH) SANDWICHES

one 25-cm (20-in) sourdough ficelle (narrow French stick)
50 ml (2 fl oz) honey mustard
125 g (4 oz) lightly smoked Black Forest ham, thinly sliced
125 g (4 oz) ripe Brie, cut in 3-mm (⅛-in) slices
3 ripe tomatoes, thinly sliced
green-leaf lettuce

1. Cut the ficelle in half lengthways using a bread knife. Spread a thin layer of mustard on all slices.

2. Fold the ham slices to the width of the bread, and lay across the entire bottom piece of bread evenly. Lay the Brie and tomatoes over the ham.

3. Lay the lettuce over the tomatoes, covering the sandwich entirely with a thin layer of leaves. Put the top half of the bread back on, and cut through the middle into two equal sandwiches.

PANINI WITH ROASTED TOMATOES, SQUASH AND MOZZARELLA

Panini are, literally, 'little breads,' or rolls. When Italians say *panini* today, they actually mean *panini imbottiti,* or filled rolls—in other words, Italian sandwiches. Ideally, one makes these sandwiches on round, crusty rolls, that have the outer texture of good French or Italian bread, along with a coarse crumb inside. If you can't find such rolls, make the sandwiches on individually sized sections of French or Italian bread. We sell lots of these every day in the shop.

MAKES 8 SANDWICHES

1 large courgette (about 350 g/¾ lb), thinly sliced lengthways
1 large yellow marrow (squash) (about 350 g/ ¾ lb), sliced thinly lengthways
8 plum tomatoes, cut into quarters
salt and pepper to taste
1 garlic clove, finely chopped
30 ml (2 tbsp) balsamic vinegar
90 ml (6 tbsp) olive oil
8 large, round rolls
450 g (1 lb) fresh mozzarella, cut in 8 slices
16 large fresh basil leaves

1. Preheat oven to 200°C (400°F).

2. Place the courgette, yellow marrow (squash) and tomatoes in a roasting tin and season with salt and pepper. Cook in preheated oven for 10 to 15 minutes, or until the courgette and marrow are very soft and the tomatoes are juicy and slightly blackened.

3. Place the garlic in a small bowl, and whisk in the vinegar and olive oil. Season with salt and pepper and let the mixture stand for about 2 hours.

4. When ready to serve, cut each roll in two and sprinkle each half with the vinaigrette. Separate the marrow (squash) and courgette and place equal portions on 8 bottom halves of rolls. To each, add 1 slice of mozzarella and 2 basil leaves. Pour the remaining vinaigrette over all. Cover each slice with the other bread half and serve.

ROASTED CATFISH SANDWICH WITH SMOKED SALMON AND ROCKET

This is a very quiet but very comforting sandwich—a real crowd-pleaser over the years. Make sure the catfish fillets are still juicy when you remove them from the oven.

MAKES 8 SANDWICHES

15 ml (1 tbsp) olive oil
30 ml (2 tbsp) lemon juice
5 g (1 tsp) chopped garlic
salt and pepper to taste
1.8 kg (4 lb) catfish fillets, cut in 8 pieces
15 g (1 tbsp) coarsely chopped fresh dill
50 g (2 oz) thinly sliced smoked salmon
5 ml (1 tsp) Amontillado sherry
125 ml (4 fl oz) mayonnaise
16 slices white sandwich loaf
32 rocket leaves
15 g (1 tbsp) toasted sesame seeds

1. Preheat the oven to 200°C (400°F).

2. Spread the olive oil on a roasting tin and add lemon juice, garlic, salt, and pepper. Rub each catfish piece with the marinade, and place in refrigerator for 2 hours.

3. Put the dill, salmon and sherry in a food processor and make a paste. Mix the salmon paste into the mayonnaise by hand. Set aside.

4. Bake the fish for 7 to 10 minutes, or until the flesh flakes easily when poked with a fork. Remove from the oven and pour the juices into a small saucepan. While waiting for the fish to cool completely, reduce the juices in the pan over moderate heat until you have about 5 ml (1 tsp) of thick glaze.

5. Add the glaze to the mayonnaise mix and spread the mixture on 16 slices of bread. Lay 4 rocket leaves on each of 8 slices of bread and place each piece of catfish

on the rocket. Sprinkle with sesame seeds, cover with remaining bread slices and serve.

PAN BAGNAT

Literally translated, *pan bagnat* means bathed bread. It's something like a salade niçoise on a roll, with the dressing seeping into the bread and making it wet. In Nice, you'll find it on every street corner. It is eaten for breakfast, lunch, on picnics and as an hors d'oeuvre— though it is most commonly eaten as a mid-morning snack.

MAKES 1 LARGE SANDWICH, ENOUGH FOR 2 PEOPLE

1 loaf of round, crusty French bread (the ideal loaf
    is about 20 cm (8 in) in diameter, 5 cm (2 in) high
    and weighs about 350 g (¾ lb); the pane di casa
    at Dean & DeLuca is perfect)
1 garlic clove, halved
50 ml (2 fl oz) extra-virgin olive oil
10 ml (2 tsp) red-wine vinegar, or more to taste
salt and pepper to taste
3 large, ripe tomatoes, cored and sliced
24 fresh basil leaves
8 fresh mint leaves
175 g (6 oz) canned tuna packed in olive oil
1 spring onion, chopped
10 g (2 tsp) drained capers packed in brine
12 niçoise (black) olives, stoned
6 anchovy fillets packed in olive oil (optional)
1 hard-boiled egg, peeled and sliced

1. Halve the bread horizontally. Remove some of the soft centre of the bread to make a hollow, rub each half with a cut side of garlic, drizzle each with about 1 tablespoon olive oil and a little vinegar and sprinkle with salt and pepper.

2. Cover the bottom slice of bread with half the tomato slices, drizzle with a bit of olive oil and top with 12 basil leaves and the mint leaves. Stir together the tuna, spring onion, capers and olives in a small bowl, then place on top of mint leaves. Top with anchovies, if desired. Make a layer of hard-boiled egg, then a layer of remaining tomato slices and remaining basil. Drizzle with remaining olive oil and vinegar. Season to taste with salt and pepper. Place top slice of bread on sandwich and wrap tightly in aluminium foil.

3. Let the sandwich stand at room temperature for at least 1 hour before serving so that the dressing may saturate the bread. Cut into halves or quarters.

Note: We like to make pan bagnat in 1 large sandwich—but you could make 2 sandwiches on 2 smaller rolls (each about 10 cm (4 in) in diameter), using the same ingredients listed above. Each sandwich would then serve 1 person. This is the way you usually find it on street corners in Nice.

DEAN & DELUCA'S TUNA SANDWICH WITH CARROTS, RED ONION AND PARSLEY

We sympathise with the purists when it comes to tuna salad sandwiches: the combo of canned tuna, just a little mayo and just good white bread is an eternal verity. But we have developed this fancier variation that is also delicious. It preserves the tuna flavour, it's not too rich, it's loaded with crunchy vegetables and it flies out of the store every day.

MAKES 6 SANDWICHES

4 x 175-g (6-oz) cans drained chunk white tuna in water
90 ml (6 tbsp) finely chopped carrots
140 g (5 oz) finely chopped red onion
90 g (6 tbsp) chopped fresh parsley
90 g (6 tbsp) finely chopped celery
3 spring onions, finely chopped
350 ml (12 fl oz) of your favourite mayonnaise
1 small garlic clove, peeled and crushed
45 ml (3 tbsp) lemon juice

salt and pepper to taste
6 rolls
lettuce and tomato as accompaniments

1. Put the tuna in a large bowl. Mash. Add the carrots, onion, parsley, celery and spring onions.

2. Place the mayonnaise in a small bowl. Add the crushed garlic clove and the lemon juice. Add the mayonnaise mixture to the tuna. Mix together. Add salt and pepper to taste. Serve on rolls with lettuce and tomato.

ROASTED LEG OF LAMB WITH ONION JAM ON BRIOCHE

Well, it is a bit of trouble to roast a leg of lamb just to make sandwiches—but you've never had sandwiches as complex and main-course-like as these. The combination of freshly roasted lamb, garlic butter and herb-scented onion jam is simply irresistible. Try to find individual brioche buns for this sandwich; that way, each diner gets lots of golden outer crust. Or, you could use brioche slices from a larger brioche.

MAKES 8 SANDWICHES

For the garlic butter
115 g (4 oz) butter
15 g (1 tbsp) garlic, finely chopped
25 g (1 oz) fresh parsley, finely chopped
15 ml (1 tbsp) fresh lemon juice
salt and pepper to taste
For the lamb
1.3 kg (3 lb) boneless leg of lamb
45 ml (3 tbsp) olive oil
15 g (1 tbsp) garlic, finely chopped
salt and pepper to taste
25 g (1 oz) butter
3 large Spanish onions, thinly sliced
5 g (1 tsp) finely chopped fresh thyme
10 g (2 tsp) finely chopped fresh rosemary

10 g (2 tsp) sugar
8 sandwich-size brioche buns or brioche slices,
   7.5 cm (3 in) in diameter and 10 cm (4 in) high
8 red lettuce leaves

1. Preheat oven to 200°C (400°F).

2. *Make the garlic butter:* Place the butter, garlic, parsley and lemon juice in a food processor. Process until smooth and season with salt and pepper. Reserve in a cool place.

3. Rub the lamb with olive oil and garlic. Sprinkle with salt and pepper, place in a roasting tin and roast for 30 minutes, checking frequently with a meat thermometer. (The inside temperature for medium-rare meat should be 51°C to 54°C (125°F to 130°F)). Remove the lamb from the pan and let cool. While the lamb is cooling, put 45 ml (3 tbsp) of water in the roasting tin, scrape with a wooden spoon and reserve the juices. These juices are highly concentrated and will add to the flavour of the sandwiches.

4. Melt the butter in a large frying pan and add the onions. Cook over high heat for 2 minutes, or until the sizzling sound starts to subside. Reduce the heat to very low and cook slowly for 20 to 30 minutes, or until the onions look medium brown and syrupy, stirring frequently to prevent the bottom from burning.

5. Add the thyme, rosemary, sugar and meat juices to the onions. Mix well and continue to cook over very low heat for 5 more minutes. Remove and cool completely.

6. Cut the cooled lamb in thin diagonal slices. Spread the garlic butter on one side of each brioche and divide the onion jam evenly among the sandwiches. Place the lamb slices on top of the onions and top with a lettuce leaf. Cover with the other side of the brioche and serve.

DEAN & DELUCA ROQUEFORT SPECIAL

Well, you may say, if I've got a great piece of Roquefort, why not eat it by itself? But you'd be at odds with all the blue-cheese lovers who keep buying this great sandwich at the store. The combination of flavours and textures is remarkable—something like a fruit and cheese and bread course in one manageable package.

MAKES 8 SANDWICHES

450 g (1 lb) Roquefort cheese (other kinds of oily
   blue cheese may be substituted)
115 g (4 oz) butter
15 ml (1 tbsp) brandy
5 g (1 tsp) finely chopped garlic
45 g (3 tbsp) chopped fresh parsley
50 g (2 oz) walnuts, coarsely chopped
2 heads chicory (Belgian endive)
30 ml (2 tbsp) lemon juice
2 Granny Smith apples
1 red pepper
16 slices of walnut raisin bread

1. Combine the Roquefort, butter and brandy in a food processor and process until smooth. Add the garlic, parsley and half the walnuts and pulse until just combined. Place in a small bowl and set aside.

2. Cut off the root ends of the endives and cut each one in half lengthways. Slice into thin strips, place in small bowl and sprinkle with 15 ml (1 tbsp) of the lemon juice. Peel the apples, cut them in half, remove the core, cut apples into thin half-moon slices and place in small bowl. Add the rest of the lemon juice. Reserve both the endive strips and apples in the refrigerator.

3. Put the pepper over an open fire or under a preheated grill. Turn and sear all sides until the skin is black. Place the pepper in a sealed paper bag for 5 to 10 minutes. Remove the charred skin from the pepper. Cut in half, remove and discard the seeds and ribs and cut the pepper into thin strips. Set aside.

4. Spread half of the Roquefort mixture on 8 slices of bread. Top each slice with an equal amount of endives, apple slices and red pepper strips. Sprinkle the remaining walnuts on each slice. Spread the remaining bread slices with the remaining Roquefort mixture and top the sandwiches.

NEW SANDWICH IDEAS

We're betting that the sandwich revolution will go even further in the coming years. Here are some brand-new recipes, inspired by the kinds of sandwiches that creative chefs around the country are making today.

ITALIAN CROQUE MONSIEUR (PAN-GRILLED FOCACCIA WITH MOZZARELLA AND PROSCIUTTO)

This new sandwich idea is based on an old sandwich idea—the pride of every street corner in Paris, that Gallic take on Welsh rarebit, the croque monsieur. We've substituted prosciutto for the usual French ham, mozzarella for the usual Gruyère and focaccia for the usual white loaf—and have come up with an even tastier hot snack. Normally, we dislike cooking with prosciutto—but the prosciutto in the centre of this sandwich barely gets cooked, thereby retaining its flavour and texture.

MAKES 4 SANDWICHES

225 g (8 oz) salt-free mozzarella, cut in thin slices
4 squares of focaccia, each one 2.5 cm (½ in) thick
   by 7.5 cm (3 in) long by 7.5 cm (3 in) wide*
115 g (4 oz) prosciutto, cut in very thin slices
5 g (1 tsp) dried oregano
olive oil for pan-grilling

1. For each sandwich, evenly place about 25 g (1 oz) of mozzarella on one square of focaccia—covering, but not overhanging, the focaccia. Top with 25 g (1 oz) of

*When you buy or make focaccia, you will find it in large pieces. Simply whittle down whatever you have to the proportions given above.

prosciutto, then another ounce of mozzarella. Sprinkle with a 1.25 g (¼ tsp) of oregano, then top with a second slice of focaccia. Continue until 4 sandwiches are made.

2. Place a cast-iron frying pan over low heat. Pour in just enough oil to film the bottom. Wait 1 minute, then add the focaccia sandwiches. Place a flat cover on the pan that fits inside the pan and press down occasionally. Cook, turning frequently, until the outsides are golden brown and the cheese is melted, about 5 minutes. Serve immediately as sandwiches, or cut into triangles, squares, or rectangles for pre-party finger food.

TABOULEH-STUFFED PITTA BREADS WITH GRILLED CUMIN CHICKEN AND YOGURT-TAHINI SAUCE

These easy-to-make delights are at their best when served warm. One bite and you'll be transported to... midtown Manhattan, where thousands of sandwiches with similar Middle Eastern flavours are sold from fancy barrows every day. But they don't have the care and finesse that this sandwich has.

MAKES 2 PITTA SANDWICHES

2 large chicken thighs, boned
20 g (1½ tsp) ground cumin
1 garlic clove, chopped
5 ml (1 tsp) extra-virgin olive oil
salt and pepper to taste
50 ml (2 fl oz) plain yogurt
20 ml (4 tsp) tahini
5 ml (1 tsp) fresh lemon juice
2 pitta breads (with or without pockets)
350 g (12 oz) classic tabouleh (recipe on page 17)

1. Rub the chicken thighs with the ground cumin, garlic and olive oil. Season well with salt and pepper. Marinate in the refrigerator for 6 to 10 hours (with more time, the cumin-garlic flavour will be stronger).

2. Mix together well the yogurt, tahini paste and lemon juice. Thin out with a bit of water to make a smooth, medium-thick sauce. Season to taste with salt and pepper.

3. When ready to make the sandwiches, prepare a hot charcoal fire. Grill the chicken thighs on both sides until just past pink, about 10 minutes. (Alternatively, you can cook the chicken thighs under a preheated grill, turning once, until just past pink.) Let the cooked thighs rest for 10 minutes, then cut into 5 mm (¼ in) thick slices.

4. Steam the pitta breads until warm; this will make them softer in texture and easier to stuff or fill. If using pitta breads with pockets, cut the breads in half and stuff each of the 4 halves with chicken, tabouleh and sauce. If using pitta breads without pockets, simply place chicken, tabouleh and sauce on each pitta and fold; you may then cut them in half.

About pittas

Americans have come to assume that these round, eastern Mediterranean breads necessarily have pockets inside them. But on their home turf they usually don't. In fact, the pocketed pitta most often sold in America, in supermarkets, is the worst, least authentic pitta of all. Try to find a freshly baked pitta, without a pocket, from a local Middle Eastern bakery; you'll be amazed by the texture and flavour. And if your pitta—any pitta—is not just-out-of-the-oven fresh, steam it for a minute or two to bring it back to life.

GRILLED SALMON ON RYE WITH SAUERKRAUT AND HORSERADISH CREAM

This sandwich tastes best when the salmon is still warm.

MAKES 4 SANDWICHES

450 g (1 lb) salmon fillet, skin removed
salt and pepper to taste
vegetable oil for grilling
125 ml (4 fl oz) sour cream
10 ml (2 tsp) grated horseradish (from a bottle)
8 large slices of rye bread, medium-thin, with
   caraway seeds
125 ml (4 fl oz) fresh, tangy sauerkraut

1. Prepare a hot charcoal fire.

2. With a long, sharp knife held parallel to the cutting board, make 4 thin salmon slices, about 115 g (4 oz) each (or ask the fishmonger to do this for you). Salt and pepper the salmon slices, moisten with vegetable oil, brush the grill of a charcoal barbecue with oil and grill the salmon quickly over the coals, turning once, until the slices are just browned on the outside and just past raw on the inside (about 4 minutes). (Alternatively, you could sear the salmon slices in a few tablespoons of very hot oil in a heavy-bottomed frying pan.) Reserve.

3. Mix together the sour cream and the grated horseradish. Season well with salt and pepper.

4. Place the salmon slices on 4 slices of bread. Top each with one quarter of the sour cream mixture. Squeeze the liquid out of the sauerkraut, then divide it among the four sandwiches. Top each sandwich with another slice of rye.

THE TLT (SMOKED TROUT, LETTUCE, AND TOMATO SANDWICH)

For some blasphemers, this sandwich may be an improvement on the classic BLT: the trout plays the same salty-smoky role as bacon, but does it with more interesting flavour and texture. Make sure you've got the best bread, the best lettuce, the best tomatoes and the best mayonnaise you can find! Good potato crisps on the side, dry vinho verde in the glass, heaven on earth.

MAKES 4 SANDWICHES

8 broad, 1-cm (½-in) slices of good bread (slices cut from a round sourdough loaf work beautifully)

450 g (1 lb) smoked trout

125 ml (4 fl oz) mayonnaise (more, if desired)

12 medium-thick slices ripe, red tomato

leafy green lettuce

Divide ingredients into four sandwiches. Season with freshly ground pepper.

VITELLO TONNATO ON SEMOLINA BREAD WITH FRESH BASIL AND SUN-DRIED TOMATOES

We think that this vitello tonnato sandwich is an improvement on vitello tonnato, or thin slices of veal served with a tuna-flavoured mayonnaise. The classic dish, for us, has always lacked exciting texture and flavour. This version supplies both.

MAKES 6 SANDWICHES

450-g (1-lb) chunk of boneless veal leg (preferably from the upper leg section that's traditionally used for scallopini)

1 large onion, chopped

2 cloves garlic, smashed

bunch of fresh basil

125 ml (4 fl oz) dry white wine

450 ml (16 fl oz) water

salt and pepper to taste

115 ml (4 oz) of canned tuna (preferably packed in olive oil)

1 egg yolk

1 anchovy fillet

10 g (2 tsp) capers

15 ml (1 tbsp) lemon juice

45 ml (3 tbsp) olive oil

1 loaf of semolina bread coated with sesame seeds

12 sun-dried tomatoes, marinated in olive oil

1. Select a saucepan in which the veal chunk snugly fits. Place the onion and garlic in the pan, along with a dozen leaves of basil (stems included). Add the white wine and the water, bring to a boil, then reduce heat to moderately low and simmer slowly for 1 hour. Season well with salt and pepper. Reduce heat to low.

2. Season the veal with salt and pepper and add it to the pan. If the veal's not covered by the liquid, add a little more wine and water. Keep the liquid below a simmer until the veal is just cooked (still slightly pink inside), about 20 minutes. Remove veal from pan and let it rest 10 minutes.

3. Drain the oil from the canned tuna and place the tuna in the work bowl of a food processor, along with the egg yolk, anchovy fillet, capers and lemon juice. Blend for about 10 seconds, or until the mixture is a smooth purée. With the motor running, add the olive oil in a thin stream; when blended, the sauce should be smooth and medium-thick.

4. Cut long, diagonal slices of semolina bread, about 1 cm (⅓ in) thick. (Alternatively, you could use any French or Italian loaf.) Cut the veal into very thin slices and place a few, in a single layer, on a piece of bread. Top with a few spoonfuls of the tuna mayonnaise. Top that with 2 sun-dried tomatoes and a few fresh basil leaves. (Reserve leftover basil for another use.) Finish with a few more slices of veal. Cover with another slice of bread and repeat until 6 sandwiches are made.

GOAT CHEESE, AVOCADO AND SMOKED TURKEY SANDWICH ON NUT BREAD

Don't fret over slicing the bread exactly in this great sandwich recipe—or even the exact proportions of ingredients. But any combination of these ingredients on any slice of nut bread is going to yield an ideal picnic sandwich, especially when a crisp, cool bottle of Sancerre or Pouilly-Fumé is at hand.

MAKES 6 SANDWICHES

350 g (12 oz) tomatoes, finely chopped

15 g (1 tbsp) finely chopped spring onion

2 heaping tablespoons finely chopped coriander

salt and pepper to taste

12 slices nut bread, each about 1 cm (⅓ in) thick, 7.5 cm (3 in) wide, 15 cm (6 in) long (this is easiest to achieve if you cut the bread from a round loaf)

350 g (12 oz) goat cheese*

12 thin slices of smoked turkey breast (about 225 g (8 oz))

2 medium avocados, peeled, stoned and cut into thin slices

1. Mix together the tomatoes, spring onion and the coriander. Season to taste with salt and pepper.

2. Spread each of the 12 bread slices with 1 ounce of goat cheese. Top 6 of the slices with a slice of smoked turkey. Top each turkey slice with one sixth of the tomato mixture, spreading evenly. Top that with a thin layer of avocado slices, seasoned with salt and pepper. Top with the remaining slices of turkey and cover with the remaining 6 slices of bread (which have been spread with goat cheese). Cut each sandwich in half and serve.

ONION FRITTATA ROLLS WITH BACON AND ROASTED RED PEPPER

We love this cross-cultural collision of frittata, egg foo yong and Western sandwich (Western as in Denver, Colorado). The sandwiches taste great when freshly made, but the flavours are even better after a few hours (which makes them perfect picnic fare).

*The trickiest part of this sandwich is finding the perfect goat cheese. We've tried various types and finally discovered that we prefer Chèvre that's easily spreadable, but rather goaty in flavour. Logs from the French producer Couturier are right on target.

MAKES 6 SANDWICHES

25 g (1 oz) butter

350 g (12 oz) very thinly sliced onions

4 whole eggs plus 3 egg whites, beaten together with a fork for about 30 seconds

6 soft rolls (golden, eggy ones are best—round or oval)

12 bacon rashers, cooked crisp

2 medium red peppers, roasted (see page 175), or 75 g (6 oz) roasted red peppers from a jar)

1. Place the butter in a flameproof non-stick skillet, 13 cm (5 in) in diameter. Melt butter over moderately high heat, then add the onions. Fry, stirring occasionally, until the onions are golden brown and quite soft, about 10 minutes.

2. Add beaten eggs to pan. Cook slowly for 10 minutes, or until the base of the frittata is well set (lift the edge to check). Pass the frittata under a grill, briefly, to set the eggs on top. Slide it out from pan onto plate or countertop and let cool for 15 minutes.

3. Cut the frittata into 6 portions that fit snugly on the rolls. Place each portion on half of a roll. Top each with 2 slices of bacon and a third of a fresh roasted red pepper, peels and seeds removed, or 25 g (1 oz) of roasted red pepper from a jar. Close sandwiches with the tops of rolls.

A TRIO OF INTERNATIONAL SANDWICH TRADITIONS

The American Sandwich Revolution was driven by very American culinary ideas. But, over the last 20 years, some international specialties that might also be described as sandwiches have become extremely popular here.

BRUSCHETTA

In the fifties, when you went to an Italian restaurant you had garlic bread. You had it all too often at dinner parties, too—those awful loaves of cottony white, smeared with butter and garlic powder, wrapped in foil and warmed in the oven. The eighties saw a new kind of 'garlic bread' spread in restaurants across the land—versions of the classic southern Italian bruschetta (called *fettunta* in Tuscany), or grilled bread that has been rubbed with garlic and anointed with great olive oil. Most of the time, the bruschetta is topped with something savoury, sort of like an open-faced sandwich. These days, home chefs are making bruschetta with regularity on their barbecues or under the grill. It's a great pass-around before a dinner party, or a great first course.

BRUSCHETTA

MAKES 12 BRUSCHETTI

1 round loaf of country bread (not too dense)
6 garlic cloves, halved
225 ml (8 fl oz) great extra-virgin olive oil
salt and pepper to taste

1. Prepare a moderately hot charcoal fire.

2. Cut the middle portion of the round loaf into 6 long slices, each one almost 2.5 cm (1 in) thick. Cut these slices in half, making half-slices that are roughly 7.5 cm (3 in) by 7.5 cm (3 in) by 2.5 cm (1 in).

3. When fire is ready, place the 12 slices over it in a single layer. Cook, turning once, until the outsides of the bread are golden brown (with grill marks, if possible). This should take about 2 minutes per side, but check frequently to make sure the bread isn't burning.

4. When the bread slices are done, rub the edges and both sides, with a cut clove of garlic—lightly or heavily, depending on your garlic preference. Place the slices on a large dish in a single layer. Sprinkle each slice with 10 ml (2 tsp) of olive oil, breaking the surface of the bread lightly with a spoon to let the oil soak in. Season with salt and pepper. Turn the slices over and repeat the procedure. Let the slices sit in the olive oil for 10 to 15 minutes. Serve as for simple bruschetta, or top with other foods.

Catalan bruschetta

There's a great version of grilled bread that's made in Catalonia, in the north-east corner of Spain. In Catalan, it's called *pa amb tomaquet*. To make it, grill and rub the bread with garlic and olive oil as indicated above (you may want to use Catalan olive oil for authenticity). Then, cut a very red, super-ripe tomato at the equator and rub it across the surface of the bread. (Reserve the rest of the tomato for another use.) The bread turns beautifully red and when a few dozen of the *pa amb tomaquet* are placed side-by-side on a platter, they make a spectacular presentation. In Catalonia they serve the bread by itself, as an accompaniment to a first course. But they also like to top it and pass it around as an appetiser. We've seen it with anchovies and with ham—but you can let your imagination run wild. Olives, Manchego cheese, thin sausage slices, roasted peppers, artichoke hearts and grilled fish are all great possibilities.

BRUSCHETTA WITH FRESH TOMATO AND BASIL

MAKES 12 BRUSCHETTI

4 ripe, medium tomatoes (about 225 g (8 oz) each, coarsely chopped
115 g (4 oz) fresh basil leaves
10 ml (2 tsp) extra-virgin olive oil
5 ml (1 tsp) red-wine vinegar
1 garlic clove, pounded into a paste with 2.5 g (½ tsp) salt

salt and pepper to taste
12 slices of bruschetta (preceding recipe)

1. In a bowl mix together the tomatoes, basil, olive oil
and vinegar. Add 1.25 g (¼ tsp) of the garlic paste and
blend well. Season to taste with salt and pepper. Let
stand at room temperature for at least 30 minutes and
up to 2 hours, if possible.

2. Place the bruschetti on a large platter in a single
layer. When ready to serve, drizzle each one with about
15 ml (1 tbsp) of juice from the bottom of the bowl
containing the tomato mixture. With a slotted spoon,
strew the tomato mixture over the bruschetti. Serve
immediately.

BRUSCHETTA WITH GORGONZOLA, KALAMATA OLIVES AND GRILLED RED PEPPERS

MAKES 12 BRUSCHETTI

4 large red peppers
1 garlic clove, pounded into a paste with 2.5 g
  (½ tsp) salt
5 ml (1 tsp) extra-virgin olive oil
175 g (6 oz) crumbly Gorgonzola
250 g (9 oz) mascarpone
12 slices of bruschetta (recipe page 91)
12 Greek olives, pitted and sliced
30 g (2 tbsp) finely snipped fresh chives

1. Place the peppers over a very hot open flame (you can
use the jets of a gas range or, even better, an open
charcoal fire). Turn the peppers every 2 minutes or so
until they are completely blackened on the outside (this
should take 6 to 10 minutes). Immediately place the
charred peppers in a paper bag. Let them sit for 20
minutes.

2. After 20 minutes, remove the peppers from the bag
and, working with your fingers, peel off the blackened

skin. (Never wash off the blackened skin; water spoils
the texture of the peppers.) Cut off the tops of the
peppers and discard. Slit each pepper down the side
and remove all seeds and membranes. Cut each pepper
into 3 equal 'fillets' along the natural separations. In a
bowl mix the pepper fillets well with 1.25 g (¼ tsp) of
the garlic paste and with the olive oil. Season to taste
and leave for between 15 minutes and 1 hour.

3. In a small bowl mix together the Gorgonzola and the
mascarpone. Blend well.

4. Spread one side of each bruschetta with the
Gorgonzola mixture. Divide the sliced olives among the
12 bruschetti, placing them evenly over the cheese
mixture. Top each bruschetta with a 'fillet' of red pepper,
grilled side up. Top each bruschetta with 2.5 g (½ tsp)
chives and serve.

GRILLED AUBERGINE BRUSCHETTA WITH PROSCIUTTO

MAKES 12 BRUSCHETTI

1 x 550-g (1 lb 4 oz) aubergine
15 g (1 tbsp) salt
50 ml (2 fl oz) extra-virgin olive oil
1 round loaf of country bread
1 large garlic clove, cut
freshly ground sea salt to taste
freshly ground black pepper to taste
175 g (6 oz) prosciutto, very thinly sliced
30 g (2 tbsp) very finely chopped fresh parsley

1. Slice the aubergine into 12 rounds. Sprinkle the salt
over them, place them in a colander, weight them and
let sit over a bowl for 1 hour.

2. Prepare a charcoal fire. When ready to cook, remove
the aubergine slices from the colander and wipe off
excess moisture and salt with a towel. Brush each side

of the aubergine slices with the extra-virgin olive oil. Grill them, turning once, for 10 to 15 minutes, or until they're brown on the outside and soft on the inside. Reserve.

3. Cut the bread into 6 slices and halve the slices (each half slice should be a little larger than the aubergine slices). Brush very lightly with extra-virgin olive oil on both sides and grill the bread for about 2 minutes, turning once. Remove from the fire and rub each slice on one side with the cut clove of garlic. Turn that side up and brush it with a little more extra-virgin olive oil.

4. When ready to serve, place a slice of aubergine on a slice of bread and spread roughly with a knife. Top with a little freshly ground sea salt and a little freshly ground black pepper. Repeat with all of the bread and aubergine. Cut the prosciutto into slices that fit neatly over the aubergine and drape the slices over the 12 bruschetti. Top with parsley and serve as an hors d'oeuvre.

QUESADILLAS

The quesadilla, in essence, is a warm Mexican cheese sandwich. It is a humble dish, a popular snack throughout Mexico, where the word *quesadilla* usually denotes some kind of Mexican cheese (that's the *quesa* part), possibly mixed with other flavourings, surrounded by a corn tortilla and fried in lard or oil.

In the United States, the word *quesadilla* today usually means nothing of the sort. For one thing, wheat flour tortillas are most commonly used to make stateside quesadillas, not corn tortillas. They are rarely fried in lard; less fatty alternatives, like dry-pan frying or baking, are usually employed. And the fillings! Our creative chefs in American restaurants have stretched their imaginations when it comes to quesadillas. Not only do they use a wide variety of international cheeses that would leave a Sonoran baffled, but they stuff their

tortillas with sun-dried tomatoes, smoked salmon, chicken breast, papaya and any other New Wave multicultural option!

Basta. We find the simple quesadilla such an immensely satisfying creation that we are less likely to tamper with it than others. Here's a basic recipe (with a few North American adjustments) . . . along with two slightly more elaborate quesadillas that don't violate the Mexican aesthetic.

In these recipes, you can either dry-fry the quesadillas in a pan, or, for a bit more luxury, fry them in a little butter or lard. Either way works fine.

BASIC QUESADILLA

This is the grilled cheese sandwich of the nineties—just as simple, just as satisfying, but ever more exotic. Great for party appetisers, or quick lunches, or first courses of Mexican meals. We make it with flour tortillas, because finding good ones is much easier than finding good corn tortillas.

MAKES 32 QUESADILLA WEDGES, PERFECT FOR PARTY
APPETISERS

unsalted butter or lard (optional)
8 x 18-cm (7-in) flour tortillas
250 g (9 oz) grated or shredded cheese

1. If using butter or lard, place about 15 g (1 tbsp) of either in a large, heavy frying pan over moderate heat. Heat until almost sizzling. If you aren't using butter or lard simply place a large, heavy frying pan over moderate heat for 2 minutes.

2. Lay out 4 of the tortillas on a counter and divide the cheese among them, making sure to spread the cheese out to the edges of the tortillas. Top with the other 4 tortillas. Lift one packet with a spatula and place in the frying pan. Cook, turning once, for 2 to 3 minutes on each side, or until the cheese is melted and the tortillas are lightly browned. (The trick is to melt the cheese before the exteriors of the tortillas become very brown and hard; you want them to remain soft.) Repeat with the remaining 3 quesadillas.

3. Cut each quesadilla into 8 wedges and serve immediately.

Note: While you're finishing the quesadillas, the ones already cooked may be kept warm on a baking sheet in a 100°C (200°F) oven.

Choosing quality tortillas for quesadillas

The key to the quality of your quesadilla is the quality of the flour tortilla you buy. In the United States, fresh flour tortillas are available in supermarkets, in the UK they are harder to find. If you can't find them use Indian or other soft, leavened flatbreads. When you buy tortillas, make sure that the packet contains fresh-looking tortillas, with no dried or crumbly edges. After you make quesadillas of them, you'll know the best tortillas by their light, flaky, layered quality; bad ones are just heavy and soggy.

Cheese for quesadillas

One of the great things about quesadillas is that all soft cheeses normally used for melting taste wonderful inside 'em. Monterey Jack, which originated in Monterey, California, is the cheese most commonly used in the United States, and is now available widely in the UK, but Cheddar, Gruyère, fontina, mozzarella, provolone, and even Danish havarti are decent substitutes. Even the rubbery and relatively tasteless cheeses turn to heart-warming ooze inside the tortillas.

In Mexico, of course, other melting cheeses are used. Gooey asadero and buttery chihuahua are soft melting cheeses and quesillo, an Oaxacan cheese, is something like fresh mozzarella. They are difficult to find outside Mexico.

It is also quite common in Mexico to stuff quesadillas with more crumbly, less gooey cheeses.

Some of them also melt extremely well. Queso panela is something like curd cheese (which may be used as a substitute); it holds its shape when melted. Queso fresco is fresh and slightly salty, like a slightly dried curd cheese. Anejo or Cotija resembles a drier feta; it is usually used for crumbling on top of food, not for melting.

Other quesadilla possibilities

Here are some other ideas we like for quesadillas:

- Cooked spinach mixed with the cheese; use about half cheese and half spinach. Amazingly delicious.
- Cooked slices of chorizo (Spanish sausage) placed over the cheese.
- Roasted poblano chillies placed over the cheese.
- Refried beans and salsa placed over the cheese.
- Tomatillo paste with coriander placed over the cheese.

You can also stack tortillas to make a double-decker quesadilla; this practice is popular in Monterrey, Mexico, where the creation is called a *sincronizada*. Simply heat 1 tortilla on both sides and remove it from the pan. Then heat another tortilla in the pan. Place filling on the one in the pan, top with the already heated tortilla, top that with more filling, then top that with a third tortilla. Cook the quesadilla on both sides, as usual.

QUESADILLA WITH CORIANDER AND PICKLED RED ONIONS

Though we're quesadilla purists, we find this embellished version to be irresistible. Once again, you can dry-fry it, or you can add some butter or lard to the frying pan if you prefer it a little slicker.

MAKES 32 QUESADILLA WEDGES, PERFECT FOR PARTY
APPETISERS

2 small red onions, very thinly sliced
150 ml (5 fl oz) cider vinegar
5 garlic cloves, halved

2.5 g (½ tsp) whole black peppercorns

2.5 g (½ tsp) coriander seeds

2.5 g (½ tsp) cumin seeds

2.5 g (½ tsp) salt

unsalted butter or lard (optional)

8 x 18-cm (7-in) flour tortillas

250 g (9 oz) coarsely or finely grated cheese

115 g (4 oz) chopped fresh coriander plus sprigs for garnish

3 slender spring onions, chopped

1 jalapeño chilli, trimmed, seeded and chopped

1. Boil the onions in a saucepan with just enough salted water to cover for 1 minute. Drain the onions in a colander and discard the water. Return the onions to the saucepan with the cider vinegar, garlic, peppercorns, coriander seeds, cumin seeds and salt. Add just enough water to cover the onions, bring to a boil and boil for 3 minutes. Transfer the onions and liquid to a glass bowl and leave for at least 3 and up to 24 hours.

2. If using butter or lard, place about 15 g (1 tbsp) of either in a large, heavy fry pan over moderate heat. Heat until almost sizzling. Or, place a large, heavy fry pan over moderate heat for 2 minutes.

3. Lay out 4 of the tortillas on a counter and divide the cheese among them, making sure to spread the cheese out to the edges of the tortillas. Divide the pickled onions, the chopped coriander, the spring onions and the jalapeño among the 4 tortillas. Top each one with another tortilla.

4. Cook a quesadilla for 2 to 3 minutes on each side, or until the cheese is melted and the tortilla is browned slightly. Repeat with the remaining 3 quesadillas.

5. Cut the quesadillas into 8 wedges each, and garnish with the coriander sprigs. Serve immediately.

Note: While you're finishing the quesadillas, the ones already cooked may be kept warm on a baking sheet in a 100°C (200°F) oven.

WILD MUSHROOM AND CHIPOTLE QUESADILLAS

Though most people don't associate mushrooms with Mexican food, fungi are an integral part of several regional cuisines. We find the smoky, woodsy flavour of the chipotle (a smoked jalapeño) to be a natural match for wild mushrooms. This recipe, by the way, demonstrates another type of quesadilla: one made with a single tortilla, folded in the pan to create a half-moon.

MAKES 4 HALF-MOON QUESADILLAS

2 dried chipotle chillies

2 rashers bacon

30 g (2 tbsp) finely chopped shallots

pinch of ground cloves

225 g (8 oz) fresh wild mushrooms,* chopped

225 ml (8 fl oz) chicken stock

5 g (1 tsp) ground coriander

125 ml (4 fl oz) single cream

4 to 6 soft 25-g (10-in) flour tortillas

50 g (2 oz) grated Mexican hard cheese or pecorino Romano

30 g (2 tbsp) finely chopped fresh parsley

1. Toast the chipotles in a large frying pan over moderately high heat, turning, for 2 to 3 minutes. Take out the chillies, remove and discard the seeds and stems and soak in hot water for 10 minutes.

2. While chillies are soaking, cook the bacon until medium crisp in the frying pan. Remove the bacon, leaving the rendered fat in the pan, and chop it into rough 5-mm (¼-in) squares.

*If wild mushrooms are unavailable, substitute regular fresh mushrooms and add 25 g (1 oz) of dried wild mushrooms. Soak the dried wild mushrooms for 20 minutes in hot water before you start preparing the recipe. Combine the strained soaking liquid with chicken stock to make 225 ml (8 fl oz) and proceed with the recipe.

3. Fry the shallots in the bacon fat over moderately high heat for 2 minutes. While the shallots are cooking, remove the chipotles from the water and chop them to a rough paste. Add the chipotle paste and the pinch of cloves to the shallots. Fry, stirring, for 30 seconds. Add the mushrooms and fry again, stirring, for 5 minutes. Add the stock, bacon and coriander and stir up the bottom. When the stock comes to a boil, reduce heat to low and simmer for 20 minutes, stirring occasionally. Add the cream and stir it in well. Cook for another 10 minutes.

4. Place a medium frying pan over moderate heat. When hot, place a tortilla in it. Shake the pan to prevent sticking. After 1 minute, turn the tortilla over. Place 30 g (2 tbsp) of the mushroom mixture on the left half of the tortilla. Top with a quarter of the cheese, spreading it out to the edge, and a quarter of the parsley. With a spatula, lift the empty side of the tortilla and turn it over onto the mushrooms, making a half-moon shape. After 2 minutes, lifting from the open end with the spatula, turn the quesadilla over. The side that is now on top should be somewhat browned. Cook for 2 more minutes, or until the second side is slightly browned. Repeat for the remaining quesadillas.

Note: While you're finishing the quesadillas, the ones already cooked may be kept warm on a baking sheet in a 100°C (200°F) oven.

SMØRREBRØD

Smørrebrød are the great open-faced sandwiches of Scandinavia. They are tremendously easy to make, but create a visual impression at a party that's all out of proportion to their actual degree of difficulty. For a New Year's Eve celebration once, we made 8 different types of smørrebrød, garnished them to the nines, presented each type on its own platter, placed the platters next to each other on a large groaning board, and had our guests swooning all night. Well, maybe the frozen

Swedish aquavit with Danish beer chasers helped a little in the swoon department.

The classic bread to use is square rye bread, but in Scandinavia today they use many different types. Just find a good, fresh, serious, squarish loaf—even bakery-made white bread yields good smørrebrød. Cut thin slices, about 3 mm (⅛ in) thick. Cut the slices in half (smørrebrød is always made from half-slices of bread). Butter the bread with lightly salted butter (use Danish butter). Then, let your imagination be your guide. Pick a main ingredient or two, and garnish with herbs, eggs, pickled vegetables, onions, etc.

The following are some of our favourite smørrebrød recipes.

RADISH AND SPRING ONION SMØRREBRØD

Simplicity itself.

MAKES 12 SMØRREBRØD

16 large red radishes (about 225 g (8 oz))
4 spring onions
50 g (2 oz) lightly salted butter
6 slices of dark bread, cut in half
freshly ground black pepper to taste

1. Wash the radishes, and cut them into fairly thin slices. Cut the spring onions, including a good deal of the green tops, into the thinnest rounds possible.

2. Spread 5 g (⅛ oz) butter on each of the bread halves. Top each slice of bread with two long rows of radish slices. Scatter the frizzle of cut spring onions over the radishes, dividing them equally among the 12 smørrebrød. Top with freshly ground black pepper.

Other smørrebrød possibilities

They're endless. Here are a few we've enjoyed in Scandinavia:
  • Room temperature slices of roast pork, garnished

with room temperature wine-braised red cabbage (see red cabbage with red wine and red apples on page 178).

- Sliced new potatoes in vinaigrette, topped with thin slices of garlic sausage and parsley.
- Egg salad on lettuce, with dill, thin slices of onion and crumbled bacon.
- A slice of Danish blue cheese, topped with a raw onion ring just large enough to hold a raw egg yolk
- Roast beef on lettuce with horseradish and cornichons (miniature gherkins).

SCRAMBLED EGG WITH SALMON ROE SMØRREBRØD

Salmon roe tastes best on this luscious sandwich, but any form of caviar or fish roe will work well.

MAKES 12 SMØRREBRØD

12 extra-large eggs
60 g (2¼ oz) lightly salted butter
6 slices dark bread, cut in half
24 thin slices of cucumber
75 g (3 oz) salmon roe or other fish roe
sprigs of fresh dill for garnish

1. Beat the eggs well in a large bowl. In a heavy fry pan, about 20 cm (8 in) in diameter, melt 10 g (2 tsp) of butter over extremely low heat. Add the beaten eggs, and cook over the lowest possible heat for 45 minutes. Stir occasionally to prevent a skin from forming on the surface. The eggs will thicken very slowly. When they begin to thicken, stir gently with a large spoon to create large flaps in the scrambled eggs. (If no flaps have formed after 45 minutes, raise the heat slightly to finish the thickening. The eggs will be darker in colour and thicker than normal scrambled eggs and should fall into large folds or flaps.)

2. Spread 5 g (⅛ oz) of butter on each of the bread halves. For each smørrebrød, at 2 corners that face each

other diagonally place 2 slices of cucumber. At the other 2 corners, place about 1.25 g (¼ tsp) of salmon roe. Cover the rest of the bread with about one twelfth of the egg mixture. Repeat until all smørrebrød are done. Garnish with sprigs of fresh dill.

Variation: If you prefer, you may eliminate the salmon roe and substitute smoked salmon. Simply lay a thin slice of smoked salmon on top of the bread and under the scrambled eggs.

PRAWN SMØRREBRØD

This is one of Scandinavia's favourite smørrebrød. Cooking the prawns in salted and sweetened water brings them closer in flavour to the sea-sweet reker that you can buy on the docks there. Also for authenticity, use small, North Sea, prawns.

MAKES 12 SMØRREBRØD

675 g (1½ lb) small prawns
3 litres (5¼ pints) water
225 g (8 oz) sugar
45 g (3 tbsp) salt
10 g (2 tsp) black peppercorns
50 g (2 oz) lightly salted butter
6 slices of firm-textured white bread, cut in half
12 lettuce leaves, washed and dried
90 ml (6 tbsp) mayonnaise
lemon slices and fresh dill for garnish

1. Peel and devein the prawns. Combine the water, sugar, salt and peppercorns in a large pot. Bring to a boil. Add all of the prawns at once, then turn off the heat and remove the pot from the burner. Let rest for 5 to 10 minutes, or until the prawns are just cooked through. Remove the prawns.

2. Spread 5 g (⅛ oz) butter on each of the bread halves. Put a lettuce leaf on each bread half so that it slightly overlaps the bread on all sides. Place two long rows of slightly overlapping prawns on the lettuce. Spoon 7.5 ml (½ tbsp) mayonnaise on to each smørrebrød, or place the mayonnaise in a forcing bag and add it to each smørrebrød in decorative squiggles. Garnish with a thin lemon slice and a sprig of dill.

HERRING SMØRREBRØD WITH APPLES AND BEETROOT

If you've turned up your nose at herring fillets, try this terrific sandwich in which the herring combines beautifully with other ingredients.

MAKES 12 SMØRREBRØD

4 thin pickled herring fillets (about 350 g (12 oz) total
1 small potato, peeled, boiled and diced
3 large slices pickled beetroot, diced
45 g (3 tbsp) chopped onion
30 g (2 tbsp) chopped gherkins
1 small apple, peeled and cored
30 ml (2 tbsp) mayonnaise
50 g (2 oz) butter
6 slices of dark bread
12 green-leaf lettuce leaves
freshly ground pepper to taste
dill leaves for garnish

1. Cut the herring fillets into pieces roughly 1 x 1 cm (½ in x ½ in). Place in a bowl, and mix with potato, beetroot, onion and pickle. Dice the apple and add to the bowl. Add the mayonnaise and mix well.

2. Spread 5 g (⅛ oz) of butter on each of the bread halves. Top each half with a lettuce leaf that overlaps slightly on all sides. Divide the herring mixture among the bread halves, and sprinkle with freshly ground pepper. Garnish with dill leaves.

GOOSE LIVERWURST SMØRREBRØD

Liverwurst made with goose liver and goose fat works best for this smørrebrød, but ordinary pork liverwurst is also fine. If you cannot obtain the goose liverwurst, use a bit less of the more pungent pork product. Another possibility is a smooth liver pâté purchased from a delicatessen.

MAKES 12 SMØRREBRØD

6 rashers bacon
115 g (4 oz) sweet onion, sliced fairly thin
50 g (2 oz) lightly salted butter
6 slices of square rye bread
12 lettuce leaves, washed and dried
350 g (12 oz) goose liverwurst
freshly ground pepper to taste
finely chopped fresh parsley

1. Gently fry the bacon rashers over moderate heat in a heavy fry pan. Remove and drain on paper towels. Pour out all but 15 ml (1 tbsp) of the rendered bacon fat, turn heat to high and add the sliced onion to the pan. Fry over high heat for 2 minutes, or until the onion just begins to turn brown. Remove onion and drain on paper towels.

2. Spread 5 g (⅛ oz) butter on each of the bread halves. Top each half with a lettuce leaf that overlaps slightly on all sides. Spread about 25 g (1 oz) of liverwurst across each lettuce leaf. Cut the bacon rashers in half, and top each smørrebrød with a half-rasher of bacon. Divide the sautéed onion rings evenly among the 12 smørrebrød, top with freshly ground black pepper, and garnish each smørrebrød with parsley

PIZZA & PASTA

PIZZA AND PASTA, TWO GREAT FARINACEOUS CONCEPTS FROM ITALY, HIT OUR
SHORES WITH THE FIRST WAVE OF ITALIAN IMMIGRATION IN THE LATE
NINETEENTH CENTURY. NO ONE KNEW AT THE TIME THAT THE TWO DISHES
WOULD BECOME MAMMOTHS OF AMERICAN CUISINE IN THE TWENTIETH
CENTURY. NOR DID ANYONE KNOW IT WOULD TAKE ALMOST A HUNDRED YEARS
BEFORE AMERICANS STARTED COOKING AND SERVING THESE FOODS IN AN
AUTHENTIC ITALIAN FASHION.

PIZZA

There's little wonder that home pizza delivery has become a huge industry in America—where we've also got the market cornered on frozen pizza and home pizza kits. It all comes down to the same root cause: to make pizza from scratch at home that tastes even a little like the real thing has always been devilishly difficult.

The home problem is twofold. First of all, the high-heat ovens used by pizza restaurants are not available to the home pizza-maker; pizzas made in a 250°C (500°F) home oven are simply not the same as pizzas made at a temperature approaching 540°C (1000° F). To make matters worse, home pizza-makers have no access to the wood-burning brick ovens that give such great flavour to the best pizzas made in Italy and America.

The other home difficulty concerns flour, pizza's basic ingredient. In pizza restaurants in Italy, pizza-makers use a kind of Italian flour that is labelled *tipo 00*. It is the softest, silkiest, most refined white flour available, with a very low gluten content. It produces ideal pizza, which is simultaneously chewy and soft. Unfortunately, American flours are not graded by this system and this type of Italian flour is difficult to find in the United States, although low-gluten flours are easier to find in the UK.

One is tempted to throw up one's hands and head for the nearest telephone. But the romance of making pizza at home persists nevertheless. On the practical level, there's the attraction of making a great, low-cost meal. On the more important spiritual level, there's the sense of joy, wonder and accomplishment that one feels when a yeast-affected product is mystically rising in one's hearth—even when that 'hearth' is an electric oven.

We tested scores of pizza recipes, juggling the dozens of factors that can make a difference in the success or failure of home pizza. And we are confident that we have come up with the best home pizza recipe available—one that, with a minimum of trouble, brings you closer to real pizza at home than you've ever been before. Even if you're not a natural-born baker—or a

Neapolitan—you will succeed if you carefully follow the instructions below.

Please note that *tipo 00* flour is now available at some specialty stores, such as ours. Far and away, this is your best choice for pizza flour—especially if you mix in 10 per cent or so of strong, plain flour. But, if you can't find *tipo 00*, substitute cake flour, a soft flour that is similar to *tipo 00*.

MASTER PIZZA DOUGH RECIPE

This dough recipe can be used for any size or shape of pizza that you wish to make. Our favourite, most manageable pizza for the home is round, approximately 15-18 cm (6-7 in) in diameter—exactly the size you're likely to find at pizzerias in Naples. This recipe makes enough dough for four such pizzas. When cooked, these round pizzas can be cut into appetiser slices, or each pizza can be served whole as a main course to one diner.

MAKES ENOUGH DOUGH FOR 4 PIZZAS

125 ml (4 fl oz) milk, at room temperature
175 ml (6 fl oz) water, almost hot to the touch
 (about 50°C (125°F)
30 g (2 tbsp) dry yeast or 40 g (1½ oz) fresh yeast
300 g (10½ oz) sifted *tipo 00* flour or cake flour
40 g (1½ oz) sifted strong plain flour
3 g (¾ tsp) fine salt
olive oil for oiling the bowl

1. *Proof the yeast:* In a small bowl or coffee cup mix together the milk and water. Sprinkle in the dry yeast, or crumble the fresh yeast in your hand and mix it into the liquid. Stir once and let sit in a warm place until there is considerable foam on top, about 10 to 20 minutes. (If your mixture doesn't foam up at least a little, the yeast wasn't fresh. Buy more and start again.)

2. *Mix the yeast with the flour:* In a large bowl combine the sifted flours with the salt. Mix well. Spill the foaming yeast mixture into the bowl and, working with a wooden spoon, mix together rapidly. Smooth out as many yeast lumps as possible during this stage. Your dough at this point will be very wet.

3. *Knead the dough:* Dust a work surface with flour. Add a little flour, about 25 g (1 oz), to the dough in the mixing bowl. This should enable you to scrape the dough together and place it on the floured surface. Add more flour if necessary. Begin kneading the dough on the work surface with your hands and adding tipo 00 flour or cake flour, 25 g (1 oz) at first, less and less as you proceed. While you're kneading, at first the dough will probably stick to the work surface and your hands. Don't worry. Keep kneading and adding more flour. But don't lose patience and add too much. Add slowly. The goal is to create a dough that is just past sticky; in fact, when it's finished, it should be threatening to stick to the work surface. You may even want to work with a spatula to remove the dough from the surface if it sticks slightly. All together, kneading time should be about 10 minutes, until the dough is smooth, silky and just past stickiness. Do not end up with a very dry, very stable dough.

4. *Let the dough rise:* Lightly oil the bottom of a large bowl with the olive oil. Form the dough into a ball. Place the dough in the bowl and cover tightly with clingfilm. Place the bowl in a spot that's room temperature, neither warm nor cool. In 2 hours or so, the dough should double in size.

5. *Shape the pizza:* Cut the dough into four quarters. Place one quarter on a floured surface, pulling it gently into a round as you place it on the surface. Your goal is a round pizza that is 15-18 c, (6-7 in) in diameter, approximately 5 mm (¼ in) thick, except at the rim where it should be about 8 mm (⅜ in) thick. Use one of the following means to achieve this:

- Pull it from the outer edges until the desired shape is reached.
- Working it with your fingertips, push the dough away from the centre towards the rim, until the

centre is 5 mm (¼ in) thick and the rim has built up to 8 mm (⅜ in) thick.
- Do it pizzeria-style by placing the dough on your two fists and revolving it on your fists until it has widened to the desired shape (be careful not to tear the dough at the centre).
- Use these techniques in combination.

Do not roll out your dough.

Don't worry if your pizza isn't perfectly round; there's much to be said for rusticity. If your pizza doesn't have much of a rim, use your fingertips to crimp the dough and build a small one around the circumference; this is called the *cornicione*. If your pizza dough has a tear in it, transplant a small piece of dough from the remaining dough, smoothing it in. Run a wide spatula under the pizza to make sure you'll be able to move it easily off of the surface later; add extra flour underneath if it's sticking.

Repeat this process until all four pizzas are shaped.

6. *Let the dough rise a second time:* Place towels loosely over the pizzas as soon as they're shaped. Let each pizza rest for at least 10 minutes and up to 60 minutes before cooking. The pizzas should puff very slightly.

Pizza equipment
You don't need much to make a pizza, but two special pieces of equipment really do make the process easier and the result better.

The first is the pizza stone, made from natural stoneware. It helps by distributing the heat evenly for a more evenly cooked pizza and by absorbing moisture and creating a crunchier crust on the underside of the pizza. To use a pizza stone, simply place it in your oven as you're preheating the oven. Just before placing the pizza on it, sprinkle the stone with cornmeal.

The second piece of equipment, the pizza peel, helps you to get your pizza onto the stone without mishap. It's just a thin wooden board with a long handle: if you've ever watched pizza being made in a pizzeria, you know exactly what it looks like. It's needed because the formed and topped pizza is difficult to transfer by any other means. To use a pizza peel, sprinkle it with cornmeal and place your shaped, un-topped pizza on it (after its second rise). Top the pizza, then lift the pizza peel and slide the pizza onto the pizza stone in the oven. The motion is intuitive, but it goes something like this: place the furthest edge of the peel on the stone at about the spot you'd like the furthest edge of the pizza to sit. Pull away the peel in such a way that the pizza doesn't bunch up as you're transferring it. A sharp yank is usually prescribed, but neophytes will feel more comfortable with a slow, easy withdrawal. The goal, of course, is to get the pizza sitting flat on the centre of your pizza stone.

PIZZA STYLES AND HOW TO ACHIEVE THEM
Before you actually top and cook your pizza, you should decide which style of pizza you're aiming for. By style, we mean the whole range of texture and tactile possibilities: thin, thick, light, heavy, crunchy, soft, wet, dry, chewy or crumbly. When it comes to pizza style, everyone has his or her own opinion.

You would expect this in America, where everyone eats pizza and where there are nearly as many pizza styles as there are lifestyles. More surprising, however, is the fact that among American pizza cognoscenti—those who seek out the best and most authentic pizza, both here and in Italy—there is little agreement about the 'best' style of pizza.

What follows are our three favourite pizza styles and the ways in which you can achieve them at home.

CLASSIC NAPLES

In Naples—which, with justification, considers itself the pizza capital of the world—the best pizzerias turn out round pizzas about 15-18 cm (6-7 in) in diameter. To first-time visitors, however, the texture is a surprise. These are not thin, crispy pizzas. They are between thin and thick, with lovely, pillowy, light, soft rims that suggest light focaccia, or very light bread. They are superb—and very difficult to make at home, because the amount of time pizzas usually spend in cooler home ovens turns the soft and tender into the hard and crunchy.

To make classic Naples at home: follow the instructions for the master pizza dough recipe (page 102). While the pizza is baking in your 280°C (525°F) oven, you must find a way to prevent the rim of the pizza from turning hard and crunchy. *The solution is the application of water.* After the pizza has cooked for 3 minutes, dab the rim with a water-moistened pastry brush. Feel free to make minute imprints on the rim with the end of the brush. If you're cooking on a pizza stone, be very careful to prevent water from spilling on to the stone. This could crack the stone. The brush you use, therefore, should be just a little moist. After dabbing, continue cooking the pizza for 3 minutes more.

CRUNCHY NAPLES

Some people buy the Neapolitan medium-thick, light-and-feathery concept, but still prefer a crunch in their outer crust. This is simple to achieve.

To make crunchy Naples at home: Follow the instructions for the master pizza dough recipe (page 102). Bake the pizza in a 280°C (525°F) oven for 6 minutes.

THIN AND CRUNCHY

Thinner pizzas are served in Rome, throughout northern Italy and in most of the American pizza restaurants that command foodie reverence (such as John's on Bleecker Street in New York City). It is a much more austere pizza animal, often made without even a rim.

To make thin and crunchy at home: Follow the master pizza dough recipe (page 102) until you divide the dough, at which point you must divide it into eighths. Make 8 pizzas approximately 15-18 cm (6-7 in) in diameter. Shape the dough of each pizza so that the dough is only 3 mm (⅛ in) thick. Rolling is permissible. You may create a rim that's 5 mm (¼ in) thick, or you may, as do some makers of thin pizza dough, ignore making a rim at all. This thinner pizza takes only about 5 minutes to cook in a 280°C (525°F) oven.

Pizza malfatti

You must never be obsessive about symmetry in a home pizza. We know this, because the best home pizza we ever made was a mess.

Working with an improvised pizza peel, we slid a small pizza onto the stone—only to see it fall apart and fall over itself. We smoothed it out the best we could, but it was still a mountainous landscape of peaks and valleys, fissures and cracks. Mozzarella was hanging over the rim. Luckily, we decided not to abort the mission.

What came out of the oven 6 minutes later had the tactile quality of wonderful country food. Yes, some spots were thicker, some were crunchier—but the trade-off of 'sophisticated' regularity for casual rustic variety was one we'd gladly make again.

It's impossible to reproduce that exact pizza. But, if you're adventurous, you might want to experiment with pizza malfatti ('badly made pizza')—weird shapes, folded dough and irregular thickness, among other things. You'll probably hit upon a configuration that pleases you mightily.

RECIPES FOR PIZZA TOPPINGS

One of the main things that divides pizza in Italy from pizza in America is the approach to toppings. Italians like them simple; as with pasta, they prize the subtle taste and texture of the farinaceous product under the sauce. Americans, on the other hand, pay less attention to the crust and lavish much more attention on the topping. This means that in America each pizza usually gets a lot more topping and that Americans have many

more topping possibilities than Italians do.

We prefer to play it the Italian way—especially with the quality of pizza crust that the recipe starting on page 102 will give you.

Note: All of the following pizza recipes are for Naples-style pizzas, 15 to 18 cm (6-7 in) in diameter, 5mm (¼ in) thick. If you wish to make thinner, 3mm (⅛-in) pizzas, decrease the amount of topping slightly.

FOCACCINA

This is the simplest pizza served in Neapolitan pizzerias—but a great way to show off your crust.

MAKES 1 PIZZA

¼ dough from master pizza dough recipe (page 102)
cornmeal for sprinkling
1.25 g (¼ tsp) coarse salt
5 g (1 tsp) finely grated Parmigiano-Reggiano
10 ml (2 tsp) extra-virgin olive oil

1. Preheat oven with pizza stone in it to 280°C (525°F).

2. Shape a pizza and let it rise a second time (see instructions in master pizza dough recipe).

3. When ready to cook, sprinkle a pizza peel with cornmeal. Carefully place the pizza on the paddle. Top pizza with half the coarse salt and sprinkle Parmigiano-Reggiano over the rim only. Sprinkle cornmeal on pizza stone in oven. Slide pizza on to pizza stone (see box, page 103). Bake 6 minutes. Remove and drizzle with the olive oil. Sprinkle on the rest of the coarse salt.

A pizza party suggestion

You can get a rhythm going in your pizzas.

Because the pizzas described in this section take only 6 minutes, they are the perfect excuse for a casual, stand-around-the-kitchen kind of party (or around the barbecue, if the weather's good). There you are—the 6, 7 or 8 of you—sipping Dolcetto, waiting for the first pizza to come out of the oven. It arrives. While it's being hoovered up, the next one is already cooking. This can continue for a good 10 pizzas.

The important thing is to get a delectable order established, a crescendo of pizza thrills. Whet the appetites with focaccina, the simplest of pizzas. Move on to the relative austerity of pizza alla Napoletana. Start the cheese sweepstakes with pizza Margherita, continue with pizza with mozzarella and rocket and conclude, perhaps, with pizza with mozzarella and Gorgonzola. You can make one or two of each, depending on the Collective Appetite.

With salads on the side and perhaps a platter of prosciutto, salami and other delicacies, you've got a major hit on your hands.

PIZZA ALLA NAPOLETANA

The 'regular' pizza served in Naples's pizzerias is topped only with fresh basil and sliced, uncooked cherry tomatoes. 'Cherry tomatoes?' you gasp, recoiling in horror. The fact of the matter is that southern Italian cherry tomatoes—called *pomodorini*—are as highly prized in Italy as they are intense in flavour. We are now seeing similarly spectacular cherry tomatoes grown elsewhere; even in late summer, they are sometimes the best tomatoes in the market. In any case, if you haven't had this simplest of tomato pizzas before, you'll be amazed at how addictive it is.

MAKES 1 PIZZA

¼ dough from master pizza dough recipe (page 102)
cornmeal for sprinkling
4-6 cherry tomatoes sliced thinly
1.25 g (¼ tsp) coarse salt
25 g (1 oz) torn shreds of fresh basil leaves
5 ml (1 tsp) extra-virgin olive oil

1. Preheat oven with pizza stone in it to 280°C (525°F).

2. Shape a pizza and let it rise a second time (see instructions in master pizza dough recipe).

3. When ready to cook, sprinkle a pizza peel with cornmeal. Carefully place the pizza on the paddle. Inside the rim, evenly distribute the slices of cherry tomato. Sprinkle with half the coarse salt. Sprinkle cornmeal on pizza stone in oven. Slide pizza on to pizza stone (see box, page 103). Bake 6 minutes. (If a softer crust is desired, dab rim with moistened brush after 3 minutes, then cook 3 minutes more.) Remove and immediately scatter the basil over the pizza. Drizzle with the olive oil and sprinkle with the rest of the coarse salt. Serve immediately.

PIZZA MARGHERITA

Hard as it is to believe, what Americans consider to be basic pizza—mozzarella and tomato sauce—is not the leading type of pizza in Italy. In Italy if you want a pizza with mozzarella and tomato sauce, you must ask for pizza Margherita. But it doesn't have a long history. It didn't get its name, or its popularity, until 1889, when Queen Margherita, wife of Italy's King Umberto I, was served three pizzas by Naples' leading pizza-maker. When she identified this variation as her favourite, the pizza's fame spread.

Actually, pizza Margherita in Naples is somewhat different from our basic American pizza. It is smaller and lighter in texture. The Neapolitans use very fresh, buffalo mozzarella. The tomato sauce is uncooked; it's just a purée of peeled San Marzano (plum) tomatoes. And, rather than our familiar sprinkling of dried basil or dried oregano, fresh basil leaves are placed on top. In this recipe, we have also suggested as an option a non-traditional sprinkle of pecorino Romano on top of the pizza; they don't do it in Naples, but we think it improves the flavour of the dish.

MAKES 1 PIZZA

¼ dough from master pizza dough recipe (page 102)

cornmeal for sprinkling

45 ml (3 tbsp) uncooked tomato purée from canned or fresh plum tomatoes*

1.25 g (¼ tsp) coarse salt

8 slices of fresh mozzarella, about 5mm (¼ in) thick and 4 cm (1½ in) in diameter

20 g (¾ oz) torn shreds of fresh basil leaves

1 teaspoon extra-virgin olive oil

7.5 g (1½ tsp) finely grated pecorino Romano (optional)

1. Preheat oven with pizza stone in it to 280°C (525°F) .

2. Shape a pizza and let it rise a second time (see instructions in master pizza dough recipe).

3. When ready to cook, sprinkle a pizza peel with cornmeal. Carefully place the pizza on the paddle. Inside the rim, spread the tomato purée evenly. Top with half of the coarse salt. Arrange the mozzarella slices on top of the tomato purée. Sprinkle cornmeal on pizza stone in oven. Slide pizza on to pizza stone (see box, page 103). Bake 6 minutes. (If a softer crust is desired, dab rim with moistened brush after 3 minutes, then cook 3 minutes more.) Remove and immediately scatter the basil over the pizza. Drizzle with the olive oil and sprinkle with the rest of the coarse salt. If using the pecorino Romano, sprinkle evenly over the pizza. Serve immediately.

*If you're using canned plum tomatoes: an 800-g (28-oz) can of whole plum tomatoes makes about 450 ml (1 pint) of tomato purée (enough for 10 pizzas or so). Remove the whole tomatoes from the can, and place them in a food processor. (Reserve tomato liquid for another use.) Process until you have a slightly chunky purée. Unless you have exquisitely ripe, peak-of-season plum tomatoes, we recommend using the canned product.
If you're using fresh plum tomatoes: 450 g (1 lb) of fresh tomatoes makes about 450 ml (1 pint) of tomato purée (enough for 10 pizzas or so). Plunge the tomatoes into boiling water, and cook until the skins loosen (about 1 minute). Remove tomatoes from the water, and, working under cold running water, remove the skins. Place the tomatoes in a food processor, and process until you have a slightly chunky purée.

PIZZA WITH ROCKET AND MOZZARELLA

This combination took us by surprise when we tried it recently at Santa Brigida di Ciro, the great Naples pizza restaurant. To a group of 25 fanatics who had just chomped through a *degustazione* of various *pizze,* this uncommon variation was everyone's hands-down winner. Just make sure that your rocket is fresh and potent.

MAKES 1 PIZZA

¼ dough from master pizza dough recipe (page 102)

cornmeal for sprinkling

8 slices of fresh mozzarella, about 5mm (¼ in) thick and 4 cm (1½ in) in diameter

1.25 g (½ tsp) coarse salt

50 g (2 oz) very firmly packed, fresh rocket

7.5 ml (1½ tsp) extra-virgin olive oil

1. Preheat oven with pizza stone in it to 280°C (525°F) .

2. Shape a pizza and let it rise a second time (see instructions in master pizza dough recipe).

3. When ready to cook, sprinkle a pizza peel with cornmeal. Carefully place the pizza on the paddle. Inside the rim, arrange the mozzarella slices evenly. Sprinkle with ⅛ teaspoon of the coarse salt. Sprinkle cornmeal on pizza stone in oven. Slide pizza on to pizza stone (see box, page 103). Bake 6 minutes. (If a softer crust is desired, dab rim with moistened brush after 3 minutes, then cook 3 minutes more.) Remove and immediately scatter the rocket on the cheese. Sprinkle on the remaining ⅛ teaspoon of coarse salt. Drizzle oil over all and serve immediately.

Why the 280°C (525°F) oven works

Most home pizza recipes call for a medium oven heat, approximately 210°C (425°F). The standard wisdom is that higher heat at home won't cook the pizza evenly. It will crunch the crust, but by the time the topping is cooked, the crust may burn. This problem is eliminated in restaurants at super-high heat, of course—because at 540°C (1000° F) the topping cooks very quickly, in perfect sync with the crust.

We discovered that the real source of the high-heat problem at home is the amount of topping that people usually put on the pizza. If you top it in the Italian style—with a very light topping—you'll find that at 280°C (525°F) the topping cooks in sync with the perfectly crunchy crust.

Pizza on the barbecue

The owners of Al Forno in Providence, Rhode Island, were the first to bake pizza over an open fire—and the world is grateful for it. There is no method in the known universe that produces a better home pizza than putting it on the backyard barbecue. And though the enterprise sounds fraught with technical stumbling blocks, it's really rather easy.

There is one big problem, however: grilling pizza is an intuitive thing. When it comes to grilling anything, in fact, so many variables exist—from types of barbecues to types of fuel to the way the wind is blowing on the night you cook—that no recipe could possibly take your hand and authoritatively guide you through the process.

So letter-of-the-law recipe readers, go bake a cake. For the rest of you, here's the big outline.

If pizza is put over a hot fire, the underside will burn by the time the topping is cooked. If pizza is put over a low-to-medium fire, it's possible that the crust will not develop the proper crunch. What's a would-be pizza-maker to do?

Simple—as long as your grill has a cover. Arrange your fire so that it has two separate temperatures. The best way to do this, we found, is to pile the coals (or lava rocks) high on one side and to place them very sparsely on the other side. Top with the grill and you're ready to go.

To grill pizza, we prefer dividing the master pizza dough into 8 pieces (smaller pizzas are easier to handle). Hand-stretch each to about 7.5-10 cm cm

(3-4 in) in diameter and let rise a second time as usual. Place as many pizzas as you can fit over the hot side of the fire. You don't need oil on the grate; the pizzas tighten up and don't stick. Grill for 1 to 2 minutes, or until the bottom of each pizza is light brown. Flip over for 30 seconds to a minute, just until the top side picks up a little colour.

Place the pizzas on the cool side of the fire, flipping them over again to place the bottom crust down. Top in whatever fashion you wish (all of the topping recipes in this section work just fine). Cover the grill and let the pizzas cook for 3 to 6 minutes, or just until the topping is cooked. Make sure that the underside is not getting burnt; if it is, you'll have to push coals away from the cool side of the fire.

The major difficulty you're likely to have is that cheese, if you're using cheese, won't brown on top and the rim of the pizza may remain somewhat doughy. If this happens and it bothers you, you can always place the pizza under your oven's grill for a minute or so before serving. But we like to avoid the extra step.

The result is ambrosial—light, tender and crunchy—capturing the sophisticated flavour of pizza made in wood-burning brick ovens.

PIZZA WITH MOZZARELLA AND GORGONZOLA

MAKES 1 PIZZA

1/4 dough from master pizza dough recipe (page 102)
cornmeal for sprinkling
70 g (2½ oz) coarsely chopped mozzarella
70 g (2½ oz) coarsely chopped Gorgonzola
5 ml (1 tsp) extra-virgin olive oil
freshly ground black pepper to taste

1. Preheat oven with pizza stone in it to 280°C (525°F) .

2. Shape a pizza and let it rise a second time (see instructions in master pizza dough recipe).

3. When ready to cook, sprinkle a pizza peel with cornmeal. Carefully place the pizza on the paddle. Inside the rim, arrange the mozzarella pieces evenly, then top them with an even arrangement of the Gorgonzola. Sprinkle cornmeal on pizza stone in oven. Slide pizza on to pizza stone (see box, page 103). Bake 6 minutes. (If a softer crust is desired, dab rim with moistened brush after 3 minutes, then cook 3 minutes more.) Remove and let cool for 2 to 3 minutes. Drizzle with olive oil, season to taste with black pepper and serve immediately.

Alternate pizzas

No, we're not into designer pizzas with duck confit and California goat cheese. But we do respect history and there are several other Old World dishes that seem to have gastronomic connections to Italian pizza. They are pissa-ladière from southern France and lahmajun, from the Middle East. Both can be made with the following dough.

ALTERNATE PIZZA DOUGH

MAKES ENOUGH DOUGH FOR 1 LARGE PIE

1 sachet dried yeast
350 ml (12 fl oz) warm water
pinch of sugar
400 g (14 oz) strong plain flour, or more as needed
5 ml (1 tsp) salt
30 ml (2 tbsp) olive oil plus additional for the bowl

1. Dissolve the yeast in 125 ml (4 fl oz) of the water with the sugar in a small bowl and let stand until foamy, about 5 minutes.

2. Place the flour and salt in a large bowl and make a well in the centre. Stir the yeast mixture, remaining warm water and oil into the well.

3. Work with your hands to form a dough, adding more

flour if necessary. Turn the dough out onto a lightly floured surface and knead until the dough is smooth, elastic and just past sticky, at least 5 minutes.

4. Let the dough rise in a lightly oiled bowl, covered with a towel, in a warm place for 2 hours, or until more than doubled in bulk.

PISSALADIÈRE

Pissaladière is a rectangular, open-faced niçoise tart, very pizzalike, which is topped with anchovies and olives. Tomatoes are rarely included and cheese is never included—but because of the similarity between the first five letters of the name and the word *pizza,* many assume some kind of historical link between the two dishes. The theory we believe is that *pissaladière* comes from the niçoise word *pissala,* which is an anchovy paste and the Italians shortened the name of the French dish to name their own now-more-famous creation. Whatever. It makes a fabulous lunch (with a green salad) or a terrific opener for a Provençal dinner party.

MAKES 1 LARGE TART, SERVING 10 TO 12

75 ml (5 tbsp) olive oil
6 large white onions, peeled and thinly sliced
10 g (2 tsp) sugar
10 g (2 tsp) salt
4 garlic cloves, peeled and crushed
50 ml (2 fl oz) beef stock (optional)
1 recipe alternate pizza dough (recipe above)
24 anchovy fillets, soaked in water for 10 minutes
24 black niçoise olives, stoned
freshly ground pepper to taste
50 g (2 oz) finely chopped fresh parsley

1. Place 30 ml (2 tbsp)of the olive oil in a large, heavy frying pan over high heat. Add half the onions and cook over high heat until they begin to soften, about 5 to 6 minutes. Remove the onions, reserve and repeat with the remaining onions and another 30 ml (2 tbsp)of olive oil.

When the second batch of onions is ready, return the first batch of onions to the frying pan and stir together. Add the sugar, salt and garlic and cook, covered, over moderate heat, for 30 minutes.

2. After 30 minutes, remove the cover, increase the heat to high and cook onions until dry, shiny and brown, about 15 minutes. If the onions start to burn on the bottom of the pan, add a couple of tablespoons of beef stock or water. Reserve and let cool.

3. When ready to bake, preheat your oven to 230°C (450°F). Put the dough on the table with a little flour under it. Roll it into a long rectangle, 5mm (¼ in) thick and about 30 x 50 cm (12 x 20 in). Coat a baking tin the same length and width as the pissaladière, or a little larger, with the remaining 15 ml (1 tbsp) of olive oil. Place the dough in the pan and push it well in the corners. Spread the onion mixture evenly over the dough, leaving a 5mm (¼ in) uncovered border around the edge.

4. Arrange the anchovies in a crisscross diamond pattern. Arrange the olives geometrically in between the anchovy crisscrosses. Sprinkle with freshly ground black pepper to taste. Put the pissaladière in the oven and cook until the crust is brown, about 12 to 15 minutes.

5. Remove from the oven and sprinkle with parsley. Serve hot, warm or at room temperature. If you choose to serve it warm or at room temperature, let it cool first on a cooling rack (otherwise the dough will be soggy).

LAHMAJUN

These pizzalike treats are popular in Turkey, Syria, Lebanon and Israel (they have many different spellings: *lahmacun, lachmanjan, lachma bi ajun and* more). They are essentially flatbreads on which a spicy lamb and tomato topping is baked. In Turkey, the underlying flatbread is called *pide,* which sounds something like pizza. Throughout the Middle East, they are served pizza-style—that is, as open-faced pies. But we prefer to eat them as we did on the street in Istanbul: rolled up in paper, like a donner kebab and munched out of the hands.

MAKES 6 INDIVIDUAL ROLLS

1 recipe alternate pizza dough (recipe on page 109)
For the topping
30 ml (2 tbsp) olive oil
450 g (1 lb) finely ground lean lamb
6 tomatoes, peeled, seeded, chopped and drained
1 medium onion, chopped
1 large red pepper, trimmed, seeded and chopped
30 g (1 oz) chopped fresh flat-leaf parsley
45 ml (3 tbsp) tomato purée
15 ml (1 tbsp) pomegranate syrup(optional)
5 g (1 tsp) crushed hot red pepper flakes
2.5 g (½ tsp) ground allspice
5 g (1 tsp) cornmeal for sprinkling the baking sheet
For the garnish
6 medium tomatoes, thinly sliced
1 large onion, thinly sliced
75 g (3 oz) coarsely chopped flat-leaf parsley

1. Turn the dough out onto a lightly floured surface and divide it equally into 6 pieces. Roll each piece into a ball with your hands and let stand, covered with a towel, in a warm place for 30 minutes.

2. *Make the topping:* Heat the olive oil in a large frying pan over moderate heat until hot but not smoking, add lamb and cook, stirring, just until it begins to brown. Add the remaining ingredients for the topping and cook over low heat, stirring, until the liquid has practically disappeared, about 5 minutes. Taste and adjust seasoning.

3. Place a large, heavy baking sheet in the oven and heat at 280°C (550°F) for at least 20 minutes.

4. Roll each ball of dough into a 2-mm ($\frac{1}{16}$-in)-thick circle (about 18 cm (7 in) in diameter) with a rolling pin. Place about 30 ml (2 tbsp) of cooked topping on each circle, spreading the mixture to the edge of the rim.

5. Sprinkle the baking sheet with cornmeal, place lahmajun on the baking sheet and cook for 4 to 6 minutes (the lahmajun should be cooked through but still stay soft and white).

6. Remove from oven and garnish each one with tomatoes, onion and parsley. Carefully roll the lahmajun, wrapping greaseproof paper or foil around one end of each one so they can be eaten in the hand. Serve immediately.

Note: You can improvise something like the Istanbul original without making your own dough. Simply purchase large, soft Armenian bread, steam it, spread the lamb filling across them, add the garnishes, roll and serve.

PASTA

A mere 25 years ago, pasta was a minor player on the American culinary scene. Most of us knew it as an occasional spaghetti dinner at home, in which an American brand of dried pasta would be served with tomato sauce—often out of a jar—and, perhaps, some meatballs or sausages. If we ate pasta at Italian restaurants, our universe of possibilities expanded only slightly: clam sauce was popular, Alfredo was creeping in (botched as that dish usually was) and something called carbonara was making its American debut.

The great regional pasta dishes of Italy were virtually unknown. More important, the fabulous, authentic 'feel' of pasta dishes in Italy was simply not available here. And, of course, almost no one had yet heard of freshly made egg pasta, something that didn't come in a box.

Then the universe exploded. By 1985, pasta was king of the American table. Italian restaurants greatly increased the variety of pasta dishes available and many of them made their own egg pasta daily. Non-Italian restaurants caught the wave and one was as likely to see 'pasta' dishes at American, French and even Mexican restaurants as at Italian ones. Americans were buying pasta machines as if they were going out of style (which may finally happen). If consumers weren't rolling their own pasta at home, they were buying fresh egg pasta at specialty stores that offered it; some stores were even wholly devoted to it. And the supermarket, that great barometer of American tastes, was loaded with new convenience foods based on ever-expanding varieties of pasta and pasta sauces.

It is a food that was in the right place at the right time. Americans were eager to eat lighter meals, to eat less meat and fish, to eat more food containing complex carbohydrates. Pasta was the right choice and became a kind of gastronomic religion.

But do its high priests and acolytes today get it right with any greater consistency than Americans did 25 years ago?

There's this much to be happy about: there are now many, many more people in our country who understand the way pasta is made, sauced and served in Italy and this means that finding an authentic bowl of pasta is at least possible in modern America. But the bad news is this: most of the pasta that is served today, both in restaurants and homes, still falls far short of the Italian standard. Some of the problems are old ones that continue to haunt us; some of the problems are new ones spawned by the pasta explosion.

Among the old problems, oversaucing is at the top of the list. There's something about an ocean of sauce on pasta that seems to inspire and satisfy American palates. Unfortunately, the pasta is literally lost in the sauce; one can't taste it or feel it as it's supposed to be tasted and felt. And as long as cooks fail to see that the pasta is the point of a pasta dish, their appreciation of intrinsic quality in the pasta itself will always be stunted. *In Italy, pasta is sauced with just enough liquid to lightly cling to the noodles; no extra sauce is seen in the bottom of the bowl.*

An old, related problem is the *way* we sauce pasta. Our methods of ladling the sauce on at the table, or even blending the sauce with the pasta in a large mixing bowl, don't adequately combine pasta and sauce. *The best Italian method is this: after draining the pasta-cooking pot, briefly combine pasta and sauce right in the still-warm pasta-cooking pot.* Simply return the drained pasta to the pot, place over moderate heat and add just enough sauce to coat. Cook for half a minute.

Of course, the draining itself has always been a problem in America; somewhere we picked up the notion that tap water should be run over the just-cooked pasta. This removes much of the pasta's flavour. And, traditionally, the pasta that we're draining has already been overcooked; it has lost both its optimum flavour and optimum texture.

Conversely, 'undercooked pasta'—the flip side of 'overcooked pasta'—heads the list of the new generation of pasta problems. We have indisputably become more sophisticated; almost everyone who eats pasta today is aware of the al dente concept, pasta 'to the tooth,' or with a little bite left in it. But, as with the cooking of vegetables, the pendulum has swung too far in the other direction. Cut open the cooked dried pasta that you're served these days and you may find a little uncooked white spot at the core. This is because many cooks today, afraid of going past al dente, stop cooking the pasta before it's done. Only repeated taste tests, every 10 to 20 seconds apart, right at the crucial almost-done stage, will let you know when the pasta has lost its uncooked core and is deliciously al dente without being undercooked.

Another modern problem is the new menu position that pasta has achieved. Oddly enough, *when* to serve the pasta is something we used to do authentically more than we do now. Once upon a time, we ate pasta in Italian restaurants as they do it in Italy: after the starter and before the main course. Today, many restaurants serve pastas that have main course prices (encouraging the consumption of pasta as a main course) and many at-home diners prepare pasta as a main course. The problem with this is that both restaurateurs and home cooks think they have to beef up their pasta dishes to make them appropriate as main courses—and the intrinsic delicacy of pasta is lost. More sauce. More stuff in the sauce. More cheese on top. Modern main-course pasta is filling, but it's often not authentic.

A related problem is the amount of pasta served in this country with cream sauce. It is relatively rare in Italy to find a cream-based sauce for pasta; even the original fettuccine Alfredo has no cream. But reduction cream sauces for pasta are everywhere in America, making pasta much heavier than it's supposed to be. And we grate way too much cheese on pasta, on way too many different pasta dishes. Indiscriminate use of grated cheese makes all pasta taste like...grated cheese. A little bit on the right dish is as far as they go in Italy.

Furthermore, now that we have a profusion of pastas made from different flours and a profusion of pasta shapes and a profusion of pasta sauces, we don't often show an authentic Italian sensibility in matching these things up. Thin, delicate fresh pasta is not good with a hearty meat sauce or an oily tomato sauce; it's much better with a delicate butter dressing. Thick, extruded dried pasta, like bucatini, is not good with a delicate butter sauce. Italian pasta chefs are masters of pasta-and-sauce compatibility and that's the next step for us in our country.

Perhaps we're too excited by our culinary freedom. We're still revelling in the variety of pasta. This, unfortunately, has led us to create sauces for pasta that have no business on any pasta type or shape; creativity's fine, as long as it respects the basic Italian tenets of saucing pasta. But much of the energy spent on finding new sauces might better be spent on researching authentic Italian regional ones.

Which brings us to the last great pasta problem of the day and probably the largest. When Americans first embraced *pasta fresca,* somewhere in the 1970s, they developed an instant disdain for the dried and boxed pasta that they'd theretofore been eating. Linguine, spaghetti, perciatelli, etc. suddenly became déclassé.

This was not an entirely unhealthy corrective. We'd been eating Italian food for many years, but living in ignorance of the great Northern Italian tradition of making pasta fresh, usually from eggs mixed with very soft flour (*pasta all'uovo*) and eating the pasta that day. When done right, the texture is unforgettable: light, feathery, resilient, elastic, very unlike the firmer texture of the dried semolina-and-water pasta of Southern Italy, the one that Neapolitan immigrants brought to America.

However, the new awareness and worship of *pasta fresca* spawned two problems.

First of all, it became so trendy so fast, that all you had to do was put a sign up saying you had *pasta fresca* and people would buy it. It didn't matter whether it was good *pasta fresca* or not. Similarly, people started making it at home, long before they had any standards for *pasta fresca*—so they too were making inferior versions. The sad truth is this: most of the *pasta fresca* being sold in restaurants and stores, to this day, is not of good quality. It's often soft, mushy, pasty, wholly unlike the delicate product found throughout Northern Italy.

And the irony is this: the dried, boxed pasta being sold in every supermarket today, even the domestically made pasta, is much, much better than most of the *pasta fresca* being sold. But, because we became conditioned to the thought that Northern Italian food is somehow finer and *pasta fresca* is somehow on a higher plane, many consumers still disdain boxed pasta.

This doesn't happen in Italy—where, increasingly, good boxed pasta is in vogue in the North—and it shouldn't happen here. The best brands of dried, boxed pasta imported from Italy are among the best guarantees you have of a spectacular Italian dinner.

DRIED PASTA (PASTA SECCA)

Just 10 years ago, it was difficult to buy high-quality dried pasta in the United States. Most of the products were made in America, few of them had much semolina (hard durum wheat) in them and, consequently, most didn't have the stiff bite or nutty flavour of great Italian dried pasta. Today, you can find great Italian dried pasta all over this country. Pasta from large Italian companies like De Cecco and Delverde is available everywhere. Even more exciting are the Italian pastas from small, artisanal producers. Generally, the tubes through which the artisans extrude their pastas are less smooth than the commercial tubes—thereby creating pasta with slightly irregular texture on the outside, not slick-smooth. This enables the pasta to better pick up the sauce. We were instrumental in bringing the great pastas of Martelli and Latini into the United States; keep your eyes open for others as well. And here's the ultimate good news: even the American-made pastas are much better today than they were 10 years ago.

DRIED PASTA SHAPES... AND THE BEST SAUCES FOR THEM

Dean & DeLuca carries a myriad of different dried pastas from Italy, in different shapes and we helped to bring some of these to America for the first time. Today, you can find a wide variety of dried pasta shapes in many shops across the country. Here are some you're likely to see, along with sauce recommendations. Keep in mind that *pasta secca*, generally speaking, is better than *pasta fresca* for sauces that contain olive oil; the dried pasta does not absorb the oil as readily, thereby maintaining the texture of the pasta.

LONG PASTA (PASTA LUNGA)

These are long strands of pasta, the ones we turn to when we're anxious to twirl something on our forks. They go particularly well with olive-oil based sauces, especially tomato sauces. Stubby little chunks of meat or vegetable are awkward with pasta lunga, but long, julienne strips of meat, fish or vegetable seem appropriate.

Bucatini These are fatter than spaghetti and have a little hole right in the middle of each strand (in Northern Italy, *buco* is dialect for 'hole'). Because of the hole, they take less time to cook than you might imagine—so test often. They are also called perciatelli. A slightly larger version is called bucatoni. We love all of these pastas with hearty, full-flavoured sauces, particularly meat sauces.

Capellini These are fine strands of pasta, rather more delicate than most pasta lunga. The finest of all are called 'angel's hair,' or *capelli d'angelo*. They cook quickly, usually taking under 5 minutes. Particularly good with light fish and vegetable sauces.

Fettuccine This is, arguably, the most famous of the Northern Italian fresh pastas. Today, however—trading on fettuccine's popularity—dried pasta companies are making a dried version of fettuccine (sometimes with egg, sometimes without) and boxing it. Its shape and dimensions are similar to fresh fettuccine: long, flat, ribbon-shaped, about 3mm (⅛ in) wide (though you'll find dried fettuccine as wide as 5 mm (¼ in). We're not usually wild about dried fettuccine; we prefer thinner dried pasta with the usual dried pasta sauces and prefer fresh pasta with the usual fresh pasta sauces. At a pinch, however, dried fettuccine with rich, buttery sauces can be satisfying. And some producers—like Cipriani in Italy—are making high-quality products of this ilk. You'll also find dried versions of green fettuccine, made with spinach.

Fusilli Lunghi When corkscrew pasta (fusilli) reaches the length of regular spaghetti, it is called fusilli lunghi. We love the chew of these curly strands and the way they hold thick sauces with large bits of tomatoes or other vegetables in them. Because they hold sauce so well, however, they are also appropriate for medium- and thin-textured sauces.

Linguine These long, flat pasta strands—the name means 'tongues'—have long been among the most popular dried pastas in America. Intriguingly, they don't enjoy the same popularity in Italy, where you'll only occasionally find them and most often in the South. We love them, however—both the chew that the flat shape creates and the way the flat shape holds oily sauces. A classic, of course, with white clam sauce. Lately, we've been seeing a thinner form of linguine called linguine piccole.

Perciatelli South of Rome, the dialect word for 'hole' is *pertuso and perciato* means 'pierced through.' These 'pierced through' pasta strands are the same as bucatini. See Bucatini.

Pizzoccheri This specialty of the Valtellina region in Lombardy—made from buckwheat flour—is usually prepared and served fresh. But we carry a dried pizzoccheri that is delicious with the traditional Swiss chard sauce served on the fresh pizzoccheri of the region. The pasta looks like a greyish-brown fettuccine.

Spaghetti These ubiquitous 'little strings' have become practically synonymous with dried pasta; this is one shape that Dean & DeLuca didn't have to discover. They match well with a wide variety of pasta sauces, though the all-time Italian-American classic is spaghetti and meatballs with tomato sauce. You'll also find a very thin version of spaghetti, which is called spaghettini; it is not as thin as capellini, but similarly likes light, delicate sauces.

Vermicelli The name means 'little worms' and, as you might imagine, vermicelli are very thin noodles, similar to capellini. Don't confuse them with Asian vermicelli, which are often made from mung bean flour.

SHORT PASTA (PASTA CORTA)
When we're hungry for a bowl of dried pasta, we more naturally turn to long shapes than to short shapes—

because it's so much fun to twirl the long strands and they chew so interestingly. But short pasta has its share of fun, too. For one thing, it comes in a dazzling variety of shapes, many of which are unusual and amusing. One large sub-category of pasta corta is *tubi* (tubes), which contains many of the shapes most popular in America today (like penne and rigatoni). The *tubi,* in particular, are great for sauce, since many sauces penetrate inside the fat hole of the tube—even thick sauces. Pasta corta, in general, is good with chunky sauces, particularly when the chunks are similar in size to the pasta itself; this gives the diner the opportunity to scoop up pasta and chunks of equal size. Interestingly, some of the pasta corta shapes—like penne—are also good with cream-based sauces.

Boccolotti These are thick little rings, usually simply sauced with butter and cheese.

Cavatappi Corkscrews, which are usually both wider and shorter than fusilli. Like fusilli, they hold sauces extremely well.

Cavatelli This is a Pugliese pasta shape, often made from a combination of white flour and semolina and eaten fresh in the region. Today, it is available dried. It's a thick, rather clumsy shape: a little lump, about 1 cm (½ in) long, with a single indentation running down the length of the lump on one side. We find that it doesn't pick up sauce as well as its regional partner orecchiette.

Chifferi This is the original elbow macaroni, though the Italian version apparently used somebody's fatter arms as its model. You'll find it with either a smooth exterior *(lisci)* or a ridged exterior *(rigati).*

Conchiglie This means 'shell,' and just as you'll find all sizes of shells on the beach, so you'll find all sizes of conchiglie in the grocer's. What's different about this pasta is that the 'shell' practically curls around itself like a conch so that any stuffing you place inside will

stay put should you choose to cover the stuffed shells with sauce and bake them. Usually, only the larger conchiglie are stuffed; the smaller ones are to be sauced simply with hearty sauces, particularly chunky tomato sauce. Conchiglie are also good sauce catchers on the outside, because they're ridged.

Denti d'Elefante This tube is a type of maccheroni that's relatively long and narrow—hence its designation as 'elephant's teeth.' It looks something like penne, but without slant-cut ends.

Elicoidali These are rigatoni with a difference: they have a pattern of fine ridges that wind around each piece of pasta. The name comes from *helix.* You'll also find these tubes to be a little narrower than rigatoni.

Farfalle These 'butterflies' are made from pasta rectangles that have been pinched in the centre to create a butterfly-like look. Sometimes they're translated as 'bow ties,' but that's because the Italian word for bow tie is *cravatta a farfalla* (butterfly tie). They may have ruffled edges. Smaller ones are called farfalline. All types are good with hearty sauces and in cheese-topped casseroles. You will most often see these as dried pasta, but they are also made fresh from egg pasta. A similar shape is called finochetti.

Fusilli Corti This means short fusilli—so called to distinguish this pasta from the fusilli lunghi discussed previously—but usually the box will just say fusilli. As with the long fusilli, these are corkscrew-shaped pastas that have a wonderful feel in the mouth and hold many different sauces, from thick to thin, very well. Because of their popularity, you will see many different variations of fusilli in the market (from spinach to beetroot to wholemeal.) One interesting variation is fusilli bucati which, in addition to the spiral, also manages to have a hole right down the middle of the pasta.

Gemelli These are twisted strands of pasta, usually 2.5-

5 cm (1-2 in) long, that look like someone forgot to twist very much. Imagine two strands of pasta twisted around each other quickly just to hold them together and you've got the idea. They're good with hearty meat sauces.

Gnocchi Strictly speaking, gnocchi, to be gnocchi, must be fresh. They are dumplings that are often, but not always, made with potato. Because they have become so well-known and popular, they are now being produced dried by pasta-makers in the form of a flour-only pasta that's shaped like a gnocchi—a cylinder about 2.5 cm (1 in) long, no hole inside, with deep, widely spaced grooves on the outside. They should be called 'sort-of-gnocchi,' but the box just says gnocchi. If they're small, it will say gnocchetti.

Lumache These 'snails' somewhat resemble chifferi (elbow macaroni), except that they're larger and have 2 little points at one end that look like a snail's feelers.

Maccheroni Ever since Yankee Doodle stuck a feather in his hat and called it macaroni, Americans have been passionate for this dried tubular pasta. Most Americans, however, associate the name with elbow macaroni. In Southern Italy, however, maccheroni was the original name for every kind of dried pasta. Today, there, it has lost its general meaning, but the word still applies to a great variety of short, tubular dried pasta shapes. If you see a dried pasta in a box labelled simply maccheroni, you will probably find it to be similar to rigatoni—though a little narrower, a little shorter and with or without ridges.

Millerighe These fat tubes are like rigatoni, except that each tube is straight, not curved. Also, there are many more ridges on each tube ('thousand ridges').

Mostaccioli The name means 'small moustaches,' which, in pasta language, translates as medium-size tubes with slant-cut ends that may or may not be ridged. They are very much like penne.

Orecchiette This is a regional pasta (from Puglia) that has achieved national and international popularity. It means 'little ears,' and looks something like them— more like little circles, actually, with a depression in the middle. That depression should make you elated, because it picks up sauce like nobody's business; it also perfectly picks up appropriately sized chunks (a pea, for example, nestles in beautifully). The classic Pugliese sauce for this pasta is sausage with broccoli. Orecchiette are traditionally made and eaten fresh in Puglia, but the market today is swimming with orecchiette possibilities. In America, there's a lot of dried, Pugliese, artisan-made orecchiette, produced from flour and water only.

Penne These darlings of our modern Italian restaurants are short tubes, thinner than rigatoni, slant-sliced at the ends to create a kind of pointed tip, reminiscent of a pen, or quill. The name is derived from the Italian word for 'feather,' which used to top a pen or quill. Penne are wildly popular in America today, though we're not exactly sure why. You'll find many variations in stores and restaurants. If the penne are smooth on the outside, they're penne lisce; if they're ridged on the outside, they're penne rigate. You'll find yellow ones made from flour alone and green ones made from flour mixed with spinach. If they're narrow, they'll be called just plain 'penne' (the narrower the better, to our taste). Fatter penne are called penne ziti and very fat penne are called pennoni. All of these are wonderful with hearty sauces, with appropriately sized chunks of vegetables and/or meat and topped with pecorino Romano. The smaller penne are good for cream sauces (like the very popular penne con vodka).

Radiatore We don't know what the inventor of this shape was smoking, but we're glad he smoked it. Who would have thought of pasta in the shape of 'radiators,' less than an inch long? Who would have imagined that the indentations of the radiators would pick up sauce so beautifully and that the whole silly shape would be such a textural delight? We love the chew of these things, believe it or not, in pasta salad.

Rigatoni Rigatoni are fat tubes, slightly curved, usually about 4 cm (1½ in) long and always ridged. They enjoy popularity both in Italy and in the United States. They're good with meaty, hearty sauces and the hole in the tube is large enough so that you can plan on chunks getting inside. They're also good in baked pasta casseroles.

Rotelle Kids do cartwheels for these curious delights which are shaped like, well, cartwheels (they are also called *ruote di carro*). The spokes of the wheel always look the same, but the rim of the wheel can be either smooth or ridged. Because there are so many spaces within this pasta shape and because the spokes are relatively thin pasta, you can use thinner, less hearty sauces with this pasta corta.

Sedanini *Sedano* means celery and these short pieces of pasta are cut to look like short pieces of cut celery. The Tuscans love to combine them with actual pieces of celery, creating a dish called *sedanini al sedano*.

Strozzapreti The name means 'priest stranglers,' and this pasta appears all over Italy in a variety of shapes (it seems that priest-strangling has occurred to a lot of Italians). In Montalcino, we were even served fresh strozzapreti (the chef went to confession soon after that). Sometimes they're long, which would explain the strangle part. But more often than not they're dried, short and roughly twisted (but not with the precision of fusilli). They're usually rather thick and perfect with hearty meat sauces.

Ziti Before there was penne, there was ziti; this shape was one of the earliest shapes to capture the American imagination. Actually, it's very similar to penne, except that the ends of the tubes are cut straight, rather than in the slanted fashion that makes the tip of the 'pen' in penne. Ziti were traditionally served in Naples at weddings and that's where they got their name; literally, ziti means 'bridegrooms.'

DRIED PASTA FOR SOUP

The dried pasta universe is rounded out by a million constellations of little pasta shapes that go into soup; they are called *pasta per minestre*. Pasta in soup, in Italy, is a very important tradition. In fact, pasta *not* in soup, but with a sauce, gets its own name—*pasta asciutta* (or dry pasta), to distinguish it from the mainstream tradition of putting pasta in soup. Some of the shapes of pasta per minestre you'll find are acini di pepe, alfabetini, anellini, ditali (smooth or ridged), farfalline, funghetti, orzi, quadrucci, risoni, stelline and many more. Remember that they don't *have* to go in soup; a bowl of thick orzo with a sauce of reduced chicken stock and grated cheese is a real winner on a cold day.

COOKING DRIED PASTA

To cook dried pasta you need a large pot of furiously boiling water; this is necessary so that the water will remain boiling after you've added the pasta. The pasta cooks better this way. Use a minimum of 4 litres (7 pints) of water, no matter how little pasta you're cooking.

Add the water, cold and fresh, to a large pot over high heat. Cover it. When the water boils, remove the cover and add some salt to it. The salt will definitely flavour the pasta, so use salt according to your taste. A famous pasta chef once told us to 'use only enough salt so that you can taste the water.' But this will not season the pasta very much; it's good for people who don't like salt. Make your pasta water about as salty as stock.

There is no need to add oil to the water.

Add all the pasta at once to the water. Never break long strands of pasta in half; part of the fun in eating is slurping long noodles. Immediately, using a pasta grabber or other implement, begin separating the pasta strands, making sure they're not sticking together. If the water does not come back to the boil at once, you can cover the pot to hasten the process. But, every minute or so, go back in with your implement to make sure the pasta's not sticking together. When the water returns to a boil, remove the cover.

It is impossible to say how long it will take to cook your dried pasta. When you believe it is nearing completion, start tasting every 10 to 20 seconds. It is finished when the pasta is al dente. This means that it's cooked through, but still firm. Cut through a piece of pasta and make sure that the centre is not starchy-white; a cross section of the pasta should look evenly cooked through.

The question of cheese

Americans are grated-cheese happy, sprinkling it with abandon on all kinds of sauces. But cheese on all of the tomato sauces for dried pasta, for example, converts a subtle range of sauces into one taste. And cheese, in Italy, is considered downright inappropriate on any pasta dish with a seafood sauce (they think the flavours clash).

We usually don't like to pass grated cheese at the table for pasta, unless we've already incorporated some cheese into the dish; then, the extra cheese becomes a seasoning adjustment for your guests. In the recipes that follow, if we think that cheese augments the dish, we'll tell you what kind of cheese to use and how to add it to the pasta. Serve extra cheese at the table, if you wish—but we think even that's not necessary.

SAUCING DRIED PASTA

As soon as the pasta's ready, skim 225 ml (8 fl oz) or so of pasta-cooking water off the top of the pot. Reserve. Then, pour the contents of the pot into a colander set in the sink. Shake the colander to make sure the strands are not sticking together. If it's appropriate for the dish, you may add a few teaspoons of olive oil to the pasta at

this point; shake the colander to distribute the oil and keep the noodles from sticking. Place half the pasta sauce in the now-empty cooking pot and put the pot over low heat. Add the pasta and blend well with some of the sauce. Add more sauce if necessary; the pasta should be lightly coated with sauce. If you think the sauce seems a little thick, you can lighten the dish by adding some of the hot pasta-cooking water. The pasta should be in the pot for no more than 30 seconds. Serve immediately, with a little more sauce ladled over the top.

If you are using an uncooked sauce, toss it with the pasta in a bowl, not in the pasta pot over heat.

FRESH PASTA (PASTA FRESCA)

If you want to serve fresh pasta at home, you can either buy it or make it yourself.

If you're buying it, be careful! Most of the fresh pasta sold outside Italy today is soft, mushy, pasty, not worth the money it costs nor even the short time it takes to cook and sauce. Of course, a small quantity of first-rate *pasta fresca* is made daily by pasta artisans and sold by them or at leading specialty shops like ours. But it is difficult to find. If you want fresh pasta, we recommend learning how to make your own.

Now, if you want to make your own, you may be tempted to use one of the newfangled pasta-making machines on the market.

Our general advice: Don't.

The new generation of electric pasta-extruding machines, which even blend and knead the dough for you, produces pasta that is passable at best; these are not for serious pasta-lovers and we don't recommend them.

That much is easy. But here comes the hard part: with the passage of time, we have even become disenchanted with the old-fashioned hand-cranked pasta machines. Why? Well, these machines are certainly convenient if you're making a large quantity of pasta; rolling and cutting will undoubtedly go faster than they would by hand. But the finished product just ain't the same. The rolling, on a pasta machine, is done by compressing the dough, squeezing it to thinness. Rolling by hand, when done properly, is a combination of compression and stretching—which makes the texture of the pasta much more resilient and interesting. Secondly, the rollers of a pasta machine give the dough a smooth, slick, shiny surface; hand-rolling creates a more mottled surface, which is better-tasting and picks up sauce better. As for cutting: we prefer the thrill of cutting pasta exactly to our own specifications, though the hand-cranked machine does a decent job. Doing the cutting on your own may take a little longer and may result in pasta that's not quite as uniform, but you'll experience a wonderful feeling in seeing the process through from beginning to end with no machines getting between you and the dough. And the hand-cut pasta is much easier to handle, after cutting, than is the machine-cut pasta.

All told, it will take you about 45 minutes of labour (not counting resting time) to prepare 450 g (1 lb) of fresh pasta from scratch. This is not much more time than it would take were you using a machine. And the only special equipment you need is a long, narrow rolling pin.

FRESH PASTA SHAPES...AND THE BEST SAUCES FOR THEM

If you're buying fresh egg-and-flour pasta, you'll find the variety of fresh pasta shapes is not nearly so great as the variety of dried pasta shapes. And the saucing situation is simpler too—because all of the fresh pasta shapes are good with delicate sauces, often based on butter or stock. They're good with cream sauces too, but, following Italian practice, we don't make a lot of cream sauces for pasta. Remember that the fresh pasta, with its softer texture, will more readily absorb sauce than dried pasta will. So, by all means, avoid oily sauces for fresh pasta; the pasta soaks up the oil, creating an unattractive texture. And don't forget butter-based meat sauces; these are very popular accompaniments to fresh pasta throughout Northern Italy. Here are some of the

fresh pasta shapes you're likely to see in American shops and restaurants, and in Britain too:

Fettuccine This is the king of fresh pasta in America, the shape that Americans first came to know and love. It is a 'ribbon' pasta—long and relatively narrow, just like ribbons. Fettuccine in Italy is usually about 3mm (⅛ in) wide, though in the United States it is often wider. It is served in every Roman trattoria and its most famous incarnation (created in Rome) is fettuccine Alfredo. This demonstrates a basic gastronomic truth: fettuccine likes butter and cheese. In Britain, this shape is better known as Tagliatelle, the northern Italian equivalent.

Garganelli This shape, once rare, is now achieving popularity. It should, because it's unique, the only tube-shaped pasta made from fresh pasta dough. Squares of about 4 cm (1½ in) are draped over a stick, then rolled over a ridged device to create the tube and its outer ridges. They are great with creamy, buttery sauces with chunks of vegetable, fish or meat.

Pappardelle Pappardelle are wonderfully wide pasta ribbons, very popular in Tuscany where they are often served with a wild rabbit sauce. Any meat sauce will do well—particularly, we find, when the sauce features tender, stringy, long-cooked pieces of meat. Pappardelle are usually about 2 cm (¾ in) wide, straight-edged or ruffle-edged and 15-20 cm (6-8 in) long. We love the way they slide against each other on the plate. They have another name in Bologna: larghissime.

Spaghetti alla Chitarra This pasta comes from the central region of Abruzzo and, though *chitarra* means 'guitar,' has nothing to do with music. The chitarra simply resembles a guitar, with wire strings set close to one another. Fresh pasta is pushed through the strings (using a rolling pin) and a shape that's long and narrow like spaghetti is created—but each strand is square, not round. In the Abruzzo region, spicy meat sauces are popular with spaghetti alla chitarra. In Rome, the same pasta is called tonnarelli.

Tagliatelle In the United States, this is synonymous with fettuccine. In Italy, there is a difference, though: tagliatelle is twice as wide as fettuccine, usually about 5 mm (¼ in) wide. It is the darling pasta of Bologna, where it is classically served with bolognese meat sauce or with a buttery-cheesy prosciutto sauce; sauces for tagliatelle are usually less delicate than sauces for fettuccine. The name, by the way, comes from *tagliare,* to cut.

Taglierini Another ribbon pasta, like fettuccine and tagliatelle. But of the holy tagliatelle-fettuccine-taglierini trio, taglierini are by far the narrowest, usually just 2 mm (¹⁄₁₆ in) wide. They are often served in stock in Italy, but we love them with light fish and vegetable sauces. Another name for them is tagliolini.

Trenette This is a Ligurian version of the Roman fettuccine. Normally, it is made with fewer eggs and sometimes has a ruffle cut on one side of the pasta strands. It is the classic pasta for pesto, in the home region of pesto, but is also sauced with a variety of vegetable sauces.

STUFFED PASTA SHAPES
Throughout Italy, cooks like to stuff fresh pasta with a myriad of flavourful things; this category of pasta is called *pasta ripiena.* You can find a number of these shapes for sale in grocers and supermarkets. Caveat emptor: most of the commercial brands are gummy and completely lack the delicacy of fine pasta ripiena. Here are the shapes you're most likely to see:

Agnolotti A Piedmontese specialty, usually larger than ravioli. Typically stuffed and sauced with meat.

Cannelloni These have been popular in the United

States for a long time, though they're usually a dreadful part of red-sauce restaurants. They are rectangular sheets of fresh pasta, stuffed with a variety of fillings, then rolled up like a Swiss roll and baked. Of Piedmontese origin, they're now popular throughout Italy (and even throughout Spain!). When in Italy, look for different regional names (*borlenghi* in Bologna, *ciaffagnoni* in Tuscany, *fregnacce* in Rome).

Cappelletti A favourite Northern Italian pasta ripiena. They are made from fresh pasta squares and rolled to form 'little hats.'

Ravioli Of course. Originally, these squares were made in Liguria.

Tortelli This is a confusingly named family of stuffed pastas. In Emilia, tortelli are large, square shapes, larger than ravioli, usually filled with spinach and cheese. The littler version, tortellini, are not a square at all, but look something like a navel; tortellini are a classic of Bologna, where they are often served with meat sauce or cream sauce—or in stock on New Year's Eve. Tortelloni, again in Bologna, are a larger version of tortellini. But here's the twist: outside of Emilia (Bologna's region), tortelloni refers to a large, *square* stuffed pasta—the same as tortelli in Emilia. Got it?

Throughout Italy, you'll find hundreds of other names to describe *pasta ripiena.*

MAKING FRESH PASTA
There are 8 steps in making great fresh pasta at home:
1. choosing the right flour
2. combining the flour and eggs
3. kneading the dough
4. resting the dough
5. rolling and stretching the dough
6. letting the stretched dough dry
7. cutting the dough
8. letting the pasta dry

1. CHOOSING THE RIGHT FLOUR

This is a confusing subject because there so many flours are available and because we hear so many conflicting things about Italian practice. For example, many people believe that authentic Italian pasta is made from semolina (or *semolino,* as they call it in Italy), a flour made from hard durum wheat. Actually, only the dried and boxed pasta of the South is usually made from semolina—but the *pasta fresca* of the North is usually made from tipo 00 flour, an exceedingly soft flour.

The pasta you make at home from one kind of flour will differ in texture from the pasta you make at home from another kind of flour. One big factor is the amount of gluten in the flour: more gluten means firmer pasta, less gluten means more tender pasta. Another important characteristic to watch for is resiliency: to us, the best fresh pasta of all is springy and slightly elastic. Ideally, if a strand of this resilient pasta is pulled, it will spring back into place.

Here is a range of flours, from soft to hard and what you can expect from them in pasta-making.

Tipo 00 This very soft, highly refined Italian flour—00 refers to the finest setting of the flour mill—is widely used in Northern Italy for pasta fresca. We carry it at Dean & DeLuca, but it is not widely available. If you can't find it, you can use plain flour or cake flour as a substitute. When you work with tipo 00, you'll find the dough grainier at first than other pasta doughs, but, after a few minutes of kneading, you'll see that it becomes smoother and silkier than other doughs! In general, it is easier to work with and knead than other doughs, because of its greater malleability. The pasta it produces is softer, lighter, more feathery than other pastas. It is not as firm as most, but it more than makes up for this by its greater resiliency; this is the springiest pasta you can make. We like it best after 24 hours of drying, when it becomes a bit firmer. Remember that it will take slightly less time to cook than other pastas. We would choose 00 pasta for fettuccine Alfredo, or, for example, for any butter-egg-cheese dish that emphasises lightness.

Unbleached Plain Flour This is a decent all-around choice. The pasta it yields is firm, but not especially resilient—appropriate for a wide range of sauces, from light to heavy.

Strong Plain Flour This flour is notable for its higher degree of gluten; this makes it stiff and slightly more difficult to knead than the previous two flours. But the effort is worth it, because strong plain flour produces a very chewy pasta that also has a decent amount of resiliency. The balance of these two textures seems even better after 24 hours of drying.

Semolina This flour, made from hard durum wheat, is, by far, the weirdest flour to work with (make sure the semolina you get is finely milled, or it'll be even weirder). First of all, there's the colour difference: it's yellow and so is the pasta it yields. Then, you'll find that you need more flour per egg than you do for other doughs, so be prepared to sprinkle on a little extra; in the initial blending, in fact, you'll find this the trickiest pasta for getting the flour-egg proportion just right, because this dough comes together so slowly. Then comes the kneading: this is, by far, the stiffest, most difficult dough to pummel. You'll work harder than with any other dough. Rolling out is also difficult; the dough tears more easily and is hardest to stretch thin. For your labours, you will get a pasta that is the knobbliest, the coarsest, the most rustic of all pastas—very tough and chewy, but not very resilient. We find that if you roll it as thinly as possible and cut it into narrow strands—like 2 mm ($\frac{1}{16}$ in)—you will have a marvellous bowl of pasta ready for some hearty, back-country meat sauce and lots of pecorino Romano. But don't use semolina pasta for delicate sauces. It has the virtue of being ready to use immediately after cutting. One other idea for semolina: blend it with other flours if you want to increase the firmness of your fresh pasta.

2. COMBINING THE FLOUR AND EGGS

This can be done right on your work surface, in the
classic Italian fashion, but it's much easier to do it in a
large, wide mixing bowl. For 115-140 g (4-5 oz) fresh
pasta, you will need 65 g (5 tbsp) flour and 1 large egg.
Place the flour in the centre of the bowl and create a
well in the centre of the flour. Beat the egg thoroughly in
a separate bowl (30 seconds or so). Pour the beaten egg
into the well. With your fingers, start pushing the flour
into the egg, which will thicken the egg. At some point,
the wall of the well will collapse, but that's no problem
in a bowl. Just keep mixing flour and egg together with
your hands until a ball is formed that's just past moist
and sticky. There will probably be some flaky crumbs left
in the bowl, as well as some finer particles of flour. At
this point, remove the ball of dough and place it on a
smooth, steady work surface. Wash your hands with hot
water to remove dough shreds and dry your hands
thoroughly. If the dough is still a little sticky, sprinkle
some of the remaining flour from the bowl through a
sieve onto the dough. Remember that the dough—which
is now called the sfoglia—should not be moist, but it
shouldn't be very dry either.

3. KNEADING THE DOUGH

With the heel of your hand, push about one-eighth of the
dough along the surface of the counter. Continue until
you've pushed all the dough in this fashion. This is a
good kneading technique that you can continue to use
throughout the kneading. But feel free to use any
movement that's comfortable for you (like rocking your
knuckles back and forth in the dough), just as long as
you're handling the dough roughly. This will develop the
gluten in the dough. Knead for approximately 10
minutes. Your dough should be smooth and elastic.

4. RESTING THE DOUGH

Sprinkle the dough very lightly with flour and wrap it
loosely in clingfilm. Let it rest, at room temperature, for

30 to 60 minutes. (Note: if you're preparing a double
recipe—using 140 g (5 oz) of flour with 2 eggs—divide
the dough into 2 balls at this stage. If you're preparing
a triple recipe, divide into 3 balls. The 1-recipe quantity
of dough is by far the easiest quantity to roll out.)

5. ROLLING AND STRETCHING THE DOUGH

After the dough has rested, remove it from the clingfilm.
Turning it in your hands, flatten it into a disk the size of
a large field mushroom cap. Place the dough on a lightly
floured work surface (if the dough sticks to the surface
at any point, dust it and the surface with more flour).
Place a long, narrow rolling pin across the equator of the
dough. Apply pressure and roll the dough away from you,
making sure to roll the pin completely across the edge. It
is important to think of this motion as a *pushing away*
motion, not as a *pressing down* motion. Without
applying any pressure at all, roll the pin back to the
equator. Repeat the movement 4 more times. Then give
the dough a slight turn (rotating it about an eighth of
the way) and repeat the 5 rolling movements to the
edge. Continue turning and rolling 6 more times, until
you've turned the dough all the way back to its original
position. Your dough should now be a smooth circle,
about 5 mm (¼ in) thick. If your dough is not a perfect
circle, don't worry about it. However, if it's too thick,
continue turning and rolling until you're reached 5 mm
(¼ in). Check for evenness as well; if any spots seem to
be unevenly thick, roll over them with your pin.

Now you're ready for the first stretch.

Place the pin on the dough, about two thirds of the
way to the top edge (or one third of the way down from
the top edge). Wrap the top third of the dough over the
pin. Grip it with one hand, curling your fingers around
the dough and the pin. Grab the bottom edge of the
dough with your other hand and, pulling gently in both
directions, stretch the dough slightly. Be careful: too
little pressure and the dough won't stretch; too much
pressure and you'll tear it. But stretch it as far as you
can without tearing it. Unroll the pin, place the dough on

the surface, give the dough a quarter turn and repeat the process, starting with the placement of the pin two-thirds of the way up to the edge. Go around the circle twice; in other words, stretch the dough a total of 8 times.

Place the stretched dough back on the board and, placing your pin again at the equator, roll over the top edge. Repeat this 4 times. Then, as before, give the dough a one-eighth turn and roll to the top edge 5 times. Keep making one-eighth turns and rolling until you've completed a circle. Your dough should be thin at this point—3mm (⅛ in) is good, 2 mm (1⁄16 in) is better.

Now you're ready for the second stretch.

Place the pin on the dough, about two-thirds of the way to the top edge (or one-third of the way down from the top edge). Wrap the top third of the dough over the pin, making sure that the top flap of the dough is under the pin. Place the balls of your hands on the dough that's rolled over the pin, right on top. Begin rolling the pin towards you, but the trick is this: while you're rolling, keep moving your palms outwards to the opposite ends of the rolling pin. This will stretch the dough sideways. When you've nearly reached the bottom of the dough, unroll the pin, give the dough on the board a quarter turn and start the motion again. Do this 2 more times, with 2 more quarter turns.

The dough should now be less than 2 mm (1⁄16 in) thick. If it's not, roll it out again with the pin, pushing away from you very hard, until the desired thinness is reached. Rotate the dough frequently and make sure that it is not sticking to the board.

6. LETTING THE STRETCHED DOUGH DRY

You will now have a thin piece of dough that's probably not a perfect circle. No problem. Lay a kitchen towel on a table so that its edge is lined up with the table edge. Place a rim of the dough on the towel on the table so that most of the dough is not on the table at all, but hanging over the table edge. Secure the rim of the dough on the towel with a weight (such as a heavy knife

or a small bowl). After 10 minutes of drying, rotate the dough 180 degrees and secure it again. Let it dry for 10 more minutes.

After 20 total minutes of drying, the dough should be slightly leathery and ready for cutting. (If it's too moist, it won't cut easily. If it's too dry, it will crack when you cut it.) Place the dough on a cutting surface.

7. CUTTING THE DOUGH

First of all, if you're hand-cutting (as we recommend), you can't be fanatical about perfection. The edges of the dough are a good place to learn this lesson; you'll have to just cut away the frilly, irregularly shaped edges of the dough. If you wish, you could cut the dough down to a perfect rectangle.

Many books recommend folding the dough at this point into a wide, very narrow rectangle—about 6 cm (2½ in) wide. This makes cutting go faster. But, after you've cut, you will have to unravel the folded strips of pasta—and they may have little fold marks in them.

Though it takes a bit longer, we prefer to cut the unfolded pasta into long strands with a long, thin knife. After you've cut a strand, just push it with your other hand to the side of the surface. It takes a steady hand and a good eye, but you can work through one recipe of pasta 115-140 g (4-5 oz) in 5 minutes.

You have your choice of pasta shapes. If you cut the strands 5 mm (¼ in) wide, you have tagliatelle. If you cut them 3 mm (⅛ in) wide, you have fettuccine. If you cut them 2 mm (1⁄16 in) wide, you have taglierini. We're especially fond of 00 pasta cut into tagliatelle and semolina pasta cut into taglierini.

8. LETTING THE PASTA DRY

You could eliminate this step and immediately place your freshly cut pasta in a big pot of boiling water. But only the 100 per cent semolina pasta is at or near its best when freshly cut. Most pasta fresca improves when it gets a little less fresca. You'll notice a difference after

8 hours (cut it in the morning; cook it at night) and an even bigger difference after 24 hours.

Drying is as simple as could be. Because the dough was dried well before it was cut into strips, it doesn't require any special treatment after cutting. You don't, for example, need to sprinkle flour or cornmeal on the pasta to keep it separate. Just spread the strands out so that the air hits as much surface area as possible and, if it's convenient, let the strands remain on the cutting surface. Or, you can transfer them, right after cutting, to another surface or a big dish.

If you're intending to store them for a long time (anywhere from a few weeks to 3 months), you can roll the strands around your hands into nests for more space-saving storage. Let them dry in the air for 24 hours, then place them carefully in boxes or bags.

For either the strands or the nests, however, the pasta does need to be handled carefully after it dries. If you are not gentle with it, you will break the pasta into shards.

COOKING FRESH PASTA

As in the cooking of dried pasta, to cook fresh pasta you need a large pot of furiously boiling water; this is necessary so that the water will remain at a boil after you've added the pasta. The pasta cooks better this way. Use a minimum of 4 litres (7 pints) of water, no matter how little pasta you're cooking.

Add the water, cold and fresh, to a large pot over high heat. Cover it. When the water boils, remove the cover and add some salt to it. The salt will definitely flavour the pasta, so use salt to taste. A famous pasta chef once told us to 'use only enough salt so that you can taste the water'. But this will not season the pasta very much; it's good for people who don't like salt. Our pasta fresca recipe does not include salt, so we like to make the water slightly salty—about the saltiness of stock—which will season the pasta a little bit.

There is no need to add oil to the water.

Keep the cover off for a moment or two to make sure the pot's at a full boil. Add the pasta all at once, stirring with a long spoon to make sure the strands remain separate. If the water has stopped boiling, cover the pot immediately to help the boil return.

Pasta fresca cooks quickly, but exactly how long it will take is impossible to say. A very fresh, very thin piece of 00 pasta may take no more than a minute. A thick piece of semolina pasta, dried for 48 hours, may take 5 minutes. The usual range of cooking time is 2 to 4 minutes, depending on flour type, thickness and freshness. Pasta is done when it has lost its raw flour taste; it should retain some firmness and a resilient texture should have developed. It's easy to go too far very quickly, turning your fresh pasta into unappealingly mushy noodles. So after 1½ minutes of cooking, taste constantly. We like to remove it from the water when it seems a few seconds away from doneness, because it will continue to cook as it is sauced.

BLENDING PASTA AND SAUCE

As soon as the pasta's ready, skim about 225 ml (8 fl oz) of pasta-cooking water off the top of the pot. Reserve. Then, pour the contents of the pot into a colander set in the sink. Shake the colander to make sure the noodles are not sticking together. Place some of the pasta sauce (about half) in the now-empty cooking pot and put the pot over low heat. Add the pasta and blend well with the sauce. Add more sauce if necessary; the pasta should be lightly coated with sauce. If you think the sauce seems a little thick, you can lighten the dish by adding some of the hot pasta-cooking water. The pasta should be in the pot for no more than 30 seconds. Serve immediately, with a little more sauce ladled over the top.

The question of cheese

Cheese blends very nicely with the eggy, buttery sauces that complement pasta fresca. But, once again, don't fall into the trap of grating cheese on every pasta fresca dish or they'll all taste similar. In the recipes that follow, we indicate which dishes are augmented by cheese, what kind of cheese to use and when to add it. For these recipes, you may pass extra cheese at the table if you wish—but we think that's not necessary.

TWO SPECIAL HAND-MADE PASTAS

If you love the idea of making your own pasta, if you really love sticking your hands in dough and transforming it into something delicious ... this section's for you. Across traditional Italy, the old-fashioned *casalinga* (housewife) would labour for hours making fresh pasta *piece by piece*! It is insanely labour-intensive, to be sure—but you can create intriguing textures that you never thought possible. Here are two individually made traditional pastas of which we're particularly fond.

GNOCCHI

Gnocchi are, in essence, Italian dumplings. Though many Americans think of them as necessarily including potato, they are often made in Italy from flour only. If you are using potatoes, select mature, starchy potatoes; these will need the least amount of flour and will make lighter gnocchi. Without a doubt, most of the gnocchi served in Italian restaurants in America are too heavy, often sodden. Sometimes chefs overcompensate and create gnocchi that have no chew at all.

POTATO GNOCCHI WITH HERBS

We think this recipe hits the nail right on the head: gnocchi that are light, but with just enough bite. A spectacular texture worth the trouble.

SERVES 4 AS A FIRST COURSE

2 large baking potatoes
1 large egg, lightly beaten
15 g (½ oz) unsalted butter, softened
15 g (1 tbsp) chopped fresh flat-leaf parsley
15 g (1 tbsp) snipped fresh chives
5 g (1 tsp) chopped fresh sage leaves
2.5 g (½ tsp) coarse salt
pinch of freshly ground black pepper
pinch of freshly grated nutmeg
225 g (8 oz) strong plain flour

1. Preheat the oven to 210°C (425°F). Pierce each potato with a fork several times. Bake potatoes directly on the oven rack for 1 hour, or until completely cooked through.

2. As soon as the potatoes are cool enough to handle, scrape the pulp into a medium bowl and mash with a fork or put the warm potato through a ricer. Add the egg and butter and mash until smooth. Stir in the herbs, coarse salt, pepper and nutmeg. Work in about half of the flour with your hands until the dough becomes thick. Knead in the remaining flour until the dough is firm and no longer sticky.

3. Divide the dough into 4 equal pieces. Roll each piece into a 1-cm (½-in)-thick, 60-cm (24-in) long rope. Working with 1 rope at a time (keeping the others covered with a towel), cut dough into pieces that are 1-cm (½-in) long. Roll a fork over each piece, pressing lightly, to create grooves.*

4. In a large pot of boiling salted water cook gnocchi until they float, about 3 minutes. Drain gnocchi completely. Serve immediately.

*As in this recipe, gnocchi are often grooved on the outside, to pick up sauce. *Cook's Illustrated*, a fine bi-monthly magazine, recently came up with a few new ideas. You can either roll them across a ridged butter paddle or across an unused plastic hair comb. Both of these instruments are longer than a fork, and provide more room for creating the grooves. The gnocchi, of course, should be perpendicular to the vertical slats. We have an even simpler idea: skip the grooves altogether, if you wish; we're not sure that the difference in sauce-carrying is worth the trouble.

Saucing gnocchi

Gnocchi work well with a wide range of sauces. In the United States, they're most often served with tomato sauce—but don't forget about meat sauces, cream sauces and pesto. We like gnocchi very lightly sauced, so for the recipe given here we would use just about 225 ml (8 fl oz) sauce. Our favourite way of saucing gnocchi is perhaps the simplest: tossing them with some melted butter (lightly browned butter is even better) and with a handful of freshly grated Parmigiano-Reggiano. You might want to add a sprinkling of herbs (sage works beautifully).

Some chefs like to prepare gnocchi gra-tinée; if this appeals to you, toss the cooked gnocchi with the sauce of your choice, spread them out in a gratin dish, top with a melting cheese (like Italian Fontina) and place under the grill for 3 to 4 minutes, or until the cheese melts. Sprinkle with parsley and serve.

ORECCHIETTE

These 'little ears' are a traditional pasta in Puglia, the heel of Italy's boot. Traditionally, they are made with a combination of semolina flour and white flour, then served fresh. Today in Puglia, there are lots of variations on the tradition. Often, the orecchiette are dried and shipped out of the region. Sometimes, the dried orecchiette even have egg in them and a more yellow colour. Dried orecchiette is available at Dean & DeLuca, but this is one pasta that's always even better to make at home.

HOMEMADE ORECCHIETTE

We've experimented with various flours in making these and find unbleached white flour to be the best. Because of the various stages of drying involved, you'll need to start making the orecchiette at least 3 hours before it's time to serve them.

SERVES 2

225 g (8 oz) unbleached flour
1.25 g (¼ tsp) salt
125-150 ml (4-5 fl oz) water

1. In a large bowl, mix together the flour and salt. Add in water until a fairly dry dough is formed. Turn out onto a floured board and knead for 10 minutes, or until smooth and firm.

2. Cut dough in 2 pieces and roll each piece into a long cylinder, about 1 cm (½ in) in diameter. Cut the cylinders crossways into small pieces, making a cut every 5 mm (¼ in) or so. With your fingers, round out each little piece of dough until it's a small circle, about 3 mm (⅛ in) thick and 1.5 cm (⅔ in) in diameter. Let stand in a single layer, for 15 minutes.

3. After 15 minutes, flip each piece of dough over. Now, working on the counter, press your thumb into the centre of each one, creating a depression. When you've finished, let them rest on the counter for 1 hour.

4. After 1 hour, pick up 1 orecchiette, place it in your palm and depress it again (in the same spot) with your thumb. You should now have a fairly deep depression. Return the orecchiette to the counter, depression-side down and continue with the rest until all of the orecchiette are done.

5. You can cook the orecchiette immediately, but we like the texture better if they dry for a few hours. Cook in a large pot of boiling water until just tender, about 7 to 8 minutes.

Saucing orecchiette

The traditional sauce in Puglia is made from sausage and broccoli, but all kinds of full-flavoured sauces are fabulous on orecchiette. The depression in each piece holds sauce well and can also hold little chunks of meat, vegetables or fish. One of the greatest orecchiette sauces we ever tasted was in Puglia—a combination of tomatoes, beans, fresh herbs and out-of-the-shell tiny mussels proved a spectacular meld of flavours. Sauces that are spicy with red pepper go very well with orecchiette.

PASTA SAUCES

Once upon a time, tomato sauce—usually from a jar—monopolised pasta in America. Those days are ancient history. Happily, many Americans have recently discovered that a variety of sauces are used for pasta all over Italy. Our talented American chefs have pushed the envelope still further, creating some new sauces that are in an Italian spirit. Despite all this, of course, you won't hear us denying that good tomato sauce, in all *its* infinite variety, is one of the most sublime ways to sauce your pasta.

Fast sauces for pasta

One of the best things to be learned from Italian practice is that pasta sauce need not be cooked a long time to be good. In fact, in some cases it need not be cooked at all. The following sauces will take you about as long to prepare as it takes to cook the pasta that you'll serve with them.

ANCHOVY, PIMIENTO AND SPRING ONION SAUCE

Based on the classic hors d'oeuvre of anchovies, pimientos (canned peppers) and spring onions, this uncooked sauce is fabulous on linguine.

MAKES SAUCE FOR 450 G (1 LB) DRIED PASTA

3 x 50-g (2-oz) cans anchovies
450 g (1 lb) coarsely chopped pimientos
45 g (6 tbsp) finely chopped spring onions
45 g (6 tbsp) finely chopped fresh parsley
5 g (1 tsp) very finely chopped garlic

45 ml (3 tbsp) lemon juice
45 ml (3 tbsp) liquid from pimientos
45 ml (3 tbsp) oil from anchovy cans

Chop the anchovies. Combine with all other ingredients in a mixing bowl. Mix well with cooked pasta. Serve immediately.

FETA, KALAMATA OLIVE, FRESH OREGANO AND CAPER SAUCE

For minimum effort, this sauce packs maximum flavour. We like it spicy, but you might want to cut back on the chilli peppers. Also, the type of feta you choose will affect the texture mightily: creamy feta (like the ones made in France) will yield a creamier sauce and drier feta (like much of the Greek feta) will yield a more crumbly sauce. We prefer the creamy texture. And we like tossing this sauce with small pieces of pasta corta, such as little penne or sedanini (little 'celery stalks').

MAKES SAUCE FOR 450 G (1 LB) DRIED PASTA

50 g (2 oz) fresh flat-leaf parsley leaves plus additional chopped leaves for garnish
10 g (2 tsp) drained capers packed in vinegar and brine
5 ml (1 tsp) packed, fresh oregano leaves
75 ml (2½ fl oz) extra-virgin olive oil
¼ to 1 small fresh, hot, red chilli pepper, trimmed and seeded
2 garlic cloves
1 very small red onion, cut into rings
115 g (4 oz) feta cheese, coarsely crumbled
12 kalamata olives, stoned and chopped

1. Chop the 50 g (2 oz) parsley, capers and oregano together, place in a serving bowl and stir in the olive oil.

2. Chop the chilli and garlic and add to the olive oil mixture. Add the onion, feta and olives.

3. Toss with hot pasta. (Add a little of the hot pasta cooking water if a thinner sauce is desired.) Season to taste and garnish with more parsley.

FRIED EGG, RED PEPPER, GARLIC AND HERB TOPPING FOR PASTA

This perfectly simple preparation makes one of our favourite pasta dishes. You just cook up some fried eggs in flavoured butter and oil, then pour the results over a dish of pasta that has been tossed with cheese. Divide carefully and serve. We love this topping on thick, long, dried pasta like perciatelli—but find it works equally well on 5-cm (2-in) squares of fresh pasta. Quality ingredients are always important in a dish as simple as this. Use eggs from free-range chickens if you can.

MAKES TOPPING FOR 450 G (1 LB) DRIED PASTA

45 ml (3 tbsp) extra-virgin olive oil
25 g (1 oz) unsalted butter
2 large garlic cloves, thinly sliced
crushed hot red pepper flakes to taste
4 large eggs (preferably free-range)
coarse salt to taste
50 g (2 oz) freshly grated Parmigiano-Reggiano
  plus additional as an accompaniment
50 g (2 oz) chopped fresh parsley
15 g (1 tbsp) chopped fresh oregano or sage

1. While the pasta for this dish is cooking, heat the olive oil and butter in a large frying pan over moderate heat. Add the garlic and cook, stirring, for 2 minutes. Add the eggs and cook, sunny-side up, basting with a spoon, for 2 to 3 minutes without turning, or until the eggs are just done (the yolks must remain runny). Remove the pan from the heat and sprinkle eggs with coarse salt and hot red pepper flakes.

2. You must time this dish so that the pasta is ready as soon as the eggs are done. Place the pasta on a serving dish and toss with the Parmigiano-Reggiano, additional red pepper flakes and parsley. Pour the contents of the egg pan, including the oil, butter and garlic, onto the pasta. Garnish pasta and eggs with oregano or sage and serve immediately. Pass the additional Parmigiano-Reggiano at the table.

GOAT CHEESE AND TOMATO SAUCE

This is not a traditional Italian sauce, but it's delicious nevertheless: pink and light, with a subtle, creamy flavour. Dean & DeLuca carries a lovely certified organic fresh mild goat cheese from Birch River, West Virginia, which is perfect in the dish. We like this sauce best with linguine.

MAKES SAUCE FOR 450 G (1 LB) DRIED PASTA

175 g (6 oz) fresh soft mild goat cheese, at room
  temperature
75 ml (5 tbsp) extra-virgin olive oil
900 g (2 lb) ripe tomatoes (about 6 medium),
  peeled, seeded and finely diced
salt and pepper to taste
60-90 ml (4-6 tbsp) oil-soaked sun-dried tomatoes,
  shredded

1. Mash together the goat cheese and olive oil in a bowl with a fork until smooth. Gently stir in ripe tomatoes.

2. Toss with hot pasta. (Add a little of the hot pasta cooking water if a thinner sauce is desired.) Season with salt and pepper. Place in bowls and top each bowl with a tablespoon of sun-dried tomatoes. Serve immediately.

CREAMY EGG AND PROSCIUTTO SAUCE

This is our improvement on the ubiquitous and usually boring Alfredo sauce. This rich sauce goes nicely on long strands of thick, dried pasta, such as bucatini. It is also a good choice for dried fettuccine.

MAKES SAUCE FOR 225 G (8 OZ) DRIED PASTA

115 g (4 oz) fatty prosciutto, sliced very thin
    unsalted butter
4 large eggs
salt and pepper to taste
pinch of nutmeg
90 g (6 tbsp) freshly grated Parmigiano-Reggiano,
    plus additional as an accompaniment if desired

1. Separate the prosciutto into fat and meat. Finely chop the fat; cut the meat into broad strips.

2. In a heavy saucepan over moderately low heat melt the butter. Add the chopped prosciutto fat. Cook, stirring occasionally, for 15 minutes, or until the fat has begun to melt and the liquid in the pan is just starting to turn brown. Remove from heat and let cool for 5 minutes.

3. Beat the eggs for 30 seconds in a mixing bowl. Season lightly with salt and pepper. Add a few drops of the butter–prosciutto fat mixture. Add a few larger drops. Keep adding more, until all is incorporated, then return the mixture to the pan. Cook over very low heat for 5 to 10 minutes, or until the egg mixture has just begun to thicken. When it's ready, beat in the nutmeg.

4. Place cooked pasta in a wide, shallow mixing bowl. Toss with the egg mixture, the reserved strips of prosciutto and the Parmigiano-Reggiano. Season to taste, adding more nutmeg if desired. (If you find the sauce too thick, thin it with 30-45 ml (2-3 tbsp) of the hot pasta cooking water.) Serve directly from the mixing bowl. Pass additional Parmigiano-Reggiano if desired.

YELLOW TOMATO AND BASIL SAUCE

This is your basic, simple, fairly fast pasta sauce—but it has an amazing twist to it. The yellow tomatoes, which are lower in acid than red tomatoes, create a sauce filled with the exotic, mysterious, ineffable aroma of wild tomatoes (the original tomatoes from South America

were probably yellow). The colour, too, is magnificent . . . and it can be made even more beautiful by mixing in a few orange tomatoes. If you can't find yellow or orange tomatoes, use fresh red tomatoes for a wonderful, though more conventional, basic sauce. We especially like it on linguine or other thin, long dried pasta. If you choose not to pass it through a food mill, you will have a fabulous summer soup that is delicious when served cold.

    MAKES ENOUGH SAUCE FOR 450 G (1 LB) DRIED PASTA

30 ml (2 tbsp) extra-virgin olive oil
2 cloves garlic, finely chopped
3 large, ripe yellow or orange tomatoes (about 550 g
    (1¼ lb) total), chopped
4 sprigs of fresh basil

1. Heat the olive oil in a large saucepan over moderately low heat. Stir in the garlic and cook, stirring occasionally, until very soft, about 5 minutes. Stir in the tomatoes and basil sprigs and simmer, stirring frequently, for 15 minutes, or until the tomatoes form a sauce.

2. Discard the basil sprigs and any stray leaves and pass the tomato mixture through a food mill.

3. Toss with hot pasta. Serve immediately.

THIN MARINARA SAUCE

This simple, delicious winner is one of our favourite pasta sauces—thin, almost stocky. Making it thinner, keeping more liquid in the sauce, is a reflection of a hot climate, like Naples's. It's also a reflection of delicate taste. You may want to thicken the sauce a bit at table by adding some freshly grated pecorino Romano. Please make sure to use top-quality canned tomatoes for this one; inferior tomatoes have nowhere to hide. We love this sauce on spaghetti or linguine.

    MAKES ENOUGH SAUCE FOR 450 G (1 LB) DRIED PASTA

30 ml (2 tbsp) olive oil

4 shallots, finely chopped

800-g (28-oz) can plum tomatoes

50 g (2 oz) chopped fresh basil plus additional
leaves for garnish

30 g (2 tbsp) fresh marjoram leaves plus additional
for garnish

1. Place 15 ml (1 tbsp) of the olive oil in a heavy saucepan over moderately high heat. Add the shallots and sauté until soft, about 5 minutes.

2. Put the canned tomatoes, with their liquid, through a food mill. Add tomatoes and liquid to pan. Simmer for 20 minutes. Five minutes before the sauce is finished, add the basil and marjoram. When it's finished, season to taste and drizzle with 15 ml (1 tbsp) of extra-virgin olive oil.

3. Toss with hot pasta. Divide among pasta bowls, top with a little more sauce and garnish with the additional fresh herbs.

SIMMERED GARLIC AND OIL SAUCE (AGLIO E OLIO)

Aglio e olio—garlic and oil sauce—is one of the all-time great fast pasta sauces. This one is a little lighter than most, because it calls for a little water to replace some of the oil. Fabulous on linguinie.

   MAKES ENOUGH SAUCE FOR 450 G (1 LB) DRIED PASTA

1 medium head of garlic, very thinly sliced

150 ml (5 fl oz) fruity olive oil

50 ml (2 fl oz) hot water

salt to taste

25 g (1 oz) very finely chopped fresh parsley

1. Place the garlic and olive oil in a small, heavy saucepan over low heat. Bring the oil to a slow, steady bubble, then cook for 15 minutes. Using a small whisk, vigorously beat in the water until a smooth sauce is

formed. Season with salt. Keep warm.

2. When the pasta is ready to serve, drain it in a colander and moisten it with a little bit of the sauce. Place pasta back in the cooking pot over low heat and toss well with the rest of the sauce and the parsley. Taste and, if necessary, season with coarse salt. Serve immediately.

FRESH TOMATO WITH FRESH GINGER SAUCE

This is not a traditional Italian sauce, but don't let that stop you—the surprise of fresh ginger in a tomato sauce is utterly delicious. This is a great sauce to make ahead and reheat when you need a really quick meal. To make this sauce even quicker, you can serve it unpuréed or unmilled—but we think the extra step of smoothing it out better distributes the ginger flavour. This sauce is superb with spaghetti or any long, thin, dried pasta.

   MAKES ENOUGH SAUCE FOR 450 G (1 LB) DRIED PASTA

75 g (3 oz) chopped shallots

10 g (2 tsp) chopped peeled fresh ginger

2 garlic cloves, chopped

50 g (2 oz) unsalted butter

450 g (1 lb) diced peeled fresh ripe tomatoes (if
necessary, you may use an equivalent amount of
canned tomatoes)

pinch of sugar

salt and pepper to taste

25 g (1 oz) chopped fresh parsley leaves

1. Cook the shallots, ginger and garlic in the butter in a medium frying pan over moderate heat for 4 minutes, stirring.

2. Stir in the tomatoes and the sugar and gently simmer, stirring occasionally, for 15 minutes.

3. Season to taste with salt and pepper. Put the sauce through a food mill or purée in a food processor or blender until smooth.

4. Toss with hot pasta and parsley leaves. Serve immediately.

GREEN OLIVE SAUCE WITH FRESH MINT

This is a new, uncooked sauce that is for olive-lovers only. The intensity of the olive flavour will vary, depending on the type of olives you use—but if you find it strong, you can always tame it by adding more cheese or more of the pasta cooking water to the sauce. You may also want to experiment with the ratio of sauce to pasta until you discover which level of flavour works best for you. We love this sauce on thick, long pasta such as perciatelli.

MAKES ENOUGH SAUCE FOR 450 G (1 LB) DRIED PASTA

175 g (6 oz) large green olives, such as manzanilla, plus a few additional olives, chopped, for garnish
7.5 g (1½ tsp) chopped garlic
25 g (1 oz) fresh mint leaves plus additional for garnish
90 g (6 tbsp) grated Parmigiano-Reggiano plus additional as an accompaniment
10 ml (2 tsp) extra-virgin olive oil

1. Stone the olives and place the olives, garlic, mint leaves, Parmigiano-Reggiano and olive oil in the work bowl of a food processor. Purée. Just before serving, add about 125 ml (4 fl oz) of pasta cooking water to the purée (add additional cooking water until desired consistency is reached).

2. In a large bowl, toss with pasta. (You may not need the full amount of sauce; the pasta should be lightly dressed. If it seems too dry, add a little additional cooking water.) Toss the pasta with the additional mint leaves, torn into large pieces. Divide the pasta among 4 to 5 individual bowls and top with the additional grated cheese. Garnish with the additional mint leaves and the additional chopped green olives, if desired.

TUNA SAUCE WITH SUN-DRIED TOMATOES AND KALAMATA OLIVES

This is a terrific uncooked pasta sauce, easy to make and brimming with flavour . We like it with linguine or spaghetti.

MAKES ENOUGH SAUCE FOR 450 G (1 LB) DRIED PASTA

115 g (4 oz) canned tuna packed in olive oil
50 g (2 oz) chopped sun-dried tomatoes*
8 kalamata olives, pitted and chopped
30 ml (2 tbsp) lemon juice plus additional for squeezing on pasta
10 ml (2 tsp) extra-virgin olive oil
30 g (2 tbsp) very finely chopped fresh parsley

1. Drain off the olive oil from the canned tuna and place the tuna in a small bowl. Add the sun-dried tomatoes, olives, lemon juice and extra-virgin olive oil. Mash together with a fork until fairly smooth. When ready to serve, blend with 175 ml (6 fl oz) cooking water from the pot.

2. In a large bowl, toss the tuna sauce with hot pasta. (If the pasta with sauce seems a little dry, add a little additional cooking water.) Divide pasta among 4 to 5 individual bowls. Squeeze a little additional lemon juice on the pasta in each bowl and top with the finely chopped parsley.

Longer-cooked sauces for pasta
We love the ease of short-cooked sauces—and the amazing flavour that vivid ingredients can quickly contribute. But, when we've got the time, we also love to let sauces spend hours on the stove—particularly if they contain meat. Compensations for the loss of freshness in the sauce are, in some cases, greater subtlety of flavour and, in other cases, greater concentration of flavour.

*Use marinated sun-dried tomatoes that are soft and sweet.

Tomato sauces

Which tomatoes to use for sauce

Some of the tomato-sauce recipes in this chapter call for fresh tomatoes and some for canned tomatoes; this reflects our judgment as to which kind is best for each individual sauce. However, at a pinch, one type can always be substituted for the other. Just remember the equivalency equation: one 800-g (28-oz) can of plum tomatoes yields 12 to 14 tomatoes, which weigh approximately 550 g (1¼ lb). Use the canned tomatoes, by weight, as you would the fresh tomatoes.

Most of the tomato-sauce recipes in this chapter that use fresh tomatoes call for plum tomatoes; they are meatier, contain less juice and yield thicker sauces. But you may use either fresh plum tomatoes or fresh round tomatoes for these sauces; whatever weight of tomatoes is called for, use that weight. And keep in mind that the sauces made from ordinary round tomatoes will be a little thinner than the sauces made from plum tomatoes.

Lastly, when buying canned tomatoes, look for the Italian brands of plum tomatoes that are marked 'San Marzano'—they are usually very high in quality. They contain either the San Marzano variety of tomatoes, which flourishes around Naples, or a closely related tomato variety called *lampadina,* which is usually designated 'San Marzano-style' on the can. Be wary of cheaper brands of canned Italian plum tomatoes; they can be watery and acidic. Also, some of the American brands of canned tomatoes are now very good, particularly Hunt's tomatoes in thick tomato purée (keep in mind that this product will make a thicker sauce).

Which are the best canned tomatoes in the market for making pasta sauce? To our taste, Muir Glen Organic Whole Peeled Tomatoes, from Sacramento, California, packed in tomato liquid, come closest to capturing the sweet and wild taste of fresh tomatoes.

LONG-COOKED TOMATO AND BASIL SAUCE

If you like the taste of long-cooked tomato sauce, you won't do better than this recipe. It does take 6 hours to reach its apogee, but it takes virtually no pot-watching. When you taste the finished product, you won't believe the intensity and concentration of tomato flavour —with a finish, like good wine, that lasts for minutes.

MAKES ENOUGH SAUCE FOR 675 G (1½ LB) PASTA

30 ml (2 tbsp) olive oil
10 cloves garlic, chopped coarsely
1 large yellow onion, diced
2.25 kg (5 lb) fresh plum tomatoes, chopped coarsely, or equal amount canned plum tomatoes, drained
4 fresh bay leaves, pulverised with butt end of knife to release flavour, or 2 whole dried bay leaves
3 whole sprigs of rosemary or 15 g (1 tbsp) dried leaves
3 whole sprigs of thyme or 10 g (2 tsp) dried leaves
15 g (1 tbsp) coarse salt
5 g (1 tsp) freshly ground black pepper
115 g (4 oz) firmly packed basil leaves, cut into chiffonnade

1. Heat olive oil in large casserole over moderate heat, add garlic and onion and cook until softened, about 5 minutes. Add all other ingredients except the basil and cook over low heat, covered, stirring occasionally, for 2 hours. Remove cover and cook for 3 more hours. If using dried bay leaves, remove them.

2. If using fresh tomatoes, pass the sauce through a food mill to remove skins and return to pot. Whichever tomatoes you're using, cook for another hour over moderately high heat until reduced by about one third. Adjust seasoning. Add basil and toss with warm pasta. Serve immediately.

Note: If using canned tomatoes, you have the option of not using the food mill as there are no tomato skins to be removed. After the first 5 hours of cooking, remove the herb sprigs and dried bay leaves and reduce sauce over moderately high heat by about one third. Adjust seasoning and add basil. This will be a chunkier sauce.

ROASTED TOMATO SAUCE WITH PANCETTA AND HERBS

Roasting the tomatoes gives the sauce a wonderful additional layer of flavour and the pancetta lends even more depth. You could make a vegetarian version by leaving the pancetta out; this yields a sweeter, more tomatoey taste. We like this sauce with long dried pasta, like spaghetti.

MAKES SAUCE FOR 900 G (2 LB) DRIED PASTA

175 g (6 oz) thick-sliced pancetta, chopped
15 ml (1 tbsp) extra-virgin olive oil plus additional for the pan
2.25 kg (5 lb) ripe tomatoes (about 14 medium), peeled and seeded
6 small shallots
4 small cloves garlic
3 bay leaves
15 g (1 tbsp) chopped fresh sage leaves
15 g (1 tbsp) chopped fresh rosemary leaves
15 g (1 tbsp) fresh thyme leaves
5 g (1 tsp) chopped fresh oregano leaves
1.25 g (¼ tsp) crushed hot red pepper flakes
25 g (1 oz) chopped fresh basil leaves
salt and pepper to taste

1. Preheat oven to 140°C (300°F).

2. Cook the pancetta in the olive oil in a medium frying pan over moderate heat, stirring frequently, until it begins to crisp, about 7 minutes. Remove the pan from heat.

3. Cut tomatoes in half. Brush a large roasting tin (at least 30 x 46 cm (12 x 18 in)) with olive oil. Arrange

tomatoes, cut side up, in a single layer in the pan. Tuck in the shallots, garlic cloves and bay leaves. Sprinkle with the fresh herbs except the basil, hot red pepper flakes and contents of pancetta frying pan.

4. Bake for 2 hours, then stir vegetables around. Bake for 1 hour more. Let the mixture cool slightly, discard the bay leaves and chop tomatoes and vegetables coarsely (discarding outer skins of shallots if they have toughened). Stir in fresh basil leaves. Season to taste with salt and pepper.

The variety of Italian tomato sauces

The possible number of Italian tomato sauce permutations is unknowable, but it's probably staggering. Here are some of the factors that can totally change the nature of a tomato sauce:

Fresh tomatoes or canned tomatoes? Fresh tomatoes lend a sunnier, brighter taste to sauces, but canned tomatoes (called *pelati* in Italy) are fine—especially for long-cooked sauces and if the canned tomatoes are of good quality.

What kind of canned tomatoes? You can find canned tomatoes in tomato liquid as well as canned tomatoes in thick tomato purée; these will make sauces of different textures. Additionally, there's tremendous quality variation in canned tomatoes: some are thin, watery and acidic; some are thick, rich and sweet.

What colour fresh tomatoes? Red tomatoes are traditionally used, but yellow tomatoes lend a wild tomato flavour and are less acidic.

Short-cooked or long-cooked? This makes a great difference in tomato sauce; shorter-cooked sauces have a fresher tomato taste, longer-cooked sauces emphasise more the cooked-in taste of all the ingredients.

Chunky sauce or smooth sauce? Another big difference. Chunkier sauces have a more interesting chew, but smooth sauces cling to some pastas better. Also: did you smooth out your sauce by puréeing it in the blender/food processor, or by putting it through a food mill? Some claim that the food mill makes a milder sauce than the blender/food processor, because it crushes the cells of the tomato less severely.

Garlic or no garlic? To some, it wouldn't be tomato sauce without garlic. But many Italians (including Giorgio DeLuca) feel that tomato sauce is better and tastes more like tomato, when garlic is not used.

Equally diverse are the names used across Italy, in Italian cookbooks and in Italian-American restaurants for tomato sauces. Here are a few of the names you're most likely to come across for sauces that are made chiefly from tomatoes:

Arrabbiata An 'angry' tomato sauce, enraged by the addition of hot red pepper flakes.

Marinara This name is widely used in the United States, but not used much in Italy. The name probably originated with Italian sailors (i.e., mariners), who had to cook their tomato sauce quickly—and many cooks use the name today to denote a chunky, quick-cooked sauce (the quick sauces are sometimes designated *alla svelta*). But other cooks use the name marinara for any tomato sauce, long- or short-cooked.

Passata This is the tomato purée that millions of Italian housewives preserve in jars every summer and fall, made from the abundance of fresh tomatoes. The name refers to the 'passing' of the fresh, washed tomatoes through a simple machine that removes skin and seeds. Into sterilised jars go the tomatoes, ready to be heated quickly, or long-cooked, in January.

Pummarola (or Pommarola) This is the fairly quickly cooked tomato sauce (about 30 minutes) that is popular around Naples. One of the key elements is the inclusion of aromatic vegetables, such as onion, carrot and celery, in the simmering stock (though they usually get sieved out later). It is thought of as a summer sauce, made from fresh tomatoes. Its winter equivalent is called *sugo scappato;* it is made from canned tomatoes and the aromatic vegetables are sautéed before the tomatoes are added.

Sugo di Pomodoro (or Salsa di Pomodoro) Literally, in each case, this means tomato sauce. You'll also see pasta dishes designated, for example, *linguine al pomodoro*. In reality, any of these names can indicate any one of the infinite tomato sauce variations. If you see one of the names on a menu, all you know is that there are tomatoes involved. If it's a good restaurant, that's all ye need to know.

ARRABBIATA SAUCE

There are spicy-hot, simple tomato sauces made all over Italy, christened with different names—but arrabbiata is the name for the sauce you're most likely to see in upscale Italian restaurants in America today. It means angry, furious and refers, of course, to the wrath of the red pepper flakes. (Feel free to add more of them, by the way, if you happen to be feeling unusually angry.) We like this sauce on penne and on spaghetti too. Lots of restaurants today are using the sauce in non-pasta dishes; 'angry lobster' has become a new staple of Italian-American restaurants (lobster fra diavolo having yielded to lobster all' arrabbiata).

MAKES SAUCE FOR 350 G (¾ LB) DRIED PASTA

1 x 800-g (28-oz) can and 1 x 280-g (10-oz) can
    peeled Italian plum tomatoes with their liquid
125 ml (4 fl oz) extra-virgin olive oil
salt and black pepper to taste
5 ml (1 tsp) crushed hot red pepper flakes
40 g (1½ oz) freshly grated Parmigiano-Reggiano
15 g (1 tbsp) chopped fresh oregano leaves

1. Stir together the tomatoes with their liquid and olive oil in a medium saucepan and cook at a low boil, stirring occasionally and breaking up the tomatoes with a wooden spoon, for 35 minutes, or until very thick. Season the mixture with salt and black pepper.

2. Pass the tomato mixture through a food mill into another saucepan, add the red pepper flakes and simmer for 10 minutes.

3. Toss with pasta. Transfer to a serving bowl and toss with the Parmigiano-Reggiano. Top with chopped oregano and serve.

TOMATO SAUCE WITH FENNEL, OLIVES AND ORANGE ZEST

Though this is not a traditional sauce, the wild array of flavours has a distinctly Sicilian tang. We like it best on spaghetti or any long, dried pasta.

MAKES SAUCE FOR 450 G (1 LB) DRIED PASTA

125 ml (4 fl oz) extra-virgin olive oil

450 g (1 lb) fennel bulb, cut into thin julienne strips

2 small red onions, peeled and sliced into thin rings

4 garlic cloves, slivered

25 g (1¼ tsp) herbes de Provence

10 plum tomatoes (about 1 kg (2¼ lb)), peeled, seeded and chopped or 10 canned plum tomatoes

two 7.5-cm (3-in) strips orange zest removed with a vegetable peeler plus 10 g (2 tsp) finely grated orange zest

salt and pepper to taste

40 g (1½ oz) packed fresh basil leaves

40 g (1½ oz) packed fresh parsley leaves

18 picholine olives (or other green olives), stoned and chopped

18 niçoise olives (or other black olives), stoned and chopped

30 g (2 tbsp) drained capers, packed in vinegar and brine

1. Heat the olive oil in a large frying pan over moderate heat. Stir in the fennel, red onions, garlic and herbes de Provence and cook, stirring frequently, for 40 minutes, or until the vegetables are very soft and golden brown.

2. Stir in the tomatoes and strips of orange zest and cook over moderate heat, stirring occasionally, for 20 minutes, or until tomatoes have formed a sauce. Discard the orange zest. Season to taste with salt and pepper.

3. Chop the basil, parsley, olives and capers.

4. Toss hot pasta with the grated orange zest, then with the tomato sauce, then with the herb mixture. Serve immediately.

PUTTANESCA SAUCE

Based on the salacious nature of this sauce's name (*puttana* means 'whore'), its origins are usually discussed in some version of the same story. 'Prostitutes in Naples,' the story goes, 'needed to make something quick and nourishing between … ahem … appointments. Thus was puttanesca sauce born.' We have no idea if there's any truth to this. We don't care. No matter who did what to whom, the sauce is a fabulous whiff of southern Italy—a chunky, intensely flavoured, sun-drenched bowlful of Naples. We like it best on thin, long pasta, like linguine piccole. The original puttanesca has tomatoes in it; there is also a sauce called puttanesca bianca (white puttanesca), which contains olives, capers and anchovies, but no tomatoes.

MAKES ENOUGH SAUCE FOR 450 G (1 LB) DRIED PASTA

¼ cup olive oil

2 tablespoons finely chopped garlic

800 g (28-oz) can plum tomatoes, drained

100 g (4 oz) pitted gaeta olives, halved
45 ml (3 tbsp) coarsely chopped anchovies
2 tablespoons capers
1½ teaspoons coarse salt
¼ teaspoon hot red pepper flakes
¼ cup coarsely chopped fresh flat-leaf parsley

1. In medium saucepan, heat olive oil over low heat. Add garlic and cook until garlic is light gold, about 10 minutes.

2. Crush tomatoes by hand, leaving juice behind and add tomatoes to pan. Add olives, anchovies, capers, coarse salt and red pepper flakes. Simmer gently over moderate heat for 20 minutes, or until the sauce is reduced by about one third.

3. Adjust seasoning and add chopped parsley. Stir to combine.

4. Make sure to mix hot pasta with a little olive oil. Stir in sauce and serve immediately.

Note: Sauce can be made several hours ahead and reheated.

Vegetable sauces
Tomato sauce, of course, is Italy's most famous vegetable sauce. But there are lots of other vegetable sauces in Italy that either use tomatoes as a minor player or use no tomatoes at all.

SICILIAN CAULIFLOWER SAUCE WITH SAFFRON, PINE NUTS AND SULTANAS

This sauce is related to the Sicilian classic pasta con le sarde, which features a sweet-and-sour sauce made with fresh sardines and wild fennel (both a little difficult to find here). In this version, cauliflower teams up with saffron and tomatoes—the tomatoes give the sauce a beautiful colour and contribute to the hint of

sweet-and-sour in the dish. In the dried fruit and nut section at Dean & DeLuca you'll find fantastic Chinese pine nuts, which are great here. We love this sauce with a long, thick pasta—like perciatelli or bucatini, both of which have a hole in the middle. By the way, this sauce tastes even better after a few days in the refrigerator.

MAKES ENOUGH SAUCE FOR 1½ POUNDS DRIED PASTA

50 g (2 oz) sultanas
150 ml (5 fl oz) warm water
2.5 g (½ tsp) saffron threads, crumbled
450 g (1 lb) cauliflower florets (about 1 small head cauliflower), each floret cut the long way into several pieces
50 ml (2 fl oz) extra-virgin olive oil
2 small red onions, cut into thin rings
4 garlic cloves, chopped
3 large ripe tomatoes (550 g (1¼ lb)), peeled, seeded and chopped
3 anchovies packed in oil, rinsed, drained and chopped
1 bay leaf
30 ml (2 tbsp) toasted pine nuts
5 ml (1 tsp) red-wine vinegar, or more to taste
salt and pepper to taste
50 g (2 oz) freshly grated pecorino Romano
25 g (1 oz) fresh flat-leaf parsley

1. Soak the sultanas in 125 ml (4 fl oz) warm water in a small bowl. Steep the saffron in the rest of the warm water in another small bowl.

2. Cook the cauliflower in a large casserole of boiling salted water just until crisp-tender, about 5 minutes. Drain in a colander and refresh with cold water to stop the cooking. Dry the cauliflower well on paper towels.

3. Heat the olive oil in a large, deep frying pan over moderate heat, add the onions and the garlic and cook, stirring occasionally, until softened, about 5 minutes.

Stir in the tomatoes, anchovies and bay leaf and cook, stirring occasionally, for 10 minutes. Stir in the sultanas with liquid, saffron with liquid, cauliflower, pine nuts, vinegar, salt and pepper and cook at a bare simmer for 10 minutes. Discard the bay leaf.

4. Toss with hot pasta. In a bowl combine with the pecorino Romano. Blend well. (Add some pasta cooking water if a thinner sauce is desired.) Add the parsley leaves. Taste for seasoning. Serve immediately.

PEPERONATA SAUCE

This is a chunky sauce that we've been making for years at the store. It features, most prominently, the bright taste of red peppers. But what we find especially interesting is the big herbal flavour, perfectly complementary to the pepper flavour, that is furnished by the last-minute addition of fresh basil and marjoram. You could substitute other fresh herbs if necessary. The sauce is delicious with either long, thick strands of pasta, like perciatelli, or short, chunky pasta, like orecchiette.

MAKES SAUCE FOR 900 G (2 LB) DRIED PASTA

50 g (2 fl oz) extra-virgin olive oil
1 aubergine (about 350 g (12 oz))
1 medium onion, peeled and chopped
1 medium green pepper
1 medium red pepper
1 medium yellow pepper
4 fresh plum tomatoes, chopped
1.25 ml (¼ tsp) balsamic vinegar
1.25 ml (¼ tsp) red-wine vinegar
225 ml (8 fl oz) tomato purée
25 g (1 oz) chopped fresh basil
25 g (1 oz) chopped fresh marjoram

1. Place 30 ml (2 tbsp) of the olive oil in a large sauté pan over moderate heat. Cut the aubergine into 1-cm (½-in) cubes and add to the hot oil with the chopped onion. Cook until aubergine softens, about 10 minutes. Remove and reserve.

2. Stem and seed the peppers. Cut each one in half. Cut half of each pepper into medium dice and the other half into julienne strips. Add the rest of the olive oil to the pan in which the aubergine cooked, set it over moderately high heat and sauté the peppers for 10 minutes. Add the tomatoes and cook for 5 minutes. Add the aubergine-onion mixture, the two vinegars and the tomato purée. Bring to a boil, reduce heat to moderate and simmer for 5 minutes.

3. Add the basil and marjoram. Remove from heat. Season to taste with salt and pepper. Let rest for 5 minutes, toss with hot pasta and serve.

FRESH AND DRIED MUSHROOM SAUCE WITH HERBS

This brown, chunky sauce doesn't mess around—it has lots of mushroom flavour. But too much dried mushroom flavour can be overwhelming—and that's why a battuto of rosemary, parsley, anchovy and garlic is added to the mushrooms, along with a little tomato. The balance of flavours is superb. We love it on orrechiette, which perfectly pick up the chunks of mushroom and tomato. But the mushroom-butter flavours also play well with a fresh ribbon pasta, like tagliatelle.

MAKES ENOUGH SAUCE FOR 450 G (1 LB) PASTA

225 ml (8 fl oz) cold water
25 g (1 oz) dried porcini (cep) mushrooms
75 g (3 oz) flat-leaf parsley leaves
1 small sprig of fresh rosemary, leaves stripped
  from stem
2 cloves garlic
2 anchovy fillets packed in oil, rinsed and drained
50 g (2 oz) unsalted butter
30 ml (2 tbsp) extra-virgin olive oil
675 g (1½ lb) fresh tomatoes (about 4 medium

tomatoes), peeled, seeded and finely chopped
175 g (6 oz) fresh chestnut or large flat field and/or
    other mushrooms, stems and caps separated,
    both thinly sliced
salt and pepper to taste

1. Put the cold water in a small saucepan with a lid and add the dried porcini. Bring the water to a simmer over moderate heat, remove the pan from heat and let mixture stand, covered, for 30 minutes. Strain the liquid through a coffee filter and reserve. Rinse the mushrooms of any remaining sand and chop finely.

2. Chop together the 125 g (4 oz) of the parsley, the rosemary leaves, garlic and anchovies.

3. Heat the butter and the olive oil in a large frying pan, add the parsley mixture and cook over moderately low heat, stirring frequently, for 5 minutes.

4. Stir in the tomatoes, the strained mushroom soaking liquid and the chopped dried mushrooms and cook, stirring frequently, over moderately low heat for 20 minutes. Stir in the sliced fresh mushrooms and cook, stirring occasionally, for 15 minutes longer, reducing heat to low if necessary to prevent sticking. Season to taste with salt and pepper.

5. Toss hot pasta with the mushroom sauce. If a thinner sauce is desired, add a little hot pasta cooking water. Top with the rest of the chopped parsley and serve immediately.

Meat sauces
Perhaps these are not at the height of fashion in America right now, but when American diners regain their senses they will be. So what if there's a little saturated fat involved? You don't put that much sauce on a portion of pasta and the glow in your belly on a cold winter's day is worth a few calories.

SAUCE BOLOGNESE

Meat sauce is on the menu of almost every Italian-American restaurant, but this classic meat sauce—from Bologna, in the great gastronomic region of Emilia-Romagna—is the granddaddy of them all. It takes hours to make, but its incomparable depth is worth the time. Its classic partner is tagliatelle, but it's also good on little stuffed pasta shapes, like tortellini. Additionally, we often embrace the Italian-American practice and serve it on long dried pasta, like spaghetti.

MAKES 6 CUPS

50 ml (2 fl oz) olive oil
350 g (12 oz) chopped yellow onions
115 g (4 oz) diced carrot
115 g (4 oz) diced celery
10 g (2 tsp) kosher salt
5 g (1 tsp) ground black pepper
450 g (1 lb) minced beef (preferably stewing steak)
225 g (8 oz) minced veal
225 g (8 oz) minced pork
115 g (4 oz) chicken livers, finely chopped
450 ml (16 fl oz) tomato sauce
400 ml (14 fl oz) beef stock
225 ml (8 fl oz) dry white wine
freshly grated nutmeg to taste

1. Heat olive oil over moderate heat in large saucepan. Add onions, stir and cover. Cook, stirring occasionally, for about 20 minutes, until onions are wilted and light golden. Uncover and continue cooking for another 15 minutes, until onions are golden and lightly caramelised. (Watch carefully, so the onions don't burn.) Add carrot, celery, kosher salt and pepper and cook for 5 minutes.

2. Add ground beef, veal and pork and crumble with the back of a wooden spoon. Cook until meat is no longer pink and add chicken livers. Cook another 5 minutes, stirring occasionally.

3. Add tomato sauce, 225 ml (8 fl oz) beef stock and white wine. Stir well and simmer, uncovered, over low heat for 1½ hours. (The sauce should barely bubble.) Add remaining beef stock, stir and continue simmering for another 1½ hours. Add nutmeg and adjust seasoning.

Note: You may be surprised at how thick and meaty this sauce is. Its heartiness makes it perfect for the lasagne verde bolognese, which appears on page 148. If the sauce is to be used on a bowl of pasta, like tagliatelle, however, it can be thinned with water during the last half hour of cooking. Some chefs even add a little cream just before the sauce is finished.

ITALIAN SAUSAGE SAUCE WITH FRESH FENNEL

Rich Italian sausage finds a perfectly light, fresh, herbal-vegetable background in this delicious sauce. You can use sweet Italian sausage from the supermarket or purchase one of the great fresh sausages made at Dean & DeLuca—or make your own Dean & DeLuca-style sausage (recipe on page 460) We like this sauce with short, relatively thin dried pasta shapes, like penne or ziti.

MAKES ENOUGH SAUCE FOR 90 G (2 LB) DRIED PASTA

450 g (1 lb) sweet Italian sausages (about 4)
50 ml (2 fl oz) extra-virgin olive oil
2 bulbs fresh fennel and the feathery fennel greens
1 onion, finely chopped
1 stalk celery with leaves, finely chopped
4 garlic cloves, slivered
1.8 kg (4 lb) ripe tomatoes (about 10 tomatoes),
  coarsely chopped
50 g (2 oz) chopped fresh basil
50 g (2 oz) chopped fresh parsley
30 ml (2 tbsp) tomato purée
salt and pepper to taste
freshly grated Parmigiano-Reggiano as an
  accompaniment

1. Prick each sausage several times with the tines of a fork. Cook the sausage in 15 ml (1 tbsp) olive oil in a large, deep frying pan over moderate heat, turning often, until well browned and cooked through, about 25 minutes. Remove sausage from frying pan with a slotted spoon and set aside. Add the rest of the olive oil. Finely chop the fennel bulb, reserving the feathery greens and add bulb to frying pan. Stir in the onion, celery and garlic and cook, over moderately low heat, stirring frequently, for 20 minutes or until the vegetables are very soft and lightly browned.

2. Stir in the tomatoes, basil, parsley, tomato purée, salt and pepper and cook, stirring occasionally, for 45 minutes. (Add a little water if necessary to prevent the sauce from sticking to the frying pan.) Put the sauce through a food mill into a saucepan.

3. Cut the sausage into medium chunks, add to the sauce and cook for 5 minutes longer.

4. Toss hot pasta with the sauce. (Add a little pasta cooking water if necessary to reach the desired consistency.) Sprinkle with fennel greens and serve immediately. Pass freshly grated Parmigiano-Reggiano if desired.

SAUCE AMATRICIANA

This wonderful, spicy, pancetta-flavoured sauce, not seen often enough in the United States, is a restaurant classic in Rome. That's because many Roman restaurant workers come from Amatrice, a town in the Sabine hills, about 80 km (50 miles) north-east of Rome. In Italy, it is often served on bucatini—dried pasta that's slightly bigger than spaghetti and with a hole in the middle of each strand.

MAKES ENOUGH SAUCE FOR 450 G (1 LB) DRIED PASTA

2 garlic cloves, finely chopped
4 medium yellow onions, diced

30 ml (2 tbsp) pure olive oil

140 g (5 oz) pancetta, diced

1.8 kg (4 lb) fresh plum tomatoes, peeled, seeded and diced (about 5 cups)

5 ml (1 tsp) kosher salt

2.5 g (½ tsp) freshly ground black pepper

2.5 g (½ tsp) crushed hot red pepper flakes (or more to taste)

25 g (1 oz) freshly grated Parmigiano-Reggiano

25 g (1 oz) freshly grated pecorino Romano

Cook the garlic and onions in the olive oil, covered, over low heat, for about 20 minutes. Remove lid and cook another 10 to 15 minutes, until onions turn golden brown. Add pancetta and cook for 10 minutes. Add plum tomatoes, kosher salt, black pepper and red pepper flakes and cook over moderate heat for 15 to 20 minutes, until tomatoes have reduced slightly. Add cheeses, mix well to melt and toss with warm pasta. Serve immediately.

TUSCAN RABBIT SAUCE

A classic pasta dish in Tuscany is pappardelle con lepre—wide ribbons of fresh pasta with a dark, meaty sauce made from wild hare. Because wild hare is not so easy to find, we make a similar dish from domesticated rabbit. The main difference in our version is greater lightness of colour and texture; we use chicken stock and white wine in place of the traditional beef stock and red wine. But there's no retrenchment in flavour—it's a delicious sauce that tastes extremely meaty, somewhere between the tastes of chicken and veal. Serve it with fresh pappardelle or with other fresh pastas, like fettuccine or tagilatelle.

MAKES ENOUGH SAUCE FOR 450 G (1 LB) FRESH PASTA

50 ml (2 fl oz) olive oil

175 g (6 oz) diced onion

175 g (6 oz) diced celery

175 g (6 oz) diced carrots

115 g (4 oz) bacon, diced

25 g (1 oz) plain flour

5 g (1 tsp) salt

2.5 g (½ tsp) black pepper

1 x 1.3-kg (3-lb) rabbit, cut into 8 pieces

225 ml (8 fl oz) dry white wine

1.2 litres (2 pints) chicken stock

225 ml (8 fl oz) water

30 ml (2 tbsp) tomato purée

15 ml (1 tbsp) chopped fresh sage

1 cinnamon stick

115 g (4 oz) grated pecorino Romano

1. In a large, heavy saucepan heat the olive oil over moderate heat. Add the onion, celery and carrots and cook until soft, about 5 minutes. Add bacon and cook until bacon is cooked but not too crispy, 5 to 7 minutes. Remove vegetables and bacon and reserve.

2. Combine flour, salt and pepper on a plate. Increase heat under pan to moderately high. Dredge rabbit pieces in flour just before cooking. Brown rabbit pieces well, a few at a time and set aside. Drain excess fat from pan.

3. Add white wine to pan and boil for 2 minutes, scraping up the browned bits that cling to the pan. Return rabbit to pan along with reserved vegetables and bacon. Add chicken stock, water, tomato purée, sage and cinnamon stick. Stir well. Partially cover pan, reduce heat and simmer gently for 45 minutes. Remove meat from pot and when cool enough to handle, remove meat from bones. Shred meat coarsely. Return to pan.

4. Simmer, uncovered, for another 45 minutes, or until the sauce is nicely thickened and the meat is stringy and tender. Remove cinnamon stick.

5. Toss with hot pasta and serve with pecorino Romano.

PORK SAUSAGE RAGÙ WITH SAFFRON

This Sardinian specialty is excellent prepared with Dean & DeLuca's homemade hot Italian sausage. The high budget–low budget confrontation of saffron and sausage is intriguing; the ingredients seem almost medieval together. We love this sauce with a short, stubby dried pasta, like malloreddus, or the Pugliese specialty cavatelli.

MAKES SAUCE FOR 900 G (2 LB) DRIED PASTA

450 g (1 lb) hot Italian sausages (about 4)
50 ml (2 fl oz) olive oil
2 small onions, finely chopped
2 garlic cloves, chopped
1 kg (2¼ lb) fresh ripe tomatoes (about 7 medium
   tomatoes), peeled, seeded, and chopped
350 ml (12 fl oz) fine quality tomato sauce
   (preferably homemade)
10 sun-dried tomato halves packed in oil, finely
   chopped
2 bay leaves
1.25 g (¼ tsp) saffron threads, crumbled
salt and pepper to taste
115 g (4 oz) freshly grated pecorino Romano
chopped fresh flat-leaf parsley leaves for
   garnish

1. Prick each sausage several times with the tines of a fork. Heat the olive oil in a large casserole over moderately low heat and in it cook the sausages, turning frequently, until well browned on all sides and cooked through, about 25 minutes. Remove the sausages with a slotted spoon. Stir in the onions and garlic and cook, stirring frequently and scraping up the browned bits on the bottom, until onions are softened, about 7 minutes. When the sausages are cool enough to handle, cut them crosswise into thin slices.

2. Add the chopped tomatoes, tomato sauce, sun-dried tomatoes, bay leaves, saffron, salt and pepper and cook over low heat at a bare simmer, stirring frequently and

carefully so the sauce will not stick, for 1 hour. Discard the bay leaves.

3. Stir hot pasta into the casserole with the sausage and simmer for 3 minutes. Remove from heat and stir in the pecorino Romano. Spoon the pasta into bowls and top with parsley.

SICILIAN LAMB SAUCE WITH PEAS

The Greeks inhabited Sicily in the ancient world and this full-flavoured, hearty, lamby, stewlike sauce is definitely on the Greek side of the Sicilian experience. Please note: the peas in this sauce do not retain their bright green colour (this is not *nuova cucina*)—but they do contribute to the sauce's deep flavour and lovely texture. We like it with ziti or rigatoni.

MAKES SAUCE FOR 900 G (2 LB) DRIED PASTA

40 g (1½ oz) unsalted butter
45 ml (3 tbsp) extra-virgin olive oil
900 g (2 lb) boneless leg of lamb (not lean), cut
   into 1-cm (1/2-in) pieces
1 small onion, finely chopped
3 garlic cloves, chopped
900 g (2 lb) plum tomatoes (about 10 tomatoes),
   peeled, seeded and chopped
125 ml (4 fl oz) water
6 sprigs of fresh flat-leaf parsley, leaves stripped
   from stem
6 sprigs of fresh thyme, leaves stripped from stem
6 sprigs of fresh marjoram, leaves stripped from
   stem
280 g (10 oz) shelled fresh peas or a 280 g (10 oz)
   package frozen peas, thawed
freshly grated pecorino Romano as an
   accompaniment

1. Heat the butter and olive oil over moderately high heat in a deep, 30-cm (12-in) non-stick frying pan with a lid. Add the lamb pieces, in batches and cook, stirring frequently, for 4 minutes each batch, until all of the pieces are browned. Stir in the onion and garlic and cook, stirring occasionally, until softened, about 4 minutes. Stir in the tomatoes and water and simmer, loosely covered, stirring occasionally, for 30 minutes. Stir in the herbs, reserving half of the fresh marjoram, and simmer, covered, stirring occasionally, for 30 minutes.

2. Stir in the peas and cook until the lamb begins to fall apart, about 20 minutes. Taste for seasoning.

3. Toss hot pasta with the sauce. (Add 125 ml (4 fl oz) pasta cooking water if necessary to reach the desired consistency). Sprinkle with the remaining marjoram and serve immediately with the pecorino Romano.

TUSCAN CHICKEN LIVER AND SAUSAGE SAUCE

This classic sauce is very chunky and very rich with liver taste—which means it marries marvellously well with pasta. It's also a treat when spooned over a bowl of creamy polenta. The original sauce was made with ground pork, but we find that sweet sausage makes it even heartier and gives it more depth of flavour. Rigatoni and ziti are great pasta shapes for this sauce.

MAKES SAUCE FOR 1.3 KG (3 LB) DRIED PASTA

50 ml (2 fl oz) olive oil
1 large onion, finely chopped
2 medium carrots, finely chopped
50 g (2 oz) chopped fresh flat-leaf parsley plus
   additional for garnish
1 celery stalk, including leaves, finely chopped
2 garlic cloves, chopped
(350 g 12 oz) mild Italian sausage, removed from
   casings
125 ml (4 fl oz) dry red wine
45 ml (3 tbsp) tomato purée
800-g (28-oz) can crushed tomatoes
25 g (1 oz) unsalted butter
4 absolutely fresh chicken livers, trimmed and cut

into small pieces (about 350 g (12 oz) trimmed)
salt and pepper to taste
freshly grated pecorino Romano as an
   accompaniment

1. Heat the oil until hot but not smoking in a large heavy saucepan over moderate heat. Stir in the onion, carrots, parsley, celery and garlic and cook, stirring frequently, for about 10 minutes, or until the vegetables are soft but not browned.

2. Add the sausage and cook, stirring and breaking up all the lumps with a wooden spoon, for 4 minutes, or until the meat changes colour but does not brown. Stir in the wine and the tomato purée and cook at a bare simmer, stirring, for 10 minutes. Add the tomatoes and cook at a bare simmer, partially covered, stirring occasionally, for 40 minutes.

3. Season the chicken livers with salt and pepper. Heat half the butter in a medium frying pan over moderate heat. When the foam subsides, add the chicken livers and cook, stirring, until they are nicely browned on the outside but still pink on the inside, about 3 minutes. Add the chicken livers and the rest of the butter to the sauce and simmer for 5 minutes. Season to taste with salt and pepper. Serve immediately. Pass pecorino Romano, if desired.

Clam sauces
We love pasta with clam sauce...but boy, does it spell controversy.

First of all, there's the question of fresh vs. canned clams. The latter ingredient does have its devotées across America. We feel, however, that unless this dish is made with fresh clams it's not worth making. But that opinion raises a raft of other controversies: what size clams? served in the shell or not? cooked how long?

Then, of course, comes the colour of the sauce. Most clam sauce fanatics swear by white, because they believe it enables more of the clam flavour to come

through. Now, we've had enough delicious bowls of
linguine with red clam sauce to lust after that other
colour too, occasionally, but we are basically in the
white-sauce camp.

Once again, flags go up. Which type of white clam
sauce? Lots of Little Italy–style restaurants serve an oily
one. Lots of upscale, white-tablecloth Italian restaurants
violate ethnic authenticity and serve a creamy one. Our
preference: a light, flavour-packed stocky one. You'll find
great recipes for all these variations here.

Finally, which type of pasta? We are partial to dried
pasta lunga for clam sauce and we've included our
specific pasta recommendations with the recipes.

There is, of course, a basic clam sauce problem: if
clams are cooked a short time, the clam texture's great
but there's not enough clam flavour; if the clams are
cooked a long time, there's more clam flavour but the
clams are tough. All of the following recipes solve the
problem neatly.

WHITE CLAM SAUCE, STOCKY-STYLE

This is our favourite clam sauce by far. Like all clam
sauces, it's good on linguine—but its delicacy marries
even better with very thin, long pasta, like capellini.

MAKES SAUCE FOR 450 G (1 LB) DRIED PASTA

8 very large chowder clams (each about 225-280 g
(8-10 oz))
a little bottled clam juice (if necessary)
30 ml (2 tbsp) olive oil
12 large garlic cloves, finely chopped
675 g (11/2 lb) small clams, scrubbed
25 g (1 oz) very finely chopped fresh parsley

1. Open the chowder clams, making sure to catch all the
clam juice. Chop the clams and reserve them. Pour the
clam juice into a large measuring cup; it should come to
about 450 ml (16 fl oz). (If it doesn't, make up the
difference with bottled clam juice.) Then add 125 ml (4
fl oz) water, making 600 ml (1 pint) liquid in all.

2. Pour the olive oil into a wide, heavy pot over moderate
heat. Add the chopped garlic and cook for 4 to 5
minutes, or until the garlic just starts to turn brown. Add
a little clam juice to loosen the garlic, then add the rest
of the juice. Simmer for 2 minutes.

3. Bring clam juice to a boil and add the clams. Cover.
Within 2 minutes or so, their shells should swing open;
remove the small clams from the pot and place them in
a bowl. Reduce heat to low under clam juice in pot and
add the reserved, raw, chopped clams. Cook very gently
for ½ minute.

4. Make sure the pasta is done at this point. Spill the
pasta into a colander and place the pasta cooking pot over
low heat. Return the pasta to the cooking pot. Add two-
thirds of the clam stock plus the liquid that has collected
in the bowl of small clams. Add 45 ml (3 tbsp) of the
chopped parsley. Stir to blend, about 1 minute. Taste for
seasoning. Divide pasta among 5 to 6 individual pasta
bowls and top with the remaining clam stock, remaining
parsley and the small clams. Serve immediately.

WHITE CLAM SAUCE, CREAMY-STYLE

This is a delicious, lemony version of creamy white clam
sauce. We like it on spaghetti and also on thin pasta
fresca, like taglierini.

MAKES ENOUGH SAUCE FOR 450 G (1 LB) PASTA

12 very large chowder clams (each about 225-280 g/
8-10 oz)
a little bottled clam juice (if necessary)
40 g (1½ oz) butter
12 large garlic cloves, finely chopped
40 g (1½ oz) flour
350 g (12 oz) shredded fresh basil plus additional
for garnish
30 ml (2 tbsp) lemon juice
½ teaspoon grated lemon rind
freshly ground black pepper

1. Open clams, making sure to catch all the clam juice. Mince the clams and reserve them. Pour the clam juice into a large measuring cup; it should come to about 350 ml (12 fl oz). (If it doesn't, make up the difference with bottled clam juice.)

2. Melt the butter over moderate heat in a heavy saucepan. Add the garlic and cook for 2 minutes. (Do not let it brown.) Add the flour and cook, whisking to blend well, for another 2 minutes. Add the clam juice all at once, whisking to blend well with the roux. Bring to a boil, add 75 g (3 oz) shredded basil, the lemon juice and the lemon rind. Reduce heat and simmer gently for 2 minutes, adding the chopped clams for the last 30 seconds of cooking. Add freshly ground black pepper, if desired and a little water if the sauce is too thick.

3. When the pasta is ready, drain it in a colander. Return pasta to its cooking pot and place over low heat. Add the rest of the shredded basil, reserving the basil to be used for garnish, and half the clam sauce. Stir well. Divide the pasta among 5 or 6 bowls and top with remaining clam sauce (you may have a little left over). Garnish with additional basil leaves and serve immediately.

The choice of clams

If you're planning to serve whole cooked clams in the shell as part of your pasta dish, you must serve quickly cooked, tender and tiny clams. Don't use cherrystones or even littlenecks, both of which get too rubbery for our taste when cooked in the shell. In many seafood markets today you can find either tiny Manila clams or tiny New Zealand cockles; both are sweet and briny, smaller than a littleneck and very tender when cooked in the shell. They are much closer to the wonderful *vongole* you find in Italy.

For chopped clams that go into the sauce, any size will do—though we find that large chowder clams (225-280 g (8-10 oz) each) are by far the most economical.

Chop up 8 of these huge quahogs and you've got 225 g (8 oz) of chopped clam bellies. If large clams are not available, use cockles and refer to the following conversion guide:

- One 225-g (8-oz) chowder clam (quahog) yields about 60 ml (4 tbsp) juice and 30 ml (2 tbsp) chopped clam.
- One 115-g (4-oz) cherrystone clam yields about 45 ml (3 tbsp) juice and 20 g (1½ tbsp) chopped clam.
- One 50-g (2-oz) littleneck yields about 15 ml (1 tbsp) juice and 10 g (2 tsp) chopped clam.
- One 160-g (6.5-oz) can chopped clams yields about 90 ml (6 tbsp) of juice and 75 g (5 tbsp) chopped clams.

WHITE CLAM SAUCE, OIL-AND-GARLIC STYLE

This sauce and al dente linguine were made for each other.

MAKES ENOUGH SAUCE FOR 450 G (1 LB) DRIED PASTA

12 very large chowder clams
50 ml (2 fl oz) good, fruity olive oil
90 ml (6 tbsp) very thinly sliced garlic
90 ml (6 tbsp) fine quality extra-virgin olive oil plus additional for drizzling
50 g (2 oz) chopped parsley

1. Open the clams, making sure to catch all the clam juice. Mince the clams and reserve them. You should have about 350 ml (12 fl oz) of chopped clams. Reserve the clam juice.

2. Add the 30 ml (2 fl oz) of fruity olive oil to a large frying pan over moderate heat. Add the garlic and cook, stirring occasionally, for 5 minutes, or until some of the garlic has turned medium-brown. Add the clams and 50 ml (2 fl oz) of the reserved clam juice. Cook, stirring to blend well, for 1 minute. Reduce heat to low and add the 90 ml (6 tbsp) extra-virgin olive oil and parsley. Remove from heat if the pasta is not ready.

5. As soon as the pasta is al dente, spill it into a colander and place the pasta cooking pot over low heat. Return the pasta to the pot. Add the clam sauce, stirring to blend well. Moisten with a bit of the reserved clam juice. Taste for seasoning. Divide among 5 to 6 individual pasta bowls and drizzle a little additional extra-virgin olive oil over each one. Serve immediately.

RED CLAM SAUCE

There are many ways to make this dish. We celebrate its Little Italy roots and make it with a megaton of garlic. The one-two punch of clams is irresistible: chopped, soft bellies of large clams mingle with the small, brittle shells and succulent little bellies of miniature clams (cockles). Great on linguine, or, even better, on linguine piccole, or narrow linguine.

MAKES ENOUGH SAUCE FOR 450 G (1 LB) DRIED PASTA

6 very large chowder clams (225-280 g (8-10 oz)) each)
800 g (28-oz) can tomatoes
30 ml (2 tbsp) olive oil
1 large head garlic, cut in thin slices, plus 15 g (1 tbsp) finely chopped garlic
700 g (1½ lb) small Manila clams, scrubbed
100 g (3½ oz) shredded fresh basil plus whole leaves for garnish

1. Open the chowder clams, making sure to catch all the clam juice. Coarsely chop the clams and reserve them. You should have about 350 g (12 oz) chopped clams and 350 ml (12 fl oz) of clam juice. Reserve the clam juice.

2. Strain out the tomatoes from the can of tomatoes, reserving both the liquid and the tomatoes. Coarsely chop the tomatoes.

3. Place the olive oil in a large saucepan over low heat. Add the sliced garlic cloves and cook gently until they start turning golden brown, about 20 minutes. Add 225 ml (8 fl oz) of the clam juice, reserving the rest. Add 225 ml (8 fl oz) of the tomato liquid to the saucepan, reserving the rest for another use. Bring to a boil, then simmer the tomato mixture gently until it is reduced to about 250 ml (9 fl oz) , about 45 minutes.

4. When ready to serve, add the small clams to the tomato-clam sauce and toss with the rest of the chopped garlic. Cover and simmer until the shells swing open, 2 to 3 minutes. Remove and reserve small clams. Add the coarsely chopped tomatoes and the shredded basil to the sauce and simmer 2 to 3 minutes.

5. Drain the hot pasta in a colander and toss with a little olive oil. Place the pasta cooking pot, now dry, over very low heat. Add about half of the sauce, along with the chopped chowder clams and the reserved chopped clams. Add the drained pasta and toss well for 1 minute. Add the rest of the reserved clam juice. Divide pasta among 4 to 6 pasta bowls. Top with the remaining sauce and the basil leaf garnish and serve immediately.

BAKED PASTA CASSEROLES

Choosing your lasagna noodle
If you want to make lasagne al forno at home, you have three lasagna noodle options to choose from.

Dried, Boxed Lasagna This is the pasta choice that American lasagna-makers have made for years. But lasagna connoisseurs are not crazy about the feel of a lasagne al forno made from these noodles. The finished product is on the heavy, doughy side, with none of the delicacy of fresh pasta. Additionally, the ingredients of the lasagne al forno (cheese, meat, tomatoes) slide off the smooth plates of pasta rather than grabbing on to them. Think of a dried-pasta version of lasagne al forno as a group of ingredients wrapped in non-stick baking paper and of a fresh-dough version as a group of ingredients wrapped in clingy clingfilm.

Sometimes, however, you don't have a choice. So if you are using dried, boxed lasagna noodles in the lasagna recipes given here, remember that a 450-g (1-lb) box contains about 20 noodles; 1 box will more than cover each of the lasagne al forno recipes that appear here. Each dried noodle is approximately 5 cm (2 in) wide and 25 cm (10 in) long. Consult the recipe to see how many noodles you need, then cook them in salted boiling water for about 8 minutes, or until almost fully cooked. It is best if you cook only 4 or 5 noodles at a time, so that the water remains boiling. Continue until all noodles are cooked (they should be quite al dente). The recipes given here call for each layer of lasagne al forno to be 3 strips wide, so choose a tin that's at least 25 x 18 cm (11 in x 7 in) (the noodles expand a bit during their initial boil).

Fresh Lasagna This is the preferred choice of lasagna connoisseurs; the noodles grab onto the filling ingredients and the whole coalesces into a tight, delicious unit. You can either make your own lasagna noodles (use pasta fresca recipe on page 132) or you can buy sheets of pasta fresca that you can cut into lasagna noodles. In either case, use fresh pasta that's no more than 2mm (1/16 in) thick. Cut into the usual lasagna noodle shapes: about 25 cm (10 in) long, about 5 cm (2 in) wide. Consult the recipes given here to see how many noodles you need. Remember that eighteen 25 x 5 cm (10 x 2-in)strips of fresh pasta for lasagna will weigh between 350-400 g (12-14 oz) (it's best to buy 450 g (1 lb) of fresh pasta for any of the recipes given here; leftovers can be cut into any other pasta shapes you like).

To prepare fresh lasagna noodles for the tin, you must cook them very briefly in a large pot of boiling water. Once again, cook no more than 4 or 5 at a time. After you place the noodles in the boiling water and the water returns to a boil, wait a few seconds and then immediately remove the pasta. Run it under cold water, then place it between sheets of paper towels to dry.

Instant, No-Boil or Oven-Ready Lasagna This is a tremendously important innovation in the world of lasagna (but not for the reason that the inventors think). These dried noodles were developed so that you don't have to boil them before you start layering them in the lasagna tin. It works, we suppose, but we're not thrilled with the texture of the finished product.

However, if you boil the noodles for 3 minutes only, then layer them in the tin, they yield a texture in the finished product that is, by far, the best dried-lasagna texture we've ever tasted. Lasagne al forno made from briefly boiled no-boil noodles is lighter, more delicate, more refined than any other lasagne al forno made from dried noodles.

The only problem is that no-boil noodles are new in the market and they are being produced in different sizes. You'll have to improvise their fit in the tin after you see what size you've purchased. However, if you're using the original no-boil noodles (Ondine, by pasta manufacturer Delverde), you can use the following guidelines. Each sheet is approximately 16 x 15 cm (6½ x 6 in). This means that if you line up 2 of them in a baking tin in the right way, you'll have a layer that's 30 x 16 cm (12 x 6½ in). This is pretty close to the 25 x 15 cm (10 x 6 in) layer that the regular dried noodles yield. To make a whole tin of lasagne al forno that calls for, say, 18 regular dried noodles (3 per layer), you'll need only 12 no-boil noodles (2 per layer). Because the size of the lasagne al forno will be a little larger, increase the proportions slightly for the filling.

LASAGNE AL FORNO

Many people misunderstand lasagna. The word *lasagna,* by itself, does not refer to an oven-baked casserole. Strictly speaking, it is a type of pasta noodle, long, very broad, rectangular, usually made with egg, sometimes wavy at the edge (lasagne ricci or lasagne reginelle), sometimes straight at the edge. Often, in Italy, the noodles are not baked together, but simply served with sauce. Any of the meat sauces are great with lasagna noodles—particularly the sauce bolognese, the pork sausage ragù with saffron and the Sicilian lamb sauce with peas. Just lay a strip of cooked lasagna on each diner's plate, ladle on some sauce, cover with another strip, ladle on some more sauce and dust with cheese.

What most people in America call 'lasagna' is, in Italy, known as lasagna al forno—or lasagna noodles cooked in the oven. This dish is perfect for parties, or large crowds, because it feeds so many and because it can be made in advance.

Here's a range of lasagne al forno dishes that we especially like.

OLD-FASHIONED ITALIAN-AMERICAN LASAGNA WITH RICOTTA AND TOMATO SAUCE

What's old-fashioned about this lasagna is that it contains the holy trinity of ricotta, mozzarella and tomatoes. However—unlike the prototypical Italian-American lasagna, which is so heavy and oozy with cheese that it sags under its own weight—this lasagna comes closer to the Italian lasagna ideal of lightness, simplicity and what Marcella Hazan calls 'deftness'. You could increase the mozzarella by 50 per cent if you want the dish heavier, or you could add sausage and/or meatballs in the classic Little Italy manner. But we prefer this vegetarian lasagna just as it is, with its great purity of tomato flavour.

SERVES 6

75 ml (2½ fl oz) olive oil
3 large yellow onions, diced
3 x 800-g (28-oz) cans plum tomatoes, drained
15 ml (1 tbsp) coarse salt
5 ml (1 tsp) freshly ground black pepper
450 g (1 lb) whole-milk ricotta
1 egg

75 g (3 oz) finely grated Parmigiano-Reggiano
15 g (1 tbsp) chopped fresh basil
pinch of freshly grated nutmeg
40 g (1½ oz) butter, melted
18 sheets lasagna, each about 25 x 5 cm
    (10 x 2 in), parboiled (see directions on
    page 146)
450 g (1 lb) mozzarella, grated

1. Heat olive oil over moderate heat in large saucepan. Add onions, stir and cover. Cook for about 20 minutes, stirring occasionally, until onions are translucent. Using a food mill, purée plum tomatoes directly into the pan. Add 5 g (2 tsp) of the coarse salt and 2.5 g (½ tsp) of the pepper and cook, uncovered, for about 30 minutes, or until sauce is reduced to about 1 litre (1¾ pints).

2. In small bowl mix ricotta, egg, 30 ml (2 tbsp) of the Parmigiano-Reggiano, basil, remaining salt and pepper and nutmeg. Stir well to combine.

3. Butter generously the bottom and sides of a baking pan, 28 x 23 x 4 cm (11 x 9 in x 1½ in). Take 175 ml (6 fl oz) of tomato sauce and spread on bottom of pan.

4. Place 3 lasagna noodles on bottom of pan, overlapping them slightly. Spread a 125 g (4 oz) of ricotta mixture evenly over noodles. Spread 175 ml (6 fl oz) of tomato sauce on top of this. Sprinkle with a *mozzarella .* heaping 125 g (4 oz). Repeat this 4 times. Then place last 3 noodles on top and sprinkle with the rest of the mozzarella and the rest of the Parmigiano-Reggiano. (The lasagna may be assembled up to this point 2 days in advance and stored in refrigerator, covered. Bring to room temperature before cooking.)

5. When ready to cook, preheat oven to 200°C (400°F). Bake on top shelf of oven for 20 to 25 minutes, or until cheese is melted. Let sit for 5 minutes and serve.

LASAGNE VERDE BOLOGNESE

The residents of Bologna claim lasagne al forno as their own and an extant fourteenth-century recipe from the University of Bologna gives their claim good authority. But they have more to brag about than historical precedence; their rich version of lasagna—loaded with profound sauce bolognese and topped off with a palate-caressing white sauce—is our hands-down favourite in the lasagna league.

SERVES 10 TO 12

100 g (3½ oz) butter
25 g (1 oz) plain flour
568 ml (1 pint) milk, heated almost to boiling
5 g (1 tsp) coarse salt
2.5 g (¼ tsp) white pepper
pinch of freshly grated nutmeg
225 g (8 oz) grated Parmigiano-Reggiano
115 g (4 oz) grated pecorino Romano
18 sheets fresh or dried green lasagne noodles,
  each one about 5 x 25 cm (2 x 10 in), parboiled
  (see directions on page 146)
1½ recipe of sauce bolognese about 1.3 litres
  (2¼ pints), page 138

1. Make a roux by melting 50 g (2 oz) butter in a medium saucepan over moderate heat. Add 15 g (1 tbsp) flour at a time, whisking well after each addition. Cook roux gently for 2 to 3 minutes, whisking constantly. Do not let the colour change. Add hot milk slowly, whisking constantly and cook for about 25 minutes over low heat. Do not stop whisking or stirring. Cook until the sauce has consistency of very thick cream. Season with salt, pepper and nutmeg.

2. Mix Parmigiano-Reggiano and pecorino Romano in a small bowl.

3. Melt the rest of the butter. Grease bottom and sides of a 23 x 28 x 4 cm (9 x 11 x 1½ in) roasting tin well. Spread 225 ml (8 fl oz) of the sauce on bottom of tin.

4. Place 3 lasagna noodles on bottom of pan; they will overlap slightly. Spread about 400 ml (14 fl oz) of sauce bolognese evenly on noodles. Sprinkle with 50 g (2 oz) of cheese mixture. Repeat this 4 times. Place last 3 noodles on top, spread remaining sauce over all and sprinkle with remaining cheese. (The lasagna may be assembled up to this point 2 days in advance and stored in refrigerator, covered. Bring to room temperature before cooking.)

5. When ready to cook, preheat oven to 200°C (400°F). Bake on top shelf of oven for about 20 minutes, until top is light golden brown. Let sit for 5 minutes and serve.

WILD MUSHROOM LASAGNA WITH SMOKED MOZZARELLA AND FRESH SAGE

You've probably never had a lasagna like this one: austere, unsaucy, devoted singularly to the flavours of one ingredient—mushrooms. And do those flavours ever come through! The smoky mozzarella only serves to underline the earthy, woodsy autumness of it all. Use the deepest-tasting wild mushrooms you can find (we've done this dish with everything from French chanterelles to Japanese mitsutake mushrooms). The key to success is slicing all of the mushrooms very thinly; the thinness of the cut is what gives the dish its delicacy. We like to use a mandoline or one of those less expensive plastic versions.

SERVES 6

350 g (12 oz) firmly packed cups dried porcini
  mushrooms
50 g (2 oz) unsalted butter
450 g (1 lb) very thinly sliced cultivated mushrooms
550 g (1¼ lb) very thinly sliced wild mushrooms
6 shallots, peeled and very thinly sliced
6 cloves garlic, peeled and finely chopped
30 g (2 tbsp) fresh sage, finely chopped (plus extra
  leaves for garnish)
125 ml (4 fl oz) double cream

salt and freshly ground pepper to taste
freshly grated nutmeg
9 sheets lasagna, each one about 25 x 5 cm
   (10 x 2 in), parboiled (see page 146)
450 g (1 lb) smoked mozzarella, shredded
75 g (3 oz) shaved Parmigiano-Reggiano plus extra
   for serving

1. Place the dried porcini mushrooms in a bowl and cover with about 450 ml (16 fl oz) of hot water. Soak for 30 minutes.

2. Place 25 g (1 oz) of the butter in a very large sauté pan over moderately high heat. When the butter has melted and is just starting to brown slightly, add the sliced cultivated mushrooms. Make sure the pan is not crowded (if it is, do this in two batches). Sauté the mushrooms over high heat for 2 minutes, or until they begin to brown slightly. Remove and reserve.

3. Add the rest of the butter to the pan over moderately high heat. When the butter has melted and is just starting to brown slightly, add the sliced wild mushrooms. Make sure the pan is not crowded (if it is, do this in two batches). Also add the shallots, the garlic and the chopped sage. Sauté the mushrooms over high heat for 2 minutes, or until they begin to brown slightly. Return the sautéed cultivated mushrooms to the pan and mix together well. Drain the porcini and add to the pan, mixing well. Add the cream and cook over high heat until the cream thickens slightly (about 30 seconds). Remove mixture from heat. Season with salt, pepper and freshly grated nutmeg.

4. Butter a lasagna tin that is roughly 23 x 28 x 4 cm (9 x 11 x 1½ in). Place 3 parboiled lasagna strips on the bottom of the tin (they may overlap slightly). Cover with half the mushroom mixture, half of the Parmigiano-Reggiano and a quarter of the smoked mozzarella. Make sure everything is spread out evenly. Top with 3 more lasagna strips. Cover with the remaining half of the mushroom mixture, the remaining half of the Parmigiano-Reggiano and the second quarter of the smoked mozzarella (reserving half of the original amount). Make sure everything is spread out evenly. Top with the last 3 lasagna strips. Place whole leaves of sage over the lasagna in a decorative pattern. Top with the remaining smoked mozzarella, spreading it out evenly.

5. Cover the lasagna pan well with aluminum foil and bake in a preheated 170°C (325°F) oven for 30 minutes. Remove from oven, remove foil and place under the grill until brown and bubbly on top, about 1 minute. Let rest 10 minutes, then cut into sections and place on plates. There will probably be a little creamy liquid at the bottom of the lasagna pan. Reduce briefly, if desired and spoon a little over the lasagna portions. Sprinkle each portion with salt and freshly grated Parmigiano-Reggiano and serve.

Note: This recipe, especially, is good with *fresh* lasagna noodles. It doesn't have as much goo in the middle as other lasagnas and the fresh noodles help pull it together.

Macaroni and fontina cheese

Lots of people consider macaroni and cheese the ultimate comfort food, but it has never enchanted us. We find the traditional American version relentless: you're lost in a sea of dairy, with no way out. But add a few bright vegetables to the casserole, use a grown-up cheese with real flavour, bind it all with a luscious browned butter béchamel packed with aromatic fresh herbs—and we think you've got something extraordinary that really may make you feel safe again. By the way, you'll find fontina at all levels of flavour we prefer a strong-tasting one in this dish.

SERVES 6

15 ml (1 tbsp) olive oil
1 medium onion, thinly sliced

1 clove garlic, chopped

4 small yellow and/or orange peppers, trimmed and
  cut into very thin strips

2 small courgettes (175 g (6 oz) total), cut
  crossways into thin slices, then into thin strips

2 small yellow crookneck squash (175 g (6 oz)
  each), cut crossways into thin slices, then into
  thin strips

salt and freshly ground pepper to taste

225 g (8 oz) imported Italian penne or another short
  tubular shape

45 ml (3 tbsp) unsalted butter

40 g (1½ oz) plain flour

2 sprigs fresh rosemary

4 fresh sage leaves

1 bay leaf

350 ml (12 fl oz) milk

280 g (10 oz) grated Italian fontina cheese

1. Preheat the oven to 210°C (425°F).

2. Heat the olive oil in a large non-stick frying pan over
moderate heat and stir in the onion. Cook, stirring, for 2
minutes. Add the garlic and cook, stirring, for 1 minute.
Raise the heat slightly and add the peppers. Cook,
stirring, for 2 minutes. Add the courgettes and yellow
squash and cook, stirring for 2 minutes. Season with
salt and pepper and set aside.

3. Cook the pasta in a large pot of boiling salted water
for 4 minutes. Drain the pasta and rinse it with cold
water.

4. Heat the butter in a medium-size heavy saucepan
over moderate to moderately high heat until it becomes
a medium nutty brown, being careful not to burn it. Stir
in the flour, rosemary, sage and bay leaf. Cook, stirring
constantly, for 2 minutes. Slowly add the milk and cook,
stirring, for 4 to 5 minutes, or until the sauce is very
thick—the consistency of sour cream. Strain the sauce
and season well with salt and pepper. Cool slightly.

5. Return the pasta to the same large pot and stir in the
sauce. Add the vegetables and 225 g (8 oz) of the
grated fontina and blend completely. Place the mixture
in a deep earthenware or glass baking dish 23 x 33 x
5 cm (about 9 x 13 x 2 in). Sprinkle with the remaining
fontina. Bake for 20 minutes, until the pasta is browned
and crusty on top.

ASIAN NOODLES

We can't close our pasta discussion without a look at
noodles from the East, which have also boomed during
the American pastamania of recent decades. If you live
near Asian markets, you're in luck. There's a profusion of
both fresh and dried noodles available today that will
also keep your meals light and healthful, while providing
a refreshing break from the Italian way of doing things.

Here are the leading noodles:

CHINESE NOODLES (MEIN)

WHEAT FLOUR
Fresh Noodles Maybe there's something in this Marco
Polo business after all; these popular noodles, made
fresh in Chinatown noodle factories across America,
bear a strong resemblance to Italian pasta. The most
common type is long, like spaghetti and about 3 mm
(⅛ in) thick. You can also find 'thin mein' (like capellini)
and 'wide mein' (like fettuccine). The noodles may
include eggs (in which case they'll be yellowish), or may
not (in which case they'll be white). These are the
noodles that are used most often in the steaming bowls
of soup, noodles, vegetables and meat (like roast duck)
that have become so popular in and out of Chinatowns;
they take just a few minutes to boil. But they are also
the noodles used for the old-time stir-fried dish lo mein;
just make sure to boil the noodles first before you cook
them a second time in a wok. Fresh Chinese wheat-flour
noodles freeze well and you may be able to find them
frozen at Chinese groceries.

Dried Noodles Our general advice in buying Italian pasta is: choose dried over fresh. The choice is not that clear when it comes to Chinese wheat-flour noodles. The fresh ones are made by people who know what they're doing and they're generally excellent. The dried ones usually don't have the spring, the resiliency, of the fresh product. But don't fret; if you can't find fresh, buy dried. They are also consistently good and are delicious in soups. Remember that you'll have to cook them longer than fresh noodles in boiling water.

RICE FLOUR

Fresh Noodles Made from ground rice and water, these may be our favourite Chinese noodles. Pearly white, glistening, slightly gummy (but in a pleasing way), slippery as can be, they are sometimes called sha he fen, meaning 'rice noodle from Sha He,' the Chinese town most famous for fresh rice-flour noodle production. They are vastly different in taste and texture from wheat-flour noodles. When cut very thin, like angel hair, they are called *mei fun*; one of our favourite Chinatown dishes is mei fun noodles stir-fried with prawns. When cut thicker, like pappardelle (about 2 cm (¾ in) wide), they are called *hor fun* or *chow fun*; the latter is the name usually used for the great Chinatown dish of quickly stir-fried noodles with meat, vegetable or fish. For mei fun and chow fun dishes, the noodles only need a brief stir-fry; no preliminary boil is necessary. When cut very wide, into wrappers about 7.5 cm (3 in) square, they are rolled around prawns, beef or other fillings, steamed and offered from the dim sum trolley.

Dried Noodles When Chinese manufacturers dry rice-flour noodles, they obtain a different product altogether. If the noodles are to be used in soups or stir-fries (for which you would initially soak them in warm water until softened), they just don't have the same glisten and chew. However, they do perform one trick that is unique. If you don't soak them, but toss them in deep oil at about 190°C (375°F), they instantly 'explode' in the oil, puffing up to 4 to 5 times their original volume. This makes a great base for saucy, stir-fried dishes.

BEAN FLOUR

Also called *fen si,* or *sai fun,* these long, thin vermicelli-type noodles look and feel like clear plastic. They are made from a paste of water and mung bean flour (yes, these are the beans that also yield the common bean sprouts). They are sometimes referred to as cellophane or transparent or slippery noodles. Though they have very little taste of their own, these noodles take on new life when tossed with strong spices or peppers in Chinese stir-fries and soups. They will keep their texture better if, rather than boiling them, you soak them in warm water before using them.

JAPANESE NOODLES

BUCKWHEAT

Soba These are thin, grey-brown buckwheat noodles with a slightly granular, rustic texture and a mild but distinctive flavour . They have tremendous cachet in Japan. Soba can be made with 100 per cent buckwheat or a combination of buckwheat and unbleached white flour. There are many varieties of soba available including *ito soba* (40 per cent buckwheat), *cha soba* (a beautiful green soba made with green tea powder), *yomogi soba* (with dried mugwort leaves), just to name a few. Soba noodles can be either fresh or dried. The noodles are often served in a bowl of hot stock along with vegetables, fish, or meat (this is called *kake-soba*). Then, of course, there's the almost ritualistic high-end soba restaurants, where the noodles are ceremoniously presented in a bamboo serving box, alongside a dipping sauce; soba may be served in this style (called *mori-soba*) either hot or cold. The best restaurants use only hand-kneaded soba (called *te-uchi*), which has a rougher, more rustic texture than machine-kneaded soba.

REGULAR WHEAT

Somen Long, thin and fragile white noodles made from hard wheat flour, oil and water. The very versatile and light somen is traditionally served in cold dishes. They are usually sold dried.

Hiyamugi Thin white noodles similar to somen. Hiyamugi are usually sold dried and are often served in a variety of cold dishes.

Udon Very long, cream-coloured noodles that look like thick linguine. Udon have an extremely mild taste and a slippery texture. They are made from 100 percent whole wheat flour or a combination of whole wheat and unbleached white flour. They are often used as a noodle for stock or served cold with a dipping sauce. Brown rice udon (a combination of rice and wheat flour) is also available. Kishimen is a wider, thicker variety of udon and can be used as a substitute, when available, in any traditional udon recipe or dish.

THAI NOODLES

RICE FLOUR

Generically called *guay tiaw,* these noodles, cut into various thicknesses, can be either fresh or dried; they are used extensively in Thai soups, sautés, salads and noodle dishes.

Sen Yaai (*sen* means 'strands' and *yaai* means 'big'). These are very much like the Chinese chow fun noodle and are used in similar ways (as in stir-fries with meats and/or vegetables). They are always fresh or frozen.

Sen Lek (*lek* means 'small'). These are thinner than sen yaai, about 3mm (⅛ in) thick (something like fettuccine in size). They differ in another way as well: though the name refers to either fresh or dried noodles, they are most often found dried, both here and in Thailand. Dried sen lek are the noodles to use in pad thai (see page 153), one of the most popular dishes in Thai restaurants in America. Soak sen lek in warm water for 15 to 20 minutes before using.

Sen Mee (*mee* means 'fine'). These are the thinnest rice noodles of all. They are also known as rice stick or rice vermicelli. They are never sold fresh, always in a dried, wiry mass. If you soak them for 15 minutes, you can use them in stir-fries or salads. Most excitingly, if you drop them into a deep-fryer of hot oil they puff up, virtually explode, quadrupling in volume almost instantly; this treatment is the basis of the popular Thai dish mee krob (see page 154).

Khanom Chine This is another type of fresh rice-flour noodle, traditionally served with Thai curries or various hot sauces. They are very thin, resembling angel hair pasta. Unfortunately, khanom chine noodles are almost impossible to find outside of Thailand.

WHEAT FLOUR AND EGG

Called *ba mee,* these are used less extensively in Thai cooking than they are in Chinese cooking. They are usually found fresh, but sometimes they are sold dried (then they're called *mee sua*). The fresh ones can be cooked in boiling water for 10 to 15 seconds, then used in soups or stir-fries. Or the fresh ones can be deep-fried for a crunchy noodle that forms a base on a platter for stir-fries.

DRIED BEAN FLOUR

Also called woon sen, silver, glass or shining noodles, these are made from mung bean flour and water. They are white before cooking but translucent, almost clear, after they've soaked in room temperature water for 15 to 20 minutes. In cold Thai salads, their bland taste and slippery texture provide a perfect canvas for hot spices and southeast Asian flavours. They can also be stir-fried, but they can get a little gooey in the wok.

THREE THAI NOODLE DISHES

Of all the great Asian noodle traditions Americans have discovered over the last 20 years, none has had as much impact as the Thai tradition. Such dishes as pad thai and mee krob became instant restaurant classics; now, with the simple recipes presented here, they can be classics in your kitchen as well.

THAI-STYLE NOODLES WITH PEANUT AND CUCUMBER SAUCE

MAKES 4 APPETISERS

60 ml (4 tbsp) Thai fish sauce

30 g (2 tbsp) sugar

5 g (1 tsp) finely chopped fresh hot chilli pepper

100 g (2½ oz) peeled, seeded, cucumber, cut in 1-cm (½-inch) dice

30 g (2 tbsp) shredded mint leaves plus extra leaves for garnish

15 g (1 tbsp) shredded coriander leaves plus extra leaves for garnish

1.25 g (¼ tsp) grated lime zest

15 ml (1 tbsp) fresh lime juice

30 g (2 tbsp) chopped peanuts

15 ml (1 tbsp) water

5 g (1 tsp) chopped inner core of fresh lemongrass (optional)

225 g (8 oz) dried noodles (you may use Thai sen lek, Japanese kishimen or dried Italian fettuccine)

1. Combine the first 11 ingredients in a mixing bowl. Mix well and let sit for a few minutes.

2. Drop the noodles in a pot of boiling water. When the noodles are al dente, drain them in a colander, divide them among 4 bowls and top each with a quarter of the peanut mixture. Garnish each bowl with a tablespoon or so of mixed mint and coriander leaves.

PAD THAI WITH PRAWNS

SERVES 4

225 g (8 oz) dried sen lek (flat rice noodles, 3 mm (⅛ in) thick)

90 ml (6 tbsp) water

5 ml (1 tsp) tamarind concentrate

50 g (2 oz) palm sugar*

45 ml (3 tbsp) distilled white vinegar

45 ml (3 tbsp) nam pla (Thai fish sauce)

1.25 g (¼ tsp) coarsely ground dried red chillies, or more to taste

30 g (2 tbsp) finely chopped dried shrimps

1.25 ml (¼ tsp) safflower or rapeseed oil

4 (preferably purple) shallots, chopped

3 garlic cloves, chopped

5 ml (1 tsp) shredded pickled salted radish (optional)

450 g (1 lb) large prawns, peeled and deveined

4 spring onions (green parts only), sliced very thin on diagonal

115 g (4 oz) peanuts, roasted and chopped

225 g (8 oz) fresh bean sprouts

50 g (2 oz) chopped coriander plus fresh coriander leaves and stems for garnish

2 limes, quartered lengthways

1. Soak sen lek in a large bowl in warm water to cover for 15 to 20 minutes or until softened; drain completely in a colander.

2. While noodles are soaking, bring the water to a boil in a small saucepan. Add the tamarind concentrate and stir well to blend. Add the palm sugar, vinegar, nam pla and dried red chillies and simmer for 5 minutes. Remove the pan from the heat, add dried shrimps and reserve.

*Palm sugar, which may have been the first man-made sugar, can be found in Southeast Asian groceries. It is brown in colour and suggests the flavours of the maple and caramel. The Indian sugar called jaggery is a good substitute. If you have access to neither, you can use good old brown sugar.

3. Heat oil in a large frying pan or wok over moderate heat. Stir in shallots, garlic and optional salted radish and stir-fry for 2 minutes. Raise heat to high, add the prawns and cook until prawns are just past translucent, about 1 minute. Remove prawns immediately and reserve.

4. Add palm sugar mixture to the pan in which the prawns cooked, along with the drained noodles, half of the spring onions and half of the peanuts. Cook, for 4 minutes, or until most of the liquid is evaporated. Stir in the cooked prawns and the bean sprouts and cook, stirring, for 1 minute longer. Place pad thai on a platter, toss with remaining spring onions, peanuts and the chopped coriander. Arrange coriander leaves and lime quarters over and around the dish. Serve immediately.

THAI CRISP-FRIED NOODLES WITH CRAB, PORK AND BEAN SPROUTS (MEE KROB)

SERVES 8

485 ml (17 fl oz) vegetable oil

1 medium onion, finely chopped

3 cloves garlic, finely chopped

6 dried Chinese mushrooms, soaked in warm water and sliced

1 green chilli, seeded and chopped

20 ml (1½ tbsp) thin soy sauce

juice of 1½ limes

20 ml (1½ tbsp) dark Chinese vinegar

60 g (2¼ oz) sugar

25 ml (5 tsp) fish sauce

45 ml (3 tbsp) tomato paste

1 egg

1.25 ml (¼ tsp) sesame oil

115 g (4 oz) finely shredded pork

4 spring onions, cut into shreds

225 g (8 oz) mung bean sprouts

115 g (4 oz) crabmeat

115 g (4 oz) sen mee (very thin dried rice noodle)

1. Place 20 ml (1½ tbsp) of the oil in a heavy saucepan over moderately high heat. Add the onion, garlic, dried mushrooms and chilli. Sauté about 5 minutes, or until the onion is lightly browned.

2. Add soy sauce, lime juice, Chinese vinegar, all but 1.25 ml (¼ tsp) of the sugar, 30 ml (2 tbsp) of fish sauce and the tomato paste. Bring mixture to a boil, remove from heat and reserve.

3. In a small bowl, beat the egg with the rest of the fish sauce and the sesame oil. Pour into a wide non-stick frying pan set over low heat and tilt the frying pan until a wide, thin omelette is formed. Cook the egg for about 10 minutes, turning several times, until it's dry and firm. Remove egg from frying pan, roll up and cut into thin 3-mm (¼-in) strips. Reserve.

4. Place 15 ml (1 tbsp) oil in a wok over high heat. Add the pork and stir-fry for 2 minutes. Add the spring onions, bean sprouts, crabmeat and reserved strips of egg. Sprinkle the mixture with the rest of the sugar. Stir-fry 30 seconds, remove and reserve.

5. When ready to serve, heat the rest of the oil in a deep-fryer or a wok. Tear the sen mee into halves (it's easiest to do this in a large shopping bag). When the oil reaches 190°C (375°F), put one eighth of the noodles in the oil; within a few seconds, they will puff up. Turn noodles over once and remove. They should be golden. Repeat with remaining noodles. Place the cooked noodles on paper towels on a baking pan and keep warm in 100°C (200°F) oven.

6. When all of the noodles are cooked, place one eighth of them on a serving platter. Heat the bean sprout mixture. Spread one eighth of the bean sprout mixture evenly over the noodles. Continue with eighths until all of the noodles and all of the bean sprout mixture are used. Heat sauce, pour it over the mee krob and mix together gently to distribute the sauce. Serve.

VEGETABLES

NO CATEGORY OF FOOD PRODUCT—NOT MEAT, NOT FISH, NOT FRUIT, NOT CHEESE—WAS ROCKED AS MUCH BY THE AMERICAN GASTRONOMIC REVOLUTION OF THE EIGHTIES AND NINETIES AS WERE VEGETABLES. IN A MERE TWO DECADES, 'VEGGIES' WENT FROM LIMP, SORRY, GREY-GREEN CULINARY MARGINALIA TO, IN MANY CASES, THE MOST EXCITING AND, SOMETIMES, THE MOST SOUGHT-AFTER COMPONENTS OF THE AMERICAN DINING EXPERIENCE.

THERE IS A WELTER OF EXPLANATIONS FOR THIS STARTLING REVERSAL.

MOST IMPORTANT, PERHAPS, HAS BEEN THE GROWING AMERICAN OBSESSION WITH HEALTH OVER THE LAST 20 YEARS. MEAT, SO LONG THE DOMINANT PART OF ANY AMERICAN MEAL, INCREASINGLY GOT PUSHED AWAY FROM 'THE CENTRE OF THE PLATE' AS MORE AMERICANS SOUGHT LIGHTER, MORE HEALTHFUL ALTERNATIVES. FOR MANY OF THESE DINERS, MEAT BECAME THE MAIN COURSE ONLY ON SPECIAL DAYS, WHILE VEGETABLES BECAME THE CENTRAL ATTRACTION ON MOST DAYS. FOR SOME OF THEM, VEGETABLES BECAME THE DAY-IN, DAY-OUT FARE.

THEN, TOO, CAME AN ADVANCE IN KNOW-HOW CONCERNING VEGETABLE COOKERY. THROUGH A BETTER UNDERSTANDING OF FRENCH TECHNIQUE AND A GROWING AWARENESS OF QUICK CHINESE COOKING METHODS, WE RELEGATED THE SADLY OVERCOOKED (AND FLAVOURLESS) VEGETABLE TO HISTORY.

THIS GENERAL SENSITIVITY TO COOKING VEGETABLES PROPERLY WAS BOLSTERED BY SPECIFIC DISHES THAT STARTED TO FLOOD IN FROM VARIOUS ETHNIC CUISINES. ONCE, 'FOREIGN' CUISINE HAD MEANT FRENCH—AND FANCY FRENCH AT THAT, WITH ITS EMPHASIS ON IMPRESSIVE MAIN-COURSE MEAT DISHES. IN THE EIGHTIES AND NINETIES, OUR CULINARY COMPASS SPUN TOWARD THE CUISINES OF 'POORER' NATIONS—WHICH ALMOST ALWAYS DE-EMPHASISED MEAT AND PAID GREATER ATTENTION TO VEGETABLES. FROM THE VEGETABLE CURRIES OF SOUTHERN INDIA TO THE BRIGHT-GREEN STIR-FRIES OF CHINA, TO THE CHILLI-AND-SWEETCORN CUISINE OF MEXICO, THE EXCITEMENT OF SPECIFIC DISHES CAUSED VEGETABLES TO TAKE SEVERAL GIANT STEPS FORWARD IN THE AMERICAN CULINARY IMAGINATION.

COMMERCE FOLLOWS TASTE IN AMERICA—AND TOP AMERICAN CHEFS SOON FOUND THAT VEGETABLES WERE BIG BUSINESS. SOME MAINSTREAM CALIFORNIA RESTAURATEURS REPORTED THAT AS MANY AS A THIRD OF THEIR CUSTOMERS ORDERED ONLY VEGETABLES. CREATIVE AMERICAN CHEFS ROSE TO THE CHALLENGE. SOON, CHEFS OF THE DAVID BOULEY/CHARLIE TROTTER STATURE WERE OFFERING COMPLETE *MENUS DÉGUSTATIONS* DEVOTED TO VEGETABLES ONLY.

OF COURSE, THESE CHEFS WERE ALSO INSPIRED BY THE INCREASING AVAILABILITY OF *GREAT* VEGETABLES. MANY CHEFS, LIKE ALICE WATERS OF CHEZ PANISSE IN BERKELEY, STARTED MAKING ARRANGEMENTS WITH FARMERS

TO GROW HIGH-QUALITY PRODUCE. SOON QUALITY WAS EXCEEDED ONLY BY VARIETY. THINGS NEVER GROWN BEFORE IN THIS COUNTRY (LIKE RADICCHIO AND LEMONGRASS) STARTED TO SPROUT IN AMERICAN FIELDS AND GARDENS. VEGETABLE VARIETIES NOT GROWN HERE FOR YEARS (LIKE OLDER, IRREGULARLY SHAPED TOMATO VARIETIES)—NOW GROUPED UNDER THE RUBRIC 'HEIRLOOM VARIETIES'—ROARED BACK.

MOST HAPPILY, THESE ADVANCES AFFECTED NOT ONLY OUR RESTAURANT CHEFS. FARMERS' MARKETS SPRANG UP AROUND THE COUNTRY, OFFERING NEW MARVELS TO ANY AMATEUR CHEF WILLING TO WANDER FROM STALL TO STALL. SPECIALTY GROCERIES GOT INTO THE ACT. AT ABOUT THE SAME TIME THAT ALICE WATERS WAS MAKING ARRANGEMENTS WITH FARMERS IN CALIFORNIA, WE WERE MAKING THE SAME ARRANGEMENTS WITH FARMERS ON THE EAST COAST. FURTHERMORE, THE SUPERMARKETS STARTED TO FEEL THE PRESSURE—AND THE RESULT TODAY IN SUPERMARKETS ACROSS AMERICA IS A DISPLAY OF PRODUCE THAT FOR QUALITY AND VARIETY MAKES THE TYPICAL SUPERMARKET FRUIT AND VEGETABLE SECTION OF THE SIXTIES LOOK LIKE A RAILWAY STATION IN SIBERIA.

AMERICA HAS INDEED BEEN GREENED AND OUR LIVES ARE BETTER FOR IT.

ABOUT GRILLING VEGETABLES

Of all the methods of vegetable cooking that Americans have embraced over the last 20 years, grilling is undoubtedly number one. It's hard to find a trendy American restaurant today that doesn't offer an assortment of grilled vegetables as a main course— and, come summer, many backyard barbecues once devoted to sirloin now give equal time to peppers and aubergines.

It may just be the meat connection that explains this grilling phenomenon. Steamed vegetables don't always satisfy reformed meat-eaters—but when the veggies come off the grill, as browned and smoky as fillet steak, the transition from full-time carnivore to sometime herbivore is eased. Cooked on a grill, vegetables seem meaty. Just as grilling forms a delicious crust on the outside of a steak, so does grilling improve the exterior of a vegetable slice—maybe even more so than a steak, because the sugar content of vegetables creates a luscious exterior caramelisation.

Unfortunately, it's not as easy to cook vegetables on a grill as it is steak. Two large problems recur in vegetable grill platters: first, the vegetables are unpleasantly charred on the outside, while still underdone on the inside, because the heat is too high; second, before the vegetables are cooked on the inside, they become irrevocably dry and tough on the outside, because the heat is too low.

Grilled vegetable recipes

For more delicious ways to serve grilled vegetables, see the recipes for smoked mozzarella salad with grilled red peppers on page 12, grilled aubergine with fresh mint and balsamic vinegar on page 20 and grilled Japanese aubergine with orange-sesame miso sauce, page 177.

Now grilling is *always* much more of an intuitive art than a prescriptive science and getting the heat right is always the trickiest part for grillers. But grilling vegetables brings another set of problems, for each vegetable has its own requirements. Many a grilled vegetable plate has been ruined by a thoughtless chef who threw every vegetable in exactly the same condition on exactly the same fire.

Dividing the vegetable kingdom into three parts will improve your vegetable grilling immediately.

1. Vegetables that need only be sliced and grilled

There aren't many in this category; most vegetables are better with some sort of pre-grill treatment. But the glory of late summer—rich, ripe, red tomatoes—can be cut in slices and placed directly over a hot fire. Cook until grilled on the outside, still intact on the inside (5 to 8 minutes, turning once, should do the trick). Tomatillos, which take a little longer to cook, can be given the same treatment.

2. Vegetables that need to be coated with oil before grilling

Many vegetables will turn dry and hard on the outside without pre-grill treatment. One of the best ways to treat them is to brush them with olive oil or even better, to marinate them for an hour or so in olive oil mixed with chopped garlic and herbs. The leading contenders for this treatment are asparagus, Belgian endive, leeks (cut in half lengthways), mushrooms, onions, radicchio, spring onions (left whole), and courgettes. Moderately high heat works best for this group.

3. Vegetables that need to be parboiled and oiled before grilling

Some vegetables are particularly susceptible to drying out on the grill. Therefore, we recommend boiling them part-way before grilling. Aubergine is tricky; sometimes it just turns to cardboard on a grill. But if you cut it into

1-cm (⅓-in) slices, simmer them for a moment in water, brush the slices with olive oil, then place the slices over a hot fire, you'll get perfect aubergine every time. Artichokes, too, so delicious on the grill, are not reliable without parboiling; remove many of the leaves, leaving behind the heart with a small crown of leaves around it, poach for 15 minutes, cut in half lengthways, oil and grill over a moderately hot fire. Potatoes and sweet potatoes must be precooked even more; boil them until two-thirds done, oil them, then place on a hot barbecue until browned and tender.

For most of these vegetables, slices about 1 cm (½ in) thick grill best.

The special case of grilled corn-on-the-cob

We are corn-on-the-cob purists, longtime lovers of simply boiled corn . . . but we recognise the charms of grilled corn, with its delicious smokiness and caramelisation. How to do it best, however, is controversial.

Some backyard chefs place whole ears, unhusked, right on the barbecue. This essentially steams the corn, without giving it much smoky grill flavour.

Some cooks like to pull the husk back, remove the corn silk, then re-cloak the ear in its husk, tying the bundle up with a few strands of silk. This gives the same steamed, unsmoky result—but corn cooked without its silk yields less flavour.

Lastly, corn kernels can be directly exposed to fire. Placing the husked ears right over the fire chars the kernels and gives them the full flavour of the grill. But, if the fire's too hot the charring can be excessive and this detracts from the corn flavour. Some chefs like to soak the corn in water or milk for half an hour before putting it on the grill, a good way to retard the char effect.

Our favourite solution is to wrap each husked ear in a slice of bacon. Simply wind the bacon around the ear, attach it with a toothpick then barbecue the corn (as you would any corn) over a moderately hot fire for about 20

minutes. The bacon bastes the corn and serves as a partial anti-char barrier to the fire—but not enough to prevent the corn from picking up a rich, smoky taste.

GRILLED AUBERGINE WITH YOGURT SAUCE

Another way to prevent aubergine from drying out on the grill is to pre-bake it whole. Slicing it and finishing it on the grill gives it a wonderful, smoky flavour. This recipe makes a great appetiser—or, along with pitta, rice and salad, a great main course.

SERVES 4 AS A FIRST COURSE

For the aubergine
2 aubergines (each about 350 g (1½ lb))
salt and pepper to taste
olive oil for brushing
25 g (2 tbsp) chopped fresh parsley
25 g (2 tbsp) chopped fresh dill
For the yogurt sauce
225 ml (8 fl oz) plain yogurt
50 g (2 oz) chopped cucumber
50 g (2 oz) chopped tomato
1 shallot, chopped
15 g (1 tbsp) finely chopped fresh parsley
15 g (1 tbsp) finely chopped fresh dill
salt and pepper to taste

1. *Make the aubergine:* Preheat oven to 200°C (400°F). Wash the aubergines and pierce each one a dozen times with a fork. Place in the oven and cook until just tender, about 30 minutes. (The aubergines should be slightly wrinkled, smaller and slightly browned.) Remove and cool.

2. When ready to serve, heat the grill. Cut off the aubergine stems, then make thick, diagonal aubergine slices. They should be about 2 cm (¾ in) thick each and there should be about 6 from each aubergine.

3. Season the aubergine slices with salt and pepper and

brush with a little olive oil. When the grill is hot, place on grill and cook for about 5 minutes per side, or until the slices are nicely browned. Arrange in single layer on platter and sprinkle with the parsley and dill.

4. *Make yogurt sauce:* Mix all of the ingredients together in a bowl. Serve over the aubergine slices or on the side.

The grilled vegetable champ: sweet peppers

We'd guess that of all the vegetables being grilled in this country on the smoky altar of more healthful eating, the pepper is the single type grilled most often. Besides its frequent appearance on the assorted grilled vegetable plate, the grilled (or roasted) pepper, peeled of its charred exterior, finds its way into innumerable modern salads, sandwiches and cooked dishes. It truly is a great ingredient to have on hand for improvisation; smoky, sweet, intensely flavoured, it enlivens virtually any dish it joins.

You don't even need a barbecue to make it. You can place whole peppers under an oven grill and, after turning them frequently, you will have peppers that are charred on the outside in 10 to 15 minutes. But because the cooking takes so long, the peppers cook too much, turn soft, lose their crunch.

A better method, if you have a gas range, is to cook them over the open fire of your range. Simply stick a fork in the stem end of each pepper, then place the peppers over the jets on high. Turn frequently; they should be charred in 5 to 7 minutes and crunchier than the grilled peppers.

Best of all, of course, is a hot, smoky charcoal fire. With this method, you get both quick cooking *and* the flavour of the grill. Simply turn the peppers with tongs until charred on all sides. If the fire's very hot, this will take less than 5 minutes.

Whichever method you use, the peppers must be peeled after charring. Before doing this, first place them in a paper or plastic bag (off the grill), seal and let them rest for 15 minutes. The steam that's created will separate the charred skin from the flesh. Remove peppers from the bag and slide the charred skin off with your fingers. Cardinal rule: *Do not wash the peppers!* Many cooks do this to 'clean' them thoroughly of the charred skin, but this 'cleans' away the oils and flavour as well. Better to have a bit of black than a lack of flavour. Stem and seed the peppers and you're ready.

One perennial favourite of ours is marinated grilled peppers: cut the prepared peppers in broad slices, toss them with olive oil, chopped garlic, herbs, salt and pepper and let them marinate for a few hours. Serve the marinated peppers on bruschetta. Simple and sublime.

THE MODERN VEGETABLE ROLL CALL

Here are some of the vegetables, both old and new, that have come to be very widely used in the eighties and nineties by restaurant chefs and home cooks. They also happen to be among our favourites.

AVOCADO

As Mexican restaurants became hot in the eighties, the avocado, once a sometime kind of thing in the supermarket, achieved new popularity. This ancient Aztec fruit (they called it *ahuacatl*) was suddenly in demand—for its buttery texture and subtle nutty taste. But the avocado presents a problem for cooks, because it turns bitter when exposed to heat. If you've got creative salad and/or cold soup plans, look for the Haas avocado; that's the smallish one with the dark, nubbly skin. The large green ones seem watery by comparison, with less flavour.

GUACAMOLE

This Mexican staple has now become an American staple. But all too often, north of the border, it's badly made. What we particularly dislike is mashed-to-death guacamole, where the avocado becomes a purée, without texture. In the following terrific version, the avocado is cut into coarse chunks and then gently folded into a flavourful purée. Serve with tortilla chips and margaritas, just as you normally would.

MAKES ENOUGH GUACAMOLE TO SATISFY 6 TO 8 CHIP-
WIELDING, TEQUILA-IMBIBING DINERS

50 g (2 oz) chopped onion
2 to 4 jalapeño chillies (depending on your heat
   tolerance), seeded
2 tomatillos (green tomatoes), quartered
juice of 1 lime plus a little additional for drizzling
   the avocados
¼ cup fresh coriander plus additional forgarnish
5 large Haas avocados
salt and pepper to taste

1. Place onions, jalapeños, tomatillos, juice of 1 lime and coriander leaves in a food processor. Purée.

2. Peel and stone the avocados. Cut the flesh into coarse chunks, drizzling the avocados with the additional lime juice while cutting to prevent them from discolouring. Toss avocado chunks very gently in a large bowl with the tomatillo purée. Season to taste with salt and pepper. The guacamole may be served immediately, but it will develop more flavour if it is kept, covered with plastic wrap, for 1 to 2 hours in the refrigerator. Garnish with the additional coriander leaves just before serving.

BEETROOT

Beetroot once meant sweet, overcooked slices out of a can or jar. But American chefs have now discovered the wonderful taste of fresh beetroot and have found all kinds of new and traditional ways to cook and present them. They're delicious when simply boiled. Don't peel them before cooking or cut the roots too close to the beetroot or they will 'bleed' into the water. They're also terrific when roasted or grilled. Yellow baby beetroot have become something of a passion in New American restaurants. They are wonderful when simply boiled, peeled, cut in half and tossed into a New Wave salad creation.

PUGLIESE BEETROOT SALAD WITH FRESH MINT

We were served this marvellous combination of flavours in Puglia, where restaurant meals always begin with more than a dozen vegetable dishes. Now, we're seeing salads like it at lots of new Italian restaurants in America. The flavour of beetroot and fresh mint together is simply sensational.

SERVES 6 TO 8 AS A SIDE DISH

900 g (2 lb) beetroot (weigh after removing roots
   and tops), unpeeled
20 ml (4 tsp) red-wine vinegar
5 ml (1 tsp) lemon juice
50 ml (2 fl oz) extra-virgin olive oil
10g (2 tsp) coarse salt
5g (1 tsp) freshly ground black pepper
50 g (2 oz) shredded fresh mint

1. Bring a large pot of salted water to a boil and cook beetroot until fork tender, about 30 minutes for small beetroot. Remove from water and set aside until cool enough to handle. Slip off skins and cut beetroot into 5-mm (¼-in) slices.

2. Whisk vinegar, lemon juice, olive oil, coarse salt and pepper together in a large bowl. Add beetroot and toss thoroughly. Gently fold mint into beetroot. Adjust seasoning and serve at room temperature.

CHARCOAL-ROASTED BEETROOT AND RED ONIONS

The flavour of these smoky roasted beetroot is spectacularly concentrated. Serve them warm as a side dish; they're rather high in natural sweetness and make a good accompaniment to duck, goose or pork.

SERVES 4 AS A SIDE DISH

6 small fresh unpeeled beetroot (about 550 g
   (1¼ lb) trimmed weight), trimmed of all but 2.5
   cm (1 in) of greens and unpeeled
2 medium red onions, unpeeled

30ml (2 tbsp) extra-virgin olive oil
100 ml (3½ fl oz) chicken stock
45 ml (3 tbsp) balsamic vinegar
7 g (1½ tsp) fresh thyme leaves
salt and pepper to taste

1. Prepare a moderately hot charcoal fire in a barbecue unit that has a cover. Place the beetroot and red onions in a 25-cm (10-in) cast-iron frying pan and drizzle with the olive oil. Place the frying pan over the fire, cover the grill unit and roast the vegetables at least 1 to 1½ hours, depending on the size of the vegetables. (You may have to leave the beetroot in a little longer than the onions. The onions should be soft to the touch and a fork should pierce the beetroot easily. Alternatively, you can roast the beetroot in the frying pan in a 200°C (400°F) oven).

2. Remove the vegetables from the frying pan with tongs. Add the stock, balsamic vinegar and 1 tsp thyme to the frying pan, place over high heat and boil the liquid, scraping the bottom of the pan, for about 4 minutes, or until dark, glossy brown and syrupy. Season with salt and pepper.

3. Peel the beetroot and onions when they're cool enough to handle. Slice the beetroot into julienne strips and the onions into thin rings. Spoon the liquid over the onions and beetroot, add the rest of the thyme and stir well to combine. Heat briefly and serve.

CABBAGE

If ever a vegetable had low-class status, it was the cabbage. But a funny thing happened on the way to the sauerkraut factory. Suddenly, in the seventies and eighties, top chefs in France began juxtaposing low-born and high-born ingredients—which meant that a lot of cabbage got served with lobster and foie gras and a lot of people started looking at cabbage in a new way. Along came the glorification of traditional peasant food in the late eighties—and cabbage, that perennial second-class citizen, was suddenly popular, even

glamorous. It is important, of course, to buy good cabbage (avoid dried-out heads), to cook green cabbage a relatively short amount of time (to prevent that stinky cabbage smell from invading your home) and to be creative in your cabbage cookery.

ITALIAN-STYLE CABBAGE WITH TOMATOES AND PECORINO ROMANO

People often think first of Germanic and eastern European traditions when it comes to cabbage. But cabbage is widely used elsewhere. There are many delicious cabbage dishes throughout Italy, for example, and diners are sometimes surprised to discover that cabbage and tomatoes go extremely well together. This robust side dish is a fabulous accompaniment to meats that have been marinated in a Mediterranean fashion and grilled. We like to use our favourite cooking cabbage for this dish—savoy cabbage, which, with its pretty curls and lacy patterns, seems lighter, less 'cabbage-y' than ordinary cabbage.

SERVES 4 AS A SIDE DISH

450 g (1 lb) savoy cabbage
45 ml (3 tbsp) olive oil
1 large onion, halved and cut into very thin rings
2 large garlic cloves, chopped
6 canned Italian plum tomatoes
125 ml (4 fl oz) tomato liquid from the can, or
   chicken stock, or beef stock
30 ml (2 tbsp) red-wine vinegar
5 g (1 tsp) dried thyme
salt and pepper to taste
15 g (½ oz) butter
pecorino Romano for grating

1. Remove the core of the cabbage and cut the remaining cabbage into 5-mm (¼-in) strips.

2. Place the olive oil in a large sauté pan or casserole over high heat. Add the onion rings and sauté until they start to soften and brown. Add the cabbage and garlic, stirring to blend well. Crush the tomatoes with your hands over the cabbage and add them to the pan. Add the tomato liquid (or stock), vinegar and thyme. Season well with salt and lots of freshly ground black pepper. Bring mixture to a boil, reduce heat and cook, covered, for 30 minutes, or until cabbage is softened and flavours are blended.

3. When ready to serve, stir butter into the cabbage. Place on plates and pass pecorino Romano for grating over the dish.

ALSATIAN-STYLE RED CABBAGE WITH RED WINE AND RED APPLES

There are two major schools of red-cabbage-cooking: quick-cooking to keep the cabbage crunchy and long-cooking to develop maximum flavour. Because red cabbage does not turn 'stinky' after long cooking, as green cabbage does, we favour the latter method. To keep things fresh-tasting, the cabbage is cooked with acidic ingredients; this also helps retain colour. The sweet apple added late in the game provides a delightful taste and texture contrast in this dish; it is terrific with roast pork, roast duck or roast goose.

SERVES 8 AS A SIDE DISH

2 heads of red cabbage (350 g (1½ lb) each)
4 Red Delicious or other dessert apples
2 lemons
1 litre (1¾ pints) dry red wine
3 medium-large onions
50 g (2 oz) unsalted butter
50 g (2 oz) sugar
225 ml (8 fl oz) red-wine vinegar
4 coriander seeds
5 g (1 tsp) freshly grated nutmeg
5 g (1 tsp) ground cinnamon
5 g (1 tsp) dried thyme
salt and pepper to taste

finely chopped fresh parsley for garnish

1. Cut the cabbages in half lengthways. Remove the cores and slice cabbages in thin strips. Peel the apples, cut them in quarters, core them and rub them with 1 lemon, quartered. Reserve apple quarters. Put the peels and cores of the apples in a saucepan with the red wine and bring to a boil. Boil for 1 minute, remove from heat and reserve.

2. Peel the onions and slice thinly. Melt 25 g (1 oz) of the butter in a large, heavy stew pot over high heat. Add the sliced onion and the sugar, stirring well. Sauté, stirring, for about 15 minutes, or until the onion is dark brown but not burned. Add the sliced red cabbage and cook until softened, about 5 minutes. Add the vinegar and cook until dry, about 5 minutes.

3. Pour the red wine through a strainer over the cabbage. Bring to a boil. Add the coriander, nutmeg, cinnamon, thyme and the juice of the remaining lemon. Taste for seasoning. Cover and bake in a 180°C (350°F) oven for 1½ hours. (Check once or twice to make sure the cabbage doesn't stick to the bottom of the pan.)

4. When the cabbage is almost done, cut the reserved apple quarters into 4 slices per quarter. Place the rest of the butter in a frying pan over high heat. When the sizzling stops, add the apple slices. Cook for a few minutes, or until the apples are nicely browned on the outside and just tender inside.

5. Remove cabbage from oven and toss with cooked apples. Season to taste with salt and pepper, sprinkle with parsley and serve immediately.

CHILLIES
> *Sin el chili los mexicanos no creen que están comiendo.* (Without chillies, Mexicans don't believe they're eating.)
> —Fray Bartolomé de las Casas, 16th century

And this may apply as well to many Americans in the latter portion of the twentieth century, who have accepted chillies in a very big way. Chillies, once a purely local phenomenon, have exploded across the United States in the last two decades. They are used by restaurant chefs and home cooks for South-western and Mexican dishes, to be sure—but they are also used increasingly in a wide range of creative international dishes. This is why even the average supermarket today boasts at least half a dozen chilli varieties; speciality shops such as ours, of course, feature many more.

FRESH CHILLIES

A simple way to use fresh chillies is to chop them, along with other flavouring agents (like garlic and onions), and then sauté them all as a base for soups, stews and sauces; this mixture is known as a *sofrito.* Hot chillies are great in salsas and milder ones may be sliced into chunks and used in stews, or stir-fried in Asian dishes (jalapeños and beef are particularly good together). Whole ones are fabulous for stuffing. However you use fresh chillies, make sure to remove the seeds and the ribs that the seeds are attached to; these are the hottest parts of the chilli. Then, make sure to wash your hands afterwards. Here are some of the varieties you're most likely to find today.

Anaheim These long, summer-green chillies—15-20 cm (6-8 in) in length—are called *chile chilaca* in southern Mexico and *chile verde* in northern Mexico. They have a wonderful vegetable flavour, can be mild to medium-hot and are excellent when roasted and added to stews or soups.

Banana (Hungarian Wax) Yellow-green, thin-skinned chillies which are about 10-12 cm (4-5 in) long. They are medium-hot with a sweet chilli flavour and are similar to the Mexican variety called *chiles largos.* They are particularly good in fish dishes, like seviche.

Cachucha Also called *Rocotillo,* these delicate little chillies (about 2.5 x 2.5 cm (1 x 1 in)) come in shades of orange, yellow and red—and can be very hot, though not nearly as hot as their habañero and Scotch bonnet cousins. Because of their fruity flavour, we use them to spice up Caribbean-style fish dishes and sweeter salsas. They are very popular in Cuban cooking.

Cayenne Long, twisted red or green chillies which taper to a point, cayennes are very hot and have a slightly sweet flavour.

Dutch Red A familiar-looking chilli with its long, smooth, curved shape and fire-engine-red colour. These peppers, also known as Holland chillies, are great for roasting and adding to sauces or salsas; they are also fine for pickling. They are medium-hot, but some can be hotter.

Habañero Originally from Brazil, these super-hot chillies are slightly larger than Scotch bonnets and come in a rainbow of colours. Be extremely careful and judicious with these. We really love experimenting with the tropical fruit flavours of the riper ones. Just in case, it helps to have a tall glass of milk close by (dairy products are your best palate-extinguishers).

Jalapeño Especially good pickled *en escabeche,* these chillies are an American favourite. Short and cone-shaped, red or green, jalapeños are relatively tame and have mild vegetable tones (the red jalapeño is a bit sweeter). We like roasting them and adding them to meaty, cheesy dishes, or frying them and adding them to tomato sauces.

Poblano Poblano chillies are named for the area around Puebla, Mexico and are one of the oldest chillies indigenous to Mexico. Also called *chile para rellenar,* or chilli for stuffing, this is a large chilli, usually 13 x 7.5 cm (5 x 3 in), with a beautiful dark, forest-green colour. The poblano is one of the most popular chillies in Mexico and one of our favourites too. A mild chilli (with an occasional, fiery surprise), the large, full poblano (it looks something like a slightly stunted sweet pepper, though darker) is most often used in chiles rellenos and in moles or other sauces. Roasted, poblanos have a wonderfully smooth, smoky flavour.

Red Cherry These small, tomato-red chillies with thick skins have traditionally been available in America pickled, in jars. Increasingly, fresh ones are in our markets—with thick skin and about the size of a small tomato. We like to use these medium-hot chillies in salads and salsas.

Scotch Bonnet Closely related to habañero chillies, these small, walnut-size chillies are full of perfumy, tropical flavours. Don't let that fool you, though. The Scotch bonnet, like the habañero, is *extremely* hot. It comes in many colours, but we think the reds and dark yellows have the best flavour. They are essential in jerk sauces and are excellent in sweet, fiery salsas with tropical fruit added.

Serrano The widely available little serrano (which means 'from the mountains') is bright green or red, with smooth skin and is about 5 x 1 cm (2 x ½ in) across. With their biting, crisp heat (they're hotter than jalapeños), they are wonderful in salsa fresca combined with tomatoes, coriander and lime.

Thai (Bird *or* Bird's Eye Peppers) These tiny, long and pointed green or red chillies are Thailand's hottest chillies and are commonly used in south-east Asian cooking. We like to use them whole in Szechuan stir-fries, slivered in Thai curries and chopped in spicy cold Asian noodle dishes. If the heat of these chillies is too much for you, they also make an attractive kitchen display.

A recipe for fresh chillies, a recipe for dried chillies

CHILES RELLENOS STUFFED WITH GOAT CHEESE AND COATED WITH BEER BATTER

Almost every Tex-Mex restaurant in America offers heavy, batter-coated, cheese-stuffed poblano chillies, or chiles rellenos; it is a marvellous way to use fresh poblano chillies. We like the classic dish well enough, but think a lighter filling and a thinner coating are improvements.

MAKES 8 CHILES RELLENOS, ENOUGH FOR 4 MAIN-COURSE SERVINGS

8 large fresh poblano chillies
225 g (8 oz) mild goat cheese, at room temperature
225 g (8 oz) Monterey Jack cheese, grated
15 g (1 tbsp) chopped fresh parsley
15 g (1 tbsp) chopped fresh coriander
15 g (1 tbsp) finely chopped toasted almonds
5 g (1 tsp) chopped garlic
10 ml (2 tsp) lime juice
5 g (1 tsp) coarse salt
2.5 g (¼ tsp) freshly ground black pepper
175 g (6 oz) plain flour
250 ml (9 fl oz) beer
vegetable oil for frying
225 g (8 oz) pico de gallo (recipe on page 483)

1. Roast chillies over open flame or under broiler, turning them to colour evenly. When chillies are black, place in a paper bag, close bag and let sit for 20 minutes. Wipe charred skins off with paper towels.

2. Make a lengthways slit in each chilli, leaving the stems intact. Carefully remove and discard the seeds. Pat the chillies dry.

3. Mix together goat cheese, Jack cheese, parsley, coriander, almonds, garlic, lime juice, coarse salt and black pepper in a medium bowl until combined. Divide the cheese mixture into 8 ovals and gently place each inside a chilli. (If a chilli accidentally tears, hold it together with a toothpick.

4. Whisk together 115 g (4 oz) of the flour and the beer. (Do not overmix; lumps are acceptable.)

5. Heat the oil (it should be about 1 cm (½ in) deep) to 180°C (350°F) in a wide frying pan. When the oil is hot, dip 4 chillies in remaining flour, shaking off any excess and then dip them in the beer batter. Put them in the hot oil and when they are browned on one side, gently turn them to brown on the other side. Drain on paper towels and keep warm in a preheated 120°C (250°F) oven. Repeat with the remaining chillies.

6. Place 2 chiles rellenos on each of 4 serving plates and serve with pico de gallo.

ADOBO SAUCE

A great way to use dried chillies is to make sauce out of them; the finished product emphasises the specific flavour of whichever chillies you're using. Adobo is a confusing term in Mexican cooking; it refers, variously, to pastes for rubbing on meat, to marinades for all kinds of foods and to sauces; all of these adobos, however, usually contain chillies and vinegar. The following adobo is a sauce—good for grilled meat, chilli con carne and many other things. It features the wonderful, pruny taste of ancho chillies, along with a little smoky heat from the chipotle.

MAKES (6 FL OZ) CUP

1 dried chipotle chilli
4 dried ancho chillies
50 ml (2 fl oz) red-wine vinegar
90 ml (6 tbsp) orange juice
30 ml (2 tbsp) lime juice
50 g (2 oz) chopped yellow onion

30 g (2 tbsp) chopped garlic
100 g (2½ oz) honey, or more to taste
10 g (2 tsp) salt, or to taste

1. Roast chipotle and ancho chillies in a preheated 220°C (450°F) oven for 2 to 3 minutes, until they've puffed up slightly. Cut chillies open with scissors and remove stems and seeds. Place chillies in a bowl and cover with hot water. Let soak for 30 minutes.

2. Remove chillies, reserving the soaking liquid. Chop chillies roughly and place in a blender with 30 ml (2 tbsp) of the soaking liquid. Purée until smooth, adding more liquid if necessary.

3. Add vinegar, orange juice, lime juice, onion, garlic, honey and kosher salt to blender. Purée until smooth. Adjust seasoning and add more honey to balance the heat if the sauce is too hot.

DRIED CHILLIES

Dried chillies exhibit an almost unbelievable range in the aromas and flavours they provide; some cooks have compared chilli types to wine-grape varieties in their complexity. Dried chillies must be softened in some way before use. Some chefs simply place them in a hot cast-iron pan for a few minutes, which softens them and lends a smoky flavour. Or you can roast them in a 230°C (450°F) oven for a few minutes, until they puff up and soften. Some chefs like to soak them in hot water, remove the seeds, then purée the softened chillies with some of the water. You could also add dried chillies to soups, stews and sauces—the chillies will flavour the dish well and will soften as they cook. Here are some of the varieties you're most likely to find today.

Ancho The ancho—a dried poblano chilli—is Mexico's most popular dried chilli and the sweetest. *Ancho* means 'wide' in Spanish and because of its size it looks something like a dried apple with thick, wrinkled, brick-red/brown skin. Anchos are wonderful in traditional Mexican moles. They are medium-hot, with overtones of prunes, chocolate and coffee.

Cascabel *Cascabel* means 'jingle-bell' in Spanish and when you shake a bag of these dried peppers, you will understand why they were given the name. Dried cascabels look like large Bing cherries; they have purple-brown, smooth skin and are about the size of walnuts. They are medium to very hot—with nutty, woodsy flavours—and are used in salsas, soups and stews.

Chipotle This is perhaps the most distinctive of the dried chillies—because, in addition to being dried, it is also smoked over a wood fire. Jalapeños are used for this process, so the finished chipotle is 5-10 cm (2-4 in) long and 2.5 cm (1 in) across, with a ridged chocolate-brown skin. Chipotles are wonderful—smoky and hot—and their uses are many; they have become the chilli darling of many New American chefs. They are usually dried, but they are also packed in cans, in an adobo sauce.

De Arbol Named for its appearance (*de arbol* means 'treelike'), the de arbol chilli is a brilliant brick red, long, thin and pointed (about 7.5 cm (3 in) long and 1 cm (½ in) across). De arbol chillies have an herbal quality and are often used in powdered form in sauces and soups. They are very hot.

Guajillo About 10-15 cm (4-6 in) long with smooth, thin skin, which ranges from orange-red to black-brown, guajillos are popular chillies for use in salsas and stews. They are piney and slightly fruity and range in heat from mild to medium.

Habanero The hottest chilli pepper around! The dried form of the fresh habañero is apricot-size or a bit smaller and has wrinkled, dark red-brown skin. Use judiciously in salsas and sauces. We like to use them in tropical fruit salsas because of their fruity overtones and because heat goes well with sweet. Dried habañeros are also available smoked.

Morita The morita is a type of small jalapeño that is often smoke-dried. About 5 cm (2 in) long with a thin, brick-red body, the morita is very hot and has a berry and plum aftertaste (the name means 'blackberry' in Spanish).

Mulato A type of dried poblano with deep rich, smoky flavours—some say tobacco and liquorice—the wrinkled, brown-black mulato is about 13 x 7.5 cm (5 x 3 in) wide. Like the ancho chilli, the mulato is an essential ingredient in mole sauces and is widely used in a variety of main course dishes.

Pasilla Translated as 'little raisin,' the pasilla chilli—also called chile negro—is named for its raisinlike aroma and shrivelled, black skin. The pasilla measures about 13-15 cm (5-6 in) long and is widely used in moles and other sauces. It is medium-hot.

Pequín Tiny, bright red chillies about the size and shape of small green olives. They are very hot and have earthy, citrusy overtones. We like to use them in flavoured oils, flavoured vinegars and spicy sauces.

CORN

The American passion for sweet corn—the official name for what most people refer to as corn-on-the-cob—is nothing new. But a couple of extremely important things have changed in the last 2 decades.

First, scientists have created new types that offer sweetness and shelf-life heretofore impossible. There are now 3 officially recognised groups of 'sweet corn':

Standard Corn This is what all corn-on-the-cob used to be, before the scientists intervened. At its best, it is wonderful: moderately sweet, with deep corn flavour and a fairly firm texture. The problem that the scientists set out to solve, of course, is that standard corn, very soon after being picked, starts converting its sugar to starch. This is why stories abound of corn-pickers setting up their pots of boiling water in the field to maximise the sweetness of their just-picked corn. Standard corn declines immediately, then goes seriously downhill after a day or two, even if it's refrigerated (which retards the deterioration a bit).

Sugary Enhancer This type of engineered corn—one of the 2 so-called 'super-sweets'—is named for the 'sugary enhancer gene' that has been added to it. The good news is this: sugary enhancer varieties are generally sweeter than standard corn varieties and can stay sweet for up to 4 days under refrigeration. That's revolutionary in the corn biz. Unfortunately, the corn flavour of sugary enhancer varieties is not as deep as the corn flavour of standard corn varieties and the kernels are soft.

Shrunken-2 The other type of 'super-sweet' on the market today also has good genes that have been manipulated in the laboratory. It is amazingly sweet— with 2 to 3 times the sugar content of standard corn. Furthermore, its texture is closer to that of standard corn and it stays sweet for up to 10 days under refrigeration; this is why you'll see it grown in the South during the winter and boldly shipped long distances across the country. Is there a problem with it? Yes . . . a big one. It's simply sweet, like confectionery, without real corn flavour.

Corn-on-the-cob in supermarkets and street markets is usually not identified by the terms 'standard corn', 'sugary enhancer' and 'shrunken-2'. But now that you know the terms, you should ask the greengrocers and stallholders to identify the type of corn you're buying.

The other great change on the corn scene has been the extent to which creative American chefs are using fresh corn in their new creations. Many chefs take corn—that mystical, ancient plant—almost as a

symbol of North American food and culture and have accordingly used it in a wide range of salads, soups, baked goods and main courses.

A trendy corn product: miniature corn

They started turning up in Asian stir-fries, those oh-so-cute whole ears of corn, not more than 5 cm (2 in) long. But they're canned and they taste watery, insipid. Great news: farmers are now harvesting some of their corn early, when it's tiny and selling it at their farm stands in early summer. Finally, baby corn that's worthy of including in a Chinese stir-fry or Thai salad.

SIMPLE CORN-ON-THE-COB

There has always been controversy about how to cook corn-on-the-cob. Some experts say put the ears in cold water, bring the water to a boil then turn the heat off (at which point the corn is ready). Others advise you to add the ears to boiling water and cook for 5 to 7 minutes. The modern school recommends a shorter cooking time; some even say that the super-sweets need hardly any time at all and recommend a 30-second dunk in boiling water. We confess this tastes raw to us.

We have one strong opinion to add to the literature: *Do not remove the husk and silk before boiling the corn.* This is heresy—but you'll be amazed at the extra corn flavour the ears pick up when they boil inside their husks. And don't worry about removing the wet silk and husks after cooking; if you let the corn cool a moment or two, silk removal is easier from wet, cooked corn than it is from dry, raw corn.

So here's our preferred method: buy just-picked corn. Get it fast to a very large pot of boiling unsalted water. Throw a few unhusked ears in at a time, so as not to break the boil. Cover if necessary, to bring water back to the boil. Taste for doneness; the corn should take no more than 4 to 5 minutes. Remove from pot, remove husks and silk and serve immediately with lots of sweet butter and salt. Repeat endlessly.

CORN KORMA

Here's an example of creative corn, a dish with global sensibility based on an old American favourite: creamed corn. But this may be the best creamed corn you've ever tasted—because, in addition to the cream, a wealth of Indian spices lends interest to the dish. But it's subtly spiced and not very hot, so it can be served as an accompaniment to a range of Western dishes. We like it best with pieces of chicken marinated in the Indian fashion and grilled. It's rich, so a little goes a long way.

SERVES 6 TO 8 AS A SIDE DISH

2.5 g (½ tsp) black cumin (ajwain)
1.25 g (¼ tsp) yellow mustard seed
1.25 g (¼ tsp) fenugreek
1.25 g (¼ tsp) coriander
45 ml (3 tbsp) plain yogurt
1.25 g (¼ tsp) ground cardamom
1.25 g (¼ tsp) cayenne pepper
5 g (1 tsp) coarse salt
15 ml (1 tbsp) vegetable oil
15 g (1 tbsp) chopped fresh ginger
15 g (1 tbsp) chopped garlic
225 g (8 oz) finely chopped onion
1 litre (1¾ pints) double cream
1 cinnamon stick
8 ears fresh corn kernels
5 g (1 tsp) white pepper

1. Grind cumin seed, mustard seed, fenugreek and coriander in a spice grinder until fine. Place yogurt in a small bowl and add 7.5 g (1½ tsp) of spice mixture plus the ground cardamom, cayenne pepper and coarse salt. Whisk thoroughly.

2. Place oil in a medium saucepan over moderate heat.

Add ginger, garlic and onion and cook until soft, about 5 minutes. Add cream and cinnamon stick and reduce by about half, about 20 to 25 minutes. Remove cinnamon.

3. Add corn kernels and cook until just tender, about 3 to 4 minutes. Remove from heat. Add yogurt mixture and stir well. Season with salt and white pepper and serve immediately.

A trendy by-product of corn: huitlacoche

Any Mexican or Southwestern restaurant with gastronomic pretensions in the United States today is serving huitlacoche—a product practically unknown here just a few years ago, but revered by Mexican chefs for thousands of years.

Huitlacoche is also known as 'night smut,'as unappetising as that sounds. But there's a reason for the nickname: huitlacoche is a fungus that grows on corn, inside the husk, turning the kernels into an unattractive grey-black or blue-black mass. But don't let the name or the look scare you: huitlacoche is wonderfully earthy and mushroomy in taste, something like the Mexican equivalent of truffles.

Formerly, huitlacoche was available only from Mexico, because American farmers have always tried to discourage its growth. Today, it is grown commercially in Florida and Pennsylvania and marketed fresh, but the flavour is not as intense as Mexican huitlacoche. It is also available frozen and canned, but neither is as good as fresh.

Nope...if you want the best huitlacoche, you'll have to look for fresh Mexican huitlacoche at peak season (winter and spring). If you can find it (you'll have an easier time the closer to Mexico you get), combine it with chillies and herbs (epazote is a traditional Mexican pairing) and stuff any type of Mexican entity with it—tortillas, mild chillies or tamales, for example. Top with cheese as you see fit. You won't be disappointed.

AUBERGINE

Aubergine was the original meat substitute for incipient vegetarians in this country: a vegetable that everyone claimed was 'meaty'. We're not so sure about that image; to us, aubergine has a mineral taste, almost like oysters. Whatever its taste profile, this already popular vegetable became even more popular over the last decade, due to the discovery on these shores of fabulous ethnic dishes that feature it from all over the globe and the willingness of American chefs to add new ideas for it to the international aubergine repertoire. This makes perfect sense: aubergine is a remarkable medium for absorbing a wide range of different flavours.

Here's a variety of ideas, both old and new, for this delicious vegetable.

RATATOUILLE

The great Provençal vegetable mélange (based on sweet peppers, tomatoes, aubergines, courgettes and garlic) is prepared in hundreds of ways. The simplest method involves throwing all of the vegetables into a large pot and cooking them together. More refined methods involve the separate cooking of each vegetable and a brief commingling at the end. Then there's the question of cooking time: short, for maximum distinctness of each vegetable; or long, for maximum development of flavour? We like 'em both. But the following recipe, our favourite, is long on time and sacrifices the distinct, bright colour of each vegetable to the greater good of communal depth. We like to serve this lusty, burnished ratatouille at room temperature as a first course, or as part of a Southern French first-course array that includes olives, cheese, anchovies and crusty bread. You could serve it warm as a side dish or, like many modern chefs, use it for sandwiches, omelettes, salads, and pizza and as a base for grilled fish. Its uses are endless.

SERVES 10 AS A FIRST COURSE OR SIDE DISH

900 g (2 lb) onions
5 garlic cloves
900 g (2 lb) courgettes
900 g (2 lb) yellow squash
900 g (2 lb) green peppers
450 g (1 lb) yellow peppers
450 g (1 lb) red peppers
900 g (2 lb) aubergine
900 g (2 lb) fresh ripe tomatoes
about 125 ml (4 fl oz) olive oil
salt to taste
4 sprigs of thyme
1 bay leaf
1 sprig of rosemary
350 ml (12 fl oz) vegetable stock (or thin tomato juice)
freshly ground pepper to taste

1. Peel the onions and chop them coarsely. Peel the garlic and crush the peeled cloves with the flat part of a knife.

2. Cut courgettes and yellow squash, unpeeled, into 1-cm (½-in) cubes. Remove the stems and seeds from the peppers and cut them into 1-cm (½-in) square pieces. Cut the aubergine into 1-cm (½-in) cubes.

3. Remove the stems from the tomatoes and criss-cross the bottoms with a small, sharp knife. Plunge in boiling water for a minute or 2, until the skin starts to fall away. Refresh in cold water and remove the skin. Cut the tomatoes in half lengthways and remove all the seeds. Chop tomatoes coarsely.

4. Put 40 ml (1½ tbsp) of olive oil in a large, heavy pan over moderate heat. Add the onions. Cook until they begin to soften, about 5 minutes and add the garlic. Reduce heat to very low. You will shortly add other vegetables to this pan and total cooking time on top of the stove will be about 45 minutes.

5. While the onions and garlic are cooking over very low heat, put another frying pan over high heat until it starts to smoke and then add 40 ml (1½ tbsp) of olive oil. Add enough courgette cubes all at once to cover the bottom of the pan. Cook over high heat until courgettes are lightly browned on all sides. Remove the courgette cubes and put them in the pan with the onions. Repeat the process until all the courgette cubes have been cooked. Do the same with the yellow squash. Make sure to add a little olive oil between each new batch. Continue with the peppers, then the aubergine cubes, adding the browned vegetables to the onion pan as soon as they are cooked.

6. When all the vegetables are browned and added to the onion pan, stir them together and increase the heat to high. Add the salt to taste, thyme, bay leaf and rosemary and stir well. Cover the pan, place in a preheated 200°C (400°F) oven and add 350 ml (12 fl oz) vegetable stock. After 1 hour, remove pan from the oven and place ingredients of pan in a colander set over a bowl. If liquid drains out of the vegetable mixture, return the liquid to the pan and reduce it to a thick glaze. While it is cooking, you can add additional juices that run out of the vegetables.

7. When all the juices have been reduced, return the vegetables to the pan. (You should have a shiny, moist ratatouille with very little liquid.) Turn the heat off. Add the chopped tomatoes and cover. If serving as a warm side dish, let the ratatouille stand for 10 minutes, just enough to 'cook' the tomatoes. If serving at room temperature, let the pan stand until it comes to room temperature. The ratatouille is even better if you let it stand overnight.

8. When ready to serve, remove the bay leaf and season to taste with salt and black pepper.

CAPONATA

Caponata is the great room-temperature mix of aubergine and other vegetables that is sometimes called an Italian ratatouille. But it differs greatly from its French cousin in one chief way; it is a member of an ancient classification of dishes called *agrodolce*—those made with sweet-and-sour flavouring. Though most Americans are familiar only with the caponata marketed by Progresso in small cans, there are many versions of caponata in Italy. Most are from Sicily, though there are many from Tuscany as well; in Sicily fresh or canned tomatoes are used, while Tuscans tend to use tomato paste and unpeeled aubergine. The following Sicilian version is utterly delicious; it tastes like a grown-up version of the stuff in the Progresso cans. It is only mildly sweet—so if you're used to the sweeter version, you can bump up the sugar a bit and add a few more sultanas. The optional hard-boiled eggs in the recipe make the dish richer. It's a wonderful appetiser, served with crusty bread and, perhaps, other antipasto items.

SERVES 8 AS A FIRST COURSE

2 medium aubergines (about 800 g (1¾ lb) total)
salt to taste
2 large red onions, peeled, halved through the root and sliced very thinly
4 celery stalks (including leaves), cut in 1-cm (½-in) dice
175 ml (6 fl oz) olive oil
6 very ripe small tomatoes (about 1½ pounds), chopped and put through a food mill
175 g (6 oz) brine-cured green and black olives (preferably Sicilian), stoned and coarsely chopped
45 g (3 tbsp) capers
45 g (3 tbsp) toasted pine nuts
50 g (2 oz) sultanas
freshly ground pepper to taste
100 ml (2½ fl oz) red-wine vinegar
15 g (1 tbsp) sugar, or more to taste
3 hard-boiled eggs, coarsely chopped (optional)
chopped fresh flat-leaf parsley for garnish

1. Remove the stems from the aubergine, peel and cut into 2-cm (¾-in) dice. Place the aubergine in a colander, sprinkle liberally with salt and let drain, stirring occasionally, for 1 hour.

2. While the aubergine is draining, soak the sliced onions in a large bowl of cold water to cover for 30 minutes. Drain the onions and dry on kitchen towels.

3. Blanch the celery in a saucepan of boiling salted water for 1 minute. Drain the celery in a sieve and dry on kitchen towels.

4. Heat 50 ml (2 fl oz) olive oil in a large frying pan with a lid over moderate heat until hot but not smoking. Add the onions and cook, stirring, for 10 minutes, until very soft but not browned. Add the tomatoes, olives, capers, pine nuts and sultanas. Season with freshly ground black pepper. Simmer, covered, for 15 minutes. Let stand, covered.

5. Rinse the aubergine to remove the salt and dry on kitchen towels. Heat the rest of the olive oil in another large frying pan over moderate heat until hot but not smoking. Add the aubergine, in batches and cook, stirring frequently, for 10 to 15 minutes, or until cooked through but still firm. Season the aubergine with salt and pepper, remove with a slotted spoon and drain on paper towels. Add the celery to the frying pan with the oil and cook over moderate heat, stirring, for 5 minutes, or until softened but not browned. Remove the celery with a slotted spoon to the frying pan with the tomato mixture.

6. Add the aubergine to the tomato mixture and cook over moderate heat, uncovered, for 10 minutes. Stir in the vinegar and the sugar and cook for 10 minutes to evaporate the vinegar. Taste and adjust the seasonings. Bring to room temperature.

7. When ready to serve, stir in the hard-boiled eggs, if desired. Place on a platter and garnish with the parsley.

AUBERGINE PARMIGIANO-REGGIANO WITH TOMATO AND CAPER SAUCE

One of the most popular aubergine dishes in America is aubergine parmigiana, which has nothing to do with Parma. It also has nothing to do with good culinary logic: why deep-fry something, only to bury it in a wet, tomato-sauce casserole? We prefer the following variation—long, deep-fried aubergine slices, served on top of a light sauce—which preserves the crispness of the deep-frying. It also brings Parmigiano-Reggiano cheese into the picture, restoring some sense to the name 'aubergine parmigiana.'

SERVES 4

3 cups olive oil for deep-frying
550 g (1¼ lb) aubergine
2 large garlic cloves
(½ tsp) salt plus additional to taste
50 g (2 oz) flour
freshly ground black pepper to taste
2 eggs, lightly beaten
50 g (2 oz) freshly made breadcrumbs(not too fine)
90 g (6 tbsp) grated Parmigiano-Reggiano plus thinly shaved slices of cheese for garnish
15 g (1 tbsp) rubbed sage (dry) plus fresh sage leaves for garnish
8 canned tomatoes
20 g (5 tsp) capers
5 ml (1 tsp) extra-virgin olive oil
dash of grated nutmeg

1. Put olive oil in a large, heavy pan over moderate heat. Bring to 185°C (365°F).

2. Cut 1 cm (½ in) off aubergine at both ends. Cut two long sides to remove the 'bulge,'turning aubergine into a fairly regular rectangular block. Cut off skin on all sides. Reserve all cuttings for another use. Slice the rectangular block lengthways into 4 long 'cutlets,'each about 1 cm (½ in) thick.

3. Smash the garlic cloves with the flat side of a knife on a counter, remove the peel and sprinkle the garlic with 2.5 g (½ tsp) salt. Rub the garlic well against the aubergine slices, then discard.

4. Season the flour with salt and pepper. Coat the aubergine slices with the flour. Dip each slice in the eggs. Mix together the breadcrumbs, the 90 g (6 tbsp) of Parmigiano-Reggiano and the rubbed sage. Coat the aubergine slices with the bread-crumb mixture.

5. When oil has reached 185°C (365°F), immerse aubergine slices, 2 at a time. (Try to keep temperature constant.) Cook for 3 minutes, or until aubergine is golden brown outside, soft inside. Drain and dab on paper towels while the other 2 slices are cooking. Remove them when done, drain and dab.

6. *Prepare sauce*: Squeeze the juice from the canned tomatoes, then place in blender, along with the capers. Purée. Pour into small bowl, whisk in the extra-virgin olive oil and season with salt and pepper.

7. Pour the sauce on to 4 dinner plates, distributing evenly. Top with aubergine cutlets. Season with salt, pepper and a dash of nutmeg. Immediately top each hot cutlet with thinly shaved slices of Parmigiano-Reggiano. Garnish with fresh sage leaves.

AUBERGINE, RED PEPPER AND GOAT CHEESE TERRINE

It started in the eighties at some trendy restaurant somewhere; within a few years, every creative chef in America was making his or her version of the aubergine, red pepper and goat cheese terrine. It's now an aubergine classic that fully deserves its status...and now deserves the attention of home chefs. Use a very sharp knife to slice the terrine when it's done. Some chefs even use electric knives and slice it fairly thin. It's delicious all by itself—but very often you'll find it drizzled with some sort of herb-infused oil, often basil oil (see page 482).

SERVES 12 TO 16 AS A FIRST COURSE

2 large aubergines (about 450 g (1 lb) each)
30 ml (2 tbsp) olive oil
1 head garlic
12.5 g (2½ tsp) coarse salt
4 red peppers
10 ml (2 tsp) balsamic vinegar
375 g (13 oz) mild, soft goat cheese, at room
  temperature
50 ml (2 fl oz) double cream
30 g (2 tbsp) chopped fresh thyme
pinch of ground black pepper
pinch of freshly grated nutmeg

1. Preheat oven to 220°C (425°F).

2. Slice aubergines lengthways into 5-mm (¼-in) strips, cutting as evenly as possible. Place strips on well oiled baking sheets and brush them with the olive oil, reserving 2.5 ml (½ tsp). Roast in oven for 20 minutes, until just tender. Set aside to cool.

3. Cut off the top of the head of garlic, exposing a cross section of each clove. Wrap garlic in aluminium foil, sprinkle with the rest of the olive oil and 2.5 g (½ tsp) of the coarse salt and roast in the 220°C (425°F) oven for 30 minutes, or until the cloves are soft. Set aside to cool.

4. Roast peppers over open flame or under the grill until the skins are black, turning peppers to char skins evenly. Place peppers in a paper bag, close the bag and leave for 30 minutes. Wipe the charred skins off with paper towels. Carefully remove stems and seeds, leaving the flesh in one piece if possible. Flatten peppers on a baking sheet (peppers will tear naturally into a few pieces). Sprinkle with balsamic vinegar and 2.5 g (½ tsp) of the coarse salt.

5. Remove garlic cloves from their skins. Place them in a mixing bowl with the goat cheese, cream, thyme, 7.5 g (1½ tsp) of coarse salt, black pepper and nutmeg. Beat well with a wooden spoon, mixing thoroughly.

6. Lightly oil a terrine (about 30 x 10 x 7.5 cm) (12 x 4 x 3 in) and line with clingfilm, leaving at least 15 cm (6 in) of clingfilm hanging over the edges on all sides. Line the bottom with about one sixth of the aubergine strips and line the sides of the terrine with another one sixth of the aubergine strips. (Try to fit the slices in as neatly as possible; a little trimming may be necessary.) Arrange a layer of red pepper pieces on top of the aubergine, using about one quarter of the peppers (trim the peppers to the width of the terrine, so they fit neatly). Spread one quarter of the cheese mixture evenly on top of the peppers. Repeat this layering process 3 times, finishing with a final layer of aubergine. Trim the aubergine to fit perfectly. Fold the clingfilm tightly over the top and cover the terrine with its lid.

7. Place terrine in a larger baking pan and bake in a preheated 200°C (400°F) oven. Before closing the door, fill the baking pan with enough hot water to come three-quarters the way up the sides of the terrine. Bake for 1 hour and 15 minutes, or until the internal temperature of the terrine is 70°C (160°F). Cool and refrigerate overnight.

8. One hour before serving, remove terrine from refrigerator. Grab the clingfilm on the sides of the terrine and carefully lift it to loosen the terrine from the pan. When it's loosened, invert terrine on to a baking sheet and carefully remove clingfilm. Allow terrine to sit out for about 1 hour, so that it warms slightly. Slice off messy ends using a very sharp knife. Discard. Slice the remaining terrine into 8-mm (⅜-in) thick slices and serve 2 slices per person.

AUBERGINE MADRAS

Aubergine deliciously soaks up the warm spices of Indian cooking.

SERVES 8 AS A SIDE DISH

2 kg (4½ lb) aubergine
50 ml (2 fl oz) vegetable oil
225 g (8 oz) chopped yellow onion
4 large garlic cloves, chopped
10 g (2 tsp) chopped green chilli
45 g (3 tbsp) chopped or grated fresh ginger
10 g (2 tsp) coarse salt
15 g (1 tbsp) fenugreek
10 g (2 tsp) coriander seeds
2.5 g (½ tsp) cumin seeds
2 x 800-g (28-oz) cans crushed tomatoes
75 g (3 oz) roughly chopped coriander
freshly grated nutmeg to taste

1. Preheat oven to 200°C (400°F). Cut aubergines in half lengthways and place, cut sides down, on an oiled sheet pan. Roast for 20 minutes, or until aubergines are tender but not mushy. Cut aubergine into 2.5-cm (1-in) cubes and reserve.

2. In a large saucepan, heat oil over moderate heat. Add onion, garlic, chilli, ginger and salt and cook, stirring occasionally, for 10 minutes.

3. While the onions are cooking, toast fenugreek, coriander and cumin in a dry frying pan over moderate heat for 2 minutes, or until spices are fragrant. Using a spice grinder or a mortar and pestle, grind seeds into a fine powder.

4. Add spices to saucepan and cook for 2 minutes. Add crushed tomatoes and simmer, covered, for 30 minutes. Remove cover and simmer for another 30 minutes, or until tomato sauce is reduced by about one third.

5. Add reserved aubergine and chopped coriander.

Simmer gently for about 10 minutes to heat aubergine through. Adjust seasoning and garnish with the remaining coriander leaves and nutmeg.

GRILLED JAPANESE AUBERGINE WITH ORANGE-SESAMEMISO SAUCE

Asian aubergine is one of the most succulent varieties; usually, it's sweeter and less bitter than its Western counterpart. You'll know it in the market by its different shape and colour: much thinner and much lighter purple than Western aubergine. There are Chinese aubergines and Japanese aubergines; the former are a little larger and a little lighter in colour (some consider them a little sweeter as well). Neither needs initial preparation (like salting or parboiling) before grilling. We like the small Japanese variety for this delicious first course. The miso sauce is creative, not traditional—it incorporates some non-Japanese ingredients—but it is hauntingly delicious.

SERVES 4 AS A FIRST COURSE

30 ml (2 tbsp) barley miso
20 ml (1½ tbsp) tahini
20 ml (1½ tbsp) honey
30 ml (2 tbsp) sake (Japanese rice wine)
30 ml (2 tbsp) water
zest and juice of 1 orange
30 ml (2 tbsp) finely chopped fresh ginger
4 Japanese aubergines (about 115 g (4 oz) each)

1. Prepare a hot charcoal fire.

2. Combine all ingredients except the aubergines in a small saucepan. Blend well and bring to a simmer over moderately high heat. Simmer for 3 minutes. Strain and reserve.

3. Leaving the stems on the aubergines, make 3 long incisions in each one, drawing your knife through the opposite end of the aubergine. Fan each aubergine out, so that the 4 'leaves' are connected at the stem.

4. Brush the aubergines with a little miso and grill 4 to 5 minutes on each side, or until aubergine is tender. Remove from grill, place each aubergine on a plate and serve at room temperature with miso sauce on the side.

LEAFY GREENS

Scarred by the national antipathy towards spinach (admiration for Popeye notwithstanding), most Americans grew up with a distaste for leafy greens. Years ago, in fact, other than spinach, there wasn't much to choose from; Americans always preferred veggies in the form of geometric solids (like peas and string beans), and preferably out of a can.

Then the magic happened. We saw platters of leafy greens being passed around in Italian restaurants, fragrant with garlic and olive oil. We sniffed as Chinese families at the round tables in the back of Chinatown restaurants chopsticked their way through amazingly emerald mounds of leafy greens. We watched. We inhaled. Finally, we responded—particularly when we learned that many leafy greens are dense with nutrients, like vitamin A and the antioxidants.

Today, leafy greens are as common on the menus of good restaurants as they are in the produce sections of supermarkets. Home cooks love them—because it takes only a quick stir-fry or steaming and a toss with garlic, ginger, olive oil, sesame oil or whatever they fancy to bring them and their families delicious, inexpensive, nutritious food.

Here are some of the greens you're most likely to find in markets today.

Leafy green recipes

For other delicious ways to cook leafy greens, see the recipes for salad of bitter greens with poached eggs and prosciutto fettunta on page 24; Japanese spinach salad on page 33; caldo verde on page 56; and steamed shad roe bundles with ginger-lemon sauce on page 356.

Beetroot Tops Beetroot tops are so beautiful and healthful, it's surprising that they're not more popular; people who buy fresh beetroot often discard the tops that are attached to them. What a pity! Remember that longer, more developed greens tend to be tough, so make sure you're getting the best: look for small, bright green leaves with vibrant purple veining and stems (if these are very thin, you can eat them too). When cooked, beetroot tops have the texture of spinach, with a similar but subtler taste. We like to steam them, then quickly pan-fry them with a little olive oil, then dress them with lemon and salt.

Broccoli rabe (*broccoli di rape, rapini* or calabrese) has been a staple for years in Little Italy restaurants and has even been available in street markets for a long time. Now, however, it is getting more attention than ever. It is sold in big, bright green bunches of leaves and medium-thick stalks (thinner than broccoli), sometimes with tiny yellow florets. The taste is reminiscent of kale, except for the clean, almost stinging bitterness—which some people love and others hate. We're in the former group, especially when the bitter bite is mediated by lots of sweet garlic. Simply sauté 7 or 8 smashed cloves in a little olive oil, toss a bunch of washed broccoli rabe in the pot, cook over moderate heat for 7 or 8 minutes, uncovered, season well and enjoy.

Collard Greens Very similar to **kale,** the large, heavy, flat, dark-green leaves and long stalks of collard greens are sold in big bunches. In traditional Southern dishes, the greens are cooked for a long time with ham hocks. Modern chefs shorten the cooking time and often toss out the pork. We like lightly cooked greens as much as the next diner... but we're all for tradition on this one. Cook in water with pork for over an hour and serve as a soulfood side dish.

Dandelion Greens A nice touch in salads, these medium-length, spiky greens are fairly thick and have a somewhat bitter, grassy taste. The largest leaves are better cooked than raw. Though similar in flavour and texture to the ubiquitous dandelion weed, dandelion greens available in supermarkets and street markets are cultivated for eating.

Escarole Somewhere between a thick green (like kale) and a romaine-type lettuce, escarole, known in the UK as Batavian endive, has large flat leaves with a slightly bitter flavour and a slightly leathery texture. It makes a nice salad green in small amounts, but we recommend it prepared in the Italian style—boiled, steamed or sautéed and dressed with lemon and olive oil. Soup made from escarole and chicken stock is also delicious.

Kale Kale has hearty, olive-coloured, curly leaves, which are great in soups. The national Portuguese soup, in fact, caldo verde, is made with a green that resembles kale. The Portuguese cut it into very thin strips and boil it rather quickly, preserving its colour; you can also leave the kale in larger, leafier pieces and stir-fry them or braise for a long time. There is also decorative kale (still edible); its very firm, beautiful leaves come in several different colours (such as purple), but the colour fades as it is cooked.

Mustard Greens Difficult to find in the UK, a fairly unusual-looking green, mustard has long, medium-thick stalks, similar to calabrese, with thin, curly bright green leaves at the top. Raw, the flavour is very much like horseradish or hot mustard; the stalks have a stronger flavour than the leaves. Use sparingly in salads as an accent, or braise for a delicious side dish to strong-flavoured main courses.

Spinach Perhaps because spinach has been with us for so long, it varies more in market quality than do other greens in this section. The spinach marketers learned years ago that the stuff sells better in plastic bags; therefore, much of the spinach sold today is prepackaged. This is one reason so many people dislike spinach; often, the stuff in those bags is tired, with an attenuated taste. Once you've had bright, healthy spinach with garden-fresh flavour, you'll never go back to the bags again. So, when buying spinach, look for loose spinach leaves; this spinach is usually even better than unbagged spinach that has been tied into bundles. Make sure the leaves are fresh-looking, light, stiff with freshness—not watery or heavy or limp—with no signs of deterioration. Some people like spinach raw—raw spinach with raw mushroom and crisp bacon salad was a big deal in the eighties—but we think this is a green that doesn't have much flavour until it's cooked. Simply tear off the stems and the thicker ribs, then wash the spinach leaves well in several changes of cold water to remove the grit (those awful bags of spinach do have the advantage of being prewashed.) Place the wet leaves in a large pot over moderate high heat. Don't worry if the leaves fill the pot; just turn the mass of leaves over every 30 seconds or so with a long spoon. Within 2 to 3 minutes, the spinach will have cooked down considerably. It should still be bright green. It's delicious just as it is, with salt and pepper—but a little garlic and olive oil couldn't hurt.

Swiss Chard Large, curly green leaves with white, Chinese cabbage-like stalks. The stalks take longer to cook than the leaves, so you can remove them or cook them separately. Chard has a mild vegetable taste and a touch of bitterness (much less so than calabrese, though). We like to experiment with chard in cheesy gratins.

Turnip Tops Very similar in flavour and texture to beetroot tops, these mild and sweet greens have flat, thin green leaves and long stems. We love to blanch them and toss them with pasta, Parmigiano-Reggiano, olive oil and salt. When you can find them, turnip tops are sold with their vegetables attached, like beetroot tops, so there's nothing to waste. Watch out for wilted, dry greens left too long on the shelves.

MUSHROOMS

Americans have always liked their mushrooms—but, until a few years ago, their favourites were the most prosaic mushrooms of all in the global mushroom forest, the smooth, regular ones with the snow-white caps that come in the blue corrugated cardboard boxes, usually from Pennsylvania. The French call them *champignons de Paris,* as if their name might make them more exciting than they are. But the truth is that they're uninteresting in texture, bland in flavour.

Many Americans have now discovered that the real excitement, mycologically speaking, is in wild mushrooms. We began hearing tales of European mushroom hunters, who combed their fields in spring, summer and autumn, gathering these wild, intensely flavoured gems. Their booty began to trickle in here—but, even more important, Americans began combing their own fertile fields for wild mushrooms. Then, impressed by the American willingness to shell out big bucks for little caps, mushroom producers starting cultivating those kinds of 'wild' mushrooms (like shiitake) that could reproduce themselves under controlled conditions. Today, in America, mushrooms are a growth industry.

Here are the serious mushroom varieties that you're likely to find in today's markets.

Mushroom recipes

For other delicious ways to cook mushrooms, see the recipes for fresh porcini with fennel, arugula and shaved Parmigiano-Reggiano on page 23; Italian lentil and wild mushroom soup on page 72; wild mushroom and chipotle quesadillas on page 95; fresh and dried mushroom sauce with herbs on page 137; wild mushroom lasagna with smoked mozzarella and fresh sage on page 148; and mushroom risotto on page 226.

Chanterelle This golden or reddish-orange, firm-fleshed wild mushroom, whose shape has been likened to a wind-blown umbrella, is well-known among fungus aficionados. It's the unusual appearance and chewy texture that causes the excitement; the flavour is quite mild, only slightly woodsy. Great for simple sautés; chanterelles pick up the flavours of butter, garlic, shallots and herbs beautifully. Pricey.

Cremini Cremini are cultivated mushrooms, the size and shape of the usual button mushrooms you find in supermarkets. In the UK they are known as chestnut mushrooms because of the brown caps. They are slightly stronger in flavour than the ordinary cultivated mushroom. Any dish calling for button mushrooms will be deepened if cremini are used but don't make the mistake of thinking that cremini have the texture or flavour interest of wild mushrooms.

Enoki (Enokidake) Though found in the wild, the enoki sold in supermarkets are almost always cultivated and sold in small, vacuum-packed plastic containers. They have white, stringlike stems, tiny caps and a slightly crunchy texture. These Asian oddities are practically flavourless, but their fanciful appearance—each one looks like spaghetti with a cap—makes them a favourite among modern chefs for garnishing salads, soups, etc.

Hen-of-the-Woods This pretty, mild-flavoured mushroom with a ruffled surface is widely found in forests in the United States but is rare in the UK. It is also called sheep's head and chicken-of-the-woods, the Latin name is Hydnum repandum. Some connoisseurs prefer the stem to the cap, because of the stem's firmer bite.

Matsutake This is the superstar mushroom of Japan, a wild one that has resisted attempts at cultivation. In a lean season, when few of them have sprung up, matsutakes can bring prices comparable to truffle prices. We think of them as Japanese porcini: resilient, earthy, delightful to chew. They are superb in sophisticated stir-fries and with grilled fish and meats.

Master recipe for sautéing mushrooms

There are many recipes for wild or cultivated mushrooms. However, if we have terrific mushrooms, we like to simply sauté them and serve as a first course, or alongside the main course. Here's a general plan for sautéing your mushrooms, no matter which kind you've got. You can use one type of mushroom or, if you cut them into similarly sized pieces, you can mix different types.

MUSHROOM SAUTÉ

SERVES 4 AS A SIDE DISH

30 ml (2 tbsp) unsalted butter
2 shallots, chopped
450 g (1 lb) wild mushrooms
½ cup rich veal or beef stock
7.5 ml (1½ tsp) demiglace (optional)
salt and pepper to taste
15 g (1 tbsp) chopped fresh parsley

1. Melt butter in large sauté pan over moderate heat. Add shallots and cook until transparent.

2. Cut the mushrooms in broad, fairly thin slices. Add mushrooms to the pan, toss with cooked shallots, reduce heat slightly and cover. Cook mushrooms, stirring occasionally, for 3 minutes, or until they have wilted. Remove cover, raise heat to high and sauté until the mushrooms have become slightly browned and crisp, about 3 minutes.

3. Add the stock. Stir and reduce over high heat until most of the liquid has evaporated. If you are using demiglace, add it for the last minute of cooking. Remove pan from heat and season the mushrooms to taste. Add chopped parsley and serve immediately.

Morel Morels are among the most unusual of wild mushrooms and among our favourites. Their shape is different from that of any other mushroom: brown honeycomb-like hives sit on top of hollow, creamy-white bases. The indentations in the 'honeycomb' wall are fabulous for picking up sauces. They grow in the spring and into the summer in the wild. Be sure, of course, that the ones you buy really are fresh; we've seen many expensive morels in the market that are either too wet (and have turned mouldy), or dried out. They should smell clean and woodsy, not funky. Actually, we have discovered that dried morels—even though the texture's not quite as interesting—are more reliable and have a much deeper flavour than fresh ones. Morels are great in a mixed sauté with their springtime partner, asparagus—and though we're not big on mushrooms in cream sauce, we don't mind it as much with morels.

Oyster Mushrooms (Pleurottes) These cream-and-oyster-coloured, fan-shaped delectables have skyrocketed in price and popularity over the past few years. They're not very dense, or bosky-smelling—but somehow they develop texture and flavour as they're cooked. Wild or cultivated, they are great simply sautéed in butter with shallots (as long as they're browned a bit)...then served as an individual course, or alongside the main course. They are sold in clusters of large to very small mushrooms; the base, where the cluster is connected, has the least interesting texture—but you can improve that by cutting the base into thin slices. Sometimes you can even find yellow or pink oyster mushrooms; the colour fades when the mushroom is cooked.

Porcini (Boletus, Cèpes) To many mushroom-lovers, this is as good as it gets. In the spring and autumn in Italy, porcini are on everyone's table—sautéed with garlic, tossed in pasta, added to risotto, served with meats and even sliced raw and added to salads. They're no less revered in France; anyone who has tasted them there in season cannot forget that Gallic combination of garlic and earthy mushroom flavour. As special as the flavour is the texture: firm, but not too firm, with a melting, velvety, almost slightly fuzzy feel. Porcini have bulbous, heavy stems with tightly fitted caps, light-beige to dark-brown. If you can't find fresh porcini, dried porcini are always available. After soaking them for an hour or so in warm water, you'll find they have a deep mushroom flavour, but nowhere near the texture of fresh porcini. The reconstituted dried will do in a pinch when tossed with pasta, risotto and other dishes. All porcini are very pricey.

Truffles

Mushrooms are beloved of gastronomes, of course—but the truffle, another fungus, is adored. Truffles sell for many times the price of even the most expensive wild mushrooms—and they pack many times the flavour if they are in good condition. Unfortunately, many of us spend many dollars for 'fresh' truffles, only to come home with attenuated fungi, too long out of the ground to offer the real thrills of a fresh truffle. So this is the first commandment of truffle-buying: make sure the truffles you buy are fresh and potent. You can tell by smelling them.

Then you'll have to decide whether you prefer black truffles or white truffles.

Black truffles are one of the glories of French cuisine. They grow in many parts of France, but the most famous ones come from the Perigord region in the south-west. They are in season from early December until late February—and, when tasted in France at that time, they are unforgettable. They're also good when handled well and shipped to America. The flavour is beyond bosky: deep, secret, quite literally sexy. They are used in many ways, but their flavour improves with a little cooking—this is the most important thing to keep in mind about black truffles. If you're making a brown sauce for meat, for example and wish a truffle taste, simply slice some truffles (very thinly) and simmer them in the sauce for about 10 minutes.

White truffles, one of the glories of Italian cuisine, have a totally different flavour. They are more pungent, almost like a cross between strong cauliflower and potent garlic (though no description does them justice). They grow in a few spots in Italy, but only one place has them in abundance: the territory around the town of Alba, in Piemonte, in the north-west corner of Italy. They start appearing in August and are finished by Christmas. Again, there are many uses for them—but the most important thing to keep in mind is that they taste best when eaten raw. This means that, in season, Italians shave them very thin over a wide range of things: pasta, risotto, eggs and polenta, for example.

Keep in mind, especially in the summer and early in the truffle season, that truffles called 'summer truffles' come into the marketplace. They are usually neither black nor white—rather, somewhere in between, like grey, or brown. They don't have the intensity of in-season black or white truffles and shouldn't cost as much. Some unscrupulous merchants call them in-season truffles and sell them at in-season prices.

Can you use truffles out of season? There's a large market for canned or jarred truffles, both black and white, which also sell at high prices. You will get some of the true flavour of truffle in these products. But they are watery, washed out and the texture is never interesting. Wait for fresh truffles in season. If you must have out-of-season truffles, you can try the rather good frozen black truffles from France that have become available recently in America. One of the best out-of-season alternatives is truffle oil—but truffle oil loses its pungency about a year after manufacture, so don't buy it unless you know it's fresh. A fresh, vibrant truffle oil, however—drizzled on salads, vegetables, pasta, risotto, seafood and meat—is a very good thing.

Are top-condition fresh truffles worth the price? In a word—yes.

Portobello This is a fancy American name for cup and flat field mushrooms. They are currently the darling of every fashionable New York restaurant for their one chief virtue: size. Because they're very thick and can be as large as 10 cm (4 in) across the cap, they become meaty when cooked. Unfortunately, flavour's another story. Portobellos are cultivated mushrooms—actually, they're full-grown cremini mushrooms—and therefore have little of the earthy taste one seeks in great mushrooms. However, if you prepare them with lots of other flavours—garlic, herbs, good olive oil, balsamic vinegar—they are perfectly acceptable background noise. If you're grilling them, as so many restaurants do today, keep in mind that they can dry out when placed on a hot fire; the trick is to marinate them first for a few hours in an oil/vinegar combination. Also: the extremely dark gills on the underside of the cap have a way of making everything they come in contact with—the grill, a pan, a sauce, your plate, your mouth—seem a little dirty, as if they've been brushed with fine brown-black earth. The only way to prevent this—and we recommend it strongly—is to cut the gills away with a small sharp paring knife before proceeding with portobellos. And, by all means, keep the portobellos whole—to cut them into pieces is to ignore their strongest point: size.

Plain old supermarket mushrooms

If you have access only to cultivated, supermarket, white-capped button mushrooms, you can deepen their flavour in a very simple way. Brush them lightly with olive oil, season well with salt and pepper and place them in a roasting pan in a fairly hot oven (anywhere from 180°C-230°C (350°F-450°F) for about 30 minutes. They will become rather dry and wrinkled on the surface, rather watery within—but their flavour will be concentrated. You can then serve them whole, as a side dish, or sliced in other dishes. If serving them whole, you may want to brown them by passing them under the grill for a few moments. If you happen to be cooking a roast, you can cook mushrooms this way right in the already occupied roasting tin.

Shiitake Shiitake—one the most widely cultivated mushrooms in the world—is that rare variety that's more exciting dried. The dense and meaty dried shiitakes, after they've been reconstituted by soaking in warm water for an hour or so, are one of the delights of Chinese and Japanese cuisine. Marketeers in this country, however, seeing an opportunity to cash in on the American assumption that fresh is better than dried, have flooded our markets, even supermarkets, with fresh shiitakes; indeed, outside of *champignons de Paris,* they are perhaps the easiest fresh mushrooms to find today. Fresh shiitakes, with their cocoa-brown caps and tough cream-coloured stems, are not bad—they're just one of the quieter fresh mushrooms in flavour and one of the least interesting in texture. We recommend going to a good grocery in any Chinatown and paying the high price for the best dried shiitake; you'll know them by the crosslike markings on the cap (these expensive shiitakes are known as 'flower' shiitakes). The dried ones, of course, are great in Asian soups and stir-fries (we especially like them alongside bean curd and green Chinese vegetables). The fresh ones can be used in the same way you'd use fresh chanterelles and fresh morels—but don't expect a big flavour.

Trompettes des Morts The rather ominous name of these mushrooms—'trumpets of death'—has caused some marketeers to call them 'horns of plenty' instead. Don't let the name throw you: these wild black mushrooms with the shape of miniature trumpets have a deep, robust flavour, delicate texture and a lot of visual appeal. Try them sautéed alongside roasted meats or poultry for a hearty side dish.

Cook's tip: cleaning mushrooms

Many wild mushrooms come to the market with dirt and grit clinging to them. You may be tempted to run water over them ... but resist! It is even more important to keep water away from wild mushrooms than from cultivated ones, because wild mushrooms generally have more crevices waiting to soak up the water (if they do this, you may get a watery plate of mushrooms). Instead, wipe your mushrooms gently with a barely damp cloth, or use a mushroom brush.

OLIVES

Once in America, 'olives' meant something positively awful: those huge, soft, stoneless, tasteless black things in cans from California, which usually ended up on a dish with celery hearts before the start of an 'important' meal. When Europeans spoke of their passion for olives, we Americans had no idea what they meant.

Who could blame us? We had simply never tasted the properly handled fruit of the olive tree—those tangy, oval delights that have been sustaining Mediterraneans and others, for perhaps as long as five thousand years.

Happily, as with so many other food products, things have now drastically changed. Scores of olive types from Europe, the Middle East and North Africa are rampaging through our specialty groceries, giving Americans a delicious chance to catch up with the rest of the olive-loving world.

There is one problem with the sudden influx, though: the variety is daunting. But help is at hand. For there are only three main things you need to know about olives before you can fearlessly make your own informed selections at the market: ripeness, method of curing and treatment after curing.

Ripeness Green olives and black olives are not two different types of olives. All olives are green when they're unripe and black when they're ripe. As they're ripening, from green to black, they go through a number of intermediate colours: red, brown and purple are all possible colours at in-between stages of ripeness. Olive producers can choose to harvest at any stage of ripeness.

What does this mean to you? A lot—because some people prefer the flavours of unripe olives (usually more vegetal, herbal, some would say more 'olive-y'), and some prefer the flavours of ripe olives (more buttery, pruny, or liquorice-like). You have to decide which you like. (We can't; we like 'em both.)

Method of Curing Perhaps even more important than ripeness in the finished taste of the olive is the method of curing.

Curing is something that *all* olives must undergo. It would be lovely if we could eat fresh olives, right off the tree, either green or black. But we can't. Just-picked olives taste horrible and are virtually inedible; a naturally occurring chemical in all olives called *oleuropein* renders them painfully bitter. Long ago, some clever European, probably serendipitously, discovered that if olives are cured in some fashion or other the bitterness diminishes and the wonderful, latent olive flavours emerge.

There are many ways to cure olives and each way yields a different taste. Half of all olives that Americans eat are the tasteless California ones, which are cured in lye. The lye works quickly, which the industry loves (as little as a few hours), efficiently stripping the olive of its bitterness—but it also strips the olive of its taste. Even the beautiful Cerignolas of Southern Italy, which are ash-cured (a related process), don't leave the factory with much flavour. We say: avoid lye- and ash-curing.

There are two major curing methods that you should seek out (you should always inquire as to curing method when you're buying olives—if you're in New York's Dean & DeLuca, make sure to talk to Carmine, our font of olive wisdom).

The first great method is brine-curing. The olives are soaked in salty water for as long as six months to become palatable. But the flavour of the olive is miraculously preserved. Usually, brine-cured olives have a smooth, shiny skin, with a moist-looking exterior.

The second great method is dry-curing. The olives are rubbed with coarse salt which leaches out the bitterness. Later on, the olives are usually washed then soaked in oil. Dry-cured olives have a dry, wrinkled look on the outside and are usually much more powerfully flavoured than the brine-cured olives.

There are other curing methods, like oil-curing and water-curing. And, often, producers will use a combination of methods to cure their olives. It's not important to know everything; most good olives will have been either brine-cured or dry-cured. If you've learned which you like better you're on your way.

Treatment After Curing Many an olive producer will 'finish' the olives by soaking them, after curing, in vinegar, or wine, or oil. Sometimes, flavourings will be added; garlic, herbs, spices, chillies and citrus peel are likely candidates. It's important to know this. You may think you like the taste of a particular olive... only to discover later that it's the added flavour you like.

The following are some of the olives you're most likely to see in good specialty shops today. When you buy them, the olives should be open to the air, on dishes or in tubs; sealed olives in cans or jars are just not as vivid-tasting or as exciting in texture. The fresh olives are your solution to the inevitable question: 'what should I serve for starters at my dinner party?' Simply place an array of top-notch olives on attractive dishes around the room, pass fino sherry or other drinks and your guests will be delighted.

An asterisk (*) indicates those olives we use most frequently.

Olive recipes

For other delicious ways to serve olives, see the recipes for salade niçoise on page 12; feta kalamata olive, fresh oregano and caper sauce on page 127; green olive sauce with fresh mint on page 131; tomato sauce with fennel, olives and orange zest on page 135; puttanesca sauce on page 135; caponata on page 173; mashed potatoes with green olive oil on page 192; roasted cod steaks with green olives and sherry vinegar on page 299; provençal rabbit stew with olives and capers on page 398; and tapenade on page 496.

Alfonso Also spelled *Alphonso,* these are large, lusty, Chilean olives, rather soft, with pale, purple-brown flesh. They are brine-cured in old wine barrels, then soaked in wine or wine vinegar. They are easy to stone and have a rich, salty-bitter Mediterranean flavour.

Arbequina Traditionally used for oil in Catalonia, these tiny but meaty Spanish olives are about the size of a fingernail, with colours ranging from pale gold to light brownish red. They are brine-cured; sometimes fresh garlic and herbs are added to the barrel to enhance the earthy, nutty, smoky, slightly bitter flavours. The texture is fairly crunchy, but the flesh is difficult to separate from the stone. Sometimes they are sold with stems and leaves attached.

Bella di Cerignola (Green) These Southern Italian olives stand out from the others because of their super-colossal size and their startlingly bright spring-green colour. But don't judge a book by its cover, or an olive by its colour; they are ash-cured—which means that they are closer in flavour to canned California olives than other European olives. The firm, sweet flesh clings to the stone—but it's practically flavourless. Those who don't like the pungent flavour of traditional European olives often fall in love with these oversized curiosities. If bigger is really better for you, there's a still larger grade of Cerignola than the Bella, called Apulian.

Bella di Cerignola (Black) The black equivalent of the olive above: gigantic size, exaggerated colour (inky black), not much flavour. Strangely enough, the black Cerignolas are a little more flavourful than the green ones and the stone is a little easier to remove.

Cracked Provençal A medium-sized, very green French olive. The olives are brine-cured and usually brought to the States packed with herbes de Provence and oil. They are easy to stone, have firm flesh and an extraordinary flavour—mild and herbal with a touch of pine. We especially like to serve these as hors d'oeuvres with other Provençal treats (like ratatouille).

*Gaeta Small Italian brine-cured olives with smooth flesh, sometimes purple, sometimes black. They are pleasantly sour and salty, but not easy to stone. They are one our favourite olives: lots of flavour, but (to most palates) not over the top. They are a bit like niçoise olives, but meatier and sometimes marinated with lemon peel.

Greek (Green) These brine-cured olives are pale-green, fat and full of juice, with a slight bitterness and mild saltiness. They are easy to stone and are often used (pitted) in soups and stews.

Greek (Black) The black variety of this brine-cured olive has brown to deep purple flesh—almost like the soft flesh of a ripe plum! The flavour's almost winey and the soft flesh is very easy to mash into a purée.

Greek Oil-Cured Wrinkled as oil-cured olives are and brown to black in colour, this olive has an almost nutty flavour. They're not firm enough for nibbling, but good for cooking.

Italian San Remo A small brown-to-purple-to-black olive, from Liguria (on the Italian Riviera), this olive is brine-cured and packed in oil. The flavour is very subtle but very pleasant. It is difficult to stone.

Jordanian Homestyle A very interesting Middle Eastern olive: they are fairly large, green-to-brown, with a pronounced fruity flavour. Firm in texture.

*Kalamata Also spelled *Calamata,* these famous Greek olives come from a place called Kalamata on Greece's Peloponnese peninsula. There, they are slit, brine-cured, then often packed in vinegar. They are usually deep-purple in colour, medium-size, pointy in shape, with just enough flavour to be interesting, but not enough aggressive flavour to interfere with other flavours in a dish. They are one of our very favourite olives for use in cooking, Greek or otherwise. They're also fabulous with feta cheese and retsina.

Lebanese (Green) These 'green' olives are usually just past 'unripe'—which means you'll find some brown and purple tint in them. They are medium in size, very meaty, with a fairly sour taste.

Lebanese (Black) This medium-sized olive is a brine-cured black; accordingly, it's smooth and glossy on the outside. It's rather soft inside, almost mealy, with a pleasing earthy-nutty taste.

*Manzanilla These large Spanish table olives have a lusty, oily, unripened flavour, with smoky overtones. They are brine-cured, range in colour from pale green to green-brown, are rich and chewy and relatively easy to pit. They are classics at tapas time in Southern Spain and are delicious with a glass of manzanilla or fino sherry.

Moroccan Green This cracked, medium-size variety has very soft flesh and a pleasingly sour taste. It's a crowd-pleasing hors d'oeuvre olive.

*Moroccan Oil-Cured Medium-size and wrinkled, these jet-black olives are staples in the Maghreb (the band of countries across Northern Africa). They are heat-dried, cured in salt and preserved in oil (the Italians call olives made this way *olives al forno*). When you taste one of these, you know you're tasting an olive. They are extremely salty, somewhat bitter, rather oily, meaty in texture, with a strong, liquorice-like, almost smoky flavour that lasts on the palate for minutes. They are very easy to pit. The classic oil-cured olive.

Naphlion This is a fairly long and pointy Greek olive, with a brown-to-green glossy exterior. It's usually cracked, brine-cured, then soaked in oil. The naphlion is quite salty and quite sour at the same time and has a lovely, crisp snap to the flesh.

*Niçoise These classic olives from Nice are near and dear to our hearts. They are very small olives, chestnut to brown-black in colour, which have ripened quickly and are then brine-cured. The downside is that they have large stones with little flesh; the upside is that we like the sharp, sour flesh. Sometimes packed with herbs. Indispensable for salade niçoise.

Nyons A delicious, medium-sized French variety from northern Provence, this olive is greenish-black to dark black in colour. Sometimes they're brine-cured, but they're usually dried and cured in a way similar to Moroccan oil-cured olives; the difference is that Nyons olives are dried for a shorter period of time and less salt is used. Therefore, they have a milder flavour than the strong Moroccan oil-cured olives. They are fleshy, fairly soft and are often sold with herbs and garlic added.

Picholine Long, pointy and brine-cured, this very crunchy green olive from France is slightly sweet and salty, with a wonderful herbal flavour. Though the stone is hard to remove, Picholines are delicious at the table as well as in cooking. Sometimes in the United States, they are packed in citric acid.

Sicilian This designation is used for lots of different olives. Most of the true Sicilian olives are brownish-green monsters: large, brine-cured, with lots of fleshy soft fruit. Sometimes hot peppers and a little olive oil are added to the olive brine. There are also Sicilian oil-cured olives, similar to Moroccan oil-cured olives but usually tossed with red pepper flakes. Unfortunately, most 'Sicilian-style' olives sold in the United States are grown in California and are not as interesting as their Italian namesakes. Often, you'll find Sicilian olives cracked.

Syrian This is a good Middle Eastern olive for cooking, or for those who don't like intensity in their eating olives. It's large, dark-green, fleshy, fairly crisp and not much more than a little sour.

Turkish Oil-Cured Black and wrinkly like the Moroccan oil-cured olive, but the Turkish oil-cured olive has a milder flavour.

ANDALUSIAN MARINATED OLIVES

The unmistakable taste of the exotic Spanish South is in this great dish of marinated olives—perfect with a glass of fino sherry.

MAKES 450 G (1 LB) MARINATED OLIVES

50 g (2 oz) pimientos or soft roasted red peppers
25 g (1 oz) capers
2 large garlic cloves
8 anchovies
20 g (4 tsp) chopped fresh oregano leaves
10 g (2 tsp) chopped fresh thyme leaves
10 g (2 tsp) chopped fresh rosemary leaves
5 g (1 tsp) ground cumin seed
90 ml (6 tbsp) red-wine vinegar
125 ml (4 fl oz) Spanish olive oil
450 g (1 lb) large green brine-cured olives, such as manzanilla

1. Place all ingredients except the olives in a food processor. Blend until just mixed, about 15 seconds.

2. Crack the olives slightly with the side of a heavy cleaver. Place the olives in a jar or bowl and cover with the pimiento purée. Cover tightly. The olives will be delicious immediately, but will develop even more flavour in 1 to 2 weeks under refrigeration.

MOROCCAN BLACK OLIVE AND CITRUS SAUCE

There is a traditional Moroccan salad: an arrangement of orange slices and black olives dressed with olive oil. We've always loved the idea and the flavours, but find the whole olives a little strange, texturally, against the orange slices. The following sauce is based on that salad—but it combines the elements better. It's

something like a Moroccan salsa and it's sensational on grilled fish or grilled chicken. Look for wrinkled, flavourful, oil-cured black olives...just make sure they're not overly bitter.

MAKES ENOUGH SAUCE FOR 6 MAIN-COURSE SERVINGS OF FISH OR CHICKEN

2 large navel oranges
1 large lemon
2.5 g (½ tsp) grated lemon rind
115g (4 oz) pitted and chopped oil-cured black olives, such as Moroccan oil-cured
1.25 g (½ tsp) finely chopped garlic
2.5 g (½ tsp) sweet paprika
pinch of cayenne pepper
5 g (1 tsp) ground ginger (make sure it's fresh)
2.5 g (½ tsp) granulated sugar, or more to taste
30 ml (2 tbsp) olive oil
30 ml (2 tbsp) finely chopped fresh parsley

1. Using a sharp knife, cut the rind and white pith away from the oranges. Then cut out the orange sections, leaving behind the fibrous white material that separates the sections. Do the same with the lemon. Chop orange sections and lemon sections into coarse chunks and place them gently in a bowl.

2. Add the lemon rind, olives, garlic, paprika, cayenne pepper, ginger and sugar to the bowl. Stir gently to combine. Pour off any citrus juice that accumulates and discard. Add the olive oil and parsley, stir gently once again, taste for seasoning and serve immediately on grilled fish or grilled chicken.

ONIONS AND GARLIC

Julia Child once said that she couldn't imagine a civilisation without onions and garlic. We can't imagine an American restaurant of the eighties and nineties without 'em.

It's not that this pair of sulphurous cousins wasn't

always present in American cooking; many a dish cooked on these shores has featured a little onion or garlic in the background. But three recent developments thrust them squarely into the foreground.

First, Americans discovered that ethnic cuisines used these flavourings to a much greater extent than we ever dreamed. While we were dutifully adding 'one medium clove of garlic' to our version of Chinese food, the Chinese were busy chopping up a dozen cloves for the same dish. We found out that quantity doesn't matter as much as cooking time; if you cook your garlic well, the flavour will be deep and mellow, not harsh and aggressive. A kind of culinary politeness stayed our hand before—but we're bolder than ever now.

Secondly, we discovered that there's more to onions and garlic than that mesh bag of copper-skinned onions in the supermarket, just next to those medium-sized heads of white, papery garlic. As with so many other vegetables, we discovered variety. First, elephant garlic captured our attention—a much larger head with a milder flavour. Unfortunately, we soon discovered that elephant garlic is often on the dry side and turns rancid quickly. Then we discovered that the small heads of purple garlic appearing in our markets are milder *and* juicier than the papery white ones.

Then came all the related members of the onion family: shallots, leeks, spring onions, rampions, chives, Japanese chives and garlic chives. After that, we realised that onions themselves come in varieties—and we fell in love with the super-sweet onions that are raised all around the country. Most famous is the Vidalia (say vie-dale-ya), from Georgia, which, during its peak season in the spring, is so sweet you can eat it like fruit. Texas Sweets follow in the spring. Walla Wallas, from eastern Washington, follow in July. The sweet onions from Maui, Hawaii are available year-round.

Many of our best chefs in the eighties realised that with the wealth of onions and garlic in our markets and with our growing fondness for them, onions and garlic themselves should play a leading role on our plates. Appetisers, soups and side dishes began to feature

these once drastically under-used ingredients.

Here are a few of the ways that chefs today are making onions and garlic shine.

DEEP-FRIED ONION RINGS

Onion rings have been popular for decades—but in the eighties and nineties they graduated from 'bar food' to one of the pet dishes of New American chefs. Thankfully, this didn't mean a new generation of 'creative' onion ring dishes (balsamic-marinated onion rings with goat cheese batter?)—but it did mean special care and attention paid to these addictive halos and lots of subtle variations in thickness and texture on the basic theme. There's one type we know we hate: the super thick crust, from which a thin, wet, stringy piece of onion slithers, leaving behind a deep-fried tunnel of dough. The following recipe has a light coating that sticks to its onion. And we've chosen to cut that onion thick, since we emphasise the onion itself by using the sweetest, most delicious onions we can find.

SERVES 6 AS A SIDE DISH

1 large sweet white onion (about 550 g (1¼ lb)), peeled, sliced 1-cm (½-in) thick and separated into rings
1 litre (1¾ pints) buttermilk
about 1.4 litres (2½ pints) vegetable oil for deep-frying
175 g (6 oz) plain flour
50 g (2 oz) stone-ground yellow cornmeal
20 g (1½ tsp) coarse salt plus additional for sprinkling, if desired
5 g (1 tsp) freshly ground black pepper
15 g (1 tbsp) smoky chilli powder (optional)*

*The chilli powder addition is about as far as we like to go in the direction of 'creative' onion rings; these chilli-spiked ones go marvellously well with any Southwest-style steak dishes. If you use a regular chilli powder, you'll get only heat; if you can find a smoked chilli powder, you'll get a wonderful flavour as well. A company in New Jersey called Chili Today, Hot Tamale makes a delicious smoked habanero chilli powder that would be dynamite on your rings.

1. Soak the onion rings in a bowl with the buttermilk, stirring occasionally, for 30 minutes.

2. Heat the oil to 190°C (375°F) in a large casserole over moderately high heat.

3. While the oil is heating, stir together the flour, cornmeal, coarse salt, pepper and chilli powder (if using) on a plate.

4. When the oil is hot enough, begin making the rings. One by one, remove the onion rings from the buttermilk (taking care to leave lots of clinging buttermilk), and coat each one with the flour mixture. (Don't shake off excess flour.) When you've coated 5 or 6, put them carefully in the hot oil. Deep-fry until they are golden brown on both sides, stirring and turning them if necessary, 2 to 3 minutes. (When you first add them, they will sink to the bottom, but should float to the top very quickly; stir the onions so they don't stick together.) Drain the onion rings on paper towels and serve immediately if possible. Otherwise, keep them warm (in a preheated 120°C (250°F) oven). Wait for the oil to get hot again and repeat with remaining onions, skimming any burned bits from the oil between batches. Serve hot, sprinkled with additional coarse salt (if desired).

WHOLE HEADS OF ROASTED GARLIC

Here's another dish that became a standard during the American revolution (the restaurant revolution of the eighties and nineties, that is). It started as a California thing, but soon chefs everywhere were roasting whole heads of garlic and using them in a variety of ways. Most simply, the cooked cloves are great to squeeze; the soft garlic that comes out is a delicious spread for bread. You can squeeze the garlic on rustic European breads, on crostini, on bruschetta—but it's surprisingly good on simple buttered toast. You can also spread the garlic on cooked food—like grilled fish, meat and vegetables. The garlic purée is lovely mixed into potato

dishes (like mashed potatoes) and bean dishes. Finally, lots of chefs like to garnish their main courses with whole pieces of roasted garlic that have been carefully extracted from the whole roasted head. Just strew with impunity.

> 4 heads fresh garlic, loose outer skin removed
> 4 x 7.5-cm (3-in) strips lemon zest, removed with a vegetable peeler
> 6 sprigs of fresh thyme plus more for garnish
> 2 sprigs of fresh rosemary
> 2 sprigs of fresh sage
> 2 bay leaves
> 50 ml (2 fl oz) extra-virgin olive oil
> warm buttered toast for serving

1. Preheat the oven to 200°C (400°F).

2. Cut off the stem and the top of one fifth of the heads of garlic. Place the garlic in a garlic roaster or on a large piece of heavy-duty aluminium foil. Place lemon zest, thyme, rosemary, sage and bay leaves across the cut top of the garlic heads and drizzle with olive oil. Place the cover on the garlic roaster or close up the aluminium foil and seal the edges tightly.

3. Roast the garlic for 1 hour. Remove the package from the oven, open carefully and let the contents cool slightly. Discard the herb sprigs and lemon zest. Serve.

POTATOES

Potatoes have always been popular in America; before everything changed, gastronomically, we were known for our 'meat and potatoes'. But the way we looked at potatoes in the eighties and nineties was radically new.

Once upon a time, a spud was just a spud; if you wanted potatoes for dinner, you went out and bought them. That was that. Neither cooks nor diners thought much about potato types.

Recently, however, chefs have realised that there is a big dichotomy in the potato world: high-starch and low-starch potatoes. Some potato dishes work best with the former, some with the latter. Here are some types of potatoes that fall into each high- and low-starch group:

High-Starch Potatoes Potatoes with a higher starch content are drier, mealier, more floury when cooked. They also tend to fall apart—so they're not a good choice for dishes in which you want whole slices of potatoes. They shine as baking potatoes, above all else, particularly if you're looking for a light, dry fluffiness. They are also good for deep-frying; the browning that they receive in the oil holds each piece together. And some chefs prefer them for mashed potatoes, since they make a lighter, fluffier product. The hands-down high-starch champion is the russet, the staple potato of Idaho. It's oval, with brown skin and white flesh. Russet Burbanks and russet Norkotahs are two leading varieties from this group.

Low-Starch Potatoes Potatoes with a lower starch content are wetter and waxier. They are recommended whenever you want a potato to hold its shape, in salads and gratins, for example. They are also good for mashed potatoes, if you prefer a denser, wetter, creamier texture.

Here are some leading types of low-starch potatoes:

Round Whites Usually low in starch, sometimes medium-starch. Round, light brown skin, white flesh.

Round Reds Low in starch. Round, red skin, white flesh. Often waxier and sweeter than round whites.

New Potatoes Not a separate group of potatoes, but the new crop of any potato. However, what we see most often in the U.S.A. as 'new potatoes' are round reds. They are very wet, very low in starch—great for potato salads.

Yellow Potatoes Usually low in starch. Usually round, with light brown skin and yellow flesh. Some varieties seem rich, almost buttery.

Fingerlings Low in starch. Usually about 2.5 cm (1 in) wide and 7.5 cm (3 in) long, like fingers. Often noticeably deeper in flavour. Ruby crescent fingerlings, purple Peruvian fingerlings, Russian banana fingerlings are typical varieties.

Blue or Purple Potatoes The original potatoes from Peru were probably blue or purple and these 'heirloom' varieties are making a big comeback today. Low in starch—and really not different in flavour or cooking qualities from other low-starch potatoes. But chefs like them because their colours are so striking. They are becoming available in the UK.

Which potato?

There is much talk about the best potato for baked potatoes. There really is a difference when you bake with russets because their starchy flesh makes a lighter, drier, fluffier baked potato. Some people prefer the wetter, creamier feel of low-starch baked potatoes, however. One thing is sure: for baked potatoes, avoid thin-skinned types, like new potatoes, which won't yield much of a crunchy skin.

FAVOURITE POTATO DISHES

Lots of chefs have gotten creative with potatoes. But when those basics of the American table—like steak, meat loaf and roast chicken—need potato mates, there's nothing like the tried-and-true companions.

BAKED POTATOES

Here's a lowly dish, very familiar to Americans, that found new status in the eighties. Just as Marcel Duchamp once put ordinary objects in a museum so that we'd see them in new ways, so did fancy restaurants of the last decade treat the humble baked potato. In the late eighties, The Four Seasons in New York served a huge, ungarnished, perfectly cooked baked potato, on a simple plate, for $12. Anointed only with extra-virgin olive oil, it was an immediate sensation—and it instantly raised the status of the baked potato.

The fact that many restaurants finally figured out how to bake potatoes also helped. The old-fashioned restaurant baked potato was a sorry sight: wrapped in aluminium foil, it never developed the crispy, crunchy skin that defines a great baked potato. Thankfully, today, the foil has been removed—in better restaurants and, we hope, in your home kitchen.

And keep this in mind, after you've cooked your perfectly crunchy baked potato: butter and sour cream are not the only possible embellishments. The Four Seasons, in addition to bringing us a high price, also brought us a great idea: the charred outside of a good baked potato and the sweet, tender flesh inside, are among the world's greatest foils for the pungency of a young, green, Tuscan extra-virgin olive oil. Simply cut open the potato, drizzle away and top with coarse salt.

PERFECT BAKED POTATOES

Cooking perfect baked potatoes requires no special equipment. Simply preheat your oven to 250°C (500°F). Wash the potatoes of your choice, place on the centre shelf of the oven, turn the potatoes once or twice during cooking and cook until crunchy on the outside, tender within.

Cooking time depends on size. Here's a handy guide:
115-g (¼-lb) potato: 45 minutes
225-g (½-lb) potato: 1 hour 10 minutes
350-g (¾-lb) potato: 1 hour 30 minutes

We prefer larger potatoes for baking, so the skin gets crunchier and the flavour of the skin permeates the potato more. One of the best baked potatoes we've ever had was an enormous, 675-g (1½-lb) red Pontiac, which cooked for 2 hours and 15 minutes.

Note: For light, dry, super-crunchy potatoes, cut the baked potatoes, after cooking, into walnut-sized chunks. Place in a roasting tin in a preheated 280°C (550°F)

oven for 20 minutes. Toss with coarse salt, extra-virgin olive oil and serve.

MASHED POTATOES

How the humble have risen! Mashed potatoes—those squishy spuds we all learned to hate at the school cafeteria, in the army, in any institution through which Americans have passed, that plebeian purée that was the nadir of culinary fashion during the frenzy of the acquisitive eighties—have resumed their rightful place as an easy road to comfort, contentment and the recoverable joys of childhood. It was the simultaneous rise in the late eighties of bistro fashion in France and the wave of nostalgia cooking here (which inevitably paired mashed potatoes with meat loaf), that brought these now-lovable spoonfuls roaring back to culinary respectability.

Making good mashed potatoes is not difficult. There are just a few key things you should know.

1. The choice of potato makes a big difference. If you prefer fluffier, lighter mashed potatoes, choose a Russet potato, like Idaho baking potatoes. If you prefer smoother, creamier, heavier mashed potatoes, choose waxy, low-starch potatoes. We especially like to make mashed potatoes from the yellow-fleshed varieties, like Yukon Gold; they make creamier potatoes … with an almost buttery flavour even before you add the butter!

2. You should boil the potatoes with their skins on; this helps retain the potato flavour. Boil them in salted water, just until tender. This rule doesn't necessarily apply if you're making flavoured mashed potatoes, in which case you may want to boil peeled potatoes with flavourings.

3. The way you mash your potatoes makes all the difference. Potato cells carry something called 'free starch,' and you want to release as little of it as possible—since it makes your mashed potatoes gummy. Mashing with a fork, or a masher, releases very little free starch, but it also results in lumpy mashed potatoes. Mashing with a food mill produces a lump-free product—but the food mill shears the potato cells open and releases some free starch. The out-and-out free-starch-spilling champion is the food processor, which creates a flood of the stuff; *do not use a food processor for mashed potatoes unless you're looking for book paste!* Our favourite tool, by far, is the potato ricer. It gently mashes the potatoes without turning them at all gummy. It has one additional virtue: it can rice unpeeled potatoes without letting the peel get through the ricer. If you're serious about mashed potatoes, buy a ricer.

4. After you've mashed your potatoes, put them back in the pot over moderate heat for a few minutes to dry them out.

5. Add room temperature butter first to the warmed-up potatoes in the pot, then warmed liquid.

6. The liquid you use makes a big difference: skimmed milk for thinnest mashed potatoes, full-cream milk for medium, single cream for richest (though some American chefs swear by canned evaporated milk). Whichever liquid you use, warm it first so that it doesn't cool the potatoes. If you want mashed potatoes that are less dairy-laden (and more potato-y), you might add some of the potato cooking water to the mashed potatoes.

7. Whip the potatoes in the pot. Mashed potatoes are really misnamed—because they should be both mashed *and* whipped. The whipping lightens them. A sturdy balloon whisk does the job well but, if you like electricity, you can use the old double-sided electric hand-beater. The newfangled sauce-making gadgets with a single rotary—like the Braun hand blender—also do a good job on mashed potatoes.

BASIC MASHED POTATOES

Here's an all-purpose mashed potato recipe—but the specific liquid and the amounts of liquid and butter are up to you, depending on how thick/thin, buttery/non-buttery you like your mashed potatoes.

SERVES 4 AS A SIDE DISH

900 g (2 lb) potatoes (we prefer Yukon Gold)
115-225 g (4-8 oz) unsalted butter, at room temperature
125-225 ml (4-8 fl oz) liquid, warmed (see discussion opposite)
salt and pepper to taste

1. Place whole potatoes in a large pot of boiling, salted water. Boil until tender, 20 to 40 minutes, depending on size of potatoes.

2. When cool enough to handle, rice potatoes in a potato ricer (if you're using another mashing device, you'll have to peel the potatoes first).

3. Place the potatoes back in the pot over moderate heat. Stir for a few minutes, until potatoes are warm and dry. (Ensure they do not burn.)

4. Beat in the butter. Beat in the warmed liquid. Whisk vigorously until potatoes are lightened (about a minute with a hand-held whisk). Season to taste with salt and pepper and serve immediately.

MASHED POTATOES WITH GREEN OLIVE OIL

Somewhere in the Mediterranean-mad eighties, chefs started substituting olive oil for butter in their mashed potatoes; the dish achieved its greatest fame at La Maison Blanche in Paris. We think it's a great alternative to buttery potatoes—especially when the greenest, most pungent olive oil is used. Young, high-quality Tuscan oils are often very green and any young oil (not more than 2 years old) made by any producer in the Laudemio consortium can be relied upon for greenness. We like to take the concept a step further and fleck the already greenish mashed potatoes with bits of good green olives. If you find this too bitter, by all means cut back on the amount of green olives.

SERVES 8 AS A SIDE DISH

> 1.8 kg (4 lb) potatoes, peeled and cut into 2.5-cm (1-in) pieces
> 10 large sprigs of fresh basil
> three 7.5-cm (3-in) strips lemon zest removed with a vegetable peeler
> salt to taste
> 125-225 ml (4-8 fl oz) very green extra-virgin olive oil plus additional for drizzling
> 225 g (8 oz) picholine or other high-quality green olives, stoned and finely chopped
> pepper to taste

1. Combine the potatoes, basil and lemon zest with enough cold water to cover them by 5 cm (2 in) in a casserole. Bring the water to a boil and add salt. Simmer the potatoes for 20 minutes, or until tender.

2. Drain the potatoes in a colander, reserving about 225 ml (8 fl oz) of the cooking water. Return the potatoes to the casserole and cook them over moderate heat until any excess liquid is evaporated. Discard basil and lemon zest.

3. Force the potatoes through a ricer into a bowl. Beat in the olive oil (exact amount depends on your taste), olives, salt and pepper to taste and enough of the reserved cooking water to reach the desired consistency. Drizzle with green olive oil and serve hot.

The Robuchon variation
Superstar Parisian chef Joël Robuchon has many signature dishes—but none has brought him more attention than his *pommes purées,* or mashed potatoes.

Mashed potatoes are classic in France as well as America—but no one has ever dared use as much butter as Robuchon. The result is incredible—almost like a potato-flavoured butter purée that makes your whole body glow. Next time you're ready for a saturated fat binge—and the best mashed potatoes you've ever tasted—follow our basic mashed potato recipe, but use 450 g (1 lb) of unsalted butter (best quality) to every 900 g (2 lb) potatoes. Also, use the best-quality cream you can find to thin the purée (approximately 125-225 ml (4-8 fl oz)). Satisfaction—and lots of calories—guaranteed.

MASHED POTATOES WITH ROASTED GARLIC
These mashed potatoes, too, became one of the hottest side dishes in creative American restaurants of the last decade. Our version uses no cream or milk, so it may remind you more of a potato purée than of mashed potatoes. That's good—because the pronounced potato flavour that results stands up nicely to the sweet roasted garlic.

SERVES 8 AS A SIDE DISH

> 12 shallots, unpeeled
> 2 large heads of garlic, papery outer skin removed (leaving the head intact) plus 8 garlic cloves, peeled
> 125 ml (4 fl oz) extra-virgin olive oil
> salt and pepper to taste
> 1.6 kg (3½ lb) potatoes, peeled and cut into large chunks
> 75 g (3 oz) unsalted butter, at room temperature

1. Preheat the oven to 220°C (425°F).

2. Toss together the shallots, heads of garlic and 15 ml (1 tbsp) olive oil. Sprinkle liberally with salt and pepper. Wrap the garlic and shallots tightly in a foil package and roast for 1 hour.

3. Unwrap the package carefully and let the shallots and garlic cool until they can be handled. Peel the shallots and the garlic and purée them in a small food processor.

4. Place potatoes in a large pot of boiling, salted water with the 8 peeled garlic cloves. Boil until potatoes are tender, 20 to 40 minutes, depending on size of potatoes. Drain potatoes and garlic in a colander, reserving about 1 cup of the cooking water.

5. When cool enough to handle, rice potatoes and garlic in a potato ricer. Return riced mixture to the pot and cook it over moderate heat until any excess liquid is evaporated.

6. Over moderate heat, whip in the garlic-shallot purée, the rest of the olive oil, the butter, salt and pepper to taste and enough of the reserved cooking water to reach the desired consistency. Serve immediately.

DEEP-FRIED POTATOES

Americans moan aplenty about the 'unhealthy' method of deep-frying; when it comes to potatoes, however, we keep ordering deep-fried ones as if they could add years to our lives. Considering the link between happiness and health, we're not so sure they can't.

Seven steps to great french fries

    1. Use russet potatoes, like Idaho potatoes.
    2. Use potatoes that are a little old (the skins should be a little wrinkled and the potatoes a little soft).
    3. Peel and cut potatoes and soak in water overnight.
    4. Use very fresh vegetable oil—or, even better, rendered beef fat or pork fat.
    5. Use the two-fry method: the first frying at 170°C (340°F), the second frying at 190°C (390°F).
    6. Coat the potatoes lightly with cornflour before

the second frying. This gives them a more interesting exterior texture. Also, the cornflour coating retards browning, so you can cook them a little longer and get them crispier.
    7. Serve immediately.

FRENCH FRIES

French fries (chips), of course, have been, are and will continue to be the most popular form of deep-fried potatoes. They even gained a new status in the eighties, when serious restaurants serving the New California cooking took French fries from the bistro and put them on fancier, more ambitious menus. But there is a problem: French fries made at home often fall short of French fries made in restaurants. The chief difference is in texture: homemade chips tend to be slick and smooth on the outside, restaurant chips tend to be more nubbly. By following the recipe below, you'll make them as interestingly textured and as good as the ones you enjoy in great restaurants.

SERVES 6

1.3 kg (3 lb) russet potatoes (about 6), peeled
1 litre (1¾ pints) vegetable oil for deep-frying
about 115 g (4 oz) cornflour for light coating
coarse salt

1. Trim potatoes in the shape of a rectangle. Cut into 5-mm (¼-in) slices and then cut into 5 mm (¼-in) chips. Put in a bowl of cold water and soak for at least 1 hour or preferably overnight. (The longer they soak, the more starch is removed and the crispier the chips will be.)

2. When ready to fry, heat oil in a deep, heavy, straight-sided pot to 165°C (340°F). Add a small batch of potatoes straight from the water. (Stand back as the oil will splatter. Make sure to separate the chips from each other, with a fork, right after you add them to the oil.) Fry the potatoes, in small batches, for about 3 to 4 minutes, until they look blistered on the surface. (This step essentially blanches the potatoes, so there should be very little colour on the potatoes.) Remove to a baking sheet lined with paper towels.

3. When ready to serve, heat oil to 195°C (390°F). Place the once-cooked potatoes in a large colander and toss lightly with cornflour. Fry potatoes, again in small batches, for about 2 minutes, until they are deep golden brown and surface is a little crinkly. (You might even see blisters on the chips.) Remove to a baking sheet lined with paper towels and sprinkle generously with coarse salt. Serve immediately for maximum crispiness.

MATCHSTICK POTATOES

If crispiness is important to you, then you might want to make matchstick potatoes (*pommes allumettes*). They are our favourite chips. They are also the crispiest... and they have the additional virtue of needing only one frying.

SERVES 4

1.3 kg (3 lb) floury potatoes, peeled (about 6)
about 225 g (8 oz) cornflour for light coating
1 litre (1¾ pints) vegetable oil for frying

1. Peel the floury potatoes and cut them into 3-mm (⅛-in) slices. Then cut the slices into long strips, 3-mm (⅛ in) wide. These are the matchsticks. Soak them in water overnight (you may soak them as little as half an hour, or you may omit this step if you don't have time).

2. When ready to cook, dust them lightly with cornflour, then fry them at 195°C (390°F) until golden brown. (Be especially diligent in separating them when they hit the hot oil.) Remove, drain on paper towels and salt liberally.

Note: After being cooked, these potatoes will stay crispy much longer than the twice-cooked potatoes; you can

hold them for half an hour or more without any loss of crispiness. They'll even be fairly crispy the next day.

GARLIC POTATO CRISPS

Garlic potato crisps have become a new classic of creative American restaurants. The following method is the simplest one we've seen, though it still provides a great fresh garlic flavour.

SERVES 4

1 large floury potato, peeled
50 ml (2 fl oz) olive oil
4 garlic cloves, finely chopped
1 litre (1¾ pints) vegetable oil for frying
10 g (2 tsp) salt

1. With a mandoline, slice potato into rounds as thinly as possible. Rinse rounds with cold water until water runs clear and dry potatoes thoroughly on paper towels.

2. In a small saucepan heat olive oil and garlic over low heat until garlic aroma is released, about 5 minutes. Place garlic and oil in blender and purée.

3. Heat vegetable oil in a large saucepan to 160°C (325°F). Fry the potato slices in several batches, stirring frequently with a slotted spoon, until potatoes are light golden, about 7 to 8 minutes. Place crisps on paper towels to dry and sprinkle immediately with salt. Brush lightly with garlic oil. Serve immediately.

Note: The crisps can be made several hours in advance and stored in an airtight container. Do not brush with garlic oil until they are reheated. If making crisps in advance, reheat them in a 200°C (400°F) oven for 2 to 3 minutes to re-crisp, then brush with garlic oil.

POTATO GRATINS

To us, one of the noblest things you can do with a potato

is slice it thinly and layer it with flavourful ingredients in a gratin dish. Bake it, brown it on top and—voilà!—a gratin is born. Contrary to popular opinion, cheese is not necessarily part of the equation; a gratin is defined by the browning on top. But we love cheese on potato gratins and are particularly partial to the cheesy versions made in eastern France, Switzerland and north-west Italy. Use waxy, wet, unstarchy potatoes for the best texture in the finished product.

Gaufrettes

One of the trendiest deep-fried potatoes in fancy restaurants of the eighties and nineties (both French and New American restaurants) was the gaufrette, or waffle-cut chip. Each round slice looks like a little waffle, with holes in the grid. Gaufrettes are served either alongside the main course, or, very often, as a garnish; what became extremely trendy for a while, in fact, was the practice of standing a single gaufrette in a mound of tuna tartare (or some other expensive, chopped raw fish).

To make gaufrettes, you need a slicer that creates the waffle shape. You can find an inexpensive plastic one; the Waffle and Fancy Cutter by Boerner, made in Germany, does the job perfectly well.

Simply peel floury potatoes evenly, so that, after peeling, the potato is a round, fairly even cylinder. Cut each potato in half, crossways and start slicing on the slicer according to the directions, making slices as thin as possible. The trick in the cutting (as your slicer's instruction book will tell you) is to turn the whole potato 90° before making each slice. Your finished gaufrettes will be best if you soak the slices in water overnight.

When ready to cook, heat several cm of oil in a deep-fryer until it reaches 155°C (320°F); a low temperature is needed to make the gaufrettes crisp and potato-crisp-like. Fry until golden-brown and crunchy, about 6 to 7 minutes. Drain on paper towels and sprinkle with salt.

GRATIN DAUPHINOIS

This is the classic potato gratin, from eastern France and from every self-respecting bistro anywhere in France or America. There are as many recipes for it as there are chefs. We are partial to the following one, however—which cooks the potato slices in milk, draining the milk away and then combines the potatoes with cream in the gratin dish. Other keys to quality are the thinness of the potato slices (as thin as possible), and the degree of doneness of the slices after the first cooking (make sure they're still slightly firm). Serve this gratin with a simple roast chicken and a bottle of Beaujolais and you'll feel like you're wearing a beret and smoking Gauloises.

SERVES 6 AS A SIDE DISH

1 litre (1¾ pints) milk
3 large garlic cloves, smashed
salt and pepper to taste
freshly grated nutmeg to taste
8 medium low-starch potatoes
unsalted butter for buttering the gratin dish
350 g (12 oz) grated Gruyère
850 ml (1½ pints) double cream

1. Place the milk and garlic in a large, heavy saucepan. Season with salt, pepper and a little nutmeg. Bring to a boil and simmer for 15 minutes.

2. Preheat oven to 230°C (450°F).

3. Peel the potatoes and slice thinly on a mandoline or plastic vegetable slicer. Place potato slices in hot simmering milk and cook very gently for 10 minutes or so, or just until the potatoes begin to soften.

4. Immediately drain the potatoes in a colander (reserve milk for another use, if desired). Butter an oval gratin dish that measures about 30 cm (12 in) long and 25 cm (10 in) wide (at the widest spot). Place half the potato slices in the dish, neatly arranged, making sure to sprinkle every single layer of potatoes with a little salt, pepper and nutmeg. When half the potatoes are placed, cover with half of the grated cheese. Place the second half of the potato slices, again seasoning with salt, pepper and nutmeg. Top with the remaining half of the cheese, evenly spread out. Pour the cream over and around the potatoes.

5. Cover the gratin loosely (with a lid or with aluminium foil). Place in the oven and cook for about 45 minutes, or until the cream has cooked away. Remove the lid and place the gratin briefly under the grill until it's brown and bubbly. Serve immediately.

POTATO GRATIN WITH MUSHROOMS, BUCKWHEAT AND FONTINA

We have never heard of a traditional use of this combination of ingredients, but we think it strikes a chord of international Alpine harmony. With ingredients drawn from cuisines all around the Alps, this delicious dish *should* be a Swiss classic, even if they haven't heard of it yet. We find that it works well as a side dish with roast pork, turkey, or game, or with braised meats. Wine-braised sauerkraut on the side of this side would round out the plate nicely.

SERVES 6 AS A SIDE DISH

450 ml (16 fl oz) chicken or beef broth
250 g (8 oz) toasted buckwheat groats (whole kasha)
50 g (2 oz) unsalted butter plus additional for buttering gratin dish
1 garlic clove, sliced thin
250 g (8 oz) coarsely chopped mushrooms
1 kg (2½ lb) low-starch potatoes, peeled, washed and sliced 5 mm (⅛ in) thick
225 g (8 oz) very thinly sliced onions
salt to taste
350 ml (12 fl oz) heavy cream
350 g (12 oz) grated Italian fontina (preferably from Val d'Aosta)

1. *Cook the buckwheat:* Bring the broth to a boil in a saucepan with a tightly fitting lid over high heat. Add the buckwheat, stir, cover and reduce heat to low. Simmer for 15 minutes, or until the buckwheat is mostly soft but with a slight crunch remaining.

2. *While the buckwheat is simmering, cook the mushrooms:* melt the 25 g (1 oz) butter in a frying pan over low heat. Add the garlic and cook until it begins to turn golden. Add the mushrooms and cook until their juices cover the bottom of the pan, about 10 minutes.

3. *Assemble the gratin:* Grease a large baking dish or gratin dish 35 x 22 x 5 cm (14 x 8½ x 2 in) with butter. Arrange a layer of potato slices on the bottom of the dish. Cover the empty spaces with more potato slices until you can no longer see the bottom and you've used about half of the potato slices. Next, arrange the onion slices over the potatoes. Sprinkle lightly with salt. Spoon the cooked mushrooms over the potatoes and onions, making sure to cover them. Top the mushroom layer with the cooked buckwheat. Layer the remaining potatoes and sprinkle lightly with salt. Pour the cream over the gratin, making sure to moisten as much of the surface as you can. Sprinkle the cheese over the top. Cover with foil.

4. Bake the gratin in a preheated 190°C (375°F) oven for 20 minutes. Remove the foil and bake for 20 more minutes, or until the cheese is brown and the cream is bubbling. Remove the gratin from the oven and let it cool for 10 minutes so that the liquids set. Serve immediately.

OTHER POTATO DISHES

ITALIAN POTATO CROQUETTES
These golden-brown logs, rich with cheese-and-potato flavour, were staples in Italian-American restaurants of

the fifties. They disappeared for a while, but are now making a comeback in restaurants that pay homage to the Italian-American cuisine of the good old days. They're fabulous accompaniments to saucy meat dishes, like chicken cacciatore; serve 2 to each diner. Make sure to season them well, using as much nutmeg, salt and pepper as you can tolerate.

SERVES 8 AS A SIDE DISH

450 g (1 lb) floury potatoes
25 g (1 oz) butter, at room temperature
2 eggs
10 g (2 tsp) very finely chopped onion
90 g (6 tbsp) very finely chopped fresh parsley
10 ml (2 tsp) extra-virgin olive oil
115 g (4 oz) freshly grated pecorino Romano
freshly grated nutmeg to taste
salt and pepper to taste
1 litre (1¾ pints) inexpensive olive oil for deep-frying
115 g (4 oz) freshly made, well seasoned breadcrumbs

1. Peel the potatoes and boil them in salted water until just cooked.

2. Working over a large bowl, put the potatoes through a potato ricer. Immediately add the butter and blend well with a fork. Beat 1 of the eggs and add to the potatoes, blending well. Add the onion, parsley, extra-virgin olive oil and pecorino Romano. Blend well. Add nutmeg to taste. Season extremely well with salt and pepper. Place mixture in the refrigerator for 30 minutes.

3. When ready to cook croquettes, place the oil in a heavy pot for deep-frying (a wok works well). Over medium-high heat, bring the oil to 185°C (360°F). Break the other egg into a wide, shallow bowl. Spread out the breadcrumbs in a second wide, shallow bowl. Divide the potato mixture into 8 pieces and shape each piece with your hands into a small log, about 7.5 g (3 in) long and

25 g (1 in) thick. (Try to keep them nicely cylindrical, like small egg rolls.)

4. Dip each croquette in the beaten egg, then roll in the breadcrumbs, making sure each croquette is coated well on all sides. Slip the croquettes, a few at a time, into the hot oil. Cook, turning occasionally so that the croquettes brown evenly, for 3 minutes. (They are done when they reach a deep, uniform, golden brown.) Drain on paper towels and serve immediately, sprinkled with salt if desired.

SPANISH POTATO OMELETTE (TORTILLA ESPAÑOLA)

'Omelette' is not exactly the right word for this unique Spanish treat . . . but we don't have a better word in English to describe it. It's a dense moist cake of potato, egg and onion, totally different from both the French omelette and the Mexican tortilla, more like a frittata than anything else. It sits on every tapas bar in Spain, at room temperature, waiting to be cut into wedges and served; it is, in fact, the most widely served tapa in that country. Soothing, homey, creamy and satisfying, when first tasted it is often thought to contain cheese. But it doesn't; much of the creaminess comes from the slow cooking of the potatoes in the olive oil. This version is a little thinner than the classic Spanish tortilla; we like it better, because it's a little more delicate. Serve it as an appetiser before a Spanish meal, or even as a light lunch with a salad on the side.

SERVES 6 AS A TAPA

125 ml (4 fl oz) olive oil
450 g (1 lb) russet potatoes
1 medium onion, halved through the root and sliced thin
6 large eggs, lightly beaten
salt and pepper to taste
coarse salt for sprinkling the tortilla
Spanish olive oil for sprinkling the tortilla

1. Heat the oil in an 20-23 cm (8-9-in) non-stick or well seasoned cast-iron frying pan over moderate heat. Peel the potatoes and slice them very thinly (we like to use a mandoline or a less expensive slicing machine made from plastic). (Do not put the potatoes in water.) Add the potatoes and the onion to the frying pan and stir until they are completely coated with the oil. Reduce the heat to moderately low and cook, stirring often so the vegetables will not colour, until the potatoes are cooked through, about 12 minutes (they should remain separate). Remove the potatoes and onion with a slotted spoon to a baking sheet lined with paper towels and let them drain.

2. Pour the oil out of the frying pan and into a cup. Wipe out the frying pan and remove any piece of onion or potato stuck to it. Add 45 ml (3 tbsp) of the oil from the cup back to the frying pan. Transfer the potato mixture to a shallow bowl, pour the eggs over them, turning to coat well, season with salt and pepper and let stand for 10 minutes.

3. Heat the oil in the frying pan over moderately high heat until very hot but not smoking and add the potato and egg mixture, spreading the potatoes evenly. Reduce the heat and shake the pan often to prevent sticking.

4. When the top is no longer liquidy (about 10 minutes), cover the frying pan with a plate and turn the tortilla out. Add 30 ml (2 tbsp) more of the reserved oil, return the tortilla, cooked side up, to the frying pan and cook for about 5 minutes longer, or until cooked through and the underside is moderately browned. Let the tortilla rest until it comes to room temperature.

5. When ready to serve, cut into 6 wedges and sprinkle each wedge with a little coarse salt and Spanish olive oil.

POTATO PANCAKES (LATKES)

Latkes are eaten in Jewish communities all over the world on the first night of the 8-day Hanukkah celebration. But you don't have to be Jewish to enjoy them—all you have to be is a good cook. For the sad fact is that many of the potato pancakes made in restaurants around the world are not good at all: they can be heavy, or greasy, or burned on the outside. At their best, latkes are light, lacy, flavourful, crisp and dry. Just use the following guide and you will whip up the best potato pancakes you've ever tasted. They are delicious as a side dish (with brisket, for example), or by themselves (served with apple sauce or sour cream).

- Use large potatoes; they contain more starch which helps bind the mixture.
- Grate the potatoes by hand: they give off less moisture. To get most of the moisture out, squeeze the potatoes by hand, or in a cloth towel, leaving behind the liquid.
- Use baking powder in the recipe: the latkes will be lighter.
- Make the batter chunky and loose textured if you want really crisp latkes. When the batter is loose, it has more rough edges to brown, which makes the latkes crunchy. Remember, however, that the looser the batter, the more oil it will absorb.
- Cook the batter as soon as possible after stirring it. Waiting may make it separate and will make it discolour.
- Make sure the oil is hot enough before adding the pancakes: if it isn't, they will be greasy.
- Cook the pancakes at the right temperature (moderate). If you cook them at too high a temperature, the outside will be done but the inside will not and at too low they will never get crisp enough.
- Turn the pancakes only once; each time you turn them they absorb oil.

MAKES 16 PANCAKES

4 large floury potatoes
1 medium onion, finely grated

1 large egg
2.5 g (½ tsp) baking powder
25 g (2 tbsp) all-purpose flour, or more if needed
15 g (1 tbsp) chopped fresh parsley or dill (non-
    traditional and optional)
salt and pepper to taste
125 ml (4 fl oz) vegetable oil for frying
sour cream and/or apple sauce as an
    accompaniment

1. Peel and finely grate the potatoes into a strainer. Add the onion and squeeze to press out any moisture. In a large bowl, stir together the potato mixture, egg, baking powder and flour (quantity of flour will vary depending on moisture of potatoes). Add parsley and season well with salt and pepper.

2. Heat some of the oil in a large, heavy frying pan over moderate heat (there should be just enough oil to pan-fry the pancakes, not to deep-fry them). The oil should be hot, but not smoking. Drop the potato mixture into the frying pan, 30 g (2 tbsp) at a time and smooth the tops with the back of a spoon to 6 x 7.5 cm (2½ x 3 in) in diameter. (Don't crowd pancakes in the pan; they should not touch each other.) Fry over moderate heat, turning them carefully once with a spatula, for 4 to 5 minutes on each side, or until dark golden brown and crisp on the outside. When they are cooked, drain the latkes on brown paper bags or paper towels. Repeat until all the pancakes are made; stir potato mixture thoroughly before frying each batch. Add more oil to the frying pan, if necessary.

3. Serve the latkes immediately with sour cream and/or apple sauce.

POTATO GALETTE

This wafer-thin, feather-light ring of potatoes became extremely popular in the old days of nouvelle cuisine. Approximately the size and thinness of a CD, the potato

ring is used as a garnish. Typically, a serving of red meat—say, a fanned-out display of rare duck breast slices—is topped by the galette, which typically slants against the meat 'casually arranged'. It is very crispy, deep in potato flavour and soaks up meat juices beautifully when it sits next to them on a plate.

MAKES 8 GALETTES

115 g (4 oz) butter
1 large floury potato, peeled
coarse salt for sprinkling the galette

1. To clarify butter, melt in a small pan and let sit for 5 minutes. Skim off the foam on top and discard. Then carefully pour off the buttery liquid (this is the clarified butter), discarding the milky solids in the bottom of the pan.

2. Using a plastic mandoline or similar device, slice potato into 2-mm (1/16-in) slices. Dry well on a kitchen towel. (Do not rinse the potatoes; the starch helps hold the potato together.)

3. Coat the bottom of a 20-cm (8-in) non-stick frying pan lightly with clarified butter and heat over moderately high heat. When butter is hot, make a ring of overlapping potato slices, leaving the centre open. (There will be about 8 potato slices in the ring which will be about 7.5-10 cm (3-4 in) in diameter.) Gently push down slices with a spatula as the galette is cooking to help the slices stick together. Cook for about 5 minutes, until underside is golden brown and crispy. Flip and cook for about another 5 minutes. (Watch carefully so that the galette does not get too dark.)

4. Remove to a baking sheet lined with paper towels. Sprinkle with coarse salt immediately. Keep warm in a 120°C (250°F) oven while the others are being cooked.

Note: If the galettes are to be held longer than 15 minutes, they should be recrisped. Lightly coat bottom of frying pan with clarified butter. When butter is hot, cook galette for 1 minute per side, remove to paper towels and sprinkle with coarse salt.

Some exotic indian spices

The spicy Indian potatoes with peas calls for a few spices which for Americans are exotic and hard to find.

Garam Masala This powder is actually a blend of ground spices, with emphasis on the 'sweeter,' more fragrant ones—such as cardamom, clove, cinnamon, nutmeg and mace. It is often added to a dish in the last few minutes of cooking, so that all the flavour may be preserved.

Black Mustard Seeds Confusingly, what are called black mustard seeds at Indian stores are actually brown mustard seeds. Not to worry. Just make sure to cook them over high heat so that their pungent flavour is released.

Asa fœtida You'll usually find this very exotic spice in powdered form. It is made from the sap of a large plant and, startlingly, tastes something like garlic.

SPICY INDIAN POTATOES WITH PEAS

Popular throughout Northern India, this dish is a lovely combination of tastes and textures. It will make you swear off prepared curry powder forever, because the blend of spices in the dish results in a remarkable layering of flavours. This version is quite hot; adjust the amount of green chillies and Indian chilli powder to your own taste.

SERVES 6 AS A SIDE DISH

3 medium-large low-starch potatoes (about
  1¼ pounds total)
2 teaspoons coriander seeds
30 ml (2 tbsp) ghee or vegetable oil
2 hot green chillies, seeded and chopped
30 g (2 tbsp) chopped peeled fresh ginger
30 g (2 tbsp) chopped fresh coriander roots and
  stems plus leaves for garnish
5 g (1 tsp) cumin
5 g (1 tsp) garam masala
2.5 g (½ tsp) black mustard seeds
pinch of ground turmeric
small pinch of asa fœtida (optional)
4 small tomatoes peeled, seeded and chopped
salt to taste
2.5 g (½ tsp) Indian chilli powder or ground red
  pepper
450 g (1 lb) fresh or thawed frozen tiny green peas
15 ml (1 tbsp) fresh lemon juice

1. Peel the potatoes and cut in 1-cm (½-in) dice. Boil the potatoes in salted water to cover in a medium saucepan until cooked through but still firm, about 15 to 20 minutes. Drain the potatoes in a colander.

2. While the potatoes are cooking, toast the coriander in a small frying pan over moderately high heat, shaking the pan, until the seeds are aromatic, about 2 minutes. Let seeds cool completely and grind to a fine powder in a coffee/spice grinder.

3. Heat the ghee or vegetable oil in a large frying pan over moderate heat until hot but not smoking. Add the chillies, ginger, coriander stems and roots, cumin, garam masala, black mustard seeds, turmeric and freshly ground coriander. Cook, stirring, until the mustard seeds pop, about 3 minutes. Add the optional asa fœtida, stirring. Stir in the tomatoes, salt well and cook, stirring, until the tomatoes release their liquid and begin to form a sauce, about 3 minutes.

4. Add the potatoes and Indian chilli powder and cook gently for 3 minutes. Add the peas and cook for 3 minutes. Sprinkle with lemon juice, garnish with fresh coriander leaves and serve immediately.

ROOT VEGETABLES AND TUBERS

Historically Americans haven't been averse to root vegetables—they just haven't thought about them much at all. The new generation of American chefs, however, has taken a shine to the sweet earthiness that root vegetables provide and has made them a regular part of the new menu (particularly in purées and gratins). We hope you do the same. Here are the root vegetables and tubers that are popular today:

Root vegetable recipes

For more delicious ways to serve root vegetables, see the recipes for ribollita on page 45, wheat beer soup with cheese croutons on page 67, steamed shad roe bundles with ginger-lemon sauce on page 356, lamb shanks braised in red wine with root vegetables on page 443 and kielbasa stew with root vegetables on page 462.

Celeriac Known in the U.S. as *celery root,* this small, knobby brown root is probably the strangest-looking of the root vegetables (it is to the vegetable world what ugli fruit is to citrus). Its caramel-white, dense flesh tastes rather like celery—without the strings! The French call it *céleri-rave* and, when cut into julienne and dressed with a mayonnaise-based sauce, it is the star of céleri-rave rémoulade, a classic French picnic item. We also like to toss raw strips of it with fresh fennel, then with olive oil, lemon and sea salt. But it's also delicious cooked—by itself, with other vegetables, or in stews. We especially like it in purées or in gratins.

Jerusalem Artichoke These small, light brown, knobby vegetables—a favourite of Native Americans in the eastern United States—have a mild, slightly sweet flavour and a dense, waxy-potato texture. They can be peeled before or after cooking and are delicious in soups, stews or on their own. The name is fascinating: they are the roots of the North American sunflower plant, which is called *girasole* in Italian and somewhere along the line *girasole* became 'Jerusalem'. Other than a very

subtle flavour resemblance, they have nothing at all to do with artichokes.

Parsnip Parsnips look like overgrown, fat white carrots and, especially when smaller and thinner, have an intensely sweet flavour. Use them in soups or stews and the rest of the dish will sweeten. The flavour of parsnips is more like cabbage or cauliflower than like carrots. They have a slightly woody texture, which disappears when they are roasted, baked, boiled, steamed or fried. Like many root vegetables, they are fantastic puréed.

Swede The Swede is also known as the yellow turnip and it is the 'neep' of the Scottish 'mashed neeps'. The French think it fit only for animals but it is popular throughout northern Europe. The French don't usually get it this wrong. Swedes—with their brownish skin and orange-yellow flesh—are absolutely delicious when cut into thin strips and cooked alongside other vegetables in vegetable stews or stir-fries. We've used them for years in our basic Indian vegetable curry and in a Provençal sauté that includes lots of garlic and fennel seeds.

Salsify Otherwise known as *oyster plant* because of a purported similarity in flavour to the mollusk, this root vegetable looks like a long, white carrot. It is often used in French and Italian dishes—softened and sautéed with prosciutto, or used in a creamy gratin. But it is delicious batter-fried, or blanched and served cold with traditional Italian condiments. Black salsify, a very long, carrot-shaped root with white flesh, has rough black skin and a mild flavour much like salsify. Also known as *scorzonera,* black salsify is usually blanched, then the creamy flesh is sliced and sautéed, or used in a gratin.

Sweet Potato Boiled, baked or mashed, sweet potatoes are a great alternative to white potatoes. One main variety of sweet potato has dry, mealy, yellow flesh and is more common in the northern part of the United States. A second main variety has moister, sweeter, more orange-yellow flesh and is preferred by Southerners—in the South this variety is sometimes mistakenly called a yam; yams are another plant entirely. The sweet, dense flesh of sweet potatoes is enhanced by spices like cinnamon or nutmeg... and, if you're veering from the savoury, a touch of brown sugar.

Turnip This classic root vegetable—with its white-and-purple exterior, it's perhaps the most familiar of them all—looks like a child's top, has a mild radish flavour and dense, cream-coloured flesh. Freshly peeled, it makes a nice alternative to radish or mooli in a salad. But we also like it in the more traditional guises: sautéed in goose fat, cubed and cooked with other root vegetables and mashed into purées with lots of sweet butter.

Yam Very often in our markets, sweet potatoes—even when canned—are identified as yams. But the true yam is very much a tropical vegetable—usually larger than a sweet potato, with rougher skin and whiter flesh. Yams may be used in cooking as sweet potatoes are—but true yams are often starchier than sweet potatoes and less sweet.

Two root vegetable gratins
Potato gratins dominate the headlines... but gratins are equally delicious when made with root vegetables. Here are two great ones.

CELERIAC GRATIN WITH SAFFRON AND GRUYÈRE CHEESE

If you like the taste of celeriac, you'll love this full-flavoured dish. Delicious with roast chicken.

SERVES 12

    1.8 kg (4 lb) celeriac, peeled and coarsely chopped
    1.3 kg (3 lb) russet potatoes (preferably Idaho),
      peeled and coarsely chopped
    225 ml (8 fl oz) double cream

    115 g (4 oz) butter
    2.5 g (½ tsp) saffron
    2 garlic cloves, finely chopped
    350 g (12 oz) Gruyère, coarsely grated
    salt and pepper to taste
    50 g (2 oz) coarsely chopped fresh flat-leaf parsley

1. Preheat oven to 200°C (400°F).

2. Place the celeriac and the potatoes in separate large saucepans with enough salted water to cover. Bring to a boil and cook until soft. Strain both the celery and potatoes and set aside.

3. In a heavy saucepan bring the cream to a boil over moderately high heat and add the butter, saffron and garlic. Reduce the heat to moderately low and cook about 5 minutes, or until the cream mixture is bright yellow.

4. Purée the celeriac in a food processor, gradually adding the cream mixture. Set aside. Place the potatoes in a bowl and mash until you have a rough texture. Add the celeriac mixture to the potatoes and add 1 cup of the Gruyère. Mix together with a wooden spoon and season generously with salt and pepper.

5. Butter a 33 x 23 cm (13 x 9 in) ovenproof dish. If you prefer to serve individual portions, you could use instead eight ramekins with a 300 ml (10 fl oz) capacity. Place the celeriac-potato mixture in the large, ovenproof dish or in the individual ramekins.

6. Sprinkle the top with the parsley and the remaining Gruyère. Bake in oven for about 15 minutes, or until the casserole is heated through and the top is golden brown.

GRATIN OF TURNIPS WITH BACON AND SAVOY CABBAGE

This is a deeply flavoured creation, a bite of rural

France. Make sure to serve it immediately, because the turnips turn bitter if the gratin sits for a few hours. Perfect as an accompaniment to garlic sausage.

SERVES 8

225g (8 oz) bacon, in 5-mm (¼-in) dice
2.2 kg (5 lb) turnip, peeled and sliced 3 mm (⅛ in) thick
6 large leaves finely shredded Savoy cabbage
salt and pepper to taste
125 ml (4 fl oz) beef stock
175 g (6 oz) Gruyère, coarsely grated
50 g (2 oz) freshly made breadcrumbs

1. Preheat oven to 190°C (375°F).

2. Place bacon in large frying pan over moderate heat and cook for 2 to 3 minutes, or until plenty of fat covers the bottom of the pan.

3. Place one quarter of the turnip slices in the pan and cook about 10 minutes, until turnips are cooked through. Remove turnips (be careful to keep most of the bacon in pan when removing the cooked turnips). Repeat until all turnips are cooked. When cooking the last batch of turnips, add the cabbage to the pan with the turnips. When finished, the turnips should be cooked through, the cabbage wilted and the bacon crisp.

4. Butter a 33 x 23 cm (13 x 9 in) ovenproof dish (about 2.25-litre (4-pint) capacity). Layer the turnip slices in the ovenproof dish and season each layer with salt and pepper. (Make each layer as even as possible; don't worry if the turnip slices fall apart.) Heat the beef stock in a small saucepan and pour over turnips. Sprinkle the Gruyère and breadcrumbs over the top and bake for 20 minutes, or until the top is crisp and golden. Serve immediately.

SQUASH AND MARROW

Squash—like tomatoes, potatoes, corn and chilli peppers—is an indigenous American food; the name 'squash,' in fact, comes from the Narragansett Indian word *askútasquash,* which means 'a green thing eaten raw'. But raw or cooked, squash and its relatives, marrow and courgette, have never been an American favourite. With the exception of the ubiquitous courgette, the sugary baked winter squash and a few squash decorations at harvest time, the native bounty of American squashes has been largely ignored by American chefs.

We can understand why: squash is not one of the world's most flavourful vegetables.

However, the new generation of American chefs has taken to squash like no generation before. Why? First of all, there *is* tremendous variety in shapes and colours, reasonable variety in textures and some variety in flavours. Secondly, squash is a wonderful background for other, more pronounced flavours. Thirdly, squash is our own ... and this appeals to chefs and home cooks trying to forge an American cuisine.

If you're interested in expanding your squash repertoire, the first thing you should know is that squash breaks into two main families: summer squash and winter squash.

Summer squash, the harvest of which in the Northeast begins in July, is infinitely more tender than winter squash. You can, in fact, eat the whole thing—both the thin outer skin and the interior flesh. The best-tasting summer squash is on the small side, not more than 4 in) long. The most familiar example of summer squash is courgette.

Winter squash, harvested in the Northeast beginning in September, is a much heartier vegetable. The flesh, though much firmer than the flesh of summer squash, is fine for eating; the thick outer skin, or rind, is not edible at all and must be cut away. Winter squashes are most delectable when fully ripe. The most familiar examples of winter squash are pumpkin, butternut squash and acorn squash.

In reality, many American squash types—whether 'summer' or 'winter'—are now available in the UK for most of the year. Here are the types you're most likely to see.

Acorn The acorn is a small to medium winter squash with forest-green or blue-green skin, often patched with yellow or orange. The mildly flavoured pumpkin-coloured flesh is best enjoyed when the squash is simply cut in half (or quartered), baked and dressed with a touch of butter and something sweet (like brown sugar, maple syrup, golden syrup or honey). Many markets are beginning to carry esoteric varieties like baby golden acorn and albino acorn.

Butternut This winter squash has an oblong, pear shape (some say 'bowling pin') and pinkish-tan skin. Large or small, butternut squashes have a large proportion of dense flesh, with a sweet, mild flavour similar to that of acorn squash. They are traditionally prepared in the same sweet way as acorns—but we like to bake halved small ones, then drizzle good olive oil and sea salt over the browned, crispy tops. Good also in risotti.

Delicata This is a cylindrical, fleshy-orange winter squash with distinctive green stripes running along the length. The flesh is yellow and has a taste reminiscent of sweetcorn—meaning that just butter and salt will make delicata a simple treat.

Hokkaido This Japanese winter squash has good flavour in its dark-orange flesh. It's great in dishes that require flavour from the squash itself.

Hubbard A winter squash that can grow up to 6.75 kg (15 lb) or so and is usually sold in pieces. Hubbard tends to be a bit stringy, mealy and a little dry—but it makes an ambrosial purée when touched with fresh cream and fragrant spices. Perfect for the Christmas holidays.

Pattypan A beautiful, scalloped-edge summer squash with bright yellow skin and sometimes a green 'eye' on either end. Pattypans can be baby-size up to the size of an acorn squash—the smaller the sweeter. They can be cooked whole, or cut in pieces and sautéed or baked.

Pumpkin Yes, some jack-o'-lanterns are edible! The pumpkins recommended for eating are roughly the size of acorn squash and are called *sugar* or *sweet* pumpkins. These are really delicious and can be prepared like any other winter squash—with sweet spices and a touch of brown sugar or honey. Carved out, the pumpkin flesh can be made into a fabulously creamy pumpkin soup—and you can use the shell for serving. Pumpkin is also traditional in Italy, often as a filling for pasta (sauce these pumpkin pillows simply with butter, cheese and sage). Pumpkin custards, flans, soufflés and gratins, have become the rage lately in creative American restaurants.

Spaghetti A large, oval-shaped, yellow winter marrow or gourd, which has stringy, yellow flesh that, after cooking, separates into strands resembling spaghetti. You can cook it either by baking it in the oven or boiling it in a large pot. Spaghetti marrow is also called *vegetable spaghetti* and it can be used in place of pasta with the full range of pasta sauces; the spaghetti marrow is not as resilient as pasta, but it is a little crunchier—and lower in calories!

Squash recipes

For more delicious ways to serve squash, see the recipes for perciatelli with a vegetable julienne on page 28; minestrone on page 44; panini with roasted tomatoes, squash and mozzarella on page 83; ratatouille on page 172; pumpkin gratin with sun-dried tomatoes on page 209; couscous with lamb, chicken, merguez, hearty vegetables and harissa on page 260; and pumpkin and pancetta stuffing on page 390.

Snake Also called long gourd, this Sicilian specialty is better known as *cucuzza,* or some similar take on the Southern Italian dialect. Long, thin and very pale green winter squash with cotton-white flesh, snake should be bought small (avoid any monster-size gourd that looks like a marrow). Though it's a winter marrow and therefore has an inedible skin—the inner flesh can be prepared as you would marrow or courgette. We like cucuzza sautéed with a little prosciutto, onion and tomato; the richness of the meat balances the tangy quality of the gourd.

Sweet Dumpling These creamy white-and-green-striped dumpling-shaped squash or marrows weigh no more than 450 g (1 lb), usually less and are about the size of large oranges. Because the orange-yellow flesh of dumpling squash is mellow, dense and sweet when cooked, it is best served *au naturel*... but it is also lovely when hollowed out and used for preparing and serving squash soup.

Turban This winter squash lives up to its name; atop the red-and-green base is something that looks like a turban, or a hat. The rich flesh of the turban squash can be used for many things... but one of the best uses is in soup, which can be poured back into the hollowed-out squash and topped with the dramatic 'turban.'

Yellow Squash About the size and shape of courgette and often prepared in the same way, yellow summer squash is a bit crunchier and sweeter than courgette. Our favourite way to prepare it: slice it thinly, grill it and pile it high on sourdough bread with mozzarella, pesto and other vegetables.

Courgette and marrow these are everywhere at every time of the year. Actually, it's in late summer that you have to be particularly careful with them because everyone and his brother will be trying to give you monstrous marrows from the garden. These baseball bats are okay for courgette bread but not especially good in vegetable dishes. For most purposes, seek out small, tender courgettes. When it comes to cooking them, you must also be vigilant. We hate the taste of raw courgette—it can almost make you gag—and 'fashionably' undercooked courgette is one of our least favourite vegetables. On the other hand, if you overcook it, it practically melts away. We like best courgette that has been salted, drained, then browned—either in a frying pan or on a grill—just to tenderness. It is fabulous with the full panoply of Mediterranean flavourings—garlic, tomato and basil being among the best.

Marrow blossoms

Ripening courgettes and marrows yield a deep-yellow blossom, which can be harvested and eaten. Jacques Maximin, in Nice, made them very trendy in the eighties and the trend has caught on here among our top restaurant chefs. But there's no reason you can't make them at home. They are a seasonal treat, usually available only in late summer and early fall at specialty groceries and farmers markets. In Nice, they like to coat them with a light, tempura-like batter and deep-fry them in olive oil. We find them particularly delicious when stuffed (crabmeat is good) and then battered and fried.

STUFFED COURGETTE GENOVESE

These courgette 'boats,'stuffed with potatoes and cheese, come from a recipe supplied by our sun-dried-tomato guru in Liguria. Served at room temperature, they are fabulous openers for a sunny Mediterranean meal.

SERVES 4 AS A FIRST COURSE

4 courgettes, about 685 g (1½ lb) total)
1 large potato
115 g (4 oz) grated Parmigiano-Reggiano
1 egg, beaten

pinch of freshly grated nutmeg
salt and pepper to taste
20 ml (4 tsp) pesto
extra-virgin olive oil for drizzling

1. Remove courgette stems and cut a thin round slice from the bottom of each courgette. Now cut the courgette in half lengthways. Using a serrated spoon, scoop out the flesh of each courgette half, leaving 5 mm (¼ in) of courgette flesh intact at both ends of each half. You will have 8 courgette 'boats,'and a mound of scooped-out courgette flesh. Reserve both.

2. Boil the potato until tender. When cool enough to handle, peel and mash in a potato ricer. Add the reserved courgette flesh, the Parmigiano-Reggiano, the egg and the nutmeg. Season to taste with salt and pepper.

3. Stuff each courgette 'boat' with the potato mixture. (The mixture should be only as high as the walls of the courgette, or a little above.) With a brush, smear about 2.5 ml (½ tsp) of pesto on each courgette 'boat.'

4. Choose a baking tin in which the courgette 'boats' fit snugly. Spread a little olive oil in the bottom of the tin and top with the courgette. Pour 5 mm (¼ in) of water into the pan, cover with foil and place in a preheated 200°C (400°F) oven. After 20 minutes, remove the foil. Continue cooking for another 25 minutes. Remove courgette, place on a platter and let cool to warm room temperature. When ready to serve, drizzle with extra-virgin olive oil.

TOMATOES

Americans have always loved tomatoes—but, given the quality of the tomatoes we've always eaten, you have to wonder why. Most of our tomatoes have been those sorry, pallid supermarket pretenders—bred to a perfect (and insipid) shape to maximise transportability, picked unripe, gassed to bring up the red colour and finally cottony and tasteless on the palate. Only in the peak months of August and September—and only from private backyard gardens—did most Americans get a taste of the real thing.

There's lots of happy news today in tomatoland. First of all, the late summer/early fall bonanza of real tomatoes has now become something we all can share, even if we don't have gardens. The profusion of farmers markets has brought great, in-season tomatoes to many urban Americans who were formerly shut out. Moreover, many farmers have gone back to growing old varieties of tomatoes, the kind that were rejected by the modern tomato shippers. Look for 'heirloom varieties'; you'll know them by their funny, convoluted shapes and their intense flavour.

But there's even better news: you don't have to circle August on your tomato calendar any longer, spending the other 11 months in tomato-deprived anticipation. A new generation of tomato shippers has understood the year-round need for quality tomatoes and is carefully shipping fabulous tomatoes from southern hothouses to markets all around the country, all year round. Of course, you have to pay the price. You'll see medium-small tomatoes, still clinging to the vine at about $4 (£2.50) a pound. And you'll see the ultra-premium cherry tomatoes—bursting with juice, flavour and sweetness—at about $7 (£4.25) a pound.

When tomatoes are this good—and there's no reason to buy anything less—you don't need a complicated recipe to make the most of them. Simply slice them, drizzle great olive oil on them and season with superb sea salt and freshly ground black pepper. Fresh herbs are optional. Great tomatoes also love bread and any type of open-faced tomato sandwich (on great, crusty loaves, possibly grilled and oiled) is going to be a winner.

What do you do, however, when you can't find fabulous tomatoes and you're craving a tomato? One solution is to concentrate the flavour and the sweetness of whatever tomatoes you've got by oven-drying them.

Tomato recipes

For more delicious ways to serve tomatoes, see the recipes for mozzarella, tomato and basil salad on page 11; penne with roasted tomatoes and fennel on page 28; pappa al pomodoro on page 55; bruschetta with fresh tomato and basil on page 91; goat cheese and tomato sauce on page 128; fresh tomato with fresh ginger sauce on page 130; tomato sauce with fennel, olives and orange zest on page 135; Ligurian stuffed tomatoes with olives, anchovies and basil on page 231; prawn marinara on page 347; and Turkish-style lamb shanks braised with vegetables on page 444.

OVEN-DRIED TOMATOES

You'll be amazed at the flavour and concentration of these tomatoes, which are simply baked in the oven at a very low temperature for many hours. Use them immediately in tomato salads, in sauces, in stews. Or, mix them with herbs and garlic, cover them with good olive oil and hold them for a few days in a container at room temperature.

MAKES 8 OVEN-DRIED TOMATO HALVES

4 ripe tomatoes
olive oil for brushing tomatoes
salt and pepper to taste

1. Preheat oven to 65°C (150°F).

2. Cut the tomatoes in half crossways and place on a baking sheet, cut sides up. Brush tomatoes with a little olive oil and sprinkle with salt and pepper. Place in oven for 20 hours or so. When finished, the tomatoes should be about half of their original size and still moist. (If you overcook them, they will shrink even further and dry out.)

OVEN-DRIED TOMATO AND AUBERGINE TIMBALES WITH PESTO

One of our favourite ways to use the oven-dried tomatoes is in building first-course timbales that also include baked aubergine and pesto. It's remarkably simple to do, but your guests will be dazzled. If you like, you can make the timbales a little richer by layering in a little goat cheese as well.

SERVES 4 AS A FIRST COURSE

1 small aubergine (about 175 g (6 oz))
extra-virgin olive oil for smearing the ramekins
8 oven-dried tomato halves (recipe precedes)
45 ml (3 tbsp) pesto (recipe on page 497)
salt to taste

1. Prick the aubergine all over with a fork. Place in a preheated 200°C (400°F) oven and cook until soft, about 30 minutes.

2. *Prepare the timbales:* Choose 4 small ramekins that hold about 75 ml (2½ oz) liquid each. Smear each one with a little extra-virgin olive oil. Place an oven-dried tomato half, skin side down, in each ramekin (the tomato should just fit the ramekin). Top with 5 ml (1 tsp) pesto. Top with a 1-cm (½-in) slice of roasted aubergine. Salt the aubergine. Top with 5 ml (1 tsp) pesto and then another tomato half, cut side down. You can serve immediately, or let sit at room temperature for several hours to allow flavours to mingle.

3. When ready to serve, run a small, sharp knife around and under the vegetables to prepare for unmoulding. Then, turn each ramekin upside down on to small serving plates. The vegetables should come out of the ramekins in stacked, perfectly round cylinders. Serve immediately, drizzled with a little oil from the pesto.

Sun-dried tomatoes

Ligurian tomato-farmers came up with a great idea very long ago: they'd spread out their excess tomatoes in the sun, every summer and thereby preserve a part of the crop that otherwise would have gone to waste. How were they to know that the smorgasbord that was the eighties in America virtually couldn't have happened without their invention?

We feel responsible for the sun-dried tomato epidemic in trendy eateries across the United States, because we were the first ones to import sun-dried tomatoes into the country. We liked them then and we like them now—but we must confess that, in our opinion, many chefs here are overdoing it a bit.

Sun-dried tomatoes have a very strong flavour—they're the vegetable equivalent of anchovies—and therefore have to be used sparingly; we've been shocked to see restaurants and hosts setting them out in bowls, as something to be nibbled, like olives or nuts! Also, because of their strong flavour, sun-dried tomatoes must be carefully paired with other foods; they can easily overwhelm, or clash with, their gastronomic playmates. We like them with other vegetables (they're great in salads), with eggs (they're terrific in frittatas) and as an accent next to starchy things (as on bread). But don't use them whole, or even in large chunks; generally, thin julienne strips of sun-dried tomatoes blend best with other foods.

As for purchasing them: be careful when you shop, because there are enormous differences of quality in sun-dried tomatoes.

You'll find sun-dried tomatoes mostly available in three different forms: dried (not reconstituted); reconstituted, in oil, in jars (sometimes with herbs); and reconstituted, in oil, in open tubs at fancy groceries, often mixed with other things (like herbs, garlic and pine nuts).

Buying them in dried form is a good way to save a little money on this pricey item. But you must be wary: there are lots of dried ones that have been dried too quickly, too brutally. You'll know them by their leathery texture—which, unfortunately, remains, even after you reconstitute them in water yourself. Watch out especially for dark ones; bright red is safest.

If you're reconstituting them yourself, you can get good-quality ones softened up in half an hour or so by pouring boiling water over them. But this speedy process removes a lot of flavour from the tomatoes. Our favourite method is to mix together seven-eighths warm water with one-eighth vinegar, pour the mixture over the dried tomatoes and let them steep for 24 to 36 hours. Then they're full of flavour and ready for any gastronomic use you intend.

If you're buying sun-dried tomatoes that have already been reconstituted and are preserved in oil, you should buy them in jars. We have tasted delicious open tubs of reconstituted, oil-soaked sun-dried tomatoes from fancy groceries . . . but only from groceries with rapid turnover. Too often, these tubs sit out for days, or weeks—at which time the sun-dried tomatoes become oxidised. Once again, look at the tomatoes carefully; you want ones that are red and plump. The safest way to buy reconstituted, oil-marinated sun-dried tomatoes is in a jar, because the closed jar preserves them well. Beyond that, of course, there are other issues. Did the producer use good oil? Did he overwhelm the tomatoes with herbs and/or garlic? Our favourite brand remains the Ligurian brand with which we started it all, Crespi; only the finest Ligurian oil is used and the tomatoes taste very fresh and very tomatoey.

Here's a recipe that shows off the ingredient well:

PUMPKIN GRATIN WITH SUN-DRIED TOMATOES

Sun-dried tomatoes are great here, since their bright acidity cuts the richness of the pumpkin. This is not as unusual a pairing as you might think; it is a very popular ingredient in Southern France and Northern Italy. This dish tastes best with a good, smoky bacon, like the applewood-smoked bacon that we sell at Dean & DeLuca.

SERVES 6

whole 1.3-kg (3-lb) pumpkin

salt and pepper to taste

50 g (2 oz) smoked bacon, finely diced

1 large red onion, chopped

225 g (8 oz) finely chopped sun-dried tomatoes (use oil-marinated type)

5 g (1 tsp) fresh thyme leaves

2 large eggs, lightly beaten

45 ml (3 tbsp) double cream

100 g (3½ oz) finely grated Gruyère or Italian fontina

25 g (1 oz) coarse fresh white breadcrumbs

1. Remove the flesh from the inside of the pumpkin, discard the seeds and cut flesh into thin slices, about 5 x 5 cm (2 x 2 in). Cook the pumpkin slices in a large casserole of boiling salted water until just tender, about 10 minutes. Drain the pumpkin in a colander and transfer to a bowl. Season well with salt and pepper.

2. Preheat oven to 190°C (375°F).

3. Cook the bacon in a large frying pan over moderate heat, stirring frequently, until it begins to crisp. Remove the bacon with a slotted spoon to paper towels to drain. Stir in the onion and cook, stirring frequently, until softened, about 5 minutes. Remove the frying pan from the heat and stir in half of the sun-dried tomatoes and the thyme; let cool slightly.

4. Stir the onion mixture, cooked bacon, eggs, cream and 30 g (2 tbsp) of the cheese into the pumpkin and season with salt and pepper. Place mixture in a 28-cm (9-in) gratin dish, smoothing the top. Sprinkle with the rest of the cheese and breadcrumbs and bake until nicely browned, about 30 minutes. Let stand for 5 minutes before serving.

5. Divide among 6 plates and strew the rest of the chopped sun-dried tomatoes over the gratin portions.

THE 'NEW' VEGETABLES

Once upon a time in America, virtually no one had heard of broccoli. Then, in the twenties Italian immigrants started to sell it at street markets in Italian neighbourhoods. In the forties, other street markets started to carry this strange stalk. It was a 'new' vegetable less than 75 years ago and is an 'old' staple today.

Well, there are new 'new' vegetables today. But they may soon be 'old' staples as well, because the 'new' vegetables of the eighties and nineties—this time largely supplied by Asian and Latin immigrants—are already moving into the mainstream.

ASIAN VEGETABLE GUIDE

BEANSPROUTS

Beansprouts began their American popularity in bad Chinese stir-fries, with the sprouts coming out of a can. But boy, has there been progress! Soon, we became used to crunchy *fresh* beansprouts in *good* stir-fries—and before you knew it, fresh beansprouts were as common in American supermarkets as in trendy, healthful salads that had nothing to do with Chinese food.

If you shop in Chinese markets, you're likely to find two main types of beansprouts. Relatively thick mung beansprouts are the most common—the ones many of us think of as beansprouts. They should be pearly white; browning indicates age. The Chinese like to pluck off the yellowish head and the stringy tail of the sprout. The other type is soy beansprouts which are longer and even thicker. Both types are great in stir-fries.

These days, you'll find lots of other sprouts in the market, intended for uses other than traditional Chinese ones. Lacy, thin alfalfa sprouts are very popular in the United States in salads, brown lentil sprouts are popular in Indian cooking and daikon sprouts are much-loved in Japan. You'll also find sprouts from cress, green peas, buckwheat, chick peas and others. Experiment with these in salads and stir-fries.

All sprouts should be fresh-looking: not dried out, not soft, not mushy. Smell them to make sure they're fresh; spoiled ones will have an unpleasant rotting vegetable smell.

BITTER MELON (BITTER GOURD)

The very strange-looking bitter melon or gourd with its light green, warty skin is very highly regarded in Asian countries, where it is said to purify the blood and cool the system. This medium-long, cucumber-shaped melon has a bitter vegetable flavour and is usually braised, steamed, or stir-fried with spices and often served with meat (skin it, cut away the seeds and the inner membrane and parboil for a few minutes). Because bitterness is not high on the American palate's hit parade, the flavour takes some getting used to for many of us.

BURDOCK ROOT

Known as *gobo* in Japan, where it is cultivated for food (it is cultivated for medicine in China), burdock root is a brownish-black root vegetable, long and thin, with fingerlike extensions and dense white flesh. It is a mild, crunchy vegetable. We like to use it, peeled, in traditional Japanese stews and hot noodle dishes; once you peel it, use it quickly to prevent discolouration. You may also come across pickled burdock root, which is orange in colour (the roots look like short, thin carrots), and is much sharper in flavour. It is delicious and has become very popular in salads at trendy Asian restaurants.

CHINESE CABBAGE (CHINESE LEAVES)

There are many types of Chinese cabbage. Here are the ones you're most likely to come across in Chinese markets in America:

Bok Choy Available all year, the cabbage variety called *bok choy* in America and the UK (actually, dozens of varieties of bok choy are grown in China) has thick white stems, a rounded base and dark-green, spinachlike leaves. It has a clean, almost watery taste, with a pleasing suggestion of cabbage on the palate (it's like cabbage *lite*). It's especially good sliced in stir-fries, leaves and all, cooked in a wok hot enough to sear the outside of the bok choy pieces.

Choy Sum A close relative of bok choy. In fact, choy sum is often called *bok choy sum*. It is smaller and thinner than bok choy and more delicate. Smaller and more delicate still is baby bok choy sum, which has moved on to adventurous New American menus. (The American designation *choy sum* is a little confusing, because *choy sum* in Hong Kong means another type of Chinese cabbage entirely, one that is slightly bitter with very narrow stems. In America, this one is known as *yow choy*.)

Chinese Leaves Originally from China, now grown in southern Europe and in northern California, Chinese leaves constitute the Big Two of Chinese cabbages in America. Chinese leaves has a tightly packed pale green head, crinkly leaves and a very mild flavour. Also good in stir-fries and in soups. Indispensable in kimchi, the Korean pickled cabbage.

Chinese Broccoli Also known as *gai larn* in Chinese produce markets, this flowering green tastes only faintly like European broccoli; the taste is less cabbagey, nuttier and decidedly more bitter. Other differences are the virtual absence of florets, the higher proportion of stalks and the much greater size and quantity of leaves (which are good to eat). Cooking softens the bitterness. We like to blanch it first, then stir-fry it in oil with oyster sauce and shiitake mushrooms. It is always served a little crunchy.

Mustard Greens These vegetables are hard to find in the UK although mustard is grown here. The flavour of the greens is similar to mustard: spicy, edgy, surprising to most who taste it. There are many varieties in China, but the mustard greens seen in the U.S. have wide, curved stalks and lots of broad, bright green leaves. We prefer the ones with straight stalks; they're a little smaller, more delicate and, after a quick boil, are great in stir-fries with lightly thickened yellow sauces (made from chicken stock, garlic and ginger).

CHINESE OKRA

Also called *luffa* or *angled luffa,* this vegetable is actually a loofah! Chinese okra can grow up to 270 cm (9 ft) long (!) but the ones you'll see in Asian groceries are generally about 45 cm (18 in). Buy Chinese okra on the young side and trim the ribs with a vegetable peeler to avoid bitterness. Steaming and stir-frying are the usual methods of cooking this unusual vegetable; it combines well with fish, meat and highly flavoured Chinese sauces.

MOOLI (DAIKON)

A long, Japanese white radish with about a 5-cm (2-in) diameter, raw mooli (daikon) has a light, delicious flavour—milder than red garden radishes and with a wonderful, crisp bite. The Japanese pickle it, cook it or eat it raw (often with sushi). Try it peeled and cut into julienne slivers for Asian-style vegetable salads. Also eaten in the West Indies, hence the name mooli, by which it is known in the UK.

LONG BEAN

One of the most beautiful vegetables, Chinese long beans (*dau gok* in Cantonese)—which look like amazingly long string beans—make a delicious side dish. They are not as intensely flavoured as string beans or haricots verts; actually, they are part of the black-eyed pea family, not the bean family. But they look intriguing and they combine beautifully with Chinese flavourings. Buy them young, thin, smooth and bright green; they can grow to a 'yard-long,' as they are sometimes called, but the best ones are no more than 45 cm (18 in) long. You may cut them to any length you desire (it won't affect the cooking time), but don't cut them too short, or they will lose some of their grace and beauty. Cutting them into halves or thirds crosswise is good—but leave them as long as you can, given the plates they will be eaten from and what else will be on the plate.

LOTUS ROOT

This oddly attractive cylindrical root has creamy white flesh and is full of round holes that make slices of lotus root look like the petals of a flower. The crunchy, opaque flesh tastes a bit like artichoke and is often sliced and stir-fried, or slow-cooked in soups and stews, or stuffed to make more elaborate dishes. One treatment of lotus root has become a trendy staple at New American restaurants: the deep-fried lotus root chip as garnish. Once you peel and slice lotus root, use it quickly—it discolours in no time.

SEAWEED

Most of the better known seaweeds are Japanese varieties, such as hijiki, kombu, nori and wakame. Each one is used differently...though all have rich, vegetal, marinelike flavours. Toasted nori, of course, is used to wrap sushi, while thin strands of hijiki are a healthful addition to salads or other dishes. Long black strips of kombu are the base for the Japanese soup stock dashi and the curly leaves of wakame are treated as vegetables and added to rich stews and soups. Though only recently popular, they are very tasty and are always full of nutrients. Hawaii (where *ogo* is the generic name for seaweed), as you might expect, is the seaweed capital of the United States.

WATER CHESTNUT

Most of us rarely get to see fresh water chestnuts; the old can, unfortunately, still holds sway. This is a shame, because fresh water chestnuts, with their rich, chocolate-brown skins, are very delicious. Additionally, they have a juicy, cooling, refreshing quality. They are extremely versatile and are commonly eaten raw as a fruit, or in dessert dishes, or in savoury stir-fries.

WINTER MELON

This well-known Chinese vegetable, also called *dong gwa* or *winter gourd,* looks like a dusty watermelon and can reach 45 kg (100 lb)—one of the largest vegetables grown! It is the snowlike covering that gives it its name; actually, peak season is in the summer. It has a neutral flavour and has flesh like pale, white marrow (to which family it belongs). It is best known for its use in traditional winter melon soup, but is also eaten as a sweet—boiled in sugar syrup and candied.

CHINESE BROCCOLI WITH BLACK BEAN SAUCE
SERVES 6 TO 8 AS PART OF A CHINESE MEAL

15 g (1 tbsp) fermented black beans
900 g (2 lb) Chinese broccoli,
  separated in stalks
75 ml (3 tbsp) peanut oil
2 large garlic cloves, chopped
2 quarter-size slices fresh ginger, chopped
5 g (1 tsp) sugar
125 ml (4 fl oz) chicken stock
5 g (1 tsp) cornflour

1. Cover the black beans with warm water. Let sit for 5 to 10 minutes.

2. Plunge the Chinese broccoli, leaves included, into a large pot of salted boiling water. Cook for 1 minute. Refresh under cold water and dry on paper towels.

3. Place the peanut oil in a large wok over very high heat. Drain the black beans and smash them with a heavy cleaver. Toss them into the hot wok, along with the garlic and ginger. Stir-fry for 15 seconds. Add the broccoli and stir to coat broccoli with oil and seasonings. Add the sugar and chicken stock. Stir, cover and cook over high heat until broccoli is just done, about 2 minutes (it should still be crunchy).

4. Mix the cornflour in a small bowl with a small amount of water (about 45 ml (3 tbsp)) to make a liquid that resembles double cream. Make sure the chicken stock is boiling in the wok, then add the cornflour mixture to it. Stir vigorously, place Chinese broccoli on a platter and serve immediately.

CHINESE LONG BEANS WITH SHREDDED PORK, GARLIC AND GINGER

The flavours in this dish are subtle—which puts the focus on the beans and transports you to a hot wok spot in Chinatown. The main supporting player in this recipe—the Chinese roast pork—is just a phone call away; you can order it from any Chinese take-away. Or you can leave it out and make the dish vegetarian. But we like it better with a little pork.
SERVES 4 TO 6 AS PART OF A CHINESE MEAL

450-g (1-lb) bunch thin Chinese long beans, ends
  trimmed and the beans cut crossways into halves
  or thirds
15 ml (1 tbsp) rapeseed or safflower oil
3 shallots, sliced crossways
20 g (1½ tbsp) very thin strips peeled fresh ginger
4 garlic cloves, sliced crosswise
50 g (2 oz) Chinese roast pork, cut into very thin
  strips
15 ml (1 tbsp) soy sauce or more to taste
7.5 ml (1½ tsp) Asian (toasted) sesame oil
1.25 g (¼ tsp) crushed hot red pepper flakes or
  more to taste

1. Bring a large casserole of water to a boil and add salt. Add the long beans and blanch for 1 minute. Drain the beans in a colander and refresh with cold water.

2. Heat the rapeseed oil in a large, well seasoned wok over moderately high heat until hot but not smoking. Add the shallots, ginger and garlic and stir-fry for 2 minutes, or until soft.

3. Add the long beans, roast pork, soy sauce, sesame oil and pepper flakes and stir fry for 3 or 4 minutes, or until beans are cooked through and very hot.

4. Place the beans on a platter and serve hot.

WINTER MELON SOUP

For maximum dramatic effect at a big-deal dinner, use a scooped-out, elaborately carved winter melon as a tureen for this delicious soup.

SERVES 4

750 ml (1¼ pints) rich pork stock
1 chicken drumstick and thigh
50 g (2 oz) diced Smithfield or York ham
3 spring onions, chopped
1 garlic clove, chopped
50 g (2 oz) sliced bamboo shoots (fresh, if possible)
50 g (2 oz) peeled and diced water chestnuts (fresh, if possible)
15 g (1 tbsp) dried shrimp, soaked in warm water for 20 minutes
6 Chinese mushrooms, soaked in warm water for 20 minutes
225 g (8 oz) diced winter melon
115 g (4 oz) diced tomato
115 g (4 oz) peas (fresh or thawed frozen)
115 g (4 oz) baby corn
45 g (3 tbsp) cornflour
50 g (2 oz) diced bean curd (firm-style)
2.5 ml (½ tsp) Chinese sesame oil

1. Bring the pork stock to a boil in a large, heavy saucepan. Reduce to a simmer, add the chicken and cook gently for 30 minutes. Remove the chicken, bone the meat, shred it and discard the bones.

2. Add the shredded chicken to the pork stock with the ham, spring onions, garlic, bamboo shoots, water chestnuts and dried shrimp. Slice the Chinese mushrooms and add to the stock. Simmer for 30 minutes.

3. Add the winter melon, tomato, peas and baby corn. Bring soup to a boil. Mix together the cornflour with enough cold water to make a liquid resembling heavy cream. Pour enough into boiling soup, stirring, to thicken soup lightly. Reduce to simmer and add the bean curd. Cook gently for 10 minutes. Swirl in sesame oil and serve immediately.

TROPICAL VEGETABLE GUIDE

Boniato (*batata*) This vegetable, sometimes called a Cuban sweet potato, does in fact have the shape, look and feel of an oblong, red sweet potato: faint purple skin covered by dusty, black patches. It has dry, starchy white flesh that is easy to cut. When boiled, the flesh tastes and feels very much like the flesh of a moist baked potato…but with a touch of nutty sweetness. Boniatos are also fabulous when mashed.

Breadfruit Breadfruit looks like a cantaloupe-size armadillo covered in Astro Turf! Its creamy-white flesh tastes smooth, sweet and slightly grassy. It is commonly used in purées. Latino cooks make a quality distinction between watery and meaty breadfruit; the latter is more prized for its dense, hard texture.

Calabaza A pumpkin variety from the West Indies, calabaza is generally large and green on the outside… though the colour can vary. The sweet, earthy flesh is yellow-orange and is delicious in vegetables stews, or mashed for fritters.

Chocho Also called *xoxo, chayote, mirliton, christophine and vegetable pear,* it is actually a summer squash that looks like a cross between a pear and an avocado; it has light green skin. When buying chayote, look for one that's hard and firm to the touch. Make sure that the skin is unblemished. The raw flesh is crisp, wet and translucent—rather like a Chinese pear—with the taste and smell of freshly mown grass (though we don't recommend eating it this way). Chayote is very versatile and can be boiled, steamed or grilled. We especially like it stuffed with meats and spices, as it's often done in Cajun country.

Jicama (pronounced KHEE-kama) This tan-skinned vegetable has the crisp, watery bite of fresh water chestnuts. It is probably the only one in this category you would want to eat uncooked (peeled, of course). While some find it bland, the crunchy flesh of jicama is fantastic when really fresh; just a touch of salt and lemon brings out its flavour. It's particularly nice in vegetable salads along with coriander, tomatoes and lime. Can be found occasionally in the UK.

Name (pronounced gná–may) This is a type of yam that is sold in pieces and resembles small logs of old wood. It has hard, cream-coloured flesh, which takes longer to cook than the flesh of other starchy vegetables in this section. We think it's also drier, a bit stringier and less flavourful than the others. It tastes best when mashed, or when baked with butter like winter squash.

Nopales Also known as cactus paddles, nopales are the 'leaves' from various kinds of the nopal cactus. They have tiny needles on the skin that are easily shaved off. These flat, round green paddles have a mildly spicy green-bean flavour and a chewy, viscous quality when cooked. These are definitely an acquired taste.

Plantains Plantains resemble bananas—but are about twice the size, with a much thicker, heavier skin. Furthermore . . . bananas are usually eaten raw, while plantains are always cooked. Plantains are unusual in that they come to the market at three different levels of ripeness—and Latino chefs do three different things with them. The unripe ones, which are dark green on the outside and rock hard inside, are usually peeled, sliced, partially fried, squashed (sometimes in a hinged paddle dedicated to this purpose), then fried again to make something like round plantain french fries. We find green plaintains to have a little less flavour than more mature ones. The medium-ripe plantains, which have a yellow-black skin, are used in many different ways; often, they are puréed and turned into mashed plantains or fufu. Ripe plantains are very black on the outside, relatively soft on the inside and quite sweet. More often than not, they are simply peeled, sliced and pan-fried—then served as an accompaniment to the main course, along with rice and beans. There is also a variety of plantain called *burrus,* which is smaller than the regular plantain, with white flesh and slightly less flavour.

Taro Also known as *dasheen, tannia, tannier,* or *eddo,* taro root is a barrel-shaped tuber that has rough, barklike skin and cottony, cream-coloured flesh. It is the basis of the Hawaiian staple, poi, which is puréed taro root—one of the most tasteless dishes in the world, with a gluey texture. However, taro is at its best when thinly sliced and deep-fried.

Tomatillo There's much confusion about tomatillos. They look like green, unripe tomatoes—but they are not! They come from a different family entirely (related to the small fruit sometimes called *cape gooseberries* or *physallis*). They have a natural parchmentlike wrapping around them and are terrific when eaten raw. The taste is fascinating: somewhere between rhubarb, apples, pumpkin and persimmons. They are absolutely vital in green salsas and Mexican salads, particularly when you want a great shortcut to real South-west flavour.

Yautia Also called *malanga,* this yam-shaped vegetable
has dark brown, hairy skin and soft, pure white flesh,
which is a little gummy on the surface. When boiled, it
has a wonderful, sweet baked potato–like texture with a
faint taste of—we're not crazy—fat, juicy lamb chops.
When fried into crispy potato-like crisps, it makes a
delicious, starchy and unusual snack, which is not at all
oily.

Yuca The yuca root, better known as cassava, manioc or
manihot, is really wonderful to cook with. Don't be put
off by the unfamiliar look and feel—dark brown,
barklike skin and a long, cylindrical shape. The skin and
pinkish layer underneath are easily peeled off with a
large, heavy paring knife. The flesh of the yuca should
be pure white without dark patches. The flesh is hard, so
be careful cutting it at first. Yuca is cooked in a variety
of ways: when boiled it is starchy and a bit sticky, with a
roasted chestnut texture and sweetness. The taste is
something like potatoes with a mineral or metal tang.
Yuca's delicious when cut into chunks resembling sauté
potatoes and deep-fried. Yuca is also used to make a
dough for tarts and pies.

RICE/BEANS/ GRAINS

IN THE NUTRITIONALLY MINDED NINETIES, IT HAS BECOME INCREASINGLY CLEAR THAT ONLY THE MODERN WESTERN NATIONS OF THE WORLD ARE IN THE HABIT OF PUTTING MEAT 'AT THE CENTRE OF THE PLATE'.

MOST OF THE REST OF THE WORLD PUTS SOMETHING ELSE AT THE CENTRE OF THE PLATE: CARBOHYDRATES, USUALLY IN THE FORM OF RICE, BEANS AND GRAINS.

AS WE AMERICANS STARTED LOOKING TO THESE OTHER CUISINES FOR OUR NUTRITIONAL MODELS—AND AS WE LEARNED MORE ABOUT THEIR CLASSIC DISHES BASED ON RICE, BEANS AND GRAINS—THE CATEGORY EXPLODED. PEOPLE WHO, 10 YEARS AGO, KNEW NOTHING BEYOND UNCLE BEN'S RICE, CAMPBELL'S PORK AND BEANS AND KELLOGG'S CORN FLAKES WERE SUDDENLY ASKING FOR BASMATI, DRIED FAVA BEANS (BROAD BEANS) AND SPELT AT THEIR FANCY GROCERIES.

PEOPLE OFTEN THINK OF DEAN & DELUCA AS A SHOP THAT CHAMPIONED ITALIAN PRODUCTS IN THE UNITED STATES—BUT THEY MAY NOT REALISE THAT WE WERE ALSO THE FIRST TO DISTRIBUTE IN THIS COUNTRY MANY OF THE RICES, BEANS AND GRAINS THAT HAVE BECOME SUCH AN INTEGRAL PART OF AMERICAN COOKING TODAY.

RICE

For millions of people around the world, rice is a daily staple. For some of them, fish, meat and vegetables are merely 'condiments' that accompany the rice; for others, rice is an everyday side dish to fish, meat and vegetables.

We see little of either practice in the United States. Though rice is sometimes served in America as an accompanying starch (especially in the South), it rarely constitutes the 'main' dish of an American meal.

But things have been changing—and again, the growth of authentic ethnic food in American restaurants has turned the tide. Many Americans have learned to eat rice as a side dish, out of a bowl with chopsticks alongside their Chinese food. Even more important, the great rice dishes of China, Thailand, Japan, India, the Middle East, Italy, Spain and Latin America have excited the American palate. A restaurant-goer in America might now have risotto instead of pasta in an Italian restaurant, paella as a main course in a Spanish restaurant and biryani as one of the main dishes in an Indian restaurant even though these dishes were once virtually unknown here.

Our national rice consciousness has also been bolstered by the growing availability of different rices from around the world. There are over seven thousand varieties and no one can keep track of them all. Here are the chief categories of available rices and some of the most important types within each category.

Brown rice and white rice

When rice is harvested, the central white part (or endosperm) has a brown coating that contains most of the rice's fibre and most of its nutrients. The people of most rice-eating nations around the world, even though they depend on rice for much of their nutrition, prefer white rice, stripped of its brown coating. Recently, in the United States, unstripped rice, or brown rice, has become popular among 'health food' fans.

We side with most of the world in most gastronomic situations. There's something clean and refreshing about white rice; a bowl of brown rice just seems wrong, for example, with a Chinese meal. However, the nuttier flavour and chewier texture of brown rice works perfectly when you're craving a 'grain' experience rather than an ethnic one.

Long-Grain Rice There are two types of starch in every grain of rice, in varying proportions: amylose and amylopectin. Long-grain rice has more of the former, which is a tougher starch to dissolve. This means that long-grain rice should be used when you want a dry and fluffy texture in your rice dish, with every grain separate. It's as good for the complicated pilafs of the Middle East and India as it is for a simple white rice side dish. It is the type that you're most likely to find in your supermarket, generically labelled 'long-grain rice'. However, there are some special long-grain rices produced around the world that you should seek out: *basmati* (the aromatic rice of India and Pakistan); *Texmati* (a Texas version of the same); *wehani* (a reddish-brown California variety); *wild pecan rice* (no pecans, but with a brownish colour and nutty flavour); *popcorn rice* (a Louisiana rice that tastes like popcorn); *jasmine rice* (a Thai rice with no jasmine in it, but a delicate jasmine flavour); and *Thai black rice* (a black, shiny rice from Thailand, usually used in desserts).

Short-Grain Rice Grains of short-grain rice, which are thicker than grains of long-grain rice and much higher in amylopectin (which dissolves in water easily), stick together more than long-grain—so this category is for making wetter, creamier, less fluffy rice dishes (like Italian risotti and Spanish paellas). Short-grain is also best when you want the rice to stick together for a second cooking, as in rice croquettes. It's available in brown or white.

Sticky Rice This is a type of short-grain rice that is stickier still. It's perfect for sushi, where the grains must hold together under their mantles of seaweed. In the rest of Asia, outside of Japan, its most common use is in dessert.

To wash, or not to wash?

There's lots of contradictory advice available about washing rice. Some cooks say always. Some cooks say never. We say: sometimes. There are two reasons why the advice varies: the type of rice varies and the dish to be made with the rice varies.

Type of Rice First of all: is the rice dirty? Most plastic-bagged rices available in British and American supermarkets are not dirty and no washing is necessary on that score. But if you buy rice from sacks at ethnic groceries, you may want to wash dirt and impurities away. Much American rice is polished and needs no washing; some foreign rices are not polished (not polishing helps retain nutrients in the rice) and these may need to be washed.

Secondly: is the rice old or young? Younger rice has more moisture to begin with and may absorb more if you wash it; this is not desirable if you're making fluffy rice. Older rice is drier and may not absorb water as you wash it. If your rice merchant is Asian, chances are he or she will know the age of the rice. If you have to determine the age yourself, check the colour: the older rice will be more opaque, with a dusty look; the younger rice will be more translucent.

Lastly, if you're cooking sticky rice, you'll need to rinse it heavily; it has an oily coating that's best removed.

Type of Dish If you're making fluffy rice (for which you'll use long-grain rice) you will improve the fluff if you wash the rice carefully—but only if the rice is old! If you wash young rice, you may make it wetter and cause it to yield less fluffy results. Remember: the ideal for fluffy rice is old, long-grain rice, carefully washed. Things are simpler if you're making creamy, risotto-style rice: no matter which type of short-grain rice you use, you will improve the creaminess if you don't wash the rice. (Please note: if your chief interest is retaining nutrients in the rice, don't wash it under any circumstances.)

MAKING BASIC FLUFFY RICE

Not only is there no Santa Claus, there's another crusher: those directions on the backs of boxes and plastic bags of long-grain rice don't always yield perfect fluffy results! If you make a lot of fluffy rice and seek perfection, you might want to invest in an electric Asian rice cooker (which does an excellent job). But Luddites too can make perfect rice.

FLUFFY RICE

The following recipe yields perfect results every time: fluffy rice that's dry and a little chewy—just like in Chinese restaurants. It's very important that during the second step of the recipe you get the heat as low as possible; you might want to use a heat-tamer on your burner (a metal pad that lowers the amount of heat under the pot).

MAKES ABOUT 550 G (20 OZ)

225 g (8 oz) long-grain rice, unwashed if young
350 ml (12 fl oz) cold water
1.25 ml (¼ tsp) salt

1. Place the rice in a heavy saucepan with a tight-fitting lid. Add the water and salt. Place the pan over high heat and bring to a boil. Reduce heat slightly, but continue to boil until the water is just about evaporated, 5 to 10 minutes.

2. Bring heat down as low as you can. Cover pan and cook rice until tender about 15 minutes. Place a clean tea towel (or dish cloth) on top of rice, cover again, remove pan from heat and let sit for 5 minutes.

3. Fluff rice with a fork and serve.

Note: If you don't use a heat-tamer, you may get a crusty layer of rice on the bottom of the pan. This is prized in many cultures—it even gets its own name, depending on what country you're in. In Thailand, they let the crusty rice dry in the sun, cut it into circles, deep-fry the circles and use them as a pick-up for dips. So do not scrape the crusty layer at the bottom of the saucepan into your fluffy rice. Instead, dry it for a few minutes, in the saucepan, in a 150°C (300°F) oven. Then, scrape it out, break it up and deep-fry the lumps for a great snack.

Two Thai methods for fluffy rice

Thai chefs know something about rice; central Thailand is one of the world's largest rice-producing areas and may have even been the birthplace of rice. In Thailand, they like to use the 'index-finger' method for cooking fluffy rice. Place rinsed long-grain rice in a heavy, flat-bottomed pot; don't fill the pot with rice any more than one third of the way. Place the tip of your index finger on top of the rice, then add cold water until the water comes up to the first joint of your finger (that's the joint with creases below the nail). Place pot over moderately high heat and, stirring occasionally, bring to a boil. Reduce heat to low, cover and simmer for 10 to 15 minutes or until the rice is dry and fluffy.

The second Thai method is an ancient one. Fill a pot with water (say, 4 litres (7 pints)) and add a good quantity of rice to it (say, 900 g (2 lb)). Bring to a boil and cook, uncovered, for 10 to 15 minutes; test the rice to see if the texture's to your taste. Spill out the water—the Thais save this nutritious liquid for use as a milk substitute. The rice will be wet—so place the pot over moderate heat and keep turning, stirring and flipping the rice until it's dry and fluffy (about 5 to 10 minutes). This rice will be especially fragrant when done.

RISOTTO

Risotto doesn't mean 'rice' in Italian; it means something like 'riced,' or cooked in the traditional way that Northern Italians cook rice (they've been doing it for about 500 years). In common parlance, risotto is the name of a creamy, oozy rice dish, made by forcing grains of rice to absorb slowly a flavoured stock . It is perhaps the greatest example in the world of short-grain rice's gastronomic potential.

Those who have sampled risotto in Italy never forget the remarkable taste and texture of this unique dish. Happily, risotto became popular in America's Italian restaurants in the eighties and, today, most northern Italian restaurants serve it; unhappily, it's a rare experience to find risotto in America as perfectly cooked as it is in Italy.

This is a shame. It's really a simple dish to prepare, with results all out of proportion to the effort expended. When it's right, it is, to us, the ultimate comfort food. Those who haven't tasted it are often surprised to learn that it has nothing in common with the fluffy rice dishes of the world. It is more like porridge—rice suspended in a creamy ooze, real stick-to-your-ribs food. Serve it instead of pasta as they often do in Northern Italy—all by itself as a first course as an in-between course, or as a main course.

If you want to make perfect risotto:

Use the right rice. The most important thing when making a risotto is to use the right rice; choose an Italian short-grain rice that absorbs the liquid it's cooked in and swells up without breaking or becoming mushy. There are four types of rice in Italy: superfino, fino, semifino and ordinario, of which only the first two are good for risotto. Arborio, from Piemonte, is a popular rice of the superfino type; other good varieties of this type are Roma, Maratelli and Carnaroli. Vialone Nano, from around Lake Garda, is good rice of the fino type; it's a little shorter than Arborio, and has a lower proportion of amylopectin, the fast-dissolving starch that makes short-grain rice sticky. This means that risotti made with Vialone Nano is looser—which is the way they like it in the Veneto. Do not use any other type of rice!

Choose the right pot. Pick a heavy-bottomed pot with even heat distribution, copper, anodised aluminium or stainless steel. No cover is necessary. We like to use a wide pot which holds the rice in as thin a layer as possible; cooking a lot of rice in a small pot makes for uneven liquid absorption.

Coat the rice with butter. The first step in risotto-making is frying onions, shallots or garlic in butter, right in the risotto pot. When onions, shallots, or garlic have melted add the rice—and make sure to stir the rice well, coating every grain with butter.

Use mildly flavoured, simmering stock. The next step is the first addition of simmering stock to the rice. Make sure to use a stock with a mild flavour, lest you overwhelm the subtle flavour of the risotto. We especially dislike strong mushroom liquid left over from soaking dried mushrooms; they overwhelm a mushroom risotto. Make sure also that the stock is not overly salty; you can always adjust the seasoning later of an under-salted risotto.

Add stock as the rice soaks it up. The first addition of stock is the largest. After the rice has absorbed this first addition, you must add another125 ml (4 fl oz) of simmering stock . When the rice soaks it up, then add another 125 ml (4 fl oz) of simmering stock . And so on , until the rice reaches the perfect degree of doneness.

Keep stirring. Though it's not necessary to stir the rice every second of the way, fairly constant stirring (with a pause of a minute here and there) will create an evenly cooked risotto.

Know the signs of perfectly cooked rice. During the cooking process, the rice absorbs stock —which finally penetrates and softens the protein surrounding the starch nucleus of the rice grain. When it hits the nucleus and is about to soften it (the nucleus will be transparent at this point), the rice is done and must be removed from the heat. The rice grains must be neither firm (undercooked) nor soft (overcooked); they should have just a suggestion of resistance at the centre as you bite them.

Adjust the texture of the risotto just before serving. Sometimes, your rice may be perfectly cooked ... but the sauce surrounding it may be too thin. We like a good, runny risotto—and, therefore, we usually add a little more hot stock to adjust the texture of the dish after the rice is done. Think of it as rice in a copious, medium-thick sauce.

Add the mantecato at the end. Italians like to 'mount' the risotto at the end by adding room-temperature butter and lots of freshly grated Parmigiano-Reggiano, both stirred in with a wooden spoon. You may not want to do this for all risotti, but you will find it brings delicious results to most. The amount of butter called for in most authentic recipes may make you gasp—but once you taste the deep, soul-satisfying flavour it gives the dish, you'll probably want to put in even more.

RISOTTO MILANESE

This is a basic risotto; its only flavouring, beyond the fundamentals, is saffron. It is also one of our favourites. In Lombardy, where it originated, it is always served as an accompaniment to osso buco (defying the risotto-as-a-separate-course rule).

SERVES 12

115 g (4 oz) unsalted butter
280 g (10 oz) finely chopped onion
500 g (1 lb 2 oz) Arborio rice
5 g (1 tsp) loosely packed saffron threads
2-2.5 litres (3½-4½ pints) light, boiling chicken
   stock
175 g (6 oz) grated Parmigiano-Reggiano

1. Melt half the butter over moderate heat in a large, heavy stockpot. Add the chopped onion and cook, stirring occasionally, until the onion is soft and golden about 7 minutes. Add the Arborio rice. Stir well to coat the rice with the butter. Sprinkle with the saffron threads. Cook, stirring, for 1 minute.

2. Increase the heat to moderately high. Add 450 ml (16 fl oz) of the chicken stock (or enough to just cover the rice, stirring constantly. When all of the stock has been absorbed add 125 ml (4 fl oz) more boiling stock, stirring until it is absorbed. Repeat this procedure, adding stock until the rice is al dente. Add stock at the end to adjust sauce. (You will need 2-2.5 litres (3½-4½ pints) of stock altogether.)

3. Stir the remaining butter into the rice along with the freshly grated Parmigiano-Reggiano. Taste for seasoning and serve hot from a large platter onto warmed plates.

LEMON-HERB RISOTTO WITH YELLOW PEPPER PURÉE

The joy of this risotto is the beautiful balance of lemon and yellow pepper. If you like chunks of things in your risotto, you might want to consider adding either cooked pieces of asparagus or cooked peas to this risotto at the last minute before serving.

SERVES 6 AS A FIRST COURSE

3 yellow peppers, trimmed and chopped
about 1.2 litres (2 pints) chicken stock (preferably homemade)
salt and pepper to taste
6 sprigs of fresh mint plus 30 g (2 tbsp) chopped leaves
6 sprigs of parsley plus 30 g (2 tbsp) chopped leaves
1 sprig of fresh rosemary
175 ml (6 fl oz) olive oil
225 g (8 oz) chopped shallots
225 g (8 oz) finely diced fresh fennel bulb
3 garlic cloves, finely chopped
280 g (10 oz) superfino rice
2.5 g (½ tsp) ground coriander
115 g (4 oz) dry white wine
10 g (2 tsp) finely grated fresh lemon zest
3 tablespoons unsalted butter, softened

75 g (3 oz) freshly grated Parmigiano-Reggiano plus additional for the table
10 ml (2 tsp) fresh lemon juice

1. Cook peppers in 90 ml (6 tbsp) water and 50 ml (2 fl oz) of the chicken stock in a frying pan , covered, over moderately low heat, stirring frequently until very soft, about 20 minutes. Purée the peppers in a food processor and strain through a coarse sieve into a small bowl. Season the purée with salt and pepper to taste. (You should have about 175 ml (6 fl oz) pepper purée.)

2. Bring the rest of the stock to a full boil in a saucepan add the mint, parsley and rosemary, reduce the heat and keep stock at a bare simmer.

3. Heat the olive oil in a heavy 2- to 3-litre (3½- to 5¼-pint) saucepan and cook the shallots, fennel and garlic over moderate heat, stirring frequently with a wooden spoon until very soft but not browned, about 8 minutes. Stir in the rice and coriander and cook, stirring constantly, until the edges of the rice become translucent, about 5 minutes. Add the wine and the lemon zest and cook, stirring constantly, until wine is absorbed, about 3 minutes.

4. Remove the herb sprigs from the stock with a slotted spoon or tongs. Add about 125 ml (4 fl oz) simmering stock to the rice and cook, stirring constantly, until all the stock is absorbed. Continue adding stock about 125 ml (4 fl oz) at a time and cooking, stirring constantly and letting each addition be absorbed before adding the next, until rice is al dente about 20 to 25 minutes; season with salt and pepper about halfway through the cooking.

5. Remove the pan from heat and stir in pepper purée, butter, Parmigiano-Reggiano, 1 tablespoon of chopped mint, the chopped parsley, lemon juice and season to taste with salt and pepper. Place the risotto on serving plates, sprinkle with the rest of the mint and serve immediately with the additional Parmigiano-Reggiano.

SHELLFISH RISOTTO WITH SAFFRON

Shellfish risotto was made originally in Venice and risotto with saffron is from Milan. This tale of two cities has a very happy ending: though in most shellfish risotti the flavour of shellfish is not strong in the rice itself, that is deliciously far from the case here. If you use the freshest shellfish you can find, the rice—as well as the shellfish—will taste of the sea.

SERVES 6 AS A FIRST COURSE

2.5 g (½ tsp) saffron threads, crumbled
225 ml (8 fl oz) dry white wine
225 ml (8 fl oz) water
18 small cultivated mussels, scrubbed and bearded
225 g (8 oz) large prawns, peeled, deveined and
    shells reserved
6 sprigs of fresh flat-leaf parsley
2 x 7.5-cm (3-in) strips orange zest
2 x 7.5-cm (3-in) strips lemon zest
2.5 g (½ tsp) fennel seeds
3 canned Italian plum tomatoes, drained and
    pressed through a sieve
40 g (1½ oz) unsalted butter
30 ml (2 tbsp) olive oil
3 large leeks (white and pale green part only),
    quartered lengthways, sliced thinly and washed
    thoroughly
1 garlic clove, crushed with the side of a knife
280 g (10 oz) superfino rice
115 g (4 oz) shelled scallops
salt and pepper to taste
chopped fresh parsley for garnish

1. Soak the saffron threads in 30 ml (2 tbsp) warm water in a small bowl for 20 minutes.

2. Heat the wine and water in a large heavy saucepan to boiling. Add the mussels, cover the pan and cook over moderately high heat just until the mussels open about 3 to 6 minutes, discarding any that do not open. Remove the open mussels with a slotted spoon, place in a bowl and reserve.

3. Reduce the heat under the saucepan to moderate and add the prawn shells, parsley sprigs, zests, fennel seeds and saffron threads with their liquid. Simmer the mixture, covered, for 15 minutes. Strain the liquid through a very fine sieve lined with damp muslin and discard the solids. Measure strained liquid and add enough water to make 1.2 litres (2 pints). Transfer the liquid to a saucepan add the sieved tomatoes and bring the liquid to a bare simmer.

4. Heat the butter and olive oil in a heavy 2- to 3-litre (3½- to 5¼-pint) saucepan and cook the leeks and garlic over moderate heat, stirring frequently with a wooden spoon, until very soft but not browned, about 5 minutes. Stir in the rice and cook, stirring constantly, until the edges of the rice become translucent, about 4 minutes. Add about 125 ml (4 fl oz) simmering liquid to the rice and cook, stirring constantly and adjusting the heat to maintain a lively simmer (not a steady boil) until all the liquid is absorbed. Continue adding liquid about 125 ml (4 fl oz) at a time and cook, stirring constantly and letting each addition be absorbed before adding the next. After 15 minutes of cooking, add the prawns, scallops, salt and pepper and continue to cook until rice is al dente (tender but still firm at the centre) about 5 to 10 minutes longer. (The risotto should be very creamy; if it isn't add more liquid). About 2 minutes before finishing the risotto add the reserved mussels with their juices.

5. Remove the pan from heat and season to taste with salt and pepper. Arrange the risotto on a serving dish, sprinkle with parsley and serve immediately.

MUSHROOM RISOTTO

Risotti that use dried mushrooms are difficult to get right. You want the full mushroom flavour to permeate the dish, of course . . . so most chefs are tempted to use lots of the liquid in which the mushrooms soaked as stock for the dish. But this can make the dish *too* intense; it often ends up tasting like concentrated mushroom soup from a dried powder. The following recipe gets it just right: mushroomy, but not overbearingly so, with a lovely buttery undertaste. We're mixing our mushrooms here to bring out the most complex mushroom flavour. This is a stick-to-the-ribs, dark-brown risotto; don't forget to lighten it a bit by adding a little extra stock right at the end.

SERVES 6 AS A FIRST COURSE

2 packets dried porcini (ceps)
about 1.2 litres (2 pints) veal or beef stock
    (preferably homemade)
8 sprigs of fresh thyme plus additional for garnish
4 sprigs of fresh sage plus additional for garnish
2 bay leaves
50 ml (2 fl oz) olive oil
3 large leeks (white and pale green part only),
    quartered lengthwise, sliced thin and washed
    thoroughly
2 garlic cloves, chopped
350 g (12 oz) cultivated mushrooms, thinly sliced
2 anchovies, drained and mashed to a paste
280 g (10 oz) superfino rice
125 ml (4 fl oz) dry red wine
40 g (1½ oz) unsalted butter, softened
70 g (2½ oz) freshly grated Parmigiano-Reggiano
salt and pepper to taste

1. Soak the dried porcini in a bowl in 175 ml (6 fl oz) hot water for 30 minutes. Remove the mushrooms with a slotted spoon, chop them finely and set them aside in a small bowl. Strain the soaking liquid through a coffee filter. (You should have about 125 ml (4 fl oz) liquid.)

2. Bring the stock to a full boil with the thyme, sage, bay leaves and mushroom soaking liquid in a medium saucepan, reduce the heat and keep it going at a bare simmer.

3. Heat the olive oil in a heavy 2- to 3-litre (3½- to 5½-pint) saucepan and cook the leeks and garlic over moderate heat, stirring frequently with a wooden spoon, until very soft but not browned about 6 minutes. Add the fresh mushrooms and the anchovies and cook, stirring constantly, for 5 minutes or until the mushrooms are softened (reduce the heat slightly if the mushrooms begin to stick). Stir in the rice and cook, stirring constantly, for 2 minutes. Add the wine and cook, stirring constantly, until wine is absorbed about 1 minute. Stir in the chopped dried mushrooms.

4. Remove the herb sprigs from the stock with a slotted spoon or tongs. Add about 125 ml (4 fl oz) simmering stock to the rice and cook, stirring constantly, until all the stock is absorbed. Continue adding stock about 125 ml (4 fl oz) at a time and cook, stirring constantly and letting each addition be absorbed before adding the next, until rice is al dente, 20 to 25 minutes; season with salt and pepper about halfway through the cooking.

5. Remove the pan from heat and stir in the butter, Parmigiano-Reggiano and salt and pepper to taste. Garnish risotto with the additional thyme and sage sprigs and serve immediately.

PILAFS

The pilaf—variously spelled *pilaff, pilau, pillau, pulao, pellao a*nd other ways—is one of the great Middle Eastern/Indian contributions to world cuisine. Chefs in those parts of the world are masters at cooking long-grain rice in flavoured stocks with seasonings and other ingredients, to create full-flavoured rice dishes that are always fluffier and lighter than Italian risotti.

LEBANESE RICE AND LENTILS WITH CARAMELISED ONIONS (MUJADARAH)

This ancient Lebanese dish has many different names and many different preparations. In its purest form— where the lentils are puréed and served with the rice— it is thought to be Esau's 'mess of pottage'. The variation we prefer (and present here) is often called *moudardara:* in it, the lentils remain whole. The same dish is called *ruz koshari* in Saudi Arabia and Egypt, where it is served with a tomato sauce. We like to serve it topped with vegetable garnishes and alongside other Lebanese vegetable dishes and salads as part of a first-course array of meze.

SERVES 8 AS PART OF A FIRST-COURSE ARRAY

225 g (8 oz) green or brown lentils, rinsed and
    picked over
1 litre (1¾ pints) cold water
125 ml (4 fl oz) olive oil
3 large white onions, thinly sliced
115 g (4 oz) basmati or other long-grain white rice
5 g (1 tsp) salt
1 teaspoon allspice
Garnishes
lemon wedges
plain yogurt
spring onions, cut diagonally
radishes, thinly sliced
olive oil for drizzling

1. Bring the lentils and the water to a boil in a large saucepan, reduce the heat and simmer, skimming, until the lentils are nearly tender, about 25 minutes.

2. While the lentils are cooking, heat the olive oil in a large frying pan over moderate heat until hot but not smoking. Stir in the onions and cook, stirring, until soft about 5 minutes. Remove 350g (12 oz) of the onions with a slotted spoon to a bowl. Continue cooking the remaining onions, stirring constantly about 5 to 7 more minutes or until nicely caramelised and beginning to

crisp. Remove with slotted spoon and set aside on paper towels.

3. Drain the lentils and reserve the liquid (the liquid should measure at least 350 ml (12 fl oz); (if it doesn't add water). Return the lentils to the pan add the 350 ml (12 fl oz) liquid, the onions that you removed first, rice, salt and allspice and cook over very low heat, covered, until the rice is tender about 20 minutes.

4. Place the mujadarah on a platter and top with the longer-cooked, crispy onions. Serve garnishes on the side.

LAMB BIRYANI

We love biryanis—those super-flavourful Indian pilafs, crammed with intriguing spices and chunks of meat, fish or vegetables. Though they're made with a long-grain rice—often the fabulous, milk-scented basmati— the texture of the finished dish is less fluffy and a little creamier than other long-grain rice dishes.

SERVES 6 AS PART OF AN INDIAN MEAL

450 g (1 lb) boneless lamb shoulder, cut in 1-cm
    (½-inch) cubes
15 g (1 tbsp) puréed fresh ginger
15 g (1 tbsp) puréed garlic plus 2 finely chopped
    garlic cloves
juice of 1 lime
7 cinnamon sticks
15 g (1 tbsp) green cardamom seeds, cracked open
40 g (1½ tsp) whole cloves
50 g (2 oz) chopped fresh coriander
25 g (1 oz) chopped fresh mint
2 green chillies, seeded and chopped
5 g (1 tsp) salt
15 ml (1 tbsp) plain yogurt
115 g (4 oz) ghee or unsalted butter
3 medium onions, chopped
350 g (12 oz) basmati rice

2 dried curry leaves (optional)
225 ml (8 fl oz) chicken stock
225 ml (8 fl oz) water
225 ml (8 fl oz) milk
5 g (1 tsp) saffron threads

1. Place the lamb in a large mixing bowl and add the puréed ginger, puréed garlic, lime juice, 5 of the cinnamon sticks, 10 g (2 tsp) of the cardamom, 5 g (1 tsp) of the cloves, the coriander , the mint, the green chillies, the salt and the yogurt. Marinate for 3 hours.

2. Place 60 g (4 tbsp) of the ghee in a frying pan over moderately high heat. Sauté two-thirds of the onions until lightly browned. Add the meat mixture with its marinade and cook over high heat for 20 minutes.

3. While meat is cooking, cook the rice. In a casserole, melt the rest of the ghee over moderately high heat. Add the 2 finely chopped garlic cloves and the remaining onion; sauté until lightly browned. Add the basmati rice, stirring well to coat with the butter. Add the rest of the cinnamon sticks, cardamom and cloves and the 2 curry leaves. Add the chicken stock and the water. Bring the mixture to the boil, then reduce heat. Cover and cook for 12 minutes (the liquid should be reduced, but the rice should still be a little firm).

4. Preheat oven to 150°C (300°F).

5. Warm the milk with the saffron threads in a small saucepan.

6. Add the lamb mixture to the rice mixture in the casserole, mixing together well. Add the warmed milk with saffron. Cover and bake in the 150°C (300°F) oven for 15 minutes or until rice is cooked and fairly dry. Serve with other Indian main-course dishes.

PERSIAN RICE PILAF WITH RAISINS, MINT AND PINE NUTS

This is not a traditional Iranian dish—but it is a delicious one that captures the essence of that cuisine. It makes a fabulous accompaniment to shish kebab or any kind of grilled or roast lamb.

SERVES 4 AS A SIDE DISH

45 ml (3 tbsp) olive oil
50 g (2 oz) chopped onion
225 g (8 oz) long-grain rice
50 g (2 oz) sultanas
2.5 g (½ tsp) saffron threads
1.25 g (½ tsp) salt
400 ml (14 fl oz) water
50 g (2 oz) pine nuts
1 tomato, weighing 175g (6 oz), chopped
50 g (2 oz) chopped fresh mint plus whole leaves
    for garnish

1. Preheat oven to 230°C (450°F).

2. Place 15 ml (1 tbsp) of the olive oil in a saucepan with a tight-fitting lid over moderate heat. Add the onion and cook until it starts to soften about 3 minutes. Add the rice, sultanas, the saffron and the salt and mix well. Cook for 3 minutes and add the water. Bring to a boil over high heat, stir with a fork, then reduce heat to low. Cover tightly and simmer for about 20 minutes or until rice is cooked and completely dry.

3. While the rice is simmering, spread the pine nuts out in a single layer on a baking sheet and bake for 15 to 20 minutes or until they have turned golden brown. Remove and cool.

4. When the rice is done, fork through it to separate the grains. Let it cool for a few minutes. When ready to serve, combine it with the pine nuts, chopped tomato, chopped mint and the rest of the olive oil (use less if desired). Arrange on a dish and garnish with mint leaves.

SPANISH RICE DISHES

SPANISH RICE DISHES

Spain is great rice country. It was actually the conduit through which rice flowed into Europe. The Arabs brought rice to Spain from Asia in the eighth century; the Italians didn't borrow the idea for at least another few hundred years; and the French didn't plant rice until the seventeenth century. Today, the east coast of Spain is one of Europe's great rice-producing regions...and the Spaniards have developed a host of ingenious ways to use the local product.

PAELLA

Paella, Spain's extraordinary rice casserole, is one of those national dishes that inspire nothing but controversy. What goes into a classic paella? We're convinced that the original paella, from Spain's Valencia region, contained snails, rabbit and string beans—but we never see these ingredients in the paellas served in Spanish restaurants in the U.S. which unfortunately rarely offer paella that tastes anything at all like paella in Spain. We tend to focus on the quantity of seafood embedded in the rice...and lose sight of the rice itself, paella's most important ingredient. The texture of the rice in the finished dish is the key to quality and authenticity: in Spain, paella is not fluffy like a pilaf or oozy like a risotto. Instead, it is somewhere in between, slightly creamy, glistening with oil and flavour. Among other things, it is the type of rice that creates the authentic paella feel: short-grained Valencian rice, thick and almost round, called *granza*. At Dean & DeLuca, we sell a good brand called Alcazaba; if you can't find Valencian short-grained rice, use Italian Arborio instead. The following recipe is one we've made at Dean & DeLuca for years and we're convinced it's the next best thing to an air ticket on Iberia.

SERVES 8

50 ml (2 fl oz) Spanish olive oil
225 g (8 oz) chorizo, mildly cured, cut in 1-cm (½-in) rounds

685 g (1½ lb) chicken thighs, cut into 16 pieces
salt and pepper to taste
450 g (1 lb) short-grain rice, rinsed
1 medium red onion, coarsely chopped
½ sweet red pepper, stemmed, seeded and cut into 2.5-cm (1-in) cubes
½ green pepper, stemmed, seeded, and cut into 2.5-cm (1-in) cubes
½ yellow pepper, stemmed, seeded, and cut into 2.5-cm (1-in) cubes
½ medium fennel bulb, coarsely chopped
25 g (1 oz) finely chopped garlic
2.5 g (½ tsp) dried hot red pepper flakes
225 ml (8 fl oz) dry white wine
7.5 g (1½ tsp) saffron threads
6 sprigs of thyme
1.5 litres (2¾ pints) chicken stock
25 ml (1½ tbsp) Pernod or another anise-flavoured liqueur
1½ lb medium prawns, peeled and deveined
225 ml (8 fl oz) water
16 mussels, scrubbed and bearded
16 small clams (cockles), rinsed
225 g (8 oz) monkfish, cut into 1-cm (½-in) pieces
115 g (4 oz) oil-cured black olives, pitted and coarsely chopped
1 lemon, sliced into wedges
coarsely chopped fresh flat-leaf parsley for garnish

1. Preheat oven to 180°C (350°F).

2. Heat 30 ml (2 tbsp) of the olive oil over high heat in a wide frying pan, preferably a paella pan, about 47 cm (18½ in) wide. Quickly cook the chorizo slices until brown about 30 seconds per side. Set chorizo aside on paper towels.

3. Add the rest of the olive oil to the pan and reduce heat to moderately high. Pat chicken dry and season both sides with lots of salt and pepper. Cook chicken until brown about 5 minutes per side. Reserve.

4. Put rice in same pan and quickly stir the rice over low heat with a wooden spoon until translucent—this should take about 2 minutes. Add onion, peppers, fennel, garlic and red pepper flakes and cook another 3 minutes. Add wine, saffron, thyme and all but 225 ml (8 fl oz) chicken stock, making sure there is about 1 cm (½ in) liquid to cover ingredients. Taste liquid for seasoning; add salt and pepper if necessary. Bring to a boil add reserved cooked chicken, browned chorizo and Pernod. Place pan in oven for 20 minutes adding more chicken stock if the rice has soaked up the stock. Remember to bury the prawns in the rice after 10 minutes of cooking time. When done, the rice should be tender and the paella slightly wet.

5. While the rice is cooking add the water to a large pot and bring to a boil. Add mussels and clams and cover, shaking the pan frequently, until mussels and clams are opened. Discard any mussels or clams that do not open. Once paella is ready, remove from oven and stir in mussels, clams, monkfish and olives. Mix well, cover with foil and let rest for 5 minutes. By serving time, the monkfish should be cooked through evenly. Garnish with lemon wedges and parsley.

Other Spanish rice dishes

Paella may be Spain's most famous rice dish, but it is far from Spain's only rice dish. All along the Mediterranean coast of Spain, local chefs make fabulous rice dishes, just waiting to be discovered by us Americans.

In Valencia itself, home of paella, there are several other classics—usually wetter in texture than paella. Arroz caldoso de monte (mountain rice) is made in a wide clay pot and has the texture of a soupy stew. Arroz al horno or baked rice (often tossed with vegetables), is traditionally cooked in a shallow clay casserole and is a little drier.

Just to the south, in Alicante, the famous arroz a banda is made; it is rice cooked in a strong fish stock , with no chunks of seafood in it, but plenty of garlic mayonnaise served on the side. Also from this region is arroz con costra alicantino; it's a rice casserole, often made with meatballs, that features an egg crust on top.

And just to the north of Valencia, in the great gastronomic region of Catalonia, you find arròs negre or black rice; it is made with squid ink. Also from this region is arròs a la cassola amb marisc; this is a fabulous rice and seafood specialty, much soupier than paella, served with garlic mayonnaise on the side.

DISHES STUFFED WITH RICE

Rice is wonderful by itself. But one of its most exciting roles, worldwide, is as a stuffing for vegetables—because it soaks up flavours so well.

DOLMADES

Dolmades are stuffed vine leaves, found in many different countries around the eastern Mediterranean—which is why the name has many different variations (including dolmas and dolmathes). The most famous are from Greece and Turkey. Turkish cooks believe that if you stuff the leaves with meat, you should make them with butter and serve them warm. If the leaves are stuffed with rice, however (the variation we favour), they should be made with olive oil and served at room temperature. This delicious recipe calls for exactly that. The brine-soaked vine leaves from jars are acceptable to use in this dish—they're probably your only option—but Mediterranean chefs often make dolmades from fresh vine leaves. Dolmades are a dynamic part of a Mediterranean appetiser assortment, with feta cheese, olives and tomatoes.

MAKES 36 DOLMADES

36 vine leaves from a jar

150 ml (5 fl oz) olive oil

1 bunch of spring onions, finely chopped

15 g (1 tbsp) finely chopped fresh parsley

175 g (6 oz) long-grain rice

15g (1 tbsp) chopped fresh dill

50 g (2 oz) pine nuts

50 g (2 oz) sultanas, soaked for 30 minutes in
  50 ml (2 fl oz) white wine

salt and pepper to taste

juice of 2 lemons

350 ml (12 fl oz) chicken stock

225 ml (12 fl oz) water

1. Scald the vine leaves with hot water, cut off the stems, pat the leaves dry and place them on paper towels with their shiny surfaces down.

2. Add 30 ml (2 tbsp) of the olive oil to a heavy frying pan over moderate heat. Add the spring onions and parsley and cook for 10 minutes.

3. Add the rice, dill, pine nuts and sultanas. Stir well. Cook for 5 minutes. Season with salt and pepper.

4. *Stuff the vine leaves:* Place about 5 g (1 tsp) of the rice mixture near the bottom edge of each leaf (the shiny side is still down). Fold about 5 mm (¼ in) of each side of the leaf over the filling, then roll the leaf up towards the tip at the top. Each one should be a small, compact, tightly wrapped cylinder.

5. Select a heavy pot that will hold 18 of the leaves in 1 layer. Add 18 stuffed leaves, then sprinkle with the juice of 1 lemon and 30 ml (2 tbsp) olive oil. Make a second layer of 18 stuffed leaves on top of the first. Once again, sprinkle with the juice of 1 lemon and 30 ml (2 tbsp) olive oil. Pour the chicken stock, the water and the rest of the olive oil over all (the liquid should cover the stuffed leaves).

6. Weight leaves with a plate, so they don't move around during cooking. Simmer the leaves, covered, over very low heat for 50 minutes.

7. When the leaves are cool enough to handle, remove them from the pot. Drain them, cool them to room temperature and serve.

LIGURIAN STUFFED TOMATOES WITH OLIVES ANCHOVIES AND BASIL

This delightful room-temperature treat is alive with the flavours of the Italian Riviera. Great ingredients are the key to this dish. Find terrific small tomatoes, just bigger than cherry tomatoes, that are sold on the vine. Use long-grain rice that has been cooked to fluffy, each-grain-separate perfection. Choose brine-cured green olives with lots of flavour; don't use the pretty but insipid Cerignolas. Serve 3 tomatoes per person as an ideal summer first course or serve 1 tomato each to 12 people as a very light starter for a dinner party. You'll find the rice a wonderful, starchy foil for the tomato and the tomato a great enlivener of the rice. Gastronomic symbiosis at its best.

SERVES 4 AS A FIRST COURSE

12 small tomatoes (each about 5 cm (2 in) in
  diameter and a scant 50 g (2 oz))

salt and pepper to taste

about 90 ml (6 tbsp) extra-virgin olive oil

3 large garlic cloves, very finely chopped

350 g (12 oz) fluffy cooked rice (halve rice recipe on
  page 221)

30 ml (2 tbsp) chicken stock

4 flat anchovy fillets

10 ml (2 tsp) lemon juice

115 g (4 oz) brine-cured, large, green olives plus a
  few additional for garnish

25 g (1 oz) very finely chopped fresh basil

1. With a small, sharp knife, cut a wide hole in the stem end of each tomato, scooping out the interior. Cut as close as you can to the tomato skin on the side and on the bottom. Scoop out all remaining seeds and pulp (reserve for another use). You will be left with 12 hollowed-out tomato shells. Salt and pepper them well, turn them upside down and reserve.

2. Place 10 ml (2 tsp) of the olive oil in a small saucepan over low heat. Add the chopped garlic and cook until it's just soft, about 3 minutes. (Do not allow the garlic to brown.)

3. Add the garlic to the rice in a mixing bowl. Combine well. Add the chicken stock and 15 ml (1 tbsp) of the olive oil.

4. Sprinkle the anchovy fillets with the lemon juice and chop them until they're practically a paste. Add to the rice mixture, blending well.

5. Crush the olives with the side of a cleaver, remove, discard the stones and chop the olive flesh very finely. Add it to the rice mixture with half the chopped basil. Blend and season the mixture extremely well with salt and pepper.

6. Stuff the hollowed-out tomatoes with the rice mixture. Serve immediately or, for maximum flavour, hold for 1 to 2 hours. When ready to serve, divide the tomatoes among 4 plates, placing 3 tomatoes at the centre of each plate. Slice the remaining olives and top the tomatoes with them decoratively. Top that with the remaining chopped basil leaves. Drizzle extra-virgin olive oil over and around the tomatoes.

ROASTED POBLANO CHILLIES STUFFED WITH CORIANDER RICE

Roast the poblano chillies for this delicious appetiser just as you would sweet peppers (see page 168); once again a charcoal fire is best. The combination of char-grilling, chilli heat, spices, lime juice—and rice to soak it all up—is irresistible.

SERVES 4 AS A FIRST COURSE

4 fresh poblano chillies, roasted and peeled
1.25 g (¼ tsp) whole coriander seeds
1.25 g (¼ tsp) whole cumin seeds
pinch of whole anise seeds
100 g (3½ oz) Texmati or
  other long-grain rice
15 ml (1 tbsp) rapeseed oil
15 g (1 tbsp) toasted pumpkin seeds, chopped
15 g (1 tbsp) chopped fresh coriander
5 ml (1 tsp) fresh lime juice
1.25 g (¼ tsp) ground ancho chilli powder or more
  to taste
225 ml (8 fl oz) pico de gallo (page 483)

1. Make a lengthways slit in each chilli, leaving the stems intact. Carefully remove and discard the seeds. Pat the chillies dry.

2. Toast the coriander and cumin seeds in a small dry frying pan over moderately high heat until very aromatic but not burned, 1 to 2 minutes. Transfer the seeds to a bowl and cool completely. Grind the toasted seeds with the anise seeds to a fine powder in a mortar and pestle or a coffee/spice grinder.

3. Cook the rice in a large saucepan of boiling salted water for about 16 minutes or until al dente. Drain in a sieve, refresh with cold water to stop the cooking and spread the rice out to dry thoroughly on a plate lined with paper towels.

4. Stir together the rice, ground spices, oil, pumpkin seeds, coriander, lime juice and ancho powder in a small bowl until combined well. Divide the rice mixture into 4 portions and gently place one inside each pepper. Serve at room temperature with pico de gallo spooned over the stuffed chillies.

RICE SALADS

If you've found rice salad insipid—don't give up! With full-flavoured, imaginative ingredients, rice salad can be a spectacular addition to any buffet table a fabulous first course or even an eye-opening main course. Try this pair of unusual ones.

PRAWNS AND RICE SALAD, SUSHI-STYLE, WITH SESAME AND AVOCADO

SERVES 4 AS A LUNCH MAIN COURSE

1 litre (1¾ pints) water
225 g (8 oz) thick slices of peeled fresh ginger
150 ml (5 fl oz) Japanese rice vinegar
1.25 g (¼ tsp) salt
16 large prawns
salt to taste
90 ml (6 tbsp) vegetable oil
20 ml (1½ tsp) Japanese soy sauce
2.5 ml (½ tsp) dark sesame oil
90 g (6 tbsp) short-grain rice
1.25 ml (¼ tsp) sugar
10 g (2 tsp) white sesame seeds
650 g (1½ lb) soft lettuce, such as butter or red oak
75 g (3 oz) watercress leaves
75 g (3 oz) alfalfa sprouts
16 thin slices avocado
2 sheets nori (black Japanese seaweed) or nori komi furikake (see box on page 234)

1. Place the water in a medium saucepan. Add the slices of ginger, 50 ml (2 tbsp) of the rice vinegar and the salt. Bring to a boil, then simmer vigorously (just below a rolling boil) for 20 minutes.

2. *While the ginger is simmering, prepare the prawns:* peel them, leaving the tail intact. Make a deep cut to devein them, then spread them open in butterfly fashion, keeping them attached at the tail. Salt them lightly.

3. *Prepare the dressing:* Place 75 ml (3 fl oz) of the rice vinegar in a small bowl with the vegetable oil, soy sauce and dark sesame oil. Whisk vigorously until smooth, then season to taste with salt.

4. When the ginger water has simmered for 20 minutes, turn off the heat. Let it cool for a few minutes. Then add the prawns to the water and let them sit until just cooked about 1 to 2 minutes. Remove the prawns. If they've curled up, uncurl them with your fingers. Toss them in a small bowl with 50 ml (2 tbsp) of the dressing. Reserve.

5. Remove the ginger slices from the water still in the pan and discard. Add the rice to the water, bring to a boil and boil, uncovered, until the rice is just cooked, about 15 minutes (you may need to add a little additional water towards the end). Remove the rice and toss with the rest of the rice vinegar and the sugar.

6. Toast the sesame seeds in a 250°C (500°F) oven until golden brown, about 5 minutes, and toss with the rice. Reserve.

7. Wash and dry the lettuce and salad greens. Toss the lettuce, watercress leaves and alfalfa sprouts in a large bowl. Add about two-thirds of the remaining dressing and blend well.

8. Divide the salad among 4 dinner plates. On each plate, place 4 slices of avocado on top of the greens in pinwheel fashion, with the tips of the avocado slices at the centre of each plate. Position 4 prawns on each plate, cut side up, tails towards the centre of the plates, nestled between avocado slices. Divide the rice among the 16 prawns, patting a bit along the length of each butterflied prawns. Drizzle the remaining dressing over the avocado slices and the prawns.

9. Hold the sheets of nori about 7.5 cm (3 in) from an open flame. Toast on both sides until they crisp, about

30 seconds. Cut into thin shreds and garnish the prawns with the shreds.

Japanese sprinkles

A great, ultra-convenient substitute for the toasted nori in this recipe is nori komi furikake—dried seaweed shreds with sesame seeds in a jar, available in Japanese groceries. All you have to do is open the jar and sprinkle. They make a great garnish for this salad or any other Japanese-inspired salad.

MEXICAN RICE SALAD WITH MUSSELS, CORN, LIME AND CORIANDER

We suggest using a long-grain brown rice for this refreshing summer dinner dish or anytime lunch. The bran that remains on brown rice serves to keep the grains separate; stickiness is the last texture you want in a rice salad.

SERVES 4 AS A LUNCH MAIN COURSE

10 ml (2 tsp) vegetable oil

30 g (2 tbsp) chopped shallots

15 g (1 tbsp) garlic, chopped

225 g (8 oz) long-grain brown rice

225 g (8 oz) drained canned tomatoes, chopped

30 g (2 tbsp) chopped green chillies

350 ml (12 fl oz) chicken or vegetable stock

5 ears of fresh corn-on-the-cob, peeled, or 225 g (8 oz) thawed frozen sweetcorn

24 mussels, scrubbed and bearded

7.5 g (1½ tsp) ground cumin

50 g (2 oz) red onion, chopped

50 g (2 oz) fresh coriander , chopped

45 g (3 tbsp) fresh oregano, chopped (optional; do not substitute dried)

50 ml (2 fl oz) extra-virgin olive oil

50 ml (2 fl oz) fresh lime juice

salt and pepper to taste

1. *Cook the rice:* Place the vegetable oil in a medium saucepan with a tight-fitting lid over moderately low heat. Add the shallots and half the garlic. Stir for 1 minute, then add the rice. Stir until each grain glistens, then add the tomatoes, green chillies and stock. Bring the mixture to a boil, stir once, cover and reduce heat to a simmer. Let the rice cook for 30 minutes (follow the directions on the rice package if the timing varies from ours). Remove the pan from the heat and let it sit, covered, for 10 minutes.

2. While the rice is cooking, steam the corn kernels and the mussels. Scatter the mussels over the corn on a steamer in a large pot containing an inch of hot water. Put the pot on a high flame and cover it. After 5 minutes, remove the corn and any mussels whose shells have opened. Cover the pot again and after another 5 minutes remove the remaining mussels. Discard any mussels that are not open or do not open easily.

3. If using fresh corn, cut the corn kernels off the cobs. Place corn kernels in a large bowl. Add the cumin, red onion, remaining garlic, coriander, optional fresh oregano, olive oil and lime juice. Toss gently. Add the cooked rice and toss thoroughly but gently. Add salt and pepper to taste. Remove and discard a half shell of each mussel and set the remaining mussels on the half shell in the bottom of a serving bowl. Lay the rice over the top. Using a large spoon, raise the mussels gently by scooping from the bottom so that some of the rice falls to the bottom. Chill, covered, for at least 2 hours. Fluff with a fork before serving.

WILD RICE

As you've undoubtedly heard by now, wild rice is not really rice, but the seed of a wild aquatic grass, native to Minnesota and other Great Lakes states; it was a staple of the Sioux and Chippewa Indians. Today, of course, it is hideously expensive; that's because traditional harvesting of wild rice is so labour-intensive. You may be comforted by the fact that newfangled production methods in Minnesota and in California, have lowered the price of some wild rices; you may be disturbed by the fact that these cheaper rices don't taste as good. We say: if you want the full, nutty, smoky crunchiness of wild rice, pay the top price for the best hand-harvested, traditional Minnesota wild rice you can find. Look for giant or long, which is the top grade and has grains up to 2.5 cm (1 in) long. Extra-fancy or medium are less expensive, with smaller grains and perfectly acceptable. Select or short may contain broken grains and unbroken grains of varying size; this is acceptable when looks are unimportant (as in a stuffing).

Wild rice is very simple to cook. If you've got great wild rice and want a pure experience of it, simply wash the rice, add it to a large pot of salted boiling water and simmer, covered, for 45 minutes to an hour, until the rice is done to your liking. We prefer it on the al dente side, but some like a more tender bowl of wild rice, in which many of the grains have burst open.

WILD RICE WITH HERBS AND APPLEWOOD-SMOKED BACON

Use any bacon you like for this great wild-rice side dish. But the applewood-smoked one we're recommending available at Dean & DeLuca, lends the dish a lovely sweet-smoky character. The star of the dish, however, is still the crunchy, nutty wild rice. If you want to emphasise the crunch, cook the rice only 45 minutes or so. If you cook it for an hour, the rice will be softer. This dish is lovely with roast poultry, especially when some kind of fruit appears on the plate.

SERVES 8 AS A SIDE DISH

6 rashers of applewood-smoked bacon, cut crossways into thin strips
225 g (8 oz) finely diced red onion
2 garlic cloves, chopped
350 g (12 oz) wild rice, rinsed well under cold water and drained

350 ml (12 fl oz) water
450 ml (16 fl oz) chicken or vegetable stock
1 small bay leaf
2.5 g (½ tsp) salt or more to taste
15 g (1 tbsp) chopped fresh parsley
15 g (1 tbsp) chopped fresh rosemary
15 g (1 tbsp) chopped fresh thyme
freshly ground black pepper to taste
50 g (2 oz) toasted pine nuts

1. Cook bacon in a large saucepan with a lid, uncovered, over moderate heat, stirring, until crisp; remove with a slotted spoon and drain on paper towels. Stir in the onion and garlic and cook, stirring, over moderate heat until golden, about 5 minutes.

2. Add wild rice, water, stock, bay leaf and salt. Cover and bring to a boil over moderate heat. Uncover and boil gently without stirring, 45 to 60 minutes, depending on desired degree of doneness. Drain add herbs, season well with freshly ground black pepper and set over lowest possible heat. Dry out for 5 minutes, shaking the pan. Stir in the bacon and pine nuts and discard the bay leaf. Serve hot.

BEANS (AND PEAS AND LENTILS)

In America's Depression years of the thirties, hoboes were always depicted sitting beside the railway, eating beans out of cans. This image neatly sums up the modern American status of this ancient product: anything of the lowest value isn't even worth a hill of you-know-whats.

The picture is entirely different in Europe and Asia, where beans play a leading role in some of those continents' leading dishes. But the irony is this: almost all the beans used in those dishes across the oceans are native to the New World. Among the great beans used in Europe and Asia today, only the broad bean (known in the US as fava bean), the chick pea, the black-eyed pea, the adzuki bean and the soy bean are native.

So what is a bean anyway? The same thing,

botanically as a pea and a lentil. All three are the seeds of vegetables that have pods. These seeds—beans, peas and lentils—are known collectively as legumes or pulses. Break open a pea pod, and those round things inside are legumes (peas). Break open a string bean (which you don't have to do to eat it) and those little light-coloured things inside are legumes (beans). In fact, those little light-coloured things in the string beans, if allowed to grow, would become kidney beans. After drying, they would be dried kidney beans.

Serious cooks use these legumes fresh *and* dried. Canned and frozen beans are usually eschewed.

FRESH LEGUMES

Fresh peas, sold in their fresh green pods are the fresh legume that's most commonly available.

Fresh beans are available inside ordinary string beans, but they're tiny and negligible; in some seasons, fresh bean pods (like those of cranberry beans) do contain large, fresh, scarlet-blotched, usable beans.

The last of the legumes, lentils, are rarely seen in fresh form.

DRIED LEGUMES

This chapter—and our kitchen!—doesn't focus on fresh legumes. For we believe that fresh beans, peas and lentils usually become even more interesting after they're dried. The Europeans seem to agree, because most of their classic bean dishes are based on dried beans. And billions of home chefs around the world seem to agree too—at least on the grounds of convenience—because dried beans, peas and lentils have become major international pantry items.

Well, the good news is this: American households have finally emerged from their anti-bean prejudice and today we join the world in prizing dried legumes. This has led to more good news: the interest in dried legumes among American consumers has created a massive increase of imports and availability, resulting in a

dizzying variety of dried bean, pea and lentil types on American grocery shelves today. We are proud to have pioneered in this country many of the currently available types (though it's not true that we are considering a name change to Bean & Beluga).

MASTER LIST OF DRIED LEGUMES

Here are some of the leading dried legumes available in American markets and specialty shops today. Because beans dominate the category—with scores of old 'heirloom' varieties that have been resuscitated by farmers—dried beans make up most of the following entries, with a few dried peas. Dried lentils are described in a single entry.

Note: Many of the dried beans on the market can be substituted for one another in various recipes. The most important thing, when substituting, is to find a bean of approximately the same size. Therefore, we have noted those beans that are interchangeable with similar beans by placing an **(I)** after the entry and have described each of these beans as small **(S)**, medium **(M)** or large **(L)**. If no symbols appear, the dried bean is not interchangeable.

Adzuki Names in English vary (including *aduki* and *azuki*), because they are all transliterations from Japanese. These are small, maroon-coloured beans with a white racing stripe. Adzuki are sweet, nutty and non-mealy. They are used mainly in Japan as a paste for desserts, but are also delicious whole in salads. Adzuki beans have thick skins and require long soaking and cooking.

Appaloosa This is a new hybrid of the pinto bean. Medium-size, long and narrow; one end is white, the other very dark with tan veins. Named for the Appaloosa horse which, like the beans, hails from the Palouse a legume-growing region of eastern Washington and western Idaho. They are fairly neutral in flavour and well suited to strong seasoning. **(I) (S)**

Black Beans These are small beans, sometimes called turtle beans. They're actually very dark purple rather than black (as the cooking liquid shows). Black beans have a distinctive, earthy flavour and are much appreciated in Latin American cuisines. They marry well with garlic, coriander, smoked meat and acidic ingredients and are a classic bean for soup and for Brazilian feijoada. Also good when tossed with salsa to make a black bean salad.

Black-Eyed Peas One of the few beans with non-American roots, black-eyed peas are thought to have originated in ancient China. They are medium-size, dull white beans, with a purple-black spot. They have a thin skin and cook rather quickly. The flavour is subtle, slightly sweet and the texture is a little mealy. Black-eyed peas are used widely today in Africa, India and the American South. They are good for soaking up meat juices, especially pork. In Britain they are often called black-eyed peas. **(I) (M)**

Calypso The calypso is a round, medium-size bean, with both black and white markings. Its earthy flavour is particularly good in hearty, slow-cooked soups. The calypso is also good for meat-and-bean stews, like cassoulet. **(I) (M)**

Cannellini These are sometimes known as white kidney beans, though they occasionally show some yellow discolouration. Their mild flavour makes them extremely versatile. White kidney beans are very popular in Italy, where the red kidney bean is used much less frequently. Cannellini are most often cooked in Mediterranean fashion, with herbs, olive oil, garlic and tomatoes. **(I) (M)**

Chick peas Called *ceci* in Italy, *pois-chiches* in France and *garbanzos* in Spain, chick peas are among our very favourite dried beans. They are one of the few beans not native to the Americas, having first been used about 7,000 years ago in the Middle East. Chick peas are medium-size, light yellow-brown, round beans, crinkled when dry, with a fairly thick, removable skin. There are a number of Middle Eastern classics based on puréed chick peas—like hummus and falafel—but their nutty flavour is also widely valued in French, Spanish and Italian soups (such as the Spanish classic *cocido*). They are also terrific in meat stews, perfectly partnering chicken, sausages and pork. Their ability to hold their shape after long cooking makes them particularly suitable for soups and stews.

China Yellow These pale yellow beans are small, plump and roundish. The colour fades when cooked. With a buttery-smooth texture and rich flavour, they are excellent for purées. China yellow beans are good with saffron and other strong flavours—and they're not from China at all. **(I) (S)**

Corona This is a commercial name for a very large, very firm and flavourful white bean that comes from Italy. The name is used by a company called Tartuferia in Weehawken, New Jersey. The Corona is a fabulous bean; even after soaking overnight, it must be simmered for 2 to 3 hours before it has softened up. If you can find it, your cassoulet is made.

Cranberry Currently fashionable in Italian restaurants and known in the UK as borlotti beans; cranberry beans also go by the names *Roman, saluggia, rosecoco* and *crab-eye*. They are medium-size, plump, round, white beans (sometimes beige or tan) with purplish veins. Pods bear same markings as beans; markings fade when cooked. They're valued in Italy as well as Latin America for their smooth texture and mild flavour. One of the few beans sometimes available fresh, cranberry beans are good with olive oil, garlic, herbs and tomatoes. **(I) (M)**

European Soldier This medium-size member of the extensive 'white bean' family has a red mark resembling the silhouette of a soldier standing at attention. The mark remains even after the bean is cooked. The European Soldier's good bean flavour stands up nicely to assertive sauces. It's fabulous in dishes that contain cheese. **(I) (M)**

Fava (Broad bean or Horse Bean) When an ancient Roman called for beans, he got favas. Favas are one of the only European beans in use today that are indigenous to the region. They are much prized in fresh form and can readily be found in American markets in the spring. Dried favas are very different and cannot be substituted in recipes for fresh ones. The dried ones are either large, flat, greenish-brown to dark-brown beans, quite sandy in texture or small and brown in which case they are known as field beans. If you've purchased unpeeled dried favas, peel the skins after soaking if the skins don't float to the top. You can also purchase peeled dried beans—and you have a further choice among large or small, whole or split. The beans are traditionally puréed and used in fritters (like falafel) and in stews (like the Portuguese manchoupa, with stringy meat and tomatoes). We recommend matching the hearty flavour and texture of these beans with strong ingredients such as fresh herbs, like thyme.

Flageolet This is an unusual French bean, in that it is harvested before maturity; this practice makes it unusually delicate in texture and flavour. It is a small, pale green bean—often so pale it's almost white. Because of its delicate nature, it works particularly well with French cuisine. In Brittany, it is the traditional partner to roast leg of lamb or it is served in a gently herbed tomato sauce. Try serving flageolets in a gratin or in a vinaigrette-dressed salad with red potatoes.

Gigandes These are very large white beans imported from Spain or Greece. Gigandes are good in bean stews, like Spanish fabada, though they're a little grainy when cooked. **(I) (L)**

Great Northern Beans A commercial name, Great Northern is the American name for the white haricot bean and is used for any number of beans from the vast 'white bean' family. They are medium-sized, flattish, slightly kidney-like in shape and very ordinary in flavour and texture. **(I) (M)**

Jacob's Cattle. Jacob's Cattle is a medium-size, long, slim member of the extensive 'white bean' family, with red-purple-maroon blotches and circles. Grown in New England since colonial times, they have an especially smooth texture and a distinctive fresh flavour. Jacob's Cattle beans are delicious with Mediterranean flavourings. Add them to sliced Italian sausages simmered in tomatoes and red wine with fresh rosemary. **(I) (M)**

Kidney Beans These classic beans come in both red and white. For the white kidney beans, see Cannellini. Red kidney beans also known as *Mexican beans, habichuelas* and *haricots rouges* are an ancient variety from south-western Mexico. They are medium-size, shaped as the name indicates, with two colour possibilities: either deep brownish-reddish-purplish (usually used for canning) or light red (usually marketed dry). Their virtues include a reasonably full, beany flavour and a rich texture. They're good in Spanish, Mexican, Latin American and South-western dishes. See Spanish Tolosana and Small Red Beans. **(I) (M).**

Lentils The lentil may have been cultivated in western Asia as early as 8000 B.C., which would certainly make it the earliest cultivated legume. With its sweet, earthy, very distinctive flavour, it is also one of our favourite legumes. It's a little difficult to keep track of, because there are many varieties cultivated in many different countries. Broadly speaking, there are five distinct groups of lentils in the marketplace. Most common are green lentils and brown lentils; the browns are a little smaller than the greens and have a slightly deeper taste. Whole red lentils are relatively large, deep-flavoured, salmon-coloured lentils that turn yellow when cooked. Red lentils are whole red lentils that have been peeled and split; they are less earthy than green and brown lentils, but a little spicy. Our favourite lentils of all are known as puy or French green lentils, though they don't necessarily come from France. Some of the best ones do come from a small area in France called Le Puy; they're firmer than other lentils, with a slightly wilder flavour. Others come from a small area in Umbria, Italy called Castelluccio; they don't hold their shape quite as well as those from Puy but the flavour is even more intense. Lentils don't need soaking, cook relatively quickly (about 20 minutes at the most) and threaten to turn into purée if you don't watch them carefully. Uses are endless: soups, stews, curries, salads, pastas, rice dishes, croquettes. See box, page 241, on Indian Dal for more information.

Lima Beans (Butter Beans) There are actually two types of lima beans with two different botanical classifications, the small lima and the large lima. They are both native to Peru and are named after its capital city in most of the US, but in the South and in the UK they are known as broad beans . We are very fond of the unique, meaty-buttery flavour of limas. The small lima bean is about 1 cm (½ in) in length and thinner than its cousin. The large lima bean is anywhere from 2 cm (¾ in) to 2.5 cm (1 in) long and is white with a slight green shade. Largest of all and most distinctive, is a type of large lima bean called the Christmas lima. It is a white bean with distinctive purple-brown, batik-like markings. The flavour is unique: sweet and chestnut-like. The Christmas lima is fantastic for soaking up accompanying flavours, but it's a little grainy when cooked. All of these beans were great favourites of the native Americans, who invented a combination of lima beans and sweetcorn called *msickquatash*—which has been transmuted into succotash. We like limas in all manner of soups, stews and purées.

Mung Beans Another non-American bean, this one is native to India. It is a small bean, greenish, somewhere between round and square. East Asians don't usually eat them in dried form; instead, mung beans are sprouted (to make the most common form of bean sprouts) or converted into 'bean thread' noodles (these are the shiny, 'cellophane' ones). Indians, however, do cook the dried ones—either whole, hulled or split. As you might expect, they are delicious in curried sauces. See box, page 241, on Indian Dal for more information.

Navy Beans Small and oval, navy beans are members of the extensive 'white bean' family. Sometimes they are even marketed as Great Northern beans and vice versa. They are rather ordinary in flavour and texture. **(I) (S)**

French Navy Beans These are in a different class altogether from the aforementioned navy beans. Small, plump and round, French navy beans are white beans with green undertones. They are velvety and smooth in texture, with a rich almost bacony flavour. Use French navy whenever navy beans are called for. They are best when cooked simply with garlic and olive oil or with meat juices. Unique.

Pea Beans These are very small members of the large 'white bean' family also called 'small whites' or 'California beans.' They are only about half the size of navy beans. **(I) (S)**

Pigeon Peas Pigeon peas are very small beans about 5 mm (¼ in) long, grey-yellow in colour, with a long 'eye'. One of the few non-American beans, the pigeon pea was originally cultivated in ancient Egypt, then brought to the Caribbean and the southern United States by African slaves. It may have been the original bean for Hoppin' John, a bean-and-rice dish of the South. The pigeon pea is said to have a slight narcotic effect. It is easiest to find in West Indian groceries.

Pinto Beans Pintos are closely related to red kidney beans, though they are a little smaller, with an oval shape and a pinkish brown background that is freckled (pinto means 'painted'). The colour fades into a uniform pink when cooked. They are not particularly deep in flavour and are a little mealy when cooked. They are the workhorses of South-western cooking and the most often used bean for chilli, should the chilli happen to contain beans. See Appaloosa and Rattlesnake. **(I) (M)**

Rattlesnake A new hybrid of the pinto bean, the rattlesnake is a medium-size, slightly elongated, light-brown bean with dark-brown veins. Its good, strong beany flavour (much more than pintos), is well suited for Mexican and South-western cuisines and for purées (like refried beans). We usually use these when pintos are called for. **(I) (M)**

Scarlet Runner This is a very large, plump, purple-black bean with distinctive markings. Its unusually crisp texture, even when cooked, makes it very suitable for salads. There are no substitutes for that texture. In Britain it is mostly eaten fresh and young, in the pod.

Small Red The small red is a member of the red kidney family, though smaller (less than 1 cm (½ in)) and slightly elongated (not quite kidney-shaped). It's fairly bland and ordinary, so it can be seasoned with a decisive hand. **(I) (S)**

Snowcap The snowcap is a medium-size white bean with tan and red veins. Its flavour is slightly tangy almost reminiscent of tomato and its texture is clean. Good in salads. **(I) (M)**

Soy (soya) beans Soy beans, the classic bean of China, come in a bewildering variety of sizes and colours. But you don't have to knock yourself out learning them all: you might think (as we do) that traditional soy derivatives like soy sauce, tofu, tempeh and miso taste a lot better than soy beans themselves. We suspect the Chinese and Japanese know this; this is why they convert most of their soy beans into something else. If you're really curious, however, buy some black soy beans

(these are the tastiest kind) at a health food shop, soak them for at least 12 hours, then boil them for 3 to 4 hours. You may find them firm but bland.

Spanish Tolosana This medium-size variant of the red kidney bean is maroon-coloured with tan veins. Texture is smoother than that of kidney beans and flavour is brighter. It's good in Latin American bean dishes with chillies. **(I) (M)**

Split Peas When fresh peas are dried, they are known as whole dried peas—but they are not that common in the marketplace. Much more common are dried split peas—peas that have been dried, peeled and split in half to facilitate quicker cooking. But because they're split, the peas don't retain their shape after being cooked. Both green split peas and yellow split peas are available; they are very similar, except that the yellow ones have a more intense flavour. Both are great in thick, stick-to-your-ribs soups and in purées. Peas are another non-American legume, probably originating in the Middle East about 6000 B.C. Today, many of them are grown in northern latitudes; western Canada is the world's largest producer.

Steuben Yellow-Eye There are several beans called yellow-eye, so named for a yellow-brown mark on the bean's white background. The beans vary mainly by the size of the 'eye'. Our favourite is this one also called 'molasses eye'—with an eye that covers half the surface. It is a mildly flavoured bean, with a thin skin and a smooth texture. The Steuben yellow-eye is probably the original 'Boston baked bean,' but it's delicious in assertive sauces. These beans are good to cook separately, then simmer for a while in a sauce, soup or stew. **(I) (S)**

Swedish Brown This is a small, roundish, café-au-lait-coloured bean. It's good in hearty stews. **(I) (S)**

Sweet White Runner Sweet white runners are very

large, plump, off-white beans, unique both in size and taste. The rich, sweet flavour stands up well on its own—so sweet white runners are great with just olive oil, salt and pepper. They're also terrific as an absorber for meaty stews and one of the best beans for cassoulet. **(I) (L)**

Indian dal
Perhaps the greatest, most inventive user in the world of dried legumes is India, where all dried legumes are known as *dal*. The category, of course, divides into three parts:

Beans Dried mung beans (moong dal) are known as *green gram* beans; when the bean is whole as it is often in northern and western India, it is called *sabat moong*. Dried black gram beans, from another plant are called *urad dal;* once again, when the bean is whole as it often is in the north, it is called *sabat urad.*

Peas A bewildering variety of split peas are used in Indian cooking, mostly to make that spicy soup/purée that is commonly called *dal* (confusingly, the same name that is used for the whole category of dried legumes). The most frequently used pea is the yellow split pea, which is called *channa dal*. Yellow split peas are an acceptable substitute, but they don't have the same flavour.

Lentils Lentils are by far the most commonly used dried legumes in India. There are many different types. Among the most common are yellow lentils or *toovar dal;* they are peeled and split yellow lentils. Another favourite is the pink lentil or *masoor dal;* they are peeled brown lentils, which are pink after peeling. In the West, we call them whole red lentils.

CHOOSING, STORING, AND COOKING DRIED BEANS
No preservatives are used in dried beans, so the age of the beans is an issue. Yes, there is a difference between older beans and younger beans. The older ones are drier and therefore require more soaking and cooking time; their flavour may also be a little duller. Generally, it's best to use dried beans that are no more than a year beyond their harvest. The best way to ensure the beans are fresh is to shop wherever the bean turnover is high.

As for storage: keep them in air-tight containers, in as cool a temperature as possible (but don't put them in the refrigerator). Make sure you don't mix batches of old beans and young beans, as their cooking times will be different.

The first step in cooking most dried legumes is soaking them. On some modern legumes the packages indicate that no soaking is necessary—but we think soaked legumes yield a better finished product than unsoaked. The only exception is lentils and split peas; they cook quickly and well, even without soaking.

The traditional method of soaking beans calls for a soak of 6 to 12 hours. After picking the beans over and washing them, you should cover them with tepid water until they're submerged far under the surface of the water. Change the water a few times, especially if your kitchen is warm. The older, drier and larger the bean, the longer it needs to be soaked.

There is a shorter way to soak your beans, if you want to be more spontaneous. Pick over and wash the beans, then cover them entirely with hot water in a large saucepan. Boil the beans for 2 minutes, then cover with a lid, remove pot from heat and let soak for an hour.

When ready to cook, rinse the beans (soaked either way) in tepid water. Cover the beans by 5cm (2 in) with *unsalted* cold water in a medium saucepan. (Do not salt the beans until you're finished cooking or they will toughen!) Bring to a boil, reduce heat and cover partially. Cook for 60 to 90 minutes or until beans are soft. The beans should be covered by water at all times; you will probably have to add more water to the beans to keep them completely immersed. Keep a large pot of water at a simmer for this purpose.

Bean counting

Okay...in a perfect world we all want to use dried beans when beans are called for in a recipe. But sometimes there's that dinner to be made on the spot a recipe at hand calling for dried beans, nary a dried bean in the house...but there are plenty of canned beans in the pantry. What are you going to do? Skip the guilt and make that dinner, using the following conversions:

225 g (8 oz) dried beans, uncooked=two 430-g (15.5-oz) cans of beans (drained)

450 g (1 lb) dried beans, uncooked=3½ x 430-g (15.5-oz) can of beans (drained)

750 g (12 oz) cooked dried beans=1 x 430-g (15.5-oz) can of beans (drained)

450 g (1 lb) dried beans =1.3 kg (3 lb) cooked beans

CLASSIC ITALIAN BEAN DISHES

The Italians—particularly the Tuscans, who are known as *mangiafagioli*—are great bean-eaters. You may well want to follow their lead and replace the pasta course with a bean course—in this case, either of the two great bean dishes that follow.

FAGIOLI AL FIASCO

In Tuscany, this traditional recipe calls for beans to be cooked overnight in a Chianti flask (a fiasco) in the embers of a hearth. We find that similar, if less evocative, results can be obtained with more conventional equipment. We also find that adding balsamic vinegar, an ingredient from the other side of the Apennines, works wonders in this recipe...so we follow Garibaldi's footsteps in continuing the unification of Italy. Good as a side dish, great as a course unto itself.

SERVES 4 AS A FIRST COURSE

250 g (9 oz) dried cannellini
25 g (1 oz) packed, chopped fresh sage

5 g (1 tsp) chopped garlic
(3 tbsp) chopped fresh parsley
125 ml (4 fl oz) extra-virgin olive oil
15 ml (1 tbsp) balsamic vinegar
7.5 g (1½ tsp) salt
salt and pepper to taste

1. Cook beans according to the basic instructions (page 241).

2. When the beans are done, drain them and place them in a large bowl. Add all the remaining ingredients and mix well. Let the beans sit for at least 30 minutes. Season with salt and pepper. Serve warm or at room temperature.

EUROPEAN SOLDIER BEANS WITH GORGONZOLA AND FRESH SAGE

Here's a recipe that never fails to astonish. When we tell people how easy it is to make at home, they raise a skeptical eyebrow. Follow this recipe and prove it to yourself. If you cook the beans in advance, this is a 10-minute miracle. Substitute cannellini or other medium-size white beans, if you can't find the European soldiers.

SERVES 4 AS A FIRST COURSE

250 g (9 oz) dried European soldier beans
175 g (6 oz) mild Gorgonzola cheese
50 g (2 oz) chopped fresh sage (you may substitute fresh rosemary, but not dried sage)
125 ml (4 fl oz) extra-virgin olive oil

1. Cook beans according to the basic instructions (page 241).

2. When the beans are done, drain them and put them in a mixing bowl. Add the remaining ingredients and stir well so that the cheese melts in and the sage is well dispersed. Season well with salt and pepper. Serve warm.

DIXIE BEAN DISHES

There are beans all over regional American cuisine. But the South is a strong candidate for Bean Capital of the United States.

LOUISIANA RED BEANS AND RICE

A plate of red beans and rice, garnished with ham hocks, is the traditional Monday lunch in New Orleans after the Sunday ham dinner. But we think this recipe's too good to be thought of as a solution for leftovers. Serve it anytime! Furthermore, the creamy ooze of red beans that this recipe will yield needs no upstaging from a whole ham hock. Simply mix the shredded ham into the beans and let the beans take their well deserved star turn.

SERVES 8 AS A MAIN COURSE

2 x 260-g (9.5-oz) packets dried red kidney beans or dried small red beans, rinsed and picked over
15 ml (1 tbsp) olive oil
1 large onion, coarsely chopped
1 stick celery, chopped
2 garlic cloves, chopped
4 spring onions, chopped
1 meaty ham bone or smoked ham hock, split (about 900 g (2 lb))
2 bay leaves
5 g (1 tsp) dried thyme leaves
5 g (1 tsp) ground red pepper or more to taste
5 ml (1 tsp) Worcestershire sauce
2 litres (3½ pints) cold water
salt to taste
900 g (2 lb) cooked long-grain white rice for serving
50 g (2 oz) finely chopped fresh flat-leaf parsley plus additional for garnish
hot red pepper sauce as an accompaniment

1. Soak the red kidney beans overnight in cold water to cover by 5 cm (2 in). Or quick-soak beans by bringing them and enough cold water to cover by 5 cm (2 in) to a boil over moderately high heat in a large casserole; boil the beans for 2 minutes, remove the pan from heat, cover and let stand for 1 hour. Drain the beans in a colander.

2. Heat the oil over moderate heat in a large casserole and add the onion, celery, garlic and spring onions. Cook, stirring, for 10 minutes.

3. Add the soaked beans, ham bone, bay leaves, thyme, red pepper, Worcestershire sauce and the cold water. Bring to a boil and simmer over very low heat for 3½ hours, adding a little more water if necessary, until the mixture is thick and the beans are very tender. Season to taste with salt. Remove the bay leaf.

4. Remove the ham bone, shred the meat still on the bone and add it to the beans. Discard the bone. Mash some of the beans together until the entire mixture is creamy. For each serving, spoon 225 g (8 oz) of beans over 115 g (4 oz) of rice. Sprinkle parsley on top and serve hot red pepper sauce on the side.

___

Phaseolus vulgaris

If there's one botanical classification of beans that you should know, it's this one. *Phaseolus vulgaris* is the official name for a large family of white beans that are often known in the U.S. as the 'classic' European beans—though, ironically, they all originally came from America. In this family are such beans as cannellini, flageolets, Great Northern beans, navy beans, pea beans and soldier beans. The category is so large that bean experts, when describing a bean, often begin by saying either 'in the *phaseolus vulgaris* family' or 'not in the *phaseolus vulgaris* family.'

___

HOPPIN' JOHN

This mildly spicy bean-and-rice combo is a classic in the low country (that's the area around Charleston,

South Carolina). Most agree that it was brought there by African slaves, but no one can figure out where it got its name. No one's even sure if the original dish contained black-eyed peas, pigeon peas or yellow-eyed beans. Our favourite theory is that it was originally made from pigeon peas, called *pois à pigeon* in the French-speaking Caribbean; if you pronounce the last two words of that French name, you get something very close to Hoppin' John. But don't worry about the etymology. Just make sure to serve the dish as soon as it's ready—and, if you want it to bring you good luck, serve it (as they do in the South) on New Year's Day.

SERVES 6 AS A SIDE DISH

225 g (8 oz) dried black-eyed peas or yellow-eyed beans, rinsed and picked over

15 ml (1 tbsp) olive oil

1 large onion, coarsely chopped

1 stalk celery, chopped

2 large garlic cloves, chopped

4 spring onions, chopped

1 litre (1¾ pints) cool water

1 smoked ham hock, split

2.5 g (½ tsp) ground red pepper (or more, if desired)

1 bay leaf

50 g (2 oz) finely chopped fresh flat-leaf parsley

5 g (1 tsp) salt

225 g (8 oz) long-grain white rice (preferably Texmati or basmati)

3 g (¾ tsp) dried thyme

pinch of ground cloves

For garnish

45 g (3 tbsp) chopped plum tomatoes

45 g (3 tbsp) chopped spring onions

30 g (2 tbsp) chopped fresh parsley

30 g (2 tbsp) chopped fresh mint leaves

1. Soak the black-eyed peas overnight in 5 cm (2 in) of cold water. Or quick-soak peas by bringing them and enough cold water to cover by 5 cm (2 in) to a boil over moderately high heat in a large pan; boil the peas for 2 minutes, remove the pan from heat, cover and let stand for 1 hour.

2. Heat oil in large casserole and cook onion, celery and garlic until slightly soft about 4 minutes. Add spring onions and cook 2 more minutes.

3. Add the cool water, ham hock, red pepper, bay leaf, parsley and peas to the casserole. Bring mixture to a boil, skim the surface to remove any fat and cook at a bare simmer for 2 hours or until peas become tender. Add the salt a few minutes before the end of the cooking time. (The peas should not be too tender or they will become mushy when combined with the rice.) Remove the ham hock and cut the meat into fine dice. Add the meat to the beans and discard the ham bones.

4. Add rice, 2.5 g (½ tsp) of the thyme, ground cloves and enough water to cover the rice completely. Stir gently and simmer, covered, over very low heat for 25 minutes or until the rice is done. Add the rest of the thyme at the last minute along with additional ground red pepper, if desired. Season to taste with salt. Remove the bay leaf. Serve steaming hot in bowls garnished with tomatoes, spring onions, parsley and mint.

BEAN CHILLIES

To chilli purists, beans do not belong in chilli. The original chilli con carne was just meat, with a few seasonings, simmered in a sauce made from hot chilli peppers. Beans and tomatoes were not welcome! This kind of bean-less, tomato-less chilli can still be found today throughout Texas. Well, we can be as purist as the next cowboy—but we do recognise that beans absorb the flavours of chilli marvellously well. And, therefore, we enjoy making bean chillies, which may or may not contain meat. Just remember that the quality of a chilli dish is seriously affected by your source of chilli flavour. There are many chilli powders available on the market and most of them are a blend of dried ground chilli peppers (usually uninteresting ones), cumin, garlic salt oregano and flour. We recommend sticking with the pure flavour of chillies by using a pure ground chilli powder made from a specific chilli, such as ancho chilli powder (which is available at Dean & DeLuca). Or you may grind your own dried chillies. The other flavours normally found in 'chilli powder' can be added directly to the chilli, in fresher form.

BLACK BEAN CHILI WITH AUBERGINES

Aubergines are not traditional in chilli, of course—but they furnish a fabulous, meaty chew next to the chew of the beans in this deep, dark, delicious chilli. Serve in bowls as a vegetarian main course.

SERVES 4 AS A MAIN COURSE

700 g (1½ lb) aubergine, unpeeled, stemmed, and cut into 2.5-cm (1-in) cubes
salt for sprinkling the aubergine plus additional to taste
15 dried New Mexican red chillies (about 85 g (3 oz))
850 ml (1½ pints) water
50 ml (2 fl oz) extra-virgin olive oil
2 small red onions, finely chopped
4 garlic cloves, chopped
800-g (28-oz) can plum tomatoes, drained and chopped
7.5 g (½ tbsp) ground coriander
2.5 g (½ tsp) ground cumin
1 bay leaf
450g (1 lb) cooked black beans
As accompaniments
white cheddar, coarsely grated
red onions, finely diced
fresh coriander , coarsely chopped

1. Place the aubergine cubes in a strainer and sprinkle generously with salt. Let stand for 1 hour and pat dry with paper towels.

2. Simmer the chillies and water in a large saucepan for 20 minutes. Purée the chillies and the liquid, in batches, in a blender until very smooth. Force the purée through a fine sieve and discard any solid pieces.

3. Heat the oil in a large, heavy casserole over moderately high heat. Add aubergine and cook, stirring, until almost tender, about 4 minutes. Remove aubergine and set aside. Add onions and garlic to the same Dutch oven adding more oil if necessary and cook, stirring, for 4 minutes.

4. Add tomatoes, ground coriander, cumin, bay leaf, aubergine and chilli purée and simmer 5 minutes.

5. Add beans and simmer over moderate heat for 15 minutes. Season to taste with salt. Remove the bay leaf. Place in bowls and top with cheese, onions and coriander .

SPICY PINTO BEAN CHILI WITH CHORIZO

This is a delicious, chunky chilli that focuses on the beans. It is mildly hot; if you wish to crank up the heat add more jalapeños or more ground red pepper to taste. You can serve this in a bowl as a lusty stew or you can brighten it up by placing it on dinner plates and passing the optional accompaniments to your guests. Serve warm flour tortillas on the side.

SERVES 4 AS A MAIN COURSE

15 ml (1 tbsp) olive oil
225 g (8 oz) fresh chorizo
1 sweet white onion, diced
2 garlic cloves, chopped
20 g (1½ tbsp) ancho chilli powder
10 g (2 tsp) ground cumin seeds
1 bay leaf
5 g (1 tsp) aniseed
5 g (1 tsp) ground coriander seeds
1 x 450-g (1-lb) can whole tomatoes in purée

450 g (1 lb) cooked pinto beans or rattlesnake
    beans
1 yellow pepper, trimmed and diced (you can
    substitute red or green)
2 jalapeño peppers (or more to taste), seeded and
    chopped
salt and ground hot red pepper to taste
30 g (2 tbsp) chopped fresh coriander plus
    additional for garnish
As accompaniments (optional)
grated queso fresco (fresh Mexican cheese)
chopped spring onions
sour cream
chopped red onion
diced fresh tomato
diced avocado
lime wedges

1. Heat the oil in a large heavy saucepan over
moderately high heat until hot but not smoking. Add the
chorizo and cook, turning often, until well browned and
cooked through about 15 minutes. Remove the sausage
with tongs to drain on paper towels. When cool enough
to handle, cut the sausage crossways into thin slices.

2. Add the onion to the pan and cook, stirring, for 5
minutes or until softened. Reduce the heat to moderate
and stir in the garlic, chilli powder, cumin, bay leaf,
aniseed and ground coriander. Cook, stirring, for 2
minutes (be careful not to burn the spices). Add the
tomatoes, the beans, reserved sausage, pepper and
jalapeños. Season to taste with salt and ground red
pepper. Reduce the heat and simmer, uncovered, stirring
occasionally and breaking up the tomatoes with a spoon,
for 30 minutes. Stir in 30 g (2 tbsp) of the fresh
coriander . Sprinkle with the additional coriander and
serve with the optional accompaniments.

MIDDLE EASTERN BEAN DISHES
The Middle East is the home of the only true
Mediterranean bean, the field bean. Today, dried field or

horse beans (*fool*) are still very popular in the region—as
are chick peas, lentils and a range of New World beans.

FALAFEL
These deep-fried balls with irresistible Middle Eastern
flavour have become street-corner staples in large
American cities, where thousands of them are sold from
barrows daily. But they're also easy to prepare at home.
You can make them with chick peas, with field beans
(as they do in Egypt) or with a combination of the two.
We like them with chick peas alone.
    MAKES 16 FALAFEL, ENOUGH FOR 4 SANDWICHESOR 4
    FIRST-COURSE SERVINGS

200 g (7 oz) dried chick peas
4 spring onions (white and green parts), cleaned
    and chopped
15 g (1 tbsp) chopped garlic
50 g (2 oz) chopped fresh parsley
15 g (1 tbsp) fresh mint, coarsely chopped
5 g (1 tsp) chopped hot green chilli (like jalapeño)
5 g (1 tsp) salt
7.5 g (1½ tsp) ground cumin
5 g (1 tsp) ground coriander
7.5 g (1½ tsp) baking powder
3 tablespoons warm water
light olive oil for deep-frying

1. Place dried chick peas in a bowl and cover with cold
water. Soak for at least 12 hours and up to 15 hours.

2. When ready to cook, drain the chick peas and place
them in a food processor. Add spring onions, garlic,
parsley, mint, chilli, salt, cumin and coriander. Mix
baking powder with the warm water and add mixture to
food processor. Process until smooth. Transfer mixture to
a small bowl, cover and refrigerate for 30 minutes.

3. Pour the oil to a depth of 5 cm (2 in) in a heavy
saucepan or wok. Heat to 190°C (375°F).

4. When falafel mixture is chilled, roll into 16 ping-pong-ball-sized balls. Slip a few at a time into the hot oil, making sure they don't stick to the bottom. Cook, turning, for about 6 minutes or until the balls are a dark, even brown on all sides. Remove with slotted spoon and drain on paper towels. Serve either in sandwiches or as a falafel first course (see box below).

Serving falafel

Here are two ways to serve falafel: in sandwiches and as a first course.

Falafel are traditionally served in pitta-bread sandwiches. To make 1 sandwich, cut a pitta-with-a-pocket in half and stuff the half with 4 falafel balls, thin slices of cucumber, onion and tomato along with chopped parsley and chopped mint. Use the other half pitta for a second sandwich. If you have soft, fresh pittas that have no pockets, simply place your ingredients on half of the pitta, then fold the other half of the pitta over the ingredients to create a half-moon shape.

Drizzle the ingredients with the following sauce:
125 ml (4 fl oz) plain yogurt
45 ml (3 tbsp) tahini paste
2.5 g (½ tsp) very finely chopped garlic
10 ml (2 tsp) fresh lemon juice
water
salt and pepper to taste

Mix together the yogurt, tahini paste, garlic and lemon juice. Thin out with water to make a smooth, medium-thick sauce. Season to taste with salt and pepper.

We like to serve falafel, without pitta as the first course of a Middle Eastern dinner. Simply place 4 cooked falafel balls on each of 4 appetiser plates, drizzle some of the yogurt-tahini sauce over and around them and strew with a rough cut of cucumbers, onions, tomatoes, parsley and mint.

HUMMUS

We're crazy about this Middle Eastern chick pea-and-sesame-paste purée; served cold with pitta, olives and raw vegetables, it makes a great start to a festive dinner party. In this dish, the best texture of all is obtained by passing the cooked chick peas through a food mill; other devices—like a food processor—are acceptable, but inferior. The following version is lighter than most, because it doesn't contain oil (but you may drizzle the finished dish with olive oil).

SERVES 4 AS A FIRST COURSE

350 g (12 oz) dried chick peas, soaked overnight
2 garlic cloves, chopped to a paste
50 g (2 oz) tahini paste
75 ml (2½ fl oz) lemon juice
salt and white pepper to taste
olive oil for drizzling
paprika and ground cumin (optional)
Arab bread, such as pitta as an accompaniment

1. Drain the soaked chick peas. Cover them with water and simmer until quite soft about 1½ hours. Drain chick peas, reserving a little of the cooking water.

2. Pass chick peas through the fine blade of a food mill. Mix chick pea purée with garlic paste, tahini paste, lemon juice and about 50 ml (2 fl oz) of the cooking water. The goal is a medium-thick spread. Season to taste with salt and white pepper. Serve on a platter, drizzled with olive oil. (You may also sprinkle paprika and/or ground cumin on the hummus.) Serve with slices of Arab bread, like pitta, to scoop up the hummus.

MAIN-COURSE BEAN-AND-MEAT CLASSICS

There's no sense denying it: some of our favourite dishes in the world are hearty casseroles of meat and dried beans, scented with the country tastes of various peasant traditions. Beans are wonderful by themselves—but they're also wonderful carriers of meat juices and flavours. Bean-and-meat classics may not have passed muster at fancy dinner parties in the eighties, of course, when someone in the kitchen was arranging everyone's tiny portions of expensive food on individual dinner plates. But we've all come to our gastronomic senses, thank God and can now find dinner-party happiness in huge, bubbling casseroles of beans and meat served directly at the table.

CASSOULET

Cassoulet, the great stew of south-western France, is probably the world's most famous bean-and-meat dish. Its popularity in America was assured in the sixties, when Julia Child published a long, involved, wonderful recipe for it in *Mastering the Art of French Cooking*, Volume I; it has been a litmus test for French-chef-wannabes among Americans ever since. The intervening decades have shown that you don't have to labour for 3 days to produce a great cassoulet. You do, on the other hand, still have to wade through all the controversy that surrounds this dish as you choose your ingredients (see box, page 249). For our dream cassoulet, it boils down to this: confit is out, lamb in a crust is out and your choice of beans is the most important variable. Dried white beans are de rigueur—but which dried white beans? In France as Julia pointed out, beans from various localities—Cayence, Pamiers, Mazères, Lavelanet—are touted by various chefs as the best for cassoulet. In the United States, Great Northern beans are usually recommended, but in our opinion they are rather small and undramatic for this great dish. We prefer to go larger—even larger, in fact, than they normally go in France. A larger dried white bean you might want to consider is the fat Christmas lima. It has a fascinating, chestnut-like flavour; unfortunately, it is a little too grainy and softens quickly. A much better bean for this job, we feel, is the sweet white runner bean; it's distinctively flavoured and will stand up to long cooking. Best of all, if you can find it, is a large, Italian white bean called Corona by the company that distributes it (see page

237). The Corona takes almost 3 hours of slow simmering to cook; when it's done, however, it's creamy yet firm, filled with the meaty flavours of a cassoulet yet still strong in its own bean flavour. A masterpiece. Whichever dried beans you choose, make sure they're relatively fresh.

SERVES 6 AS A MAIN COURSE

450g (1 lb) dried white beans, soaked overnight in cold water to cover
125 ml (4 fl oz) tomato purée
1.8 kg (4 lb) lamb bones
2 litres (3½ pint) chicken stock
2 bouquets garni (parsley stems, bay leaves, peppercorns and thyme sprigs wrapped in cheesecloth)
350 ml (12 fl oz) dry white wine or vermouth
450g (1 lb) boneless lamb, cut from the leg into 4 cm (1½-in) cubes (the older the lamb the better; or use mutton)
450 g (1 lb) pork shoulder cut into 4 cm (1½-in) cubes
3 pig's trotters, split (optional)
salt and pepper to taste
flour for dusting
45 g (3 tbsp) goose , duck or bacon fat or lard
225g (8 oz) onions, chopped
12 garlic cloves, smashed, plus 50g (8 oz) finely chopped garlic
2 carrots, chopped
800-ml (28-oz) can plum tomatoes, drained and chopped
115g (4 oz) thick bacon rashers
900 g (2 lb) French garlic sausage (several different types if possible)
50 ml (2 tbsp) Armagnac

1. When ready to prepare dish, preheat oven to 200°C (400°F).

2. Brush the tomato purée over the lamb bones and

bake, turning bones frequently, for 45 minutes. Remove bones.

3. Place bones in a large stockpot and cover with the chicken stock. Add 1 bouquet garni. Add the wine or vermouth to the lamb roasting tin and deglaze the tin over high heat until the wine is reduced to about 150 ml (5 fl oz). Add to the stockpot. Simmer stock gently for 1½ hours. Pour stock through colander into a large casserole, discarding bouquet garni and bones.

4. Generously season the lamb cubes, pork cubes and pig's trotters (if using) with salt and pepper. Dust lightly with flour. Heat 15 g (1 tbsp) goose or other fat in a large sauté pan over moderately high heat. Making sure the pan is not too crowded, quickly sear the lamb cubes in batches until brown on all sides about 3 minutes. Add to the casserole with the lamb stock. In the same pan, sear the pork cubes until golden on all sides about 3 minutes. (During this process, you may need to add more fat to the pan.) Add pork cubes to the casserole. Do the same with the pig's trotters, if using and add to the casserole.

5. In the same sauté pan, cook the onions, garlic and carrots (adding more fat, if necessary) over moderately high heat for 10 minutes. Add vegetables to the lamb stock and meat in the casserole along with the remaining bouquet garni. Add the canned tomatoes and their juice to the casserole, breaking up the tomatoes. Drain the beans and add them to the casserole. Mix well. Simmer all over very low heat until meat is tender, about 1½ hours. (Make sure the stew never boils or the meat will become tough.) When meats are tender, strain stock from the casserole, degrease and reserve. Remove the pig's trotters, if used, and discard the fatty skin; divide the trotters into meaty chunks and return to the pot.

6. Cut the bacon slices into 2.5-cm (1-in) pieces. Drop into simmering water for 2 minutes, then refresh bacon pieces with cold water. Drain and add to the casserole.

Add the garlic sausages. Add enough reserved cooking liquid to the casserole to just cover the beans and meat. Simmer very gently, partially covered, for 1 hour or until beans are tender and flavours are amalgamated. Every few minutes, distribute a little of the finely chopped garlic through the stew. You will also need to check the liquid level every so often and add reserved liquid as needed; the 'sauce' around the meat and beans should be ample and medium-thick—neither pasty nor soupy.

7. When almost ready to serve, remove the sausages and cut into 1-cm (½-in) rounds. Return to the casserole and mix well, being careful not to break the beans. Stir in the Armagnac, season with salt and pepper and bring to boil on top of the stove. Reduce heat to low and simmer for 5 more minutes. (Add more liquid if necessary to make a medium-rich sauce.) Divide cassoulet among 6 dinner plates, sprinkle with parsley and serve with crusty bread.

The cassoulet controversies

The most serious cassoulet controversy concerns the type of meat that goes into the stew along with the beans. Decades ago, food historian Waverly Root sorted out the three main styles of cassoulet in France: cassoulet from Castelnaudry, he said, is a 'pure' cassoulet with only pork alongside the beans; in Toulouse, to the pork and beans are added preserved duck or preserved goose (confit); in Carcassonne, the pork is joined not by confit but by mutton. Now, we are lovers of confit, but appreciate it most when it comes sizzling, crisp-skinned, out of a sauté pan; texture-wise, in a cassoulet, we find confit a wet, stringy disappointment. Mutton, however, is another story: long-cooked cubes of mature lamb add fabulous flavour and texture to a cassoulet. We even like to use a lamb stock for cooking the beans. Call us Carcassonniènne on this one.

The other major controversy involves the cassoulet crust. According to legend, chefs used to add breadcrumbs to the top of a cooking cassoulet, wait for them to harden into a crust, break the crust, mix it in with the sauce in the stewpot, then start again with more breadcrumbs to build the crust again; supposedly a cassoulet that didn't have its crust 'broken' 7 times wasn't worth beans. In reality, in France today, you almost never see a crust on a dish of cassoulet. That suits us fine, because making a crust prevents the chef from remaining vigilant as the stew is finishing. Here's what we mean: at the end of the cooking process, the beans are absorbing liquid like mad and threatening to turn the cassoulet dry; to prevent this you have to keep adding more braising liquid as the cassoulet finishes. But you can't add more liquid if you've built the Great Wall of Carcassonne on top of your cassoulet. Think of the crust as an excrescence as we do and just serve your fabulous uncrusted cassoulet right out of the pot.

COCIDO

There are cocidos made all over Spain and each region has its own variation. Basically, it is a pot of stewed chick peas with lots of meat and vegetables added—kind of a Spanish pot-au-feu. The most famous cocido comes from Madrid—cocido Madrileño—where the main meat is beef. But the best one we've ever had was in Galicia, where pork products stole the show (this would be a shock to the medieval Jews, who are said to have invented this dish). In any variation, however, it is the luscious Spanish chick peas that are the soul of the dish. Cocido is normally served in several courses, but the following recipe simplifies that practice; simply serve each diner a large bowl of broth, vegetables, meat and chick peas. It is an immensely satisfying winter meal. By the way, we like to stray from tradition and throw a chilli pepper into the pot; we think it adds another level of interest to the dish.

SERVES 6

450 g (1 lb) dried chick peas, soaked in water overnight
1 x 1.8-2.25 kg (4-5 lb) stewing chicken, skinned and cut into 6 pieces
450 g (1 lb) pork loin cut into 7.5-cm (3-in) chunks
450 g (1 lb) ham hock
450 g (1 lb) slice of veal shank
16 fl oz (2 cups) dry white wine
1 litre (1¾ pints) chicken stock
1 litre (1¾ pints) water
6 chorizo sausages
1 large onion, chopped
3 large garlic cloves, chopped
4 medium waxy potatoes, peeled and cubed
3 parsnips, peeled and coarsely diced
3 carrots, coarsely diced
1 bay leaf
1 fresh red hot chilli pepper (optional)

1. Drain the chick peas and place them in a large stockpot. Add the chicken, pork loin, ham hock, veal shank, wine, chicken stock and water. Bring to a boil, remove froth, reduce heat to moderate and simmer gently, uncovered, for 2½ hours.

2. Add the chorizos, onion, garlic, potatoes, parsnips, carrots, bay leaf and chilli. Simmer gently, uncovered, for 1 hour more.

3. When ready to serve cocido, remove ham hock and veal shank. Cut meat off of the bones, discard bones and return shredded meat to stockpot. Remove the bay leaf.

4. To serve, either place the cocido in a large tureen and serve from the tureen at table or divide the cocido among 6 large soup bowls, making sure each person gets 1 piece of chicken and 1 chorizo. Serve hot.

Fabada

Spain has fabulous main-course bean dishes. The Cocido Madrileño is the most famous of the classics, but a strong candidate for international attention is Fabada. Made in the gastronomically undiscovered region of Asturias along Spain's northern coast, Fabada is a combination of dried beans, sausages and an assortment of funky porcine cuts. It's firmly in the cassoulet tradition—though, unlike cassoulet, no crust ever appears on top. Furthermore, the beans themselves are incomparable. They use white beans called *judías del barco de Avila*—which are large, succulent and creamy, perhaps the most delicious beans in any international main-course bean classic we've ever tasted. It's rare to find beans of this name outside Spain, but gigandes and Coronas are good substitutes.

FEIJOADA

This bean-and-meat classic is the national dish of Brazil; though it's never going to be a national dish in the United States the growing popularity of South American food is making feijoada better-known here every day. It's a dazzling array of pork items and black beans that certainly deserves wider international attention. It was originally devised by the African slaves who toiled in the north-east of Brazil. The owners of the sugar plantations would eat high on the hog and leave the lesser cuts of pork for the workers; the slaves would finally get the upper hand by making tastier food than the owners could ever imagine. Alongside the beans and meats, the traditional accompaniments are white rice, couvé (a Portuguese cabbage very like our kale), farofa (a couscous-like dish made from manioc flour, which is sprinkled on and served alongside the feijoada) orange slices and hot sauce. In modern Rio de Janeiro, life practically stops on Saturday afternoon as the cariocas sit down in restaurants and homes to enormous platters of feijoada, which they linger over for hours. It's a great idea as well for your next dinner party. Go authentic, if you can handle it and add all the porcine parts that the Brazilians do; they're actually delicious. Or leave out the meats below that are listed as optional. Either way, the dish is a revelation.

SERVES 12 AS A MAIN COURSE

The meats

450 g (1 lb) carne seca or salted corned beef

450 g (1 lb) salted pork ribs

1 smoked beef tongue (about 700 g (1½ lb))

1 cured pork butt (about 700 g (1½ lb))

225 g (½ lb) fresh pig's ear (optional)

225 g (½ lb) fresh pig's feet, split lengthwise (optional)

2 fresh pig's tails (optional)

450 g (1 lb) linguiça sausage

450 g (1 lb)smoked calabrese sausage (or kielbasa)

225 g (½ lb) paio or other fatty blood sausage (optional)

The beans

1.3 kg (3 lb) dried black beans (preferably Brazilian, but you may use any dried black bean)

1 large onion

2 bay leaves

50 ml (2 fl oz) vegetable oil

3 garlic cloves, chopped

50 ml (2 fl oz) white vinegar

The rice

50 g (2 oz) butter

1 large onion, chopped

550 g (1¼ lb) raw white long-grained rice, washed

700 ml (1¼ pints) water

The farofa

225 g (8 oz) butter

115 g (4 oz) chopped onion

15 g (1 tbsp) chopped garlic

225 g (8 oz) smoked bacon, sliced thick and then cut into small cubes

6 eggs

1 kg (2¼ lb) manioc flour (available at ethnic groceries)

50 g (2 oz) chopped fresh parsley

The kale

900 g (2 lb) kale leaves, stems removed

30 ml (2 tbsp) vegetable oil

3 garlic cloves, finely chopped

The hot pepper sauce

30 ml (2 tbsp) vinegar from a bottle of malagueta
    peppers marinated in vinegar (see box, page 253)

malagueta peppers (depending on your heat
    threshold)

115 g (4 oz) cooked black beans

125 ml (4 fl oz) stock from black beans

4 large navel oranges, peeled and separated into
    sections

1. The day before serving the feijoada, soak the carne seca and pork ribs in water to cover. Change water 3 times in 24 hours. Wash and pick over the black beans to remove impurities. Soak beans in water to cover by 4 inches overnight (or at least 6 hours).

Obtaining the meats

It may take a little extra effort to procure all of the meats required for an authentic feijoada. When we make feijoada, we visit the following stores that make up our 'feijoada itinerary.'

Dean & DeLuca At our own store, you can find delicious smoked calabrese sausage, linguiça and paio (blood sausage).

Esposito (500 Ninth Avenue, New York City) This is a 'pork butcher's', with an Italian ethnic spin. But it's the perfect place to find pig's ears, pig's tails and pig's feet.

Emporium Brasil (15 West 46th St., New York City) This store is dedicated to Brazilian products. It's not a butcher shop, but you will find packages of Brazilian carne seca here.

2. On the day of serving, drain the beans and add them to a large stockpot. Add the large onion (whole) and the 2 bay leaves. Add enough water to cover beans. Bring to a boil and boil for 10 minutes.

3. Reduce heat so that the liquid is gently simmering and add the drained carne seca, beef tongue, pork butt and pig's ear, trotters and tails. Add enough additional water so that meats are almost covered. Simmer gently for a total of about 3 hours. After 2 hours, begin to check the doneness of the meats. Some of the meats will be tender at this point; remove tender pieces and place them in a baking tin. Cover the tender meats with some of the bean cooking liquid to prevent dryness and cover the pan. Place the pan in a 100°C (200°F) oven to keep the meats warm. Over the next hour as you near a total of 3 hours cooking, remove any meats from the bean pot that become tender and add them to the baking pan in the oven.

4. Also at the 2-hour mark add the drained pork ribs and the sausages to the bean pot. Simmer them for the last hour of the 3-hour cooking in the bean pot.

5. After a total of 3 hours' cooking time, everything (meats, sausages, beans) should be tender. Remove all of the meats to the baking tin in the oven; add some more bean stock if necessary to keep them moist. Remove and discard the whole onion and bay leaves. Keep the beans and liquid warm in the bean pot.

6. *Make the rice:* Melt the butter over moderate heat in a heavy saucepan with a tight-fitting lid. Add the chopped onion and cook, stirring, for 3 minutes. Add the rice and stir to coat with the butter. Add the water, bring to a boil, reduce heat to very low and cook until rice is done about 20 minutes.

7. *Make the farofa:* Melt the butter in a heavy stockpot over moderately high heat. Add the onion, garlic and bacon. Sauté until the bacon starts to brown slightly about 3 minutes. Reduce heat to moderate and stir in the eggs. Cook like scrambled eggs, gently scraping the bottom of the pot. As the eggs begin to scramble add the manioc flour in a steady stream, stirring constantly. Continue to cook the farofa for 4 to 5 minutes, breaking up any lumps. Add the fresh parsley and keep warm in a serving dish.

8. *Make the kale:* Roll up the kale leaves tightly from one side of a leaf to the other; cut each rolled leaf, working from tip to stem, into thin shreds. Blanch shreds quickly in salted boiling water and drain. In a large frying pan, place the vegetable oil over moderate heat. Add the garlic and cook for 3 minutes, stirring. Add the blanched kale and toss it well with the oil and garlic. Cook for 4 minutes, until kale is just wilted. Keep warm.

9. *Make the hot pepper sauce:* In a food processor or blender, combine the vinegar from the malagueta peppers, the malagueta peppers, the 115 g (4 oz) cooked black beans and the 125 ml (4 fl oz) stock from black beans. Purée until a smooth sauce is formed. Adjust for seasoning and/or heat and/or thickness (the sauce should be medium-thick). Keep warm until serving time.

Malagueta peppers

The tiny, incendiary peppers of Bahia, in north-eastern Brazil are some of the most flavourful chillies in the world. Every supermarket in Brazil carries bottles of malagueta peppers (green or red) soaking in vinegar; it is this chilli-flavoured vinegar that is often sprinkled over the black beans of a feijoada. You can find these bottled treasures at Portuguese and African groceries.

10. To finish preparing the beans, remove 225 g (8 oz) cooked beans from the pot and purée them in a food processor or blender. Return purée to the pot, stir in well, bring to a boil and add the 50 g (2 oz) vegetable oil and

chopped garlic. Simmer for 10 minutes, then add the vinegar. Taste for seasoning. The beans are now ready to serve.

11. To serve the meats arrange them on a large platter so that each type of meat gets its own 'corner' of the platter. Shred the carne seca. Cut the pork ribs in pieces. Remove the outer layer of skin from the beef tongue and slice the tongue in thick pieces. Slice the pork butt. Cut the sausages on the bias into thick slices. Make thin slices from the pig's ear, if using. Serve the pig's feet intact, if using. Carve the tail meat from the bone, if using. Just before serving, ladle a little hot bean liquid over the meats on the platter to moisten them.

12. Serve the following in separate serving bowls: the beans, the rice, the farofa, the kale, and the hot pepper sauce. Serve the orange slices arranged on a flat plate. Serve extra malagueta peppers in vinegar, if you have them, for sprinkling over the feijoada.

What to drink with feijoada

Though beer and fruity red wine go well with feijoada, no self-respecting Brazilian would consider drinking anything other than a caiparinha with the dish. Tangy and super-refreshing, it's like a Brazilian margarita, except that no tequila is used; instead the drink is made from cachaça a Brazilian sugarcane distillate which is not generally available in the UK. To make one, simply cut a small lime into a dozen pieces, place them in a heavy tumbler, mash them with a wooden spoon add sugar to taste (opinions vary as to the ideal sweetness of this drink), cachaça, lots of shaved ice, stir and serve.

BEAN DISHES ON THE SIDE

Americans always been meat-and-potatoes people, but that hasn't stopped them from relishing beans with their viennas. And when Americans discovered that the

Normans serve beans with lamb, Tuscans serve beans with steak and hundreds of regional cuisines emphasise beans on the side, there was virtually no stopping them in the eighties and nineties.

GARLICKY BEAN AND POTATO PURÉE

What's particularly interesting about this bean purée is that it's not made with olive oil; instead, cream and butter are used to give it extra richness. This makes the dish absolutely exquisite as an accompaniment to all manner of French and Italian entrées, from grilled fish to sausages. Think of it as mashed potatoes with a surprise.

MAKES ABOUT (1 LITRE) 1¾ PINTS

450 g (1 lb) dried white beans
2 bay leaves
2 sprigs of thyme or 1.25 g (¼ tsp) dried thyme
1 large onion
2 cloves
1 carrot
2 garlic cloves plus 2 whole heads garlic
450 g (1 lb) russet potatoes (preferably Idaho)
115 g (4 oz) unsalted butter
125 g (4 oz) cream
15 g (1 tbsp) salt or to taste
5 g (1 tsp) black pepper or to taste
22ml (4½ tsp) lemon juice or to taste (if serving at room temperature)

1. The night before serving, rinse the beans and soak them in cold water, making sure beans are totally immersed. Let them sit, uncovered at room temperature overnight.

2. The next day, rinse the beans and put them in a large pot of clean water to cover by 5 cm (2 in). Pierce the onion with the cloves. Add the bay leaves, thyme, onion, carrot and the 2 garlic cloves. Bring to a boil, reduce heat and simmer about 2 hours or until beans start to

fall apart. (Add more water if beans start to dry up before they are cooked.) Once beans are cooked, drain and let sit in colander. Remove bay leaves, thyme sprigs and cloves.

3. While the beans are simmering, peel potatoes and cut in half. Place in a medium-size pot of cold salted water. Simmer for about 20 minutes or until the potatoes begin to fall apart. Strain and let potatoes sit in a colander for 5 minutes. Place in a large bowl.

4. Preheat oven to 180°C (350°F). Place the 2 garlic heads in oven and roast for 20 minutes or until soft when lightly pressed. Remove from oven and let cool. When the garlic has cooled, squeeze each garlic clove into a small bowl. Set aside.

5. Add butter and cream to a small pan. Bring to a boil. Add half of the mixture to potatoes. Mash together until small chunks remain. Set aside.

6. Place drained beans in a food processor. Add other half of cream and butter mixture and purée until mixture is smooth.

7. Finally add bean mixture and roasted garlic to potatoes. Add the salt and pepper.

Note: If you allow this dish to come to room temperature, you will have a great dip for bread and crudités or a great spread as the base for a sandwich. Add 15-30 ml (1-2 tbsp) of lemon juice and mix well.

CHANNA VAZI

Chick peas are the one legume that comes in a canned form that is good enough to recommend. Using canned chick peas in this richly flavoured Indian recipe makes it weeknight heaven. Just make sure to rinse the beans under cold water before using.

SERVES 4 AS A SIDE DISH

15 ml (1 tbsp) ghee or vegetable oil

2 medium onions, sliced paper thin

2 medium garlic cloves, chopped

15 g (1 tbsp) ground cumin

5 g (1 tsp) toasted ground fenugreek

15 g (1 tbsp) ground coriander

pinch of ground cloves

350 g (12 oz) chopped fresh tomatoes

400-g (14-oz) can chick peas, rinsed and drained

30 g (2 tbsp) chopped fresh coriander

In a medium saucepan, warm the ghee or vegetable oil over moderate heat. When it is hot add the onions and cook them, stirring occasionally, until they brown about 10 minutes. Add the garlic, cumin, fenugreek, coriander and cloves and stir them in well. Add the tomatoes, cover and reduce the heat. Simmer the mixture for 15 minutes or until the tomatoes are broken down. Add the chick peas, cover the pan and simmer for 10 more minutes. Add a little water, if desired, to make a thin gravy. Serve hot or warm. Top each serving with coriander .

FLAGEOLETS À LA BRETONNE

There is a classic north-western French pairing of flageolets with lamb, in which the pale young beans are cooked with plenty of garlic and served in their own sauce. Less well known is the following dish, which is the other customary use in Brittany for flageolets: beans in an herbed tomato sauce. There is, of course, no reason not to serve it with roast lamb anyway; it's delicious.

SERVES 6 AS A SIDE DISH

2 medium onions

2 whole cloves

250 g (9 oz) dried flageolets, soaked for 6 hours
and drained

45 ml (3 tbsp) olive oil

1 garlic clove, smashed and chopped

5 g (1 tsp) dried rosemary, rubbed between your

fingers

5 g (1 tsp) dried thyme

1 bay leaf

450 g (1 lb) drained canned tomatoes, broken into
chunks

salt to taste

1. Peel 1 of the onions and stud it with the 2 cloves on opposite sides. Put the studded onion along with the beans and water to cover by 5 cm (2 in), in a medium saucepan. (A narrow diameter saucepan is preferable to a wide one.) Bring to a boil, reduce heat to low, cover partially and simmer for 1 hour or until beans are soft. Skim off any foam that rises to the top.

2. *While beans are cooking, make the sauce:* Heat the olive oil in a medium saucepan over moderate heat. Chop the remaining onion coarsely and add it to the pan along with the garlic, rosemary, thyme and bay leaf. Cook until onion is just translucent, but not too soft. Add the tomatoes and season well with salt. Cover, reduce heat to low and simmer for about 45 minutes.

3. When beans are ready, drain them in a colander, discarding the clove-studded onion. Add the drained beans to the sauce and stir them together. Adjust salt and pepper before serving.

STEUBEN YELLOW-EYE BEANS IN CREAMY CUMIN SAUCE WITH MUSHROOMS

The south Indian character of this vegetarian dish is highlighted by the generous sprinkling of coriander it receives at the end. The dish tastes best when served warm.

SERVES 4 AS A MAIN COURSE

250 g (9 oz) dried Steuben yellow-eye beans or
black-eyed peas

30 ml (2 tbsp) vegetable oil

115 g (4 oz) finely chopped onion

5 g (1 tsp) grated fresh ginger

250 g (9 oz) sliced mushrooms

1 garlic clove, chopped

20 g (1½ tbsp) ground cumin

15 g (1 tbsp) ground coriander

450 g (1 lb) drained canned tomatoes, broken into
chunks

225 ml (8 fl oz) plain yogurt

70 g (2½ oz) packed, chopped fresh coriander

15 g (1 tbsp) grated lime zest

10 g (2 tsp) salt or to taste

pepper to taste

1. Cook beans according to the basic instructions (page 241).

2. While the beans are cooking, heat the oil in a medium saucepan over moderately high heat. When the oil is hot add the onion and sauté it, stirring occasionally, until it turns brown. Add the ginger, mushrooms, garlic, cumin and coriander. Cook, stirring occasionally, for 10 minutes or until mushrooms are wilted. Add the tomatoes, stir up the bottom of the pan, reduce heat to low, cover and simmer for about 1 hour.

3. When beans are done, drain them in a colander and add them to the sauce. Stir well, remove the pan from the heat and let it sit, uncovered, stirring occasionally, for at least 15 minutes and up to 1 hour. Add the yogurt, coriander and lime zest and stir well. Season with salt and pepper.

APPALOOSAS IN ANCHO SAUCE

This dish features the chocolatey flavour of ancho chillies. To get that flavour, you can either use the dried whole chillies or—because several purveyors are now offering chilli powders made from specific chillies—you could use ancho chilli powder. The dried chillies take a little more work, but provide a richer flavour. You can enjoy these beans as a vegetarian main course over rice or as a filling for burritos or tacos. They also go well with grilled meats.

SERVES 4 AS A MAIN COURSE

250 g (9 oz) dried Appaloosa beans or pinto beans

4 ancho chillies or 3 tablespoons ancho powder

15 ml (1 tbsp) vegetable oil

1 medium white onion, sliced very thinly

2 garlic cloves, chopped

1 dried chipotle chilli

10 g (2 tsp) ground cumin

450 g (1 lb) drained canned tomatoes, broken into
chunks

7.5 g (1½ tsp) salt

25 g (1 oz) packed, chopped fresh coriander

225 ml (8 fl oz) sour cream

1. Cook beans according to the basic instructions (page 241).

2. *While beans are cooking, prepare the ancho chilli purée:* If you're using whole chillies, toast them in a 100°C (200°F) oven for 5 minutes, remove seeds and stems and soak in 225 ml (8 fl oz) hot water for 15 minutes. In a food processor, process the chillies to a thin purée with half the soaking water. If you're using the ancho chilli powder, mix it with 125 ml (4 fl oz) water.

3. In a medium saucepan over moderate heat, heat the vegetable oil. Cook the onion and garlic for 5 minutes. Add the chilli purée or the chilli powder-water mixture, chipotle and ground cumin. Add the tomatoes, stir up the bottom of the pan, reduce heat to low, cover and simmer for about 40 minutes.

4. When the beans are done, drain them in a colander and add them to the sauce. Stir well. (If the dish seems dry add a little water and simmer for another 2 minutes). Remove the chipotle and add the salt. Top each serving with coriander and sour cream.

BEAN CURD

Bean curd is also a bean product! When soy beans are boiled, they yield a foam or curd, which is gathered and pressed into bean curd. Bean curd (or tofu) is extremely mild in flavour—which makes it a good carrier for other flavours. To most aficionados, however, the real treat is the texture. 'Soft' bean curd (ask your merchant or look at the labelling if the tofu is in a package) has a silken texture almost custardlike. It may be used in steamed dishes or soups—but in many dishes (like stir-fries) it falls apart. 'Firm' bean curd has a tougher, chewier texture; it's the one to use if you wish to stir-fry or deep-fry bean curd.

STIR-FRIED BEAN CURD WITH GROUND PORK AND OYSTER SAUCE

Use firm-textured bean curd for this spicy Szechuan treat.

SERVES 4 AS PART OF A CHINESE MEAL

225 g (8 oz) ground pork

1 egg, beaten

25g (1 oz) cornflour

2.5 g (½ tsp) Chinese 5-spice powder

115g (4 oz) finely chopped spring onions (white and green parts)

15 g (1 tbsp) sugar

7.5 g (¾ tsp) sesame oil

7.5 g (¼ tsp) salt

1.25 ml (1 tbsp) vegetable oil

115g (4 oz) finely chopped red pepper

2.5g (½ tsp) finely chopped hot green chilli (or more to taste)

20 g (4 tsp) finely chopped garlic

20 g (4 tsp) finely chopped ginger

225 ml (8 fl oz) chicken stock

30 ml (2 tbsp) thin soy sauce

30 ml (2 tbsp) oyster sauce

450 g (1 lb) firm bean curd, cut in 2-cm (¾-inch) cubes at room temperature

1. Mix together the pork, egg, 15 g (1 tbsp) of the cornstarch, 5-spice powder, 15 g (1 tbsp) of the spring onions, 2.5 g (½ tsp) of the sugar, 1.25 ml (¼ tsp) of the sesame oil and salt. Place the vegetable oil in a hot wok over very high heat, then add small, thumbnail-size clumps of the pork mixture. Stir-fry for about 1 minute or until the clumps are browned and cooked through. Remove from wok and reserve, leaving oil behind.

2. Reduce the heat to moderate. Add to the wok 90 g (6 tbsp) of spring onions, chopped red pepper, chopped green chilli, chopped garlic and chopped ginger. Stir-fry for 30 seconds. Add the browned pork and stir well, tossing with the rest of the sugar. Increase the heat to high and add the chicken stock, soy sauce and oyster sauce. Stir well and bring to a boil. Mix the remaining 10 g (2 tsp) of cornflour with a little cold water in a cup, then stir into the wok. Gently stir in the bean curd cubes, taking care not to break them up.

3. As soon as the bean curd is heated through, remove contents of wok and place on serving platter. Sprinkle with the rest of the chopped spring onion and the remaining half teaspoon of sesame oil.

STEAMED TOFU RAMEKINS WITH SOY SAUCE, SPRING ONIONS AND NORI

And this lightning-fast Japanese meal-opener shows off the loveliness of soft tofu: inside their ramekins, the chunks of jiggly bean curd turn to virtual velvet. Combined with the vapours of the steamer, the tofu yields a delicious stock in the ramekin—making this a perfect starter. If you don't have the small ramekins, you can easily transpose this recipe to plates or bowls. Make the 450 g (1 lb) of tofu on one plate, if you wish; just keep the proportions of the other ingredients intact.

MAKES 8 SMALL FIRST-COURSE SERVINGS

450 g (1 lb) soft bean curd, broken into coarse chunks

4 teaspoons Japanese soy sauce
10 g (2 tsp) finely chopped spring onion
20 g (4 tsp) aji nori furikake*
few drops Japanese sesame oil

1. Divide the bean curd among 8 small ramekins that each have a capacity of 50 ml (2 fl oz). Drizzle each one with 2.5 ml (½ tsp) of soy sauce. Place on a steamer rack over boiling water and steam until hot about 3 minutes.

2. Remove from steamer and sprinkle each ramekin with spring onion and aji nori furikake. Drizzle a drop or 2 of sesame oil on each one and serve immediately.

GRAINS

In a sense, grains have always been wildly popular in America. What comestibles have been more widely consumed over the years than bread (made from wheat), breakfast cereal (made from a variety of grains) and sweetcorn (maize), in all the manifold forms in which it is eaten in the USA?

But Americans have rarely thought of these products as grains or as grain-based. We have always taken our grains transformed, not straight. If, 20 years ago, you'd mentioned whole, untransformed grains to the average American consumer—grains like bulgur wheat, kamut, quinoa and spelt—you would have met blank stares.

Enter the health-food people, who—using the initially isolated health-food shop as a base—started exploring the fabulous diversity of the world's whole grains. Serious diners—those who live to eat, rather than the other way 'round—paid little or no attention to this 'nutritional fringe'. By 1985, when new vegetables, new beans and new cuisines were already making

*Aji nori furikake is a fabulous Japanese convenience food: crisp strips of nori (black-green seaweed sheets), tossed with toasted sesame seeds. It's a great sprinkle for many Japanese dishes, and available at Japanese groceries.

significant inroads on our gastronomic complacency, the mainstream turnaround on grains had barely begun.

You'd have to say that that turnaround has not yet reached seismic proportions. Americans still don't seek out the most exotic of whole grains, nor with any regularity do we give them a central position in our meals. But in the latter portion of the eighties some of America's top restaurant chefs starting using whole grains much more widely—the rather exotic quinoa definitely had its 15 minutes of fame—and this highly visible restaurant activity is bound to have the usual trickle-down effect. Groceries such as ours—that are definitely *not* health-food stores—are already carrying a wide range of whole grains.

What are grains? Webster's Dictionary defines a grain as '1) a small, hard seed or seedlike fruit, especially that of any cereal plant . . . 2) cereal seeds in general . . . 3) any plant or plants producing cereal seeds'. That pretty much covers the waterfront . . . and demonstrates that it's difficult to pinpoint the definition of a grain; in common usage as you can see, grain refers to several different things. Furthermore, we often call certain commodities 'grains', even if they fall outside this rather broad Webster's definition (couscous, buckwheat, kasha, for example).

We say: let's not be botanists on this one. We all mean something similar these days when we culinarily discuss grains: those little granules from an array of different plants, often in whole form, that can be cooked to yield delightful mounds of starch, which can be great substitutes for potatoes and beans as a side dish or the basis of creative main dishes.

But there are some further difficulties in attempting to discuss grains as a group. For one thing, grains cook in various ways, for different lengths of time. Some are best cooked in lots of water, while some are best cooked in a minimum amount of water; some may take as little as 20 minutes to cook, while others may need an hour and a half. Some grains are very strong in flavour, while some are not assertive. Some grains taste decidedly nutty, some taste decidedly earthy. And some grains, when cooked, have a delightfully chewy texture—while some are properly cooked only if they're soft and yielding.

There are several things you can usually count on, however. Whole grains need a good rinsing before you cook them. Then, if you dry them out in a frying pan over moderate heat, you can be sure of enhancing their nutty, toasty characteristics. Finally, think of these whole grains as you think of rice: cook them in water and, if you wish to prevent blandness, salt the water (this is where grains deviate from beans, for bean cooking water should never be salted.)

Here are some of the grains most in favour with restaurant chefs and home cooks today.

BARLEY

Barley is a very old grain—and one that has been in American restaurants for some time, in the form of mushroom-and-barley soup! Outside of that use, however Americans have rarely cooked with it. Today, chefs are making up for lost time. If you want to join them, you'll find that barley comes in several different forms: unhulled (this is chewy stuff), hulled, pearled (polished), black barley and hull-less white barley. The pearled form is the most common, but hulled barley is the best compromise between taste and chewability, we find.

SPRINGTIME BARLEY SALAD WITH MORELS ASPARAGUS AND FRESH MINT

This salad really shows off the pleasing texture and subtle flavour of barley. As currently constituted, it's a celebration of spring—but other green vegetables can be substituted for the asparagus and other wild mushrooms for the morels, in other seasons. Whenever you make it, you'll find it simultaneously hearty and fresh-tasting. It's also fresh and delicious the next day, right out of the refrigerator.

SERVES 6 AS A SIDE DISH

225 g (8 oz) hulled barley
175 g (6 oz) (trimmed weight) pencil-thin
   asparagus, cut diagonally into 1-inch lengths
175 g (3 oz) plus 3 tablespoons extra-virgin olive oil
2 shallots, chopped
85 g (3 oz) fresh morel mushrooms, stems
   discarded and the morels sliced thin crosswise
   (about 115 g (4 oz)) or 25 g (1 oz) dried morels
   soaked for 30 minutes in hot water and sliced
2 fresh lemons, juiced
15 g (1 tbsp) chopped fresh flat-leaf parsley
salt and pepper to taste
15 g (1 tbsp) chopped fresh mint

1. Cook the barley in a large pot of boiling salted water for 30 minutes or until tender. Add the asparagus and cook for 4 minutes or until bright green and crisp-tender. Drain the barley and asparagus completely in a colander and transfer to a bowl.

2. While the barley is cooking, heat 45ml (3 tbsp) of the olive oil in a small frying pan over moderate heat until hot but not smoking. Cook the shallots, stirring, until softened about 2 minutes. Add the sliced morels and cook, stirring, until the mushrooms have given off their liquid and it has evaporated and the mushrooms are softened about 3 minutes. Stir in 15 ml (1 tbsp) the lemon juice and the parsley. Remove the frying pan from the heat and season mixture to taste with salt and pepper.

3. Let the barley and the mushroom mixture cool to room temperature. When ready to serve, whisk together the rest of the olive oil with the remaining lemon juice (from about 1½ lemons). Stir the dressing into the barley with the morel mixture and mint. Season to taste and serve immediately.

COUSCOUS

We place couscous in the grain section, because most people think of it as a whole grain. But couscous is not a whole grain; it is, in fact a type of pasta (which has been made, of course, from grains). Couscous is made by combining some kind of starch with water and then breaking the dough up into granules. The result resembles the kind of tiny pasta that the Italians would use for soup. And the pasta connection is strengthened still further by the fact that modern North Africans almost always make the couscous granules out of semolina flour.

There's a little further confusion about couscous. The name also refers to a cooked dish, served across North Africa, which contains the couscous granules. It is the classic Islamic Sabbath luncheon dish and also the celebration dish for weddings and feast days. Typically, some kind of meat and/or vegetable stew bubbles away in the bottom tier of a special two-tier pot called a *couscoussière*. Over the stew, in the top tier, the couscous granules are steamed by the fumes of the stew; it is said that the word *couscous* actually refers to the sound made while the whole contraption is cooking. Then the steamed, fluffy couscous grains are placed on plates and topped with the stew ingredients. A sauce is made by mixing the stew's stock with a hot pepper sauce called *harissa*. Couscous is often eaten with the thumb and first two fingers of the right hand; you grab a bit of the couscous and compress it into a ball, pass it through the stew and pop into your mouth.

In Morocco, when couscous is served at a feast, it is always the last dish presented before dessert.

One shopping note: virtually all couscous sold in this country is labelled quick-cooking couscous; the box will inform you that it takes only 5 minutes to steam it. This is true—however, the granules will not expand to their maximum capacity after only 5 minutes. Your quantity yield will be low... and, even worse, the granules will continue to expand in your stomach! This is why some people feel bloated after eating couscous. By all means buy the box labelled quick-cooking couscous, but steam it for at least 30 minutes. You get more of it, it tastes better and there's no tummy trouble.

The hottest new couscous
A different kind of couscous has hit our shores and become a trendy restaurant dish in recent years. Variously called *moughrabia, maftoul, Israeli toasted pasta or couscousou,* it is simply larger grains of couscous, usually made from semolina flour. It is much heartier than the regular tiny couscous and is often cooked in a highly seasoned stock. This larger type of couscous is popular in Israel and Lebanon.

COUSCOUS WITH LAMB, CHICKEN, MERGUEZ, HEARTY VEGETABLES AND HARISSA
There are many versions of couscous across North Africa. British and Americans are probably most familiar with the Algerian/Tunisian style, because this is the type of couscous dish served at the couscous restaurants of Paris. It is spicy-hot and often contains spicy merguez sausage. The most refined couscous dishes of all, however are made in Morocco, where there are many regional variations. The following recipe, in party-size proportions, is an amalgam—but, for all its mongrel nature, it's the deepest-tasting, most delicious couscous we know. The spiciness suggests Algeria, while the sweet raisins suggest the Moroccan city of Fez. *We* suggest you stop reading and start cooking immediately.

SERVES 8 AS A MAIN COURSE

30 ml (2 tbsp) olive oil

450 g (1 lb) fresh merguez sausage, pricked with a
   fork (you can substitute hot Italian sausage)

900 g (2 lb) lamb neck (with bones), cut into 5-cm
   (2-in) pieces

10 chicken legs

2 large red onions, coarsely chopped

70g (2½ oz) chopped fresh flat-leaf parsley

70g (2½ oz) fresh coriander

2 cinnamon sticks

5 g (1 tsp) ground ginger

2.5 g (½ tsp) saffron threads, crumbled

1½ litres (2¾ pints) chicken or vegetable stock

6 slender carrots, halved lengthways and cut into
   7.5 cm (3-in) lengths

3 small turnips (about 350 g (¾ lb)), peeled and
   cut into 1-cm (½-in)- thick wedges

3 fresh green chillies, seeded and finely chopped

salt and pepper to taste

350 g (¾ lb) pumpkin, peeled, seeded and cut into
   2.5-g (1-in) pieces

900 g (2 lb) couscous

85 g (3 oz) unsalted butter

225 g (8 oz) cooked chick peas, warm

85 g (3 oz) sultanas, soaked in warm water for 15
   minutes and drained

125 ml (4 fl oz) harissa sauce (see page 496)

125 ml (4 fl oz) tomato purée

450 ml (16 fl oz) stock from the stew

1. Over moderate heat, place the olive oil in the bottom of a couscoussière or a casserole over which you can fit a steamer top. Heat oil until hot but not smoking. Add the merguez and cook, turning with tongs, until well browned and cooked through about 15 minutes. Remove the sausage to a plate, cut into 2.5-cm (1-in) lengths and reserve. Add the lamb and the chicken legs to the pot in batches and cook, turning, until well browned, about 10 minutes. Remove the lamb and the chicken legs to the plate with the merguez.

2. Stir in the onions, parsley, coriander, cinnamon sticks, ginger and saffron and cook, stirring and scraping up the browned bits from the bottom of the pan, until the onions are softened and lightly browned about 6 minutes.

3. Return the lamb and the chicken (not the sausage) to the pot add 1.2 litres (2 pints) stock and cook, stirring occasionally, for 1 hour or until the lamb is tender. Stir in the carrots, turnips and chillies and cook, stirring occasionally, for about 30 minutes or until the vegetables are tender. Season to taste with salt and

pepper. Cook the pumpkin separately in boiling salted water until tender, drain and reserve.

4. While the stew is cooking, place the couscous in a large bowl, wash quickly with cool water and drain immediately (use about 1.3 litres (2¼ pints) water for every 450 g (1 lb) couscous). Allow the couscous to sit for 15 minutes; the grains should expand. Work them through your fingers to separate each grain. Place half of the couscous over the stew in the steamer top of the couscoussière. Alternatively, you may place the couscous in a steamer top that you have fitted over the casserole. Or, if you have a regular steamer, you may transfer the stew to the bottom of the steamer and place the couscous in the top part. Cover the top part with the couscous and bring the stew below to a boil. When the steam from the stew begins to pass through the couscous add the remaining grains of couscous to the top. Seal tightly with foil where the couscous pan meets the stew pot. Steam for ½ hour (the grains should be soft but not mushy). When the couscous grains are done, transfer them to a bowl and mix in the remaining 225 ml (8 fl oz) of stock (heated), the butter and salt and pepper to taste.

5. Add the reserved merguez and pumpkin to the stew pot with the chick peas and sultanas. Taste stew for seasoning.

6. In a bowl, mix together the harissa sauce and the tomato paste. Beat in 450 ml (16 fl oz) of hot stock from the stew pot.

7. Arrange the couscous piled high on a large platter. Top with the solid contents of the stew pot arranged decoratively. Drizzle with a little of the harissa tomato-purée-and-stock mixture and serve immediately. Pass the remaining harissa tomato paste stock mixture as a sauce.

FARRO (SPELT GRAINS)

The Italians call this important ancient grain *farro*—but in English it's more likely to be named *spelt* or *emmer*. It is a member of the wheat family, but can be eaten by people who are allergic to wheat (which is one of the reasons it's having such a renaissance today). We know that over 2,000 years ago the Romans cultivated it and made a thick soup of it; over the centuries, its use diminished in most of Italy—though in parts of Puglia it has always been popular and still is. When farro is cooked, the hearty texture most resembles that of barley—though it has a slightly nuttier flavour.

FARRO 'RISOTTO' WITH WILD MUSHROOMS AND PARMIGIANO-REGGIANO

One of the hottest restaurant trends today is making risotto without rice: that is, making dishes that resemble risotto with grains other than rice. We stumbled upon this use for farro when we tested our first sample of it—at the same time we were also testing a sample of dried porcini. There was the plain, cooked farro and there were these plump, pungent soaked mushrooms. What else were we to do? This recipe worked so well with our imported Italian sample because the grains had been scarred in the milling process, leaving a rough surface; that type of surface texture gives a soupy, glutinous consistency to the cooked product, like that of Arborio rice. We've since found that American grown and milled spelt grains have a smoother surface of unscarred bran and as a result cook up separate and distinct from one another, like American long-grain rice. In order to arrive at the desired texture for this recipe, you must use imported farro. It's great as a side dish to braised meat.

SERVES 6 AS A SIDE DISH

450 g (1 lb) spelt grains
1 litre (1¾ pints) water
25 g (1 oz) dried wild mushrooms (preferably porcini)

25 g (1 oz) unsalted butter
30 ml (2 tbsp) olive oil
225 g (8 oz) finely chopped onion
225 ml (8 fl oz) dry white wine
salt and pepper to taste
50 g (2 oz) grated Parmigiano-Reggiano

1. Boil the farro in the water, salted, in a large saucepan, partially covered, for 45 minutes or until it is soft. Drain it in a colander or strainer.

2. While the farro is cooking, soak the dried mushrooms in a bowl with 225 ml (8 fl oz) of hot water for 15 minutes. Remove them from the bowl with your fingers, squeezing the water back into the bowl. Reserve the soaking liquid. Chop the mushrooms coarsely.

3. Melt the butter in the olive oil in a frying pan over low heat. Add the onion and cook until soft. Stir in the mushrooms and then add the wine. Simmer for 10 minutes. Strain the reserved mushroom soaking liquid through a cheesecloth or fine strainer into the frying pan. Simmer for 10 minutes. If the farro is not yet cooked, remove the frying pan from the heat and set aside.

4. When the farro is cooked and drained, put it back into the empty pan and add the contents of the frying pan . Mix well and season to taste with salt and pepper. Top each serving with grated Parmigiano-Reggiano.

KAMUT

Kamut (pronounced kah-moot) is a type of wheat that's been around since ancient Egyptian times; the word *kamut,* in fact, comes from the ancient Egyptian word for wheat. Its kernels are 2 to 3 times the size of ordinary wheat kernels. Available in health-food stores—and now in fancy groceries—kamut has a higher protein value and generally a higher nutritional value than other varieties of wheat but it is hard to find in the UK and can be replaced with spelt. As with spelt, people who are allergic to wheat may find that they don't have the same allergic reactions to kamut. Gastronomically, it's a real winner: it combines a nutty taste with a chewy, dense texture that's extremely satisfying to the tooth.

KAMUT AND FETA SALAD

Kamut is lovely as a warm side dish—but it's especially good in this room-temperature salad, which can be served alone as a first course. It combines the great tastes and textures of kamut with a series of Greek and Middle Eastern flavour explosions that, if you're tasting with imagination, seem to emphasise the ancient nature of this grain. If you wish to serve it as a room-temperature side dish, you might want to pair it with grilled meat or fish that has Greek or Middle Eastern flavours.

SERVES 4 AS A FIRST COURSE

225 g (8 oz) kamut grains
50 g (2 oz) diced feta cheese
115 g (4 oz) thinly sliced red onion
115 g (4 oz) julienne strips of cucumber, seeds removed
50 ml (2 fl oz) extra-virgin olive oil
50 ml (2 oz) julienne strips of roasted red or orange pepper
45 g (3 tbsp) chopped fresh flat-leaf parsley
15 g (1 tbsp) chopped fresh mint leaves plus mint sprigs for garnish
45 ml (3 tbsp) fresh lemon juice or more if desired
15 g (1 tbsp) chopped pitted brine-cured black olives
5 g (1 tsp) ground cumin seed
1 garlic clove, chopped or more to taste
crushed hot red pepper flakes to taste
salt to taste

1. Cook the kamut grains in a large pot of boiling salted water for 1 hour or until they are tender and drain completely.

2. Stir together the warm kamut grains, the feta, onion, cucumber, olive oil, roasted pepper, chopped herbs, lemon juice, olives, cumin, garlic and red pepper flakes in a large bowl. Season to taste with salt. Serve salad at room temperature, garnished with mint sprigs.

KASHA

Kasha is made from the kernels of the buckwheat plant (these kernels are often called groats), which have been hulled, roasted and cracked into coarse, medium or fine pieces. Technically, neither kasha nor buckwheat are grains. Buckwheat is an herbaceous plant from the family of rhubarb and sorrel, not a grain at all . . . although it looks a lot like cereal grains and is nutritionally comparable to grains. Additionally, the look, texture and flavour of kasha—deep tan, chewy, nutty—are extremely grainlike. Buckwheat is an excellent source of complex carbohydrates and it contains all 8 of the amino-acids (which makes it the closest to a perfect protein of any plant source). It is probably from Asia originally and most likely was later introduced to Eastern Europe and the Mediterranean by migrating tribes.

KASHA VARNISHKES

This combination of kasha and noodles came to America by way of the Eastern European shtetl, where it once provided a cheap, nutritionally balanced meal. Today, of course, it's usually served as a side dish to the main course. Originally, fresh, flat noodles were used—but the standard in America is bow-tie noodles out of a box; in fact, it wouldn't seem like kasha varnishkes without the bow-ties. This version is even further from the shtetl, because it contains such upscale ingredients as red onions, shiitake mushrooms and chives. So who's complaining? It still tastes authentic and it is the most delicious version we've ever tasted. If you've never had this wonderful, nutty-tasting ethnic treat, there's no time like the present....

SERVES 8 AS A SIDE DISH

350 g (12 oz) kasha (buckwheat groats)

2 large eggs

90 g (3¼ oz) chicken fat, rendered (you may substitute rapeseed or safflower oil)

2 medium red onions, finely diced

225 g (8 oz) fresh shiitake mushrooms, stems discarded and caps sliced thin

350 ml (12 fl oz) chicken stock

salt and pepper to taste

115 g (4 oz) farfalle (bow-tie pasta)

45 g (3 tbsp) chopped fresh flat-leaf parsley leaves

45 g (3 tbsp) snipped fresh chives

1. Stir the kasha and eggs together with a fork in a small bowl.

2. Heat a large non-stick frying pan over moderate heat and cook the kasha mixture, stirring constantly, until the eggs have dried and the kasha grains are separated, about 5 minutes. Transfer the kasha mixture to a bowl.

3. Heat the fat or the oil in the same frying pan, wiped clean, over moderately high heat. Add the red onions and mushrooms and cook, stirring frequently, until the onions are softened about 4 minutes. Reserve.

4. Bring the stock to a boil in a large saucepan. Stir in the kasha mixture and bring to a boil. Season stock to taste with salt and pepper. Reduce heat to low and simmer, covered, for 15 minutes or until kasha is tender.

5. While kasha is cooking, cook farfalle in a large kettle of boiling salted water for about 8 minutes or until al dente and drain. Stir farfalle and reserved mushroom mixture into cooked kasha add parsley and let stand, uncovered, for 2 minutes. Place on a platter and serve hot sprinkled with chives.

POLENTA

Polenta means 'mush' in Italian and in the twentieth century polenta in Italy almost always means a mush made from dried-and-ground corn (corn kernels are classified as 'grains'). It is a remarkably versatile and delicious mush that is capturing wider attention around the globe.

Polenta, however, didn't always mean *cornmeal* mush. Polenta is an ancient food in Italy, predating the arrival of corn in Europe (polenta actually, predates pasta, rice and bread as a starchy staple). What the Romans called *pulmentum* was not made from corn; it was a mush made from other grains (like spelt and millet) a porridge that probably resembled semolina pudding. After the discovery of corn in the New World, the Italians got the idea to convert dried, ground corn into their beloved mush. The corn practice probably began in Friuli and spread rapidly to the Veneto. For centuries now, Northern Italians have been known as *polentoni a* disparaging Southern Italian name for eaters of corn polenta—a dish that carries the stigma of 'poor people's food'.

It is far from 'poor people's food' in America today; in fact, many an Italian restaurateur has noted the irony of serving to patrons the mush that sustained his poor family 50 years ago—for $17 a bowl in New York or Los Angeles! Polenta became very trendy in the 'Northern' Italian restaurants of the eighties and nineties and as it becomes better understood, it will likely grow even more popular.

Basically, it is great comfort food. In its simplest preparation (the one we like best, by far) polenta is a warm, soft bowl of tender cornmeal porridge, eaten with a spoon, fabulous with little more than cheese and butter. It's great—especially on a winter night—to surprise your guests with this, just when they're expecting a bowl of pasta in your Italian meal sequence. Usually, unfortunately, polenta is not served this way in American restaurants. More commonly, chefs cook the polenta until it's firmer, then spread it out on a board, or in a tray, let it harden, then cut it into shapes (circles and triangles, for example), which get one further cooking (grilling, shallow-frying or grilling). This, too, can be very good.

There's much polenta-making lore and many home chefs are intimidated by it. But making polenta is really a simple matter.

According to the purest Italian tradition, polenta should be cooked in a large copper pot that's shaped like a pail, with a flared rim; it's called a *paiolo*. Actually any wide, heavy-bottomed pot or saucepan will do just fine. Tradition also calls for a long wooden stick for stirring, called a *tarello*—which must be made, they say, from either chestnut or acacia! We say: your regular wooden spoon will get the job done very nicely (we like a spoon on the wide side, though).

Next, which type of cornmeal to choose? You'll find coarse-ground, medium-ground and fine-ground bags of cornmeal. Some chefs prefer the fine-ground, because it produces a creamier bowl of polenta. But we miss in this the attractively rougher texture of coarse-ground meal . . . and also believe that coarse-ground meal produces a cornier flavour. Please note: coarse-ground meal spoils more quickly than fine-ground, so don't plan to store it more than 4 months. You'll also have the choice of yellow or white cornmeal. We have not found much flavour difference, but we lean towards the yellow colour that the yellow meal produces in the finished dish. One type of cornmeal we definitely don't recommend: instant polenta, which cooks in 5 minutes but unfortunately gets the lowest marks for texture and flavour.

Cooking real polenta doesn't take that much time or trouble anyway. It is simply a matter of stirring the cornmeal into hot liquid in such a way that the meal does not produce clumps; then, the polenta is stirred and cooked for a fairly short time. Here are some general guidelines:

- For most polentas, you should use 225 g (8 oz) of cornmeal to 700 ml (1½ pints) of liquid. Depending on the recipe, the liquid may be water, milk or stock. If you want to make an extremely soft and runny polenta, you'll need to use more liquid—say, 600 ml (1 pint).

- Salt is important to polenta, otherwise the mush will be bland. And it's best to add the salt at the beginning of the cooking process. We like 5 g (1 tsp) salt for every 225 g (8 oz) of cornmeal used.

- The blending of the cornmeal and the liquid is all-important. We like the classic method: bring the liquid to a boil, reduce the heat to moderate, then slowly stir in the cornmeal in a fine stream. Classicists insist that stirring in one direction only will prevent lumps. If lumps do start to develop, they can be obliterated if they are crushed against the side of the pot.

- Most classic recipes call for a wooden spoon as the stirring implement, but we like to begin the process with a whisk. After we whisk in all the cornmeal, we then switch to a wooden spoon. It is important to keep stirring the polenta until it's done; this prevents those dreaded clumps.

- Temperature? Remember: boil the liquid first, then reduce the heat to moderate as you add the cornmeal. After you've whisked in the cornmeal, reduce the heat to low.

- Cooking time? The classic prescription for doneness is 'when the polenta pulls away from the side of the pot.' The exact time varies with every pot and with your taste. Polenta can be done in as little as 10 minutes; it will be runnier, but have a grainier texture at that point. If you cook and stir it for 20 to 40 minutes, the graininess will smooth out as the polenta firms up. If you want to cool your polenta and cut it into shapes, you'll need this longer cooking time in the pot.

- Must you stir continuously? Some chefs insist that if the temperature is extremely low, constant vigilance is not required for the prevention of clumps. Try it out on your own stove, with your own pot. Or try the invention of Carlo Middione a San Francisco restaurateur, who came up with the idea of cooking polenta in the top of a double boiler. He uses liquid to cornmeal in a ratio of 4 to 1, cooks the mush for 1½ hours over gently simmering water and gives it a stir only every half hour. Here is a range of polenta recipes.

BASIC SOFT POLENTA

This is the classic, meltingly soft bowl of mush, just waiting for its crown of butter and cheese.

SERVES 8 AS A FIRST COURSE

450 ml (16 fl oz) water
1 litre (1¾ pints) milk
10 g (2 tsp) salt
450 g (1 lb) yellow cornmeal (preferably coarse-ground)
40 g (1½ oz) unsalted butter
75 g (2½ oz) freshly grated Parmesan
freshly ground black pepper to taste

1. Bring the water, milk and salt to a boil in a large saucepan and reduce the heat to moderate so that water comes to a simmer.

2. Pour in the cornmeal by the handful in a thin stream *very slowly*, stirring constantly with a whisk to prevent lumps. Keep the mixture at a bare simmer and stir constantly. Cook the polenta, stirring and crushing any lumps that might form against the side of the pan, for 10 minutes. (As it cooks the polenta will thicken considerably.) The polenta is done when it comes away effortlessly from the side of the pan.

3. Remove the pan from the heat and whisk the butter, Parmesan and black pepper into the polenta. Turn polenta out on a serving platter and serve hot.

SOFT POLENTA WITH GORGONZOLA AND MASCARPONE

This dish features very, very soft polenta, thinner in texture than basic soft polenta—it's almost like a soup!—with the creamy goodness of mascarpone and a subtle whiff of blue cheese blended in. Serve this in wide soup bowls at a winter dinner party instead of pasta after a salad and before a main course; your guests will swoon.

SERVES 4 AS A FIRST COURSE

600 ml (1 pint) water
450 ml (16 fl oz) chicken stock
3 large sprigs of fresh sage
5 g (1 tsp) salt
225 g (8 oz) yellow cornmeal
115 g (4 oz) mascarpone cheese
50 g (2 oz) Gorgonzola dolce
25 g (1 oz) unsalted butter
freshly ground black pepper to taste
10 sage leaves, slivered
Parmigiano-Reggiano for grating

1. Bring the water, chicken stock, sage sprigs and salt to a boil in a large saucepan and boil, covered, for 3 minutes. Discard sage sprigs. Reduce the heat to moderate so that the liquid comes to a simmer.

2. Pour in the cornmeal by the handful in a thin stream *very slowly*, whisking constantly in one direction. When all the cornmeal is added, begin stirring with a long-handled wooden spoon. Keep the mixture at a bare simmer and stir frequently. Cook the polenta, stirring and crushing any lumps that might form against the side of the pan, for 15 to 20 minutes. (As it cooks the polenta will thicken considerably.) The polenta is done when it comes away effortlessly from the side of the pan.

3. Remove the pan from the heat and whisk mascarpone, Gorgonzola and butter into the polenta. Pour polenta into serving bowls and sprinkle with pepper and sage. Pass Parmigiano-Reggiano at the table for grating.

POLENTA TARAGNA ALLA VALTELLINESE

Dean & DeLuca and other specialty food shops carry a product called *polenta taragna,* which is loosely translated on the package as Indian cornmeal with buckwheat flour. Italians have been making polenta out of buckwheat as well as barley and other grains, for centuries and this product mixes cornmeal with the buckwheat because many find that the buckwheat alone is too bitter. Polenta taragna is exactly what you need for this classic dish from Valtellina (a valley in the Alps of Lombardy); it is always prepared with buckwheat, cornmeal, butter and cheese. The Taleggio gives the dish a wonderful, earthy taste. It's a creamy, but not super-soft bowl of polenta, grainlike in flavour, ideal as a side dish with something saucy—like beef braised in Barolo wine.

SERVES 6 AS A SIDE DISH

850 ml (1½ pints) water
2.5 g (½ tsp) salt
225 g (8 oz) polenta taragna
85 g (3 oz) unsalted butter, cut into pieces
115 g (4 oz) Taleggio cheese, sliced
freshly ground black pepper to taste

1. Bring the water and salt to a boil in a large saucepan, then reduce the heat to moderately low so that the water comes to a simmer.

2. Pour in the polenta taragna by the handful in a thin stream *very slowly,* stirring constantly with a long-handled wooden spoon to prevent lumps. Keep the mixture at a bare simmer and stir frequently. (It is not necessary to stir constantly if the polenta is cooked on low heat.) After all the polenta is added, stir in half the butter and cook the polenta, stirring and crushing any lumps that might form against the side of the pan, for 20 to 25 minutes. (As it cooks the polenta will thicken considerably.) The polenta is done when it comes away effortlessly from the side of the pan.

3. Remove the pan from the heat and stir in half the cheese, the rest of the butter and the pepper. Season to taste. Add remaining cheese and stir quickly, leaving some of the cheese unmelted. Transfer the polenta to a serving platter and serve immediately.

Uses for polenta cut-outs

The possibilities are endless. Here are a few things we especially like to do.

Use polenta as you would crostini. Cut the polenta into triangles, grill them, then top them with a chicken-liver spread or a raw tomato-and-garlic salad or slices of prosciutto.

Melt cheese over the cut-outs. Cut the polenta into circles, sauté them in butter, place them on a baking sheet, top with mozzarella then melt under a grill.

Use the cut-outs in place of pasta in lasagna-like dishes. Spread the polenta out a little thinner in the baking tin, then cut into long rectangular strips. Build a lasagna-like casserole, with tomato sauce and cheese, using the polenta strips in place of pasta.

FIRM POLENTA CUT-OUTS

By cooking polenta longer, you will achieve a firmer mass—which can then be spread out, cooled and cut into shapes that have a springy, resilient texture. There is a classic Northern Italian board, called a *tagliere,* on which the polenta is spread. But you can do it on any flat surface or in a baking dish. The key question is: what thickness do you like in the finished product? We're partial to polenta cut-outs that are about 1 cm (½ in) thick, so we spread our just-cooked polenta out into a large, smooth rectangle that's 1 cm (½ in) thick. The polenta shapes may be cut out after a half hour of cooling, but the texture's much better if the slab is refrigerated for 24 hours.

450 ml (16 fl oz) water
1 litre (1¼ pints) milk

10 g (2 tsp) coarse salt
450 g (16 oz) yellow cornmeal (preferably coarse-
    ground)

1. Bring the water, milk and coarse salt to a boil in a large saucepan and reduce the heat to moderate so that the liquid comes to a simmer.

2. Pour in the cornmeal by the handful in a thin stream *very slowly,* stirring constantly with a whisk to prevent lumps. After the cornmeal is whisked in, keep the mixture at a bare simmer and stir constantly with a wooden spoon. Cook the polenta, stirring and crushing any lumps that might form against the side of the pan, for 30 minutes. (As it cooks the polenta will thicken considerably.)

3. Quickly turn the polenta into an oiled 30- x 23-cm (13- x 9-in) pan or on to a baking sheet, depending on the desired thickness. Smooth out the polenta. Refrigerate for 24 hours, if possible. Cut the polenta into slices or pieces of any shape you desire (such as triangles, stars, rectangles, circles or squares). The cut-outs can then be reheated by grilling or baking (brush with olive oil first for any of these methods). Or you may sauté the cut-outs in olive oil or butter.

MOULDED POLENTA

Another great traditional way to treat firm polenta is to make a mould of it and then scoop out the centre. The hole in the centre may be filled with any kind of stew; we're especially partial to a hearty, chunky sausage-and-pepper stew with polenta. The polenta you scoop out may be reserved for another use.

SERVES 4

450 ml (16 fl oz) water
1 litre (1¾ pints) milk
10 g (2 tsp) kosher (coarse) salt

450 g (1 lb) yellow cornmeal (preferably coarse-
    ground)

1. Bring the water, milk and kosher salt to a boil in a large saucepan and reduce the heat to moderate so that the liquid comes to a simmer.

2. Pour in the cornmeal by the handful in a thin, steady stream, whisking constantly to prevent lumps. After the cornmeal is whisked in, keep the mixture at a bare simmer and stir constantly with a wooden spoon. Cook the polenta, stirring and crushing any lumps that might form against the side of the pan, for 30 minutes. (As it cooks, the polenta will thicken considerably.)

3. Quickly turn the polenta into a large oiled mixing bowl with a 2.5-litre (4½-pint) capacity, whose base has a diameter of about 10 cm (4 in). Let the polenta stand for 20 minutes until firm. Flip the polenta out onto a platter and scoop out about 450 g (1 lb) of polenta from the centre, forming a ring (the central hole will be about 10 cm (4 in) in diameter.) Fill the hole with a stew of your choice. Let the stew spill out over the edge.

POSOLE

Just another example of corn's infinite variety as a grain, posole has origins that are shrouded in ancient American prehistory. It may have been the Mayans or the Aztecs who first discovered that if corn kernels are boiled in water that has ashes in it, it will be easier to remove the tough hulls of the kernels. The ashes contributed the chemical lime; today, producers skip the ash routine and simply slake the kernels with lime. These are not tender kernels of sweet corn, mind you; these are big, tough kernels, otherwise inedible. Making posole is a nearly pan-American tradition; in Peru, they call corn treated this way *mote blanco* or *maise gigante.* Alabamans call it *hominy.* Vermonters and Long Islanders call it *samp.* In New Mexico—site of the lime-slaked-corn tradition—it's called *posole.* The product is available in dried form and requires a long soak before cooking; cooked posole is sold in cans, but neither the taste nor the texture is as exciting. To get an idea of this taste, think of the earthy, deserty taste of corn tortillas; they are made from masa —which is made from posole.

POSOLE SALAD WITH AVOCADO, GREEN CHILLI, LEMON AND CORIANDER

Posole is often paired with pork and pork fat in New Mexico's chilli-laden soups and stews. We find that pairing posole with avocado in this delicious salad adds the richness that the pork usually provides. This yellow, green and red salad is easy to make in large quantities so it's ideal for entertaining.

SERVES 8 AS A SIDE DISH

225 g (8 oz) dried posole (or 450 g (1 lb) canned
    hominy, drained)
2 bay leaves
2 ripe avocados
50 g (2 oz) packed fresh coriander leaves, chopped
2 lemons
8 small pickled green chillies, chopped
70 g (2½ oz) red onion, finely chopped
7.5 g (1½ tsp) salt
30 g (2 tbsp) chilli powder
10 g (2 tsp) ground cumin
coriander sprigs for garnish

1. Soak posole for at least 3 hours or overnight. Drain, add fresh water and the bay leaves and boil in a medium saucepan until soft enough to chew comfortably (some people like it at 30 minutes, some prefer it at 2 hours). Drain again. Remove and discard bay leaves. (Alternatively, if you're using canned hominy, begin with step 2.)

2. Halve and stone the avocados. Scoop the pulp out and chop it into 1-cm (½-in) cubes. Place in a large bowl with the coriander . Squeeze the juice of the lemons onto the avocado and coriander. Add the cooked posole (or

drained, canned hominy) and the remaining ingredients to the bowl. Mix the ingredients thoroughly but carefully (try not to mash the avocado). Garnish with the coriander sprigs.

QUINOA

Quinoa is remarkable a standout grain: the soft but crunchy texture of the cooked product is unique, comparable only to the finest-textured caviar. But quinoa (pronounced *keen*-wah, with the accent on the first syllable) has a remarkable story as well. It is a very ancient grain, cultivated over 5,000 years ago by the Incas, who considered it sacred and called it 'the mother grain'. It is a very small seed and comes from an annual herb that's in the same family as our weed called lamb's quarters. It grows where other grains fear to tread: at high altitudes (like the Andes of Peru), in poor soil at frigid temperatures and under very dry conditions. An American 'discovered' it in the seventies and by 1983 was growing several strains of it in Colorado. Today, it is the trendiest of the trendy whole grains, valued as much for its nutritional qualities (it's rich in calcium, protein and phosphorus) as for its phenomenal texture and nutty flavour. Quinoa is available at health food shops in the UK

QUINOA PILAF WITH MUSTARD SEEDS

This recipe applies Madras style to the ancient Andean grain. The pilaf pairs well with meat or fish cooked with Indian or Middle Eastern spices; it might be best to avoid serving it with dishes that feature Mediterranean herbs.

SERVES 6 AS A SIDE DISH

225 g (8 oz) quinoa
30 ml (2 tbsp) vegetable oil
5 g (1 tsp) black mustard seeds
75 g (2¾ oz) chopped onion
75 g (2¾ oz) chopped carrot
5 g (1 tsp) chopped green chilli

2.5 g (½ tsp) ground cumin
30 g (2 tbsp) chopped coriander stems
450 ml (16 fl oz) chicken stock
coriander leaves for garnish

1. Toast the quinoa by warming it in a dry pan over moderate heat for a couple of minutes, shaking the pan to ensure that all the grains make contact with the bottom. (The quinoa should turn just a shade darker.) Remove the quinoa from the pan and set it aside.

2. Warm the vegetable oil over moderately high heat in a heavy bottomed saucepan with a tight-fitting lid. Add the mustard seeds. (As they get hot, they will begin to splutter). Reduce the heat to moderate and add the onion and carrot. Cook until the onion turns golden. Add the green chilli, cumin and coriander stems and cook for another 2 minutes. Add the toasted quinoa and stir well to make sure each grain glistens with a trace of oil.

3. Add the chicken stock. (It will sizzle for a second or two.) Increase the heat to high. When the mixture begins to boil around the edge, stir it well, cover the pan, reduce the heat as low as possible and cook the quinoa for 17 minutes. Remove the pan from the heat. Garnish with the coriander leaves.

TRITICALE
Triticale (pronounced trit-i-kay-lee) is the first truly man-made grain—a hybrid of wheat and rye developed in the sixties. The flavour is a little stronger than wheat and a little milder than rye; it has a great nutty taste. The name comes from the Latin, *triticum* for wheat and *secale* for rye—and the hybrid is exactly that a combination of both grains, but with a much higher protein content and a better balance of essential amino acids than either one. It is a beige-coloured grain with the shape of rice. After boiling in water for an hour or so, triticale cooks into plump separate grains with a marvellous texture: chewy skin and a starchy core. You'll

be tempted to break each one slowly between your teeth. Triticale can be served as is or can be tossed quickly in a pan with additional seasonings.

TRITICALE WITH PEANUTS AND ASIAN SEASONINGS
This recipe makes a delicious and unusual side dish for any saucy stir-fry or any roasted meat served with a sauce.

SERVES 4 AS A SIDE DISH

225 g (8 oz) triticale grains
30 ml (2 tbsp) rapeseed or safflower oil
2 spring onions, sliced very finely on the diagonal
10 g (2 tsp) chopped peeled fresh ginger
2 garlic cloves, chopped
salt to taste
1.25 ml (¼ tsp) sesame oil or more to taste
45 g (3 tbsp) chopped salted roasted peanuts
fresh coriander leaves for garnish

1. Cook the triticale grains in a large pot of boiling salted water for 1 hour or until they are tender.

2. About 5 minutes before the triticale is done, in a large, deep frying pan or a wok heat the oil over moderately high heat until it is hot but not smoking. Stir in the spring onions, ginger and garlic and cook, stirring frequently, for 2 or 3 minutes or until the mixture is very fragrant.

3. Drain the triticale and add it to the spring onion mixture. Season to taste with salt and cook, stirring, for 2 minutes or until heated through. Stir in the sesame oil and 2 tablespoons of the peanuts and transfer to a serving bowl. Sprinkle with the remaining 15 g (1 tbsp) peanuts and the coriander .

WHEAT GRAINS
Wheat grains are one of our favourite whole grains; the

big, round grains fairly pop in the mouth, providing an extremely exciting chew. Wheat grains are simply whole kernels harvested from the wheat plant and hulled.

WHEAT GRAIN SALAD WITH DRIED CRANBERRIES AND FRESH HERBS

Winter or summer, our customers can't get enough of this salad. It's ridiculously good for you, of course, but it's also one of those rare dishes with an impeccable nutritional profile that does not prevent it from being absolutely addictive. We use hard red winter wheat for this salad to obtain a chewy texture and a russet background colour. For the herbs, use whatever is available fresh; we've found that tarragon, chervil, rosemary and chives are a particularly felicitous combination. The salad makes a great accompaniment to grilled fish or chicken.

SERVES 8 AS A SIDE DISH

450 g (1 lb) dried wheat grains
3 litres (5¼ pints) water
115 g (4 oz) dried cranberries
50 g (2 oz) chopped red onion
60 g (2¼ oz) packed, chopped mixed fresh herbs
15 g (1 tbsp) salt
50 ml (2 fl oz) raspberry vinegar
30 ml (2 tbsp) light, fruity olive oil
salt and pepper to taste

1. Boil the wheat grains in the 3 litres (5¼ pints) salted water, for 60 minutes or until they are soft but still chewy. Drain them in a strainer.

2. Add the drained wheat grains to a large mixing bowl with the cranberries, red onion, and chopped herbs. Dissolve the salt in the raspberry vinegar and pour the vinegar over the wheat grains along with the oil. Let the salad sit, covered, for at least 30 minutes and up to 2 hours. (The flavour is enhanced the longer the salad sits.) Season to taste with more salt and pepper. Serve.

FISH &
SHELLFISH

AMERICAN WATERS ARE TEEMING WITH SOME OF THE GREATEST SEAFOOD IN THE WORLD. HOWEVER, FOR MOST OF THIS CENTURY IT WAS NOT EASY FOR CONSUMERS IN MOST PARTS OF THIS COUNTRY TO OBTAIN GREAT FISH; OUR RATHER CLUMSY DISTRIBUTION SYSTEM SAW TO THAT. AS A RESULT, MANY AMERICANS ALIVE TODAY GREW UP WITH DISLIKE FOR, OR AT LEAST INDIFFERENCE TO, FISH ON THE TABLE.

OVER THE LAST TWO DECADES, THINGS SLOWLY BEGAN TO CHANGE.

ONCE AGAIN, THE NEW-FOUND AMERICAN PASSION FOR HEALTHY EATING WAS THE PRIME MOVER. AS FAR BACK AS THE FIFTIES—EVEN BEFORE AMERICANS STARTED TO CONSIDER VEGETABLES, GRAINS AND LEGUMES AS MEAT ALTERNATIVES—FISH WAS BEING PROMOTED AS A WHOLESOME SUBSTITUTE. IT STARTED WITH TALK ABOUT 'BRAIN FOOD'; WITH TIME, THIS METAMORPHOSED INTO THE STANDARD DISCUSSION ABOUT LOWER CHOLESTEROL AND LOWER SATURATED FAT; TODAY, WE HEAR MUCH ABOUT THE ABILITY OF THE FATTY OMEGA-3 FISH OILS TO RAISE HDL, THE 'GOOD' CHOLESTEROL AND LOWER LDL, THE 'BAD' CHOLESTEROL. THE DETAILS CHANGE EVERY FEW SEASONS, BUT THE FUNDAMENTALS REMAIN: AMERICANS HAVE COME TO BELIEVE THAT FISH IS GOOD FOR YOU.

THIS, OF COURSE, HAS LED TO GREATER DEMAND FOR FISH—WHICH, IN TURN, HAS LED TO BETTER FISH DISTRIBUTION. IN VAST STRETCHES OF THE MIDWEST, CONSUMERS ONCE HAD THE CHOICE OF MRS. PAUL'S FISH STICKS OR NOTHING; TODAY, FRESH FISH FROM BOTH COASTS AND THE GULF IS FLOWN INTO THE MIDDLE OF THE COUNTRY WITH REGULARITY. MOREOVER, FISH MARKETERS HAVE DISCOVERED—ALONG WITH FRUIT AND VEGETABLE MARKETERS, CHEESE MARKETERS AND WINE MARKETERS—THAT 'LOCAL' SELLS; MANY AMERICAN CONSUMERS TODAY FANCY THEMSELVES THE FOUNDING PALATES OF NEW 'REGIONAL' CUISINES. THEREFORE, ALL OVER THE COUNTRY RIGHT NOW—FROM THE LAKES AND STREAMS OF THE MIDWEST, TO THE BAYOUS OF LOUISIANA, TO THE INLETS OF PUGET SOUND IN WASHINGTON STATE, TO THE DEEP-SEA OFFSHORE CATCHES OF NEW ENGLAND—LOCAL FISH FINDS ITS WAY MORE QUICKLY, MORE REGULARLY AND WITH MORE PRECISE NAMING AND IDENTIFICATION INTO THE LOCAL FOOD CHAIN. WE RECALL WITH SOMETHING BETWEEN HORROR AND AMUSEMENT THE MOMENT WHEN, 10 YEARS AGO, ON A VISIT TO NANTUCKET—AN ISLAND 48 KM (30 MILES) OFF THE COAST OF MASSACHUSETTS, WITH ITS SURROUNDING WATERS CONSTANTLY BEING PLIED BY COMMERCIAL FISHING VESSELS—WE WERE TOLD AT A LOCAL FISH MARKET THAT NO LOCAL SEAFOOD WAS AVAILABLE. WHATEVER WAS CAUGHT OFF NANTUCKET WENT INTO THE NATIONAL DISTRIBUTION CHAINS, ONLY TO RETURN TO THE ISLAND, PERHAPS A WEEK LATER, IN THE COMPANY OF OTHER OLD FISH

FROM GOD-KNOWS-WHERE. TODAY, FISHMONGERS ON NANTUCKET PROUDLY PROCLAIM 'ISLAND CLAMS,' 'ISLAND SWORDFISH,' 'ISLAND' THIS AND 'ISLAND' THAT.

RESTAURANT CHEFS, OF COURSE, HAVE BEEN IN THE FOREFRONT OF THIS MOVEMENT. THEY'VE EVEN TAKEN IT A STEP FURTHER—BY WORKING WITH AREA FISHERMEN TO GET FISH EVEN FRESHER THAN WHAT'S AVAILABLE TO THE PUBLIC. IN SOME CASES, LOCAL FISHERMEN CALL CHEFS ON THE TELEPHONE— SOMETIMES FROM THEIR INCOMING BOATS—TO MAKE DEALS FOR WHAT THEY'VE JUST CAUGHT. THE ELAPSED TIME BETWEEN FISH ON THE LINE AND FISH ON THE PLATE CAN BE MERE HOURS.

AND THIS HAS HAD FURTHER RAMIFICATIONS. THE PRISTINE, SPANKING FRESH FISH INSPIRES CHEFS TO . . . DO LITTLE WITH IT! WHEN FISH IS THIS GOOD, WHY COVER IT UP WITH HEAVY SEASONINGS AND SAUCES? AMERICANS HAVE LEARNED TO SAVOUR THE SIMPLICITY OF GREAT RAW FISH AT SUSHI BARS. THEY'VE BEEN TREATED TO A NEW GENERATION OF 'IMPORTANT' FRENCH RESTAURANTS, LIKE LE BERNARDIN IN NEW YORK, DEDICATED TO THE FAST, SIMPLE COOKING OF IMMACULATE SEAFOOD. AND THEY'VE FLOCKED TO RESTAURANTS, FIRST IN CALIFORNIA, THEN IN THE REST OF THE COUNTRY, WHERE CHEFS ARE SIMPLY PLACING GREAT FISH OVER CHARCOAL, PARTICULARLY MESQUITE CHARCOAL, AND CREATING THE FAIRLY NEW AMERICAN COOKING CATEGORY OF 'GRILLED FISH'.

IN EACH OF THESE CASES, SIMPLICITY IS THE KEY. A NEW GENERATION OF FAMILY COOKS HAS BEEN INSPIRED TO MIRROR RESTAURANT CHEFS AT HOME. FIRST THEY FIND SUPER-FRESH FISH, IN GREAT CONDITION; THEN THEY COOK IT SIMPLY—VERY OFTEN ON THE SAME BACKYARD BARBECUE THAT ONCE COOKED ALL THOSE HOT DOGS AND HAMBURGERS.

OF COURSE, THINGS ARE NOT PERFECT YET IN WATERWORLD. WE RECALL THE VISIT TO NEW YORK, A FEW YEARS BACK, OF A GREAT SPANISH CHEF FROM THE COSTA BRAVA IN CATALONIA. WHEN HE VIEWED AMERICA'S FRESHEST SEAFOOD, AT 4 O'CLOCK IN THE MORNING, AT THE FULTON FISH MARKET IN LOWER MANHATTAN, HE SAID, 'THIS IS THE KIND OF FISH THAT RESTAURANT CHEFS IN SPAIN WOULD REJECT AS TOO OLD'. HE SHOULD HAVE SEEN THE WAY THINGS WERE 10 YEARS AGO.

ANOTHER PROBLEM IS THAT CLASSIC AMERICAN GASTRONOMIC PENCHANT FOR PRODUCTS UTTERLY TRANSFORMED FROM THEIR NATURAL STATES—WHICH, IN THIS PISCINE CASE, MEANS FISH FILLETS RATHER THAN WHOLE FISH. THE SCALING, SKINNING AND DEBONING PRESENT PROBLEMS AT THE MARKET—BECAUSE IT'S EASIER TO JUDGE THE FRESHNESS OF WHOLE FISH THAN IT IS TO JUDGE THE FRESHNESS OF FILLETS. NOW THAT WE'RE GETTING MUCH FRESHER FISH IN OUR MARKETS, WE'D LIKE TO SEE A GROWTH IN POPULARITY OF WHOLE FISH. AND THERE'D BE AN ANCILLARY BENEFIT, TOO: IN MOST CASES, WHOLE FISH TASTE BETTER THAN ANTISEPTIC FILLETS.

THE BASIC CHOICE: TO FILLET OR NOT TO FILLET?

COOKING WHOLE FISH

Around the world, fish-lovers are daffy for fish served whole. From the poached salmon of northern Europe to the great fennel-grilled loup de mer of the Mediterranean to the steaming platters of whole garoupa from the South China Sea served with fermented black beans, whole fish are one of the grandest gastronomic treats in restaurants and homes virtually everywhere.

Americans, however, have never quite taken to the category. With a few exceptions we've come to accept, we recoil when a once-alive creature is presented to us in its entirety; as a culture, we have historically preferred neat little geometric cuts with no messy evidence of life (such as bones, skin and a head). It is true that, occasionally, in our grandest French restaurants, Americans have ordered whole Dover sole—but the head waiter, historically, has removed the fillets at tableside and returned the messy parts of the fish to the kitchen. In France and other parts of the world, this would usually be viewed as ruining the fun; one of the greatest joys in fish-eating, to most people around the world, is taking the fish apart yourself, discovering secret pockets of sweet meat, actually sucking some of the meat off of the bones in spots inaccessible to knife and fork.

And there's more good gastronomic sense in the practice of cooking and serving whole fish: whole fish taste better. This is so for two reasons. First of all, when the fish cooks on the bone and under the skin, additional natural flavour from the bones and skin cooks into the flesh. Secondly, the outer coating of skin on a whole fish can pick up flavour from the cooking process in a way that the outside of a fillet could not; imagine the difference between a whole flounder, its skin puffed up and crunchy from the grill and a white flounder fillet.

Here's a quartet of recipes demonstrating various ways to cook whole fish.

How to judge if fish is fresh

One reason Americans have been reluctant to cook fish at home, we speculate, is that so much of the fish available at retail markets has been substandard. Happily, fish quality at retail has improved in the last ten years—and is bound to get even better.

So...it's out there. Now, how do you find it? How do you pick out the best and the freshest?

It's not difficult at all, if you use your common sense. Start with a skeptical attitude; assume that most of the fish you're going to see won't come up to your standards. And your standards are these: only fish that seem practically alive, that plausibly came out of the water in the last 48 hours and that certainly have been kept cold will give you the sweetness and delicacy that you seek on your table.

There are a few key things to look for.

For all fish Your nose is your most powerful weapon when you're shopping for fish. Don't be afraid to get in there and sniff your prospects! Fresh fish have very little smell; if anything, you'll find a pleasant, briny whiff of the sea. If fish smell fishy, don't buy them. If they smell ammoniac, certainly don't buy them: this comes from a bacterial presence that clearly indicates the fish are over the hill.

And all fish (except shellfish) should be resilient to the touch. When you poke a fresh fish (whole or in pieces), your finger shouldn't leave a depression in the fish; the poked spot should spring right back. If it doesn't, poke another fish.

Lastly, make sure the fish you buy is cold. Better yet, find a trustworthy fishmonger and get his guarantee that it has been kept cold. Fish stored at too-high temperatures deteriorate much more rapidly than fish kept cold. In the display case, the fish should be sitting on ice—not in the ice or in a pool of water.

For whole fish These are the easiest to judge, because they give you the most clues. Consider these criteria:

Eyes Standard wisdom is to look for clear, not cloudy, eyes. But standard wisdom forgets that the eyes of some fish cloud as they die, or as the fish are pulled up to the surface. Forget limpidity. Just make sure the eyes fill the eye sockets and are not sunken.

Gills Standard wisdom has it right on this one; the freshest fish have the reddest gills. In the seafood markets of Istanbul (a great fish town), the gills are turned out so that prospective buyers can see just how red they are; they look like ruby necklaces round the throats of the fish. Unfortunately, we rarely get to see that bright red colour here. Pink is acceptable; muddy brown means over the hill. Look for wetness, too; dried-out gills are old.

Scales The scales of a fresh fish cling tightly to the skin. Make sure the scales of the fish you intend to buy don't come sliding off with a light brush of your hand.

Feel of the skin Sticky, slimy skin is a sign of age; really fresh fish have a clean, wet feel on the outside.

For fish pieces (steaks and fillets) These are harder to judge for freshness than whole fish are and—often—less likely to be fresh. If you want to buy fish this way, try to find a market that's willing to cut your fillets or steaks to order. Precut fish that sits in the store deteriorates more rapidly than fish on the bone. Once again, use your common sense. Fresh steaks and fillets should look wet and firm; older ones dry out (especially around the edges) and show separations (or cracks) in the flesh. Don't be fooled by fishmongers who spray their old pieces of fish with water to make them look wetter; if you look carefully at the flesh, you can see whether it's plump and firm or starting to fall apart.

For shellfish See individual fish, starting on page 317.

WHOLE SAUTÉED DOVER SOLE

Cooking whole fish in a pan, in butter, is a wonderful way of encouraging a crisp, buttery exterior and a perfectly moist interior. And we think it just doesn't get any better than doing it with whole Dover sole—especially if you have very fresh Dover sole. Happily, we often see them in the United States, today from Holland. Each fish weighs less than 450 g (1 lb)—about 350 g (12 oz) or so after gutting and the removal of the black skin on the upper side—so one Dover sole makes a perfect portion for one diner. This is one fish we wouldn't play around with: the sweet, resilient flesh responds so well to the classic sauté method (in clarified butter), why look for something better? Serve with boiled potatoes, or just a crisp glass of white wine. If you've never had this fish prepared this way and the whole proposition sounds boring to you—would you please just try this once so you can see why a classic is irrefutably a classic?

SERVES 2

2 Dover soles (each about 12 oz (¾ lb) after gutting)
30 ml (2 tbsp) milk
salt and pepper to taste
flour for coating
140 g (5 oz) unsalted butter
chopped fresh parsley for garnish
lemon wedges for garnish

1. To remove the black skin on the top side of each fish, cut off the dorsal fins and anal fins with scissors. Then, with the dark side up and holding the tail in one hand, make a small incision just above the tail with a sharp knife. Cut a small flap of the skin at that point—just enough to grab the skin with your hand. Then pull the skin in the direction of the head, pulling the skin away from the flesh. The dark skin should come off easily. (Alternatively, you could ask your fishmonger to perform this operation.)

2. Sprinkle the fish on both sides with the milk. Season well with salt and pepper. Place a bed of plain flour on a large platter (about 225 g (8 oz) of flour altogether) and place a fish in the flour. Turn several times to coat, shake off excess flour and place the fish on a rack to dry. Repeat with the second fish. Dry both fish for 10 minutes.

3. Place 115 g (4 oz) of the butter in a small saucepan with a spout over moderately low heat. As soon as the butter has melted, skim off and discard the foam on top. Then pour the butter, in one motion, into a small dish, leaving behind the milky solids at the bottom of the pan. (The clear liquid in the small dish is clarified butter.)

4. If you have one frying pan large enough to cook both fish simultaneously, pour all of the clarified butter into it over moderately high heat. If you don't, divide the clarified butter between 2 pans over moderately high heat. As soon as the butter is very hot, add the fish, skin side up. After 1 minute or so, slide a spatula under to make sure the fish is not sticking. After a total of 3 minutes, check the underside; it should be golden brown. If it is, carefully turn the fish onto its other side. Cook another 3 minutes, or until the underside is golden brown. Remove fish and place on 2 large individual plates.

5. Wipe out most of the clarified butter in one pan with a paper towel and remove pan from heat. Quickly toss the rest of the butter into the pan. Within a few seconds, it should be melted and foamy. Immediately pour it over the cooked fish. Top with chopped parsley, place lemon wedges on the side and serve at once.

How to eat a whole fish

Once you master this easily learned craft, you'll love eating whole fish at the table. If you're a righty, place the fish with its head to your right. For most fish, you simply take a knife in your right hand (a 'fish knife' is designed for this purpose, but any table knife will do), make a cut just under the gills and slide the knife along leftwards, underneath the flesh that sits on top of the fish's central bone, cutting it from that bone. You'll end up with a neat, skin-on fillet that you can lift right off the bone and eat. Then, you'll be looking at a whole fish on your plate with a large central bone exposed, covering another fillet that sits under it. Simply lift the bone with your hands; it should come immediately away from that underlying second fillet. Now you've freed 90 percent of the meat. The only complications arise with the other bones in the fish. The parts of the skeleton near the top fin of the fish (the dorsal fin) and the bottom fin (the anal fin) contain smaller, more intricate bones—so getting the flesh around them may take a little work. This is especially complicated with flatfish, like Dover sole; round fish, like bass, have far fewer bones on the bottom side supporting the anal fin. But probing the fish on your plate for its secret compartments of meat is part of the adventure.

BAKED RED SNAPPER IN A SALT CRUST

When you're cooking whole fish in the oven, sealing it inside a tough, impenetrable crust is the best way to retain the delicate fish flavour and keep the fish very moist and juicy. Traditionally in France, the crust is made of salt—which congeals and holds during the baking process and is then shattered and removed before serving. But we've found that adding cornmeal to the salt does an even better job of sealing in the fish— plus the shell is much easier to remove when the fish is done. For all the salt in the coating, the fish emerges not salty at all . . . and it makes a beautiful presentation if you slip it from its crust in full view of your dining partner. Just make sure your companion doesn't eat the salty crust. The sauce that accompanies the fish supplies a wonderful New American emphasis.

SERVES 2

350 g (12 oz) all-purpose flour

225 g (8 oz) cornmeal

280 g (10 oz) coarse salt

15 g (1 tbsp) fresh rosemary leaves

2 large egg whites

175 ml (6 fl oz) water plus additional if necessary

900-g (2-lb) whole red snapper (with head and tail
 intact)

50 ml (2fl oz) olive oil

2 shallots, chopped

125 ml (4 fl oz) dry white wine

2 garlic cloves, chopped

1 medium tomato, peeled, seeded and chopped

15 g (1 tbsp) chopped fresh flat-leaf parsley

salt and pepper to taste

1. Preheat oven to 190°C (375°F).

2. Whisk together the flour, cornmeal, coarse salt and
rosemary in a large bowl. Add the egg whites and 125
ml (4 fl oz) of the water and stir with a wooden spoon
until combined well. Add the rest of the water plus
additional water if necessary to form a stiff dough. Roll
out the dough on a lightly floured surface to a size just
large enough to enclose the fish and transfer the dough
to a baking sheet.

3. Wrap the fish completely in the dough, pressing the
edges together to seal them and bake for 25 minutes.

4. While the fish is baking, heat 45 ml (3 tbsp) of the
olive oil in a small saucepan over moderately low heat,
add the shallots and cook, stirring, for 2 minutes, or
until slightly softened. Add the wine and garlic and boil
the mixture until the liquid is reduced by half. Stir in the
tomato and parsley and simmer for 3 minutes. Remove
the pan from the heat and whisk in the rest of the olive
oil. Season to taste with salt and pepper.

5. Using a sharp knife, make a slit in the crust across
the fish and just below the head. Then, make a long slit
that goes along the centre of the fish from that first cut

straight down to the tail (you will now have a long T-cut
on the upper side of the crust). Peel the crust away from
the fish. Fillet the fish, divide it evenly between 2 plates
and spoon the sauce over and around the fish.

CANTONESE STEAMED FLOUNDER

Steamed whole fish is a Cantonese classic, almost
always served at an important banquet, or to an
important guest, or for a New Year dinner. Steaming is a
very 'pure' way of cooking whole fish; it's the best way to
retain the delicate flavour and texture, without losing
any of the precious juices. It is not necessary to add
flavours to the steaming liquid, since the fish cooks too
quickly to allow the flavours to penetrate the flesh; it's
much better to put any flavourings on, in, or under the
fish sitting on its plate in the steamer. Bamboo
steamers are favoured by the Chinese because they
absorb condensation and prevent the juices of the fish
from becoming diluted. Flatfish, like flounder or fluke,
are delicious cooked this way, though a little tricky to
bone. Black sea bass is a good and widely used
alternative.

SERVES 2

1 x 900-g (2-lb) whole fresh flounder, scaled, gills
 removed and gutted (head left on)

30 g (2 tbsp) very finely shredded peeled fresh
 ginger

30 g (2 tbsp) very finely shredded spring onion plus
 additional for garnish

30 ml (2 tbsp) vegetable oil

30 ml (2 tbsp) thin soy sauce

30 ml (2 tbsp) Chinese rice wine

10 ml (2 tsp) toasted sesame oil

(1½ tsp) distilled white vinegar

salt and pepper to taste

1. Wash and pat dry the fish inside and out. Score the
fish diagonally almost to the bone 3 times on each side
with a sharp knife. Place the fish on a lightly oiled 22-

cm (9-in) plate deep enough to contain the steamed juices. Fill the cavity of the fish with the ginger and 30 g (2 tbsp) of the spring onion.

2. Stir together the vegetable oil, soy sauce, rice wine, sesame oil and vinegar in a small bowl. Add salt and pepper to taste. Drizzle half of the soy mixture inside the fish and the remaining half on top of the fish; rub it into the fish with your hands, especially where the fish is scored. Let the fish stand at room temperature for 30 minutes.

3. Put the plate into a 25-cm (10-in) bamboo steamer and cover with the steamer lid. Fill a wok one-third full of water. Bring the water to a simmer and place the bamboo basket over the water. Steam over moderate heat for about 10 to 12 minutes per 2.5 cm (1 in) (measuring at the thickest part), or until the fish is opaque throughout. Spoon the juices that have accumulated in the plate over the fish just before serving. Serve the fish in the basket sprinkled with the remaining finely shredded spring onions.

THAI CRISPY SEA BASS WITH SPICY TAMARIND SAUCE

Deep-frying whole fish is very popular in all parts of Asia; it creates a lovely, crunchy crust that goes well with strongly flavoured sauces. The practice is particularly widespread in Thailand, where the whirling Thai palette of hot-sweet-sour-salty flavours comes into play.

SERVES 4 AS PART OF A THAI DINNER

25 g (1 oz) dried tamarind pulp
30 ml (2 tbsp) vegetable oil
2 shallots, thinly sliced
4 large garlic cloves, thinly sliced
2 small red chillies, finely sliced
1 small green chilli, finely sliced
125 ml (4 fl oz) chicken stock

15 ml (1 tbsp) Thai fish sauce
15 g (1 tbsp) light brown sugar
pinch of salt
vegetable oil for frying
125 g (4 oz) plain flour
2.5 g (½ tsp) freshly ground black pepper
1 whole sea bass, cleaned and gutted (about 700 g (1½ lb))
1 spring onion (white and green parts), thinly sliced on an angle
30 g (2 tbsp) finely chopped lemongrass
fresh coriander for garnish

1. Put tamarind pulp in ½ cup warm water for 15 minutes. Mash the pulp with a fork occasionally to help break it down. Strain liquid through a fine mesh strainer, pushing down hard on the solids. Reserve liquid.

2. Heat vegetable oil in a medium saucepan over moderately high heat. When hot but not smoking, add shallots and garlic and sauté, stirring once or twice, for 3 to 4 minutes. (They should have a deep caramel colour but not be burnt.) Add 1 of the red chillies and the green chilli and cook, stirring, for 3 minutes.

3. Add reserved tamarind liquid, chicken stock, fish sauce, brown sugar and salt. Stir well and cook, uncovered, for 15 minutes. (The sauce should be thick enough to coat the back of a spoon.) Reserve.

4. Pour vegetable oil into a large, deep skillet or wok. The oil should be about 2 cm (¾ in) deep. Heat to 190°C (375°F).

5. Combine flour and black pepper and spread out on a plate. Rinse fish in cold water and dry well. Make 3 deep slashes on each side of the fish. Dip the sea bass into the flour and coat well on both sides. Let fish sit for 5 minutes.

6. When oil is hot, carefully slide the fish into it. Cook for 5 minutes, until the underside is deep golden brown. Turn the fish over with a spatula and a pair of tongs and fry for another 5 minutes. Remove the fish and drain on paper towels.

7. Put fish on a serving platter and cover with sauce. Garnish with the spring onion, remaining sliced red chilli, lemongrass and coriander.

GUIDE TO WHOLE FISH
These are some of our favourite fish to cook whole. Not all are available outside North America.

Black Sea Bass There's a lot of confusion about this name—*black sea bass, black bass and sea bass* are all used these days to describe the same fish, the one with the iridescent black-webbed skin that Chinese restaurants steam whole and Thai restaurants deep-fry whole. Strictly speaking, the name of this fish—which comes only from American waters—is *black sea bass* (*sea bass* is a European fish). *Black bass* is an acceptable alternate name. Whatever it is called, the white, fairly fatty, fairly firm flesh is delicious—and the fish is a perfectly manageable size for cooking whole.

Dover Sole Very expensive and not easy to find—but this is probably the greatest fish in the world for cooking whole. One fish makes a perfect portion for 1 diner and the texture of the sweet flesh—amazingly springy, resilient, yet tender—is unparalleled in the fish world. Do not be fooled by unscrupulous fishmongers passing off other soles (lemon, witch) as Dover sole. There's even a Pacific flounder that is officially called Dover sole. The real thing comes from Europe (though not just Dover) and has a black spot at the rear of the upper fin. Grill it over or under heat or sauté it in butter.

Flounder From the flatfish family, flounder is sometimes called 'winter flounder'. Chinese-Americans like to marinate this fish briefly in rice wine and salt, dry it thoroughly, then deep-fry it whole (it usually weighs just over a kilogram (under 3 lb)). If you have a wok large enough to accommodate this operation, you'll love the crispy results. Serve with a black bean sauce, if desired. It's also good steamed with Chinese flavourings.

Fluke Fluke is another flatfish, very much like flounder, though usually a little larger. Because it's most available in summer months, it's often called 'summer flounder'. Look for smaller ones (1.3 kg (3 lb) or so) and use in Chinese dishes as you would flounder.

John Dory This great Mediterranean fish—it's known as *St. Pierre* in France—is, happily, also fished in the waters of the western Atlantic. It's a peculiar fish—very flat, with a large head and therefore difficult to fillet. It is, therefore, a natural for cooking whole. The sweet, firm white flesh takes particularly well to grilling.

Pompano There are many reasons to eat pompano whole—not the least of which is that it's easy eating, because the meat is very accessible. Also in its favour is its size; the fish is usually sold weighing 350 g (¾ lb) to 900 g (2 lb), perfect for individual portions. The shiny, silvery skin adds visual appeal and the meaty, slightly oily, sweet flesh is great over or under a grill or shallow-fried in butter. A member of the 'jack' family.

Porgy Porgy's another fish that's ideal for cooking whole; because they're rather small (usually under 450 g (1 lb)) and because they have a tough skin, they're not easy to fillet when raw. Of course, they're not so easy to deal with after cooking whole, either, as they contain many small bones. But this difficulty has kept the price down, making porgy a favourite 'poor' fish. We think the taste—especially when the fish is grilled whole, in the Greek olive-oil-and-lemon style—is easily worth the trouble; 'poor' porgy feeds on 'rich' crustaceans and therefore develops unusually good flavour. By the way, porgies are often caught in the saltwater inlets of the eastern United States coast—but there are many related fish in the Atlantic and Mediterranean also called 'porgy'.

Red Snapper 'Snapper' is another fish family with many relatives; there are hundreds of 'snapper' varieties all over the world. This poses a problem when it comes to red snapper—because this is an expensive fish and there are other snappers that look something like the true red snapper. Unfortunately, they don't taste as sweet and meaty—so make sure you're getting the real thing before you pay the price. When you've got the real thing, with its deep-red but silver-tinged skin, why do anything other than show off that beautiful coat by serving the fish whole? Red snappers usually come to the fishmonger weighing between 900-2.7 kg (2-6 lb); get one as close as you can to 900 g (2 lb) for cooking whole. The firm flesh takes well to grilling and roasting; the flesh will be especially succulent if you bake it in a salt crust.

Rouget To our taste, the only fish that gives Dover sole a run for its money as world's greatest whole-cooked fish is rouget. It's totally different, however. Rouget (*red mullet* in English, *triglia* in Italian) is a small (often 115 g (¼ lb)), narrow, bright-red member of the goatfish family that is prized in the Mediterranean for its firm flesh and almost shellfishlike flavour. A standard restaurant dish in the south of France is whole grilled rouget (usually 4 to 5 to an order). Intriguingly, there's a custom there of not gutting this fish, so it comes to the table with an even more intense taste. In France, rouget de roche—or red mullet caught around the cliffs in the sea—is especially prized.

Salmon If you have a large fish poacher and a large crowd coming to a festive springtime buffet, there's little that's more impressive than a whole salmon, poached in court-bouillon, served cold on a beautiful platter and garnished to the nines. Serve with a flavoured

mayonnaise or sour cream that's been thinned with buttermilk and greened with fresh herbs.

Sardines If you like everything about eating whole fish at the table, you'll love eating whole sardines. For one thing, you get lots of them in a main-course portion (usually 5 or 6), so you get to practice your filleting skills over and over again. The oily flesh is delicious on the barbecue and the silvery skin cooks up to a wonderful, fishy crunch; sardines are so flavourful, little dressing or seasoning is needed. Be warned, though: some describe the flavour as 'strong'. These are fish for fish-lovers only. For a more complicated look at sardines—and one that masks the fishy flavour a bit—see the recipe for grilled sardines with Moroccan preserved lemons and olive oil on page 307.

Smelt One of the world's great small fish, perfect for flouring and throwing in deep oil. Best to use smelt on the smaller side, not more than 7.5 cm (3 in) in length.

Striped Bass Striped bass has always been one of the most prized fish caught in American waters. Unfortunately, overfishing and pollution wreaked havoc on the supply of wild striped bass and today most striped bass on sale are farmed. The good news here is that the farmed ones tend to be on the small side (as little as 900 g (2 lb)) and this makes them perfect for whole-cooking; they are especially popular in Greek and Turkish seafood restaurants, where they are grilled. The bad news is that they're very mild in flavour, lacking the distinctiveness of wild striped bass (they actually have a mixed parentage). If you see a smaller wild striped bass on the market (though, sadly, this is unlikely) grab it and grill it. All striped bass share the same, unique texture—kind of ropy, or stringy, somewhere between firm and tender.

Trout If you have the chance to catch wild trout and cook it immediately in a cast-iron pan in lots of butter over an open fire and savour it under tall pines and an

August moon—you will have one of the finest fish-eating experiences in the world. If you have access only to shop-bought farmed trout and to the overhead fluorescent of your own kitchen, you'll still enjoy this treat—though we guarantee it won't be the same.

Whitebait This is a general name for the kind of tiny fish that are superb when floured, deep-fried and eaten whole; many different kinds of fish come to the market as 'whitebait'. Cook them as quickly as possible after purchasing and serve them as appetisers with champagne.

COOKING FISH FILLETS

Cooking fish fillets makes a good deal of sense when you're strapped for time; though they're intrinsically less interesting than whole fish, there could hardly be a more quickly cooked source of protein. Dot them with butter and place under the grill—you'll have dinner in 4 minutes. Or season them well and slip them into a frying pan—you'll break the 4-minute record. Or arrange them on a steamer tray and place over boiling water—3 minutes is a possibility here. As for saucing and seasoning: because the inherent delicacy of most fish fillets is easy to overwhelm, the key is finding complementary flavours that support the fish, but don't ride roughshod over it.

Which fillets to choose? It is much easier to make distinctions among whole fish than it is to do so among fish that have been filleted. Stripped of their skeletal structures, separated from their heads, tails and fins, deprived of their essential shapes, many fish fillets are alike—in appearance, in preparation requirements, in taste. The main differences you'll find are in texture: some fish fillets are hearty, some are delicate; some fish fillets are oily, some are lean. Know your hearty from your delicate, especially, as you set out to cook fillets.

GUIDE TO FISH FILLETS

Here are some fillets that are common in the market—and a few uncommon ones that we love.

Black Cod Not a cod at all and sometimes called *sable*, black cod has wonderful fatty flesh. Hearty.

Bluefish A distinctive fillet for its blue-grey colour and its strong fish taste, bluefish is oily. Hearty.

Catfish Catfish has white, lean, delicate flesh. It's one of the only fish that's better farmed than wild, because the former have less of the characteristic 'petrol' taste. Superb fillets for deep-frying. Now imported into the UK.

Flounder Many different types of fish go by this name. They are usually lean, fairly delicate fillets, but a little coarser in texture than the more delicate fillets of types of sole. Good for fried fillets.

Halibut Halibut is a fabulous, creamy-textured fish. Serve in thick fillets. Hearty.

Lingcod The name comes from 'greenling'; lingcod is not a member of the cod family. It has sweet, lean flesh with large flakes. Delicate.

Opakapaka This is a pink snapper from Hawaii. It's leaner in summer, fattier in winter. Delicate.

Monkfish Monkfish, also called *lotte*, is very distinctive: it has very firm flesh but is fairly lean and watery. Hearty. Good for roasting.

Orange Roughy This newly popular import from New Zealand has lean and tender fillets. Delicate.

Petrale Sole Petrale sole is a West Coast fish, and one of the best flounders. It's tender and lean, with larger flakes than most flounder or sole. Delicate.

Red Snapper We prefer red snapper as a whole fish, but skin-on fillets are still pretty. They're fairly lean, with large flakes. Delicate. Don't buy red snapper without the skin on; it may well be another fish.

Salmon Very distinctive for its pink-orange flesh, salmon is one fish we often prefer in fillets, as opposed to steaks: the fish seems to flake better when it's cut this way. Fatty and hearty.

Sole There are many different ones in the market (including lemon and witch) and many of them are just flounder. All are mild-flavoured, lean and delicate. Only the true Dover sole is different—much heartier, more resilient in texture.

Skate Skate is very distinctive for its thick, ropy bands of flesh. Sweet and fatty. Hearty. Fabulous in many different preparations.

Spanish Mackerel (Horse Mackerel) A member of the mackerel family worth remembering, because the flesh—though fatty—is less oily and less fishy than the flesh of regular mackerel. Slightly red in colour when raw. Hearty.

Sturgeon Sturgeon is so firm and hearty, it almost seems like chicken or veal. Fatty. Delicious.

Tillapia Tillapia is an important fish worldwide and newly popular in America. Farmed tillapia is cleaner tasting than wild tillapia. Lean, tender, delicate fillets.

Tuna Very distinctive: tuna is so red it looks like beef. Serve in thick fillets, but make sure they're no more than rare in the middle (we think raw's even better). Lean and hearty.

HEARTY FISH FILLETS

The hearty fillets can take rougher treatment than the delicate ones (see Guide to Fish Fillets). They are especially good for grilling and in stews.

MERLUZA A LA VASCA

Hearty fillets are needed for this stew or the fillets may fall apart. In the Basque region of Spain, where this dish originates, hake (merluza) is used; it's a long, grey-skinned fish and the most widely used in Spain, but you may substitute cod or similar. In the Basque region, the dish is often served at table right out of its casserole; in fancier restaurants, a decorative arrangement of the ingredients is made on each plate. We prefer the latter method, because the white fillets, green vegetables, yellow egg yolks and black mussels look so strikingly Spanish together on a white plate.

SERVES 4

900 g (2 lb) hearty fillets, cut into 12 pieces
50 g (2 oz) seasoned flour
30 ml (2 tbsp) olive oil
1 medium onion, chopped
5 large garlic cloves, chopped
225 ml (8 fl oz) dry white wine
225 ml (8 fl oz) clam juice
12 asparagus tips
12 small clams (cockles)
12 small mussels, scrubbed and debearded
115 g (4 oz) frozen peas
3 hard-boiled eggs, cut into 4 round slices each
30 g (2 tbsp) arrowroot
50 g (2 oz) chopped fresh parsley for garnish
lemon slices for garnish

1. Preheat oven to 180 °C (350°F).

2. Dredge fish fillets in seasoned flour. Place olive oil in large frying pan over moderately high heat. Fry for 1 to 2 minutes, just until they start to change colour on the outside. Place fillets in a baking dish large enough to hold them comfortably in a single layer. Add onion and garlic to the frying pan and cook, stirring, over moderately high heat for 2 minutes. Transfer the onion and garlic to the baking dish, distributing them evenly.

3. Add the white wine and clam juice to the frying pan over high heat. Scrape up any brown bits clinging to the pan. Boil for 1 minute, add the asparagus and cook for 2 minutes. Add the asparagus and the liquid to the baking dish.

4. Nestle the clams and mussels in the liquid in the baking dish. Cover and bake for 8 to 10 minutes, or until the shellfish have opened. Remove clams and mussels and reserve, keeping them warm. Place peas and egg slices in baking dish, cover and bake in oven for an additional 2 minutes, or until peas have cooked through.

5. Strain contents of baking dish through a sieve (do this gently, so as not to break up the fish). Place 350 ml (12 fl oz) of the liquid in a saucepan and quickly bring to a boil. Mix the arrowroot in a cup with enough cold water to make a mixture that resembles double cream in texture. Whisk in arrowroot until a medium-thick sauce is formed. Season with salt and pepper.

6. Divide fish fillets, clams, mussels, asparagus, peas and egg slices among 4 dinner plates, arranging decoratively if desired. Coat with sauce. Garnish with parsley and lemon. Serve immediately.

DELICATE FISH FILLETS

With the delicate fillets (see Guide to Fish Fillets), obviously, you worry more about fish falling apart. Grilling, shallow-frying and steaming are all good ways of keeping your delicate fillets together—particularly if you don't overcook them.

STEAMED FISH FILLETS WITH DELICATE VEGETABLES

It's hard to decide what this recipe's highest virtue is: it is made up of healthful ingredients; has a fresh and stunning taste and a fine visual presentation. Perhaps the best thing is that you can have it on the table 30 minutes after you walk in the door.

SERVES 4

15 ml (1 tbsp) olive oil
225 g (8 oz) thinly sliced onion
5 g (1 tsp) chopped garlic
2 medium carrots, shredded with a peeler
1 small courgette (about 225 g (8 oz)), cut into
    julienne strips
1 bay leaf
15 g (1 tsp) dried basil
2.5 g (½ tsp) dried savoury
salt and pepper to taste
125 ml (4 fl oz) water
4 flat fish fillets (about 150 g (5½ oz) each, skin
    on, if possible), washed and dried

1. Heat the olive oil in a large frying pan with a tight-fitting lid over moderate heat. Add the onion, garlic and carrots. Fry for 5 minutes, or until onion and carrots are soft. Add the courgettes, bay leaf, basil and savoury. Stir well and sauté for 5 minutes. Season well with salt and pepper and then add the water. Bring the water to a boil, reduce the heat and cover. Simmer for 5 minutes.

2. Lay the fillets, skin side down, on the vegetables. Season lightly with salt and pepper. Cover the pan and simmer for 3 to 7 minutes, depending on the thickness of the fish. (When just past the translucent stage, the fish is done.)

3. To serve, slide a metal fish-slice under each fillet's bed of vegetables, discard the bay leaf and deposit each portion on its bed on each plate.

THREE FAVOURITE METHODS FOR COOKING FISH

METHOD A: FISH ON THE GRILL

More than any other cooking method, grilling—wildly popular since the emergence of grill restaurants in California in the early eighties—has transformed fish in America. Many Americans grew up with grilling as the major restaurant cooking method for fish, but not many were moved to reproduce that at home (lacking the firepower of overhead restaurant grills). But cooking fish over, rather than under, heat is another matter; every Joe has a backyard barbecue.

Happily, the cooking itself is easy as can be. Here are the few things you need to think about.

GRILLING WHOLE FISH

We love grilling whole fish, because the skin of the fish usually picks up a smoky goodness from the heat. Small whole fish, like sardines, work wonderfully well over a hot fire. Medium whole fish, like black sea bass or red snapper, are great when cooked over medium-hot coals; slash them a few times on each side so that the heat penetrates better. Larger fish may char on the outside before the inside is done; we avoid them. To facilitate the cooking of any whole fish, place it in a hinged grilling basket before placing it on the fire so you can easily flip the fish and remove it. (For selection, see Guide to Whole Fish, page 282.

Whole grilled fish, Greek- and Turkish-style

Restaurants in California started the recent craze for barbecue-grilled fish—but those restaurants rarely cook whole fish; the classic California grill is a thick steak or fillet. When we think whole grilled fish, we think Greek and Turkish—due to a new generation of upscale, in-vogue, Greek and Turkish restaurants across the country that sometimes identify themselves as seafood restaurants. Their cooking is based on ancient Mediterranean practice: hauling fresh fish out of the sea, seasoning them simply with olive oil and salt and cooking them quickly over wood fires. Perhaps the greatest grilled fish we've ever tasted was at a seafood grill restaurant in Istanbul, where we tasted the outstanding local fish lüfer (usually translated, incorrectly, as bluefish). Served with a simple salad, the great European-style bread of Istanbul and an icy glass of raki (an anise-flavoured liqueur), it was grilled fish heaven. In the United States, lots of Greek restaurants specialise in porgy (for a less expensive menu choice) and striped bass (for a more expensive menu choice). You can easily reproduce these restaurant experiences at home by grilling these very fish, anointing them with great Greek olive oil and serving fresh pitta on the side along with a tomato and feta salad with kalamata olives. And don't forget the retsina.

GRILLING FISH FILLETS OR STEAKS

Generally speaking, the easiest fillets or steaks to cook over a grill are thick ones from firm-fleshed fish; this kind helps ensure that the fish will hold together as you move it around on the grill. Salmon, tuna, halibut, sturgeon and swordfish are ideal candidates. Interestingly, however—and counter to all classical advice—if you select thin fillets of firm-fleshed fish and oil them and the grill well and place them over a very hot fire, they will cook beautifully in about 2 minutes *and* will come right off the grill with a metal fish-slice; try this 'paillard' technique with bluefish, salmon, or monkfish.

SHELLFISH ON THE BARBECUE

We are wild about shellfish on the grill; the smokiness of a good wood fire marries better with the strong, sweet flavours of shellfish than it does with any other type of fish.

Hard-shelled Bivalves A super-hot grill, covered, is a

great way to spring open bivalves such as clams, mussels, scallops and oysters. The shellfish only need to be washed before you put them on the hot fire and cover. Check in 2 minutes to see if the shells have swung open; all shells should be open within 6 minutes. (Do not overcook.) Serve with garlic butter and lemon for a simple, sublime treat.

Crustaceans with Shells Crustaceans such as prawns and lobster are fabulous on the grill—but they're even better if you leave some of the shell on during the cooking process. The reason is that the hot fire caramelises the shell, providing an intense shellfish flavour that spreads to the flesh itself. You may be tempted to remove the shells from prawns before grilling or to buy shelled prawns. But don't! Simply butterfly the prawns, shell on, devein them if you wish, spread them open and place them over a hot fire; cook about 2 to 3 minutes per side, turning once. Leaving the shell on comes more naturally for lobster and crab, because you're not likely to pick raw meat out of the shells before grilling. Both of these crustaceans must be raw or they will not grill successfully; get your fishmonger to split them open for you. Lobsters should be grilled, split side up, covered, for about 8 minutes, or until the tomalley and roe (if any) are set; then brush with butter, or olive oil and turn the lobsters over so the cut side faces the fire. They should be done within 2 more minutes. Crabs cut in half should be turned once and will take about 8 minutes to cook. For an unusual treat, try cooking cleaned soft-shell crabs over a hot fire; they'll take just 3 to 4 minutes per side.

Cephalopods This is one of our favourite grill categories, particularly when the squid or octopus are small (they're more tender this way). If your squid are medium-sized, after cleaning them you may cut open the body sac, splay it and thread it on skewers; this prevents it from curling up as you cook it. Cook the tentacles separately. If the squid are tiny—our favourite—just cook them whole. Ditto for one of the

sea's finest treats: tiny octopuses, no bigger than a Ping-Pong ball (about 20 to the pound), are best when cooked whole on the grill for just a few minutes. Both grilled squid and grilled octopus are particularly delicious with Thai dipping sauces (see page 500).

Delicious marinated and grilled prawns

GRILLED PRAWNS WITH TURKISH SPICES
SERVES 4 AS AN APPETISER

450 g (1 lb) (16 to 20) large prawns
2.5 g (½ tsp) ground cumin
pinch of cayenne pepper
salt to taste
¼ lemon
4 large garlic cloves, finely chopped
olive oil for drizzling over the prawns
30 g (2 tbsp) chopped fresh parsley
30 g (2 tbsp) chopped fresh dill

1. Remove the legs from the underside of each prawn. Cut through the shell on the back, butterflying each prawn and removing the black vein. Leave the shell intact. Spread the prawns out, cut side up, on a platter. Sprinkle with the cumin, cayenne pepper and salt. Squeeze the lemon juice over the prawns, then scatter the garlic evenly over the prawns. Marinate in the refrigerator for 3 to 4 hours.

2. When ready to cook, heat a barbecue grill. Drizzle a little olive oil on both sides of each prawn. When the grill is medium-hot, place the prawns on it. Cook about 3 minutes on each side, or until the prawns are just past translucent. Remove prawns from grill, place on platter and sprinkle with the parsley and dill. Serve immediately.

MARINADES AND COATINGS FOR GRILLED FISH

If you wish to preserve the delicate flavour of fish—which is already being assaulted by a smoky fire—there's no need to marinate. However, the subtle tang of soy sauce marinades works nicely with fish, because not much distraction is added and lemon-olive oil-garlic combinations also seem very natural. Marinades work best on pieces of fish, such as steaks, fillets and chunks for shish kebab; large whole fish don't absorb the flavours as well. All fish, whole and in pieces, will need some kind of oil brush before grilling to prevent them from sticking to the bars of the grill.

Shellfish don't need to be marinated before grilling either—but their strong flavours stand up better to marinades, if you're marinade-minded, than do the mild flavours of regular fish. Asian flavours are especially exciting with grilled shellfish, we find, but Mediterranean flavours and Mexican-South-west-Caribbean flavours also seem to combine well. For prawns and cephalopods, make sure to brush lightly with oil before grilling; this will prevent the fish from sticking to the grill. For lobster, make sure to brush the cut and exposed meat with oil while cooking to prevent it from drying out.

HEAT AND FUEL FOR GRILLED FISH

Fish cooks quickly, which means that a hot fire will not harm the fish (a hot fire for food that take a long time to cook, like chicken legs, will char the outside before the inside is cooked). We like to use hardwood lump charcoal which burns at a high temperature. If you're using briquettes or a gas grill, you can get a smoky flavour by soaking wood chips in water for a few minutes then adding them to the fire just before cooking.

DEGREE OF DONENESS

There are no hard-and-fast rules concerning degree of doneness for grilled fish. To our taste, the answer depends on the fish. Tuna, for example, is dreadful if cooked past raw (or, at the most, rare) in the centre. Moving up the doneness scale, salmon works best, we feel, when it's still 'medium-rare' in the centre, still slightly translucent; swordfish can be a shade more done. A thick slab of halibut, to our taste, is best when ever-so-slightly underdone in the centre. Most white fish, however—anything from thin paillards of bluefish to thick slabs of monkfish to whole striped bass—tastes best when fully cooked through. Ditto for shellfish; it's just not attractive when uncooked in the centre. But for white fish and shellfish both, it's of great importance to remove the fish from the fire *as soon as it's cooked through*—lest it dry out on the grill.

The classic prescription for fish degree of doneness is 10 minutes of cooking time per 2.5 cm (1 in) of fish; we find that 8 minutes usually works better. There's one other doneness criterion for fish on the grill: outer charring. For pieces of fish, we like golden brown grill marks on the outside; for whole fish, we like browned, puffy, crunchy skin on the outside; for shellfish, golden brown is perfect for prawns, squid, octopus and the cut side of lobster.

SAUCES AND CONDIMENTS FOR GRILLED FISH

Coarse salt is about as far as fish purists go in saucing their grilled fish; on a particularly creative day, they might consider freshly ground black pepper, a squeeze of lemon juice, or even—gasp!—olive oil. We are somewhat sympathetic to this position, actually; when the fish is fabulous, why mask it? But in the California grill restaurants that fuelled the Grilled Fish Ascendancy—like the Hayes Street Grill in San Francisco—a plethora of sauces was always available on the side for your grilled fish. And they tasted damned good, too. So you might want to consider serving your family or guests a little side dish of sauce so they can play—anything from French butter sauces to Mediterranean olive oil sauces to Latino salsas to Thai dipping sauces. See Chapter Nine for further ideas.

METHOD B: FISH IN HOT WATER

We'd guess it was the whole steamed fish at Chinese restaurants that turned Americans on to the great practice of cooking fish in, or with, water; that Cantonese steamed flounder, or whichever fish, under its light mantle of soy sauce, sesame oil, spring onions and ginger, was always perfectly cooked, perfect in texture, perfectly appropriate in the wet medium from whence it originally came. But it's not only the Asians who realised the after-life affinity of fish for water; the French, after all, have been 'poaching' whole fish, like salmon, in flavoured broths for centuries.

For home chefs just beginning to experiment with these techniques, there are several big advantages.

The first one is practical: water-cooking fish (steaming or poaching) is extremely easy and, apart from a steamer, requires no special equipment. The second advantage is nutritional: it's the cleanest form of fish cookery available, with absolutely no fat needed to keep the fish moist. Even more important, to us, are the taste benefits.

Classic texts tell you that water cookery is recommended for lean fish, because it adds juiciness to them. And it is true that water-cooking adds juiciness to any fish, keeps it moist. But we also find that it works beautifully for fatty fish because the hot water dissolves some of the fat in the fish, making them taste cleaner and lighter. Moreover, when the flavour of the fish itself is really prized, there's no technique that interferes less with the flavour of the fish than water-cooking. In Norway, for example, a great salmon nation, you'll never find a traditional salmon dinner that doesn't feature salmon cooked in a pot of water—and they usually don't even add seasonings to the poaching water!

Here are the two main methods of fish-and-water cookery:

STEAMING

The principle couldn't be simpler: you place fish over boiling water and the hot steam rises to cook the fish.

But there are a few nuances.

First of all, there's the steamer. We like a big one—it gives us more room when we're steaming and, sometimes, we can cook different fish simultaneously. The Chinese make very large steamers from inexpensive aluminium that work very well; the bottom section is a large pot that holds water, the top sections are perforated containers for the fish that allow the steam to rise and circulate. The Chinese also like to use bamboo steamers—large containers with slots—which are traditionally wedged into large woks that contain boiling water. Both the metal and the bamboo steamers can be arranged so that multiple containers sit on top of each other, with one cover over all; this way, you can cook multiple fish at the same time. You can, of course, always rig your own steamer: just place a tall metal can in a shallow pot of boiling water (make sure the can rises above the water) and balance a wide plate on top of the can. Place the fish on the plate, cover the pot—and you've got a steamer!

Next question: steaming the fish right on the slotted trivet or rack, or steaming the fish on a plate? You can place your fish right on the rack, if you wish, but the lovely juices that seep out of the fish will drain right down to the boiling water and be lost. Steaming the fish on a plate retains the juices. Furthermore, on a plate you can retain any liquids that you choose to steam with the fish—such as soy sauce, Thai fish sauce and olive oil.

The plate, however, raises a few questions. First of all, it has to be large enough to hold your fish—but small enough to allow enough room around the perimeter of the plate for the steam to rise over the fish (this is why large steamers are good). Then there's the question of removing the plate; when the fish is cooked, it's difficult to withdraw the hot plate from the steamer. To the rescue, however, are the Chinese: they've invented a fabulous three-pronged, retractable device (very inexpensive) that allows you to grip the plate with the three hooks and evenly lift it out of the steamer. No serious fish chef should be without one; it's available at grocers in Chinatown.

What's best for steaming: whole fish or pieces of fish? They're both good, but we are partial to whole fish cooked in this way. When the fish is allowed to stay together, everything in the fish (bones, head, skin) flavours the flesh.

Should you steam fish plain or seasoned? Very bland fish—such as pollock—that's not spanking fresh and is cut into fillets, will emerge from the steamer tasting bland. This kind of steamed fish should definitely be seasoned. But with whole, flavourful, very fresh fish, seasoning is optional.

If you're seasoning the fish—and whether you're using whole fish or fish pieces—be creative; combine a range of dry seasonings, chunky seasonings and liquids to flavour the fish. Here are a few ethnic possibilities:

Mexican Steamed Fish Scatter fresh chilli slices and coriander over the fish; season with good chilli powder (like ancho chilli powder); and drizzle fish when cooked with lime juice.

Thai Steamed Fish Scatter fresh chilli slices, thin lemongrass slices and shredded kaffir lime leaves over the fish; and drizzle fish when cooked with lime juice and Thai fish sauce.

Spanish Steamed Fish Scatter finely chopped garlic and bits of chorizo over the fish; season with Spanish paprika, saffron, salt and pepper; and drizzle when cooked with Spanish olive oil and sherry vinegar.

POACHING

Poaching—or cooking food briefly in gently simmering water—is a classic French fish-cooking method. It is distinguished from 'boiling' by the temperature of the liquid; a poaching liquid never boils, because the violent action of the water might tear the fish apart. Also, out of their concern for maintaining the shape of the fish, the French, classically, have poached whole fish, such as salmon, in long, fish-shaped pans known as 'poachers';

when whole fish come out of the poaching liquid (lifted out on an ingenious panel that's part of the fish poacher), they are beautifully intact.

The problem for the rest of us is in the equipment and assembling the crowd needed to devour a 4.5-kg (10-lb) salmon; most American home chefs, cooking for small families and with nary a classic poacher in the cupboard, tend to stay away from all those whole-fish French poaching classics.

But there's no need to! Poaching yields simply delicious results for fish . . . and you can do it in a regular pot, with regular pieces of fish. The key is using thick, unboned, unskinned fish steaks; the structure of the fish works perfectly to the chef's advantage in keeping the pieces together—as long as the water's not boiling furiously. Choose fish that are firm-fleshed, such as salmon and halibut; soft-textured fish, such as bluefish, don't stand a chance of standing up.

In classic French cooking, the poaching liquid is always flavoured; it's called *court bouillon*. The flavourings vary a bit. Usually, carrots, leeks and onions are in the pot, along with some kind of acidity—which can be provided by white wine, vinegar or lemon juice. One classic court bouillon is made from milk, which is said to keep the fish very white as it cooks. If the poaching liquid is flavoured with fish (usually bones and head), then it's called a fish fumet. Frankly, we've found that neither the traditional court bouillon nor the traditional *fish fumet* adds significant flavour to a piece of poached fish—certainly not enough flavour to make the classic poaching liquids worth the trouble.

But here's a new wrinkle: if you apply other, stronger ethnic elements to the basic French technique, you'll end up with poaching liquids that really do add significant flavour to the fish.

For the following international ideas, create a poaching liquid with a high proportion of flavouring agents. Simmer the liquid for at least 45 minutes before adding the fish. Choose thick steaks (or thick chunks) of firm-textured fish, with skin and bones intact if possible. Cook the fish at a very low temperature and allow about 8 minutes of cooking for every 2.5 cm (1 in) of thickness. When the fish is done, drizzle it, if desired, with an appropriate sauce; your simplest sauce option is to place 450 ml (16 fl oz) of the poaching liquid in a saucepan and reduce it to a thin sauce.

Norwegian poached salmon

The traditional Norwegian method of poaching their incredible wild salmon must be the world's simplest cooking method—but if you do have great salmon, the results are superb.

Fill a large pot with cold water and bring it to a simmer. Salt it lightly. Carefully lower salmon steaks into the water (each steak should be about 4 cm (1½ in) thick). Simmer steaks gently for about 10 minutes, or until just cooked through. Remove and serve with a salad of cucumber slices tossed with sour cream, fresh dill and a little sugar.

Malaysian Poached Fish Make poaching liquid with thin coconut milk, fresh ginger, tamarind juice and good curry powder; and drizzle fish when cooked with reduced poaching liquid.

Greek Poached Fish Make poaching liquid with water, tomatoes, marjoram, garlic and cinnamon sticks. Drizzle fish when cooked with Greek olive oil and fresh herbs or reduced poaching liquid.

Mexican Poached Fish Make poaching liquid with water, flavourful dried chillies (like ancho or chipotle), coriander, garlic and lime juice; and top the fish when cooked with raw salsa or reduced poaching liquid.

Indian Poached Fish Make poaching liquid with water, toasted whole spices (like cumin, coriander, mustard seeds, cloves and cinnamon stick), ginger, onions, garlic, curry leaves and tamarind juice; and drizzle fish when cooked with mustard oil and lemon juice, or reduced poaching liquid.

METHOD C: FISH IN THE FRYER

We love deep-fried fish. We don't care what anyone says. 'Fried' is such a bad word to modern Americans that one of the country's most successful fast-food chains— Kentucky Fried Chicken—decided to call itself KFC instead. Why? So that potential customers won't be turned off by that unspeakable *F* word. Of course, they continue to sell tons and tons of fried chicken. And that's the situation in a nutshell: Americans hate the idea of frying—but boy do they love fried food itself! And why not? Encasing any food—like fish!—in a crisp shell preserves the taste of the food inside and keeps it unbeatably moist. The mild taste and crunchy texture are further reasons to love fried fish.

And here's the topper: recent scientific tests have shown that when food is properly fried (at a heat between 160°C and 190°C (325°F and 375°F)), only a tiny amount of the cooking oil is absorbed by the food.

So don't worry. Be happy. Enjoy without guilt a tried-and-true method of cooking fish that had universal appeal before the Fat Police appeared and will have universal appeal after they go away.

Here are our five favourite ways of coating fish for deep-frying.

1. FLOUR COATING

The easiest coating of all for fried seafood is simply flour. It works particularly well with very small fish— because a coating that's any heavier would overwhelm the little critters. The simple flour coating doesn't work as well, however, on thicker or larger fish; then, it seems too delicate.

DEEP-FRIED WHITEBAIT WITH CRUNCHY PARSLEY

This is a great dish for the start of a dinner party. As soon as the tiny fish are crisp, you place them on a platter that is lined with a white napkin—and then pass the platter, enabling your guests to pick up fish as you go by. Each tiny fish, of course, is eaten whole.

SERVES 12 AS AN APPETISER

225 g (8 oz) plain flour
7.5 g (1½ tsp) salt
5 g (1 tsp) freshly ground black pepper
450 g (1 lb) whitebait (tiny fish)
1 litre (1¾ pints) vegetable oil
1 bunch fresh curly parsley, stems removed and the leaves washed and dried
lemon slices for garnish

1. Place the flour in a large paper bag. Add the salt and pepper and shake well.

2. Dry the fish and add them to the bag. Shake until the fish are well coated with flour. Pour them into a sieve set over a bowl and shake, reserving the excess flour. Spread the whitebait out on a baking sheet and let them rest for 15 minutes.

3. Place the reserved flour back in the paper bag. Add the whitebait to it once again, shake and place them in a sieve. Toss to remove excess flour.

4. Heat oil in a deep-fryer, large wok, or Dutch oven to 190°C (375°F). Working in small batches, add whitebait to the hot oil. Cook 1 to 2 minutes, or just until the whitebait are golden brown. Drain on paper towels. Add the parsley leaves in batches and fry for 10 seconds or so, or until the parsley is crisp. Drain parsley on paper towels. Toss parsley with fish, place on platter, garnish with lemon and serve.

2. REGULAR CRUMB COATING

This is the simple coating most often seen among home cooks in America—you wet the fish with egg, to make the coating stick, then you coat the fish with some kind of crumb. The results are wonderful: a thin, crisp, fragile

coating surrounds juicy fish. It is a coating particularly recommended for delicate fish; because it's so thin and light, it doesn't mask the delicacy of the fish. Breadcrumbs are the ones most often used (the fresher and finer the better)—but we think that cracker meal makes an even finer coating. Cornmeal is a very popular coating, especially in the South, after an egg bath—but we usually find the cornmeal coatings to be unappealingly stiff and dry. Matzo meal works in the same way. Here are two variations of the 'regular crumb coat'.

Techniques for perfect crumb coatings

Lots of little things add up to perfect deep-fried fish. Here are the main ones to keep in mind.

You'll be dipping your fish into eggs, and into breadcrumbs or cracker meal—and probably using a fork to do so. It is very important to use one fork for the egg bowl and another fork for the crumb bowl! Otherwise, the moisture from the egg will clump up the crumbs and make the coating heavier.

Similarly, it is important to lift the fish out of the egg bath and hold it over the egg for 30 seconds or so before crumbing it, so that excess egg can drip back into the bowl. Otherwise, the fish will be too wet and will clump up the crumbs.

Keep a vigilant eye on the crumbs. If they start to clump up, remove the clumps. Also keep a vigilant eye on your crumb fork; if it starts to develop clumps on the tines, remove the clumps.

Always place more crumbs on the crumb plate than you need; this helps to prevent the crumbs from clumping up. The quantities given in the recipes here are plenty; keep in mind that you will have leftover crumbs after coating.

Crumb coatings yield the best results if you allow the coated fish to dry in the air for at least 15 minutes. Arrange the fish so that as much air as possible circulates around them (for example, place on a rack without letting the fish pieces touch one another).

FRIED FLOUNDER FILLETS WITH CRACKER MEAL COATING

Any thin, white-fleshed fillets will do for this delicate fry—but flounder has the perfect texture for this coating. The same method can be applied to almost any fish or shellfish you wish to fry, including prawns and oysters. Great with the classic accompaniments: lemon wedges, tartar sauce, coleslaw and chips.

SERVES 4

1 litre (1¾ pints) vegetable oil
2 very large eggs
350 g (12 oz) cracker or matzo meal
5 g (1 tsp) fine salt plus additional to taste
5 g (1 tsp) freshly ground black pepper
900 g (2 lb) flounder fillets, cut into 16 thin pieces

1. Place the vegetable oil in a deep-fryer, wok, or casserole. Heat to 170°C (360°F).

2. Beat the eggs well in a wide, shallow bowl. Toss the cracker meal with the salt and pepper and place on a wide dish. Dip the fillets, 1 at a time, in the egg, then in the cracker meal. Turn each fillet around in the cracker meal until well coated. (The fillets will cook best if you dry them for at least 15 minutes; it is best to do this on a rack, so that the air can circulate.)

3. When ready to cook, lower the coated fillets, in batches, into the hot oil. (It is best to do just a few at a time, so that the heat of the oil doesn't decrease.) Cook 2 to 3 minutes, or until the fillets are golden brown. Remove, drain on paper towels and salt to taste. Serve immediately.

FRIED SCALLOPS WITH CRACKER MEAL COATING

Scallops are a special case when it comes to deep-frying; if not treated properly, they tend to 'bleed' a milky liquid through the coating, spoiling the crispness of the fry. Therefore, a quick salt soak (to remove moisture)

and an extra layer of coating (flour) are recommended. This recipe will work well for any scallop—but the small bay scallops work best, to our taste. And if you can get the incredibly sweet and succulent scallops of Peconic Bay, Long Island, New York or of Nantucket, Massachusetts, your scallop fry will be truly memorable.

SERVES 4

450 g (1 lb) scallops (preferably Peconic Bay or Nantucket bay scallops)
8 g (1¾ tsp) salt plus additional to taste
1 litre (1¾ pints) vegetable oil
50 g (2 oz) all-purpose flour
3 ml (¾ tsp) freshly ground black pepper
2 very large eggs
225 g (8 oz) cracker or matzo meal

1. Toss the scallops with 2.5 g (½ tsp) of the salt and place in a colander to drain. Let sit at room temperature for 30 minutes.

2. When ready to fry, heat the vegetable oil in a deep-fryer, wok, or casserole to 170°C (340°F).

3. Mix the flour well with 1.25 g (¼ tsp) of the salt and 1.25 g (¼ tsp) of the pepper. Place seasoned flour on a wide dish. Beat the eggs well in a wide, shallow bowl. Toss the cracker meal with the rest of the salt and the rest of the pepper. Place on a wide dish. Dust the scallops, a few at a time, in the flour. Dip the scallops, a few at a time, in the eggs, then in the cracker meal. Turn each scallop around in the cracker meal until well coated. (The scallops will cook best if you dry them for at least 15 minutes; it is best to do this on a fine-meshed grid, so that the air can circulate. If you're drying them on a plate, turn them over after a few minutes.)

4. When ready to cook, lower the coated scallops, in batches, into the hot oil. (It is best to do just a few at a time—7 or 8 small scallops—so that the heat of the oil doesn't decrease.) Cook 2 to 3 minutes, or until the scallops are golden brown. Remove, drain on paper towels and sprinkle with the additional salt. Serve immediately.

3. PANKO CRUMB COATING

Our favourite crumb coating of all is a special one from Japan, available at Japanese groceries. Panko crumbs are light, crispy, air-shot crumbs that yield an amazing texture on fried fish—crunchy, light and kind of frilly all at the same time. If you've had tonkatsu (deep-fried pork fillets) in a Japanese restaurant, you're familiar with the feel. You can use Panko crumbs on a wide range of seafood items, but you'll find they work best with fish that have at least a little heft (prawns and soft-shell crabs are especially good).

FRIED SALMON FILLET WITH MUSTARD AND PANKO CRUMBS

Try this unusual deep-fry with Panko crumbs. Salmon is often eschewed for deep-frys because it's an oily fish. But slicing it thinly and coating it with dry-and-light Panko crumbs, makes all the difference. Lovely as an appetiser, especially when served atop a lightly dressed tangle of frilly greens.

SERVES 8 AS AN APPETISER

1 litre (1¾ pints) vegetable oil
450 g (1 lb) salmon fillet (not salmon steak)
salt and pepper to taste
50 ml (2 fl oz) Dijon mustard
2 eggs
225 g (8 oz) Panko crumbs

1. Place oil in deep-fryer, wok, or casserole and heat to 167°C (365°F).

2. Using a long, sharp knife and cutting practically parallel with your kitchen counter, shave off about 16

thin slices of salmon, each one about 5 mm (¼ in) thick and 5 x 7.5 cm (2 x 3 in).

3. Season the salmon slices well with salt and pepper. Smear 1.25 ml (¼ tsp) of Dijon mustard on each side of each salmon slice.

4. Beat the eggs well in a wide, shallow bowl. Place the Panko crumbs on a wide dish. Slip the salmon slices, 1 at a time, in the eggs, then embed the slices, 1 at a time, in the crumbs, pressing lightly all around to make the crumbs adhere. Let dry for at least 15 minutes.

5. When ready to cook, place the salmon slices, a few at a time, in the oil. Fry for 1 to 2 minutes, or until the exterior is golden brown and the salmon is just cooked. Drain on paper towels and serve immediately.

Cajun popcorn: a special New Orleans deep-fry
Though we're not keen on cornmeal coatings, cornmeal is necessary for this now-classic dish to have authentic flavour. Paul Prudhomme, Cajun culinary god, made the dish famous: deep-fried crawfish (crayfish) tails in a spicy batter, so-named because they're eaten by the handful, just like popcorn. Because crawfish tails are not widely available, this dish is more likely to be made with prawns (popcorn shrimp, it's usually called). We prefer the original critters, but have made a few changes in the classic recipe. For starters, we like to season both the crawfish and the coating. Then, Prudhomme's original called for an egg batter made with cornmeal, yielding something like a fritter—but we feel that a flour coating with a little cornmeal, no eggs please, makes a lighter, crunchier 'popcorn'.

CAJUN POPCORN

SERVES 8 AS AN APPETISER

For the crawfish seasoning mixture

10 g (2 tsp) salt

10 g (2 tsp) sweet paprika

10 g (2 tsp) garlic powder

5 g (1 tsp) onion powder

5 g (1 tsp) sugar

5 g (1 tsp) freshly ground black pepper

5 g (1 tsp) cayenne pepper

5 g (1 tsp) dried thyme

5 g (1 tsp) dried oregano

900 g (2 lb) partially cooked, shelled crawfish tails
 (see Finding Crawfish on page 42)

1 litre (1¾ pints) vegetable oil

For the coating

450 g (1 lb) plain flour

115 g (4 oz) finely ground cornmeal

30 g (2 tbsp) sweet paprika

10 g (2 tsp) dried oregano

10 g (2 tsp) sugar

10 g (2 tsp) garlic powder

5 g (1 tsp) cayenne pepper

1. *Make the crawfish seasoning mixture:* In a bowl blend together all ingredients.

2. Toss the crawfish with the seasoning mixture. Cover and refrigerate for 2 hours.

3. When ready to cook, heat the oil in a pot, deep-fryer, or wok to 190°C (375°F).

4. *While oil is heating, make the coating:* Place the flour, cornmeal, paprika, oregano, sugar, garlic powder and cayenne pepper in a large paper bag and shake well. Dampen the crawfish with about 50 ml (2 fl oz) water. Add the crawfish to the paper bag and shake well.

5. Fry the crawfish in batches (it may take as many as 6 batches.), making sure the oil doesn't dip below 190°C (375°F). Fry each batch for 1 to 2 minutes, or until the crawfish are golden brown and crunchy. Remove with a slotted spoon, drain on paper towels and sprinkle with

coarse salt. Serve immediately. with green Tabasco and a bottle of Dixie beer.

---

4. REGULAR BATTER

Batter is a thickish paste, made of flour and some type of liquid (water, milk or beer). Eggs may or may not be included. Fried fish, coated with batter, is very popular all around the world; it is batter, in fact, that coats the fish in the British specialty fish and chips. We must confess, however, we're not great fans of conventional batter; though it seals the fish beautifully and keeps it very moist, batter coating is often too thick for the delicacy of most fish. Sometimes, the fish gets lost in the coating.

That caveat established, we hasten to point out that batters on the light side can be wonderful coatings for fish—particularly fish that are hearty-textured and thickly cut.

Here's a pair of batters that are lighter than the usual. Hold both of them for an hour before using; this helps the flour absorb the liquid and lets the batter stick to the fish better.

LIGHT FISH BATTER

This crunchy batter will remind you of the coating on British fish and chips—though you'll find it lighter and drier than most. Try it on thick fillets of cod (about 1 cm (½ in)) or any firm-fleshed fish that's similarly cut. With thick cuts of fish, it's a good idea to make small cuts about 1 cm (⅓ in) deep on all sides of the fish before battering; this promotes more even cooking.

MAKES ENOUGH BATTER FOR 900 G (2 LB) FISH FILLETS

115 g (4 oz) plain flour

5 g (1 tsp) baking powder

2.5 g (½ tsp) salt

250 ml (9 fl oz) water

Place the flour in a large mixing bowl and blend in the

baking powder and salt. Whisk in the water until the batter is smooth. Let the batter rest, uncovered, for 1 hour.

Note: When ready to cook, dry fish fillets well, salt them, coat lightly with flour and then dip them in the batter. Let excess batter drip off, then fry fillets in 170°C (360°F) vegetable oil until they're golden brown outside, just cooked within. Serve immediately.

BEER-MILK-AND-BUTTER BATTER

This batter—though still on the light side—has more of everything: it's heartier, with more crunch, more flavour and a little more oiliness. It's great for full flavoured shellfish, like prawns or for very lean fish that could use a little lubrication.

MAKES ENOUGH BATTER FOR 900 G (2 LB) FISH OR SHELLFISH

175 g (6 oz) plain flour
2 g (¾ tsp) salt
2.5 g (½ tsp) freshly ground pepper
50 ml (2 fl oz) milk
175 fl (6 fl oz) beer
1 egg
15 g (½ oz) melted butter

1. Place the flour in a large mixing bowl and blend in the salt and pepper.

2. Place the milk in a small bowl and whisk in the beer and the egg, whisking until smooth. Whisk in the melted butter.

3. Whisk the beer mixture into the flour, whisking until smooth. Let rest for 1 hour.

Note: When ready to cook, dry fish or shellfish well, salt, coat lightly with flour and then dip in the batter. Let excess batter drip off, then fry fish in 185°C (360°F)

vegetable oil until golden brown outside, just cooked within. Serve immediately.

5. TEMPURA

Our favourite batter of all is Japanese tempura, which makes extremely light and lacy fried seafood. The key to a good tempura is undermixing the batter; by leaving it lumpy, you don't develop the gluten in the flour. This means a lighter coating. Another trick is using a low-gluten flour, not a strong plain flour. Lastly, mixing the flour with ice-cold water is another way of slowing down the formation of gluten.

TEMPURA BATTER

This batter is best with seafood that is on the thin side; a thick chunk of halibut would not showcase the delicacy of tempura. Thin fillets (like flounder fillets) and small pieces of shellfish (oysters, mussels and prawns that have been shelled and butterflied) work best. Make the batter immediately before using; do not let it rest.

MAKES ENOUGH BATTER FOR 900 G (2 LB) OF SEAFOOD

2 medium eggs
ice water
140g (5 oz) sifted flour

1. Break the eggs into a measuring cup and beat lightly. Pour in enough ice water (leaving the ice behind) to measure 250 ml (9 fl oz) of egg-water mixture; blend the water and egg very lightly, with just a few strokes of a fork.

2. Turn mixture into a mixing bowl and add the entire amount of flour to it. Working with chopsticks, combine liquid and flour very lightly—a few strokes should do it. (You want a lumpy batter—even a batter with some unmixed flour clinging to the side of the mixing bowl.) Use immediately.

Note: When ready to cook, dry fish or shellfish well, coat lightly with flour and then dip in the batter. Let excess batter drip off, then fry fish in 180°C (360°F) vegetable oil until golden brown outside, just cooked within. Serve immediately.

A few deep-frying tips

Never deep-fry at less than 160°C (325°F); the food will soak up oil. Don't deep-fry over 190°C (375°F); the food will burn. If you're looking to cook something small extremely quickly, 195°C (395°F) is absolutely the upper limit.

- Never cook too much at once; this reduces the oil temperature.
- An electric deep-fryer is a good investment; its virtue is that it maintains an even temperature during frying.
- If you don't have an electric fryer, you must get a deep-frying thermometer to clip on to the side of your cooking vessel so you can monitor the heat.
- Deep-frying works well in any heavy pot that enables you to create a wide pool of oil, at least 5 cm (2 in) deep, that doesn't come more than halfway up the sides. Woks work very well. Appropriately shaped cast-iron pots are also good, because they hold heat very well.
- Oil with a high smoking point is good for deep-frying. Vegetable oils, such as rapeseed, sunflower and safflower, work just fine. Peanut oil has a particularly high smoking point. Extra-virgin olive oil is not a good choice, because it has a low smoking point. Once an oil has reached the smoking point—the smoke will be visible—it has been damaged and should be discarded.
- Use wide skimmers (wire mesh are best) to put food into the oil and to remove it from the oil. Always drain fried food on absorbent paper towels immediately after removing it from the oil.

SOME PARTICULARLY DISTINCTIVE FISH AND THEIR RECIPES

FIN FISH

FRESH COD

Poor cod. Though it has played a crucial role in many cultures, at many points in history, it is, today, in America, a tremendously undervalued, underappreciated fish. 'Oh, it's just cod,' some finny snobs might say—as if its abundance in our waters had anything to do with its intrinsic deliciousness. We love the snowy white flesh of fresh cod, which separates into large, moist, creamy flakes. Furthermore, cod is low in fat and available all year round. There are many, many ways to prepare fresh cod. Keep in mind that fresh cod is usually sold either as fillets or steaks—and that the fillets are better for delicate dishes, the steaks for heartier dishes.

CREAM-POACHED COD FILLETS WITH WHITE WINE, MUSHROOMS, ONIONS AND TOMATOES

Cream sauces, like cod, are not the height of fashion . . . but cod and cream taste so delicious together you may want to swim against the stream for one night only. This dish has a wonderful, comforting, *cuisine-bourgeoise* quality; it's like something out of a prewar kitchen in northern France. And the cream sauce is on the light side, cut further by the enlivening acidity of tomatoes and onions. Serve fluffy rice or boiled potatoes on the side.

SERVES 6

15 g (½ oz) unsalted butter
350 g (¾ lb) shiitake mushrooms, stems discarded and the mushrooms sliced thin
1 medium onion, halved, sliced thin
2 medium tomatoes, peeled, seeded and chopped
2 large shallots, sliced thin
50 ml (2 fl oz) dry white wine

30 g (2 tbsp) chopped fresh flat-leaf parsley plus
   additional for garnish
5 g (1 tsp) fresh thyme
250 ml (9 fl oz) crème fraîche
salt and pepper to taste
700 g (1½ lb) fresh cod fillets (about 1 cm (½ in)
   thick), cut into strips 2 cm (1½ in) wide

1. Divide the butter between two 10-inch frying pans.
Place the frying pans over moderately low heat and
divide the mushrooms, onion, tomatoes, shallots, white
wine, 30 g (2 tbsp) of the chopped parsley and thyme
between them. Cook, stirring occasionally, for about 8
minutes, or until the vegetables are softened and the
liquid is almost evaporated.

2. Divide the crème fraîche between the frying pans and
bring to a bare simmer. Season to taste. Stir in the cod,
dividing it between the frying pans and cook very gently,
turning once, for 5 to 8 minutes (when the centres of the
fish are milky white, the cod is done).

3. Transfer the cod to a platter. If you wish the sauce to
be a little thicker, boil it for 1 to 2 minutes, or until it is
reduced to the desired consistency. Pour the sauce over
the fish, garnish with the additional parsley and serve
hot.

ROASTED COD STEAKS WITH GREEN OLIVES AND SHERRY VINEGAR

Cod is a remarkable canvas against which bright
colours may be splashed; in this recipe, the mild, snowy-
white firm flesh is a perfect foil to the strong,
Mediterranean flavours of the sauce. Despite the swirls
of flavour around it, the cod always retains its subtle
character.

SERVES 6

50 ml (2 fl oz) extra-virgin olive oil
1 medium onion, finely chopped
3 shallots, chopped
2 large garlic cloves, chopped
50 ml (2 fl oz) sherry vinegar
2 plum tomatoes, peeled, seeded and finely
   chopped
8 large brine-cured green olives, stoned and
   coarsely chopped
7.5 g (1½ tsp) fresh thyme leaves plus sprigs for
   garnish
30 g (2 tbsp) chopped fresh flat-leaf parsley
salt and pepper to taste
1 kg (2¼ lb) cod steak, cut into 6 pieces
30 ml (2 tbsp) dry white wine
50 ml (2 fl oz) fish stock or water

1. Preheat oven to 220°C (425°F).

2. Heat 15 ml (1 tbsp) of the olive oil in a medium frying
pan over moderate heat until hot but not smoking. Add
the onion, shallots and garlic and cook, stirring, until
the onion is pale golden, about 15 minutes.

3. Stir in the vinegar and simmer gently, covered, for 5
minutes. Stir in the tomatoes and 20 ml (1½ tbsp) of
the olive oil and cook, covered, stirring occasionally, for
10 minutes. Stir in the olives and the thyme leaves and
cook, uncovered, stirring, for 2 minutes. Stir in parsley
and the rest of the olive oil, remove the frying pan from
the heat and keep warm. Season to taste with salt and
pepper.

4. Oil a baking dish just large enough to hold the cod in
one layer. Add the cod, season with salt and pepper,
then and add the wine and fish stock or water. Cover
with a lightly oiled piece of greaseproof paper. Bake the
fish for 10 to 15 minutes, depending on the thickness of
the fish (allow 10 minutes per 2.5 cm (1 in)).

5. Transfer the fish to a large plate and keep warm. Pour
the cooking liquid into the frying pan with the olive
mixture and cook, stirring, over moderate heat, until

heated. Serve the cod with the sauce, garnished with the thyme sprigs.

SALT COD

Salt cod, which is simply cod that has been salted and dried for preservation, has a long and noble history throughout the world. Today, in America, it's something of an ethnic curiosity which few people have ever purchased and cooked. That's unfortunate, say we. Happily, a number of trendsetting restaurant chefs around the country have worked up the courage to feature it and we hope that home cooks follow their lead.

After salt cod is soaked, cooked and sauced, it bears a resemblance to fresh cod; the large flakes of fish slide sensuously against each other and a good balance between tender and firm is struck once again. But dried cod is a little chewier than fresh—and the flavour is a little richer, so is an ideal medium for full-flavoured sauces.

When buying salt cod, look for pieces that seem evenly dried and of even thickness; this makes it easier to prepare. Best of all (if you have a choice) is the thick 'middle,' sometimes called the 'loin' or the 'captain's cut'.

Soaking time depends on many factors. How heavily has the cod been salted? If it's stiff as a board, it may need 2 to 3 days of soaking; if it's very flexible, it may need only a few hours. Generally, figure on 24 hours of soaking, in several changes of water; then boil up a small piece to see if the salt is sufficiently reduced. If not, keep soaking.

BRANDADE DE MORUE

Probably the most famous of all salt cod dishes is brandade de morue, the great Provençal purée that tempers the saltiness of the fish with potatoes, milk and olive oil. Serve warm or at room temperature as a dip for garlicky toasts, or as a scoop atop a Provençal-flavoured salad. We discovered that drizzling white truffle oil over

brandade adds a little delicious luxury to this traditional peasant dish.

MAKES 450 G (16 OZ)

450 g (1 lb) salt cod
2.5 g (½ tsp) fennel seeds
10 black peppercorns
2 bay leaves
1.2 litres (2 pints) water
4 garlic cloves, peeled
2 baking potatoes, peeled
50 ml (2 fl oz) Provençal olive oil
125 ml (4 fl oz) warm milk
lemon juice to taste
white pepper to taste

1. In a large bowl cover the dried cod with cold water and let soak 12 to 48 hours (depending on saltiness of cod), changing the water frequently.

2. In a medium saucepan combine the fennel seeds, peppercorns, bay leaves and water. Smash 2 of the garlic cloves and add. Bring to a boil, reduce the heat and simmer 30 minutes. Strain the liquid into a saucepan through a fine sieve and set aside to cool.

3. Remove the cod from its soaking water and place it in cooled liquid. Bring to a boil, turn off the heat and let stand for 15 minutes. Remove the cod and reserve.

4. Cook the potatoes in the broth in a saucepan over moderately high heat until they are soft, about 20 minutes.

5. Add the reserved cod and the potatoes to the work bowl of a food processor. Chop the remaining 2 garlic cloves and add. With the machine running, add the olive oil and warm milk in a stream. Process until the brandade has the consistency of mashed potatoes (try to accomplish this as quickly as possible). If the brandade seems too thick, add a little more warm milk or poaching liquid.

6. Season the brandade with the lemon juice and white pepper. Serve immediately or let come to room temperature.

ESQUEIXADA

Think of this fabulous Catalan dish as Spanish sashimi or Spanish carpaccio. The really neat and surprising thing, however, is that the raw flesh of choice is salt cod! You'll be delighted at how deliciously it blends with the traditional tomatoes, onions, red-wine vinegar and olive oil. About the latter: make sure to use only the greatest, youngest extra-virgin Spanish olive oil you can find; we recommend Nuñez de Prado from Andalusia. About the salt cod: make sure to use the highest-quality, thickest, moistest salt cod you can find. We sell a terrific piece at the store that needs only 24 hours of soaking; if yours is saltier and drier, you might want to soak it for 48 hours. We have tweaked the tradition of this dish by adding the sweetness of roasted red peppers to it; you may leave them out if you wish a more austere creation. Either way, it's a great liftoff for a Spanish dinner party.

SERVES 6 AS A SMALL FIRST COURSE

225 g (½ lb) salt cod, thick middle cut
1 sweet red pepper (about 115 g (¼ lb))
125 ml (4 fl oz) Spanish extra-virgin olive oil
2 small tomatoes (about 115 g (¼ lb))
50 g (2 oz) firmly packed, extremely thinly sliced
  onion rings
10 ml (2 tsp) red-wine vinegar

1. Soak the salt cod for at least 24 hours (more, if it's especially salty) in several changes of cold water.

2. When ready to prepare dish, cook the red pepper over an open flame, turning, until charred on all sides. Place in paper bag and leave for 20 minutes. Remove blackened skin, stem and seeds. Cut pepper into long, thin strips. Reserve.

3. With a very sharp knife, cut the salt cod into very thin slices, approximately 2.5 cm (1 in) x 1 cm (½ in) x 2 mm (1/16 in). (It may shred as you cut; that's okay. Try cutting slices from all sides, to see which side yields the neatest slices.)

4. Toss slices with 30 ml (2 tbsp) of the olive oil in a large bowl. Cut each tomato in half lengthways, then cut lengthways into very thin slices. Add the tomato slices to the salt cod and toss gently. Let rest for 10 minutes.

5. Just before serving, add the onion rings, reserved red pepper strips and vinegar to the cod. Toss gently. Divide among 6 plates and top each mound of esqueixada with a teaspoon of olive oil, or more to taste. Serve immediately.

CURRIED SALT COD AND SHRIMP

This fabulous Caribbean recipe for salt cod comes from Geoffrey Holder, one of our customers. You can serve it either in large soup bowls or on dinner plates; if you take the latter path, a mound of fluffy rice on the same plate, on the side, will help absorb the delicious juices.

SERVES 6

450 g (1 lb) salt cod
30 ml (2 tbsp) olive oil
25 g (1 oz) unsalted butter
3 medium-large tomatoes, peeled and chopped
2 fresh chives, chopped
3 medium onions, finely chopped
2.5 g (½ tsp) garlic powder
2½ oz (5 tbsp) good curry powder
2 medium waxy potatoes, peeled and sliced
350 ml (12 fl oz) water
900 g (2 lb) large prawns, shelled and deveined

1. Soak the salt cod in several changes of water for 24 to 48 hours, depending on saltiness of cod.

2. When ready to cook, place the oil and butter in a casserole over moderate heat. Add the tomatoes, chives, onions, garlic powder and curry powder. Cook for 1 minute. Add the potatoes, stir well and add 350 ml (12 fl oz) water. Cover and simmer until the potatoes are almost tender, about 10 minutes.

3. Drain the salt cod and cut into broad slices. Add to the simmering mixture. Cook until the cod is heated through and tender, about 10 minutes. Add prawns and simmer until they are just cooked, 5 to 6 minutes. Adjust seasoning and serve.

HALIBUT

We'll never forget our visit to Ray's Boathouse, in Seattle, just as famed local fisherman Bruce Gore was bringing in a huge catch of halibut from cold Pacific waters. When we sampled a thick, sumptuous fillet, we were amazed. The halibut was firm-fleshed, but it quivered, nevertheless—its texture was something like a firm custard. It was one of the finest pieces of fish we'd ever tasted.

When you get super-fresh, top-quality halibut (for which you'll have pay top dollar), you can reproduce that texture at home. We think halibut is a vastly underrated fish that can't possibly remain a secret for too much longer.

When buying halibut, you'll see lots of variety in the marketplace—because halibut, the largest member of the flatfish family, weighs in at between 23 and 136 kg (50 and 300 lb). From the largest fish, steaks are out of the question; these big fish are cut into fillets (the loins of halibut used for fillets are called 'fletch'). From the smaller fish, either steaks or fillets are available. Both are excellent. If you can find it, spring halibut from Alaska is a special treat.

GRILLED HALIBUT STEAKS WITH MUSTARD COATING

This is a supremely simple way to cook halibut—perfect for showing off the intrinsic quality of the fish. Make sure you get a thick, ultra-fresh, first-rate steak from your fishmonger. It may be served simply, with boiled potatoes. Or, you may drizzle a little oil over the cooked steaks—extra-virgin olive oil works nicely, as does mustard oil, as does white truffle oil.

MAKES 4 BEHEMOTH MAIN-COURSE PORTIONS

250 ml (9 fl oz) Dijon mustard
175 ml (12 fl oz) extra-virgin olive oil plus
   additional for rubbing the broiler pan
salt and pepper to taste
4 halibut steaks (each about 7.5 cm (1½ in) thick)

1. Preheat the grill.

2. Place the mustard in a bowl and slowly whisk in the olive oil. (The mixture should be smooth.)

3. Rub a grill pan with a little olive oil. Salt and pepper the halibut steaks to taste, then place them on the pan. Brush the mustard mixture on to the tops and sides of the steaks, using about two-thirds of the mixture (it will make a fairly thick layer).

4. Place the steaks 7.5-10 cm (3-4 in) below the heat and grill until the tops are browned and puffy, about 6 to 8 minutes. Turn the steaks, brush the remaining mustard mixture over the tops and grill until fairly brown and puffy, about 6 minutes. Remove steaks, place on individual plates and serve immediately.

MAHIMAHI

We learned to love mahimahi in Hawaii, where the catch from local waters is spanking fresh; today—especially with catches off Florida and California—mahimahi on the mainland can also be very fresh. This fabulous fish has never had the attention it deserves, probably because of its other name: dolphinfish. Once Americans started finding out, however, that mahimahi is *not* a dolphin, nor is it related in any way to dolphin, its popularity on restaurant menus took off. We like it in fillet form, with the tough skin removed. It's great sautéed or grilled.

MAHIMAHI SANDWICH ON GRILLED SOURDOUGH BREAD WITH SAFFRON MAYONNAISE

In Hawaii, at the best restaurants, mahimahi is often the star of upscale lunchtime sandwiches. And it is a perfect sandwich fish: meaty enough to stand up to the texture of contiguous slabs of good bread, flavourful enough to shine through a bundle of add-on delights.

SERVES 4

4 skinless mahimahi fillets (each about 1 cm (½ in) thick)
salt and pepper to taste
8 large slices of sourdough bread (each about 2cm (⅓ in) thick)
extra-virgin olive oil for brushing
2 large garlic cloves, smashed
4 green-leaf lettuce leaves
125 ml (4 fl oz) saffron mayonnaise (see page 493)
thin tomato slices
very thin raw onion slices
15 g (1 tbsp) capers

1. Prepare a medium-hot charcoal fire.

2. Season the mahimahi fillets well with salt and pepper. Brush fillets and the bread slices with the extra-virgin olive oil.

3. Place mahimahi on grill and cook until just done, about 2 to 3 minutes per side (the flesh on the inside will be white when the fish is cooked). Grill the bread slices until just lightly toasted, about 1 minute per side.

Rub bread with garlic cloves as you remove it from the grill.

4. Spread out 4 slices of the grilled bread. Top each one with a leafy piece of lettuce. Top each lettuce leaf with a piece of grilled mahimahi, then spread about 30 ml (2 tbsp) of saffron mayonnaise on the fish. Top with tomato slices, raw onions, capers and the remaining slices of bread. Serve immediately.

MONKFISH

Twenty years ago, monkfish was nonexistent in the United States market. Though it was much-prized in Europe—especially in France, where it's called *lotte*—American retailers simply didn't offer it. It was known as a trash fish and most fishermen simply heaved it overboard. When it finally started to appear in markets, it was dirt cheap. Helped along, however, by its virtual subtitle—the 'poor man's lobster,' every fishmonger newly carrying it used to proclaim—monkfish rose dramatically in popularity. Today, it costs as much as any other trendy fish.

So . . . if it's not for poor men anymore, does it at least taste like lobster? We have to say 'no' to that one as well. It does have a meatier, puffier texture than most fish, bringing it a bit closer to lobster, but it's nowhere near as dense. Additionally, the taste doesn't compare to the rich and sweet taste of lobster. If you pour lots of melted butter on monkfish and if you have a bad cold, you might see some resemblance. . . .

But monkfish is just fine in its own right, without any reference to high-priced crustaceans. It's an unusual fish, for starters: only the tail is used, though most of the body weight is in the rest of the fish. And, though it's not as firm as lobster, it does have a spongy consistency that sets it apart from most other fin fish.

Of course, the specific texture of monkfish creates cooking problems that few chefs or home cooks solve. First of all, there's a tight-clinging membrane around the fish that doesn't cook up very attractively; either remove that membrane with a very sharp knife or have your fishmonger do it. Secondly, when monkfish is cut into fillets (that's the way you're most likely to see it) and sautéed (that's the way most people cook them), the fillets curl up in the pan and exude copious quantities of water (which ruins the sauté.)

The two recipes that follow solve the watery/curly problem in two different ways.

ROASTED MONKFISH TAIL WITH BACON, POTATOES AND FRESH THYME

One good way to solve the watery/curly problem is to roast whole chunks of monkfish at a high temperature, until they're browned on the outside. Use the thinnest part of the tail, the end of the tail where the bone is also thinnest. This section yields the most tender and delicate monkfish fillets—perfect for roasting in whole chunks. This is a wonderful country French treatment of monkfish, perfectly at home in a bistro or at your house during an informal dinner party.

SERVES 4

100 g (3½ oz) thick bacon rashers, cut crossways
  into 1-cm (½-inch) pieces
4 little red potatoes or new potatoes, scrubbed and
  sliced 5 mm (¼ in) thick
4 shallots, sliced thin
15 g (1 tbsp) fresh thyme leaves plus sprigs for
  garnish
salt and pepper to taste
700 g (1½ lb) fillet of monkfish tail, membranes
  removed and the fish cut into 4 thick serving
  pieces
30 ml (2 tbsp) dry white wine
20 g (¾ oz) butter at room temperature

1. Preheat oven to 230°C (450°F). Cook the bacon in a 25-cm (10-in) heavy, ovenproof frying pan over moderately high heat, stirring, until the bacon begins to crisp. Remove the bacon with a slotted spoon, drain on

paper towels and reserve.

2. While the bacon is cooking, add the potatoes to boiling salted water, return to a boil and boil for 4 minutes. Drain the potatoes completely in a colander.

3. Cook the shallots in the frying pan with the bacon fat over moderate heat, stirring, for 2 minutes. Stir in the potatoes, 5 g (1 tsp) of the thyme leaves and salt and pepper to taste and cook, stirring for 1 minute. Push the potato mixture to the side and add the monkfish to the centre of the frying pan. Drizzle the white wine over the monkfish fillets. Roast the monkfish in the oven for 10 minutes, then place under a hot grill until it is just cooked through and very browned on the outside.

4. When ready to serve, remove the monkfish from the frying pan, place on a dish and cover with aluminium foil. Place the frying pan over moderately high heat and add the reserved bacon pieces and the remaining 10 g (2 tsp) of thyme leaves to the potatoes and shallots. Toss until the bacon is heated through.

5. Place each monkfish fillet on a dinner plate, reserving the juice that has collected around the fillets. Top each fillet with a knob of butter. Surround the fillets decoratively with potato slices, leaving behind as much of the shallots and bacon as possible in the pan. Salt and pepper each fillet and the potato slices. Top the monkfish fillets with the remaining shallots and bacon. Pour the monkfish liquid over the fillets and garnish with fresh thyme sprigs. Serve immediately.

SAUTÉED MONKFISH FILLETS WITH BUTTERY TOMATO AND GARLIC SAUCE

This combination of techniques adds up to our favourite way to solve the watery/curly problem. First of all, you lay the monkfish fillet out on the kitchen counter, membrane side down. Then, working with a sharp knife and holding that knife at a 45-degree angle to the counter, you begin slicing off 5-mm (¼-in) thick slices of monkfish, leaving behind the tough membrane on the bottom of the fish fillet. When you have finished, you'll have approximately 16 membraneless monkfish slices and a tough membrane to discard. Then, a combination of cutting and salting (see below) removes the potential for wateriness and curling. Finally, a dip in flour seals the job. The fillets, after cooking, are crisp, dry, straight as a board and phenomenal with this simple butter sauce, which really moves the monkfish in a lobstery direction.

SERVES 4

700 g (1½ lb) monkfish fillet, cut into 16 slices, each about 5 mm (¼ in) thick (see directions in headnote)
10 g (2 tsp) coarse salt
70 g (2½ oz) unsalted butter
4 garlic cloves, very finely chopped
4 canned tomatoes
flour for dredging fish
50 ml (2 fl oz) olive oil

1. With a small, sharp knife, cut little nicks all around the circumference of each fillet (about 8 nicks per fillet). Divide the coarse salt among the fillets, sprinkling on each side. Place the fillets on a rack so that water can drip away. Let drain for 1 hour.

2. *While the fillets are draining, prepare the sauce:* Place 15 g (½ oz) of the butter in a small saucepan over very low heat. Add the garlic cloves and cook until softened, about 10 minutes. (Do not allow the garlic to brown.) Squeeze the juice out of each tomato, then squeeze the tomatoes into the pan, breaking them up with your hand. Stir well and cook over moderate heat for 1 minute. Remove from heat and reserve.

3. When almost ready to cook, wash the fillets under running water. Dry thoroughly. Place flour on large dish and dredge fillets in flour, coating them thoroughly.

Return fillets to rack for 10 minutes to dry.

4. When ready to serve, place the olive oil and 25 g (1 oz) butter in a large frying pan over moderately high heat. Cook until butter melts and foam has subsided. Add the monkfish fillets in a single layer. (Do not crowd. If you don't have a large enough frying pan, cook the fillets in 2 batches.) Cook, turning once, until each side is golden brown, about 2 minutes per side. Remove monkfish fillets to paper towels and then place on dinner plates, 4 to a plate.

5. Return the reserved tomato mixture to low heat. Whisk in the rest of the butter and heat until just melted. Pour sauce over fish and serve immediately.

OILY FISH

We're grouping a number of fish together here, because fish with a high oil content appeal to only a dedicated band of fish-lovers. Bluefish, sardines, shad, mackerel and herring share the quality of intense flavour—which is simultaneously described by detractors as 'fishy' and advocates as 'delicious'. We like oily fish, particularly when they're cooked with acidic ingredients that cut through the rich fish oil.

BAKED BLUEFISH FILLETS WITH LEMON AND ONIONS

Bluefish is for people who want to know that they're eating fish, not for those who feel that milder is better when it comes to seafood. Its strong hearty flavour, oily texture and beautiful silvery appearance are distinctive. The key to great bluefish is freshness; it's at its absolute best when just caught. After a day or two out of the sea, it begins to be unattractive, even to fish-lovers. Use the freshest fish you can find for this utterly simple, utterly delicious dish, in which the lemon is a perfect foil for the richness of the bluefish.

SERVES 4

30 ml (2 tbsp) olive oil

700 g (1½ lb) thick, skinless bluefish fillets, cut
 into 4 pieces

2 medium onions, halved through the root and
 sliced thinly

2 bay leaves

4 g (¾ tsp) chopped fresh oregano leaves plus
 sprigs for garnish

10 ml (2 tsp) red-wine vinegar

24 paper-thin lemon slices

salt and pepper to taste

1. Preheat oven to 230°C (450°F). Heat the olive oil in
an ovenproof frying pan just large enough to hold the
bluefish over moderately high heat until hot but not
smoking. Stir in the onions, bay leaves and oregano and
cook, stirring frequently, until the onions are golden,
about 15 minutes. Stir in the vinegar, season with salt
and pepper and cook for 1 minute longer.

2. Lay the bluefish fillets on top of the onions, arrange
the lemon slices on the bluefish and sprinkle with salt
and pepper. Bake the bluefish until it is just cooked
through (it will be white throughout, test it with a paring
knife), about 15 minutes, depending on the thickness of
the fillets. Place the onions on a serving plate, top with
the bluefish fillets, garnish with oregano sprigs and
serve hot.

SEARED SHAD FILLETS WITH GRANNY SMITH VINAIGRETTE

Tart Granny Smith apples act as the acidic agent here,
lightening the richness of shad with a marvellous
vinaigrette. And we employ an unusual technique to get
the most out of your shad fillets: cooking the 'dark meat'
of the fillet separately, until it's crunchy. The result is an
almost baconlike quality that enables the shad itself to
stand in for the real bacon that's often paired with this
fish.

SERVES 4

2 whole filleted shad (about 450 g (1 lb) each)

salt and pepper to taste

potato flour for dredging

½ Granny Smith apple, cored and finely diced (skin
 on)

100 ml (3½ fl oz) white-wine vinegar

100 ml (3½ fl oz) hazelnut oil

10 g (2 tsp) chopped fresh tarragon plus tarragon
 leaves for garnish

1. Place a cast-iron frying pan over high heat and heat
until very hot, about 5 minutes.

2. Cut the shad fillets into light-meat sections (no skin)
and dark-meat sections (skin attached). The light meat
is an inner flap of the boned shad fillet that separates
easily. (You should have about 450 g (1 lb) of light meat
and an equal amount of dark meat with skin attached.
You will need only 115 g (4 oz) dark meat with skin
attached for this recipe; reserve 350 g (12 oz) of the
dark meat with skin attached for another use.)

3. Cut the 450 g (1 lb) of light-meat shad fillets into 4
portions. Season it and the 115 g (4 oz) of dark meat
with salt and pepper, then flour lightly with instant flour.

4. When the pan is hot, add all the shad. Cook the light-
meat fillets, turning frequently to make sure they don't
stick, about 2 minutes per side. Remove when just
cooked (they should be browned on the outside, just past
pink on the inside). Continue to cook the dark-meat
pieces with skin, pressing down with a spatula to make
them as crunchy as possible. Remove when crackling
brown.

5. *Make the vinaigrette at the last minute:* Beat together
the apple, the vinegar, the hazelnut oil and the chopped
tarragon.

6. To serve, divide the light-meat fillets among 4 plates.
Top with diced apples removed from the vinaigrette with

a slotted spoon. Mince the crunchy dark meat finely and top the apples with that. Pour the remainder of the vinaigrette over and around the fish. Garnish with fresh tarragon leaves.

GRILLED SARDINES WITH MOROCCAN PRESERVED LEMONS AND OLIVE OIL

One of our favourite fish-eating experiences ever was at the harbour in Essaouira, Morocco. Charcoal grills are set up on the docks and when the fishing boats come in the fish goes directly from the boat to the grill. There is a huge variety of fish available, but nothing is better than the sardines—served outside at picnic tables with an assortment of salads, bread and bottled water. With this dish you can pretend you're there.

SERVES 8 AS A FIRST COURSE OR 4 AS A MAIN COURSE

900 g (2 lb) fresh sardines (about 24), scaled, eviscerated, boned and dorsal fin removed (we like to keep the head and tail, but you can remove them if desired)
3 Moroccan preserved lemons (see page 497)
salt and pepper to taste
125 ml (4 fl oz) fresh lemon juice
125 ml (4 fl oz) extra-virgin olive oil
fresh coriander for garnish

1. Prepare a moderately hot charcoal fire.

2. Wash the sardines well and soak them in cold salted water for 10 minutes. Dry on kitchen towels.

3. Grill the sardines on an oiled rack set about 10 cm (4 in) above glowing coals for 3 to 5 minutes on each side, depending on size of fish. (Carefully check for doneness; do not overcook.)

4. Cut each preserved lemon into 8 thin slices. Arrange the 24 slices on a large platter and top them with the grilled sardines. Sprinkle sardines with salt and pepper,

lemon juice and olive oil, garnish with coriander and serve immediately.

SALMON

Maybe it's the colour. Maybe it's the high fat content. Maybe it's the fact that you don't have to deal with a lot of little bones in order to enjoy it. Whatever the reason, salmon—either fresh or smoked—has long been one of America's favourite fish. With the recent advent of salmon-farming—and the now-ubiquitous presence of fresh, high-quality salmon in fishmonger's at very reasonable prices—salmon is more popular than ever. Add to this the penchant of modern American chefs for finding creative ways with salmon (both fresh and smoked) and you've got a national piscine phenomenon.

FRESH SALMON

The story starts at wholesale fish markets ... where, in some parts of the country, you can find a very wide range of fresh salmon choices.

To most salmon connoisseurs, wild salmon has more flavour and better texture than farmed salmon. Unfortunately, wild salmon is hard to come by in fishmongers; if you can find it, grab it. Of special note is the spring run of Copper River salmon from Alaska, which appears in June and the spring run of Columbia River salmon, which appears for just a few weeks at the end of February/beginning of March. Most of the time, the salmon you'll find at the fishmonger is farmed salmon; the good news is that the quality of this product is uniformly acceptable.

Next question: steaks or fillets? Salmon is most frequently cut into steaks, with a round bone sitting at the centre of each steak. Because we like fish cooked on the bone, we find salmon steaks delicious. However, we're also tremendously fond of the way fillets flake, the way the pieces of salmon flesh slide off each other in skin-on fillets. You might want to alternate steaks and fillets at your salmon dinners, for variety's sake. We especially like steaks for grilling, poaching and steaming; fillets for grilling and shallow frying.

Lastly, there's the question of cooking styles and the related question of simplicity versus complexity.

'Brown' treatments of salmon—grilling and shallow frying—are the favourites among most American chefs and home cooks. The high heat crusts the skin nicely on the outside, bubbles up the fish oil and leads to rich, deeply flavoured pieces of fish. But don't forget about water treatments, such as steaming or poaching. They leave a lighter finished product, with more of the natural salmon flavour in the foreground.

And if it's that natural flavour you're after, don't follow the practice of most American chefs in inventing all kinds of creative add-ons to cooked salmon. We love simple grilled salmon, simple sautéed fillets and simple poached steaks.

We must confess, however, that even the fussiest American chefs are on to something good; the rich, mineral taste of salmon does combine well with other flavours, even other strong flavours. Sometimes we like to get creative ourselves with this marvellous fish. Here are three of our favourite 'complex' salmon dishes.

GRILLED SALMON FILLET WITH BACON, WILD MUSHROOMS AND OYSTER SAUCE

Here, the bacon and grill combine to drive even more 'brown' flavour into salmon fillets—making this dish an especially good candidate for fruity red wine, like a young California Pinot Noir.

SERVES 4 AS A FIRST COURSE

450-g (1-lb) salmon fillet (about 2.5 cm (1 in) thick)
salt and pepper to taste
5 thin slices of smoky bacon
200 g (7 oz) very firmly packed, diced fresh shiitake
  mushrooms
5 g (1 tsp) finely chopped garlic
30 g (2 tbsp) chopped fresh flat-leaf parsley plus
  whole parsley leaves for garnish

30 ml (2 tbsp) Chinese oyster sauce
pinch of freshly grated nutmeg

1. Preheat grill. Season the salmon fillet well with salt and pepper. Wrap 3 of the bacon slices, evenly spaced, around the salmon fillet. Place fillet on a roasting tin and grill until just done, about 10 minutes.

2. *While the salmon is grilling, prepare the sauce:* Cut the remaining two slices of bacon into small squares. Place in a heavy frying pan over high heat. Cook until medium-brown, about 2 minutes. Drain away all but 5 g (1 tsp) of the bacon fat. Reduce heat to moderately high. Add the shiitake mushrooms, stir well and sauté until mushrooms become golden brown, about 3 minutes. Reduce heat to medium, stir in garlic and chopped parsley and cook for 1 minute. In a bowl, combine the oyster sauce with 50 ml (2 fl oz) hot water. Blend and add to frying pan. Cook 1 minute and season with the nutmeg.

3. To serve, remove the wrapped bacon from the salmon (discard it or use it as a garnish). Delicately slice the salmon along the natural separations and divide among 4 plates. Top each with sauce and with a flat parsley leaf for garnish.

GRILLED SALMON CUBES WITH TAWNY PORT-TARRAGON SAUCE

Made from cubes that are cut from salmon steaks, this dish features a slightly sweet, incredibly deep-tasting sauce. The total effect is so rich we advise serving it in small, appetiser portions only.

SERVES 8 AS A FIRST COURSE

350 g (¾ lb) salmon steak (3 cm (1¼ in) thick)
salt and pepper to taste
75 ml(2½ fl oz) tawny port (as dry as possible)
50 g (2 oz) firmly packed, fresh tarragon leaves (no
  stems)

1 large shallot, chopped
30 ml (1 fl oz) beef stock
115 g (4 oz) cold butter
5 ml (1 tsp) vegetable oil
coarse salt for sprinkling the salmon

1. Skin and bone the salmon steak. Cut into 8 cubes, each one approximately 1¼ inches square. Season well with salt and pepper. Place in a mixing bowl and add the tawny port. Stir in the tarragon leaves, reserving a few for garnish. Cover and marinate in the refrigerator for 2 to 6 hours (try to marinate it as long as possible).

2. When ready to cook, prepare a charcoal fire. While the fire is getting hot, prepare the sauce. Remove the salmon cubes from the marinade and reserve cubes. Pour the marinade into a small saucepan. Add the shallot and beef stock. Bring to a boil over high heat, skimming off any foam that forms on the surface. Boil the liquid until it is reduced to a glaze. Reduce the heat to low and begin whisking in the cold butter, 1 tablespoon at a time. (Make sure that the sauce doesn't 'break'. When all the butter is incorporated, you'll have a smooth, medium-thick, tan-coloured sauce.) Strain it into a clean saucepan and keep warm over very low heat, stirring occasionally.

3. *When the sauce is almost ready, grill the reserved salmon cubes:* First dry them very well, then toss them with the vegetable oil to prevent sticking. Place them on the grill and cook, turning them with tongs, until charred on the outside, still rosy-pink on the inside, about 5 minutes. (Alternatively, you could place the oiled cubes under a preheated grill, turning, until just done.)

4. Place each salmon cube on a small plate. Sprinkle with coarse salt. Drizzle each cube with 2.5 ml (½ tsp) of the sauce (reserve the leftover sauce for another use). Sprinkle each cube with a few flecks of the reserved tarragon leaves, finely chopped.

STEAMED SALMON STEAKS WITH TAMARIND-GINGER SAUCE

Steaming times for fish are totally dependent on the thickness, not the weight . . . so measure your fish carefully. This delicious, Thai-influenced recipe yields perfect, medium-rare steaks after 10 minutes of steaming.

SERVES 4

25 g (1 oz) dried tamarind pulp
50 ml (2 fl oz) rapeseed or safflower oil
4 shallots, slivered lengthways
30 g (2 tbsp) julienne strips fresh ginger
4 garlic cloves, slivered lengthways
50 g (2 oz) palm sugar or light brown sugar
45 ml (3 tbsp) nam pla (Thai fish sauce)
4 salmon steaks (each about 3 cm (1¼ in) thick)
fresh coriander for garnish

1. Place the tamarind in a small bowl and pour 125 ml (4 fl oz) boiling water over it. Let sit for 30 minutes. Break up the tamarind in the water with your fingers. Put water and tamarind in a small saucepan and simmer for 30 minutes. Strain through a sieve into a bowl, pressing on the tamarind solids with a wooden spoon.

2. Heat the oil in a medium frying pan over moderately high heat until hot but not smoking. Stir in the shallots, ginger and garlic and stir-fry for 1 minute, or until very aromatic. Stir in the palm sugar, nam pla and strained tamarind liquid and cook, stirring, for 5 minutes. Reserve.

3. Lay the salmon steaks on a lightly oiled plate that will fit into a Chinese bamboo steamer basket. Spread about 15 g (1 tbsp) of the reserved ginger-tamarind sauce on each side of each steak and let marinate for 20 minutes.

4. Bring enough water to sit just below (but not touch) the steamer basket in a wok to a simmer. Place the plate in the basket, cover with the basket lid and steam the salmon just until opaque, about 10 minutes for medium-rare. Remove the basket from the wok and the plate from the basket. With a spatula carefully remove the salmon steaks to serving plates. Pour enough liquid from the steaming plate into the reserved sauce to reach the desired consistency.

5. Quickly reheat the sauce and spoon over the salmon. Garnish with the coriander and serve hot.

SMOKED SALMON

Smoked salmon is one of the most popular 'luxury' foods in America—though, 40 years ago, it was most likely to be seen at the unluxurious appetising counters of Jewish delicatessens, referred to as 'lox' or 'nova'. It's still at those counters, of course, now bringing astronomical prices. But it's also at fine groceries of all types, at fancy French restaurants, trendy Italian restaurants, creative New American restaurants, buffets galore and expensive Russian-style emporia devoted to the delectation of caviar and smoked salmon. In a word, it's everywhere—and the choice of product is far wider than ever. Confusing, even.

So if you want to enjoy this delicious product at home . . . how do you cut through the maze and identify the very best?

Our primary consideration is the national or regional origin of the smoked salmon. We look to northern Europe first. And we find Scottish salmon, at its best, from artisanal smokehouses, coming closest to our ideal smoked salmon criteria: rich fattiness, springy resiliency, complex and haunting flavour. The more industrial Norwegian producers turn out a more consistent product, though it rarely reaches the heights of the finest Scottish salmon. Irish smoked salmon is in another league altogether: it takes a heavier cure than the other two, with more smoking, leading to a drier, smokier finished product. But it too, in the best examples, can be excellent.

For many decades, the eastern seaboard of America, up through Canada, has been a hub of smoked salmon production ('nova,' after all, was named after Nova Scotia). And today the same large companies continue to turn out decent smoked salmon (though rarely with the distinction of the best European products). There's a new wrinkle in the old game, however: small, boutique producers (like Perona Farms in New Jersey) are now turning out some top-notch smoked salmon in the northern European style.

Most smoked salmon connoisseurs agree that Atlantic salmon (intrinsically fattier) makes better smoked salmon than the leaner Pacific salmon—even when the fattiest Pacific sub-variety, called king or Chinook salmon, is used. Nevertheless, there's some good smoked salmon today coming out of the Pacific North-west that bears watching. Don't be fooled, however, into buying another type of smoked salmon that is traditional in that region: hot-smoked salmon, which is really more like cooked salmon than it is like smoked salmon. Only cold-smoked salmon (that's the European method) produces the luxuriant silkiness we associate with smoked salmon.

Next: in what form has the salmon come to the shops?

We believe that the best way to buy smoked salmon for use at home is to buy a whole side; by cutting it at home, at the last possible moment before serving, you insure the freshest and moistest slices of smoked salmon. Cutting, of course, is something of an art. You'll need a very long, thin, very sharp knife to do it properly. And you'll have to practise cutting the fish into see-through slices, with your knife practically parallel to the cutting board, if you want to get the best out of your side. This 'parallel' method yields wide, broad slices, which show off the bands of fat to elegant advantage in a great smoked salmon.

Surprisingly, presliced sides can also be good. They certainly save a lot of trouble. The angle of the slicing, however, is much sharper than the angle we're recommending and slices can be on the thick side.

If you need less than a whole side, you can always ask the counter person at a good shop, such as ours, to cut fresh slices for you. Be specific: 'I want broad, thin slices, cut with the knife parallel to the board'. If the shop assistant doesn't know what you're talking about, find another shop. The downside of this approach is that the salmon must be consumed quickly, lest your fresh-cut slices start becoming un-fresh (carefully wrapped, your purchase should be good for a few hours).

One last option is small packages of presliced smoked salmon. These vary widely in quality. Taste to see which brand appeals to you. At their best, they can cover the subject well—but never do they have the excitement of fresh smoked salmon cut right from the side.

So . . . you're ready to serve your smoked salmon. What do you do now?

The rest couldn't be simpler. Make sure that your salmon rests for 30 minutes outside the refrigerator before you serve it; this allows the fat to 'melt' a little, creating a lusher impression. Fill dinner plates with broad slices of the salmon, in single layers; it'll take just one beautifully rendered slice to fill a whole plate. Never overlap slices. Encourage people to eat the salmon with a knife and fork. This is the best way to apprehend the salmon's texture; slices of bread get in the way of the 'chew'. You can serve the salmon just as it is, or supply lemon wedges and capers. But we think a great slice of smoked salmon deserves to be savoured all by itself.

Of course, lots of inventive American chefs, over the last 20 years, have not agreed. They have unleashed on the world the new genre of smoked salmon dishes . . . many of which compromise the intrinsic quality of the product. If, however, the quality of your salmon is not extraordinary to begin with, a complicated dish may be just what you need.

Our favourite 'smoked salmon dish' that has emerged from this era is smoked salmon tartare: chopped smoked salmon with sympathetic seasonings. Some chefs mistakenly make something like it with fresh raw salmon; even sushi chefs are trained to avoid raw salmon, a common carrier of parasites. But the following smoked salmon variations are safe and delicious.

SMOKED SALMON TARTARE WITH OYSTERS AND CHIVES

Smoked salmon releases its oils when it's chopped and the resulting mound of salmon can seem a little heavy. The lemon juice and the chopped oysters both serve to bring a lighter, more refreshing quality to the dish. We find that smokier, slightly drier Irish salmon is best for smoked salmon tartare. This variation features little ovals of the tartare arranged elegantly on plates as a first course. An alternative way to serve the tartare as a starter is to spread it on toast triangles or on round croûtes; the mixture will make about 32 of those. Or, you could serve the mixture in a decorative chilled bowl with toasts or croûtes on an adjacent plate, allowing your guests to top their own toasts and croûtes. Or, you could make potato gaufrettes (see page 196) and top them with the tartare mixture . . . as many a creative American chef has done.

SERVES 4 AS A FIRST COURSE

450 g (1 lb) smoked salmon, thinly sliced
8 raw oysters, chopped to a paste
10 g (2 tsp) finely chopped fresh chives plus additional for garnish
10 g (2 tsp) finely chopped fresh tarragon plus additional for garnish
10 ml (2 tsp) freshly squeezed lemon juice
5 ml (1 tsp) Dijon mustard
salt and pepper to taste
lemon wedges for garnish

1. Chop the smoked salmon coarsely. Combine with the oysters, 10 g (2 tsp) of the chives, 10 g (2 tsp) of the tarragon, lemon juice and mustard, and continue chopping the mixture until the salmon is in small bits. Season to taste.

2. Scoop up 20 g (¾ oz) of the mixture in a large soup spoon. Wet another soup spoon and use it to shape the mixture in the first spoon into an oval. Carefully drop the oval on to a dinner plate. Arrange a total of 3 ovals on each plate (you will have enough mixture to make 12 ovals). Garnish with the additional chives, additional tarragon and lemon wedges and serve.

BUNDLES OF SMOKED SALMON TARTARE WITH OYSTERS AND CHIVES

There's yet another way to serve this mixture…fancier, fussier and more elegant, if you're in that mood. The mixture gets surrounded by a thin slice of smoked salmon, which is balanced by the presence of a whole oyster at the centre of the bundle. If you're especially fond of the interplay between smoked salmon and oyster—which we are—this one's for you.

SERVES 8 AS A FIRST COURSE

32 chives
8 thin slices of smoked salmon (each approximately 10 x 10 cm (4 x 4 in)
½ recipe tartare mixture (recipe precedes)
8 raw oysters, shucked

1. Wash the chives and keep them wet. Place 1 chive across the bottom of a 50 ml (2 fl oz) ramekin, positioning it dead centre. Working with your fingers, tuck the chive in where it meets the ramekin wall on the side, so that the chive ends come straight up the wall. Lay another chive across the first, making an X, also tucking this one against the wall. Place 2 more chives over the others, symmetrically, tucking against the wall and creating a spoke-like pattern in the bottom of the ramekin with 8 ends of chives hanging over the top edge of the ramekin.

2. Carefully lay in a slice of smoked salmon over the chive design, pressing it down onto the chives (the salmon should overlap the ramekin's top edge on the side). Now place 15 ml (1 tbsp) of the tartare mixture on top of the smoked salmon slice. Top that with an oyster. Top that with another 15 ml (1 tbsp) of tartare mixture. Fold the overhanging smoked salmon in over the mixture. Fold the overhanging chive ends in over the smoked salmon slice. (If the top is not picture-perfect, it doesn't matter; this will be the bottom of the mould.)

3. Invert the ramekin onto a serving plate. It should make a perfectly neat salmon mould with a perfectly symmetrical pattern of chive spokes on top. (If edges are a little ragged or if some chive ends are poking out from the bottom, you can use a sharp knife to push things into their proper place.)

SKATE

Skate wings (or ailes de raie) are in that group of fish (along with monkfish) that have been revered for years by the French and ignored by Americans. Happily, skate started turning up on French bistro menus in America in the eighties, then spread to less French-focused restaurants. They are not in every fishmonger's in America yet, but they are gaining in popularity.

Skate is an unusual and delicious fish: clinging tightly to a broad, flat, ridged piece of cartilage, fillets of skate wing have a ridged look, with firm, ropy strands of meat. Poaching whole wings, cartilage and all, is a traditional treatment, after which the fillets may be removed from the cartilage. But you (or the fishmonger) can easily remove the fillets from the cartilage before cooking and then proceed to grill them or sauté them.

SAUTÉED SKATE WITH CABBAGE AND SHERRY-VINEGAR CAPER SAUCE

The traditional sauce to serve with skate is browned butter. But in the eighties, fashionable restaurants in France—led by L'Ambroisie in Paris, which now has 3 stars—began serving skate with cabbage and with a buttery sauce enlivened by sherry vinegar. Today, you'll find versions of this dish in France both at fancy restaurants and at bistros; this is our version, perfect for casual family dining *or* high-end entertaining.

SERVES 4

2 onions, coarsely chopped
2 carrots, coarsely chopped
1 celery stalk (including the leaves), coarsely
  chopped
6 parsley stems
4 thyme sprigs
fennel sprigs from 1 bulb
10 black peppercorns
2 bay leaves
6 coriander seeds
225 ml (8 fl oz) white wine
850 ml (1½ pints) water
1 small cabbage, cut into thin strips
175 g (6 oz) butter, cold and cut in small pieces
30 ml (2 tbsp) sherry vinegar
1 small tomato, peeled, seeded and finely chopped
20 g (4 tsp) capers, finely chopped
salt and pepper to taste
1.3 kg (3 lb) skinless skate fillets
plain flour or potato flour for coating skate
50 g (2 oz) clarified butter plus additional if cooking
  skate in batches
3 shallots, chopped

1. Place onions, carrots and celery in a large piece of cheesecloth and tie up tightly. Tie the parsley, thyme, fennel, peppercorns, bay leaves and coriander in another piece of muslin.

2. Place the vegetable and herb bundles in a large saucepan and add the wine and water. Bring to a boil, covered, reduce the heat and simmer for 10 minutes. Add cabbage and simmer over low heat for 20 minutes, or until tender. Drain liquid from pan, reserving 450 ml (16 fl oz). Remove and discard vegetable and herb bundles. Keep cabbage, covered, in pan and set aside.

3. In a small saucepan, boil the reserved liquid until it is reduced to about 125 ml (4 fl oz), measuring frequently for accuracy. Turn off heat and whisk in the butter, a few pieces at a time, whisking until the butter is completely dissolved. (The sauce should be thick enough to coat the back of a spoon.)

4. Add 90 ml (6 tbsp) of the sauce to the cabbage and gently reheat the cabbage over very low heat. Add 10 ml (2 tsp) of the sherry vinegar to cabbage, mix well and set aside. To the sauce add the tomato, capers, the rest of the sherry vinegar and salt and pepper. Keep warm over very low heat, stirring occasionally to make sure the sauce is not separating.

5. Season the skate generously with salt and pepper and coat lightly in the flour. In a large frying pan heat the clarified butter over moderately high heat until hot but not smoking. Add the shallots and cook until translucent. Add skate and fry, in batches and adding additional clarified butter if necessary, until golden and cooked through, about 4 to 5 minutes per side.

6. Divide the cabbage among 4 dinner plates and arrange the skate fillets carefully on top. Spoon the sauce over and around the skate and serve immediately.

SWORDFISH

Swordfish has always been popular in the United States and with the rise of seafood grilling, it has become even more so. Why has this particular fish always been among the best-loved of seafood dishes here? We suspect it has to do with the inherent un-fishiness of swordfish; even fish-haters can enjoy the meaty, almost chickenlike solidity of a slab o' sword.

We like it for a different reason. Because it is so quiet in flavour, the cook doesn't have to tiptoe around, trying to preserve a 'subtle' taste that's not really there. Add to that the heartiness of the texture—and you've got a fish that you can go wild with in the kitchen, adding any brash seasonings you want without fear of spoiling something naturally good. Then, after you've boldly flavoured your swordfish, you can grill it or sauté it—but we think the further flavour that a good, smoky grill brings is by far the best way to cook this beast.

And what a beast it is. Swordfish can run up to 4 metres (13 feet) long and can weigh close to 455 kg (1000 lb). It is sold almost exclusively as steaks and has a firm, dense, compact structure, with white flesh that has a tan or coral shade. There are dark spots in swordfish steaks and many people like to avoid them. This makes good health sense, because these spots are fattier and would be the repository of any chemicals that the fish has ingested during its natural life. However— if you're a bit of a gambler and you don't mind the taste of fish—there's lots more flavour in those dark spots and they're delicious when eaten in tandem with the 'white meat'.

GRILLED SWORDFISH STEAKS SLATHERED WITH TAPENADE

This recipe holds nothing back, flavour-wise: grilled, marinated steaks—with a last-minute addition of a Provençal paste made from olives, anchovies and garlic.

SERVES 6

135 ml (4½ fl oz) olive oil
20 ml (4 tsp) balsamic vinegar
3 garlic cloves, crushed with the side of a knife
6 x 2.5-cm (1-in)-thick swordfish steaks (175-225 g (6-8 oz) each)
300 ml (10 fl oz) tapenade (see page 496)
15 g (1 tbsp) chopped fresh parsley leaves plus parsley sprigs for garnish

1. Stir together the olive oil, balsamic vinegar and garlic in a shallow baking dish just large enough to hold the swordfish in a single layer. Add the swordfish steaks, turn them in the marinade and let them marinate,

covered, at room temperature, turning once, for 30 minutes.

2. Prepare a moderately hot charcoal fire. Remove the swordfish steaks from the marinade and grill them over grey, ashy coals for 4 to 5 minutes on each side, or until they are just cooked through. Transfer the swordfish to a platter. Slather the swordfish with the tapenade, sprinkle with the chopped parsley and garnish with the parsley sprigs.

MOROCCAN SWORDFISH KEBABS

Swing to another portion of the Mediterranean—the North African coast—for this swordfish-compatible blast of flavour. The double marination (first dry, then wet) helps to drive the spice flavour into the fish.

SERVES 4

700 g (1½ lb) swordfish steaks, cut 2.5 cm (1 in) thick
20 g (4 tsp) orange zest
5 g (1 tsp) sweet paprika
5 g (1 tsp) ground cumin
25 g (5 tsp) finely chopped garlic
2.5 g (½ tsp) salt
1.25 g (¼ tsp) freshly ground black pepper
125 ml (4 fl oz) fresh squeezed orange juice (juice of about 1 large orange)
30 ml (2 tbsp) olive oil
25 g (1 oz) chopped parsley
orange wedges for garnish

1. Trim the swordfish, removing skin, gristle and bone. Cut fish into 2.5-cm (1-in) cubes (you should have about 20 cubes). Place in a medium bowl.

2. In a small bowl combine 15 g (1 tbsp) of the orange zest, paprika, cumin, 15 g (1 tbsp) of the garlic, 1.25 g (¼ tsp) of the salt and a pinch of the black pepper. Mix well. Sprinkle mixture over swordfish cubes, tossing the fish as you sprinkle, making sure that the pieces of fish are evenly covered with the spice mixture. Cover bowl and refrigerate for 1½ hours.

3. Whisk together well the orange juice, olive oil, remaining orange zest and remaining garlic. Pour this over swordfish, stirring to coat fish and marinate at room temperature for 1 hour.

4. Prepare a moderately hot charcoal fire.

5. Remove swordfish pieces from marinade and dry well. Divide cubes among 4 skewers, about 5 cubes per skewer. Just before putting skewers on the barbecue, sprinkle swordfish with remaining salt and pepper.

6. Grill the swordfish kebabs over grey, ashy coals, turning, for about 10 minutes, or until the swordfish is medium-rare. Let sit for 5 minutes, remove from skewers, sprinkle with parsley and serve immediately. Garnish the platter with the orange wedges.

TUNA

Twenty years ago, fresh tuna was practically unheard of in America. But that doesn't mean we didn't eat tuna. Far from it. Tuna in cans—white fillets of it, packed in oil—has always been one of the most popular foods in this country. In fact, that's what most of us thought tuna was; it came as a surprise to most Americans when they learned that tuna is usually blood-red. The first taste of cooked fresh tuna for many Americans was often not a happy experience—because even the slightest overcooking of this very lean fish makes it dry and unappealing. Slowly, however, things began to change. We fell in love with the meaty texture of raw tuna at sushi bars—and smart American chefs starting leaving cooked tuna raw at the centre, so the delight of that sushi experience could be re-created in other culinary contexts. Nowadays, tuna that's seared on the outside and raw within is one of the most popular seafood

choices at important American restaurants. Happily, it's easy to reproduce this treat at home.

Tuna types

Purchasing raw, fresh tuna has become ever more complicated with the appearance of different members of the tuna family in our fishmonger's. Here's a quick guide to the clan:

Bluefin This is the largest member of the family, sometimes weighing in at 680 kg (1,500 lb). The name comes from the deep-blue colour on the top side of the fish. It is caught in the Atlantic, much of it off New England—from whence it regularly makes its way to sushi bars in Tokyo. This is currently the most prized tuna in the world, loved for its deep red colour and its relatively high degree of fat.

Bigeye Bigeye is generally smaller than bluefin, with the heaviest creatures under the 180 kg (400 lb) mark. As the name implies, this member of the family has unusually large eyes, set in an unusually large head. At its best, in Hawaii (where, along with yellowfin tuna, it is called *ahi*), it can rival bluefin for succulence. However, it is usually a little leaner than bluefin; some bigeye advocates applaud this, claiming that oily Atlantic bluefin can taste a little fishy when raw. Bigeye season in Hawaii is October to April.

Yellowfin Yellowfin is usually smaller than bigeye, though it can also hit the 180 kg (400 lb) mark. It is characterised by a bright yellow stripe along its sides and yellow fins. Generally, it prefers water that's a little warmer. Its meat is lighter than bluefin or bigeye meat and a little leaner; it's also milder in flavour. Sushi aficionados consider it third-best. Yellowfin season in Hawaii is May to September.

Albacore This is a considerably smaller tuna (it never exceeds 20 kg (50 lb)) and the only tuna with ivory-coloured flesh (which turns white when cooked). Therefore, since Americans like light-coloured tuna in cans, it is the tuna of choice for canned tuna manufacturers, the one that brings the most money. It is available around the country as fresh raw tuna—ironically, often at a lower price than other kinds. Unfortunately, it can be quite dry when cooked—though during the winter albacore is a little fattier.

Skipjack This is the world's most abundant member of the tuna family. It is also the smallest tuna; though it can reach 18 kg (40 lb), it's usually 2.7-3.6 kg (6-8 lb) when caught. Skipjack has a bright blue back, with red slashes in it. It is often used for 'chunk light' canned tuna and not too widely available as fresh tuna. If you find it, however, you may wish to grill it barbecue it or shallow-fry it. Like albacore, it is fattier in winter.

SEARED GINGER TUNA WITH BUTTERED OYSTER SAUCE

This is one way of creating the seared/raw effect: shallow frying in a very hot frying pan. Seared-and-raw tuna has become especially popular in restaurants with East-meets-West themes...and the Eurasian sauce for this dish owes something to the spirit of Roy Yamaguchi in Hawaii, who continues to merge butter and Asian ingredients into fantastic backdrops for main ingredients.

SERVES 4 AS A FIRST COURSE

30 g (2 tbsp) grated fresh ginger (with juice)
10 g (2 tsp) sugar
5 ml (1 tsp) thin soy sauce
5 ml (1 tsp) sesame oil
450 g (1 lb) tuna steak (1½ inches thick), very fresh
50 ml (2 fl oz) bottled Chinese oyster sauce
50 ml (2 fl oz) shao-hsing (Chinese rice wine)
115 g (4 oz) unsalted butter, cold
10 ml (2 tsp) Dijon mustard

peanut oil for shallow frying
chopped fresh chives for garnish
radish sprouts for garnish

1. Combine the ginger, sugar, soy sauce and sesame oil. Blend well. Coat the tuna with the mixture, place in a small bowl, cover tightly and marinate in the refrigerator for 24 hours.

2. *When ready to cook, make the sauce:* Combine the oyster sauce and the rice wine in a saucepan over high heat. Bring just to a boil, then reduce heat to low. Whisk in the butter, 15 g (½ oz) at a time and whisk until a glossy sauce is formed. Whisk in the mustard thoroughly. (If too thick, thin out with a little hot water.) Keep warm.

3. Place peanut oil in a very hot frying pan to a depth of 5 mm (¼ in). Dry off the marinated tuna thoroughly. Make sure the oil is smoking heavily over very high heat, then place the tuna in it. Sear the tuna for about 30 seconds on each side, or until a dark brown crust has formed. Remove from heat immediately. (Most of the tuna steak's interior should still be raw.)

4. With a very sharp knife, cut the tuna steak into slices that are approximately ⅓ inch thick. (You should have about 16 slices.) Place a puddle of the sauce on each of 4 dinner plates, top with tuna slices, then drizzle a little more sauce over the tuna. Top with chopped chives and/or radish sprouts and serve immediately.

MEDITERRANEAN TUNA BURGERS WITH AÏOLI

Tuna's resemblance to beef is really emphasised when you make 'hamburgers' out of it; like beef burgers, tuna burgers should be cooked rare to medium-rare. Unlike beef burgers—which have a wonderful, intrinsic flavour—the relatively tasteless tuna burgers are great when piqued by strong flavourings. This flavourful dish goes in a Mediterranean direction. It's delicious with aïoli—or one of the other mayonnaises (such as lemon or saffron) that appear in Chapter Nine.

MAKES 4 TUNA BURGERS

700 g (1½ lb) fresh tuna steaks or fillets
30 ml (2 tbsp) Dijon mustard
10 g (2 tsp) chopped fresh thyme
5 g (1 tsp) fennel seeds, ground in spice grinder
1.25 g (¼ tsp) cayenne pepper
2.5 g (½ tsp) salt
olive oil for coating the frying pan
4 sesame buns or muffins, toasted
90-120 ml (6-8 tbsp) aïoli (see page 494)

1. Trim tuna, removing skin, gristle and any dark meat. Chop by hand until tuna is the texture of coarse mince. Chop it as evenly as possible. Place in a large mixing bowl.

2. Combine mustard, thyme, ground fennel, cayenne and salt in a small mixing bowl. Stir well to combine. Add to the chopped tuna and fold together carefully, making sure the mustard is evenly distributed. Divide tuna into 4 balls and gently flatten into 2.5-g (1-in) thick patties.

3. Heat a large frying pan over moderately high heat. Coat bottom of frying pan with a thin film of olive oil. When oil is hot, cook patties for about 2 minutes per side, until golden on the outside and rare to medium-rare on the inside.

4. Serve on toasted buns or muffins, slathered with aïoli.

SHELLFISH

The shellfish family has three main groups: *crustaceans* (such as shrimp, lobster and crabs); *molluscs* (such as clams, mussels and oysters); and *cephalopods* (literally, creatures whose 'feet' come out of their heads—such as squid and octopus). Cephalopods don't have outer shells, like other shellfish, but they have hard inner parts that are vestiges of their shells.

In America, the crustaceans have always been wildly popular when cooked, though the cooking has always been simple; the latest crustacean trend is to cook them in more complex dishes, with more ethnic influences. The molluscs have always been wildly popular too, both cooked and raw. Lately, health concerns have led to a drop-off in popularity of the raw forms—but Americans have made up for this by embracing a wide range of ethnic ideas for cooked molluscs. The biggest change has been in cephalopods, which couldn't get arrested 20 years ago. Today, squid is very popular and octopus—led by sushi bars, Greek restaurants and Spanish restaurants—is starting to gain a tentacle-hold on our culinary imagination.

Here are some of our favourite shellfish.

CLAMS

Centuries before Americans had even heard of sushi bars, they were wolfing down their own brand of raw fish: clams. An abundance of clams in American waters made them a popular Native American food and they've been popular ever since. However, many Americans are not aware that there's a basic dichotomy in the clam world. Now more than ever, with American fishmongers featuring a wider variety of molluscs than ever before, it pays to know your clams.

The two groups of clams are hard-shell clams and soft-shell clams. It is the former group, the hard-shells, that have always been handed across the raw bars of America; soft-shell clams are never eaten raw. The soft-shells clams, particularly in New England, have been reserved for steaming and frying. However, cooks don't seem to mind substituting hard-shells for soft-shells in pots of steamed clams and other cooked dishes. This is often disastrous—because hard-shell clams, great as they are in a raw state, can easily turn to rubber when cooked.

Here's a guide to hard-shells and soft-shells and what you can do with each.

How to tell if clams are fresh

There's no getting around this basic fact: clams must be alive when you buy them. If they're not, don't buy them.

Hard-shell clams should be tightly shut. If they're slightly open, tap them; if they don't close, pass 'em by. Once they do close, try to move the top shell sideways across the bottom shell. If the clam resists, it's alive; if you can move the shell, the clam's not alive.

Soft-shell clams are never closed all the way, because the siphon sticks out. But when you touch the clam, you should see some movement in the siphon (usually, the clam retracts it). If the siphon doesn't move, don't buy the clam.

Your last line of defence is your nose. Dead clams usually have a foul, rotten odour. Fresh clams smell like the sea.

HARD-SHELL CLAMS

Quahogs Quahog is a confusing word, all-around. First of all, there's the pronunciation: despite the second vowel, quahog is pronounced CO-hog. Then: what does it mean? Some use it to mean any round, hard-shell, East Coast clam of the *Mercenaria mercenaria* family; in this usage, chowder clams, cherrystones and littlenecks are all quahogs. But in New England, the word is more commonly used to denote only the largest clams of the *Mercenaria mercenaria* family, which are also called chowder clams or ocean quahogs; these monsters can measure 10-12 cm (4-5 in) across and weigh over 225 g (8 oz) each. Chowder clams are far too large for eating raw, but—because they provide more clam for the buck than any other clam—are an excellent choice for dishes in which you need quickly cooked chopped clams. Shell 'em, chop the bellies and heat them no more than a minute or two (after that they toughen up).

Cherrystones Named after Cherrystone Creek, Virginia, these are the largest East Coast hard-shell clams that are eaten raw. Some clamheads prefer their heft at the raw bar; others find them too large to enjoy (we're in the latter group). For cooking, they perform similarly to quahogs (see above)—but, because they're much more expensive than quahogs, it's wiser to use quahogs when you need to quickly cook chopped clams. Not good for steamers.

Top Necks These are a step down in size from cherrystones and (to us) a perfect size for eating raw. Unfortunately, they're not as widely available as littlenecks. Not recommended for cooking. Not good for steamers.

Littlenecks These are the smallest clams of the *Mercenaria mercenaria* family. They are the most expensive, by weight, of clam meat; they're in demand because many people prefer to take their raw clams in the smallest doses. We marginally prefer top necks at the raw bar, if we can find 'em. We don't recommend littlenecks for cooking. Not good for steamers. Note: On the West Coast, another small hard-shell clam (*Protothaca staminea*) is also called a 'littleneck'. This is a better cooking clam than the East Coast littleneck.

Manila Clams Manila clams (*Tapes japonica*) came to the U.S. by accident; they were mixed in with a shipment of oysters from Japan that came to the West Coast about 100 years ago. Now, they are wildly popular on the West Coast and are turning up in good fishmongers in the rest of the country. With their colourful, ridged shells, they are among the most exciting clam discoveries you can make. Whenever you need to cook whole clams in their shells (as in paella or linguine with clam sauce), these are the ones to turn to; they're very sweet and very tender even after a few minutes of heat. They are possible for any steamed clam preparation—though we still prefer to use soft-shell clams as steamers.

New Zealand Cockles Also from across the Pacific, New Zealand cockles are smaller than Manila clams, but may be used in exactly the same ways. They are the only clams for which there is British equivalent—the cockle.

SOFT-SHELL CLAMS

Steamers People in the North-east call the *Mya arenaria* clam a steamer because they would never dream of using anything else for steamed clams. It looks entirely different from the hard-shell clam. Instead of a greyish shell, the shell is quite white. As the name implies, the shell is soft, brittle (though not soft enough to eat, as in a soft-shell crab). And a siphon sticks out of the shell, which the clam may unnervingly choose to retract—but at least this demonstrates that the clam's alive. Most important: steamers remain very tender when cooked, never turning rubbery. And, if you've got a good batch, they are the sweetest of all clams. In addition to steaming these clams, you can also remove them from the shell, flour them and deep-fry them (as they do in New England).

Razor Clams Razor clams are long clams, so named because they resemble an old-fashioned, long-handled barber's razor. The shells are not as brittle as steamer shells, but they are much softer than the shells of hard-shell clams. The East Coast variety (*Ensis directus*) and the West Coast variety (*Siliqua patula*) are not related to each other, but they are similar in taste and texture. They are good clams for steaming. We're especially fond of them in quickly cooked, stir-fried Asian dishes with strong-flavoured sauces (like razor clams with green chilli and black bean sauce). On the West Coast, chefs like to dredge their razor clam bellies in flour and deep-fry them.

Geoducks Also known as the King Clam (*Panopea generosa*), this monstrous clam (pronounced, oddly, g00-ee-duck) can grow up to 90 cm (3 ft) long and weigh up to 2.2 kg (5 lb). It has an enormous siphon, the only part of the clam that's eaten (it's very popular at sushi bars in slices). The siphon can also be chopped and used in cooked dishes.

When it comes to cooking clams, using soft-shell clams is a safe route to tenderness. All of the following recipes call for them. However, if all you have are the cockles available in the UK, you can make some selective substitutions.

CLASSIC STEAMED CLAMS

This great pile of shellfish makes a terrific light meal. After the clams are steamed, each diner gets a mound of them in a bowl, a mug of clam broth and a small dish of melted butter (if you wish). Serve some bread, or potatoes and a pitcher of beer. If your steamers seem gritty, a few hours before cooking them you should fill a pot with water, add a cup of cornmeal to it and place the clams in the water. This will force them to disgorge some grit.

SERVES 4

4 celery stalks with leaves
1 bunch parsley
2.7 kg (6 lb) soft-shell clams
225 g (8 oz) unsalted butter (optional)

1. Place 2 litres (3½ pints) water in a large, wide pot over high heat. Add the celery and parsley and bring water to a boil. Add the clams, all at once (the water should not cover them). Cover the pot and cook until the clams swing open, about 5 to 10 minutes. Every 2 minutes or so, shake the pot gently so that the clams have even exposure to the heat. (Do not overcook.)

2. Using a skimmer or a large slotted spoon, place the clams in 4 large serving bowls. Strain the clam broth into 4 large mugs. Melt the butter, if using and pour into 4 small dishes. Serve immediately.

How to eat steamed clams

The main concern is ridding the clams of any remaining dirt or grit, which would be unpalatable to chew. This is why mugs of clam broth are served. You open a clam and remove the meaty part. Then, grabbing the siphon (or the 'squirter'), you pull the firm outer rim away from the centre of the clam; now, while you're holding the unfurled rim by the squirter, the rest of the rim runs down like a ribbon to the soft belly. The soft belly should dangle, like a yo-yo on a string. There may be grit throughout the rim. So you dunk the whole clam, belly and rim, several times, in the hot clam broth. This should clean the clam immaculately.

Next question: how much of the clam are you going to eat? Some people just pop the whole thing in their mouths. Some people bite everything up to the siphon, leaving the siphon behind. We say: the siphon's good eatin'—except that it has an unattractive skin around it. Simply peel off the skin and pop everything that remains, including the peeled siphon, in your mouth.

Before doing so, some people like to dip the clam in butter. As with lobster, it does add a wonderful extra taste. But if your clams are wonderful to begin with, you may want to forgo the extra dunk.

There's no reason, however, not to sip the clam broth right from the mug as the meal progresses. Just avoid the grit at the bottom of the cup.

THAI STEAMERS

In Thailand, tender little clams are often served with a coconut milk-and-basil sauce. Those flavours transpose well into this remarkable version of steamed clams. We like it best when made with the traditional soft-shelled steamer clams, but it's also delicious with cockles.

SERVES 4 AS A FIRST COURSE

350 ml (12 fl oz) chicken stock
30 ml (2 tbsp) Thai fish sauce
30 ml (2 tbsp) lemon juice

45 g (3 tbsp) chopped lemongrass
5-cm (2-in) piece galingale, peeled and cut into
    slivers
1 small fresh red chilli , finely sliced
350 ml (12 fl oz) coconut milk
2 kaffir lime leaves, rolled up and finely sliced
32 soft-shell clams
50 g (2 oz) firmly packed small fresh basil leaves

1. Combine chicken stock, fish sauce, lemon juice, lemongrass, galingale and chilli in a large saucepan and bring to a boil. Reduce heat and simmer for 10 minutes. Add coconut milk and lime leaves and simmer, stirring occasionally, for another 5 minutes.

2. Scrub clams under cold running water and discard any that are open. Put them into the coconut broth and simmer gently, adding the basil leaves about halfway through the cooking, until clams open, about 6 minutes. Shake the pan occasionally so the clams cook evenly.

3. Place 8 clams in each of 4 bowls. Ladle broth into bowls and serve immediately.

CLAM HASH

This is an old-time American comfort-food classic that achieved new popularity in the eighties with the rise of high-level, informal American dining—and the discovery that 'hash' is 'cool' (but watch out for 'foie gras hash,' and others of that forced-concept ilk). We love the play here of the soft steamer bellies against the crunchy potatoes. To turn this into a great brunch or luncheon main course, slip a few poached or fried eggs on top.

SERVES 4 AS A FIRST COURSE

350 g (12 oz) diced potatoes
1.3 kg (3 lb) soft-shell clams
25 g (1 oz) unsalted butter
10 g (2 tsp) finely chopped garlic

45 g (3 tbsp) finely chopped yellow onion

7.5 g (1½ tsp) salt

2.5 g (½ tsp) ground black pepper

30 g (2 tbsp) diced red pepper

30 g (2 tbsp) diced green pepper

pinch of cayenne pepper

pinch of paprika

1. Boil the potatoes in salted water until just tender, about 15 minutes. Drain in a colander and run cold water over the potatoes. Reserve.

2. Put 2 cm (¾ in) water in the bottom of a deep casserole and place a steamer rack over it. Bring water to a boil, put one third of the clams on the rack and cover with a tight fitting lid. Cook for about 4 to 5 minutes, until clams have opened wide. Remove clams from rack and set aside. Cook the remaining clams in 2 batches. When cool enough to handle, remove the meat from the shells, chop coarsely and reserve. (You will have about 225 g (8 oz) clam meat.)

3. Melt 15 g (½ oz) of the butter in a large frying pan over high heat. When butter is hot, add garlic, onion and salt and sauté for 2 minutes, until light golden. Add the rest of the butter and, when melted, add the reserved potatoes and black pepper. Sauté for about 6 to 7 minutes, shaking the pan occasionally, until the potatoes are crisp and well browned.

4. Add red and green peppers, cayenne, paprika and the reserved clam meat. Stir and cook for 2 minutes. Adjust seasoning and serve immediately.

Note: If you prefer a crispier top, you could pass the hash under a preheated grill for a few minutes.

CRABS

Wherever oceans are near, crab-eating abounds. And we in America, with our access to two large oceans and one large gulf, are particularly blessed in the fresh crab department; we'd go so far as to say that North America is the world's greatest crabby continent.

Of course, the actual eating of fresh crabs in America, out of the shell, has been more or less confined, historically, to the coastal areas; the rest of the country has traditionally made do with various types of frozen, refrigerated and canned crab. In fact, most Americans have always been reluctant to roll up their sleeves and get on with the messy business that is real crab-eating: cracking shells, extracting meat, sucking the remains for juice.

However, with the rise of seafood savvy—not to mention the infusion of cooking ideas from various ethnic cuisines—the distribution and consumption of fresh whole crab all around the country is on the rise. The idea of the Maryland crab house has caught on, with many restaurants in major cities now presenting that shell-crackin', finger-lickin' phenomenon. Cajun restaurants, newly popular in the eighties, often present New Orleans–style crab boils. And Chinese restaurants around the country feature a range of Cantonese crab dishes, which require the American diner to follow the lead of those Chinese families at the large round tables who are extracting crab meat like surgeons.

We are foursquare behind this whole-crab movement, as is every real crab-lover in America. But one major controversy divides this group: which is the best crab from American waters? Here's the roster of candidates.

Blue Crabs There's no controversy among us at Dean & DeLuca—*this* is America's greatest crab. In fact, we nominate it for greatest crab in the world. No crab that we've ever tasted matches the sweetness of blue crab meat at its best—or the deep flavour that blue crab tomalley and roe add to the experience. Of course, the crab is relatively small—usually no more than 7.5 cm (3 in) up the middle of the crab—and this makes the pickin' a little difficult. But it's worth the trouble. Blue crabs—named for the colouration of the shell before cooking (they turn red after)—are caught all the way from north-eastern Canada down to the Gulf of Mexico. The epicentre of the industry, of course, is the Chesapeake Bay in Maryland, where the best crabs come from. Good for steaming and boiling whole, or for cutting up and frying in full flavoured dishes. Incidentally, these are the crabs that become soft-shell crabs when they moult (see page 326).

Dungeness Crabs Most West Coast crab-lovers just laugh when you say Maryland blue crabs are America's best. Frustrated by the micro-picking process, they always proclaim the superiority of the West Coast's much larger Dungeness crab (often 15 cm (6 in) across the back). But is bigger better? The quality of the Dungeness meat is very, very good—but it lacks the extra measure of sweetness and fattiness that blue crab has at its best. Dungeness crab is named after the small town of Dungeness on Washington State's Olympia Peninsula where the commercial industry began. Very little comes from Dungeness today, however; the crab is caught from northern California all the way up to Alaska. The best of all comes from Alaska; its meat seems slightly sweeter. Good for steaming and boiling whole, or for cutting up and sautéing in full-flavoured dishes.

Stone Crabs These popular crabs, always associated with Florida, are actually caught from the Carolinas all the way around to Texas. You probably won't get the opportunity to cook them, however. After they're brought on board, the large claw of each crab is twisted off and usually cooked on the spot; it is the cooked claws of stone crabs that come to the fishmonger. The rest of the crab is thrown back into the water, where it will regenerate the claw. Stone crab claws feature meat that's easy to get at; a pile of them, chilled, makes a good appetiser. Frankly, however, stone crab claw meat is not the most exciting crab meat: it tends to be on the stringy-watery side, often lacking in sweetness and flavour.

King Crabs Now here's a Western crab we'd get really excited about—if its availability throughout the United States were wider. In fact, fresh king crab is available only in Alaska. They're just too big to ship elsewhere; though king crabs average 4.5 kg (10 lb) or so, they can go up to 12 kg (25 lb) and 180 cm (6 feet) across! The vast majority of king crab is cooked in Alaska and frozen; the large, meaty legs are then shipped around the country. These sweet, easy-to-eat frozen legs give you some idea of how wonderful this crab would be if you could get it fresh.

Snow Crabs Much smaller than king crabs (about 1.3 kg (3 lb) on average), snow crabs are the northern Pacific member of the spider crab family that also provide good, frozen leg meat. But again, like king crabs, they are not easy to find fresh.

If you can't find fresh crabs at your fish market and wish to use this marvellous crustacean in its other commercial forms, here's what you'll encounter.

Refrigerated Cooked Crabmeat This can be a very fine substitute for fresh crab—and much easier for making crab cakes, because the meat is already picked out of the shells. *But you must find a recently packed tin or plastic container of high-quality crabmeat.* The best is from Maryland blue crab and the best designation on these containers is *lump meat,* which means the meat comes from the body and is in large chunks; this is the crème de la crème of picked-over crabmeat and will cost you at least $20 (£12) a pound. *Backfin* means that the chunks are smaller. *Flaked* means that the pieces can come from anywhere in the crab and are smaller and less desirable still. Combinations of all of the above may carry idiosyncratic designations, like 'mixed' or 'special'. How do you know if the refrigerated crabmeat is fresh? Ask your fishmonger. If it's not, the first whiff after opening the container will tell you.

Frozen Cooked Crabmeat There are many forms of frozen, shell-less crabmeat in commercial distribution.

Generally speaking, they are inferior in taste and texture to refrigerated cooked crabmeat.

Frozen Cooked Crab Legs These usually come from Alaskan king crab and are very tasty for frozen crabmeat. Heat before using; grilling or steaming both work well. Expensive.

Refrigerated Cooked Crab Claws These will most likely be from stone crabs. A decent choice for crab cocktails.

Canned, Cooked, Unrefrigerated Crabmeat Forget it.

Pasteurised Crabmeat This is an attempt to bring 'fresh,' picked-over crabmeat to the consumer—but the crabmeat has been immersed in a hot-water bath. We're not fond of it.

Surimi Properly speaking, this doesn't even belong in this list—because it's not crabmeat. Many sushi bars brazenly call it 'crab' but it should be called 'imitation crab'. It's in supermarkets, too, sometimes labelled as 'crabsticks'. It is cheap fish—usually Alaskan pollack—that has been flash-frozen, chopped and turned into a paste through the addition of egg white, sugar, salt, starch and a few industrial ingredients. Sometimes, a concentrate made from cooked crab shells is added to it for a little crab flavour. Then it's luridly dyed, so the outside mimics the red of a cooked crab's shell. When finished, it's a bland, over-sweet, stringy imitation of crabmeat (now it even comes in other shellfish 'flavours'). Well, we must confess it tastes okay in a California roll at a sushi bar—but if you've ever had one made with real crab, you won't go back. We generally avoid it.

WHOLE CRABS

In the whole crab universe, there's nothing like whole crabs. Yes, there's some time and inconvenience involved in cracking them open and extracting the meat.

But you must learn to look at that process as part of the fun. With a newspaper-covered table, an army of mallets and crackers, a few jugs of beer and a lazy summer afternoon—what better way could there be to spend your time?

PLAIN BOILED CRABS

This is the simplest way imaginable to cook blue crabs—in water only, with no seasoning. Some may miss the fire of Maryland or Cajun spicing, but this method really allows the delicate flavour of the crabs to come through. Serve them at room temperature a few hours after cooking, if you like the tenderness of the meat. Or, refrigerate them overnight and serve the next day, if you like the additional flavour added by congealed crab juices. We marginally prefer the latter.

MAKES ENOUGH CRABS FOR 4 MODERATELY HUNGRY DINERS AT A CRAB DINNER

24 large, live blue crabs

1. Bring an enormous pot of salted water to a boil. As quickly as you can, put the live crabs into the water. You can do this with tongs or, if the crabs are in a bag or crate, you can try spilling the contents directly into the pot. (With claws snapping all around you, it's a messy process.)

2. Cover the pot immediately. Return to a boil, reduce the heat and simmer crabs until the meat is done, about 8 minutes after the water has returned to a boil.

3. Remove crabs from pot and chill in refrigerator a few hours (if you like them not very cold) or overnight (if you like them cold).

SPICED STEAMED CRABS, MARYLAND-STYLE

This is another simple recipe—but very different from the plain boiled crabs. Here, the crabs get a thick, spicy paste on the outside and, so that the paste sticks, the crabs are steamed rather than boiled. This is the way they're done in the great crab houses of Maryland. Then, the crabs are served hot, right out of the steamer— which means they're as juicy as can be. Our recipe includes our own homemade seasoning mixture for the crabs; if you prefer, however, you could substitute 180 g (12 tbsp) of Old Bay's widely available spice mixture for crabs.

MAKES ENOUGH CRABS FOR 4 MODERATELY HUNGRY DINERS AT A CRAB DINNER

water and vinegar
For the spice mixture
45 g (3 tbsp) black peppercorns
2 small dried red chillies
10 g (2 tsp) cayenne pepper
30 g (2 tbsp) coriander
20 g (4 tsp) brown mustard seeds
50 g (½ tsp) allspice
8 cloves
8 bay leaves
30 g (2 tbsp) celery seed
20 g (4 tsp) dill seed
5 g (1 tsp) salt
24 large, live blue crabs

1. Place enough water and vinegar, in equal proportions, in the bottom of a large, wide steamer. Place steamer over high heat and bring the liquid to a boil.

2. *While the liquid is coming to a boil, make the spice mixture:* Place all the ingredients for the spice mixture in a spice grinder and grind until a coarse powder is formed.

3. Place one quarter of the live crabs in the sink and douse them with cold water. Sprinkle one quarter of the spice mixture over all, making as much of the mixture as possible stick to the crabs. Place the crabs in a steamer rack and place rack over boiling liquid. Cook until just

done, about 15 minutes. Repeat with the remaining crabs, either by piling up more steamer racks on the same steamer base or by reusing the same steamer rack.

4. Serve immediately.

CUT CRABS

Another fabulous way to deal with raw crabs is to cut them into pieces (or have the cruel fishmonger do it) and sauté the shell-on pieces with strong accompanying flavours. This can be the basis of many a fabulous Chinese, Thai, Korean, Malaysian, Indian, Cajun, or Mexican dish. You can use either raw blue crabs or raw Dungeness crabs.

CRABS CANTONESE

This is one of our favourite dishes in Cantonese restaurants, where it is also called *crab soong*. Basically, it's made with the same sauce as prawns with lobster sauce: a rich, pork-flecked, egg-thickened creation that tastes great with shellfish. In the crab dish, the sauce is usually darkened by a little soy sauce.

SERVES 4 AS PART OF A CHINESE DINNER

(3 tbsp) fermented black beans
4 oz (¼ lb) ground pork
8 large garlic cloves, chopped
10 ml (2 tsp) thin soy sauce
4 g (¾ tsp) sugar
2 large dried Chinese mushrooms, soaked in warm
 water for 1 hour
2.5 g (½ tsp) monosodium glutamate (optional)
30 ml (2 tbsp) peanut oil
2 spring onions, chopped
30 g (2 tbsp) grated fresh ginger
6 raw blue crabs
30 ml (2 tbsp) shao-hsing (Chinese rice wine)
125 ml (4 fl oz) pork or chicken stock

20 g (1½ tbsp) cornflour

2 eggs, loosely beaten

1.25 ml (¼ tsp) Asian sesame oil

1. Place the black beans in a small bowl and cover with hot water. Soak for 15 minutes.

2. Place the ground pork in a mixing bowl. Take 2.5 g (½ tsp) of the chopped garlic, mash it to a paste and add it to the pork. Add 5 ml (1 tsp) of the soy sauce and 1.25 g (¼ tsp) of the sugar. Remove the mushrooms from the soaking water and mince to a fine paste. Add to the pork mixture with the monosodium glutamate, if using. Blend well and reserve.

3. Place a large wok over the highest heat. After 1 minute, add the peanut oil. After another minute, add the remaining chopped garlic, half the chopped spring onions and the grated ginger. Stir-fry for 1 minute. Remove the black beans from their soaking liquid, smash them with the side of a cleaver and add to the wok.

4. Push the black bean mixture to the side of the wok and add the reserved pork mixture, breaking it up into small lumps. When the pork is just cooked through (about 1 minute), push to the side of the wok.

5. Twist off the large crab claws and remove the broad top shell of the crabs. Cut the remaining crab bodies into 2 halves (or have the fishmonger do this just before you bring them home). Add all crab pieces (including the top shells) to the wok and stir-fry over high heat until crabs are just cooked, about 2 to 3 minutes.

6. While the crab is cooking, heat the shao-hsing, the stock, the rest of the soy sauce and the rest of the sugar in a small saucepan until boiling.

7. When the crab is cooked, stir everything together in the wok and add the boiling stock mixture. Return to a boil. Mix the cornflour in a small bowl with just enough water to make a liquid with the consistency of double cream. Swirl some of it in to the wok—just enough to make a medium-thick sauce.

8. Remove wok from heat and add eggs. Stir well until eggs are heated but still runny, just lightly thickened. Add the sesame oil. Turn out onto a serving platter, sprinkle with remaining spring onions and serve immediately.

CRABMEAT

PERFECT CRAB CAKES

The key to a great crab cake is the crab. You want it to be top-quality lump crabmeat and you don't want a lot of filler in the cake to interfere with the crab's subtle taste. But holding back on the filler creates a cooking problem, because crabmeat by itself (without binder) tends to fall apart in the frying pan as you're cooking it. This miraculous recipe offers the solution: there's no bread of any kind in it, but the crab cakes stay together because they're cooked on a baking sheet in the oven. These crab cakes have the additional virtue of being lighter than the usual cakes, because they don't soak up butter or oil in a frying pan . And if you use wonderful, fresh crabmeat, you'll get nothing but a wonderful, fresh crabmeat flavour. Make sure that when you pick over the crabmeat you do it gently and carefully, leaving the crab in the largest pieces possible. We like these beauties served with lemon wedges only. But if you want more dazzle on the side, use either the pico de gallo on page 483, the tarragon tartar sauce on page 494, or the lemon mayonnaise on page 493.

SERVES 4

rapeseed or safflower oil for oiling the baking sheet

175 ml (6 fl oz) thick mayonnaise

50 ml (2 fl oz) sour cream

30 ml (2 tbsp) whole-grain mustard
1 large egg, lightly beaten
900 g (2 lb) lump crabmeat, picked over to remove
  cartilage
lemon wedges as an accompaniment

1. Preheat oven to 200°C (400°F) and lightly oil a
baking sheet.

2. *Prepare the crab cakes:* Whisk together the
mayonnaise, sour cream, mustard and egg in a mixing
bowl until combined well. Gently fold in the crab with a
rubber spatula until just combined.

3. Shape the mixture into eight 2.5-cm (1-in) thick
cakes and transfer to the baking sheet.

4. Bake the crab cakes for 15 minutes or so, or until
lightly golden. Run a spatula under them once or twice
to make sure they're not sticking. When the cakes are
ready, place them under a preheated grill for 2 to 3
minutes, or until they're lightly browned on top. Remove
from grill and let stand on the baking sheet for 5
minutes. Serve with the lemon wedges.

SOFT-SHELL CRABS

This is one of the great American treats. We've seen
something similar in only one other place: in Venice,
Italy, where an Adriatic crab with a rounded body is
brought to the market soft. But it is our soft-shell crab
that's famous to seafood-lovers around the world.

The blue crabs of the Eastern seaboard shed their
shells about 20 times during their lives. Just a few hours
after shedding (or 'moulting'), the crab begins to grow a
new hard shell if it remains in the water. So an East
Coast industry has grown around the prevention of that
new growth: just-moulted blue crabs are plucked from
the water and sent live to the market. That entire soft-
shell crab is edible.

When you purchase them, make sure they're alive;

soft-shells survive for only a few days out of the water.
You can choose from small ones (called 'hotels' in the
trade) to very large ones (called 'whales'); we think the
small ones have better texture and flavour. Have the
fishmonger clean them—or do it yourself by cutting off
the eyes and mouth with a scissor, removing the gills on
both sides of the crab under the shell and removing the
'apron' from the underside (it looks something like a
catcher's chest protector). Cook them immediately for
maximum flavour, or hold cleaned ones for as long as 2
days in the refrigerator. You can also freeze soft-shell
crabs that you've cleaned. They freeze reasonably well;
in fact, you can buy frozen soft-shells at any time of
year. But we like the fresh ones best, in season (which
used to be May through June and now seems to be
February to September).

Cooking them is a little tricky. The main problem is
that, unless treated properly, they can be kind of
formless and watery after cooking. We like methods that
crisp up that soft shell. Grilling them works extremely
well. Deep-frying is another fabulous method—
especially if you use Japanese Panko crumbs (see page
295 for the coating). Our favourite way to cook them in a
pan is a bit unusual, but works wonderfully well: it's
cooking them under a brick.

BRICK-WEIGHTED SOFT-SHELL CRABS WITH LIME-GARLIC MOJO

The brick squeezes out all the excess water in the crab
and forces the side of the crab that's against the hot
pan to become extremely crisp. When you cut into a
brick-weighted soft-shell crab, it's like cutting into a
crispy piece of lobster meat. You can serve the crabs
just as they are, or with melted butter—or with this
delicious garlic-and-citrus sauce, adapted from Cuban
cuisine.

SERVES 4

12 small soft-shell crabs
salt and pepper to taste

450 ml (16 fl oz) buttermilk

For the mojo

15 ml (1 tbsp) olive oil

4 garlic cloves, finely chopped

100 ml (3½ fl oz) freshly squeezed lime juice

salt and pepper to taste

30 g (2 tbsp) chopped fresh coriander

butter for shallow-frying

flour for dredging

1. Season the crabs with salt and pepper and place in the buttermilk. Soak for 1 hour. Remove and pat dry.

2. *While the crabs are soaking, prepare the mojo:* Place the olive oil in a small, heavy saucepan over moderately low heat. Add the garlic and cook slowly for 5 minutes, or until golden, not brown. Add the lime juice, stir and bring to a boil. Remove from heat, season with salt and pepper and add the coriander. Refrigerate until cool.

3. *To prepare crabs:* Lightly dredge the crabs in the flour. Melt the butter in a pan or pans large enough to hold the crabs in a single layer over moderately high heat. (There should be a thin layer of butter in each pan.) After the foam subsides, add the crabs. Immediately place a heavy weight (like a brick or a heavy pan) over them. Cook for 3 minutes, turn each crab over and again top with the weights. Cook for 3 minutes more. Remove from heat. Dab each crab with some of the mojo. Serve immediately, 3 to a portion.

LOBSTER

Compared to other areas of seafood activity in the United States, the lobster game has remained relatively stable: we still love lobsters, we still consume lots of them simply cooked in restaurants and we still have perhaps the finest lobsters in the world (*Homarus americanus,* sometimes called Maine lobster).

Two new wrinkles have been introduced, however.

For one thing, innovative American chefs—inspired chiefly by the shellfish repertoire of Asian cuisines—have been taking advantage of lobster's rich flavour by pairing it with other bold tastes. And Americans have generally become more savvy about the condition of live lobsters in the market. Once upon a time, many of the 'live' ones were nearly dead; today, most shoppers know to look for strong vital signs (claws waving and tails flapping) before making a purchase. Additionally, there is a growing awareness that the treatment of lobsters in the last days of their lives affects their flavour at the table; some chefs go so far as to insist that their lobsters not be overcrowded, or 'stressed out' in any way, as they await their dates with culinary destiny.

Here are a few more tips for lobster buyers:

- 'Maine' lobsters are harvested all the way from Newfoundland down to the Carolinas. Should you expect better quality from the ones actually harvested in Maine? No one has ever proved that this is the case. More important than origin, we feel, is lobster freshness. So if you're in New Jersey, near the shore and you're offered a just-caught local lobster, do not hold out for one from Maine.
- We prefer female lobsters to male lobsters. The main difference is the roe (red when cooked) that's present in females; it's great to eat. Some also feel that females are a little sweeter and more tender. You can tell which ones are females by looking at the underside of the lobster, at about the midpoint of the lobster; the females have a wider girth, with little legs that are softer and furrier than male legs. Ask your fishmonger for a positive ID.
- There's a persistent rumour that small lobsters (around 450 g (1 lb)) are sweeter and more tender than large lobsters. We don't believe it; some of the 1.3 kg (3 lb) we've consumed have been among the best we've ever tasted. By the way, though many people seem to find a 550-g (1¼-lb) lobster a decent portion for one person, we always opt for 1 kg (2½ lb) per person if the pocketbook allows.

- If you're buying live lobsters to obtain lobster meat for a recipe, on average it takes about 6 pounds of live lobster to yield 450 g (1 lb) lobster meat. Keep in mind, however, that lobsters are meatier in the winter, at which time only 2 kg (4½ lb) of lobster may yield a 450 g (1 lb) meat. In the late summer, it may take as much as 4 kg (9 lb) of lobster to yield a 450 g (1 lb) of meat.
- There is a significant difference in the quality of the meat between lobsters that have recently moulted, or discarded their shells (these are known as 'soft-shell' lobsters) and lobsters with hard shells. The meat from soft-shell lobsters is generally sweeter and more tender—though the lobster may be more watery. You can simply press the lobster at the fishmonger with your fingers to find out if the shell is hard, or if it gives a little.
- Once you've purchased live lobsters, you should use them as quickly as possible. Until you do, keep them in the refrigerator, preferably covered with a damp cloth. Do *not* immerse them in water. Most live lobsters will survive for 24 hours in the refrigerator, but should be used within 12 just in case. Cooked lobster meat will last for 4 days in a cold refrigerator.

Lobster sizes
Here are the terms used by the Maine Department of Marine Resources to describe lobster size:

450 g (1 lb) : chickens
450-500 g (1 lb to 1⅛ lb): heavy chickens
525 g (1¼ lb): quarters
650-800 g (1½-1¾ lb): selects
900 g (2 lb): deuces
900 g-1 kg (2-2¼ lb): heavy selects
1 kg-1.1 kg (2¼-2½ lb): small jumbos
1kg-1.8 kg+ (2½ lb-4 lb+): jumbos

WHOLE LOBSTER
To hard-core lobster-lovers, there's simply no choice: lobsters must be purchased live, cooked whole and unadorned and eaten out of the shell. This is the primal lobster experience and many lobster-lovers go through life eating lobsters in no other way.

However, these lobsterites are divided by one major issue: should you boil or grill the creature? To New Englanders, grilling a lobster is something only a crazed New Yorker would consider. But in the steakhouses of New York City, which also do a lively trade in whole lobsters, the way to go is invariably under the grill.

BOILED LOBSTER
Lobsters cooked in water, or over water, *are* delicious. They remain optimally moist and juicy this way and no flavours derived from the cooking process impose themselves on the pure flavour of lobster. Moreover, it's easy as pie to do. We like to add lots of salt to the water, approximating the tang of seawater (in which roadside Maine lobster shacks cook their lobsters); seawater contains 2½ to 3 percent salt. French fries, lemon wedges and coleslaw are perfect accompaniments.

SERVES 4

10 litres (17½ pints) water
150 g (5 oz) salt
4 live lobsters (each 550 g-1.3 kg (1¼ to 3 lb))

1. Place the water and salt in a very large pot (it should be no more than three-quarters full of water). Cover and bring to a very rapid boil.

2. Add the lobsters, 1 at a time and cover. Bring the water back to a boil as quickly as possible. After the water returns to a boil, reduce the heat, cover and simmer the lobsters gently. For soft-shell lobsters, it will take about 12 minutes to cook a 550-g (1¼-lb) lobster after the water has returned to a boil. For lobsters that are 700 g (1½ lb) to 900 g (2 lb), allow 15 to 18 minutes after the return. For lobsters that are 1 kg (2½ lb) to 2.25 kg (5 lb), allow 20 to 25 minutes after the return. (If you're cooking hard-shell lobsters, plan to cook them a few extra minutes.)

3. Remove lobsters from the pot and let cool for a few minutes. Serve 1 lobster per person.

GRILLED LOBSTER, NEW YORK RESTAURANT STYLE

Perhaps we're influenced by our New York environment—but we have to admit that grilling a lobster and charring the shell, does add an attractive extra measure of crustacean flavour. Unfortunately, many cooks who try to achieve this result end up drying out the lobster in the process. But a technique we learned from the New York steak houses offers the best of both worlds: by boiling then grilling the lobster, you get juicy lobster *with* that extra measure of grilled flavour.

SERVES 4

4 live lobsters (each about 700 g (1½ lb))
melted butter
115 g (4 oz) buttered breadcrumbs (optional)

1. Preheat grill.

2. Fill a large pot with salted water. Bring to a boil and immediately add the lobsters. Cook for 7 minutes.

3. Remove the lobsters, split them and brush with melted butter. Grill the lobsters, sprinkling the tomalley with buttered breadcrumbs during the last minute of cooking, for 7 to 8 minutes or just until the meat is cooked and the top is nicely browned.

CUT LOBSTER

Live lobster that's cut into serving pieces, then sautéed or stir-fried with bold flavours, is a great way to enjoy lobster—though it would be anathema in Maine. For the rest of the world, the only problem this method poses is cutting up the live lobster; it's a job that makes even the non-squeamish squirm. However, if you're relatively comfortable with your position in the food chain, you can always ask your fishmonger to perform the task for you. Just make sure to use the freshly cut lobster pieces within a few hours.

STIR-FRIED SZECHUAN LOBSTER WITH CHILLI SAUCE

This spicy number is one of our favourite dishes in the whole Chinese repertory. It's also delicious when made with crab or prawns—but we like it best with lobster.

SERVES 4 AS PART OF A CHINESE DINNER

30 ml (2 tbsp) hoisin sauce
30 ml (2 tbsp) chilli sauce*
10 ml (2 tsp) shao-hsing†
5 ml (1 tsp) thin soy sauce
5 ml (1 tsp) fish sauce
5 ml (1 tsp) chilli paste with garlic
2.5 g (½ tsp) sugar
2.5 g (½ tsp) monosodium glutamate (optional)
2.5 ml (½ tsp) sesame oil
2.5 ml (½ tsp) chilli oil
75 ml (2½ fl oz) peanut oil
2 live lobsters (each about 550 g (1¼ lb) each,
    each cut into 8 serving pieces
salt to taste
30 g (2 tbsp) finely chopped fresh ginger
4 fat spring onions, white and green parts, chopped
45 g (3 tbsp) finely chopped garlic
3 dried red chilli peppers

*You can use good old American supermarket chilli sauce for this dish, the stuff that's very much like ketchup; they use something similar in Chinese cooking.

†Shao-hsing is rice wine, and is available in Chinese liquor stores. Dry sherry is a good substitute.

1. *Prepare the sauce:* mix together the hoisin sauce, chilli sauce, shao-hsing, soy sauce, fish sauce, chilli paste with garlic, sugar, monosodium glutamate (if desired), sesame oil, hot chilli oil and ½ teaspoon of the peanut oil. Reserve.

2. Add the remaining ¼ cup of peanut oil to a large, very hot wok over very high heat and heat until the oil is smoking. Salt the cut lobster pieces lightly and add them to the hot wok. Sear the cut surfaces until the lobster is just about cooked, 3 to 4 minutes. Remove the lobster pieces and place them on a platter. (Or, place them on paper towels to drain some of the oil.)

3. To the oil remaining in the wok, add the ginger, spring onions, garlic and dried chillies. Stir-fry for 1 minute. Add the lobster pieces and toss to blend well. Add the reserved sauce and toss to blend well. Turn the mixture out onto a platter and serve immediately.

LOBSTER MEAT

Fresh-cooked lobster meat is delicious and blends very well with all kinds of other flavours. Though some diners miss the joy of extracting the meat from the shells at table, others find the ease of shell-less lobster meat a great relief.

NEW ENGLAND LOBSTER ROLLS

The name of this dish suggests something complicated, architectural. But first-time visitors to New England are always amazed to discover that a lobster roll . . . is just lobster salad on a roll! And usually a hot dog roll, at that! But don't underestimate those Yankees; they know that when you've got great, fresh lobster, you don't need a fancy dish. We suggest boiling your own live lobster for this Maine treat: 2 hard-shell lobsters that are about 1 kg (2¼ lb) each will give you approximately 450 g (1 lb) lobster meat. You could buy cooked lobster meat, but it probably won't be as fresh-tasting; it might even have

been made from lobsters that died in the tank, in which case it won't taste good at all. You could, of course, one-up the Down-Easters by gussying up the dish a bit. We know a place on eastern Long Island that adds capers to its lobster roll; we have a friend who puts tomato and fresh basil on hers; and we have been known to substitute a tasty lemon-mayonnaise from California called Lemonaise (made by The Ojai Cook and carried at Dean & DeLuca) for good old Hellman's. Mostly, though, we're cranky Yankees who like it just the way they do it in Maine: simple cold lobster on a simple hot bun.

MAKES 4 LOBSTER ROLLS

450 g (1 lb) cooked lobster meat, cut into coarse
   chunks
50 g (2 oz) celery cut into the size of gambling dice
50 ml (2 fl oz) mayonnaise (preferably Hellman's)
salt and pepper to taste
pinch of sweet paprika
butter for greasing the griddle and the buns
4 hot dog buns

1. Blend the lobster meat in a bowl with the celery and mayonnaise. Add a few drops of cold water to smooth out the mixture. Season well with salt and pepper and add the paprika. Place in refrigerator until mixture is very cold.

2. Grease a griddle or a cast-iron frying pan over moderate heat with a little butter. Open the hot dog buns (without separating the two halves of each one). Smear a little butter on the outside of each bun, then place them on the hot griddle or in the hot frying pan , spread open, exterior side down. Place a weight on the buns (a heavy pan will do). Cook until the exteriors are golden, about 1 minute. Remove buns.

3. Fill each bun with one quarter of the lobster mixture, sprinkle with paprika and serve immediately.

LOBSTER SAUSAGE

Sausage made with lobster meat became one of the hot restaurant items of the eighties—though so many restaurant sausages we've tasted have been pebbly, without the necessary juiciness or richness. This is a delicious version of the dish and not hard to make. If you're not used to preparing homemade sausage, read the sausagemaking instructions on page 459.

MAKES 4 LINKS, 6 INCHES EACH

225 g (8 oz) scallops, shelled
1 large egg white
3 g (¾ tsp) salt
pinch of ground white pepper
pinch of freshly grated nutmeg
105 ml (7 tbsp) double cream
1 kg (2¼-lb) lobster
225 g (8 oz) shiitake mushrooms, stems discarded
    and the mushrooms wiped clean
8 ml (½ tbsp) olive oil
50 g (2 oz) finely diced black forest ham
5 g (1 tsp) chopped fresh tarragon
75 cm (30 in) pork casing

1. Put scallops and egg white in the bowl of a food processor and pulse until just combined, about 10 seconds. (Do not overprocess or the scallops will be tough when cooked.) Add 1.25 g (¼ tsp) of the salt, white pepper and nutmeg and stir. Cover and refrigerate for 1 hour, so that the scallops firm up slightly. After an hour, gently fold the cream into the scallops, a little at a time. Cover and refrigerate for another 2 hours.

2. Preheat oven to 180°C (350°F).

3. Steam the lobster, covered, for 8 minutes, until the shell is bright red. (The meat will be slightly undercooked.) When the shell is cool enough to handle, crack open the claws and tail and remove the meat. Discard the tomalley or coral. Coarsely chop the meat .

4. Place shiitake mushrooms on a roasting tin and brush lightly with the olive oil. Sprinkle with 1.25 g (¼ tsp) of the salt. Roast in the oven until tender, about 15 to 20 minutes. When cool, cut into 3-mm (⅛-in) slivers and then coarsely chop. (The mushrooms should be chopped slightly finer than the lobster meat.) Set aside.

5. In a large bowl combine the scallop mousse with the lobster meat, the mushrooms, the ham, the tarragon and 1.25 g (¼ tsp) of the salt. Gently stir together. To test for seasoning, poach 15 g (1 tbsp) of the mixture in gently simmering water for about 2 minutes. Taste and adjust quantities of salt, pepper and nutmeg accordingly.

6. Fill pork casing according to the instructions that come with the equipment you are using. Twist or tie the casing every 175 g (6 in) to form each link. Make sure that the ends are tied shut.

7. Bring a large pot of water to a boil, reduce the heat and bring the water to a bare simmer. (The casing will burst if the heat is too high.) Poach the sausage for 7 to 8 minutes, until a skewer inserted into the centre of the sausage is hot to the touch. Remove and cool for 5 minutes. Cut each link into 1-cm (½-in) slices and serve.

LOBSTER MEDALLIONS WITH HERBED AND TRUFFLED BUTTER SAUCE

This very simple preparation makes a dazzling starter for a fancy dinner party.

SERVES 4 AS A FIRST COURSE

700-g (1½-lb) lobster
1 bottle (750 ml (1⅓ pints) dry white wine
85 g (3 oz) unsalted butter
15 g (½ oz) fresh black truffle
5 g (1 tsp) chopped fresh tarragon (or you may use
    any fresh herb of your choice)

1. Choose a pot in which the lobster fits snugly and fill it halfway with cold water. Add the wine and bring mixture to a boil. Add the lobster, cover, return water to a boil, reduce to a simmer and cook until just done, about 12 minutes.

2. While the lobster is cooking, melt the butter in a small saucepan over low heat. Add the truffle and tarragon. Heat for 1 minute.

3. Remove the tail meat from the lobster and cut into 5-mm (¼-in) slices. Arrange the slices on 4 plates and intersperse them with slices of warmed black truffle. Remove meat from the lobster claws, cut meat in half horizontally and arrange, cut side down, next to the tail meat. Drizzle all with herbed butter. Serve immediately.

MUSSELS

Though mussels have long been wildly popular in Europe—they're a special favourite in Belgium—they've never attained the same popularity in America. However, with our newly expanded food-consciousness—and especially with the rise of cultivated mussels in the marketplace, which require virtually no scrubbing and cleaning by the home cook—we Americans have finally begun to embrace this delicious mollusc. We hope, frankly, that the embrace doesn't go too much further; at $1 per 450 g (1 lb), they are the only bargain left in shellfish.

There are several kinds of mussels available these days to the American consumer. The most familiar variety is the Atlantic blue mussel; this is the size, shape and colour most people think of when they think of mussels. There's a West Coast cousin of the blue mussel which, when grown in Penn Cove, Washington, is one of the most delicious mussels in America. Also in Washington State, cultivation has recently begun of the Mediterranean mussel, which is larger than the blue mussel but, miraculously, not flabby. In the UK, and increasingly in the U.S., you'll also find the large green-lipped mussels from New Zealand, with their beautiful shells. They vary in quality, we find , but at their best offer a very intense mussel flavour.

Here are some further mussel tips:

- Despite everyone's natural tendency to equate 'bigger' with 'better,' we're generally suspicious of big mussels. Too often, in our tasting experience, big mussels have also been soft and flabby in texture. The best mussels we ever tasted were in Normandy, right on the coast; they were almost thumbnail-tiny—with an intensely sweet flavour and remarkably firm texture we'll never forget. Since that sensitising experience, most of the smaller mussels we've tasted have seemed sweeter and firmer than their larger counterparts. Most mussels in the United States market are 2.5-7.5 cm (1-3 in) long; we invariably seek out the small ones.

- Another factor contributes to flabbiness: the mussels' spawning season. During this time, the texture turns mushy and the shelf life of the mussels is shortened. Each mussel variety has a different spawning season. Avoid Atlantic blue mussels in the summer; they are often disappointingly flabby then. The Mediterranean mussels from Puget Sound, however, are on a different schedule; they spawn in winter.

- How can you tell if a mussel is fresh? It should be tightly closed—though it may open a little at warmer temperatures. Simply tap the mussel in doubt, to see if the shell closes up. If it doesn't, slide the top and bottom shells between your thumb and forefinger; if they're easy to slide, it's quite possible that the mussel is dead. Pass it by. Also, reject any light ones, any with broken or chipped shells, or any that do not smell fresh.

- Here's a surprise: we far prefer wild mussels to the easy-to-clean cultivated mussels. The wild ones, with their thick, rough shells, take much longer to grow than the cultivated ones do; this results in a more concentrated mussel, with much better texture and flavour. Additionally, most of the cultivated mussels come to market shiny-smooth, stripped of the 'beard' that mussels grow to cling to rocks, docks and poles. But the beard helps the mussel stay alive after harvesting, When we see wild mussels available, with their beards still attached, we don't mind the work involved in debearding them; we know the mussel will be fresher-tasting.

- If you're lucky enough to find mussels with the beards attached, simply pull them off with your fingers. If the mussels have beards, it's very likely they'll also have grit surrounding them. Working under running water, scrub off the grit with a stiff brush.

- Mussels are the simplest things in the world to cook. If you want the pure mussel experience, follow the classic French method. Just put a few centimetres of combined water and white wine in a large pot, bring to a boil and toss the mussels into the liquid. If you want additional flavour, you can add butter, lemon juice, chopped shallots and fresh herbs. Cover the pot and cook over high heat until the mussels swing open (3 to 5 minutes). If some mussels don't open, remove the opened ones and cook the recalcitrant ones a few minutes longer. If they still don't open, they may well be healthy—but it's not worth taking a chance. Discard them. Serve the opened mussels in large bowls with the broth, crusty bread and crisp white wine.

- There are many ways to prepare mussels beyond the classic steaming method. First of all, you can add interesting, non-French flavours to the steaming pot (most everyone loves Italian steamed mussels, with tomatoes and garlic; also see the Spanish and Chinese versions that follow). Or, you can remove the mussel meat from steamed mussels and toss the bellies into stews, pasta dishes and rice dishes. Another delicious possibility is to open the mussels with a clam knife, coat the raw bellies with flour and deep-fry them. Lastly, mussels make a baked-clam kind of dish that is a hundred times better than baked clams, because the mussels don't turn rubbery in the baking, as clams often do.

Here are a few of our favourite mussel recipes.

MUSSELS AND CHORIZO IN SAFFRON-GARLIC BROTH

We love this Iberian version of steamed mussels, especially when good, strong-tasting New Zealand green-lipped mussels are at hand; in addition to standing up to the chorizo and garlic, their colour is beautiful against the saffron and tomato. There's not a lot of broth in this dish, but you'll be amazed at how rich and intense it is. Serve with crusty bread to soak up the broth.

SERVES 4 AS A FIRST COURSE

30 ml (2 tbsp) extra-virgin olive oil
1 medium onion, finely chopped
6 garlic cloves, coarsely chopped
large pinch of saffron threads, crumbled
115 g (4 oz) chorizo sausage, cut crossways into very thin slices
225 ml (8 fl oz) fish stock (you may substitute water)
125 g (4 fl oz) Pomi brand strained tomatoes or 125 g (4 fl oz) tomato purée
dried hot red pepper flakes to taste
900 g (2 lb) mussels, cleaned, scrubbed and debearded (about 25 large New Zealand mussels or 40 to 60 regular mussels)

1. Heat the olive oil in a large casserole over moderately low heat until hot but not smoking. Add the onion, garlic and saffron and cook for 5 minutes, stirring, until onion is softened but not browned. Stir in the chorizo and cook, stirring, for 2 minutes.

2. Add the fish stock and tomatoes and bring to a boil. Add crushed hot red pepper flakes to taste. Add the mussels and cover tightly. Cook over high heat, shaking the pot once or twice during the cooking to move the mussels around, or stirring the mussels quickly with a large spoon, for 4 to 5 minutes, or until the mussels have opened. (Discard any that have not opened.)

3. Spoon the mussel mixture into deep soup bowls and serve hot with crusty bread.

CANTONESE MUSSELS WITH BLACK BEAN SAUCE

This great version of steamed mussels is often made with clams in Chinatown restaurants—but it's just as delicious with mussels. Maybe more. Sometimes Cantonese chefs like to add a most un-Cantonese touch to the dish: hot green chillies. In your kitchen, the heat's up to you.

SERVES 4 AS PART OF A CHINESE DINNER

10 ml (2 tsp) peanut oil
30 g (2 tbsp) grated fresh ginger
15 g (1 tbsp) garlic, finely chopped
3 spring onions, chopped
1 hot green chilli, or more to taste, seeded and
 chopped (optional)
24 mussels, cleaned, scrubbed, and debearded
50 ml (2 fl oz) shao-hsing or dry sherry
15 ml (1 tbsp) oyster sauce
5 ml (1 tsp) thin soy sauce
2.5 g (½ tsp) sugar
30 g (2 tbsp) salted black beans, crushed with a
 cleaver
10 g (2 tsp) cornflour
2.5 ml (½ tsp) sesame oil

1. Place the peanut oil in a wok over moderately high heat. Stir-fry the ginger, garlic, spring onions and chilli for 1 minute. Add the mussels and stir well to blend. Add the shao-hsing or dry sherry and a scant 175ml

(6 fl oz) water. Cover and boil until the mussels swing open, about 3 to 4 minutes.

2. Remove mussels and place in colander; shake over the wok to let the juices run off into the wok. Set mussels aside. To the wok, add the oyster sauce, soy sauce, sugar and black beans. Stir well. Cook over high heat for 30 seconds.

3. Mix the cornflour in a cup with a little cold water until a creamy liquid is formed, then add to the boiling liquid in the wok (which will thicken immediately). Add the mussels, stir well for 10 seconds, then remove wok from heat. Stir in the sesame oil and serve immediately.

SIZZLED MUSSELS WITH GARLIC AND PARSLEY À LA VAUDEVILLE

Here's a smart variation on the 'clams oreganata' theme: this dish uses mussels, which never have the rubbery texture of baked clams. This recipe is modelled on a Parisian favourite, served at the Brasserie Vaudeville—and there's a wonderful Gallic sublety to its flavours. You'll also find the texture of the crumbs in this dish a revelation. Neither mushy nor oily—as the crumbs in stuffed molluscs so often are—these crumbs are dry, light, airy and refined.

SERVES 6 AS A FIRST COURSE

36 medium mussels, cleaned, scrubbed, and
 debearded
1 bottle (750 ml (1⅓ pints) dry white wine
70 g (2½ oz) butter
10 g (2 tsp) shallots, very finely chopped (almost a
 paste)
15 g (3 tsp) garlic, very finely chopped (almost a
 paste)
75 g (2¾ oz) fresh, not-too-fine breadcrumbs
85 g (3 oz) fresh parsley, very finely chopped
salt and pepper to taste
lemon wedges

1. Place the mussels in a large pot and pour in enough white wine to come halfway up the mussels (you may have some wine left over). Cover tightly and place over high heat. When the wine starts to boil, shake the pot to redistribute the mussels, holding the lid down. Continue cooking just until the mussels open, about 4 to 5 minutes. Remove the cooked mussels immediately and place them on a large roasting tin. Remove the top shell of each mussel, discard the shells and with a sharp knife separate each mussel belly from the remaining shell. Leave the cut mussels on the half-shell and set aside.

2. Preheat grill.

3. *Prepare the stuffing:* Melt the butter over moderately high heat in a heavy frying pan . (It will foam up, but do not let it burn.) Add the shallots and garlic. Cook, stirring, for about 2 minutes, or until the shallots and garlic soften. (Do not let them brown.) Turn off the heat and add the breadcrumbs and parsley. Blend well. Season with salt and pepper.

4. Top each mussel in the roasting tin with 5 g (1 tsp) of the breadcrumb mixture. Place the tin under the grill for about 1 minute, or until the mussels start to sizzle and brown. Serve immediately, 6 to a portion, squeezing a little lemon juice on each mussel.

OCTOPUS

If more Americans only knew how easy octopuses are to cook—and how delicious they are at table (with their sweet, mild shellfish flavour)—this odd-looking cephalopod would be a lot more popular than it is. We suspect its time is coming.

Part of the 'octopus problem' stems from the fact that many of us have only tasted rubbery octopus; the purple-cloaked rounds at sushi bars are invariably reminiscent of Pennsy Pinkys. And this is compounded by the fact that most cookery books that cover the subject exaggerate the point by detailing the various strategies of international cooks to tenderise octopus: hurling it against a wall, rubbing it with grated mooli (daikon), dipping it 3 times in boiling water.

We don't get it. The octopus we sell—and cook—is beautifully tender after a simple 45- to 60-minute simmer in a flavoured stock. Maybe some chefs boil the octopus furiously, which can toughen it.

Another possibility is that some octopuses are too large and therefore rubbery. When buying octopus, don't take any home that are above 1.8 kg (4 lb); 700 g (1½ lb) to 900 g (2 lb) is a nice size, almost certain to be tender. And sniff before you buy, to check for freshness; the octopus should smell clean.

Another octopus problem may be that we Americans don't know how to clean them and we don't know which parts to eat.

First of all, you can always ask your fishmonger to clean an octopus for you. If you want to do it yourself, it's relatively easy; you just turn the small head sac inside out and clean out the innards. Then you cut the head from the body and remove the hard part (the beak) and the ink sac right where the head meets the body; both head and body are edible. If you're confused about all this—cleaning out the head, finding the beak—you can simplify this process still further. Just cut off the head an inch or so below the eyes and discard the part you cut off. You'll be left with 90 per cent of the octopus, all of it edible.

Here are 2 terrific recipes drawn from 2 of the world's greatest octopus-loving cuisines.

GALICIAN-STYLE OCTOPUS (PULPO GALLEGO)

They love octopus in the north-west corner of Spain, in Galicia, where every tapas bar features a dish of boiled, paprika-scented octopus with potatoes. But this dish is a little bland and austere for most American palates—so we have pumped it up with garlic and olive oil.

SERVES 4 AS A FIRST COURSE

700-900 g (1½-2 lb) octopus, cleaned
350 ml (12 fl oz) fino sherry
850 ml (1½ pints) water
2 large garlic cloves, smashed and peeled, plus 4
    large cloves, peeled and finely chopped
5 g (1 tsp) black peppercorns
½ lemon, sliced
12.5 g (2½ tsp) paprika
450 g (1 lb) waxy potatoes, peeled and cut in ⅓-
    inch slices
15 ml (1 tbsp) olive oil
45ml (3 tbsp) extra-virgin olive oil
coarse salt to taste

1. Place the octopus in a medium saucepan and cover with 225 ml (8 fl oz) of the sherry and the water (the liquids should just cover the octopus). Add the 2 smashed garlic cloves, peppercorns, lemon and 10 g (2 tsp) of the paprika. Bring to a simmer and simmer gently, covered, adding the potato slices during the last 20 minutes of the cooking, until the octopus is tender, about 45 minutes. When the octopus is cooked, remove from heat and keep covered.

2. While the octopus is cooking, place the 15 ml (1 tbsp) of olive oil in a small frying pan over moderately low heat. Add the remaining garlic cloves to the pan. Cook, stirring, for 5 minutes, or until garlic is softened. Increase heat to high and add the rest of the sherry and the rest of the paprika. Boil the liquid until it is reduced to about 30 ml (2 tbsp). Remove from heat and whisk in the extra-virgin olive oil.

3. Remove octopus from cooking liquid and slice into serving pieces (shapes are up to you). Arrange with potato slices on 4 individual plates, drizzle the sauce over all and top with coarse salt to taste. Serve immediately.

GREEK-STYLE GRILLED OCTOPUS WITH OUZO AND FRESH THYME

One of the nice things about cooking octopus is this: after it's tenderised through a 45-minute simmer, you can then cook it further in other ways, adding new dimension to it. Greek chefs love to grill it—and the smoky essence contributed by an open fire is a wonderful marriage with the inherent octopus flavour. Add to this the great anise-flavour of ouzo, a fiery Greek distillate and you've got a sure winner. Serve with ice-cold glasses of ouzo, of course.

SERVES 4 AS A FIRST COURSE

650-900 g (1½- to 2-lb) octopus, cleaned
400 ml (14 fl oz) ouzo
850 ml (1¼ pints) water
4 large garlic cloves, smashed
1 medium onion, sliced
3 cloves
8 sprigs of fresh thyme plus thyme leaves for
    garnish
50 ml (2 fl oz) freshly squeezed lemon juice plus
    lemon wedges for garnish
olive oil for brushing on octopus
25 g (1 oz) unsalted butter

1. Place the octopus in a medium saucepan. Add 350 ml (12 fl oz) of the ouzo and the water (the liquid should just cover the octopus). Add the garlic cloves, onion, cloves and sprigs of thyme. Bring to a simmer and simmer gently for 45 minutes, or until the octopus is tender.

2. Remove octopus from the liquid, cut into serving portions (keep the tentacles whole, cut the top part into slices) and place in a small bowl. Cover with the remaining ¼ cup of 50 ml (2 fl oz) ouzo and the lemon juice. Cover and refrigerate for 24 hours.

3. Boil the liquid in which the octopus was cooked until it is reduced to about 125 ml (4 fl oz). Strain into a small saucepan, cover and refrigerate until ready to grill octopus.

4. When ready to grill octopus, prepare a hot charcoal fire. Remove octopus from marinade, brush with olive oil and place on fire. Cook until nicely grilled on the exterior of each piece, about 4 minutes per side. Place grilled octopus pieces on a platter and sprinkle with a few drops of ouzo.

5. Bring the reduced cooking liquid to a boil in the small saucepan. Add 15 ml (1 tbsp) of the octopus marinade and boil for 1 minute. Reduce heat to low and swirl in the butter. As soon as the sauce has thickened, pour it over grilled octopus and scatter thyme leaves over all. Garnish with lemon wedges and serve immediately.

OYSTERS

North America is one of the world's great oyster sites. And we Americans have had a long and celebrated oyster-eating history; Diamond Jim Brady sitting down to a gross of raw oysters (that's 144 of 'em) before dinner is among our most venerable culinary apocrypha.

Something happened, however, as we reached the midpoint of the twentieth century; the oyster bars that had been established successfully near oceans and gulfs all over the country began to close down, in response to diminished demand. The hale-and-hearty tradition of downing live, raw oysters survived in New England and New Orleans—but for the rest of the country, in the fifties, the closest most people got to raw shellfish was shrimp cocktail.

Then the magic wand that swept across the culinary landscape in the last 20 years touched the American oyster scene. The Oyster Bar at Grand Central Station, in New York City, after being shuttered for several decades, was reopened. Other, smaller operations devoted to raw shellfish began springing up in New York and in other major American cities. The term 'raw bar' became part of the lingo—and restaurants and even catered parties,

began offering them. The New Orleans oyster-eating tradition kicked into national gear and the concept of raw oysters in a glass, with hot sauce—the oyster 'shooter'—spread like wildfire. Most important, the oyster industry in the Pacific North-west expanded tremendously in the seventies, eighties and nineties—making Seattle the new epicentre of American oyster-eating and the source of America's finest oysters.

We view this turn of events with pure, untrammelled mirth—because we are oyster fanatics. Until a few years ago, unfortunately, we were frustrated oyster fanatics, because the sluggish American oyster industry was not able to supply consistently super-fresh oysters to those who wanted them. Many times we'd find oysters that didn't smell fresh, or had dried out considerably in their shells. These problems still plague oyster-buyers in America—but things are much, much better today than they were 10 years ago.

Perhaps more with oysters than any other seafood item, the variety of what's now available in America is simply staggering; there are so many different oyster names in the market and in restaurants, that many people simply give up before they begin to understand what's out there. But the field is much easier than it seems. There are only 5 species of oysters available in our markets. Unfortunately, oysters are not usually identified by these names; rather, most oyster names tell you where the oyster came from—and these names tend to be obsessively specific, right down to the individual tidal flat. Good news, however: it's not hard to recognise the 5 species and then figure out which species a Quilcene or an Apalachicola belongs to; after that, you've got it made.

Here's a guide to the 5 species, with some of our specific favourite oysters in each group.

Crassostrea Virginica Practically every oyster produced on the East Coast—from Eastern Canada, down through New England, Long Island, the mid-Atlantic states, the Chesapeake Bay, Florida and into the Gulf of Mexico—is of the species *Crassostrea virginica*. For people who grew up in these areas, this is what an oyster is. The most famous name for them is Blue Point—but that was a proprietary name owned by a company that has been out of business for 50 years; today, many people use the name 'Blue Points' generically, to refer to *Crassostrea virginica,* also known as the Atlantic oyster, or the Eastern oyster. At its best, *Crassostrea virginica* is a good, not great, oyster. We like them especially from the coldest possible waters; some of the Eastern Canadian versions of *Crassostrea virginica,* like Malpeques, or Prince Edward Islands, can be delightfully crisp and salty, almost coppery in flavour. Quality is variable down through New England (where Wellfleets and Cotuits are the most famous *Crassostrea virginica*). The New York area has been taken by storm by the eponymous Fishers Island oysters, a small oyster-producing island in eastern Long Island Sound; for some reason, Fishers Islands seem to be fresher and crisper in the New York market than any other *Crassostrea virginica.* Chincoteagues, from Virginia, can be good at midwinter (try to get Chincoteagues from the ocean side, not from the bay side). As for Gulf oysters—such as Florida's Apalachicolas, Louisiana Gulf oysters and Texas Gulf oysters—these are *Crassostrea virginica* at their worst. Often muddy, bland and mushy, sometimes downright dangerous, they are oysters we generally avoid eating raw anywhere, anytime—except in New Orleans in the winter, with hits of Tabasco bringing them to life. Gulf oysters, however, are our oysters of choice for fried oysters and for many cooked oyster dishes.

Ostrea edulis Oysters of this species are round and flat (not oblong and deep-cupped, as most oysters are). The taste is also distinct: salty and sweet simultaneously, with a pronounced metallic finish that can linger on the palate for minutes. And *Ostrea edulis* are special in texture, as well: rich and creamy as oysters can get without seeming unattractively fatty. The most famous *Ostrea edulis* is the Belon, which comes from the Belon River in France's Brittany region; it is the most expensive oyster at France's oyster bars. Similar oysters

(sometimes known as European flats) are now being cultivated in Maine and New Hampshire (very metallic from these states) and on the West Coast (somewhat milder). Sometimes they're marketed as Belons—just as California sparkling wine is marketed as champagne. But champagne can only come from the Champagne region of France and Belons can only come from the Belon River. One Washington State producer markets an especially reliable and delicious Belon-type called the Westcott European Flat. Generally speaking, if you're looking for a bright, light-textured oyster hit, don't order flats; if, however, you're looking for a big oyster that makes a statement, you can't do any better than *Ostrea edulis.*

Crassostrea Gigas Of Japanese origin and sometimes known as the Pacific Oyster, *Crassostrea gigas* is the reigning star of two world oyster hotbeds: the North-west United States and the North-west of France; almost all the oysters produced and consumed in those two places (and that includes Paris) belong to this species. They vary wildly in size and shape, but they do have a family resemblance in flavour: an oddly delicious quality known as 'fruitiness'. How can an oyster be fruity? Not from fruit, of course—but for some reason *Crassostrea gigas* tastes like watermelon rind, or cucumbers (which are actually in the melon family). Whenever you see the panoply of Pacific North-west oyster names on an oyster bar menu, almost all of those oysters will be the fruity *Crassostrea gigas.* Some of the specific ones that we've found to be most reliable and delicious over the years are Quilcenes, Hama Hamas, Willapa Bays, Totten Inlets and oysters from Crescent Beach. All things considered, we hold top-rate *Crassostrea gigas* from Washington, Oregon, California and Alaska to be the best oysters for eating raw.

Kumamoto (Crassostrea Sikamea) Just a few years ago, the textbooks gave Kumamotos an unusual place in the oyster taxonomy: they were said to be a subspecies of *Crassostrea gigas.* This was unusual because no other

American oyster was described as a subspecies of something else. Now, oyster experts have revised their collective opinion: the Kumamoto, we are told, is its own species, called *Crassostrea sikamea.* Though it can have a fruity taste reminiscent of *Crassostrea gigas,* it is very believably a species unto itself. To begin with, its looks are different: it's smaller than most Pacific oysters, but with a much deeper shell. Taste-wise—though Kumamotos are relatively mild—they can offer an intriguing earthiness, somewhat reminiscent of a damp cellar. Then there's the texture: they're often softer and creamier than other Pacific oysters, but can feature an unusual amount of briny liquid in their deeply cupped shells. Oyster-savvy consumers have taken to saying 'Kumamoto' in the same way American wine-drinkers once took to saying 'Pouilly-Fuissé'; it's now a very trendy oyster at all sorts of creative American restaurants. Kumamotos come from Washington State and the Tomales and Humboldt Bays of northern California.

Olympia (Ostrea Lurida) This very distinctive oyster is the only species that's indigenous to the West Coast; once upon a time, before its population declined, it was the favourite oyster of California and the Pacific Northwest. It defies the American 'bigger-is-better' sensibility; *Ostrea lurida* is one of the world's smallest oysters, usually no larger than the tip of your thumb. Yet it packs a big flavour—and this is why home oyster shuckers are willing to put up with opening dozens to make a single satisfying portion. The taste is complex: metallic, earthy, nutty and sweet, all at the same time. Often, they're a little creamier than we like oysters, but crisp ones can be found. An outstanding American specialty.

BUYING FRESH OYSTERS

Be unforgiving when you buy oysters, especially if you're going to eat them raw: live, healthy oysters will be closed shut. Don't consider buying oysters that are gaping open.

Beyond that clear-and-simple caveat, oyster-buying gets a lot more confusing.

For some reason, the French have a much better handle on the task of getting fresh oysters to markets and restaurants. In America, even the 'freshest' of oysters, once opened, can prove that they're a week away from the oyster bed. There's virtually no way to know this, unless you open one oyster from a batch you're considering. We say: go for it. Buy one from your fishmonger, or convince him to open a sample. Does it smell clean? Is the oyster very wet? Don't buy dry ones. Is the oyster shrinking away from its shell? Don't buy it. Is the oyster sitting in a small pool of briny liquid (sometimes called 'love potion')? Don't buy oysters that don't have this liquid.

Can you buy raw oysters year-round? We all remember the old 'R' month dictum for oysters—but many people are confused by it. There's only one reason not to buy oysters in months that don't have an 'R'— many oysters spawn in the summer months and spawning oysters have a mild, soft, milky quality that's not appealing to oyster connoisseurs. Hard-line oyster mavens prize crispness and salinity—two qualities not usually present in summer oysters. In fact, these qualities are emphasised by cold water, so many oyster lovers limit their consumption of oysters to the coldest winter months only. We stop short of making a hard-and-fast rule, because we have occasionally been surprised, both here and in France, by the quality of some oysters at odd times of the year. If you're playing percentages, however—stick to winter.

SERVING RAW OYSTERS

One of the wonderful things about raw oysters is that they're really very easy to open—much easier than clams. All you need is a sturdy oyster knife, with dull sides and a pointy but dull tip. Working with gloves or with a towel (because a slip of the knife can become a gash in the hand), simply turn the oyster cupped-side down on the counter; the flatter half of the shell will be on top. Then find the tiny spot at the smallest tip of the oyster where there's a small break in the joining of the two shells. Stick the tip of the oyster knife in the break and start twisting until you pry the flat shell open. When you get it, the oyster practically 'pops'. Then, simply run your knife under the flat, top shell to sever the oyster from the shell. Make sure to retain as much juice in the shell as possible and never, ever wash out the opened oyster.

Cultural difference here: before the oyster comes to the table, the French never sever the oyster from the cupped shell in which it now sits. They believe that this keeps the oyster fresher. American oyster chefs, however, traditionally run their knives around the oyster sitting in the cupped shell, severing it completely so that the oyster can just be poured out of the shell at the table. We go with the French method on this: less work for the chef, better result. By the way, you should never open oysters until the moment you're ready to serve them/eat them.

You can make a fabulous presentation of oysters as a first course for a dinner party. Spread crushed ice on a large platter (round is the traditional shape in France) and strew the ice with some fresh seaweed, if available. Then, lay the opened oysters on the ice in such a way that they're perfectly balanced, so that none of their precious juice spills out of their shells.

Serve with lemon wedges, dark bread, butter, crisp white wine and you've got it made. Some purists don't even drizzle the lemon on the oysters, considering it an intrusion. And no oyster connoisseur would ever compromise his oysters with cocktail sauce. Some, however, do like the tang of a mignonette sauce with oysters (just a combination of very fruity red-wine vinegar—say, 125 ml (4 fl oz)—a few teaspoons of finely chopped shallot, coarse salt and pepper). In New Orleans, of course, it is perfectly acceptable to enliven your Gulf oysters with hot sauce (we're especially fond of the relatively new green Tabasco on oysters).

COOKING WITH OYSTERS

No. Don't do it.

Well . . . sometimes, maybe, if you don't have great oysters. We think Gulf oysters make fabulous fried oysters (which can go on Po' Boy sandwiches) and are delicious when added late to gumbos. We've even had, on occasion, a high-quality oyster (like a Belon) that survived a 30-second dip in some kind of creamy soup or sauce. But the idea of cooking one of nature's perfect foods is an abomination to most oyster connoisseurs.

SCALLOPS

Scallops are among the tastiest creatures in the sea. Reflecting this fact, they have always been fairly popular in the United States. However, a few factors have prevented them from achieving the near-cult status here that they have in other countries.

First of all, some American scallops are steam-blasted open, to facilitate the removal of the scallop meat (actually, the scallop's large adductor muscle) from the shell. This practice partially cooks the scallop and makes it much less tasty when it finally reaches your kitchen.

Second, scallop distributors have long had the awful habit of soaking raw, market-destined scallops in a phosphate bath to lengthen their shelf life. This transforms their natural, raw, translucent look to a cooked white look—and destroys their fresh-from-the-sea taste. Furthermore, these phosphate-soaked scallops pick up liquid, which you pay for at scallop-high prices when your scallops are weighed at the market.

Finally, it is the almost universal custom in the United States—whether through steam-blasting or shucking—to remove the scallop meat from the scallop shell before the scallop goes to market. The state of Maine, in fact—a major scallop producer—forbids fishermen to bring scallops on the shell to shore. This is in bold contrast to European custom; there, scallops are sold in the shell at fish markets. Not only does this mean that European consumers get the delicious orange scallop roe that sits alongside the adductor muscle (which we rarely see in the U.S.), but it also means that the in-shell scallops are still alive in the market (like clams, mussels and oysters), at their optimum freshness. All things considered, scallops in Europe (in northern France or in Spain's Galicia region) seem like real food from the sea, as oysters and mussels do. The shelled dots of meat in American markets, by comparison, seem like white abstractions without a history.

There hasn't been much change in America regarding the availability of scallops-in-the-shell problem. Very rarely on the East Coast and a little more often on the West Coast, do you see live scallops in the shell—the overwhelming preponderance of scallops sold in the United States are still sold shucked. However, there is good news: there has been a major improvement in the general handling of scallops and in the quality of shelled scallops that are now coming to market.

There are over 400 varieties of scallops in the world, but almost none of them are available in this country. Compared to some other shellfish, scallops are fairly easy to keep track of. For all intents and purposes, there are just 3 major groups of scallops that you need to know. And one you can forget.

Bay Scallops *(Argopecten irradians)* These small scallops (thumbnail-sized after shelling) are harvested in close-to-land bays and inlets from New England down to North Carolina. Most of them, however and the best of them, come from Massachusetts and Long Island. In fact, two of the world's greatest scallops come from those places. The island of Nantucket, off the coast of Massachusetts, produces bay scallops of almost astonishing intensity and sweetness. And scallops from Peconic Bay, off Long Island, are, if anything, even sweeter; at their best they're literally like candy. Both of these are hard to find and amazingly expensive. But if you can find fresh, authentic ones in season (fall through early spring), you are in for the bay scallop treat

of your life; just make sure not to juxtapose them with strong, competing flavours. Other bay scallops can be good, but they pale in comparison to Nantuckets and Peconics.

Sea Scallops Once upon a time in America, sea scallops—much larger than bay scallops, the adductor muscles as large as 5 cm (2 in) across after shelling—were clearly inferior to bay scallops. Sea scallops have always cost less in the market and have almost always seemed less sweet and less intense. The culprit was their place of harvest: the deep sea, where boats would stay for many days before returning to shore with their over-the-hill harvest. Recently, however, the quality of some sea scallops on the East Coast *(Pecten magellanicus)* has improved dramatically. For we have now entered the era of 'diver' scallops, or 'day-boat' scallops. For these delectable, sweet-as-sugar scallops, divers hand-harvest large scallops within 3 miles of the Maine shore and get them to distributors within 24 hours. In fact, some of the best ones are touted as 'night-harvested' scallops—and many top restaurants brag that the sea scallops you're having for lunch today were harvested 'last night,' less than 24 hours ago. Unfortunately, these large, fabulous scallops rarely make it to the fishmongers—but if you put pressure on your fishmonger, he may be able to get them for you. Only one word of caution with these great sea scallops: they're so sweet and intense, they should be cut into slices before they are used. Other sea scallops in the market these days seem better than they used to be, but taste before you buy in quantity (you can tell sweetness right at the store by tasting a slice of raw scallop). The West Coast has a version of the sea scallop too *(Pecten caurinus)*, often called the weather-vane scallop. It is similar to the Atlantic sea scallop.

Calico Scallops We don't advise buying these. For one thing, they're often erroneously labelled in markets as 'bay scallops'. Be wary: the calico is another type of scallop entirely, harvested in warm waters from the

Carolinas, into the Gulf of Mexico and down through Central and South America. They have nowhere near the flavour or sweetness of true bay scallops. Furthermore, if any scallops in the marketplace are likely to be steam-blasted and phosphate-dunked, it's these. Next time you see calico scallops at the fish market—or 'bay scallops' that cost only $4 (£2.40) a pound—pass them by.

Pink Scallops or **Singing Scallops** These are a great Pacific North-west specialty. They are so named for their lovely pink shells, or for the sound they make as their shells swing open in the pot. What's that, you say? Shells? Yes! Pink scallops are the only scallops in America that *never* come to market out of the shell. Unfortunately, they're rare in markets outside of the Pacific North-west—but certainly worth a question or two of your fishmonger. They have a terrific sweet mollusc flavour, a little in the clam direction.

Here are some of our favourite recipes for the 3 very special types of scallops we advise you to find. If you can't locate great bay scallops, great sea scallops, or pink scallops for these recipes—they'll still be delicious with whatever substitutes you can find.

NANTUCKET BAY SCALLOPS WITH BEURRE BLANC AND CAVIAR

This is a fantastically elegant opener for a dinner party. Just make sure you use a top-quality bay scallop—either Nantucket or Peconic Bay. If your scallops aren't up to snuff, you might want to choose another dish, or increase the caviar. We have been moderate in the amount of caviar required . . . because even great caviar can't steal the thunder from a plate of perfectly sautéed, unbelievably sweet Nantucket scallops.

SERVES 6 AS A FIRST COURSE

350 g (12 oz) unsalted butter
6 large shallots
45 ml (3 tbsp) dry white wine
60 ml (4 tbsp) white-wine vinegar

45 ml (3 tbsp) warm water
2.5 g (½ tsp) salt
pinch of ground white pepper
900 g (2 lb) Nantucket bay scallops
115 g (4 oz) flour, spread out on a plate
25 g (1 oz) osetra caviar
45 g (3 tbsp) finely chopped fresh chives

1. Clarify 125 g (4½ oz) of the butter by putting it in a small saucepan and melting it over low heat. When melted, turn off heat and let pan sit for 5 minutes. Skim off and discard any foam that collects on top. Then, pour the yellow liquid into a small bowl, leaving the milky, white solids in the bottom of the pan. Discard them.

2. Put shallots, white wine and vinegar in a medium saucepan. Over moderate heat, cook until liquid is almost completely evaporated, about 5 to 7 minutes. (There should be about 15 ml (1 tbsp) of liquid left in the bottom of the pan.) Add water and stir. Turn off heat.

3. Cut rest of the butter into small pieces. Turn on the heat under the pan to low and slowly add butter, a few pieces at a time, whisking constantly. (Do not stop whisking or turn up the heat, because this could cause the butter to separate.) When all butter is incorporated, season with the salt and white pepper. Strain beurre blanc through a strainer into a cool saucepan and place saucepan in a roasting tin filled with hot water. Set tin aside.

4. Preheat oven to 250°C (500°F). Heat a large frying tin over moderately high heat. Coat the bottom of the frying pan with a thin film of clarified butter. Dry the scallops in a towel and lightly coat some in flour. (Coat only as many scallops as will fit in the frying pan without overcrowding it.) Shake scallops in a strainer, set over a bowl, to remove any excess flour.

5. When the butter is hot, gently place scallops in pan, making sure that they are not touching each other. (If they are too close together, the scallops will steam rather than sear and the flour will become gummy.) Sear on each side until golden, about 2 minutes total. Move the seared scallops to a baking sheet and cover loosely with foil while you finish the rest.

6. Over moderate heat, reheat beurre blanc, whisking constantly, until hot. Turn off heat and adjust seasoning. Place scallops in hot oven for just about 30 seconds to make sure they're hot.

7. Drizzle about 15-45 ml (2 to 3 tbsp) beurre blanc on to each of 6 plates. Divide scallops into 6 portions and put 1 portion in the middle of each plate. Gently scatter 5 g (1 tsp) caviar over and around scallops and then sprinkle with chives. Serve immediately.

PEPPER-GRILLED SEA SCALLOPS WITH ROASTED MEXICAN GREEN SAUCE

Large, luscious, diver-harvested sea scallops work particularly well when cut into slices; biting into a whole one would be almost too intense. And everything's better still if you can brown the outsides of the scallop slices in some way. The following recipe calls for a hot grill, or a hot pan (the latter choice recalling Paul Prudhomme's 'blackened redfish' method) and a hot coating. Now, given the highly flavoured crust and the full flavour of the scallops within, a strong-flavoured sauce is appropriate. In this recipe, the cooked, pepper-encrusted scallops are paired with a Mexican sauce made of cooked tomatillos. The pepper on the scallops and the chillies in the sauce marry well. Use regular sea scallops if you can't find the diver-harvested ones.

SERVES 4 AS A FIRST COURSE

6 fresh tomatillos, husked and washed
1 large poblano chilli
115 g (4 oz) chopped white onion
about 8 sprigs of fresh coriander (including stems), chopped, plus fresh leaves for garnish

2 serrano chillies, stemmed, seeded and chopped
salt to taste
450 g (1 lb) sea scallops (about 28 scallops)
25 g (5 tsp) ground coriander seed
20 g (1½ tbsp) very coarsely ground black pepper

1. Preheat oven to 230°C (450°F).

2. Roast the tomatillos on a baking sheet in the oven for 10 minutes. When cool enough to handle, peel and cut into quarters.

3. Meanwhile, place the poblano over an open flame and cook until charred on all sides. Place the poblano in a paper or plastic bag for 20 minutes, then peel off the charred skin. Remove the seeds and chop the poblano.

4. Place the tomatillo quarters, chopped poblano, onion, coriander sprigs and serranos in a blender and blend to a coarse purée. Transfer the purée to a serving dish and thin to a medium-thick sauce consistency with about 45 ml (3 tbsp) water, or more if needed. Season to taste with salt.

5. Cut scallops into round slices, about 2.5 cm (½ in) thick. Roll slices in the ground coriander, then in the cracked pepper. Grill over a hot fire, or sear in a cast-iron pan that has been heating over a hot fire for 10 minutes. Turn scallops once and remove from heat when scallops are just cooked, about 1 minute per side.

6. Serve the scallops hot on pools of the green sauce. Top with a little more green sauce and garnish with the fresh coriander leaves.

STEAMED SINGING SCALLOPS WITH THAI YELLOW CURRY BROTH

We love this bowlful of shells in broth. But if you can't find singing scallops for this light but super-flavourful dish, you can substitute 24 large sea scallops. Even better—to get the delightful shell-in-broth effect—combine the shell-less scallops with a few dozen steamers.

SERVES 4

7.5 g (½ tsp) coriander seeds
7.5 g (½ tsp) cumin seeds
1 clove
15 g (1 tbsp) finely chopped lemongrass
15 g (1 tbsp) chopped fresh ginger
50 g (2 oz) chopped shallots
15 g (1 tbsp) chopped garlic plus 3 medium garlic
   cloves, sliced thin
1 green chilli, destemmed and chopped
pinch of ground cardamom
pinch of turmeric
15 g (1 tbsp) sugar
5 g (1 tsp) Thai shrimp paste
15 ml (1 tbsp) Thai fish sauce
600 ml (1 pint) chicken stock
600 ml (1 pint) water
vegetable oil for frying
24 singing scallops (about 900 g-1 kg (2 to
   2½ lb)), rinsed in cold water
fresh coriander for garnish

1. In a small frying pan over moderate heat, dry-toast coriander and cumin, shaking frying pan frequently so seeds don't burn, for 3 to 4 minutes, until fragrant. Let seeds cool and grind in a mortar and pestle with the clove. Reserve.

2. Put the lemongrass in mortar and pestle with the ginger and grind into a paste, scraping side often. Add shallots and the chopped garlic and continue to grind mixture until paste is quite smooth. Add the green chilli with the ground cardamom, turmeric, sugar and the reserved ground spices and mash into the paste. Add the shrimp paste and fish sauce and blend, scraping the side of the mortar and making sure that the sauce doesn't splash out.

3. Scrape the curry paste into a medium saucepan and add chicken stock and water. Stir to blend. Cook over moderately high heat for 10 minutes.

4. While broth is cooking, heat 1 cm (½ in) of vegetable oil in a small saucepan until hot but not smoking. Add sliced garlic and cook, stirring, 2 to 3 minutes, until garlic is light golden in colour. Drain garlic slices on paper towels.

5. Reduce the heat under the broth to moderate so that the broth simmers. Add the scallops and cook for about 2 minutes, until shells are wide open. Remove scallops as they open.

6. Ladle 225 ml (8 fl oz) of broth into each of 4 bowls. Put 6 scallops in each bowl and garnish with the garlic chips and the coriander.

PRAWNS

Not too much has changed in prawns in America. Prawns (known in the U.S. as shrimp, in both singular and plural) have always been tremendously popular and, after canned tuna, they continue to be America's most heavily consumed seafood. The new wrinkles are new ways to consume mass quantities of them (for instance, at salad bars, in Cajun shrimp boils, at restaurants that can prepare even more of them because they leave the shells on). And then there's the new ethnic factor: we've been recently gobbling up prawns (which take wonderfully well to strong sauces) at Chinese, Thai, Indian, Italian, Spanish and Mexican restaurants and dabbling with those recipes at home.

Prawn quality has always been good and there has been no major upgrade. What's behind the history of good prawn quality is the fact that prawns freeze extremely well and virtually all prawns in the United States market have been frozen. There is no movement to change this.

There is also no movement to provide variety to the

consumer (as in the mushrooming variety of oysters in the market). There are many different kinds of prawns in the world, both wild and farmed—but our markets carry on business as usual, trumpeting no catch of 'South China Sea wild white shrimp,' or the like, simply offering, as always, 'small,' 'medium,' 'large,' and, occasionally, 'jumbo'.

Nevertheless, there are a few key things to know that will make you a better prawn buyer.

- 'Fresh prawns' in the market are almost always defrosted prawns—and, if they were defrosted a while ago, they can seem anything but 'fresh'. Touch them and make sure they feel firm, with firm, intact shells, fully filled by the prawn; loose, soft prawns, with broken shells sliding off the prawn, are to be avoided. Look for a shine on the prawn; older ones have only a dull sheen. Avoid prawns with yellowing shells, which is a sign of age. And prawns should be fresh-smelling; if they're not, they may have iodinelike odours (which, though unpleasant, don't mean the prawns are spoiled), or ammonia-like odours (which do mean the prawns are spoiled).

- A key to good health in prawns is the absence of black spots on the shells; the presence of black spots means that the prawns have begun to deteriorate. Some unscrupulous prawn handlers try to bleach black spots off the shells of unfresh prawns, by using sodium bisulphite; this gives the prawn a gritty feel outside their shells. Avoid them.

- We think the very best prawns to buy are live prawns (out of tanks); they're the freshest and sweetest—plus, they have their heads on, which, when sucked for their juices, provide great eating. You probably won't be able to find these, but regular defrosted prawns with heads on at least provide the prawn-head experience.

- Don't buy peeled and deveined prawns. Sometimes they sit in ice or water, which—with no shell to protect them—can make them taste bland and watery. To add insult to injury, they cost more than peel-on prawns.

- Because most prawns are frozen in large blocks and defrosted by individual shops (raising all kinds of questions about the timing of the defrosting), one of the best ways to buy prawns is in frozen blocks and then defrost them yourself. Five-pound blocks are commonly available. Defrost in the refrigerator. All of the defrosted prawns should be consumed within a few days. The frozen block, however, will last for months in the freezer.

- Prawns are always sorted by size. Lacking government regulation, however, the size categories in fish stores (small, medium, large) are arbitrary. The best way to get some consistency in your prawn-buying life is to start thinking of prawns in a pieces-per-kilogram (lb) way. If 1 kg (2lb 4 oz) of prawns has fewer than 10 prawns in it, the prawns are enormous. Under 20 per 450 g (1 lb) means very large prawns. At the other end of the scale, 70 prawns per 450 g (1 lb) means pretty small prawns. Once you're comfortable with this and know what you're looking for, you can say to the fishmonger 'How many prawns per 450 g (1 lb) in those 'medium' prawns?' If you're looking for 30 per 450 g (1 lb) and he says 'seventy,' you'll probably need 'large' prawns.

- What's the best size? That depends on your taste, your pocketbook and how you're using the prawns. Smaller prawns are least expensive, but take the most trouble to peel; the largest prawns are the most expensive, but take the least trouble to peel. Smaller prawns are sometimes in the worst condition; the largest prawns sometimes seem bloated, flesh and flavourless. All things considered, we generally opt for prawns that come about 30 per 450 g (1 lb) (call them what you will).

- As to prawn varieties: there are many and many ways of grouping them. One good thing to know is that most prawns are either white, pink, or brown; generally speaking, white offer the highest quality, brown the lowest.

- Brown prawns from the Gulf of Mexico are most likely to have a medicinal, iodine aroma. This is not an indication of spoilage, but it's unpleasant nevertheless; it comes from the high iodine content in their diet.
- White prawns from the Gulf of Mexico, on the other hand, are the prawns in American markets that are usually considered best, both in flavour and texture. Unfortunately, they are almost never identified as Gulf Whites; get to know your fishmonger and ask to see the packing information he gets upon receipt of the prawns.
- A debate rages concerning farmed prawns versus wild prawns. The usual issues prevail: farm-raised are more consistent, wild are more flavourful. On those rare occasions that you can determine whether your prawns are wild or farm-raised, you may find the farm-raised to be a little milder in flavour, a little more watery.

Prawn recipes

For other delicious ways to cook prawns, see the recipes for grilled prawn salad with sun-dried tomatoes, capers, fresh basil and toasted pine nuts on page 25; mild okra-thickened green gumbo with chicken, prawns and fresh herbs on page 40; posole with shellfish on page 43; Thai hot and sour soup on page 58; Indian split pea soup with seared prawns and fresh tomato relish on page 70; pad thai with prawns on page 153; paella on page 229; and prawn and rice salad, sushi-style, with sesame and avocado on page 233.

PRAWN COCKTAIL WITH THREE SAUCES

This has long been America's favourite way to eat prawns—and, therefore, doesn't usually score points among serious 'foodies'. No matter—you should never be ashamed of serving prawn cocktail, because it's an absolutely delicious way to get a party off the ground.

This is particularly so if you've got great, springy prawns and if you've cooked them perfectly (mushy prawn cocktail *is* something to disdain). Our radical cooking method actually involves no cooking at all; the prawns just kind of steep in hot water. This makes them crunchy and absolutely delicious. The whole effort, of course, will be further strengthened if you have a terrific homemade cocktail sauce to offer. In fact, if you're entertaining, why not make 3 cocktail sauces, so your guests can have a choice?

MAKES ENOUGH FOR 12 AS A PARTY STARTER

3 litres (5¼ pints) water
45 g (3 tbsp) coarse salt
900 g (2 lb) large prawns (4 to 5 dozen), unpeeled

1. Place water in a large, heavy saucepan. Add coarse salt and bring to a boil. Add prawns and turn off heat. Stir. Test after 2 to 3 minutes. Remove prawns when they seem just cooked.

2. Chill in the refrigerator until ready to serve (at least 1 hour), then let them warm slightly before serving. Serve unpeeled, or peeled, with 1 or more sauces.

How to handle prawns

Generally speaking, we like to cook prawns with their shells on; this protects the flesh from heat, retains juice and intensifies flavour. Peel-on prawns take nicely to boiling, steaming, grilling (where the charred shell picks up tremendous flavour) and sautéing. The only drawback to using peel-on prawns in these methods is that any accompanying sauce won't come into contact with the flesh of the prawns.

That's why, on saucy occasions, we often split the prawns down the back and butterfly it. This is the best of both worlds: the shell is still on to intensify flavour, but some of the flesh is exposed to a sauce.

If you want to peel the prawns before cooking, it's a simple process: simple tear off the little legs at the centre of the prawn, then pull the peel away. Some people like to leave the last section of peel and the tail on, making kind of a handle for the prawn. Save the prawn shells for making prawn stock!

Lastly, there's the question of deveining. It is not true that the black vein running down the back of the prawn is harmful; it is completely innocuous. However, some find it aesthetically objectionable. We don't. If you do, simply cut a small shallow channel in the back of each prawn and remove the black vein.

CLASSIC PRAWN COCKTAIL SAUCE

MAKES ENOUGH SAUCE FOR 4 TO 5 DOZEN PRAWNS

175 ml (6 fl oz) ketchup
45 g (3 tbsp) grated horseradish in vinegar
15 ml (1 tbsp) freshly squeezed lemon juice
a few drops of hot sauce (optional)

Mix ingredients together in a bowl. Serve.

RUSSIAN DRESSING FOR PRAWNS

MAKES ENOUGH SAUCE FOR 4 TO 5 DOZEN PRAWNS

175 ml (6 fl oz) mayonnaise
45 ml (3 tbsp) ketchup

Mix ingredients together in a bowl. Serve.

MUSTARD SAUCE

MAKES ENOUGH SAUCE FOR4 TO 5 DOZEN PRAWNS

125 ml (4 fl oz) mayonnaise
150 ml (5 fl oz) Dijon mustard
10 g (2 tsp) sugar
a few drops of hot sauce (optional)

Mix ingredients together in a bowl. Serve.

PRAWN MARINARA

This is one of the world's greatest examples of prawn-sauté—with-a-sauce. It has been a staple of Italian-American restaurants for decades and its popularity has never faded. Restaurant chefs make it with peeled prawns and we follow their practice—because this encourages the maximum blending of shellfish and tomato sauce flavours.

SERVES 4 AS A FIRST COURSE

450 g (1 lb) large prawns
15 g (1 tbsp) finely chopped garlic
45 ml (3 tbsp) olive oil
½ teaspoon salt, plus more to taste
1 recipe marinara sauce (recipe follows)
30 ml (2 tbsp) rich chicken stock
dried hot red pepper flakes to taste (optional)
salt and black pepper to taste
finely chopped fresh parsley

1. Shell, devein and butterfly the prawns. Mix well in a bowl with the garlic, 15 ml (1 tbsp) of the olive oil and the salt. Marinate, refrigerated, for 1 hour.

2. When ready to cook, place the remaining 30 ml (2 tbsp) of olive oil in a large frying pan over high heat. When the oil is hot, add the marinated prawns, spreading them out so that the cut surfaces lie flat in the bottom of the pan. Place a weight on the prawns (a slightly smaller frying pan works nicely) and press down for 30 seconds to sear the prawns. Remove prawns and reserve. Add the marinara sauce with the chicken stock. Boil rapidly over high heat until no liquid remains, about 5 minutes. Add the reserved prawns, toss well and cook until the prawns are just warm. Add the red pepper flakes, if desired and season with salt and pepper. Sprinkle parsley on top and serve immediately.

GARLICKY MARINARA SAUCE

MAKES ENOUGH SAUCE FOR 450 G (1 LB) PRAWNS

20 ml (4 tsp) olive oil
70 g (2½ oz) very thinly sliced garlic
2 x 800-g (28-oz) cans tomatoes
50 g (2 oz) firmly packed fresh basil leaves, torn

1. Place oil in heavy saucepan over moderately high heat. Add the garlic and sauté, stirring occasionally, until it just starts to brown, about 5 minutes.

2. Empty contents of tomato cans into a sieve, reserving tomato liquid, if desired, for another use. Squeeze the juice out of the tomatoes with your hands, letting the juice run through the sieve. (The remaining tomatoes should be a coarse, chunky pulp). Add tomatoes to pan with the basil. Simmer for 10 minutes, season and serve.

GRILLED PRAWNS WITH LIME-CORIANDER MARINADE

Prawns on the grill are extraordinary; as the shell and flesh brown, they pick up wonderfully sweet additional flavours. In this recipe, partially peeled prawns are used so that both flesh and shell contribute. And prawns are magnificent with the lime-and-coriander flavours of Mexican food; a cold margarita will only reinforce that bond.

SERVES 6 TO 8 AS A FIRST COURSE

1 large bunch of fresh coriander
8 medium-large chopped spring onions
2 green chillies (the heat is up to you)
10 g (2 tsp) chopped garlic
15 ml (1 tbsp) lime juice
10 g (2 tsp) ground cumin
pinch of turmeric
1.3 kg (3 lb) large prawns (about 48)
For garnish
coarse salt

freshly ground black pepper
good chilli powder (like ancho chilli powder)
lime quarters
fresh coriander

1. In a blender or a food processor place the coriander leaves and stems, spring onions, chillies, garlic, lime juice, cumin and turmeric. Purée, adding a little water if necessary to achieve the desired consistency.

2. Peel the prawns, leaving the tail intact. Devein them. Place them in a bowl and toss with the coriander purée. Marinate for 8 to 12 hours.

3. Prepare a moderately hot charcoal fire. When ready to cook, scoop up the prawns so that more of the marinade remains on one side of each one. Place the prawns marinade-side up on the grill. Cook until almost done, about 2 minutes. Turn prawns over and cook quickly on marinade side, about 1 minute. Remove prawns from grill.

4. Divide prawns among serving plates. Pass garnishes at table. Each guest should sprinkle the prawns with coarse salt, pepper, chilli powder, a squeeze of lime juice and a few coriander leaves.

SPANISH PRAWNS IN GARLIC SAUCE (GAMBAS AL AJILLO)

A classic tapa, served in every region of Spain, is also classically simple to prepare. Make sure you use the freshest prawns available; it really makes a difference. This recipe works best when cooked in an earthenware casserole.

SERVES 4 AS A TAPA

350 g (12 oz) fresh medium prawns
coarse salt to taste
50 ml (2 fl oz) extra-virgin olive oil
6 large garlic cloves, chopped

1 bay leaf

1 small hot dried red chilli pepper, seeded and crumbled

3 g (¾ tsp) sweet paprika

freshly ground black pepper to taste

15 g (1 tbsp) chopped fresh parsley

1. Devein the prawns by cutting through the back with the shell still on. Spread them open, but leave the shell attached. Salt lightly and reserve.

2. Heat the oil in an 20-cm (8-in) flameproof earthenware casserole over moderate heat until hot but not smoking. Stir in the garlic, bay leaf and chilli pepper and cook, stirring, until the garlic just begins to colour. Immediately add the prawns, paprika and freshly ground black pepper; cook, stirring constantly, until the prawns are just cooked through, being careful not to overcook. Taste for seasoning and sprinkle prawns with coarse salt if desired. Discard the bay leaf, sprinkle with parsley and serve very hot in the earthenware casserole, with crusty bread on the side.

SQUID

Squid are delicious and much-loved all around the world—but they've never been a favourite in the United States. For many years, squid (usually fried) was only available at Italian restaurants. But enough people tried fried calamari for squid to establish a beachhead here. Then came the Asian invasion: a profusion of squid dishes in restaurants (particularly Thai squid salad, see page 32) finally convinced many Americans that squid is great eating.

As one can see from the low price of squid in fishmongers, however, squid is still not a popular item for home cooks; like its fellow cephalopod, octopus, squid is still more of a restaurant item.

Why? Because people think it's tricky to cook and difficult to clean.

First of all, there is only one trick to squid cookery:

don't cook squid very much at all. Depending on the cut and the heat, 1 minute may be enough; more than 5 minutes is usually too much. A quick blast of heat turns squid from chewy to tender; too much heat turns it from tender to rubbery. You can, of course, save the day by cooking rubbery squid still further; after an hour or so, squid becomes tender again. But we far prefer the chew of squid that have been tenderised by just a few minutes of heat.

As for cleaning squid—why even worry about it? Fish markets have plenty of precleaned squid, at a reasonable price. And the quality doesn't suffer from precleaning. However, if you do want to clean it yourself (which does mean you'll pay next to nothing for your squid), it's really very easy. Here's how to do it:

- Simply lay the squid out on a counter. You'll see, at one end, the tentacles protruding from the squid sac (also called the 'body' or 'hood'). Grasp them firmly and pull them out; you will have removed the head with eyes and this head section will have some of the squid's innards clinging to it.

- Gently probe the point where the head meets the tentacles to locate the beak, a hard and round ball. Then cut the tentacles from the head just on the tentacle side of the beak; this separates the tentacles from the eyes, the beak and the ink sac. Discard all of the latter (unless you're saving the ink for a sauce). Save the tentacles.

- Stick your fingers into the body sac and remove any remaining innards, as well as the 'quill' (a transparent 'spine' that looks like plastic). You now have a clean body sac and tentacles to cook.

- Many chefs like one further refinement: peeling the fine, purple skin away from the body sac.

After cleaning, squid can be treated and/or cut in several ways. You may finely chop the tentacles, combine them with other ingredients and stuff the body sac—which can then be cooked whole. Or, you can cut the body sac into slices and fry it or sauté it along with the tentacles.

There are many different ways to cut the body sac. You can slice it into rings (very common in fried calamari). Or, you can slit it open, spread it out and cut it into strips; horizontally cut strips will curl a bit more in the pan than vertically cut strips. Asian chefs like to score their squid strips in a diamond pattern, by lightly cutting crisscrosses across the surface; this makes them prettier, more tender and better at picking up sauces.

Selecting squid at the fishmonger

First of all . . . squid freezes well. So don't be afraid to buy whole squid from a frozen block. Also don't be afraid to buy precleaned squid; make sure, however, to get an amount of tentacles that's proportionate to the amount of body sacs (or you can ask for more tentacles, if you especially like them . . . as we do).

If you're buying whole fresh squid, you should look for a few things. A creamy white colour, alongside the purple skin, is an indication of freshness; if the white part has become pinkish or, worse yet, brown, don't buy the squid. The skin of fresh squid should glisten and, like all seafood, squid should have a fresh aroma of the sea (with no fishy or cheesy notes).

Squid can grow to enormous size, but the ones that come to market usually come 2 or 3 per 450 g (1 lb). We prefer the smallest ones; you can sometimes find baby squid that are just 5 cm (2 in) in length. They're the sweetest and most tender squid of all.

FRIED CALAMARI

Flash-frying squid in deep oil is one of the best squid-cooking methods. Once upon a time, fried squid could only be found in Little Italy-style red-sauce joints—and they didn't spare the red sauce! Today, all kinds of chefs across the country love to present these crispy little morsels as a meal opener. And, happily, most people have discovered that the flavour and texture of the fried squid are ruined by a heavy blanket of sauce. The

following simple recipe yields the crispiest squid you'll find. We like it with salt alone, maybe a little lemon. But if you crave a sauce, serve on the side one of the mayonnaises you'll find in Chapter Nine (recipes begin on page 492).

SERVES 4 GENEROUSLY AS A FIRST COURSE

700 g (1½ lb) squid, cleaned
225 g (8 oz) plain flour
1.25 g (¼ tsp) cayenne pepper
vegetable oil for frying
salt to taste

1. Slice squid bodies into 5-mm (¼-in) rings. Keep tentacles whole or cut in half lengthways. Dry thoroughly with paper towels.

2. Combine flour with cayenne pepper in a deep bowl. Mix well and have a strainer nearby.

3. Heat 7.5 cm (3 in) of the oil in a deep, straight-sided saucepan or kettle to 190°C (375°F). When oil is hot, dip a few pieces of the squid in the seasoned flour, place squid in strainer and shake off any excess flour. Drop the squid into the oil. (It is important that you do not fry too many pieces of squid at once or the oil temperature will drop.) Fry squid, turning them once, for 3 to 4 minutes, until they are deep golden brown. Remove squid and place on a tray lined with paper towels to drain. Sprinkle with salt immediately.

4. Serve squid immediately, or move cooked squid to baking sheet and keep warm in a preheated 150°C (300°F) oven while you fry the rest.

FRIED SQUID WITH BEER BATTER

This tweaked version of fried squid also yields a crispy result, with a little extra flavour and texture in the coating.

700 g (1½ lb) squid, cleaned
225 g (8 oz) flour
1.25 g (¼ tsp) cayenne pepper
350 ml (12 fl oz) beer
vegetable oil for frying
salt to taste

1. Slice squid bodies into 5-mm (¼-in) rings. Keep tentacles whole or cut in half lengthways. Dry thoroughly with paper towels.

2. Combine 115 g (4 oz) of flour with cayenne pepper in a deep bowl. Mix well and have a strainer near the bowl.

3. Place the rest of the flour in a second bowl and slowly pour in the beer. Whisk only until flour and beer are combined (do not whisk until smooth).

4. Heat 7.5 cm (3 in) of the oil in a deep, straight-sided saucepan or casserole to 190°C (375°F). When oil is hot, dip a few pieces of the squid in the seasoned flour, place squid in strainer and shake off any excess flour. Dip the squid in the beer batter, making sure that you evenly coat each piece, and then carefully drop the squid into the oil. (It is important that you do not fry too many pieces of squid at once or the oil temperature will drop.) Fry squid, turning them once, for 3 to 4 minutes, until they are deep golden brown. Remove squid and place on a tray lined with paper towels to drain. Sprinkle with salt immediately.

5. Move cooked squid to baking sheet and keep warm in a preheated 150°C (300°F) oven while you fry the rest. Serve immediately.

VIETNAMESE STUFFED AND GRILLED SQUID

Many chefs around the world like to stuff squid. This recipe, inspired by Vietnamese treatments of this idea, makes a great barbecue party: as the stuffed squid come off the grill, guests roll up their own portions of squid and garnishes in lettuce leaves. If you wish, you can offer the Vietnamese dipping sauce on page 502.

you can offer the Vietnamese dipping sauce on page 502.

SERVES 8 AS AN APPETISER

10 g (¼ oz) dried shiitakes (2 to 3 medium
    mushrooms)
8 whole, small squid (about 450 g (1 lb))
115 g (4 oz) raw prawns, peeled and cleaned
10 g (2 tsp) chopped garlic
15 g (1 tbsp) chopped fresh ginger
10 ml (2 tsp) nuoc nam (Vietnamese fish sauce)
2.5 g (½ tsp) sugar
2.5 ml (½ tsp) sesame oil
pinch freshly ground black pepper
15 ml (1 tbsp) peanut oil plus additional for
    rubbing the squid
broad, soft lettuce leaves (green-leaf lettuce is
    perfect)
For garnish
julienne strips of carrot
julienne strips of spring onion
fresh coriander leaves
fresh mint
crushed peanuts
Vietnamese fish sauce
fresh lime juice

1. Prepare a hot charcoal fire.

2. Cover the shiitakes with warm water and soak for 30 minutes, or until soft. Cut off the stems and discard. Chop the caps and reserve.

3. Clean the squid, leaving the purple membrane attached. Discard the head, beak and body organs. Reserve the body sacs and tentacles. Chop the tentacles coarsely and add to the work bowl of a food processor. Chop the prawns coarsely and add to the food processor with the garlic, ginger, fish sauce, sugar, sesame oil and black pepper. Add the reserved chopped shiitake mushrooms. Process for about 10 seconds, or until a coarse paste is formed.

4. Place the 15 ml (1 tbsp) of peanut oil in a wide, heavy frying pan over very high heat. Add the paste, spreading it out into a single layer. Brown it for about 1 minute on one side. Turn it and brown for 1 minute on the other side. Remove and let cool until cool enough to handle.

5. Stuff the body sacs with the paste. (Do not overstuff; there should be about 1 cm (½ in) of space near the opening of each squid sac.) Close the openings by pushing a few toothpicks through each one. Rub each sac with a little peanut oil.

6. Place the stuffed squid on the grill. Cook, turning frequently, about 10 minutes. (The squid should be browned on all sides.)

7. To serve, place each stuffed squid on a lettuce leaf. Top with garnishes and roll up.

Note: If you want a more elegant presentation at a sit-down dinner: place a lettuce leaf on a dinner plate. Slice a cooked, stuffed squid sac into 5 or 6 rounds and place on the lettuce. Cover with garnishes and sprinkle with fish sauce and lime juice.

RAW FISH DISHES

In the days of old, raw fish in America meant two things only: clams and oysters. Then came the sushi bar explosion . . . and the idea of raw 'anything-that-swims' flooded restaurants of all kinds. Here are some of the most popular raw fish ideas in restaurants that are easy to make at home.

SASHIMI

The basic division of dishes at a sushi bar is twofold: first there are slices of raw fish (called sashimi), then there is vinegared rice combined with pieces of raw fish, cooked fish, egg or vegetable (this is called sushi).

Making sushi at home is difficult, because it takes a great deal of practice and precision to emulate sushi-bar sushi. We don't recommend making your own sushi at home.

Making sashimi, however—slices of raw fish—is another kettle of you-know-what; making it at home is much easier than making sushi.

The hardest part is finding fish that's ultra-fresh and unquestionably safe. This is not easy at a fish store that expects you to cook your fish before eating it. Talk to your fishmonger and let him know that you intend to make sashimi of what you buy. Better yet, buy fish for sashimi at a Japanese fish store, where the fishmonger is trained to know which fish is safe to eat raw.

Generally speaking, fish from deep waters (though not all of them) are the best candidates for sashimi; fathoms down, they have less chance to ingest the parasites that plague shallow-water fish. Do not make sashimi from salmon and swordfish, unless they have been marinated or frozen. Raw herring and mackerel are also to be avoided. Some of your safest choices are tuna, sea bass, Spanish mackerel and tilefish—but remember: they must be spanking fresh. And make sure to use the fish the same day that you buy it.

The main cut for sashimi that you can easily do at home is called *hira-zukuri*. To make it, you need a rectangular block of fish—say, tuna—that is roughly 3 cm x 5 mm (1¼ in wide by ¾ in high) (have your fishmonger prepare this for you). The length of the block depends on how much sashimi you're making; to make 16 pieces of traditionally cut tuna sashimi (a good portion for 4 people), you'll need a (175-g (6-in)) long block of tuna. Dipping your sharp, long knife in a solution of rice vinegar and ice water (125 ml (4 fl oz) rice vinegar to 450 ml (16 fl oz) water) and holding the knife at a 90-degree angle to the board, cut the block of tuna straight down into ⅜-inch thick pieces (firmer fish can take a 3 mm (⅛ in) cut and softer fish can be cut as thick as 2 cm (½ inch).

Arranging and serving the sashimi is up to you. In a sushi bar, of course, the fish slices would be placed up against each other, domino fashion, in the order in which they were cut. They may be resting against a mound of seaweed or freshly cut strips of mooli (daikon) (Japanese white radish). Garnishes are minimal, but a small mound of wasabi (green horseradish paste) and a pile of gari (pickled ginger) are mandatory. You can easily buy both at specialty shops and Japanese groceries. Serve the gari as is; mix wasabi powder with a little water, as in making dry English mustard (let it sit for 20 minutes after mixing).

Of course, in the New Age kitchen, anything is possible. You can serve your sashimi next to a tangle of greens. You can pour a sesame-oil dressing over it. You can dot it with hot sauce, in the style of sushi maverick Nobu Matsuhisa. Raw fish is a wonderful, light meal-opener; let your imagination be your guide.

SEVICHE

Raw fish marinated in lime or lemon juice is popular all over Latin America; in the eighties, its popularity spread to Latin restaurants, then to all kinds of restaurants in North America. Why not? It was perfectly in tune with our times—light, clean, low in fat. A kind of south-of-the-border sashimi. Moreover, one didn't have to worry about harmful microorganisms in the fish, because the citrus juice 'cooks' the flesh. It does this by lowering the pH level of the fish, creating an environment that kills off most micoorganisms. And the fish even tastes a little cooked, because the acid coagulates the protein, just as heat does; raw, translucent fish is turned whitish by the citric acid.

Lots of different fish are used in South America, Central America, Mexico and the Caribbean for seviche (which is also spelled *ceviche*). Spanish mackerel is popular in Mexico, bass in Peru, prawns and lobster in Ecuador—and almost everything that swims has been tried by inventive American chefs.

We like firm-fleshed white fish for seviche, cut into thin slices. Too often, we feel, thick chunks of soft-fleshed fish are used and the resulting chew is unappealing. Also, we trust our fish department for the safety of our fish—and thereby cut down the 'cooking' time drastically, resulting in a much better texture in our seviche. Also, it's important to drain the liquid off and add the vegetables late—lest you get a watery, unappealing seviche.

QUICK HALIBUT SEVICHE WITH GRAPEFRUIT AND CHILLIES

This fabulous seviche solves all the problems. Halibut is a perfect seviche fish (if you prefer shellfish, you may substitute thin slices of sea scallops). Marinating time is very short, keeping the fish at a resilient, almost carpaccio-like state. The dish will vary depending on the heat of the chillies, so adjust the recipe to taste. We like to leave room for a little more heat—which comes in the form of a hot sauce applied at the end. Choose a good, flavourful one that's more than just hot; a great brand is West Indies Creole Hot Pepper Sauce, made in the West Indies. And a drizzle of fabulous Andalusian extra-virgin olive oil, green and herbal-tasting, will crank things up even further.

SERVES 6 AS A FIRST COURSE

450 g (1 lb) halibut fillet
125 ml (4 fl oz) freshly squeezed lime juice
150 ml (5 fl oz) freshly squeezed grapefruit juice
1 whole grapefruit
2.5 g (½ tsp) very finely chopped garlic
30 g (2 tbsp) very finely chopped red chillies
15 g (1 tbsp) very finely chopped green chillies
30 g (2 tbsp) chiffonade of fresh mint
coarse salt to taste
hot sauce to taste
extra-virgin olive oil for drizzling the seviche

1. With a very sharp knife, cut the halibut into thin, broad slices. Place in a bowl and toss with the lime juice and grapefruit juice. Let sit at room temperature for 15 minutes.

2. While the halibut is sitting, cut the grapefruit in half crossways and, using a grapefruit knife, cut out pieces of grapefruit. Slice each piece in half lengthways.

3. When ready to serve seviche, drain the liquid completely from the halibut and discard liquid. Add grapefruit pieces to the fish with the garlic, red chillies, green chillies and mint. Toss gently. Divide among 6 plates, laying out the strips of halibut flatly on each plate. Season with coarse salt, sprinkle with hot sauce and drizzle with extra-virgin olive oil. Serve immediately.

TUNA CARPACCIO

First came the trendiness of raw beef carpaccio in American restaurants of the eighties—fuelled by tales of Harry's Bar in Venice—but not long after that came the lighter raw tuna version. Soon, it was being served at fancy French seafood restaurants, then Fancy French any-restaurants, as well as sophisticated New American restaurants.

TUNA CARPACCIO WITH MESCLUN AND PARMIGIANO-REGGIANO

This recipe is especially light thanks to lots of lemon and clean greens. Make sure you buy very fresh tuna from the fishmonger and don't forget to tell him you plan to serve it raw. Your safest route is buying the tuna from a market that caters to a Japanese clientele.

SERVES 8 AS A FIRST COURSE

10 basil leaves
1 garlic clove
125 ml (4 fl oz) extra-virgin olive oil
2 lemons
salt and pepper to taste
450 g (1 lb) raw tuna

115 g (4 oz) mesclun
115 g (4 oz) chunk of Parmigiano-Reggiano

1. Rinse the basil leaves to remove all traces of dirt, then dry well. Put the basil in a food processor with the garlic and purée. Add the olive oil in a thin stream in order to get a thick mixture. Add the juice of 1 lemon and salt and pepper to taste. Set dressing aside.

2. Cut the tuna fillet into thin slices with a very sharp knife, or have your fishmonger slice it for you. Cut the slices into small pieces so that you end up with a total of 24 pieces. Place each piece between two sheets of clingfilm or waxed paper and, using the flat side of a large knife or a heavy pan, pound into very thin pieces. (They should be approximately 5 x 7.5 cm (2 x 3 in)).

3. Drizzle some of the dressing on each of the plates. Put 3 pieces of tuna on each plate and drizzle with more dressing, reserving 45 ml (3 tbsp) of dressing. Wrap each plate with a piece of clingfilm and chill in the refrigerator until just before serving.

4. Wash and dry the mesclun and store in a bowl in the refrigerator until ready to use.

5. When ready to serve tuna, remove plates and mesclun from the refrigerator. Toss mesclun with the reserved 45 ml (3 tbsp) of dressing and season with salt and pepper. Put a small amount of the dressed mesclun on the centre of each thin slice of tuna. Sprinkle some juice from the second lemon over the mesclun and tuna. Cut the cheese into thin slices using a vegetable peeler and divide among the 8 plates. Sprinkle with salt and pepper and serve immediately.

GRAVLAX

Gravlax means 'buried salmon'—and that's exactly what the Vikings did to their catch, centuries ago, in order to preserve it. They chose the cold beach; you can just bury it in your refrigerator for a couple of days and get a splendid result. Lots of chefs did just that in the eighties and nineties, as cold gravlax became super-hot in all kinds of restaurants.

GRAVLAX WITH JUNIPER AND GIN

This gravlax has a terrific interplay of sweet and salty elements—plus a lot more flavour than usual, thanks to the delicious addition of juniper and gin. Serve it on dark bread as an opening pass-around at a party, or make a main course of it—broad gravlax slices, accompanied by mustardy potato salad, tart cucumber salad, dark bread and a bottle of frozen aquavit.

MAKES ABOUT 80 SLICES, A GOOD PARTY DISH FOR 20 TO 40 PEOPLE

1.8-kg (4-lb) fillet of very fresh salmon
25 ml (4 fl oz) gin
8 to 10 juniper berries, crushed
175 g (6 oz) coarse salt
175 g (6 oz) sugar
10 g (2 tsp) black peppercorns, crushed
1 large bunch dill, stems removed

1. Remove any bones from the salmon and wipe any scales off with a paper towel. Line a large glass dish, at least 2.5cm (1 in) high, with two layers of clingfilm that overhang the sides of the dish. Place the fillet on the clingfilm, skin side down.

2. Pour the gin evenly over the salmon. With the back of a heavy knife, break the juniper berries into coarse pieces. Spread the broken berries on the salmon and press in lightly so they do not fall off.

3. Combine the coarse salt, sugar and peppercorns together in a small bowl. Mix with fingers until well blended. Spread the mixture evenly over the entire surface of the salmon.

4. Take three-quarters of the dill and scatter it over the entire surface of the fish. Reserve the remaining dill.

5. Wrap the overhanging clingfilm around the fillet. Place a heavy frying pan on top of the fillet to weight the fish down evenly. Add additional weight, such as tin cans, to the frying pan . Place all of this on the bottom shelf of the refrigerator and let sit for 3 days.

6. When ready to serve, take the salmon out of the clingfilm. Wipe off the dill, the salt mixture and the juniper berries. Chop the reserved fresh dill finely and spread evenly on the fillet. Place the fish on a cutting board. Using a long, narrow, sharp knife and keeping the knife at a 30-degree angle, cut the salmon into thin slices (don't include the skin). The traditional cut starts diagonally at one corner of the salmon, then works back towards the centre of the fillet.

FISH EGGS

Fish eggs have long played a role in American gastronomic life, as cheap, horrible 'caviar' and as poorly cooked shad roe. But with the rise of the Quality Revolution, chefs everywhere have learned how to select the best roes and how to place them in the best contexts at the table.

One of the great things about fish eggs, despite the prohibitive price of the most famous ones, is that the 'best' doesn't necessarily mean the most expensive. There's lots of good egg-eating out there that's not beluga, osetra or sevruga.

INEXPENSIVE FISH ROE

If you like the salty, sea-bright, crumbly texture of fish roe but can't pony up the big caviar prices, you can be comforted at least by the great European practice of working inexpensive fish roes into memorable dishes. All over the continent, hard roes from such fish as carp, herring, tuna and cod are extracted and sometimes smoked. A favourite of ours is the bottarga of southern Italy, especially of Sardinia; this is grey mullet or tuna roe that has been salted and sun-dried. The tuna version is a little stronger in flavour, but both are used in pastas and salads.

TARAMASALATA

This is one of the great Greek 'dips' that so often begin a meal in Greece, accompanied by ouzo; it comes directly from the ancient Greeks, by way of later Christians who served it as a meatless dish during Lent. It is made from tarama, or carp roe; the roe is whipped into a paste with some kind of starch (bread or potatoes or both), seasoned with lemon juice and mounted with olive oil. It's on every Greek menu in America, but during the last decade has achieved crossover status in some Mediterranean, even New American restaurants. To make it at home, you must buy a refrigerated jar of tarama (usually 280 g (10 oz)). The roe will probably be a rich pink; this indicates that food colouring was used. If you can find a pale pink tarama, it's likely to taste better. We sell a very good one made by Fantis. Serve with pitta, olives, cucumber, spring onions and lemon wedges as a great party-opener. Good with ouzo or retsina.

SERVES 8 AS AN APPETISER

1 large floury potato
140 g (5 oz) tarama
50 g (2 oz) very finely chopped onion
350 ml (12 fl oz) Greek olive oil
juice of 2 lemons

1. Peel the potato and boil until tender. When cool enough to handle, force through a sieve. Reserve.

2. Immerse the tarama in lukewarm water and soak for 10 minutes.

3. Drain the tarama and place it in a large mixing bowl. Beat with an electric hand mixer until creamy. Beat in

the reserved potato and the onion. Still beating, alternately add the olive oil in a fine stream and the lemon juice. Taste for seasoning and serve.

SHAD ROE

The eggs of the bony female shad have long been regarded as a treat in the United States —though we wonder why, because the traditional cooking methods spoil shad roe. It's a rich item to begin with—so why poach it in butter (!), as most cookery books recommend? Why pair it with fatty bacon? And then, for error 3: why destroy the lovely, creamy richness that shad roe has by overcooking it until the soft eggs turn into a hard, grainy mass? If you've never been wild about shad roe, try the following recipe.

Buying shad roe

Shad roe is highly perishable, so the trick is getting roe that's as close as possible to being in the water. Best of all, of course, is having the fishmonger remove the roe of a freshly caught shad for you, right in front of your eyes. Failing that, you need to ask when the roe you're considering buying was extracted from the fish; if the answer isn't 'today' or 'yesterday,' move on.

You have several visual clues to freshness. Shad roe come in pairs, connected by a fine membrane; make sure the pair is intact and the membrane is undisturbed. Colour should be bright orange to deep red; brown is a bad sign. Look for moistness; dry shad roe is not fresh. Then, of course, use your nose, to make sure the roe doesn't smell fishy.

STEAMED SHAD ROE BUNDLES WITH GINGER-LEMON SAUCE

There are 3 important elements in this recipe. First of all, the shad is cooked in a water treatment (steaming), which helps to melt its fat. Secondly, it's cooked quickly, which helps it to retain its lovely texture. Lastly, a light, citric, Asian-influenced sauce cuts through the richness of the shad roe, lightening it considerably.

SERVES 8 AS A FIRST COURSE

450 g (1 lb) shad roe
salt and pepper to taste
32 large, unbroken spinach leaves
115 g (4 oz) julienne of parsnip
1 knob of ginger, about thumb-size
20 ml (4 tsp) freshly squeezed lemon juice
20 ml (4 tsp) nam pla (Thai fish sauce)
5 g (1 tsp) granulated sugar

1. Cut the shad roe into 8 pieces. Salt and pepper well.

2. Remove heavy ribs from spinach leaves. Dip the leaves in hot water for a few seconds, or until just soft. Overlap the edges of four leaves, making one wide sheet of spinach and place 1 piece of shad roe in the centre. Sprinkle with a little lemon juice and top with 15 g (1 tbsp) of parsnip. Fold the spinach over the shad roe, making a neat bundle. Continue until 8 bundles are made.

3. Place the bundles in a steamer over boiling water and steam for 6 minutes.

4. *Make the sauce:* Grate the ginger until you have 10 g (2 tsp) of shreds with juice. Mix it in a small bowl with the lemon juice, fish sauce and sugar. Let stand 10 minutes.

5. Place 1 steamed shad roe bundle on each of 8 small plates. Pour the sauce through a fine strainer and drizzle it evenly over and around the bundles.

Note: If you wish a slightly prettier, but fussier, presentation, you could slice the bundles and fan them out on the plates. Also, if you wish to make a main course of this, serve 3 bundles a person, with rice on the side.

CAVIAR

Though many foods are carelessly given the name 'caviar,' to the connoisseur 'caviar' means only one thing: the lightly processed eggs of 3 types of sturgeon that swim in the Caspian Sea, which is currently ringed by Russia, Kazakhstan, Azerbaijan, Turkmenistan and Iran.

Anything else called 'caviar' is an impostor. This is not just culinary posturing or a game for snobs. The caviar from the Caspian Sea really is the finest in the world—or at least one can say that no other 'caviar' tastes anything like it. Is it worth the price? Once people get addicted to its haunting flavour and texture, it most certainly is.

But there's a caveat here. Only *top-quality* Caspian Sea caviar is worth the price. The recent breakup of the Soviet Union created chaos in an already chaotic caviar market and there's a wide disparity of quality among caviars available in the United States today.

To buy intelligently (or should we say 'invest'), it's important to know the differences among the 3 types of caviar:

Beluga sturgeon yield the most expensive eggs, bringing close to $2,000 (£1,200) at retail for a top-grade kilogram. This does not necessarily mean that they are the best eggs. They come from the scarcest fish of the 3, which partially explains their high price. The beluga is also the largest fish of the 3, sometimes as long as 6 metres (20 feet), which means that the beluga eggs are larger than other eggs. The market prizes this too—though egg size, to our taste, is irrelevant when it comes to caviar quality. Beluga caviar is usually light grey to dark grey and, often, the least intensely flavoured of the three caviars. At its best, however, it has a haunting buttery quality that the other caviars can't match.

Osetra sturgeon yield eggs that are one rung down in size (osetra sturgeon don't usually exceed 2 metres (6½ feet) in length) and one rung down in price 1 kg (2¼ lb) top-grade osetra goes for under $1,000 (£600).

But osetra caviar has a special distinction. Because the osetra sturgeon swims at a deeper level than the other fish and accordingly has a different diet, the flavour of the eggs stands out; you can catch a nutty and/or herbal nuance in osetra caviar. The eggs range in colour from nearly yellow-grey to brown-black. Osetra, in our opinion, is the best value in the market. And if all 3 caviars cost exactly the same, we'd still buy mostly osetra.

Sevruga sturgeon are the smallest (only 5 feet long) and the smallish eggs they yield bring the lowest price (usually around $650 (£390) a kilo for top-grade). Sevruga caviar is often the darkest of the three caviars, ranging from medium grey to nearly black and, to our taste, seems the briniest, the most intensely flavoured. It is often the choice of European connoisseurs and it's important to remember that when one buys 'just' sevruga, one is not getting an inferior product by any means.

For all 3 caviars, the word *malossol* should appear on the label. This means 'lightly salted' in Russian and indicates a lower salt content than non-malossol caviars.

The best advice in getting value for money when you buy caviar is: buy from a reputable store. There are some shady operations that offer caviar at cut-rate prices—but the quality of their caviar is often as low as the price. There can be many things wrong with caviar; things can go awry at many different points in the caviar 'chain'. Think of the extra money you spend on buying caviar from a reputable purveyor as an insurance policy for your caviar.

If at all possible, taste before buying. Every 1.8-kg (4-lb) tin of caviar (the customary shipping size) is different. Make sure the caviar eggs are not broken or dried out. Good caviar is not salty, or fishy, or bitter, or sour. The best caviar has subtle layers of flavour. Don't be alarmed if the eggs don't seem individual, or don't 'pop' in your mouth; firm eggs are a sign of pasteurisation, which kills the uncooked flavour of great caviar. The texture of great caviar is something like a gooey jam.

If it's possible, have the store pack your portion of caviar right on the spot, right out of its 1.8-kg (4-lb) tin. If the caviar has been prepacked, take it home and consume it within a few days. Once the jar has been opened, the caviar should be eaten as soon as possible.

How should you serve caviar? To the connoisseur, there's no debate: great caviar should be served by itself, on a spoon, without any eggs, onions, or crackers.

Because so much inferior caviar has been foisted on an unknowing public over the years—we're talking really inferior caviar, like little salt pellets called lumpfish caviar sitting at room temperature in a jar on a supermarket shelf—people have had to devise ways to get this 'gourmet' food down. So our parents and grandparents served their 'caviar' with a host of add-ons that masked the flavour.

When you have real caviar and certainly when you have top-grade caviar, you don't have to do that. In fact, to do it is to commit a crime against good taste. Caviar is magnificent just by itself. Nothing beats sinking your spoon into an embarrassingly large tin of caviar, extracting a glistening mound and directing it, ungarnished, straight into the receiving department.

There are multiple serving options. If you give each guest his or her own tin, things are very simple. A 25-g (1-oz) tin is considered a decent taste, a 50-g (2-oz) tin for each person is generous and a 115-g (4-oz) tin for each person is very eighties. You may wish just to pass these tins out, if the occasion's informal, or you may place each tin on a bed of cracked ice on a plate and serve each plate at table.

If you have purchased one large tin of caviar—say, 400 g (14 oz)—you may, if the company's right and the mood requires it, simply pass out spoons and encourage dive-bombing. Or, in a more formal setting, you may divide the caviar among little dishes, egg cups, or ramekins, possibly placing each one on a bed of cracked ice. If you're really serious about serving caviar, you can buy individual-serving caviar plates that rest on receptacles designed for cracked ice.

We usually use the divide-into-small-ramekins

technique. But these details don't significantly affect the taste of the caviar. What does have an effect is the spoon you choose. The classic theory is correct: avoid silver. This can adversely alter caviar's taste, turning it metallic. Much better are spoons made out of horn, mother-of-pearl, or ivory. Caviar specialists sell these in a wide variety of shapes, sizes and styles. Some look like spoons, some look more like paddles; we like the invitation to indulgence that the latter issue.

Though we are caviar purists, every once in a while someone comes up with a great idea for combining caviar with other foods that are low-key in flavour. Two restaurant ideas for caviar became very trendy in the eighties and they are not difficult to reproduce at home.

Caviar substitutes

First of all, there *is* no substitute for caviar. But if you wish to serve simple, unenhanced fish eggs to your guests and if you're not willing to pay the caviar prices, there are a number of roes that you may want to consider. Here's what we think of the roes you're likely to find:

Kaluga This is a species of sturgeon that's found in the Amur and Liman rivers of China. It yields a roe that can be almost as good as Caspian Sea caviar, though it's inconsistent and occasionally salty. We'd be more excited about it if it didn't cost almost as much as the real thing.

American Sturgeon Caviar Be careful with this one. Sometimes the quality is extremely poor. Sometimes the roe doesn't even come from sturgeon, but from a fish called the paddlefish. When it's good, it most resembles sevruga caviar—though saltier and with firmer eggs. It sells for about half the price of the cheapest Caspian Sea caviar.

Trout Roe This one doesn't look a thing like caviar—but it is, by far, our favourite caviar substitute. The eggs are

orange-gold and very small—but the flavour is sublime. It combines salty and sweet elements, with a subtle smoky undertone. It crunches a lot more than caviar, but we don't hold that against it. The best comes from the Carolinas and a pound costs about the same as an 25 g (1 oz) of top-quality sevruga.

Salmon Roe Many people first became familiar with salmon roe at the sushi bar, where it is called *ikura*. The eggs are large (about twice the size of trout eggs), orange-pink, intense and eggy in flavour and often quite sticky. We love serving it as well in non-Japanese contexts, when it becomes one of our preferred caviar substitutes. If you can locate Russian salmon roe (which is available in the United States), you'll find it a little firmer and a little less salty than American salmon roe.

Golden Whitefish Roe This is an extremely mild-flavoured roe, as its pale-yellow colour might suggest. Pleasant, but not profound. Usually from the Great Lakes.

Lumpfish Caviar Ugh! The lumpfish is found chiefly in Scandinavian waters and offers roes of different colours that are usually dyed lurid black or lurid red before being shipped in little jars, unrefrigerated, to American supermarkets. The 'caviar' is grainy, artificially crunchy, fishy and very salty. Lumpfish 'caviar' is primarily responsible for making millions of Americans think they don't like caviar. We don't recommend it

---

BEGGAR'S PURSES

This opulent bite was made popular by Barry Wine at The Quilted Giraffe in New York City. Freshly made crêpes are filled with caviar and crème fraîche, then bunched to resemble the kind of purse that someone in Robin Hood's day might have been carrying through Sherwood Forest. They look just great when placed side by side on a silver platter and passed as hors d'oeuvres at the start of an elegant dinner party. The amount of batter called for below is more than enough for 12 crêpes—which gives you plenty of margin for crêpemaking error.

MAKES 12 PURSES, OR ENOUGH FOR 6 AS AN HORS D'OEUVRE

350 ml (12 fl oz) milk

2 eggs

115 g (4 oz) potato flour

25 g (1 oz) butter, melted and warm

50 fl (2 oz) clarified butter, melted

12 fresh chives

50 ml (2 fl oz) crème fraîche

200 g (7 oz) beluga, osetra or sevruga caviar, chilled

1. Combine the milk, eggs, potato flour and a pinch of salt in a mixing bowl. Whisk until completely incorporated. Pour through a chinois into another bowl. Just before you cook the crêpes, add 15 g (½ oz) of warm melted butter.

2. Heat a non-stick, 12.5- to 18-cm (5- to 6-inch) omelette pan (or round frying pan) over moderately high heat, then brush with some of the clarified butter. Add 50 ml (2 fl oz) of crêpe batter. Working very quickly, swirl the pan around to spread out the batter into a very thin crêpes. Cook until set, about 40 seconds. Turn the crêpes and cook for another 10 seconds or so. (Crêpes should be paper-thin and white; for beggar's purses, you should avoid the brown spots that are desirable in crêpes destined for other uses.) Place the crêpes on a plate and set aside. Brush the pan with some of the clarified butter again and repeat the process until 12 crêpes are made. You may stack the crêpes directly on top of each other, but keep the pile covered with a cloth.

3. Bring a pot of salted water to a boil and dip the chives in the water for 5 seconds. Place under cold water and reserve chives on paper towels.

4. Lay a few crêpes out and place 5 ml (1 tsp) crème

fraîche and 15 g (1 tbsp) caviar in the centre of each one. Pull the edges of the crêpes toward the centre until they meet. Then, working with thumb and forefinger, create small pleats all around the top of the purse (where the crêpe edges meet). You'll have a ruffle at the top. Tie a reserved chive around the top and make sure the purse is tightly secured. (The beggar's purse should look like a small purse, or sack, with the chive functioning as the tie-string. This technique takes a little practice, so don't be frustrated with the first one.) Continue making beggar's purses in the same manner until 12 purses are made.

5. Brush the top of each purse with a little clarified butter and serve immediately.

Variation

RUSSIAN FILLING

In this delicious variation of the now-classic beggar's purse, you get a wider range of flavours in every bite. It's not the pure caviar decadence of the classic—but it does require a lot less caviar, in case you're watching the budget. The purses are made exactly the same way, except that each one is stuffed with 5 g (1 tsp) caviar, (that's only about 60 g (2¼ oz) caviar for 12 beggar's purses), 2.5 ml (½ tsp) crème fraîche, 2.5 g (½ tsp) finely chopped red onion, 2.5 g (½ tsp) finely chopped egg and 2 capers.

PARFAIT OF CAULIFLOWER PURÉE AND CAVIAR

This amazing amuse-gueule (which means something like 'palate-opener' in French) was devised by Joel Robuchon at the great Parisian restaurant Jamin (now closed). The dish has been copied, but not too widely— because the original recipe was pretty complicated, having included lobster jelly along with everything else. But we think the jelly is not necessary, that the soul of this dish is the brilliant blending of airy cauliflower

purée with caviar; the mostly bland, slightly earthy
cauliflower creates one of the best backdrops for caviar
that we know. Serve it to 8 lucky guests at the start of
your next dinner party; it should be the first thing they
eat after sitting down. You may serve it in little egg
cups, or any pretty tiny cups—even cracked egg halves
will do. Or you may serve it it in tiny glasses, which will
enable your guests to see the layering of the ingredients
from the side.

SERVES 8 AS A VERY SMALL FIRST COURSE

175 g (6 oz) firmly packed raw cauliflower florets
¼ medium waxy potato, peeled and cut into large
   chunks
salt and pepper to taste
50 ml (2 fl oz) double cream
175 g (6 oz) top-grade caviar (we like osetra)

1. Bring a pot of salted water to a boil. Add the
cauliflower and potato. Boil until cooked through, about
25 minutes. Drain the vegetables, then pass them twice
through a very fine sieve (like a *tamis*).

2. Place the mixture in a small, heavy saucepan over
moderately high heat and dry it out for 2 to 3 minutes.
(Do not allow it to burn.) Season to taste with salt and
pepper. Chill until very cold.

3. Whip the cream until it's light and firm. Fold whipped
cream carefully into cold cauliflower mixture, preserving
the airiness of the cream if possible. Chill until very
cold.

4. When ready to serve, place one-sixteenth of the caviar
in each of 8 cups or glasses. Top each with one eighth of
the cold cauliflower cream. Top each with the remaining
one-sixteenth of caviar. Chill until very cold and serve.

MEAT

IF FISH, GRAINS AND VEGETABLES ARE THE REIGNING GOOD GUYS OF THE MODERN AMERICAN FOOD SCENE, MEAT IS DEFINITELY THE BAD GUY—AT LEAST WHERE LIP SERVICE IS PAID.

HOWEVER, THE TYPICAL AMERICAN DOES NOT PUT HIS GROCERY MONEY WHERE HIS MOUTH IS; DESPITE THE CONTINUAL BUZZ AGAINST MEAT, AMERICA CONTINUES TO BE ONE OF THE WORLD'S MOST ZEALOUS MEAT-CONSUMING NATIONS.

THE GOOD NEWS IN ALL OF THIS CULINARY SCHIZOPHRENIA IS THAT IN THE EIGHTIES AND NINETIES WE LEARNED TO EAT MEAT A LITTLE MORE SENSIBLY— AND TO MAKE A TRANSITION FROM INDISCRIMINATE SLABS-OF-ANYTHING-RED TO HIGHER-QUALITY VERSIONS OF A WIDER RANGE OF MEAT COOKED IN MORE INTERESTING WAYS.

WHEN, DURING THIS PERIOD, THE FEDERAL GOVERNMENT MADE A DISASTROUS REARRANGEMENT OF ITS BEEF-GRADING CRITERIA (ESSENTIALLY ALLOWING WHAT WAS ONCE LOWER-QUALITY CHOICE-GRADE BEEF TO BE DESIGNATED AS HIGHER-QUALITY PRIME), SOME MEAT CONNOISSEURS TOOK IT

AS A CLARION CALL: IF WE WANT GREAT MEAT, WE HAVE TO PAY MORE CAREFUL ATTENTION TO OUR SOURCES. IN THE WAKE OF THIS, QUALITY BUTCHER SHOPS EVERYWHERE INTENSIFIED THEIR SEARCH FOR GREAT MEAT TO SATISFY THEIR TOP CUSTOMERS. BOUTIQUELIKE MEAT-RAISING OPERATIONS SPRANG UP, OFFERING HIGHER-QUALITY OPTIONS IN ALMOST EVERY CATEGORY, FROM POULTRY TO VEAL TO VENISON. AND THE PURCHASE OF MEAT THROUGH THE MAIL FROM HIGH-END PRODUCERS AND DISTRIBUTORS BECAME ONE OF THE QUALITY-CONSCIOUS CONSUMER'S MEAT-BUYING OPTIONS.

INTRIGUINGLY, AT THE SAME TIME THAT CONSUMERS WERE SEEKING HIGHER QUALITY BEEF, LAMB AND VEAL, THEY WERE ALSO LEARNING TO APPRECIATE CHEAPER CUTS OF MEAT FROM THESE SAME ANIMALS. BEEF-EATING IN RESTAURANTS, FOR EXAMPLE, ONCE MEANT GREAT STEAKS FOR MOST PEOPLE; WHO COULD HAVE PREDICTED THAT IN THE NINETIES BRAISED SHORT RIBS WOULD BECOME A HOT RESTAURANT DISH? OR LAMB SHANKS, RATHER THAN EXPENSIVE LAMB CHOPS? OR OSSO BUCO OVER VEAL CUTLETS? AMERICANS TOOK A PAGE FROM THE EUROPEAN COOKBOOK, IN THIS REGARD; BISTROS, TRATTORIAS AND TASCAS THERE HAVE LONG FOCUSSED ON SLOWLY COOKED CUTS OF INEXPENSIVE MEAT. EVEN SAUSAGES BECAME TRENDY FOOD IN AMERICAN RESTAURANTS.

ALONG WITH THESE DEVELOPMENTS, SOME AMERICANS LEARNED TO EXPAND THE MEAT-EATING REPERTOIRE TO 'OTHER' MEATS. BEEF IS STILL AT THE TOP OF

OUR CHARTS AND PORK IS ANOTHER NATIONAL FAVOURITE. HOWEVER—THOUGH IT'S NOT YET REFLECTED IN SUPERMARKET SALES—FOR YEARS TRENDY RESTAURANTS HAVE REPORTED AN INCREASE IN THE SALE OF SUCH ITEMS AS GAME (ESPECIALLY VENISON), SMALL BIRDS (LIKE QUAIL AND PIGEON), EVEN OFFAL (LIKE SWEETBREADS) AND EXTREMITIES (LIKE PIGS' TROTTERS).

THIS EXPANDED REPERTOIRE OF MEAT ITEMS GREW HAND IN HAND WITH OUR EXPANDED ETHNIC CONSCIOUSNESS IN MEAT PREPARATION. FRENCH AND ITALIAN RESTAURANTS IN AMERICA BECAME MORE AUTHENTIC—WHICH MEANT MORE KINDS OF MEAT FROM MORE PARTS OF ANIMALS. AND NEW ETHNIC RESTAURANTS—SOUTH AMERICAN RESTAURANTS, VIETNAMESE RESTAURANTS AND SPANISH RESTAURANTS—FEATURED THE SAME CARNAL EXPANSION.

PERHAPS THE GREATEST LESSON THAT AMERICANS LEARNED IN THIS TRANSITIONAL PERIOD WAS THAT MEAT DOESN'T HAVE TO BE AT 'THE CENTRE OF THE PLATE.' IN TRADITIONAL AMERICAN DINING, IF THE MEAL INVOLVED MEAT, THEN MEAT DOMINATED THE MEAL (A HUGE STEAK SURROUNDED BY LESSER QUANTITIES OF STARCHES AND VEGETABLES, FOR EXAMPLE). BUT THIS IS AT ODDS WITH THE WAY MOST OF THE WORLD EATS; THROUGHOUT THE THIRD WORLD NATIONS PARTICULARLY, MEAT IS TREATED AS A 'CONDIMENT', SOMETHING TO BOOST THE FLAVOUR OF VEGETABLES, GRAINS, BEANS OR RICE. AS A NATION, WE HAVE NOT YET ARRIVED AT THAT SENSIBILITY—NOR WOULD IT BE A GREAT GASTRONOMIC THING IF WE DID AND RELENTLESSLY STUCK TO IT—

BUT WE HAVE MADE STRIDES TOWARD A BETTER UNDERSTANDING OF HOW MEAT CAN WORK IN COOPERATION WITH OTHER INGREDIENTS TO YIELD DELICIOUS FOOD.

AND THEN, OF COURSE, THERE WAS ONE FURTHER MEAT DEVELOPMENT OF THE EIGHTIES AND NINETIES, THIS ONE PURELY AMERICAN IN ORIGIN: THE ABSOLUTE RAGE, BOTH IN RESTAURANTS AND HOMES, FOR ANYTHING CARNAL SLAPPED ON A BARBECUE GRILL OVER HOT COALS. FIRST IN CALIFORNIA, THEN IN EVERY STATE OF THE UNION, GRILLED MEAT IN RESTAURANTS BECAME A NEAR-OBSESSION.

GRILLING AND SMOKING

Grilling meat had always been a national passion... but in the eighties and nineties this long-established hot practice got even hotter. And, for many Americans, it was joined in the backyard by another, related cooking method: home-smoking.

GRILLING MEAT

Grilling meat has had an interesting reversal in recent decades. Originally a home practice (*the* way of cooking meat for many of our parents), meat-grilling was not something you expected to find in restaurants. Then, in the eighties and nineties—led by California grill restaurants—chefs everywhere started to offer a wide range of grilled meat. And because they did more to these meats, gussying them up as restaurant dishes, they changed the character of our home barbecues.

It's not that hot dogs and burgers ever went out of style, but more kinds of meat went onto our home grills, with more kinds of marinades, rubs and sauces. Our growing awareness of real Southern and Midwestern barbecue played a big role here. Also important were the borrowings from grilling traditions as widespread as Asia's, Latin America's and the Mediterranean's.

Add to this the explosion of grills and grilling paraphernalia newly available to the home cook: everything from lava-rock gas grills to professional long-handled spatulas to a bewildering assortment of fuels and chips.

It's all better than it used to be... but it certainly isn't as easy and intuitive. Here then is our basic guide to New Age grilling.

Grilled meat recipes

For great grilled-meat recipes, see jerk chicken on page 380; Memphis dry-rub ribs on page 407; grilled veal chops with sage jus on page 417; grilled porterhouse steak on page 427; and grilled lamb kofta on page 445.

WHICH GRILL?

To us, the ideal grill is one that permits you to shift the level of the grilling rack so that you may place the food closer to, or farther from, the heat source. The art of grilling is contingent on many factors (including the wind and the relative dryness of your fuel) but adjusting the distance of the meat from the fire is essential. Unfortunately, this type of movable grill is not so easy to find.

America's favourite backyard grill, the Weber, with its domed cover, is good for long, slow, indirect cooking. But the type of restaurant grilling that has become so popular needs no cover and on the Weber you can't adjust the position of the grilling rack.

Oddly enough, the ubiquitous hibachi is one of the few commonly available grills that allow you to adjust positions. Its chief drawback is its small size.

What is arguably the best adjustable grill does not appear in local kitchenware shops. It is called the Grillery and is manufactured by Grillworks, Inc., in Ann Arbor, Michigan. Made of stainless steel, the regular model costs $895 and a super-large one costs $1,600. Grillworks will ship the Grillery anywhere in the United States.

In the eighties the gas grill, with its bed of lava rocks set over gas-fuelled flame, became extremely popular. We have never been crazy about this type of grill. Granted, it's easier to start and to clean than most conventional charcoal grills—but we're talking about cooking here, not starting and cleaning. The heat from the lava rocks never gets as high as we sometimes like heat to be and the flavours of grilling never seem to be as interesting in gas-grilled foods.

WHICH FUEL?

If you're eschewing the gas grill with its lava rocks, as we urge you to do, you are confronted with a basic fuel choice: charcoal or hardwood? Almost everyone in America, except in some restaurants, chooses the former.

What is charcoal? It is burned wood. But if manufacturers burned the wood in the open air, the wood would turn to ash. So they burn it in the absence of oxygen—which creates the hard, black chunks known as charcoal. It is an excellent fuel for grilling, because it burns fairly hot, fairly evenly and fairly long.

Of course, the type of charcoal you choose makes a great deal of difference. America's favourite charcoal, without question, is charcoal briquettes... but to us this is the least attractive charcoal option. Briquettes are made with sawdust and wood chips, which are bound together with other substances (such as petroleum derivatives and sodium nitrate). There's little wood flavour in briquettes and they give off a relatively low heat. Two things are in their favour, however: they burn very evenly and for quite a long time.

A big step up from briquettes, in our opinion, is lump charcoal made from hardwood. These irregularly shaped chunks burn much less evenly and some of them turn to ash before the briquettes have done so. But they furnish a hotter fire, a cleaner fire and a much 'tastier' fire. Lump charcoal was widely available in the fifties, virtually disappeared during the briquette surge of the sixties, seventies and eighties and, happily, is making a comeback in the nineties. Look for it at gourmet specialty shops. If you want an especially hot fire, look for lump charcoal made from mesquite wood.

But charcoal's not the only game in town. An interesting option—in fact, the only option for thousands of years, until charcoal was invented—is hardwood itself. The advantages of cooking with wood are better 'flavour' and a hotter fire. But chunks of wood are not easy to work with. They take longer to light than charcoal and burn much less evenly. Wood is good for nostalgic, obsessive purists who like looking at the fire every few minutes and making adjustments. Oak and hickory are the easiest to find; once again, mesquite wood is good for the hottest fires.

By the way, we avoid like the plague anything that has to do with lighter fluid. Our favourite way to start a charcoal or hardwood fire is with the chimney starter, an inexpensive device available at hardware stores. The electric coil starter is also good if you have an electric power source near your grill.

Marinades and sauces for grilled meat

The new art of home-grilling owes much to the many ethnic ideas currently in vogue for marinating and saucing grilled meat. Keep in mind this cardinal rule, however: sugar in a marinade raises the possibility that meat soaked in that marinade will burn when it comes into contact with a direct fire. Exercise caution. Consult Chapter Nine for a wide range of saucing ideas.

WHICH MEAT?

Cooking over fire is a bewildering art—made much more so by the fact that every type of meat has its own cooking requirements. Here are a few observations on some of the more popular grilling meats.

Chicken Many home cooks make the mistake of thinking that chicken, because it's 'lighter' than steak, will take less time to cook on the grill. But this is completely wrong and for one very simple reason: while steak is done at rare or medium-rare (for most people's taste), chicken should be cooked all the way through. Because chicken takes a relatively long time to cook, the fire should be no hotter than moderate and the chicken should be a good 13-15 cm (5-6 in) from the fire; a hotter fire and chicken closer to it, may result in a burnt chicken. Breasts take the least time to cook of any chicken parts; allow about 20 minutes. Wings may take 20 to 30 minutes and dark meat, both legs and thighs, will take from 30 to 40 minutes. If you've boned and flattened any of these parts, of course, you can shorten the cooking time.

Pork Like chicken, pork also needs relatively long cooking time, because most people are uncomfortable with underdone pork. For our taste, when grilled pork goes beyond juicy pink it gets dry and unattractive, so we like it less done than most people; we're confident that all danger of trichinosis is removed at only 59°C (137°F), just medium-rare. The best cuts of pork for the grill are thick ones and they should be cooked over a moderately hot fire. We like pork chops cut 4 cm (1½ in) thick and they'll take about 15 minutes to cook. A boneless loin roast is also a great option; figure about 12 minutes per 450g (1 lb) over a medium fire. Another favourite on the grill is spare ribs—particularly the meaty cut known as 'country-style ribs'; figure about 15 minutes over a medium-hot fire (for grilled country-style ribs *not* in the slow-cooked 'barbecue' style).

Veal Veal is also in the slightly longer cooking chicken/ pork camp. We avoid thin slices of veal, like scallops, on the grill. Best of all is a super-thick veal chop (loin or rib), cooked to medium-rare (or just beyond); grill chops that are 5 cm (2 in) thick about 13 cm (5 in) from a moderately hot fire for about 15 minutes. Another favourite veal cut for grilling, much less expensive, is veal breast cut into riblets; you'll get about 6 riblets out of 900 g (2 lb) of breast. This cut needs to be cooked a little longer; after marinating the riblets well, cook them about 15 cm (6 in) from a moderately hot fire for about 20 minutes.

Lamb With lamb, we move into the realm of the rare (or medium-rare); this means hotter fires and shorter cooking time. The basic cut for the grill is the lamb chop; you'll obtain best results with loin chops that are thick (about 3 cm (1½ in)). Cook these chops less than 13 cm (5 in) from a hot fire for 10 to 12 minutes. A lamb cut that has become a very popular party item on the grill and rightly so, is butterflied leg of lamb; because it's thicker in some parts and thinner in others, it provides a crowd of people with a variety of degrees of doneness. Because it's not as tender as, say, loin chops, a tenderising marinade (like one made from yogurt) is a good idea. Cook 15 cm (6 in) away from a moderately hot fire for at least 40 minutes for a whole leg. Lastly, few people consider the grill when cooking rack of lamb—but this is a great way to cook a rack. Place it less than 13 cm (5 in) from a moderately hot fire and cook for at least 30 minutes; make sure that the fatty side gets lots of heat exposure so that it browns well.

Beef Nothing needs quick cooking over a super-hot fire as much as steak; the high temperature of restaurant grills is one reason that steak at a steakhouse usually tastes so much better than steak at home. A perfect grilled steak, to us, is 5 cm (2 in) thick, severely browned (almost charred) on the outside and very rare on the inside; the combination of the juicy, underdone, inner meat with the highly flavoured, crunchy exterior is unbeatable. There are many different cuts that you can use—but our favourite of all is a porterhouse steak, which features a filet mignon side (for buttery tenderness) and a shell steak side (for deeper beef flavour). Have it cut 5 cm (2 in) thick, of course, place it less than 10 cm (4 in) from a hot fire, turn it only once and check it for doneness after 15 minutes.

Hamburgers As with steak, we like hamburgers rare on the inside, crunchy-brown on the outside. But hamburgers can't be as thick as a steak, because thick ones are too difficult to cook evenly. So we recommend well-seasoned burgers that are no more than 2 cm (¾ in) thick, cooked 7.5 cm (3 in) from a hot fire, for a total of 5 minutes or so.

Sausages There's one major dichotomy in the world of sausages-for-the-grill: some are already cooked and some are raw. The former just need to be heated, the latter need to be cooked. The most popular already-cooked sausage, of course, is the hot dog; it's easy to heat up on a grill, though we've seen many a dog ruined by an excessively charred exterior. Actually, we prefer thicker precooked sausages, such as kielbasa, to thin, precooked hot dogs; kielbasa is a winner when cooked for about 10 minutes at 15 cm (6 in) from a moderately hot fire.

Among the uncooked sausages, the most popular is fresh Italian sausage, either hot or 'sweet' (mild); it's made from raw pork, so you must make sure to cook it to at least 59°C (137°F). We find that 20 minutes at 15 cm (6 in) from a moderately hot fire does the trick. Lastly, there's a new generation of New Wave sausages being made for the grill, particularly in California. They can be made from chicken, turkey, veal, beef, lamb, pork, venison, or other meat. Understand the ingredients and cook accordingly (chicken will take longer to cook than veal).

SMOKING MEAT

A wide range of factors led to the recently increased interest in home-smoked meats. Undoubtedly, the new availability and high profile of home smoking units had the greatest effect. But, once again, watching what chefs were doing in trendy restaurants mightily affected the practice of home cooks.

Paradoxically, the restaurant smoking method that stirred the most interest nationwide in the eighties and nineties was not a practice that could be emulated by home cooks: real Southern barbecue. To do this properly, meat has to be cooked very slowly at about 98°C (210°F) in the presence of smoky wood (but not directly over it) for a very long time (many barbecue restaurants cook their meats for more than 15 hours). Only this treatment gives meat the unparalleled tenderness—and the depth of smoky flavour—that is the hallmark of great barbecue.

True barbecue restaurants use enormous closed pits—so big and so expensive as to be totally impractical for the home enthusiast. There are several 'home' versions of pits which provide an offset firebox at one end and a chimney at the other. But they, too, are larger and more expensive than most home cooks would wish. Furthermore, using them would require constant surveillance of the fire over the long cooking period and not many home cooks are willing to watch wood burn for 15 hours at a stretch.

If you want real Southern barbecue, you should go to a barbecue restaurant. But if you want the great taste of smoke in your meat, for much less trouble, here are some ways to obtain it.

Favourite meats for quick home-smoking

We love real Southern barbecue, but leave this arduous task to the professionals. However, you can do a quick smoke at home of many different meats, then slather them with great homemade barbecue sauce at the end (see sauces starting on page 488). The results won't be the same, but they will be delicious.

Try this technique especially with chicken legs and thighs, duck breasts, pork chops, rack of lamb, rib steak and homemade sausage. Smoking times will vary, depending on the degree of doneness desired. By the way, other sauces (such as Asian dipping sauces or Latin American salsas) may be substituted for the barbecue sauce.

Chips in a Covered Grill The simplest way to flavour your meat with smoke is to use wood chips, charcoal and a regular, covered grill (like a Weber). Build a low-temperature fire with the charcoal and let the coals turn to ash. Make sure the coals are off to one side of the grill. Soak a few handfuls of wood chips in water for half an hour. Place the soaked chips on the ashen coals, then place the meat on the grill—but not directly over the fire. Cover immediately and smoke until the meat is done.

The Water Smoker This is the widely marketed device that brought home smoking to lots of people in the eighties and nineties. It's a stack of grates and pans, in a metal housing, with a large domed lid that makes the whole thing look something like R2D2. Heat and smoke are generated on the bottom and a water pan above helps to keep the heat low. Furthermore, the water serves to keep the meat, which is smoking on grates at the uppermost levels of the smoker, very moist. There are many different variations on the basic design, but the type we recommend is the electric water smoker. You simply place soaked wood in the bottom, add the water pan and plug the smoker in; the wood is kept at a low, even temperature for hours.

The Smoking Box The smallest, least expensive and least elaborate smoking arrangement is a little metal box, in which you can smoke meat right on top of your range. You place soaked wood chips in the bottom of the box, then place your meat on a rack over the chips. The box is tightly closed with a lid. You place the box over a low fire on your range and the smoke very nicely permeates the meat. A fine one is the Max Burton Stove Top Smoker (made in Tacoma, WA, 206 627-2665).

Woods and chips for smoking

Smoking aficionados make much of the type of wood that's used. In reality, the differences among woods are very subtle. But there are differences and here are the ones we've found. Use these woods either as hardwood chunks or as chips.

Alder The main smoking wood of the Pacific North-west produces a delicate smoky flavour, which makes it good for poultry.

Apple Wood Used a lot in the North-east. Mild, slightly sweet, slightly fruity. Good for poultry and ham.

Hickory The wood of Southern barbecue, hickory produces a strong, hearty flavour similar to that which it imparts to bacon. Good for any meat, as long as you like it smoky. Hickory wood burns for a long time.

Maple Not as smoky as hickory and slightly sweeter. Good for poultry and pork.

Mesquite The 'hot' wood of the eighties, mesquite is better for grilling than it is for smoking; that's because it makes such a high-temperature fire. Another drawback is that mesquite smoke can create a bitter taste.

Oak Oak's only drawback is that it doesn't make a lot of smoke, so you have to use more of it. But it is assertive, like hickory, though slightly milder. Good in combination with woods that yield more smoke. Great for beef.

Pecan Wood Many Southern chefs use the wood from pecan trees, because it creates a relatively cool fire. This also yields a rich, subtle, mellow smoke, with a slightly nutty character. A great wood for many types of meat.

THE MOST POPULAR MEATS TODAY

POULTRY
The perception that poultry is more healthful than other types of meat—lower in fat, lower in calories, lower in antibiotics—has driven it to the top of the American meat menu in the nineties.

Chicken
Chicken has had a cyclical history in American gastronomic life. Many years ago, it was expensive—and therefore somewhat exalted. For most of our lifetimes, however, it has been the cheapest meat—which means that in the fifties and sixties it got little respect. 'Chicken again?' complained many a diner in low-budget households . . . and many a high-budget household kept it off the dinner-party menu.

Then the worm turned, once again. For the last few decades chicken has been recognised as one of the best sources of protein among all meats and this has made its popularity soar. As many health-conscious diners turned away from red meat, they turned to chicken. Today, there's nothing downscale in image about a grilled chicken Caesar salad; you're likely to see the trendiest, most glamorous types in Beverly Hills lunching on it.

The rise of ethnic food gave a further boost to the Chicken Resurgence. Tandoori chicken leads all Indian restaurant foods in popularity. The French bistro way with roast chicken has become almost holy. The fashion for neglected American regional classics has given fried chicken new glitter, even in this age of oil avoidance. And chicken's wonderful ability to pick up marinades and sauces has made it a headliner at everything from California grill restaurants to Cantonese noodle shops to Mexican tortilla stands.

As with most other once-standard gastronomic products of the modern era, chicken has also spawned a 'luxury' category. Recognising that the production practices on large chicken farms—keeping chickens cooped up, not allowing them to exercise—were producing tasteless chickens, a number of chicken producers starting raising 'free-range' chickens, or un-cooped chickens that were allowed to move around the barnyard. These chickens gained weight more slowly, but the proportion of meat to fat was higher. The theory is that a chicken that comes to market weight normally, without antibiotics or hormones, tastes better. But choose your free-range producer carefully. Sometimes free-range chickens (which are always more expensive) are virtually indistinguishable from mass-produced chickens in taste. Sometimes they are either similar or slightly deeper in flavour, but much tougher. Sometimes, however, they combine a pleasing texture with truly deep flavour; these, of course, are the free-range chickens to watch for. We like Murray's free-range chickens grown in Pennsylvania.

Chicken terminology

Once upon a time, chicken was a seasonal treat. Hens would start laying eggs only when the weather turned warmer and the first birds brought to the market were small ones that were just a month old or so; given their arrival in May or June, they were called 'spring chickens'. Today, there is no 'spring chicken' category. Thanks to modern poultry science, there are categories aplenty, all of them available at all times of the year. Here are some you're likely to see in markets today.

Poussin A small bird, very popular in California. Usually only 35 days old and not above 700 g (1½ lb). Available whole. Good for roasting at high heat.

Grill A little larger: under 900 g (2 lb), about 40 days old.

Fryer Between 900-1.8 kg (2 and 4 lb), about 45 days old. Fryers and roasters are available either whole, or in parts and both are good for all kinds of cooking techniques: frying, grilling, roasting, or stewing.

Young Roaster Between 1.8-2.25 kg (4-5lb), about 48 days old.

Roaster Between 2.25-3.6 kg (5-8 lb), about 60 days old. Roasters and young roasters are usually sold whole, not in parts and are good for roasting at moderate heat.

Capon A male chicken that has been made tender by castration. Usually 3.6-5.45 kg (8-12 lb) and about 75 days old. Sold whole and good for roasting at low heat.

WHOLE CHICKEN

We feel about chicken as we do about fish: cooking it whole—that is, forcing the contact of flesh, bone and skin under fire—seems to develop more of the essential flavours. Happily, Americans are far less squeamish about whole chickens than they are about whole fish.

Now, there are many ways to cook a whole chicken—but the way that really captured the attention of America in the bistro-mad eighties and nineties is roasting. Anyone who has experienced the magnificence of a properly roasted chicken at a great bistro in France—such as L'Ami Louis in Paris—forever dreams of duplicating these results at home. It's not that hard to do.

The key is coordinating the size of your bird with the heat of your oven. Moderate-temperature roasting is the surest way to maintain juiciness in the chicken—but if the bird's too small, the outside won't become golden brown and crisp. On the other hand, if you cook a large bird in a hot oven, the skin will burn before the meat cooks through. Therefore, our rule of thumb is: small birds in hot ovens, large birds in moderate ovens.

Another important roast chicken issue concerns flavouring. All kinds of ingredients, from ginger to chermoula, are stuffed into roast chicken. We go along with the trend, as long as we're aiming for an exotic bird. But if it's a bistro bird we're after, we become positively austere: no garlic or lemon in the cavity, no herbs, no spices. Bistro roast chicken should taste like chicken.

Lastly, there's the trussing issue. Classic texts tell you to truss—but we think the authors were only copying other classic texts. Tying up the bird does make a slightly neater presentation—but the parts tied to the body don't get crisp and they don't cook evenly. We say, along with a new generation of chicken roasters: no strings.

SLOW ROAST CHICKEN, BISTRO-STYLE, WITH GOOSE FAT

This recipe represents several important chicken-roasting principles. First of all, it calls for a big bird roasted at only moderate temperature; the chicken emerges from the oven as juicy as can be and—because the large bird takes longer to cook—beautifully golden brown. Secondly, it contains no flavourings—with the exception of rendered goose fat; this marvellous product is used by bistros in France for basting chickens and adds an amazing depth of poultry flavour to your roast chicken. Fresh rendered goose fat can be purchased at good butchers, particularly at Christmastime. But we carry a terrific product in a can, imported from Sarlat, France, made by Rougie. We'd recommend using it for any bistro-style roast chicken,

no matter what size chicken you choose.

SERVES 6

1 large roaster, about 3.2-3.4 kg (7-7½ lb)
90 g (6 tbsp) rendered goose fat, at room
   temperature
salt and freshly ground pepper to taste

1. Preheat oven to 150°C (300°F).

2. Brush the chicken skin all over with the goose fat. Salt the chicken fairly heavily and season with freshly ground black pepper. Place the chicken, breast side up, on a rack, in a roasting tin and place in oven.

3. Roast the chicken, basting occasionally with fat that has collected in the roasting tin, until done, about 2 to 2½ hours (the bird should be a rich golden brown). Remove chicken from oven, let rest 10 minutes, carve and serve immediately.

COMBINATION-HEAT ROAST CHICKEN WITH ROSEMARY, SHALLOTS AND GARLIC

Here's a method for a medium-size chicken that uses both high heat and lower heat; it is adapted from the findings of food scientist Harold McGee. It is the best basic roast chicken recipe we know of for medium-size birds. With this particular highly flavoured recipe, of course, we move away from the classic bistro and closer to the trattoria—but if you wish to roast a medium-size bird, bistro-style, just skip the flavourings and use this oven technique anyway.

SERVES 4

45 g (3 tbsps) chopped fresh rosemary or 15 g
   (1 tbsp) dried
5 g (1 tsp) salt
2.5 g (½ tsp) freshly ground black pepper
50 ml (2 fl oz) olive oil
1 young roaster, about 1.8 kg (4 lb)

12 shallots, peeled
20 cloves garlic, peeled
225 ml (8 fl oz) chicken stock
125 ml (4 fl oz) white wine

1. Preheat oven to 240°C (475°F).

2. Mix the rosemary, salt, pepper and olive oil together in a small bowl. Wash and pat dry the chicken inside and out. Place it in a roasting tin, making sure there is enough room to let hot air circulate around the bird. Disperse evenly the peeled shallots, the garlic cloves and the giblets, if you have them, around the pan. Using your fingers, rub the oil and rosemary mixture onto and under the skin of the entire bird, in the cavity and on the shallots, garlic and giblets. Every surface should be covered. Position the bird breast side up in the middle of the roasting tin.

3. When the oven is hot, put the roasting tin in sideways on the middle rack. After 20 minutes, remove the bird from the oven, shutting the door quickly behind it so the oven temperature does not drop. Baste the chicken, giblets and inside the bird using juices from the pan. (If there are no juices in the pan, add 50 ml (2 fl oz) water.) Turn the bird over, breast side down, propping the wing tip up with a crumpled piece of aluminium foil. Put the pan back in the oven and reduce the temperature to 230°C (450°F).

4. After 15 minutes, baste the bird thoroughly again. This time, reduce the heat to 190°C (375°F). Turn the bird breast side up. Continue cooking and basting every 15 minutes until chicken is cooked and golden brown, about 1 hour. Let the chicken rest for 10 minutes, then carve and serve.

5. While the chicken is resting, add 225 ml (8 fl oz) chicken stock and 125 ml (4 fl oz) white wine to the pan, place it over high heat and scrape up the browned bits in the bottom of the pan. Reduce to 225 ml (8 fl oz).

Remove giblets, shallots and garlic and place the pan juices in a blender. Blend until smooth, taste for seasoning, heat and serve over chicken.

When is a roast chicken done?

The perfect roast chicken is cooked through on the inside (though we, like the Cantonese, don't recoil from a touch of pink) and golden brown on the outside.

There are several ways of testing the doneness. The classic test is piercing the thigh and observing the colour of the juices; if there's no pink or red in them, the chicken's done.

Another test has you tugging the drumstick; if the chicken's done, the thigh joint should feel loose.

The best test of all, of course, is to insert a quick-read meat thermometer in the fleshy parts of the chicken. If no part is under 77°C (170°F), the chicken is done.

FAST ROAST CHICKEN, TANDOORI-STYLE, WITH SPICED ONION SAUCE

Indian chefs are fantastic chicken roasters because they make use of that great clay oven, the tandoor. The super high heat of the tandoor sears the chicken quickly, keeping the bird moist inside. Of course, marination also contributes to the juiciness. Tandoori chicken is usually cooked in parts—but why not apply all the basic principles to whole birds at home, marinating them Indian-style, then cranking the heat way up? Just make sure to use birds on the small side, lest the high heat burn a larger bird that takes longer to cook through. This recipe yields a roast chicken with the subtle flavour of Indian spices but it would be equally at home with mildly spiced Indian accompaniments or more Western-style side dishes.

SERVES 4

1 medium fryer, about 1.3 kg (3 lb)
225 ml (8 fl oz) plain yogurt

45 g (3 tbsp) chopped garlic

75 g (5 tbsp) chopped fresh ginger

5 g (1 tsp) ground coriander

5 g (1 tsp) garam masala

2.5 g (½ tsp) ground cumin

1.25 g (¼ tsp) ground allspice

1.25 g (¼ tsp) ground cinnamon

1.25 g (¼ tsp) Indian chilli powder

1.25 g (¼ tsp) ground cardamom

1.25 g (¼ tsp) ground fenugreek

7.5 g (1½ tsp) coarse salt

2.5 g (½ tsp) freshly ground black pepper

3 medium yellow onions, thinly sliced

350 ml (12 fl oz) chicken stock

pinch of saffron threads

1. Rinse chicken in cold water, inside and out. Pat dry with paper towels and place breast side up in a roasting tin.

2. Make the marinade by placing yogurt and the next 10 ingredients in a food processor or blender. Purée until smooth. Spoon marinade all over the chicken, cover and refrigerate at least overnight and up to 2 days. Bring to room temperature before proceeding.

3. Preheat oven to 250°C (500°F). Wipe the marinade off the chicken and pat chicken dry. Rub the kosher salt and pepper all over the bird. Place in·a clean roasting tin, breast side up and scatter onions around it. Pour 175 ml (6 fl oz) of the chicken stock into the bottom of the pan and add the saffron.

4. Put the chicken into the oven legs first and roast for 40 to 45 minutes. (After the first 15 minutes, baste the chicken and the onions with the remaining stock and make sure that nothing is sticking to the bottom of the pan. After another 15 minutes, baste everything again, stir the onions and—if the chicken is getting too browned—cover the chicken with foil.)

5. When the chicken is done, remove it from the tin, allowing all the juices to run back into the tin. Leave the chicken to rest for 10 minutes. With a slotted spoon, remove onions.

6. Carve the chicken and arrange pieces on a serving platter. Spoon caramelised onions over each piece and serve immediately.

Crisping the skin

If you're looking for especially crispy skin on your roast chicken, there are three extra measures you can take. Use any one of them for crisper chicken, or use them together.

1. A day before cooking the chicken, dunk it for 20 seconds in a large pot of boiling water. Remove and keep the chicken, uncovered, in your refrigerator overnight.

2. Twelve hours before cooking the chicken, dry it thoroughly and hang it in front of an electric fan. Turn the chicken occasionally, so all parts of the skin are exposed to the drying effects of the wind. Or use a hair dryer.

3. After your chicken is carved, place the pieces on a roasting tin and run them under a hot grill until they crisp up.

CHICKEN IN PARTS

Most of the chickens purchased in American supermarkets and cooked in American homes, are already cut up. Though chicken parts rarely develop the deep essence of poultry that whole birds do, they are formidably convenient and they take marvellously well to a wide range of sauces.

If you're buying chicken parts, the biggest question is this: should you buy whole cut-up chickens (that is, with all parts represented), or should you focus on one part only?

MIXED PARTS

There's good head-of-the-household sense in buying mixed parts: some people like white meat, some people like dark meat and by serving mixed-part dishes you can please them all. You can cook the parts all together which benefits the sauce by adding different types of chicken flavour. . . or you can cook the parts individually, as in the American South's outstanding contribution to world gastronomy.

SOUTHERN FRIED CHICKEN

This is one of the great American classics, the Saturday-picnic, Sunday-dinner, church-supper mainstay of a whole generation of Americans from the South-east. Unfortunately, it suffered a dip in popularity during the health-crazed eighties and many young Southerners have never tasted a good version. Happily, the nineties have brought a renewed excitement in American regional foods—and people, both in the South and around the country, are talkin' fried chicken once again. What they're talkin' 'bout, as always, are the perennial fried chicken controversies:

Which flavouring? If you're making traditional Southern fried chicken, you don't want much flavouring at all. Old-time chefs rarely go beyond salt, pepper and paprika. Of course, if you're 'updating' fried chicken (as we do in 2 cases below), the sky's the limit for flavourings. By the way, for the traditional dish we like to soak the chicken first in evaporated milk, which makes it juicier. And if you add beaten eggs to the milk, the chicken will hold its coating better.

Which coating? Some chefs dip the chicken in batter and some Northern chefs have been known to use oddities like cornflakes—but any traditional Southern

chef will tell you that only seasoned flour can provide the kind of light crunchiness for which Southern fried chicken is so justly famous.

Which cooking medium? This debate rages on. Hard-liners insist on lard, for the wonderful flavour it brings. Old-timers who have rejected lard as too heavy insist on solid vegetable shortening (Crisco). A new generation prefers vegetable oils, particularly light oils like rapeseed. We think lard tastes best—but the recipes that follow leave the choice up to you. If you are using lard, eschew the tasteless stuff sold in supermarkets and try to get fresh-rendered lard from a good butcher.

Which pan? Old-fashioned fried chicken aficionados insist on heavy-duty cast iron to fry their chickens. We think that heavy-duty is all that matters; you want even distribution of the heat. But other materials, in our experience, work equally well. Just avoid aluminium.

Here it is: our favourite version of the traditional dish. Note the drying time after the chicken is coated, which helps to promote a shatteringly chunky crust.

SERVES 4

1.3-kg (3-lb) frying chicken, cut into 8 pieces
350 ml (12-fl oz) can unsweetened evaporated milk
175 g (6 oz) flour
10 g (2 tsp) salt
2.5 g (½ tsp) ground black pepper
2.5 g (½ tsp) cayenne pepper
5 g (1 tsp) paprika
lard, vegetable shortening or vegetable oil for frying
   (at least 450 g (1 lb) or 450 ml (16 fl oz))

1. Put chicken in a glass dish large enough to hold it in a single layer and pour evaporated milk over it. Cover and refrigerate overnight, turning the chicken occasionally.

2. When ready to cook, combine the flour, salt, black

pepper, cayenne pepper and paprika in a paper bag and mix thoroughly. Put the chicken, 2 pieces at a time, into the flour mixture; shake until well coated with flour and place the pieces on a baking rack. Allow the pieces to dry on the rack for 30 minutes to 2 hours. (Don't dry for 2 hours if your kitchen isn't cool.)

3. Heat the fat in 2 deep, straight-sided frying pans to 180°C (350°F); the shortening should be about ¾ inch deep. When it is hot, carefully place half of the chicken in each pan. Fry chicken for 8 to 10 minutes on each side, about 20 minutes total, until it is deep golden brown and cooked through. (If the oil threatens to smoke at any point, reduce the heat; if the oil stops bubbling around the chicken pieces, increase the heat.)

4. Remove chicken and place on a rack to drain. Serve hot, warm, or at room temperature.

Alternative fried chicken recipes

CORNMEAL-MOLASSES FRIED CHICKEN
If you want to stray from tradition but you're feeling a little timid about your journey, why not prepare this creative variation of Southern fried chicken? The molasses adds a haunting sweetness; the bourbon and cornmeal let you know that you're in Dixie.

SERVES 4

425 ml (¾ pint) full-cream milk
125 ml (4 fl oz) molasses
45 ml (3 tbsp) bourbon
1.3-kg (3-lb) frying chicken, cut into 8 pieces
175 g (6 oz) plain flour
10 g (2 tsp) salt
5 g (1 tsp) black pepper
350 g (12 oz) yellow cornmeal

lard, vegetable fat or vegetable oil for frying (about 450 g (1 lb) or 450 ml (16 fl oz)

1. In a large bowl combine the milk, molasses and bourbon and mix well. Add the chicken pieces, cover tightly with clingfilm and refrigerate overnight.

2. When ready to cook the chicken, season the flour with salt and pepper in a large mixing bowl. Place the cornmeal in a separate bowl and place a rack next to the bowls.

3. Remove the chicken from the marinade and reserve the marinade. Heavily coat the chicken with the seasoned flour and let sit on rack for 5 to 10 minutes.

4. Heat shortening in 2 deep, straight-sided frying pans to 180°C (350°F); the shortening should be about ¾ inch deep. When it is hot, dip the chicken back into the marinade and then immediately coat with cornmeal. Carefully place half of the chicken in each pan. Fry chicken for 8 to 10 minutes on each side, about 20 minutes total, until it is deep golden brown and cooked through. (If the oil threatens to smoke at any point, reduce the heat; if the oil stops bubbling around the chicken pieces, increase the heat.)

5. Drain the chicken on paper towels and serve hot, warm, or at room temperature.

SPICY FRIED CHICKEN WITH JALAPEÑO, GARLIC AND GINGER
This dish tastes great with steamed rice and a leafy Asian salad tossed with rice-wine vinegar and a few drops of sesame oil.

SERVES 4

125 ml (4 fl oz) buttermilk
half a lemon, sliced very thin crosswise
30 g (2 tbsp) chopped fresh garlic

30 g (2 tbsp) grated peeled fresh ginger
1 or 2 jalapeños, trimmed, seeded and chopped
1.3-kg (3-lb) frying chicken, cut into 8 pieces
lard, vegetable shortening, or vegetable oil for
   frying (at least 450 g (1 lb) or 450 ml (16 fl oz)
350 g (12 oz) all-purpose flour
10 g (2 tsp) coarse salt
5 g (1 tsp) freshly ground black pepper

1. Stir together the buttermilk, lemon slices, garlic, ginger and jalapeño in a large bowl until combined well. Poke 20 holes in each piece of chicken with a fork and add the chicken to the bowl. Marinate the chicken, covered, stirring occasionally, for 4 to 8 hours in the refrigerator (depending on intensity of flavour desired). Remove the chicken from the refrigerator 1 hour before frying and let stand at room temperature. Discard the lemon slices.

2. Heat oil in 2 deep, straight-sided frying pans to 180°C (350°F); the oil should be about 2 cm (¾ in) deep.

3. When ready to cook, combine the flour, coarse salt and black pepper in a paper bag and mix thoroughly. Shake the chicken in the bag, 2 pieces at a time, until it's well coated; shake off the excess flour. Transfer the chicken to a rack and let it sit for 5 to 10 minutes.

4. Carefully place half of the chicken in each pan. Fry chicken for 8 to 10 minutes on each side, about 20 minutes total, until it is deep golden brown and cooked through. (If the oil threatens to smoke at any point, reduce the heat; if the oil stops bubbling around the chicken pieces, increase the heat.)

5. Drain the chicken on paper towels and serve hot, warm, or at room temperature.

CHICKEN CACCIATORE

Chicken 'hunter's-style' was one of the mainstays of Italian-American restaurants back in the red-sauce days of Italian dining; it has never had the fame in Italy that it has had here. Moreover, the Italian versions are simpler than our own: 'cacciatore' there simply indicates a long-cooked tomato sauce with vegetables like carrots and celery; 'cacciatore' here often indicates the presence of mushrooms and peppers. Deep as our nostalgia is for the Little Italy food of the 1950s, we prefer the chickeny purity of the Italian version.

SERVES 4

1.8-kg (4-lb) chicken, cut into 8 pieces
45 ml (3 tbsp) olive oil
5 g (1 tsp) salt
1.25 g (¼ tsp) ground black pepper
1 medium onion, cut into slivers
3 garlic cloves, sliced thin
2 large carrots, sliced into ¼-inch pieces
2 stalks celery, sliced into 1-cm (½-in) pieces
175 fl (6 fl oz) red wine
10 g (2 tsp) chopped fresh thyme
2.5 g (½ tsp) chopped fresh rosemary
1 bay leaf
pinch of dried red pepper flakes (optional)
800-g (28-oz) can crushed tomatoes
15 ml (1 tbsp) lemon juice
25 g (1 oz) chopped fresh flat-leaf parsley

1. Wash and dry the chicken pieces. Leave the breasts on the bone and split each half breast in half; you will now have 4 breast pieces, 2 wings, 2 thighs and 2 drumsticks.

2. In a deep frying pan , large enough to hold all the chicken, heat 30 ml (2 tbsp) of the olive oil over moderately high heat. When oil is hot, sprinkle chicken with 5 mm (¼ tsp) of salt and the pepper and sauté until golden brown, about 3 to 4 minutes per side. Set chicken aside.

3. Add remaining oil and then the onion, garlic, carrots, celery and another 5 mm (¼ tsp) salt. Sauté vegetables, stirring occasionally, until nicely browned, about 5 minutes. Increase heat to high and slowly add red wine, scraping the bottom of pan with a wooden spoon to remove any caramelised bits. Cook until about three-quarters of the red wine has evaporated, about 5 minutes. Add thyme, rosemary, bay leaf, red pepper flakes, crushed tomatoes, the lemon juice and the remaining salt. Stir well, bring to a boil and then reduce heat so that the sauce comes to a gentle simmer.

4. Return chicken to the pan, spooning sauce over each piece. Cook, covered, for 12 minutes and then remove the breasts, which should be cooked through but still tender. Continue to cook remaining chicken, covered, for another 15 minutes. Remove chicken and add to the breasts. Cover with foil. Reduce sauce over high heat for about 6 to 8 minutes, until it has a nice, thick consistency. Remove bay leaf. Return chicken to pan for 3 to 4 minutes to reheat. Adjust seasoning.

5. Arrange chicken pieces on a large serving platter. Cover generously with sauce. Sprinkle with chopped parsley.

COQ AU VIN

When Americans began to familiarise themselves with French cooking, coq au vin—the ancient, long-cooked chicken stew of France's Burgundy region—was one of the first dishes they took to. The delicious version here makes sense today for two reasons. First, the cooking time is considerably cut down—yielding chicken pieces with more texture and a dish that can be prepared at the end of the day. Second, no longer do we have to spend money on expensive red Burgundy to make an 'authentic' coq au vin; these days, delicious young wine is being produced in California from the red grape of Burgundy, Pinot Noir. The wine is as good in the stew pot as it is in the glass.

SERVES 4

1.8 kg (4-lb) chicken, cut into 8 pieces
280 g (10 oz) pearl onions
175 g (6 oz) bacon rashers, cut into 1.25 g (½-in) pieces
2 garlic cloves, thinly sliced
1 medium yellow onion, halved and cut into thin slivers
4 large carrots, thinly sliced
10 g (2 tsp) salt
2.5 g (½ tsp) ground black pepper
75 ml (2½ fl oz) cognac
6 parsley stems
5 g (1 tsp) herbes de Provence
1 bay leaf
4 cloves
1 litre (1¾ pints) fruity red wine (preferably California Pinot Noir)
85 g (3 oz) unsalted butter
5 g (1 tsp) sugar
450 g (1 lb) small cultivated mushrooms (fresh button mushrooms), wiped clean and quartered
30 g (2 tbsp) plain flour
25 g (1 oz) chopped fresh flat-leaf parsley

1. Wash and dry the chicken pieces. Leave the breasts on the bone and split each half breast in half; you will now have 4 breast pieces, 2 wings, 2 thighs and 2 drumsticks.

2. Drop pearl onions into a small pan of boiling water for 1 minute. Remove and, when onions are cool enough to handle, peel off the skins.

3. In a deep frying pan, large enough to hold all the chicken, sauté bacon over moderately high heat until well browned and crispy, about 7 to 8 minutes. Remove bacon and set aside on paper towels to drain. Leave fat in pan. Pat chicken pieces dry and sauté until golden brown, about 3 to 4 minutes per side. Remove chicken and set aside. Discard all but 45 g (3 tbsp) of fat and return pan to the heat.

4. Add the garlic, yellow onion, 225 g (8 oz) of sliced carrots, 5 g (1 tsp) of salt and the pepper. Sauté vegetables, stirring occasionally, until nicely browned, about 8 minutes. Reduce heat to low and then, using a bulb baster, remove as much fat as possible from the bottom of the pan. Put chicken back in pan and pour in the cognac. Carefully light the cognac with a match, then gently shake pan so that the flaming cognac coats all the chicken.

5. When the flames have subsided, add parsley stems, herbes de Provence, bay leaf, cloves, remaining salt and red wine. Bring to a boil, scrape bottom of pan to deglaze it, cover pan and reduce heat. Simmer gently for about 12 minutes, until chicken breasts are cooked through but still tender. Remove them and cover with foil. Continue cooking dark meat, covered, for another 8 to 10 minutes. Then remove it and reserve with chicken breasts.

6. Strain the liquid, pressing down on the solids to extract as much sauce as possible. Degrease the liquid and return to the pan. Over high heat reduce the liquid for 10 minutes, until thickened slightly. Turn off heat.

7. In another pan, melt 25 g (1 oz) of the butter over moderately high heat. Add pearl onions, remaining carrots, sugar and enough water to just cover the vegetables. Cook until water is evaporated and vegetables are tender, about 20 minutes. (The vegetables should be coated with a light buttery glaze.)

8. Melt 25 g (1 oz) butter over high heat in a large frying pan. When butter is hot, sauté the mushrooms, until nice and golden, about 5 minutes total. (Do not overcrowd pan or mushrooms will not brown properly.) Set aside.

9. Knead remaining butter together with flour, forming a smooth paste. Bring the reduced wine sauce up to the boil and slowly whisk in the paste, a little at a time. Continue

cooking over high heat, stirring constantly, until the sauce has reached a desirable thickness, about 5 minutes. Reduce the heat to moderate and return chicken, bacon and onions, carrots and mushrooms to the sauce. Reheat for 5 minutes.

10. Arrange chicken pieces and vegetables on a large serving platter. Cover with sauce. Sprinkle with chopped parsley. Serve immediately.

JERK CHICKEN

Thanks to Vernon, owner of Vernon's Jerk Paradise in New York City (now defunct), the Jamaican marinade-and-grill method called 'jerking' has become very popular in U.S. restaurants. It's a method that was invented by the Arawaks of Jamaica and later perfected by the Maroons, who were runaway Jamaican slaves. They would rub a seasoning paste on wild boar and other meats, principally as a means of preventing spoilage. Today, we don't worry about spoilage—but meat (typically chicken, but pork is also popular in Jamaica) is still marinated in a mixture that contains lots of incendiary Scotch bonnet peppers and fragrant allspice (both grown in Jamaica). On the home turf in Jamaica, ripe green pimento berries—fresh allspice, actually—are used, but you can substitute ground allspice. To get real 'jerk' flavour, cook the meat slowly over fragrant, smoky wood and charcoal; you're trying to approximate the flavour that comes from the smoky tin shacks on Boston Bay in Jamaica, where the meat is smoked over allspice wood. This recipe comes from a chef in our kitchen whose Jamaican grandmother is a jerk wizard. The quantities are for a big crowd, perhaps a summertime patio party. We like to serve it with a spicy green pepper-and-tomato sauce, but you can leave that part of the recipe out if you wish. By the way, Jamaicans prefer dark meat and wings for their jerk chicken—but you'd be wise to please all your guests by serving whole chickens cut in parts.

SERVES 16

For the marinade:

450 ml (16 fl oz) vegetable oil

3 onions, coarsely chopped

7 spring onions, coarsely chopped

4 green Scotch bonnet peppers, stems and seeds
  removed

30 g (2 tbsp) grated fresh ginger

45 g (3 tbsp) coarsely chopped garlic

30 g 2 tbsp) fresh thyme

45 ml (3 tbsp) red-wine vinegar

30 g (2 tbsp) brown sugar

2.5 g (½ tsp) ground cinnamon

2.5 g (½ tsp) freshly ground nutmeg

2.5 g (½ tsp) ground cloves

15 g (1 tbsp) ground allspice

5 g (1 tsp) salt

2.5 g (½ tsp) freshly ground black pepper

15 ml (1 tbsp) lime juice

45 ml (3 tbsp) Meyers rum

30 g (2 tbsp) tamarind concentrate

4 whole chickens (each 1.3-1.8 kg (3-4 lb) and cut
  in 8 pieces)

175 ml (6 fl oz) olive oil

For the sauce:

175 ml (6 fl oz) chicken stock

2 green peppers, thinly sliced

4 large plum tomatoes, seeded and thinly sliced

a few tablespoons Jamaican hot sauce, or to taste

1. Add marinade ingredients to food processor and purée until almost smooth.

2. Pierce the chicken pieces with the tip of a knife to make many tiny holes. Rub marinade into chicken and refrigerate for 24 to 48 hours, depending on desired intensity.

3. When ready to cook, prepare a slow and smoky charcoal fire. Remove chicken from marinade. Transfer the marinade to a small saucepan. Brush chicken with oil and grill over low heat until done, about 30 minutes.

4. *While chicken is cooking, make the sauce:* add stock to saucepan that contains the marinade and reduce over high heat to a saucelike consistency. Add peppers and tomatoes and cook 2 minutes. Stir in Jamaican hot sauce. Place chicken on warm platter, pour sauce over chicken and serve.

CHICKEN BREASTS

If there's one chicken part that Americans favour, it is the breast. This is a nutritional preference, we suspect: white meat has less fat than dark meat. But—nutritional concerns aside—we've never understood the culinary reasons behind this knee-jerk selection. White meat is drier than dark meat and certainly doesn't offer the same richness of flavour. Nevertheless, if you emphasise the delicacy of chicken breast by preparing it in soft, subtle, golden ways—and if you make sure to avoid drying it out—you will make a delectable chicken choice with the chicken breast.

GOLDEN CHICKEN BREASTS WITH PROSCIUTTO, FONTINA AND FRESH SAGE

Of the many Italianesque pounded chicken breast sautés with melted cheese, this one's our favourite. The reason is the coating: just egg (no flour or crumbs), which gives the chicken a wonderful, golden colour, as well as a heartwarming flavour. Use mellow, relatively unsalty, nicely fatty Italian prosciutto for wrapping the breasts. And use a full-flavoured, nutty Fontina from the Val d'Aosta for melting on top. The dish is lovely just as it is—but we like to gild the lily by adding to it a tart, light, wine-and-butter sauce that's made in moments in the frying pan.

SERVES 4

4 skinless, boneless chicken breast halves (each
  about 115 g (4 oz))

freshly ground pepper to taste

225 g (8 oz) unsalted butter

8 whole fresh sage leaves

115 g (4 oz) (very thinly sliced prosciutto

2 eggs, beaten

8 thin slices Italian Fontina
   (about 50 g (2 oz))

For the sauce (optional)

225 ml (8 fl oz) dry white wine

15 g (1 tbsp) chopped fresh sage

50 g (2 oz) unsalted butter, chilled

1. Remove the 'flap' of chicken from the underside of each breast fillet and reserve for another use. Cut each breast across the centre into 2 pieces, each piece roughly square in shape. Place the 8 pieces of chicken breast on a large piece of greaseproof paper and cover with another piece of greaseproof paper. Pound the chicken pieces with a mallet, or a heavy cleaver, until each one is approximately 3 mm (⅛ in) thick. Season with freshly ground pepper and reserve.

2. Heat the butter over moderate heat in a very large omelette pan. When it's foaming, add the sage leaves and cook them on each side for 1 minute. Remove immediately and place each leaf on one of the reserved chicken pieces. Then, wrap each piece completely in a layer of prosciutto.

3. Dip the wrapped chicken pieces, one at a time, in the beaten eggs, coating them well. Make sure the butter in the omelette pan is foaming, golden and not browned. Then place the chicken pieces in the pan. (Do not crowd. If your pan is not large enough to hold the chicken in one layer, cook it in 2 batches.) Cook chicken pieces about 2 minutes on each side, or until just past pink on the inside, golden on the outside. Remove.

4. Place chicken pieces on a flat baking sheet and cover each piece with a slice of Fontina. Place under a preheated grill until the cheese melts, about 1 minute. Divide chicken among 4 plates and serve immediately, with or without sauce.

5. *If making sauce:* While the cheese is melting, pour out the butter from the omelette pan. Add the white wine to the pan, place over high heat and reduce to about 125 ml (4 fl oz). Add the chopped sage about a minute before the reduction is complete. Reduce the heat and whisk in the chilled butter. Adjust seasoning and pour over and around the chicken.

SPINACH-STUFFED CHICKEN BREASTS WITH COGNAC AND TARRAGON

Quick-cooking chicken breasts in a hot oven—then passing them under a grill—is another way to keep them juicy. In this recipe, the spinach under the skin makes them juicier still.

SERVES 4

450 g (1 lb) fresh spinach

salt and pepper to taste

freshly grated nutmeg to taste

4 boneless chicken breast halves, skin on (about
   175 g (6 oz) each)

1 large garlic clove, smashed

50 ml (2 fl oz) cognac

40 g (1½ oz) unsalted butter at room temperature

fresh tarragon leaves for garnish

coarse salt for sprinkling the chicken (optional)

1. Preheat oven to 230°C (450°F).

2. Cut off the root ends of the spinach leaves, about 5 cm (2 in) up from the root. Discard roots. Wash the spinach leaves in several changes of water. Without drying the leaves, place them in a large pot over high heat. Cook about 3 minutes (they should be soft, but still bright green). Place wilted spinach in a colander and immediately refresh with cold water. When spinach is cool, squeeze out the water with your hands. Place dried spinach in a bowl and season very well with salt, pepper and nutmeg.

3. Rub the chicken breasts with the garlic clove, then discard it. Season the breasts well with salt and pepper on both sides and under the skin. Sprinkle breasts on both sides and under the skin with most of the cognac. Divide the spinach mixture into four and stuff each breast under the skin with a quarter of the spinach, smoothing it out so that it's distributed evenly over each breast. Smear 5 g (1 tsp) of butter on the skin of each breast.

4. Place the breasts in a roasting tin and place pan in the oven. Cook for 5 minutes. Remove breasts and place under a hot grill. They are done when the skin is golden and the white meat is just a trace rosy-pink, about 5 minutes more.

5. Place the breasts on dinner plates. Sprinkle each one with a few drops of cognac. Top each one with a knob of butter (about 5 g (1 tsp)) per breast) and garnish the butter with fresh tarragon leaves. Sprinkle with coarse salt, if desired and serve immediately.

CHICKEN WINGS

Ever since 1964, when Frank and Theresa Bellismo, at the Anchor Bar in Buffalo, New York, came up with their now ubiquitous version of bar food, chicken wings have not been the same in America. Once a culinary afterthought, chicken wings are big business today—in restaurants as well as home kitchens. What made the wings 'fly', more than anything else, is the way they're cut. Left whole, they are difficult to eat. But hack off and discard the bony tip, then cut the remaining wing into 2 pieces and you've got a juicy shank (resembling a frog's leg in texture) and a meaty 'drumette' or small drumstick. Any type of marination and high-heat cooking (like grilling or barbecueing) makes them irresistible, but, like Frank and Theresa, we think that deep-frying is best.

Taking wings
Buffalo is not the only way to cook chicken wings. Wings are remarkable in any number of ethnic guises.

Chinese: Marinate the wings in soy sauce, garlic, ginger, sugar and Chinese rice wine. Coat with cornflour, dip in egg, roll in Panko crumbs (see page 295) and deep-fry.

Indian: Marinate the wings in a chicken tandoori marinade (see page 374) for 1 to 2 days. Cook over hot coals or under grill.

Greek: Marinate the wings in fruity olive oil, retsina, fresh marjoram and fresh oregano. Grill over hot coals and serve with the yogurt sauce on page 247.

Deep South: Season wings well with salt and pepper, smoke over low heat, slather with barbecue sauce (see p. 489) in the last 10 minutes of cooking.

ORIGINAL BUFFALO CHICKEN WINGS

This is the most famous chicken wing in the world, of course. Today, lots of people are misguidedly baking the wings to save a little fat—but the dish, to us, tastes right only when the wings are deep-fried, as in the original, to a crunchy golden brown. The juxtaposition of hot wings, blue cheese dressing and celery sticks may seem a bit odd and arbitrary when you first taste it— but after you get used to classic Buffalo wings, with their classic accompaniments, you find that the dish isn't the same without them. Frank and Theresa never fully divulged their secret recipe for the dish, but a Buffalo, New York, journalist swears that the following is as close as anyone can come.

SERVES 8 AS AN APPETISER

24 chicken wings (about 1.8 kg (4 lb)), tips removed
salt and pepper to taste
1 litre (1¾ pints) vegetable oil

50 g (2 oz) unsalted butter
50 ml (2 fl oz) Louisiana hot sauce, or more to taste
15 ml (1 tbsp) white vinegar
celery sticks as an accompaniment
blue cheese dressing (recipe follows) as an
   accompaniment

1. Cut wings in half and season them well with salt and pepper.

2. Heat oil to 190°C (375°F). Fry the wings in 2 batches until crisp and brown, about 10 minutes a batch. Remove and drain on paper towels.

3. Melt the butter in a saucepan and add the hot sauce and vinegar. Stir to blend. Dip the wings into the sauce and place wings on a serving plate. Pour any extra sauce over wings. Serve with celery sticks and blue cheese dressing.

BLUE CHEESE DRESSING
MAKES 600 ML (1 PINT)

225 ml (8 fl oz) mayonnaise
2 tablespoons finely chopped onion
5 g (1 tsp) finely chopped garlic
25 g (1 oz) finely chopped fresh parsley
125 ml (4 fl oz) sour cream
15 ml (1 tbsp) lemon juice
15 ml (1 tbsp) white vinegar
225 g (8 oz) crumbled blue cheese

Mix ingredients together. Season to taste with salt and pepper.

CHICKEN THIGHS

If we had to choose our single favourite chicken part, we would pick the thigh. This delectable dark meat has more flavour than any other part of the chicken and, by far, the most appealing texture: rich, smooth and velvety. If we're preparing a cut-up chicken dish and we know that all our guests like dark meat, many's the time we'll use chicken thighs exclusively in the dish. For any kind of braised or stewed chicken, we like chicken thighs with the bone in; for any kind of quick-cooked chicken (shallow-fried or grilled) we like boneless chicken thighs.

BONE-IN CHICKEN THIGHS BRAISED WITH BALSAMIC VINEGAR AND PORCINI

These fabulous thighs get browned in a pan, then simmered with balsamic vinegar, tomatoes and porcini; use inexpensive balsamic for the braising and a little of the expensive stuff for finishing the sauce. The dish is superb with any side-dish starch that features a bit of Parmigiano-Reggiano (such as polenta, rice or potatoes).

SERVES 6

25 g (1 oz) dried porcini mushrooms
6 large chicken thighs, bone-in
salt and pepper to taste
5 garlic cloves, peeled
plain flour for dredging
two 5-mm (¼-in) thick slices of slab bacon (about
   115 g (¼ lb), cut crosswise into 1-cm (⅓-in)
   pieces
15 ml (1 tbsp) olive oil
125 ml (4 fl oz) fruity red wine, such as young
   Beaujolais
125 ml (4 fl oz) beef stock
45 ml (3 tbsp) industriale balsamic vinegar
5 g (1 tsp) arrowroot dissolved in 10 ml (2 tsp) cold
   water
175 g (6 oz) drained and chopped canned tomatoes
15 ml (1 tbsp) traditional balsamic vinegar
chopped fresh parsley for garnish

1. In a small bowl let the porcini soak in 225 ml (8 fl oz) hot water for 10 minutes or until soft. Drain them well, strain the liquid and reserve.

2. Season the chicken with salt and pepper. Chop 2 of the garlic cloves, adding a little salt, until a rough paste is formed. Cut a horizontal slit in each thigh, just above the bone and divide the garlic-salt paste evenly among the 6. Dredge the chicken thighs in the flour, shaking off the excess. In a large, heavy frying pan, cook the bacon over moderately high heat, stirring, until it is golden and crisp. Transfer it with a slotted spoon to paper towels. To the frying pan, add the chicken, skin side down and cook it, turning occasionally, for about 15 minutes, or until it is golden and crisp. Transfer the chicken to a plate, season it with salt and discard the fat in the frying pan.

3. Chop the remaining 3 garlic cloves. Add the olive oil to the frying pan and cook the garlic over moderate heat for 1 minute. Add the reserved porcini liquid, wine, broth and the 45 ml (3 tbsp) of industriale vinegar. Increase the heat to high and boil for 5 minutes. Add the arrowroot mixture in a stream, stirring. Stir in the tomatoes and add the chicken, turning it to coat with the sauce. Reduce the heat to moderately low and simmer the mixture, covered, for 10 minutes. Stir in the porcini and bacon and simmer, covered, over low heat for about 10 more minutes (do not allow the sauce to become too thick).

4. When ready to serve, stir in the 15 ml (1 tbsp) of traditional balsamic vinegar, season to taste and sprinkle the dish with the chopped parsley.

BONELESS GINGER-HOISIN CHICKEN THIGHS

Boning chicken thighs is really a snap. You turn them skin side down, then cut along both sides of the bone with a sharp knife. Work your fingers under the bone, lift it up and cut it free of the tendons holding it at both ends. Marinate the thigh and cook quickly.

SERVES 8 AS PART OF A CHINESE MEAL

115 g (4 oz) coarsely chopped peeled fresh ginger
15 g (1 tbsp) coarsely chopped garlic (about 2 large cloves)
125 ml (4 fl oz) hoisin sauce
30 ml (2 tbsp) soy sauce
30 g (2 tbsp) sugar
50 ml (2 fl oz) water
8 large chicken thighs, boned

1. Place the first six ingredients in the work bowl of a food processor. Process for a few minutes, or until you have a smooth purée.

2. Score the underside of each chicken thigh with a knife, 5-mm (¼-in) deep, in 3 or 4 places. Rub the ginger-hoisin purée all over the chicken thighs, place them in a bowl, cover tightly and refrigerate for at least 6 hours and up to 24 hours.

3. When ready to cook, place the thighs in a roasting tin, skin side up and put them under a preheated grill for 7 to 8 minutes, or until the skins are crunchy-brown. Turn the thighs over and grill for 3 to 4 minutes more, or until the chicken is just cooked through. Transfer the chicken thighs to paper towels and then to serving plates.

CHICKEN DRUMSTICKS

Drumsticks are almost as pleasing as chicken thighs: similarly deep in flavour, with the same kind of velvety feel on the palate. However, drumsticks contain more ligament and cartilage, which makes them a little more difficult to eat. Two good solutions make them easier to handle, either braise them or cut away all bones, ligaments and cartilage before cooking.

MOROCCAN BRAISED DRUMSTICKS WITH RAS EL HANOUT, CHICK PEAS AND RAISINS

Ras el hanout, which translates as 'the best in the shop',

is a warming blend of herbs and spices from Morocco. Sometimes flowers are added; try adding 5 rosebuds and/or a pinch of lavender flowers, if you wish, to the following mixture. Some variations of ras el hanout have been known to contain belladonna and aphrodisiacs; this one does not. The quantities given make more than you'll need here, so plan on saving some for other Moroccan dishes. Ras el hanout is used in Morocco to flavour a wide range of dishes and it certainly does its job in this richly spiced creation. The drumsticks, chick peas and raisins are terrific over a big platter of steamed couscous.

SERVES 4

For the ras el hanout
1 stick cinnamon, broken up
15 g (1 tbsp) sesame seeds
15 g (1 tbsp) ground ginger
15 whole black peppercorns
5 g (1 tsp) freshly ground nutmeg
5 g (1 tsp) fennel seeds
5 g (1 tsp) coriander seeds
8 whole cloves
8 allspice berries
seeds from 8 cardamom pods
2.5 g (½ tsp) whole cumin
2.5 g (½ tsp) ground red pepper
a pinch of ground mace
For the chicken
45 ml (3 tbsp) olive oil
8 chicken drumsticks
salt and pepper to taste
1 large onion, chopped
50 g (2 oz) chopped fresh coriander
15 g (3 tsp) garlic, chopped
5 g (1 tsp) coriander seeds
450 ml (16 fl oz) chicken stock
350 g (12 oz) cooked chick peas
115 g (4 oz) sultanas
2.5 g (½ tsp) harissa (page 496) or more to taste
a pinch of freshly grated orange zest

1. *Make the ras el hanout:* Grind all the ingredients to a fine powder in a coffee/spice grinder. (You will have about 50 g (2 oz)) Reserve.

2. *Make the chicken:* Heat the oil in a casserole over moderate heat until hot but not smoking. Pat the chicken dry and season generously with salt and pepper. Add the chicken and cook, in batches, turning with tongs until golden brown, about 10 minutes each batch. Remove to a plate.

3. Stir in the onion, 45 g (3 tbsp) of the coriander, garlic, coriander and 5 g (1 tsp) of the reserved ras el hanout and cook, stirring up any browned bits on the bottom of the pan, until the onion is softened, for about 5 minutes (add a bit of the stock if necessary to prevent sticking). Stir in the stock and return the chicken to the casserole. Cook at a bare simmer, covered, stirring occasionally, for 30 minutes, or until the chicken is cooked through.

4. Add the chick peas, sultanas, harissa and orange zest to the casserole and simmer, uncovered, for 5 minutes longer. Serve hot over steamed couscous, if desired and sprinkle with the remaining 15 g (1 tbsp) fresh coriander.

GRILLED BONELESS DRUMSTICKS WITH GREMOLATA

In our minds, there's not much in this world that a sprinkle of gremolata won't make better. Once reserved only for osso buco, it can enhance the flavours of a great many dishes.

SERVES 4

8 chicken drumsticks (about 1¾ pounds)
30 ml (2 tbsp) olive oil
salt and pepper to taste
30 g (2 tbsp) roughly chopped fresh flat-leaf
     parsley

20 g (4 tsp) fresh lemon zest, finely grated
1 medium garlic clove, finely chopped

1. Preheat the grill.

2. Bone the drumsticks: run a sharp knife vertically down the centre of each drumstick, cutting straight through to the bone. Then, scrape the flesh away from the bone on all sides until the bone is released. Trim away any excess cartilage. (You should have a flat, gristle-free, skin-on chicken cutlet. Alternatively, you can ask your butcher to do this for you.)

3. Brush the boned drumsticks with the olive oil and season well with salt and pepper.

4. Place the drumsticks on a lightly oiled grill rack. Place the rack 5 to 15 cm (2-6 in) from the heat source and grill for 10 minutes. Turn the drumsticks, brush with olive oil and grill for about 10 minutes longer, or until cooked through, testing often for doneness (watch the drumsticks carefully so that they do not burn; because of the differences in grills, the cooking time may vary).

5. While the drumsticks are grilling, make the gremolata. Chop together the parsley, lemon zest and garlic.

6. Transfer the drumsticks to a platter, sprinkle with the gremolata and serve immediately.

Turkey

Turkey took a giant step forward in the eighties and nineties. Once viewed in the U.S. exclusively as a Thanksgiving dish, turkey slowly grew into the 'everyday' category. The key factors were the public perception that turkey meat is lean and healthful and the growing availability of turkey parts (you no longer have to commit yourself to an enormous bird in order to serve turkey).

ROAST TURKEY
No matter how many newfangled turkey burgers and turkey stews creep into American kitchens, there's little indication that Americans will ever give up their roast turkey on Thanksgiving day. Yet millions of people who are served Thanksgiving turkey grumble about the inferiority of turkey to other birds. We used to grumble too—until we realised that the problem is in the cooking, not in the bird itself. Because the turkey's dark meat takes longer to cook than the turkey's white meat, most roast turkeys in the United States, we daresay, come to the table with dry, stringy white meat that has been overcooked while the chef's been waiting for the dark meat to cook. It's a great shame, because the white meat, if cooked just past pink (about 65.5°C (150°F)), when it still retains a great deal of juice, can be delicious indeed.

Another white-meat solution: brining turkey

Some chefs have discovered that by soaking turkey in a saltwater bath for 12 hours or so, the white meat comes to the table much juicier. There's a recipe for just such a brine on page 405, which we recommend as a preliminary soak for pork chops. But you might want to try it on your turkey as well.

PERFECT TWO-STAGE ROAST TURKEY
The solution to the white meat/dark meat roast turkey problem is simple: remove the bird from the oven as soon as the white meat is cooked, slice off the copious turkey breast and return the rest of the bird to the oven to finish cooking the dark meat. If you like displaying the whole bird on a platter, do so, but remove the breast at the table and return the dark meat to the oven. While the rest of the bird is cooking, slice the breasts on a carving board at the table and consider them a first course. One idea is to serve them with a light gravy and a white wine; when, 20 minutes later, the dark meat is

ready, serve it with a darker gravy and a red wine as a
second course. The following recipe is calibrated for a
6.3-kg (14-lb) turkey; add or subtract time depending on
the size of the bird. Remember that a quick-read meat
thermometer is the roaster's best friend.

SERVES 12

whole 6.3-kg (14-lb) turkey
butter
salt and pepper to taste

1. Preheat oven to 220°C (425°F).

2. Smear the turkey with butter, then season well with
salt and pepper. Place the turkey on a rack in a roasting
tin in the lower portion of the oven, legs towards the
back. Roast until the turkey starts to turn golden, about
15 to 20 minutes. Reduce the heat to 160°C (325°F) and
roast the turkey for about 1½ hours, basting with the
pan juices every 20 minutes or so. (The white meat is
done when a quick-read thermometer reaches 65.5°C
(150°F)).

3. Remove turkey from oven and (at table, if desired),
remove the large breast fillet from each side of the
turkey. Let the fillets rest a few minutes before carving
into thin slices.

4. Meanwhile, return the rest of the bird to the 160°C
(325°F) oven. Cook until the dark meat reaches 80°C
(175°F), about 20 minutes more. Remove, let rest a few
minutes and serve the dark meat.

TURKEY STUFFINGS

Americans expect a stuffing with their roast turkey—
but we think that the usual, heavy, wet, flavourless
mass of bread is not worth the trouble just because it
answers to the description of 'stuffing'. There are many
marvellous flavours you can bring together in
stuffings . . . and we have come to love lighter-textured

stuffings, in which the pieces of flavoured bread are
barely held together.

Furthermore, we have found that the traditional
method of roasting the stuffing inside the bird causes
several problems. First of all, stuffing your turkey before
roasting—even as little as an hour before roasting—
can promote the growth of bacteria. It's safer to bake
your 'stuffing' in a separate pan (at which point it's not
really a 'stuffing' any longer). Second, cooking your
stuffing inside the bird means you relinquish control
over the cooking time of your stuffing—a practice that
often leads to soggy, overcooked stuffing. For this reason
as well we prefer to bake the stuffing separately,
because we can remove it from the oven when it's at
perfect readiness.

BREAD AND BUTTER STUFFING WITH FRESH SAGE

We like to cook this stuffing, in particular, outside of the
bird, in a separate pan; the chunks of bread achieve a
crunchy, chewy texture that way. In fact, the dish seems
more like a delicious bread pudding than a stuffing. The
amount of butter in the recipe may raise an eyebrow or
two, but at holiday time, who's counting? The dish ends
up tasting intensely buttery without being greasy. If you
love the taste of butter, this stuffing is for you.

MAKES ENOUGH STUFFING FOR A 6.3-7.3-KG
(14-16-LB) TURKEY

900-g (2-lb) loaf white bread, sliced
225-g (8-oz) loaf wholemeal bread, sliced
700 g (1½ lb) unsalted butter
350 g (12 oz) chopped celery
450 g (16 oz) chopped onions
225 g (8 oz) peeled and chopped apple
850 ml (1½ pints) chicken stock, turkey stock or
water
8 sprigs of fresh thyme
30 sage leaves, stems removed and the leaves cut
into thin strips
225 g (8 oz) raisins

30 g (2 tbsp) salt

10 to 12 turns of freshly ground pepper

1. The night before cooking, spread all the bread out in a single layer on baking sheets or towels and allow to dry out overnight.

2. The next morning, in a large bowl roughly break the bread into coarse 4-cm (1½-in) pieces.

3. Melt the butter in a large saucepan over low heat, making sure not to burn it. Add the celery, onions and apple and cook over low heat for 5 minutes. Add the stock or water. Increase the heat to moderate and bring to a boil. Turn off the heat and allow to cool for 3 minutes.

4. Pour the mixture over the bread. Remove the leaves from the thyme sprigs and add the leaves to the bread mixture. Add the sage to the bread mixture. Add the raisins, salt and pepper and mix well.

5. Either stuff a 6.3-7.3-kg (14-16-lb) turkey with the mixture and roast immediately, or put the mixture in a large roasting tin and cover with foil. If baking separately, bake the stuffing in a 190°C (375°F) oven, covered, for 30 minutes. Remove foil, bake for another 30 minutes and serve alongside roast turkey.

CORNBREAD AND OYSTER STUFFING

This light-textured, dry and airy stuffing has tremendous depth of flavour, Southwestern-style.

MAKES ENOUGH STUFFING FOR A 6.3-7.3-KG (14-16-LB) TURKEY

70 g (2½ oz) butter

225 g (8 oz) chopped sweet onion

50 g (2 oz) finely diced celery

5 garlic cloves, finely chopped

3 jalapeño peppers, finely chopped

50 g (2 oz) red pepper, finely chopped

430 g (18 oz) cornbread, crumbled

10 g (2 tsp) fresh thyme

salt and freshly ground pepper to taste

36 fresh oysters, cut in half if large

1. Place the butter in a large omelette pan over moderately high heat. When it's melted, add the onion and celery and cook them until translucent, about 5 minutes. Add garlic cloves, jalapeños, and red pepper and cook for another 3 minutes. Remove from heat and allow the mixture to cool slightly.

2. In a large bowl combine the onion mixture with the cornbread and mix well. Add thyme and season generously with salt and freshly ground pepper. Add the oysters (not the oyster liquid) to the cornbread mixture

3. Either stuff the turkey with the mixture and roast immediately, or put the mixture in a large roasting tin and cover with foil. If baking separately, bake the stuffing, covered, in a 180°C (350°F) oven for 30 minutes. Serve with roast turkey.

SAUSAGE AND PECAN STUFFING WITH RAISINS

This is a meat stuffing with something extra: the pecans add a great texture and the raisins add a lovely sweetness.

MAKES ENOUGH STUFFING FOR A 6.3-7.3-KG (14-16-LB) TURKEY

450 g (1 lb) sweet Italian sausage, removed from casings

115 g (4 oz) butter

650 g (1½ lb) chopped yellow onions

450 g (1 lb) diced celery

10 g (2 tsp) salt

2.5 g (½ tsp) freshly ground black pepper

650 g (1½ lb) cubed, stale cornbread

20 g (4 tsp) chopped fresh thyme

15 g (1 tbsp) chopped fresh sage
225 g (8 oz) raisins
115 g (4 oz) chopped pecans

1. In a large frying pan over moderately high heat, cook the sausage, breaking it up with a wooden spoon, until well browned, about 8 minutes. Remove sausage with a slotted spoon to a plate lined with paper towels, leaving grease in frying pan. Set sausage aside to drain.

2. Add the butter to the frying pan and melt over moderate heat. Add onions, celery, salt and pepper and cook until soft, about 10 minutes.

3. Add cornbread, thyme, sage, raisins, pecans and sausage and stir to mix well. Adjust seasoning if necessary. Cool fully before stuffing bird.

Note: If the stuffing is not to be cooked inside the bird: after blending the cornbread and sausage, add 70 g (3 oz) butter, melted and 350 ml (12 fl oz) chicken stock. Stir well. Place in a large buttered roasting tin and cover. Bake at 180°C (350°F) for 15 minutes; remove cover and bake for another 20 minutes.

PUMPKIN AND PANCETTA STUFFING

MAKES ENOUGH STUFFING FOR A 6.3-7.3-KG
(14-16-LB) TURKEY

650 g (1½ lb) 1-cm (½-in) white bread cubes, crust included
1 small pumpkin (about (1½ lb))
30 ml (2 tbsp) olive oil
115 g (4 oz) pancetta, chopped
4 large shallots, sliced
50 g (2 oz) celery, diced
45 g (3 tbsp) chopped garlic
50 g (2 oz) mixed fresh herbs (such as parsley, thyme and rosemary)
50 g (2 oz) dried figs, halved

25 g (1 oz) shelled and lightly toasted pumpkin seeds
40 g (1½ oz) butter
salt and pepper to taste
50 ml (2 fl oz) chicken stock

1. Preheat oven to 180°C (350°F). Spread the bread cubes on an oiled baking sheet and bake until light brown, about 20 minutes.

2. Split the pumpkin in half and bake at 180°C (350°F) for about 30 minutes, or until tender but not mushy. Cut pumpkin flesh away from rind and cut flesh into 2.5-cm (1-in) cubes. Measure out 450 g (1 lb) in a large bowl and set aside. Discard rind.

3. In a large omelette pan, heat olive oil over moderate heat. Add the pancetta and cook for 5 minutes, until lightly crisp. Add shallots and celery and cook until translucent, about 5 minutes. Add garlic and cook another 3 minutes. Reserve.

4. Mix together pumpkin cubes, baked bread cubes, herbs, dried figs, pumpkin seeds and butter and season with salt and pepper. Add the pancetta mixture and chicken stock and mix well.

5. Either stuff the turkey with the mixture and roast immediately, or put the mixture in a large, buttered roasting tin and cover with foil. Bake, covered, at 190°C (375°F) for 15 minutes. Uncover and bake for 15 more minutes. Serve with roast turkey.

TURKEY PARTS

GUATEMALAN TURKEY MOLE

For this authentic Mayan crowd-pleaser (recorded by our world-travelling friend and customer Copeland Marks), you'll need about 3.6 kg (8 lb) of turkey parts; you may

use legs, breasts, wings, or a combination. In
Guatemala, turkey is an honoured bird and an expensive
one; this dish is prepared on special occasions such as
fiestas, weddings and important family gatherings.
Serve with rice and Latin American salads and salsas.

SERVES 8 WITH 3.6 KG (8 LB) TURKEY PARTS

1 ripe tomato, halved
2 fat spring onions, chopped
10 garlic cloves, peeled
1 dried chilli pasilla
1 dried chilli guajillo
50 g (2 oz) pepitas (raw hulled green pumpkin
    seeds)
50 g (2 oz) sesame seeds
1 cinnamon stick, broken into 3 pieces
1 large onion, peeled and halved
5 g (1 tsp) dried hot red pepper flakes
450 g (1 lb) canned tomatoes
25 g (1 oz) unsweetened baking chocolate
5 g (1 tsp) sugar

1. Bone the turkey parts, reserving the meat. Place the
bones (you should have at least 900 g (2 lb)) in a
stewpot. Add 1.8 litres (3¼ pints) of water, the tomato,
the spring onions and 4 garlic cloves. Bring to a boil
and skim off the foam that rises to the surface. Reduce
heat and simmer, covered, for 1 hour.

2. Cut the reserved turkey meat into 5-cm (2-in) cubes.
Add to the turkey broth and simmer for 20 minutes.
Remove meat and set aside. Strain the broth and
reserve.

3. Place the chilli pasilla in a small saucepan with 125
ml (4 fl oz) water. Simmer for 10 minutes.

4. Put the chilli guajillo, the pumpkin seeds, the sesame
seeds and the cinnamon into a heavy omelette pan over
low heat and toast, stirring, for 15 minutes.

5. While the seed mixture is toasting, place the onion
and remaining 6 garlic cloves on a roasting tin and char
lightly on all sides under grill (about 8 minutes).

6. In a food processor, place the chilli pasilla with its
cooking liquid, the toasted chilli guajillo, pumpkin
seeds, sesame seeds and cinnamon, the charred onion
and garlic, the pepper flakes, the canned tomatoes and
450 ml (16 fl oz) of the reserved turkey cooking liquid.
Purée until smooth. Add the chocolate and sugar and
bring the mixture to a boil.

7. When the chocolate has melted, add the turkey cubes
and enough of the reserved liquid to cover the turkey.
Simmer over low heat for 45 minutes. (The turkey should
be tender and the sauce medium-thick. Add extra broth
if necessary.) Season to taste and serve.

STUFFED DRUMSTICKS WITH BACON, BRANDY AND THYME
You'll be amazed at the deep flavour in these wonderful
turkey-and-meat bundles. It's a great dish for autumn
and winter entertaining; serve with a potato gratin. Be
sure to use fresh, not frozen, turkey drumsticks.

SERVES 6

6 turkey drumsticks
450 g (1 lb) minced pork (not too fine)
6 rashers bacon, finely chopped
7.5 g (1½ tsp) dried thyme, crumbled
3 g (¾ tsp) very finely chopped garlic
175 g (6 oz) fresh breadcrumbs
3 eggs, beaten well
15 ml (1 tbsp) brandy
3 g (¾ tsp) salt
3 g (¾ tsp) freshly ground black pepper
big pinch of ground allspice
450 ml (16 fl oz) brown stock (preferably made from
    poultry)
50 g (2 oz) chilled unsalted butter plus butter for

basting

finely chopped parsley for garnish

1. Bone the drumsticks or ask your butcher to do so. There should be no bone left, not even the tip of the drumstick. Make sure that all of the cartilage and tendons are removed and that the skin is left intact. Season the boned drumsticks well with salt and pepper and reserve. Preheat oven to 190°C (375°F).

2. In a mixing bowl, combine the next 10 ingredients. Mix thoroughly. Divide stuffing among the six boned drumsticks, stuffing each drumstick under the skin. Place the drumsticks in a roasting tin, skin side up, and place the tin in the preheated oven. Roast for 15 minutes, baste the skin with a little butter and roast for an additional 15 minutes, or until the skin is golden brown. The drumsticks may also puff up at this point. Remove from oven and keep warm.

3. Add the brown stock to the roasting tin and place over high heat. Deglaze the tin, scraping up the brown bits. Boil until a little more than half the stock remains. Just before serving, whisk in the chilled butter, 15 g (½ oz) at a time. Taste sauce for seasoning.

4. Place the stuffed turkey drumsticks on 6 dinner plates, surround with the sauce and sprinkle with chopped parsley.

Duck

Duck underwent its own revolution in the eighties—this one caused by 3 culinary ideas from France.

First of all, duck on an American table used to mean one thing only: long-cooked roast duck, with tender, grey meat inside. If you were lucky, the outside of the duck was crackling-crisp, and the whole bird was relatively unfatty. Then came the revolution: word arrived that French chefs were cooking duck breast rare, like steak and a new generation of American chefs began to do the same. It took a while for home chefs to follow

their lead, because duck breasts, by themselves, were not available at the supermarket.

Then the second French idea hit. The reason the French had so many duck breasts at their disposal was foie gras: after the livers were extracted from French ducks, one of the ways to use the rest of the bird was to market the large, meaty breasts. In the eighties, America launched its own foie gras industry—and, similarly, the large, meaty breasts of those ducks began to arrive in gourmet food stores and a few better supermarkets.

The third French idea also indirectly involved foie gras. Traditionally, the legs and thighs of the foie gras–producing ducks in France were used for preserved duck, or confit de canard. This is a great south-western French dish that was very rarely seen here before the eighties. But American chefs became keenly aware of it in the eighties and started making their own. This was backed up, once again, by our American foie gras industry making legs and thighs available and by America's chief foie gras distributor—D'Artagnan, in New Jersey—preserving thousands of ducks a year and selling the confit to restaurants and markets around the country.

The Frenchification of American duck was complete.

Types of ducks

Once upon a time, the only duck available to the average American consumer was whole frozen duck. This wasn't such a terrible thing, because frozen duck, if defrosted properly (24 hours in the refrigerator), is a decent substitute for fresh duck.

But the American duck scene has now expanded to the point where not only can you easily find fresh ducks in markets, but you sometimes have your choice of types of ducks. Here are the ducks you're most likely to see.

Pekin Duck Originally called the Peking duck when it arrived here from China in the nineteenth century, the white Pekin is the breed of the famous Long Island duck. In fact, most of the ducks raised in the United States—there are large industries in Indiana, North Carolina and

Pennsylvania as well—are of this breed. In many ways, it's not an ideal duck for duck-lovers: it is very mild in flavour, very fatty and relatively un-meaty, with a thin skin and light-coloured meat.

Muscovy Duck Also called Barbary duck, this bird is sometimes available in United States, particularly in autumn and winter. It is meatier than the Pekin duck and with a much stronger flavour—in fact, some find it almost too strong, or 'musky'. Duck-lovers love it.

Moulard This is the duck that is used in France and New York State to make foie gras; it is actually a cross of the Pekin and Muscovy ducks. It is a splendid duck: large, full-flavoured, with dark meat and wonderfully rich skin. Unfortunately, it is not easy to find whole Moulards in the American marketplace. Happily, however, the large, meaty breasts of Moulards that have been used for foie gras are available; it is these breasts that are cooked rare for the dish known as magret de canard.

Wild Ducks In addition to the raised Pekins, Muscovys and Moulards, there are many wild ducks taken by hunters in America; they are generally leaner and stringier than their domesticated cousins. Don't ever confuse Moulard with mallard; the latter is a wild duck that's particularly lean. The most famous and, perhaps, delicious, of the American wild ducks is the canvasback, which was extremely popular in the nineteenth century.

ROAST DUCK

When the rare-duck-breast phenomenon hit, American chefs all but abandoned the old idea of long-cooked, tender roast duck with a crisp skin. Rare duck was oh-so-trendy and roast duck became a culinary dinosaur. Happily, our national taste for dinosaur seems to be returning; we've seen a number of restaurants going back to the old duck-cooking method and a number of home cooks wanting to do the same. And why not? A well-done duck has much more ducky flavour than a rare-cooked breast (which, truth be told, often doesn't taste like duck at all). Furthermore, the interplay of crisp skin and tender meat in a well roasted duck is mightily satisfying.

OLD-FASHIONED CRISPY ROAST DUCK

One reason home cooks may have abandoned roast duck is that they perceived a high degree of difficulty in getting it right. But the following recipe, though it calls for many hours of roasting, is simple as can be—and leads to perfectly crisp skin and meltingly tender duck meat. To serve the ducks, you could simply cut each one in half and serve each person half a duck with the bone in. Or, you could fillet the breast and legs (making sure to keep the crisp skin intact), cut the fillets into 1-cm (½-in)-wide pieces and arrange the slices attractively on dinner plates. Either way, it's an out-and-out winner.

SERVES 4

2 large ducks (fresh or thawed frozen, each about
    2.7 kg (6 lb))
salt and pepper to taste

1. Preheat oven to 120°C (250°F).

2. *Trim the ducks:* With a sharp knife, cut away excess fat and skin that hangs at both ends of the ducks. Trim thoroughly (you should end up with about 450 g (1 lb) of excess skin and fat, which can be discarded or rendered).

3. Salt the cavity of each duck and prick each duck very thoroughly with a fork on both sides (25 to 30 pricks for each duck). Make sure to prick through the skin and subcutaneous fat only; do not prick the flesh of the duck.

4. Place the ducks on a rack set in a large roasting tin. Place pan in the oven and roast ducks at 120°C

(250°F). After 1 hour, prick ducks thoroughly on one side, turn them over and prick thoroughly on the other side. Continue to roast with the newly turned side up. Repeat this procedure every hour.

5. After 4 hours of roasting, prick and turn once again. Increase oven temperature to 180°C (350°F). Continue roasting, pricking and turning once, for an additional 30 to 90 minutes (see Note below).

6. When the ducks are done, let them sit for 15 minutes before carving. Season well with salt and pepper before serving.

Note: The amount of additional roasting time at 180°C (350°F) is up to you. Do you want a juicier finished product or a crisper finished product?

If you roast the ducks at 180°C (350°F) for 15 minutes on one side, prick and turn, then roast for 15 minutes on the other side, they will be very juicy and slightly crisp.

If you roast them for 30 minutes on one side, prick and turn and 30 minutes on the other side, they will be juicy and crisp.

If you roast them for 45 minutes on one side, prick and turn and 45 minutes on the other side, they will be pretty juicy and very crisp.

We prefer the middle path: 1 hour additional roasting time at 180°C (350°F).

DUCK BREAST

MAGRET DE CANARD WITH APPLES AND MAPLE, QUEBEC-STYLE

Although commonly misused, the French term *magret* refers strictly to the breast meat of the fattened Moulard duck—but only if its liver has been used in the production of foie gras. The Moulard is a big duck, weighing up to 3-3.6 kg (7-8 lb) dressed and its breast is very large, weighing up to 900 g (2 lb); it can easily

serve 4 people. This delicious dish has French roots, in a sense. Many elements of Quebecois cooking can be traced to Quebec's original French settlers, who were from Normandy; that would account for the use of apples. The sweet maple syrup is a Quebecois staple— they've even been known to cook their breakfast eggs in maple syrup—but the juxtaposition of something sweet with duck is very French. In any event, if you don't like mixing your sweet with your savoury, pass by this dish.

SERVES 4

30 g (2 tbsp) rendered duck fat or vegetable oil
1 magret (Moulard duck breast, about 900 g (2 lb));
 cut into 2 breast halves
2 cooking apples, peeled, cored, and cut into 3-mm
 (⅛-in) slices
3 large shallots, chopped
1 bay leaf
5 g (1 tsp) fresh thyme
salt and pepper to taste
125 ml (4 fl oz) cider vinegar
350 ml (12 fl oz) duck or chicken stock
125 ml (4 fl oz) pure maple syrup (or less, if a less
 sweet dish is desired)
15 g (½ oz) unsalted butter

1. Heat the duck fat in a heavy, 25-cm (10-in) frying pan over moderately high heat until hot but not smoking. Add the breast halves and quickly brown it on both sides, about 5 minutes total.

2. Remove the breast halves to a plate and set aside. Stir in the apples, shallots, bay leaf, thyme, salt and pepper and cook, stirring, for 3 minutes, or until lightly browned. Increase the heat to high, stir in the cider vinegar and cook until the mixture is almost dry, about 3 minutes.

3. Add the stock and maple syrup and bring to a boil. Reduce the heat, bring the liquid to a bare simmer and add the breast halves and any accumulated juices.

Braise the breast halves slowly for about 10 to 12 minutes, turning it once with tongs, until it's medium-rare. Remove the breast halves and the apples (use a slotted spoon) to plates and keep warm separately. Discard the bay leaf.

4. Over very high heat reduce the sauce until slightly thickened, about 10 minutes. Whisk in the butter. Season with salt and pepper.

5. Holding your knife at a 45-degree angle to the cutting board, slice the breast halves crosswise into 16 pieces. Place the apples on 4 serving plates and top with the breast halves fanned over the apples. Spoon the sauce over and serve immediately.

DUCK CONFIT

Confit means 'preserved'—and *confit de canard,* or duck confit, means 'preserved duck'. It is one of the most delicious creations in the whole French repertoire, it has become popular in restaurants on this side of the Atlantic and—best news of all—the home cook can easily make a version that's even better than what's commonly available in restaurants.

The dish started out, in south-western France, as a way to use the legs and thighs of Moulard ducks that were being raised for foie gras production. Thousands of ducks were being slaughtered for foie gras, but no one could use so much fresh duck meat so quickly—so preserving the meat saved the day. The legs and thighs are salted and marinated, then slowly simmered for hours in duck fat. The 'preserving' takes place when the cooked meat is placed in large crocks and completely covered with the duck fat and cooled; under the thick, white, congealed, protective layer of duck fat, the duck legs and thighs remain edible for as long as 4 months. Do they improve with age? You bet they do—every week that passes by makes them a little richer tasting, a little more velvety in texture.

The reason you can make better confit at home than

they do in restaurants is that restaurant confit is rarely confit at all. Restaurant chefs go through the early stages of the process, but usually don't hold the duck for more than a day or so for lack of storage space. Confit that's barely preserved at all still tastes good, but nothing like the confit you can really preserve at home.

Here are a few more 'confit issues'.

Which Duck? You can preserve the legs and thighs of Pekin duck—but they won't be nearly as succulent as the legs and thighs of Moulard duck.

Pink or Natural? When confit is made in France, chefs usually add a touch of saltpetre or potassium nitrate, which turns the duck flesh pink; without it, the flesh will be grey-brown. The French think the pink colour is more attractive; Americans usually avoid adding saltpetre. The choice is yours. If you wish to add saltpetre, you can find it at some pharmacies or look for a product supplied to professional chefs called Selrose.

How Long? Though confit tastes good the day you've made it, it won't have the melting, velvety quality that only time can confer. You'll notice a difference in your confit after a week of preservation and even more after a month. If, however, you really want the full confit experience, you should plan on 3 months of preservation. Make it in September and it'll be ready for Christmas!

How to Store? Strangely enough, the ideal storage conditions for confit are the same as the ideal storage conditions for wine: approximately 10-13°C (50°-55°F), in a dark cellar. Your confit will be at its best if you can give it those conditions. The refrigerator, which is colder, retards the 'velvetising' a bit, but is an adequate substitute.

What to Store it in? Wide-mouthed ceramic crocks are the classic storage vessels, but you can improvise here. Glass jars work just fine, as do enamelled cast-iron cooking pots.

How to Cook? When you're ready to serve your preserved duck, you have to heat it up. Various chefs use various methods to do so. We love it crispy-brown on the outside and favour a quick sizzle in duck fat over very high heat.

PRESERVED DUCK (CONFIT DE CANARD)

This recipe yields one of the best confits we've ever tasted. Serve it with garlicky potatoes sautéed in duck fat and a stout red wine.

SERVES 6

3 ducks
50 g (2 oz) coarse salt
5 g (1 tsp) mixed spices*
pinch of saltpetre (optional)
6 sprigs of fresh rosemary
1.8-2.25 kg (4-5 lb) rendered duck fat†

1. Cut the ducks into pieces, removing from them pieces of leg and thigh that are still attached to each other. You will have 6 leg-thigh assemblies. (The duck breasts can be reserved for another use; the rest of the ducks can be used to make rendered duck fat—recipe follows.)

2. Sprinkle the leg-thigh portions with coarse salt on both sides. Turn them skin side down and sprinkle with the mixed spices and saltpetre (if using). Place a rosemary branch on each portion and press together pairs of portions so that you have 3 'packages' of thigh-leg portions with the skin on the outside. Marinate in the refrigerator for 24 hours.

*French chefs usually keep a blend of spices in their pantries, for use in pâtés, confits, and other dishes. Sometimes this is called quatres épices, four spices, though it may have more than 4 spices in it. Today, you can find quatres épices in stores in America. There's a terrific product made in Strasbourg by Georges Bruck called Mixed Spices, which is also available. Or, you can make your own blend by combining equal amounts of ground cloves, nutmeg, and white pepper with smaller amounts of ground cinnamon, cayenne pepper, and dried thyme.

†Rendered duck fat can be purchased today in specialty food stores. You will need to buy some to make this dish, because the amount of fat rendered by 3 ducks is not enough to cover the 6 leg-thigh pieces. But you can render your own fat anyway, and add it to the fat you've purchased (recipe follows).

3. When ready to cook, remove the herbs from the duck and scrape away most of the salt. Coat the pieces lightly with a little rendered duck fat and place under a grill until the skin has browned lightly, about 3 to 4 minutes. Remove from grill and dry duck pieces thoroughly.

4. Place duck pieces in a large stewpot and cover them completely with rendered duck fat. Place over low heat and bring the fat to just below the simmering point. Cook over low heat for 2½ hours, making sure the fat doesn't boil. Remove duck pieces from fat.

5. Pour boiling water into a wide-mouthed ceramic crock (or whatever storage vessel you've chosen) and pour it out. Dry the vessel well. Place a few sticks (like chopsticks, if they fit) on the bottom of the vessel, to keep the duck elevated above the juices that will collect. Then place the duck pieces on top of the sticks, either on one level or stacked up on several levels. Pour enough of the duck fat in which the duck cooked through a fine sieve to completely cover the duck. Let the duck come to room temperature, then place it in storage (a 10°C (50°F) room or a refrigerator).

6. After the confit has chilled and the duck fat has hardened, you can improve the longevity of your confit by pouring vegetable oil over the top of the crock to a depth of 1 cm (½ in). Return to cold room or refrigerator.

7. When you're ready to cook your confit (3 months later, we urge), let the crock warm up a bit to facilitate removal of the duck pieces. Take out the duck (it should still have some fat clinging to it). Place enough duck fat in one or two omelette pans (large enough to hold the duck in one layer) to reach 5 mm (¼ in) of depth. Increase the heat to high. When the fat is very hot, place pieces of confit in the pan (or pans), skin side down. Cook until confit becomes very brown and crisp, about 5 minutes. Turn over, and brown the other side briefly, about 2 minutes. Return to skin side for final browning, about 2 minutes. Drain on paper towels and serve.

RENDERED DUCK FAT WITH WINE

Here's a delicious way to render your own duck fat.

MAKES ABOUT 450 G (1 LB) DUCK FAT

3 ducks, leg-and-thigh portions removed
350 ml (12 fl oz) dry white wine

Work over the ducks, removing as much fat and skin as you can find (save breasts, if desired, for another use and bones for stock). Cut the skin and fat into 2.5-cm (1-in) pieces and place in a large, heavy saucepan. Add the wine and 350 ml (12 fl oz) water. Bring to a boil, reduce the heat and bring to a simmer. Cook until the water and wine have evaporated, leaving pure rendered duck fat behind, about 1 hour. Strain the duck fat through muslin.

Note: The duck 'chain' never ends! After straining out the pieces of duck skin, you can return them to the pot and crisp them over moderate heat. Cool them, salt them and use them as 'duck croutons' in salad.

Rabbit

Rabbit has been a steady presence in American gastronomic life, but fell into relative disfavour in this century; for some reason, rabbits got singled out as 'cute' critters that you wouldn't want to eat.

In the eighties and nineties, many chefs—and some culinary civilians—lost their squeamishness and rabbit started turning up on trendy menus across the country. This is a good thing, as far as we're concerned—because rabbit can be delicious and tastes quite different from chicken, to which it's often compared. Rabbit is leaner than chicken, with a shinier, translucent look to the meat and a slightly firmer texture.

Because of its leanness, rabbit needs either to be cooked quickly or cooked with moisture for a long time. Sometimes, in classical European preparations, rabbits are larded or barded (two ways of adding fat). An oil-based marinade is another way of fighting the lean

problem. Generally speaking, quick-cooking smaller rabbits (1.3 kg (3 lb)) are best. If you have a larger rabbit 1.8-2.25 kg (4-5 lb), stewing or braising is your best option; quick-cooking a large rabbit could result in tough meat.

GRILLED RABBIT WITH AÏOLI

Lots of restaurant chefs participating in the 'rabbit revival' are marinating rabbit, then cooking it quickly over hot coals.

SERVES 4

2 x 1.3-kg (3-lb) rabbits, each cut in 6 pieces
700 ml (1¼ pints) dry white wine
75 ml (2½ fl oz) olive oil
50 g (2 oz) chopped fresh rosemary
70 g (2½ oz) chopped fresh marjoram
30 g (2 tbsp) finely chopped garlic
10 g (2 tsp)salt
3 g (¾ tsp) freshly ground black pepper
45 g (3 tbsp) bacon fat (rendered from 4 to 6
   rashers bacon)
4 sprigs of rosemary, for garnish
175 ml (6 fl oz) aïoli (page 494)

1. Rinse rabbit pieces under cold running water and pat dry. Place them in a large bowl.

2. In another bowl, whisk together the white wine, olive oil, rosemary, marjoram, garlic, salt and pepper. Pour marinade over the rabbit, cover and refrigerate, stirring occasionally, for 2 days.

3. Two hours before grilling, remove the rabbit from the refrigerator and bring to room temperature.

4. Prepare the grill. When grill is ready, remove rabbit from marinade and pat dry.

5. Over grey, ashy coals, grill rabbit for about 10

minutes per side, basting several times with the bacon
fat. The loin pieces will cook in about 15 to 17 minutes
total. (The rabbit should be cooked like chicken—it will
be rosy near the bone but the juices should run clear.)
When rabbit is done, let it rest for 5 minutes.

6. Arrange on a platter, garnish with rosemary sprigs
and serve with aïoli on the side.

PROVENÇAL RABBIT STEW WITH OLIVES AND CAPERS

It's not for nothing that old-timers used to talk of 'rabbit
stew'; slow-cooking the lean rabbit is a great way to
tenderise it. Now that rabbit's growing in popularity, we
hope the stew idea will come back. When stewed, the
rabbit meat is moist and tender, like chicken, but with
an extra layer of flavour. That flavour stands up perfectly
to the strong-tasting mustard, olives and capers in this
delicious, winter-weight party dish. Decide on the
thickness of the sauce yourself; we like it somewhere
between a soup and a stew, but you can make thicken
the sauce by adding potato flour or beurre manié.
Delicious with rice.

SERVES 6

3 rabbits (about 1.3 kg (3 lb) each)
30 ml (2 tbsp) olive oil plus additional if necessary
   for cooking vegetables
50 g (2 oz) flour, plus additional if necessary
50 ml (2 fl oz) Dijon mustard
450 g (1 lb) coarsely chopped onions
225 g (8 oz) coarsely chopped carrots
225 ml (8 fl oz) white wine
1 sprig of thyme
1 bay leaf
7.5 ml (1½ tsp) tomato paste
2 garlic cloves, finely chopped
a few pints chicken stock
7.5 g (1½ tsp) salt, or to taste
450 g (1 lb) fresh plum tomatoes

350 g (12 oz) brine-cured green olives
175 g (6 oz) capers
50 g (2 oz) finely chopped fresh parsley

1. Preheat oven to 190°C (375°F).

2. Cut the rabbits in 6 pieces each (the meaty hind legs,
the bonier forelegs, plus the centre loin, called *rable* in
French, cut in two). Or have your butcher do it for you. In
an ovenproof omelette pan wide enough to hold the
rabbit pieces in one layer, add the olive oil and place
over moderate heat. (If you don't have a pan big enough,
you can use 2 and divide the ingredients.)

3. Put flour in a flat dish. Brush the rabbit pieces with
the mustard and then dip into the flour, shaking off any
excess. Add the rabbit pieces to the hot oil and cook until
golden brown on both sides. Remove rabbit from the pan
and set aside.

4. Add the onions and carrots to the pan (or pans) and
cook over moderately high heat until onions are lightly
browned. (You may need to add 5 ml (1 tsp) of olive oil if
the pan is too dry.) Sprinkle the leftover flour, if there is
any, into the pan and stir well to blend with the onions.
Deglaze the pan with the white wine over high heat and
mix well. Add the thyme, bay leaf, tomato paste and
garlic and mix well.

5. Return the rabbit to the pan (or pans). Add enough
chicken stock to cover the meat and vegetables by 2.5 g
(1 in) (you may combine the stock with water, if desired).
Bring to a boil and add the salt. Cover and braise in the
oven for 1½ hours, or until the meat is just cooked
enough to start falling from the bone.

6. While the rabbit is cooking, bring a small pot of water
to boil. Remove the stems from the tomatoes with the
tip of a small knife. Make a small crisscross on the
other side of the tomato. Plunge the tomatoes into the
boiling water for about 30 seconds, or until skin begins

to pull away. Refresh under cold water and remove the peel. Cut in half lengthways and remove the seeds. Chop coarsely and reserve until needed. Rinse the olives in cold water. Reserve.

7. When the rabbit is ready, carefully remove the pieces from the pan and set aside. Strain the sauce through a colander. Discard the vegetables and herbs.

8. Return the sauce to the pan and bring to a boil over moderate heat. Add the tomatoes, olives and capers. Reduce the heat and simmer the sauce until it is reduced by about half. Thicken with flour, if desired.

9. When the sauce is ready, check the seasoning. Add the pieces of rabbit back to the pan to warm. Sprinkle with the chopped parsley and serve right from the pan, on a platter, or divided among 6 individual dinner plates.

MISCELLANEOUS SMALL BIRDS

Twenty years ago, consumption of birds other than chicken, turkey and duck in America was practically nil. Then things changed. It may have been caused by the growing sophistication of American diners, who were experiencing the great game birds of Europe on their home turf. Or it may have been caused by the growing American quest for flavour—a quest not satisfied by the flavourless chickens that we were raised on. Whatever the cause—game farms sprang up, dedicated to the production of specialty birds and cutting-edge restaurant chefs began featuring these birds on their menus. Today, a new generation of home cooks is waiting to take advantage of the newly available birds—and take advantage they should, because cooking these birds at home is not difficult at all.

By the way, terminology for these birds is tricky; pigeon is called squab and guinea fowl is called guinea hen in the U.S. Pigeon, quail and guinea fowl are often called game birds, though—because they're usually

raised on farms—they're not really game birds at all.

Squab (Pigeon)

Squab, or domesticated pigeon, is one of our favourite 'game birds'. It is much prized in France, where a young one is called *pigeonneau* and an older one is called *pigeon*. We like the young, tender ones best, usually 450 g (1 lb) or under. What's special about squab is the colour of the flesh (dark) and its meaty, juicy quality. Squab is distinguished from other 'game birds' by its delicious flesh when cooked rare or medium-rare. Texturally, it's like filet mignon at this stage; flavour-wise, it's deep, gamey, earthy, with a subtle hint of liverlike flavour.

SIMPLE ROASTED SQUAB

These are the basic directions for cooking squab. Simple roasted squab is delicious when served with a dark-brown wine sauce and with any of the potato dishes so often served in country French cuisine (like gratin dauphinoise or mashed potatoes).

SERVES 4

¼ cup olive oil
4 x 450-g (1-lb) squabs (pigeon)
10 g (2 tsp) salt
3 g (¾ tsp) fresh ground black pepper

1. Place oven rack in lower third of oven. Preheat oven to 230°C (450°F).

2. Place olive oil in a large, heavy omelette pan over moderately high heat. Dry the squabs well with a towel, then place them in hot oil. Brown the squabs on all sides, about 5 minutes total. Remove.

3. Sprinkle the squabs evenly with the salt and pepper. Put them on their sides in a medium roasting tin with all legs facing in the same direction. Cook for 4 minutes on one side, then 4 minutes on the other side. Finally, turn the squabs breast side up and cook for 4 minutes more. The squabs should be rare to medium-rare at this point. Some people like the dark meat a little well done. To accomplish this, cut off the legs and thighs and return them to the oven for a few minutes.

Quail

Quail has zoomed to the top of the charts in small-bird popularity. And do we mean small! Each bird weighs about ¼ pound and it takes 2 or 3 of them to make a single serving. We always encourage our quail-eating guests to use their fingers, rather than knife and fork.

One of the attractions of quail is the relative meatiness of the breast, considering the bird's size. Another feature is attractive to some, disappointing to others: mild flavour.

There are many type of quail, but the market so far hasn't broken out into quail varieties. No matter: quail are consistently good, whether fresh or frozen. If you're using frozen quail, just make sure to defrost them properly (overnight in the refrigerator).

Other quail options

Quail have very subtle flavour; you can go in several directions with that basic fact.

You can choose to keep things simple, in hopes of emphasising the mild flavour. The roast quail is lovely with a simple brown sauce and a mild-flavoured starch on the side.

Another great mild option is boned quail. Have your butcher remove the quail's bones (leaving the leg bones intact, if desired), and stuff the little birds with something sympathetic (like the bread and butter stuffing on page 388 or the pumpkin and pancetta stuffing on page 390). Proceed with the searing and roasting directions for simple roasted quail.

But you can mirror the quail-cooking practices of most modern American chefs, if you wish—and boost the flavour by forcing the quail to take on other strong tastes. This will obliterate the quail's own subtle flavour, but the finished dish can be delicious (the quail serves as a meaty background). Cut up the quail and try a powerful Asian marinade; then deep-fry the quail pieces to a crunchy brown. Serve with an Asian dipping sauce. Or slit the quail down the middle, butterfly them and use a Latin marinade; then grill the quail for about 5 minutes per side and serve with a salsa and warm tortillas.

SIMPLE ROASTED QUAIL

While we prefer our squab rare, we—along with many others—prefer quail that's fully cooked through.

SERVES 4

45 g (1½ oz) butter
30 ml (2 tbsp) vegetable oil
8 rosemary sprigs, broken in half
8 quail
10 g (2 tsp) salt
3 g (¾ tsp) freshly ground black pepper

1. Place oven rack in lower third of oven. Preheat oven to 230°C (450°F).

2. In a large frying pan melt butter with vegetable oil over moderately high heat. Put two rosemary sprigs inside the cavity of each quail. Rub outside of quail with the salt and pepper. When fat is hot, sear quail on each side until golden, about 5 minutes total.

3. Remove quail from frying pan and place in a medium roasting tin with breasts up and all legs facing the same direction. Put the quail in oven, legs first. Cook for 15 to 18 minutes. (To check for doneness, prick between the leg and the breast with a knife. If the juices run clear, the bird is done.) Let rest 5 minutes and serve.

Note: Some diners prefer their quail rare; if you're one of them, start checking the birds after only 10 minutes in the oven.

Guinea Fowl

Guinea fowl, a native of Africa, is another of our favourite small birds. It is much beloved in France, where small ones (under 450 g (1 lb)) are called *pintadeaux* and large ones (they can be as large as 1.3 kg (3 lb) dressed) are called *pintades*. There are males as well—the species of this bird, in fact, is the guinea fowl—but it's the female, the hen, that's preferred by most connoisseurs for its tender meat.

The cachet of the guinea fowl is that it provides some of the delicacy one normally associates with pheasant, but it doesn't dry out as easily as that larger bird. Its meat is fattier, darker and more flavourful than pheasant meat. A good, well-cooked guinea fowl provides a fabulous blast of poultry essence. If you're choosing between a guinea fowl and the bland poussin, known in the U.S. as Rock Cornish game hen—well, in our eyes, there's no choice at all.

ROAST GUINEA HEN WITH BACON AND CHICORY

This is a terrific basic recipe for guinea hen. Cooking guinea fowl is not like cooking squab; the idea is to cook it all the way through.

SERVES 2

1 kg (2½ lb) guinea hen
5 g (1 tsp) salt
2.5 g (½ tsp) black pepper
4 slices bacon
4 chicory head, cut in half lengthways
25 g (1 oz) butter
75 ml (2½ fl oz) chicken stock

1. Place the oven rack in lower third of oven. Preheat oven to 200°C (400°F).

2. Rinse the bird inside and out under cold running water. Pat dry and rub with the salt and pepper. Lay the strips of bacon lengthwise over the breasts. Secure the bacon by loosely tying with pieces of string around the girth of the bird, as if it were wearing two belts.

3. Choose a roasting tin just large enough to hold the bird and the endive. Butter the bottom of the tin with 15 g (1½ oz) of the butter. Place the 8 chicory halves around the edges of the tin and then place the hen in the centre. Break the remaining butter into little pieces and dot these pieces over the endive. Pour the chicken stock over the endive.

4. Roast the hen for 20 minutes. Remove it from the oven and baste it with any juices that have collected. Move the hen with a spatula to make sure that it is not sticking to the bottom of the pan. Flip the endives over so that they caramelise evenly. Roast the hen for another 20 minutes and baste again. Baste the endives as well. Roast another 20 to 30 minutes. (Test for doneness by piercing the thigh with the tip of a paring knife—the juices should run out clear. The endive should be tender when the stem end is pierced with a knife or fork.)

5. Untie the bacon strips and crumble coarsely, returning bacon to the roasting tin. Place roasted endives on a serving platter. Carve the bird and arrange the pieces on the endive. Degrease any juices left in the tin and pour them, with or without the bacon, over the fowl. Serve immediately.

WHITE MEAT

Pork

Pork is the world's most popular meat. Almost every culture—with the exception of those that are predominantly Muslim or Jewish—finds myriad uses for the rich-tasting meat and fat of the pig.

In America, in the eighteenth and nineteenth

centuries, pork was as prominent as it was in other cultures. However, after the Civil War beef began to soar in popularity—and pork became known as the food of the poor. It has never really recovered from this stigma; to this day, beef connotes luxury while pork connotes necessity.

Pork took an even more devastating blow in the health-crazy years of the latter twentieth century: because of its rich fat content (which, in part, is what made it taste so good), pork started to be perceived as the most fattening and unhealthful of meats.

Pork producers saw this one coming decades ago and began breeding leaner pigs; unfortunately, the producers have been wildly successful. The pig that 40 years ago would have yielded 58 kg (127 lb) of meat and 18 kg (40 lb) of fat, today yields 76 kg (167 lb) of meat and only 4.5 kg (10 lb) of fat. Today, a 3-oz (85-g) serving of pork has 6 g of fat in it; compare this to a half chicken breast, which weighs in at 8 g of fat! Pork is now one of the leanest meat options in the market.

At the table, this is a disaster. Leaner pork means pork with less flavour. Even worse, it means pork that dries out easily, that lacks the rich, juicy, luxurious chew of the old-fashioned pork. Some of the most expensive cuts of pork—like the loin—are the leanest of all and really need special treatment these days to make them palatable.

The following recipes help to put flavour and texture back into the lean, mean, modern generation of pork.

PORK ROASTS

Pork roast is a magnificent dish—its crunchy, browned outer layer holding a juicy payload of meat within. Unfortunately, the leaner pork that's everywhere these days is harder to nurse into juiciness. The first place you can fight back is at the butcher shop; let your butcher know that you'd like the least lean pork available. And don't let him shave away too much of the white fat that enrobes the roast; that fat helps to baste the roast while it's cooking.

GERMAN-STYLE PORK ROAST

If you crave the pure flavour of pork, you will enjoy this dish—no herbs, no spices, not even any garlic or onions to distract you from the pork essence. We've taken several measures here to counteract the lean-pork problem. First of all, we've called for a roast that's cut closer to the somewhat fattier rib end than the loin end. Then, we've added a layer of bacon to this roast for a little extra taste and lubrication. Finally, we've called for a very slow oven—140°C (275°F)—which helps to preserve whatever fat the poor pork has left. It all works out beautifully and the dish is a great wintertime crowd-pleaser—especially when served with its bacon gravy and mashed potatoes (see page 191) and sauerkraut (see box, page 403).

SERVES 8

one 8-rib centre cut pork roast, rib end (about
   2.7 kg (6 lb)), chine bone cracked between the
   ribs
salt and pepper to taste
8 rashers bacon
For the gravy
700 ml (1¼ pints) pork or chicken stock
45 g (1½ oz) butter at room temperature
45 g (3 tbsp) flour

1. Preheat oven to 140°C (275°F).

2. Season the pork roast well with salt and pepper. Place it in a roasting tin, fat side up. Drape the bacon rashers over the roast so that it is completely covered by the bacon.

3. Place the pork in the oven and roast until the meat reads 60°C (140°F) on a quick-read meat thermometer. If you want the outside of the roast to be especially brown, remove the bacon about 5 minutes before the roast is done, reserving the bacon and place the roast under a preheated grill until it's crispy brown.

4. Remove pork from the oven and, if you haven't already done so, remove bacon slices. Place pork on a cutting board and let it rest for 15 minutes.

5. *While the pork is resting, make the gravy:* Chop bacon coarsely. Place chopped bacon in the pork roasting tin and place the pan over high heat on top of the range. Sizzle the bacon until it's very brown. Add the pork or chicken stock and simmer for 10 minutes. While stock is simmering, mash the butter and flour together in a bowl to make a beurre manié. Just before serving the gravy and while the stock is simmering, add the beurre manié bit by bit, in pea-sized drops. Whisk the pan gravy; it should form a medium-thick sauce. Season to taste and keep warm.

6. When ready to serve, cut the pork roast through the cracked bone into meaty ribs. Serve immediately with gravy.

The ideal roast pork accompaniment

SAUERKRAUT WITH ANISEED AND BEER
A German-style pork roast begs for lightly sweet-and-sour sauerkraut. This recipe, with a subtle touch of aniseed, is just the ticket.

SERVES 8 AS A SIDE DISH

50 g (2 oz) unsalted butter
25 g (1 oz) flour
1.8 kg (4 lb) fresh sauerkraut, drained of most of its brine
450 ml (16 fl oz) lager
15g (1 tbsp) aniseed
85g (3 oz) sugar or more to taste

1. Melt the butter in a heavy pot over moderate heat, then stir in the flour. Cook, stirring, for 2 minutes.

2. Increase the heat to high. Add the sauerkraut all at once. Stir the sauerkraut well, so it's coated by the butter-flour mixture. Bring to a boil. Add the beer, the aniseed and the sugar. Return to a boil, then reduce heat to low, cover pot and cook for 30 minutes. Season and serve with pork roast.

ANCHO- AND CHIPOTLE-RUBBED PORK LOIN
Boneless loin of pork is an extremely elegant cut and was always a joy to serve. However, because it's also one of the pig's leanest cuts, in these days of extra-lean pork it's a cut that dries out especially easily. Here's a little more pork magic: we've found that by using a clay pot, you can nearly guarantee a flawlessly moist pork loin. Serve this great hunk of pork with fresh corn tortillas, chipotle salsa (page 484) and black bean chilli with aubergine (page 245).

SERVES 4

3 dried ancho chillies
2 dried chipotle chillies (or 2 chipotles canned in adobo)
5 g (1 tsp) chopped garlic
15 g (1 tbsp) lard (you may substitute 1 ml (1 tbsp) vegetable oil)
15 g (1 tbsp) ground cumin
pinch of ground cloves
10 g (2 tsp) salt
5 g (1 tsp) freshly ground black pepper
1 boneless loin of pork (about 900 g (2 lb))
1 medium white onion, very thinly sliced

1. Toast the dried chillies by putting them in a preheated 100°C (200°F) oven for 3 minutes; you should smell them toasting when you open the oven door. (If using canned chipotles, toast only the ancho.) Remove the toasted chillies from the oven and open them up. Remove and discard the seeds and stems. Place the chillies in a bowl and cover with hot water.

2. When chillies are soft (after about 15 minutes), remove them from the water and place them (or the ancho and the canned chipotle) in the work bowl of a food processor, along with the garlic, lard, cumin, cloves, salt and pepper. Pulse to make a rough paste. Rub the paste all over the pork loin with your fingers. Cover the pork and refrigerate for 8 hours. Remove it from the refrigerator 1 hour before cooking.

3. Make a bed of half the sliced onion in the clay pot. Lay the marinated pork loin over it. Cover the pork with the remaining onion.

4. Most clay pots call for soaking the lid and then placing the entire pot, with food inside, in a cold oven before turning on the heat. Follow the instructions for your pot. In any case, the oven should be set at 150°C (300°F). Once the oven is hot, cook the roast for 1 hour. Do not open the pot. After 1 hour, remove the roast from the oven. Let it sit in its liquid for 10 minutes. Slice the roast thinly and serve.

CUBAN ROAST PORK SHOULDER

Cubans love roasting pork, especially a whole suckling pig. You're much more likely to make the following dish, which features the same delicious marinade that's used for suckling pig. Actually, in Cuba they use bitter Seville oranges for the marinade; if you can find them, substitute their juice for the orange, lime and lemon juice in this recipe. Serve the pork with the usual suckling pig accompaniments: rice, black beans, boiled cassava and deep-fried ripe plantains.

SERVES 6 GENEROUSLY

2.7-kg (6-lb) pork shoulder, trimmed of excess fat
45 g (3 tbsp) finely chopped garlic
5 g (1 tsp) grated orange zest
15 g (1 tbsp) dried oregano
15 g (1 tbsp) ground cumin
15 g (1 tbsp) salt
5 g (1 tsp) ground black pepper
225 g (8 oz) thinly sliced onion
75 ml (2½ fl oz) orange juice
50 ml (2 fl oz) lime juice
50 ml (2 fl oz) lemon juice
125 ml (4 fl oz) dry sherry

1. Make tiny slits all over the pork shoulder with the tip of a paring knife. Combine garlic, orange zest, oregano, cumin, salt and black pepper and mash together to form a paste. Smear it all over the pork shoulder. Place the onion slices in a bowl large enough to hold the pork snugly and top with the pork.

2. Combine the fruit juices with the sherry and pour over the pork. Cover and marinate in the refrigerator, basting several times, overnight.

3. Bring to room temperature before proceeding. (Allow 2 hours for the pork to come to room temperature.)

4. Preheat oven to 160°C (325°F). Remove pork from marinade and dry well. Strain marinade and discard solids. Place pork in a clean, dry roasting tin and roast in oven, basting every half hour with the marinade, for 2½ hours, or until internal temperature is about 77°C (170°F). (It is traditional for this Cuban roast to be well-done.) Allow the roast to rest 15 minutes before carving.

5. Carve and arrange on a platter, spooning pan juices over the meat.

PORK CHOPS

Pork chops, in particular, have suffered in the lowered-fat sweepstakes; it has become actually difficult to cook up chops that are juicy and tender. And the choice between rib chops and loin chops has become ever more agonising: the rib chops are a little fattier, but the loin chops (in a T-bone shape) offer a side nugget of 'fillet' that is very tender. The problem with the loin chop, however, is that the rest of it threatens to dry out.

Add-ons for pork chops

Though the brined pork chops are delicious by themselves, you could serve them with an accompaniment or a sauce. Here are some possibilities:

- Cook down sliced onions and apples in butter until meltingly soft. Add sage. Place on pork chops.
- Cook down red and green peppers with onions and garlic. Add fresh herbs. Place on pork chops.
- Add mustard and a touch of cream to tomato sauce. Pour over chops.
- Stir-fry chopped bok choy with garlic, ginger and spring onions. Add chicken stock, soy sauce and a little sugar and thicken with cornflour. Add a few drops of sesame oil and pour over chops.
- Add unsweetened coconut milk to Thai green curry paste (page 473). Simmer for 20 minutes and pour over chops.
- When chops are done, paint with a barbecue sauce (select one from pages 488 to 491).

BRINED PORK CHOPS

Here's one 'solution' that will make any pork chop, even loin chops, more appealing in texture: soak 'em in brine. This particular brine also adds some subtle garlic-and-spice flavour to the chops. We've called for very thick chops, because the thick middle of the chop remains juicier longer when the chops are cooked. (The heat should be no more than moderate, lest you dry the chops out quickly.) Pan-fry these delicious chops and serve them unsauced—or choose an add-on from the sidebar on this page.

SERVES 4

2.25 litres (3¼ pints) water
50 g (2 oz) coarse salt
45 g (3 tbsp) sugar

3 bay leaves
2 cloves
1 cinnamon stick
10 g (2 tsp) black peppercorns
1 garlic clove, smashed
4 loin pork chops (each about 3 cm (1½ in) thick)
50 ml (2 fl oz) olive oil or vegetable oil

1. Mix together the water, coarse salt and sugar in a large pot. Bring to a boil over high heat. Add the bay leaves, cloves, cinnamon stick, peppercorns and garlic. Simmer for 5 minutes. Remove from heat and let cool.

2. When mixture is at room temperature, strain it over the pork chops (they must be completely immersed in the brine). Marinate chops in the refrigerator for at least 8 hours and up to 12 hours.

3. When ready to cook, remove chops from brine and dry them with a towel. Place oil in a heavy omelette pan that's large enough to hold the chops in a single layer without crowding; place the pan over moderate heat. Add the chops. After a minute or so, using tongs, shift them slightly in the pan to make sure they're not sticking. Cook until well browned on the first side, about 8 minutes. Turn over and brown on the other side. Cook further, turning occasionally, until the chops reach an internal temperature of 58°C (137°F). Remove from pan, season and serve immediately.

TONKATSU-STYLE BUTTERFLIED PORK CHOPS WITH WATERCRESS SALAD

This dish is a Japanese-Italian hybrid of two great ideas. In traditional Japanese cuisine, tonkatsu are deep-fried boneless pork cutlets served with a sweet brown sauce; we love the cutlets, but are less than enamoured of the sauce. A new Italian classic of the eighties—in America's Italian restaurants, anyway—is a butterflied rib veal chop that's deep-fried and served with an rocket salad on top; we love the concept, but always end up

THE DEAN & DELUCA COOKBOOK

dreaming of what that veal chop would taste like on a grill. Put the recipes together, tweak 'em—and you've got a butterflied, deep-fried rib pork chop, marinated first in rice-wine vinegar, with a refreshing watercress-and-bean sprout salad on top. The quick deep-frying gives a juiciness they don't normally have. Serve this dish to hungry diners only; each portion is very large.

SERVES 2

2 rib pork chops (each about 2 cm (¾ in) thick and
  about 280 g (10 oz))
50 ml (2 fl oz) rice-wine vinegar
5 ml (1 tsp) soy sauce
5 g (1 tsp) sugar
a few drops of Japanese sesame oil
1 litre (1¾ pints) peanut oil or vegetable oil
flour for dredging
1 very large egg, beaten
225 g (8 oz) panko crumbs*
For the watercress salad
225 g (8 oz) watercress leaves
115 g (4 oz) chopped tomato
15 g (1 tbsp) finely chopped spring onion
50 g (2 oz) mung beansprouts
25 ml (5 tsp) rice-wine vinegar
a few drops Japanese sesame oil
coarse salt to taste

1. *Butterfly the chops:* Lay them flat on a cutting board and, holding your knife parallel to the board, cut through the meat along the side of each chop until you reach the bone. This cut should evenly divide the meat of each chop into 2 equal flaps, which remain attached to the bone. Spread each chop out in the shape of a butterfly.

2. Place the chops between sheets of greaseproof paper and pound each flap with a mallet or a heavy cleaver. Pound until each flap is an even 5 mm (¼ in) thick.

*Panko crumbs are Japanese bread crumbs—light, airy, remarkably crisp. They are available as Japanese groceries.

3. Mix together the 50 ml (2 fl oz) rice-wine vinegar, soy sauce, sugar and a few drops of Japanese sesame oil. Place the pounded pork chops in a wide, shallow dish and pour the marinade over them. Marinate in the refrigerator, turning occasionally, for 2 hours.

4. When ready to cook, heat the peanut oil in a wok, deep-fryer, or deep, wide pot to 185°C (365°F).

5. While the oil is heating, remove pork chops from the marinade and shake off liquid. Dredge chops in flour, making sure to cover all spots of the meat and bone. Then dip the chops in the beaten egg and let the excess egg drip off. Finally, dip the chops in the panko crumbs, making sure to cover the entire meat and bone.

6. When the oil is hot, add the pork chops (if your frying vessel is not large enough, you should do this in 2 batches). Deep-fry until chops are golden brown on the outside, just cooked through on the inside, for 3 to 4 minutes altogether. Remove and drain on paper towels.

7. *While the pork chops are cooking, make the watercress salad:* Toss together the watercress, tomato, spring onion, bean sprouts, rice wine vinegar and sesame oil. (Make sure the salad has a light taste of the sesame oil; if not, add a little more.) Season with salt.

8. Place each chop on a large dinner plate and season with coarse salt. Strew each chop with the watercress salad and serve immediately.

PORK RIBS

Hallelujah for pork ribs! The porcine scientists haven't found a way to remove the fat from this great cut and the home cook doesn't need a degree in physics to keep them juicy and moist.

When cooking ribs, you have your choice of three main cuts.

Spareribs come from the lower rib cage of the pig. You will find them in slabs that weigh 1.3 kg (3 lb) or a little less, each slab containing 13 ribs. Spareribs don't feature a high meat-to-bone ratio, but to barbecue aficionados the little meat there is—against that bone—is particularly succulent.

Baby back ribs do not come from baby pigs. Rather, they are taken from the upper end of the rib cage. They are smaller than spareribs and therefore a little more delicate.

Country-style ribs are a different thing altogether. They are more like pork chops, with a very high meat-to-bone ratio. Like baby back ribs, they come from the upper end of the rib cage, but from the part where the rib section modulates into the loin. If you like meaty ribs, you'll like these.

Ribs have always been popular in American restaurants, but what has been served has usually been a burlesque version of real Southern and Mid-western barbecued ribs: the ribs are smothered in gloppy bottled barbecued sauce then fast-cooked over a hot grill. In the eighties and nineties, the true flavour of smokey, slow-cooked barbecued ribs turned up in BBQ restaurants across America. Unfortunately, it's not so easy to reproduce at home, but the following 2 recipes deliver maximum flavour for minimum work.

MEMPHIS DRY-RUB RIBS

Though the term 'barbecued ribs' conjures up images of sauce-splattered slabs of meat, many rib connoisseurs believe that the finest barbecue of all are dry-rub ribs from Memphis—ribs that lack barbecue sauce altogether. This method emphasises whatever smoky flavour you're able to coax out of your home grill. Purists also keep sauce off the table—but you should feel free to serve these delicious ribs with your favourite barbecue sauce. The following recipe yields ribs that are quite spicy, so reduce the amount of chilli powder and ground peppers if you like.

SERVES 6

For the dry rub
15 g (1 tbsp) whole cumin
1/4 cup fine-quality sweet paprika
30 g (1 oz) top-quality chilli powder*
30 g (1 oz) packed dark brown sugar
15 g (1 tbsp) granulated sugar
15 g (1 tbsp) coarsely ground black pepper
5 g (1 tsp) cayenne pepper
15 g (1 tbsp) chopped garlic mashed to a paste
    with 15 g (1 tbsp) coarse salt
3 slabs pork spareribs (about 1.3 kg (3 lb) each)

1. *Make the dry rub:* Heat a small frying pan over moderately high heat, add the cumin and toast until very fragrant, but not burned, 1 to 2 minutes. Remove and cool completely. Grind to a fine powder in a coffee/spice grinder. Transfer to a bowl and stir in the remaining dry rub ingredients, mixing with your hands, if necessary, to completely incorporate the garlic.

2. The night before serving the ribs, coat them with half of the dry rub. Cover the ribs tightly and refrigerate overnight.

3. About 4 hours before serving, prepare your fire. You'll need a large grill with a cover, good hardwood charcoal and about 2.7 kg (6 lb) of wood chips (we like hickory). Build a stack of charcoal on one side of the grill, ignite it and let it cook until the coals have turned to fine grey ash. (A thermometer is a great thing to have for this type of cooking; the ideal temperature for the inside of the covered grill is 99°C (210°F)).

4. About 1 hour before cooking the ribs, remove them from the refrigerator. Half an hour before cooking ribs, cover about a sixth of the wood chips with water.

*Try to avoid supermarket chilli powder. A good powder made from one specific type of chilli, or a blend of specified chillies, would work well here; smoky dried chipotles in the blend would be great. One surprising product we sell—a smoky, hot paprika from Spain called Carmencita would be ideal for this dish.

5. When ready to cook ribs, place the soaked wood chips on top of the coals. Transfer the meat to the grill, putting the ribs on the opposite side of the grill from the heat source. Cover. Total cooking time will be about 3 hours. Monitor the heat, ideally maintaining it at 99°C (210°F); you will need to add more charcoal during the course of the cooking. Every half hour, place another sixth of the wood chips, soaked, on top of the coals. Turn the ribs over every hour. Half an hour before the meat is done, coat it with the remaining dry rub. The meat is done when it is falling off the bones. Let the ribs stand for 10 minutes before cutting them into individual ribs.

FAST COUNTRY-STYLE RIBS WITH KANSAS CITY BARBECUE SAUCE

Producing authentic-tasting, smoky ribs takes time and trouble. The following recipe supplies some of that great flavour in a lot less time, with a lot less trouble. It employs country-style ribs, which feature much more meat than other types of ribs. Why aren't these meaty ribs used more often in barbecue? Because hard-core aficionados are used to bony ribs and don't want too much of a good thing (meat). In Kansas City, spareribs would be used instead of these. By all means, however, slather a great Kansas City barbecue sauce on these meaty ribs for a quick and satisfying treat. Just make sure to slather late in the game; slathering early prevents the smoky flavour from developing in the ribs and also leads to burned ribs.

SERVES 4

1.8 kg (4 lb) country-style ribs
450 ml (16 fl oz) Kansas City–style barbecue sauce
   (see recipe on page 489) plus additional, if
   desired, for serving

1. Preheat oven to 180°C (350°F).

2. Place ribs on a baking sheet and heat in oven for 15 to 20 minutes, or until ribs are light grey.

3. While heating ribs, prepare a slow charcoal fire. When the coals have turned to light grey ash, throw a couple of handfuls of soaked wood chips (like hickory) on the coals.

4. Place the precooked ribs fattier side up on the grill over the slow-burning coals. Put the lid on the barbecue and adjust the drafts, if any, to keep fire burning slowly. Grill the ribs, turning once or twice, for 30 minutes. Slather the ribs with 2 cups of the sauce and cook for an additional 15 minutes. Serve with additional sauce, if desired.

PORK STEWS

Pork can be delicious when long-stewed: meltingly rich and very deeply flavoured. Once again, however, the trick is finding pork that's fatty enough. There's good news when it comes to stewing pork: boneless pork butt (which is actually pork shoulder), though tough when quickly cooked, is an ideal stew meat that becomes extremely tender after long cooking.

SPICY HUNGARIAN PORK GOULASH WITH PEPPERS

A proper Hungarian goulash (or gulyás) is a great way to cook pork, because the amount of liquid used in the cooking abets the juiciness of the meat. Goulash is often misunderstood in America; it is not a thickened stew with a brown sauce. The original goulash was more of a soup (gulyásleves) and this delicious recipe holds to that tradition. If you'd like this dish to be more stewlike, either use less liquid or thicken it at the end with some arrowroot mixed with water. But if you do the latter… don't tell a Hungarian!

SERVES 6

45 ml (3 tbsp) lard or vegetable oil
1 large onion, chopped
3 garlic cloves, mashed to a paste with 1.25 g
   (¼ tsp) coarse salt

45g (1½ tbsp) Hungarian hot paprika
2.5 g (½ tsp) caraway seeds
2.5 g (½ tsp) ground cayenne pepper or more to taste
900 g (2 lb) boneless pork butt, trimmed and cut
   into 1-inch pieces
1 litre (1¾ pints) warm water (or more if needed to
   cover pork)
2 large, ripe tomatoes, peeled and chopped
1 large red pepper, seeded and chopped
2 large potatoes (about 550 g (1¼ lb) total), peeled
   and diced

1. Heat the lard in a large casserole over moderately low heat until hot but not smoking. Cook the onion, garlic, paprika, caraway seeds and cayenne until the onion is softened, but not browned, about 8 minutes. Increase the heat to high, add the pork and brown, stirring occasionally, for about 8 minutes. (Don't crowd the pork; if your pan is not large enough, brown the pork in 2 batches.)

2. Add the warm water and cook at a bare simmer, covered, for 1 hour, or until the pork is tender. Stir in the tomatoes and red pepper and simmer gently, uncovered, for 30 minutes. Stir in the potatoes and simmer until they are cooked through, about 20 minutes. Season to taste and serve in deep soup bowls.

PORTUGUESE PORK WITH CLAMS

This fabulous specialty of the Alentejo region is cooked there in a special hinged copper pot called a *cataplana;* its beauty is that it can be turned on either side on top of the stove, which enables the cook to shake the clams in the pan so they open evenly. If you can find one, by all means use it to cook this dish. But if you can't, don't fret; proceed with a regular casserole. The dish will be just as delicious. By the way, the Portuguese would use presunto (their cured ham) and chouriço (their spicy sausage) in this dish; you may substitute the more available prosciutto and chorizo. Serve with Portuguese

bread, a green salad and vinho verde.

SERVES 6

50 ml (2 fl oz) olive oil
550-g (1¼-lb) boneless pork butt, cut into 2.5-g
   (1-in) pieces
450 g (1 lb) onions, finely chopped
6 large garlic cloves, chopped
1 large green pepper, seeded and finely chopped
1 bay leaf
800-g (28-oz) can tomatoes in tomato purée
225 ml (8 fl oz) dry white wine
50-g (2-oz) chunk of fatty prosciutto (top-quality
   not necessary)
175 g (6 oz) chorizo
72 small clams (cockles), scrubbed
50-g (2-oz) chopped coriander

1. Place the olive oil in a heavy casserole over moderately high heat. Add the pork pieces and sauté until lightly browned on all sides, about 10 minutes. Add the onions, garlic, green pepper and bay leaf and sauté, stirring occasionally, for 10 minutes more.

2. Add half the tomatoes with all their purée, breaking the tomatoes into small chunks with the back of a wooden spoon. (Save the other half of the tomatoes for another use.) Add 175 ml (6 fl oz) of the wine and bring to a rapid boil. Reduce heat to low and simmer, covered, for 30 minutes.

3. Cut the prosciutto into tiny dice and add to the stew. Simmer, covered, for 30 minutes.

4. Add the chorizo to the stew. Cook, covered, until tender, another 15 to 30 minutes.

5. When almost ready to serve, add the clams to the pot, stir them into the tomato sauce and sprinkle them with the rest of the white wine. Increase heat to moderately high, cover the casserole and cook until the clams open.

While the clams are cooking, grasp the casserole with both hands and shake it a few times.

6. When the clams have opened, reduce heat to low, cover casserole and cook for 5 minutes more, allowing the clam juices to blend with the stew. While the clams are cooking, remove the chorizo, cut it into thin slices and return to the casserole. Taste sauce for seasoning. Sprinkle stew with coriander and serve in a tureen.

Ham

Ham is a confusing term, because it's used to describe so many different hamlike entities. Technically, the word 'ham' (which is from Old English) refers to the meat that's at the back of the thigh of a pig. This meat doesn't need to be cured or smoked in order to be known as 'ham'; you will sometimes find at your butcher shop a cut of pork known as 'fresh ham', which is the uncured, unsmoked 'ham' of a pig. Cooked long and slow in your home oven, it makes a delicious, white-meat roast.

But confusion creeps in because the word 'ham' is almost always used to refer to this cut of the pig *after* it has been cured with salt; 'a ham sandwich', in common parlance, refers to pinkish slices of cured meat, not to white, fresh-cooked pork.

But there's even more confusion—because the methods used to convert the thigh of a pig into something commonly called 'ham' vary widely. Some 'ham' is simply cured; some 'ham' is cured and cooked; some 'ham' is cured and smoked; some 'ham' is cured, smoked and cooked. Despite the production differences, the meat is all called 'ham'. Furthermore, the divergence in quality among 'hams' that are available in the market is staggering.

The quality hams of Dean & DeLuca

Dean & DeLuca prides itself on its enormous selection of quality hams from all over the world. Most of these exclusive hams are best for slicing and eating as they are—either plain, garnished, or on bread. A few take well to cooking.

To make it easier to understand the complexity of the ham universe, we have divided our leading hams into three categories based on the production methods used.

HAMS THAT ARE CURED ONLY

This important category of ham is called 'raw' ham by some; this means that, aside from salt-curing, no cooking or smoking is involved. Then, typically, the ham is sliced thin and eaten without further cooking. The result is a rich, silky, velvety slice of ham, the most opulently textured of all hams.

Prosciutto di Parma Italy's most famous exported ham. Salt-cured around Parma, in Emilia-Romagna, in north-central Italy. Our prosciutto di Parma is usually around 1 year old; in Italy, you can find older examples (up to 3 years old) that are silkier and deeper-tasting than the young ones. We usually carry the prosciutto di Parma of one producer only: Galloni, whose prosciutti are very consistent. After the prosciutto is thinly sliced, it should be served within a few hours just as it is. Some like to serve it with fruit, or with a drizzle of great, green, extra-virgin olive oil.

Prosciutto di Carpegna Similar to prosciutto di Parma, but made on a less industrial scale by artisanal producers in the Marches. Generally sweeter and a little finer than prosciutto di Parma.

Domestic Prosciutto Some decent prosciutto is being produced in North America, but it's usually saltier, less silky and less complex than the version. Use it for cooking (as in pasta sauces made with prosciutto). The Canadian brand we carry is the best industrially made North American prosciutto we've found.

Molasses-Cured Prosciutto This is the best North

American prosciutto, period. It is made by Salumeria Biellese, a tiny factory and storefront in New York City. Its flavour is complex and deeply porky, like the best prosciutto from Italy; despite the molasses cure, it doesn't seem sweet or 'American'. This ham has the additional virtue of being made without nitrates. Serve as you would Italian prosciutti.

Capicola Real capicola, which we carry, is a cured ham like prosciutto that has also been heavily spiced. It is made from a different part of the ham—what's called the 'picnic' ham—and, therefore, has a different shape from prosciutto; it is smaller and rounder. Unlike prosciutto, capicola doesn't have its own skin—so the producers put it in a bung casing, along with spices (like red pepper and black pepper). The result is a spicy ham, quite a bit drier than prosciutto. Great on sandwiches in combination with moister, fattier meats. By the way, 'ham capicola' is an American invention; it's something like standard American boiled ham with a red pepper coating. We don't consider it a quality ham.

Jambon Cru du Beaujolais This terrific ham is made in California, but picks up its French name because Beaujolais wine is part of the cure. Furthermore, despite the French reference, it is most like a famous Italian ham: culatello, or 'little arse', which is made near Parma and is usually described as the 'heart' of prosciutto. It's smaller, more compact than prosciutto, less striated with fat, an altogether more refined product. However, unlike culatello or prosciutto di Parma, this Jambon Cru du Beaujolais has a complex cure, with many flavourings, which results in a complex-tasting ham. Slice thin and serve as a first course.

Serrano Ham Unbeknownst to most Americans, Spain is regarded by Europeans as the greatest ham country in the world. Unfortunately, ham made in Spain has long been illegal in the United States (we're finally starting to see a trickle of it). Serrano is the prosciutto-like ham produced throughout Spain—but a ham named 'serrano'

in this country almost always has been made here, in the Spanish style. American-made serrano is usually aged a shorter time than Italian-made prosciutto. And, in the Spanish style, there's a thin spice coating that includes paprika.

HAMS THAT ARE CURED AND COOKED

A light salt cure and then cooking (usually boiling) is the combination of processes that yields what Americans normally think of as ham for ham sandwiches—i.e., boiled ham. But we offer several cured-and-cooked hams that have more distinction than the usual deli-counter boiled ham.

Jambon Cuit This 'cooked ham' from France, though it has the pinkness of American boiled ham, differs from it in several ways. First of all, it is steamed, not boiled. Secondly, the steaming does not take place under pressure (most American boiled hams are boiled under pressure, which makes them tougher, more rubbery, less soft and tender). Thirdly, it has a natural skin, not an artificial casing. Lastly, spices (mostly juniper) are hand-rubbed into it for a subtle flavour. There's nothing made in the United States that matches this beauty for delicacy and for its haunting porky, almost gamey undertaste.

Prosciutto Cotto Though 'regular' prosciutto (what the Italians call 'prosciutto crudo') is much better known in the United States, 'cooked prosciutto' is also very popular in Italy. The one we sell comes from Parma and is unusual in that, after curing, it is roasted (they are usually boiled or steamed). Roasting causes the fluids to run out of the ham and the result is a smaller product—but one with concentrated flavour.

HAMS THAT ARE CURED AND SMOKED

This lovely combination of processes can yield a wide range of results, depending on how the processes are handled. Even a minimal amount of smoke adds something hauntingly delicious to cured ham.

Hickory Smoked Ham This basic American ham has a real cured texture—meaning it's silky, not fresh and porklike. Add to that the pronounced smokiness that comes from placing the ham over a hickory fire and you've got a delicious product.

Applewood Smoked Ham And this ham's at the other end of the spectrum. A very light curing yields a ham that seems almost fresh and porklike in texture; a very light encounter with sweet applewood smoke yields a ham with barely a trace of smokiness.

New York State Ham This one is similar to the applewood ham—except that it comes from enormous animals, which makes each ham almost 10 kg (22 lb) in weight. The lightly smoked meat is very fatty and moist.

Smithfield Ham This is the great American contribution to the world of ham. Our manager Carmine calls it 'wagon-train food'—because it's so heavily cured, so salty, that it seems to last virtually forever. This very dry, almost stiff ham is not pleasant on sandwiches—but it does add great flavour to cooked food. It is regularly used by Chinese chefs in America, for example, as a substitute for the salty cooking ham of Yunnan, which is not available here. For a real Virginia breakfast, cut the ham into 5-mm (¼-in) slices, pan-fry them and serve with grits (which cuts the saltiness on your palate).

Tasso Cajun-Style Ham This one is called 'Cajun-style' because it's not made in Louisiana, where tasso is traditionally made. But this is a delicious version of tasso nevertheless. The cut of ham itself comes from near the Canadian bacon region of the pig, so it's a small chunk of ham. It's heavily coated with hot Cajun spices and is rather dry in texture. This is a cooking ham and chunks of it add an enormous depth of flavour to Cajun dishes.

Black Forest Ham (domestic) Domestic Black Forest ham differs greatly from the German product. It is from a different cut of the pig, which is larger and rounder. It is brine-cured (the German one is dry-cured) and altogether moister and less intense. It's a better ham for ham sandwiches.

Black Forest Ham (imported) The German Black Forest ham is not a true ham, but cut from a section that's closer to bacon; therefore, it is longer and flatter than the domestic Black Forest ham. It is drier, more intense, saltier and smokier; it tastes best if you slice it very thin and serve it on a platter as a first-course meat.

Speck This delicious ham, which looks like smoked prosciutto, is one of the great hams of the world, produced with care all around the Alpine region. The one we carry, however, is domestic—made by Salumeria Biellese in New York City. Frankly, it's the best speck we've ever tasted. Porky, sweet and fatty, with a perfect touch of smoke, it makes an outstanding first course, thinly sliced and served alone, at the start of a German, Swiss, Eastern French or Northern Italian meal.

BAKED HAM

When Americans think of serving ham at home for dinner, their first choice is ham that has been cured, cooked (fully or partially), smoked and often coated with something sweet. The home cook typically reinforces this sweet coating with more sweet flavours (sugar, cloves and pineapple, for example) then 'bakes' the ham in the oven until it's hot all the way through. This is the great American favourite 'baked ham' or 'Virginia ham'.

Things haven't changed much in decades—except that the quality of ready-to-eat hams has improved dramatically in recent years. Most Americans, of course, still buy industrial, cheaply made, brine-injected hams that are pumped up with water. Sometimes, they're even made of chopped ham that has been re-formed into a hamlike shape. Avoid these. Look for a ham that has been dry-cured, or brine-cured and remains intact on the bone. Avoid pre-applied sweet glazes and flavourings. Find a producer whose product you like; Tobin's, for example, in upstate New York, produces very good bone-in cooked hams that are perfect for 'baked ham' dinners.

BAKED HAM WITH COFFEE AND BROWN SUGAR GLAZE

Though it does sound a little unusual, the glaze in the recipe lends a lovely colour and flavour to the exterior of the ham; after all, ham with red-eye gravy (made with coffee) is a Southern classic. And there's another creative element in this dish: though this is baked ham, it spends most of its cooking time poaching in water on top of the stove. This keeps the ham very moist (it heats to the centre more quickly than in a dry oven). Additionally, the water method draws out the salt in the ham, rather than concentrating it. Just make sure that you keep the water below the boiling point—say, 82° to 88°C (180° to 190°F). Also make sure, of course, that the ham you choose is the best ham you can find.

SERVES AT LEAST 20

5.4-6.3 kg (12- 14-lb) smoked, ready-to-eat ham
115 g (4 oz) brown sugar
125 ml (4 fl oz) cider vinegar
15 ml (1 tbsp) Dijon mustard
225 ml (8 fl oz) strong black brewed coffee
225 g (8 oz) breadcrumbs

1. Place the ham in a very large stockpot and place water in the pot until it just covers the ham. Put the pot on the stove and turn the heat on high. When the water begins to boil, reduce heat to low and let the ham poach for 1½ hours.

2. *While the ham is cooking, prepare the glaze:* Combine the brown sugar, vinegar, mustard and black coffee in a bowl and stir with a fork until the sugar is dissolved. Add the breadcrumbs and blend in. (The glaze will become somewhat pasty as the breadcrumbs absorb the liquid.)

3. Preheat oven to 200°C (400°F).

4. Remove the ham from the pot of water and place it in a large baking pan. Carve away the excess fat, if desired and some of the rind. Spread the glaze evenly over the surface of the ham. Reduce the oven heat to 190°C (375°F) and bake the ham in the oven for 20 to 30 minutes, or until the crust is hot and dark brown. Remove the ham from the pan and place on a cutting board. Allow to rest for at least 15 minutes before carving.

Veal

Veal has long been one of the most prized meats in European cooking—playing an especially important role in the cuisine of Italy, where its delicacy is considered to be a perfect foil for sauces. Americans have never taken an especial shine to veal, traditionally preferring heartier meats with more flavour.

Once again, however, good ethnic restaurants changed the way that Americans think about food. In this case, it was Italian restaurants that did the trick: after several decades of veal scaloppini in 'Northern Italian' restaurants, we are now conditioned to accept the idea of thin veal slices, cut from high-quality veal, quickly cooked and interestingly sauced. We are also prepared to pay the price at the butcher shop for veal of this kind: often $15 (£9) per 450g (1 lb) for pale, tender, milk-fed, gristle-free, top-quality scaloppini. Interestingly, this is one meat that has been of high quality in good American butcher shops for decades and continues to be so.

Though Italian-style 'veal scaloppini' was the wedge that opened up the veal category for Americans, no longer does it dominate the field. Curious chefs have discovered that veal plays an important role in French, Spanish and Central European cuisines as well. Innovative American chefs have found their own New Wave approaches to cooking veal. And, most important, cuts other than thin, expensive scallops have begun to achieve popularity in top restaurants and butcher shops.

VEAL SCALLOPS

There is something magnificent about a high-quality veal scallop, simply cooked and deliciously sauced. The meat is tender, gentle and subtle—but only if you get top-quality veal, from the right part of the animal, that has been sliced properly.

Veal 'scaloppini', distressingly, has no legal definition; it simply means thin slices of veal. Unscrupulous butchers can sell any thin slices of veal as 'scaloppini', at 'scaloppini' prices. In Italy and France (where scaloppini are called *escalopes de veau*), chefs and butchers consider the topside to be the very best source for veal scallops; Italians call it the *noce,* the French call it the *noix,* both of which translate as the 'nut'. It is a beautifully smooth and tender piece of veal, quite lean, with no muscle separations or gristle. The bottom round is a second choice: a little less smooth, though there are good spots from which scallops can be cut. Sometimes scallops are cut from the rib-chop section, which can also be good—though the size of the scallop will be smaller. And, very often, butchers try to pass off shoulder cutlets as scaloppini; this much less tender cut should be avoided.

When buying scallops, follow the classic veal advice and look for pale meat; this will insure the delicacy that you're paying for in a great veal scallop.

One other thing can go wrong. If you're getting veal scallops from the topside, make sure that the butcher cuts the meat *against* the grain, *against* the muscle fibres. If he cuts *with* the grain, the veal scallops will seize up and turn wavy as soon as they hit the heat of a pan. Only scallops cut against the grain remain flat when cooked.

After cutting, of course, pounding is in order. Your butcher can do this for you, or you can do it at home. Simply place the scallops between pieces of greaseproof paper or clingfilm and pound them with a veal pounder (or a mallet, or a heavy cleaver, or the bottom of a pan). They should be of uniform thickness, about 5 mm (¼ in).

Saucing the sautéed scallops

Here are a few ideas for finishing off sautéed veal scallops.

CREAMY BROWN BUTTER SAUCE WITH CAPERS AND PIMIENTOS

Place 450 ml (16 fl oz) rich brown veal stock in a saucepan. Add 1 small green pepper, coarsely chopped and 125 ml (4 fl oz) Amontillado sherry. Reduce quickly to 75 ml (2½ fl oz). Strain out the green pepper, return stock to saucepan. Add 25 g (1 oz) diced pimientos and 60 g (4 tsp) capers. Begin adding chilled tablespoons of butter, beating with a whisk, until 120 g (8 tbsp) butter are incorporated into the sauce. Place the cooked scallops in the sauce and heat for 1 minute. Place scallops and sauce on plates and sprinkle with chopped parsley.

DRIED MORELS

Before cooking scallops, place 50 g (2 oz) dried morels in very warm milk to cover; soak for half an hour. When scallops are cooked, sauté a few tablespoons of finely chopped shallots in 25 g (1 oz) butter over moderate heat. Drain the morels and add to softened shallots. Cook for 2 minutes. Season with salt and pepper and strew morels over scallops on dinner plates. (Note: another possibility is to add 450 ml (16 fl oz) cream to the sautéed morels, reduce it over high heat to about 300 ml (10 fl oz) and sauce the scallops with morels and cream.)

PEPPER AND TOMATO SAUCE WITH BALSAMIC VINEGAR

While scallops are cooking, sauté 2 julienned peppers (mixed colours, if possible), a few tablespoons of chopped garlic and 1 medium onion, thinly sliced, in a few tablespoons of olive oil over moderately high heat. When the vegetables have softened and browned slightly, add 4 medium plum tomatoes (fresh or canned, seeded and cut into strips). Add 75 ml (2½ fl oz) balsamic vinegar and a few tablespoons of chopped fresh herbs. Place the scallops in the sauce and cook for 1 minute. Place scallops and sauce on dinner plates and sprinkle with finely chopped parsley.

MASTER RECIPE FOR SAUTÉED VEAL SCALLOPS

Veal scallops are quick and easy to cook. In the simplest method, they are coated in flour and sautéed in butter. After sautéing them, you may either dip them in a sauce for a few moments, or plate them and simply pour a sauce over the scallops.

SERVES 4

115 g (4 oz) flour
5 g (1 tsp) salt
2.5 g (½ tsp) ground black pepper
75 g (2¾ oz) unsalted butter
450 g (1 lb) veal scaloppini (about 8 scallops)
  pounded evenly to 5-mm (¼-in) thickness

1. Combine flour, salt and pepper and spread out on a plate.

2. In a large frying pan melt half the butter over moderately high heat. When butter is hot, but not brown, dip 2 or 3 veal scallops into the flour mixture. Coat both sides well and shake off any excess. Place them in the hot pan and cook about 2 minutes on the first side, until well browned. Flip them and cook about 1 minute on the other side. Set aside and keep warm while you finish the others. Add more butter as the butter burns.

Saucing the pan-fried scallops
Here are a few ideas for finishing off pan-fried veal scallops.

VEAL MILANESE

This is Italy's most famous fried veal, usually made with a rib chop. If you wish, soak your pounded scallops in milk for 30 minutes or so before coating with egg and breadcrumbs. Garnish cooked scallops with lemon wedges.

SCHNITZEL À LA HOLSTEIN

Another famous, wide cutlet is Wiener schnitzel (fried veal cutlets in the style of Vienna). But if you garnish the pan-fried veal scallops in the master recipe with fried eggs, anchovies and capers, you'll have a famous German schnitzel, à la Holstein. Make wider scallops and place 1 sunny-side up egg, 4 flat anchovies and a few capers on each one. Great with braised red cabbage and a frosty glass of beer.

MELTED CHEESE AND A LIGHT WINE SAUCE

When the scallops are cooked, top each one with a slice of melting cheese (such as mozzarella, Italian fontina, or Gruyère). Place under a preheated grill. While cheese is melting, spill butter out of the frying pan and add 350 ml (12 fl oz) chicken stock, 125 ml (4 fl oz) dry white wine and 2.5 g (½ tsp) very finely chopped garlic. Reduce over high heat to about 225 ml (8 fl oz). Add a few tablespoons chopped herbs. Thicken to desired consistency with beurre manié, broken into pea-sized pieces (to make beurre manié, blend together equal portions of cold butter and flour; you'll need about 15 g (1 tbsp) of each). Whisk in beurre manié, then pour sauce around scallops on dinner plates. Garnish with herbs.

MASTER RECIPE FOR PAN-FRIED VEAL SCALLOPS WITH BREADCRUMBS

Many of the most famous veal-scallop dishes are made with crumb-coated scallops. Little is done to them. Sometimes, before coating and cooking, the veal scallops are soaked in milk for an hour to make them even more succulent. Usually, however, scallops are prepared very plainly. If you wish to bump up the flavour, you can marinate the scallops for an hour or so in oil, herbs, spices and mustard.

SERVES 4

1 egg
5 ml (1 tsp) water
5 g (1 tsp) salt
2.5 g (½ tsp) ground black pepper
115 g (4 oz) unsalted butter
450 g (1 lb) veal scaloppini (about 8 scallops),
    pounded evenly to 1/4 inch thickness
280g (10 oz) dry breadcrumbs, spread out on a
    plate

1. In a shallow bowl lightly whisk the egg with the water, salt and pepper.

2. In a large frying pan melt half the butter over moderately high heat. When butter is hot, but not brown, dip 2 or 3 of the veal scallops into the egg, coating both sides well. Then, dip the scallops into the crumbs, one side at a time, pressing firmly down so that the crumbs adhere. Place the veal scallops in the hot pan and cook about 2 minutes on the first side, until well browned. Flip them and cook about 2 minutes on the other side. (They should have a golden brown, crunchy crust, but be juicy and tender inside.) Set aside and keep warm while you finish the others. Add more butter as the butter burns.

Some tips for breaded veal scallops

- To get the best breadcrumbs, make them yourself. Cut the crust away from a fresh white loaf of French or Italian bread. Cut the remaining bread into thin slices and let the slices stand, exposed to the air, for several days until quite stale. Break them up with your hands or in a food processor. The crumbs should be fine, but not super-fine; super-fine crumbs yield a heavier crust.
- For an even coating of crumbs, place the crumbed scallops on a flat surface that has been sprinkled with more breadcrumbs. Press lightly against the cutlets on each side with a wide, heavy knife.
- To insure that the crumbs will stick evenly to the scallops, press the thin, dull side of a heavy knife against the scallops (on both sides) in a diamond pattern across the surface of each scallop. You will make a light, attractive imprint in the surface of the crumbs.

VEAL CHOPS

Years after American veal consciousness was raised by scaloppini in Italian restaurants, it was raised further by an even more exciting cut of meat: the veal chop. Starting slowly in the seventies, then booming in the eighties, the thick, grilled, top-quality veal chop became one of the standard dishes of upscale Italian restaurants in the United States. Many diners today treat it as they do great steak at a steakhouse, as a restaurant specialty, not something to make at home.

But it's a snap to do well in your own kitchen.

The hardest part is finding great veal. You'll need to buy from a top-quality butcher or from a specialty store like ours. For this cut, don't be scared off by veal that's not absolutely pale; great veal chops can have a little redness to them (this may indicate a slightly older animal, with a little more flavour).

There are three types of veal chops. For Italian restaurant-style grilled chops, do not use veal shoulder chops; they are better for braised dishes. Your choice comes down to loin chops or rib chops. Loin chops are classier looking, because they're the veal equivalent of a T-bone steak, with a 'shell' side and a 'fillet' side. But rib chops tend to be a little fattier and juicier, with a bit more flavour and tenderness. If the veal is great, both loin chops and rib chops must be terrific.

GRILLED VEAL CHOPS WITH SAGE JUS

Veal chops are fantastic on the grill. There is a problem, however: the grill doesn't give you the opportunity to collect pan juices that can be poured over the veal as a light sauce. So the following method, used by many Italian restaurants, satisfies all needs. Serve with garlicky potatoes or creamy polenta.

SERVES 4

about 50 ml (2 fl oz) fruity olive oil
4 garlic cloves, smashed
50 g (2 oz) fresh sage leaves,
  plus additional for garnish
salt and pepper to taste
4 veal chops (each about 5 cm (2 in) thick)
225 ml (8 fl oz) veal stock, chicken stock or water

1. Place 30 ml (2 tbsp) of olive oil in a heavy saucepan over low heat. Add the garlic and the fresh sage leaves. Cook very slowly for 30 minutes.

2. While the olive oil-garlic mixture is cooking, salt and pepper the chops, then brush them with a little olive oil. Place over a moderately hot charcoal fire and cook, turning them, until medium-rare inside, about 15 minutes.

3. Place 15 ml (1 tbsp) of olive oil in a large, heavy frying pan over high heat. Add the chops to the pan and cook, turning, until just pink inside, another 5 minutes or so. Remove chops and place on 4 dinner plates.

4. Add the stock or water to the pan, deglaze and reduce over high heat to about 125 ml (4 fl oz). Reduce heat to moderate. Add the olive oil-garlic-sage mixture to the juices. Cook for 1 minute. Taste for seasoning. Strain the

juices over the veal chops and top each chop with the additional fresh sage leaves. Serve immediately.

STEWED AND BRAISED VEAL

One of the great developments in American veal consumption has been the recognition that not just the expensive cuts make delectable eating. When cheaper cuts of veal are properly cooked a long time in a moist medium, the result is tender, subtle, fall-off-the-bone meat that blends deliriously well with a wide range of flavours.

For bone-in meat, the best choice of all may be the fabulous, cartilaginous 'false ribs' of the veal breast. Julia Child wrote that these tendons are the favoured veal cut in France for stews. Less bony meat can be obtained from the neck and the shoulder. The latter, in fact, features a section that is relatively easy to bone and offers good chunks of boneless meat for stew, if that's your preference.

Many feel that a combination of cuts makes the most delectable veal stew. But avoid the more expensive cuts from the back legs of the calf; these are leaner and will simply dry out after long cooking.

OSSO BUCO

In the eighties and nineties, this was the dish that really popularised the concept of long-cooked veal. The name means 'bone with a hole', and it refers to thick, circular slices of cross-cut veal shank that feature a gaping, marrow-filled round of bone in the centre. Though most Americans didn't grow up with this dish, they embraced it in later life as a newfound comfort food. Not everyone, of course, goes for the dish's sexiest feature: the melting mass of fatty marrow at the centre of the bone. But we think it's delicious and possess our own marrow spoons to get at it. Another controversy concerns the traditional garnish of gremolata, a fine mince of parsley, lemon zest and garlic. Some feel it gives the dish zing, while others feel it's an excrescence that steals thunder from the veal. We're voting for it—and have even removed the excrescence charge, by building some lemon flavour into the dish. Make sure to try osso buco with its traditional partner (risotto Milanese, page 223); serve big plates of both to a wintertime crowd of hungry diners.

SERVES 4

50 g (2 oz) flour
7.5 g (1½ tsp) salt
2.5 g (½ tsp) ground black pepper
75 ml (5 tbsp) olive oil
4 centre-cut slices veal shank (each about 4 cm
  (1½ in) thick and tied with string)
225 g (8 oz) diced yellow onion
225 g (8 oz) diced carrot
225 g (8 oz) diced celery
12 g (2½ tsp) finely chopped garlic
2 bay leaves
350 ml (12 fl oz) white wine
10 g (2 tsp) grated lemon zest
175 ml (6 fl oz) beef stock
800-g (28-oz) can plum tomatoes, drained
5 g (1 tsp) chopped fresh thyme
5 g (1 tsp) chopped fresh rosemary
20 g (4 tsp) chopped fresh flat-leaf parsley

1. Preheat oven to 180°C (350°F).

2. Mix flour with 2.5 g (½ tsp) of the salt and the pepper and put on a plate. Over high heat, heat 45 ml (3 tbsp) of the oil in a deep, heavy, straight-sided, ovenproof frying pan with a tight-fitting lid large enough to hold the veal shanks in a single layer. When oil is hot but not smoking, dredge veal shanks in flour, coating each side well. Brush off any excess flour. Place in oil and sear until well browned, about 3 minutes on each side. Remove and set aside.

3. Add remaining oil and when oil is hot add onion, carrot, celery, 10 g (2 tsp) of the garlic, bay leaves and another 2.5 g (½ tsp) of salt. Cook until golden, stirring occasionally, about 8 minutes. (Make sure that the vegetables don't burn.) Add the white wine and 5 g (1 tsp) of the lemon zest. Stir and scrape the bottom of the pan to deglaze it. Cook until wine is reduced by half, about 5 minutes. Add beef stock and cook until liquid is reduced by half, another 5 minutes.

4. Put drained plum tomatoes into the frying pan with thyme, rosemary and the rest of the salt. Break up the tomatoes with the back of a spoon. Cook, stirring occasionally, for 5 minutes. Return shanks to the pan. (The tomato mixture should come about two thirds of the way up the shanks. If it does not, add some more beef stock or water.)

5. Cover with the lid and braise in the preheated 180°C (350°F) oven, turning shanks every 30 minutes, for 2 hours. (Add extra stock or water if liquid is getting too thick or too low. When shanks are done, they should be extremely tender and the meat should be starting to pull away from the bone.) Place shanks on a large platter and cover with foil until ready to serve. Cook the sauce until it is reduced to the desired consistency and adjust seasoning.

6. Make the gremolata. Mix the rest of the lemon zest, garlic and parsley. Stir well.

7. To serve, remove strings from shanks, coat with sauce and sprinkle with gremolata.

BLANQUETTE DE VEAU

Introduced to many Americans in the sixties by Julia Child and featured early on at many French restaurants in America, this white stew with mushrooms and onions was the first clue to many American diners that stewed veal can be glorious. The following recipe owes much to Julia's technique. Serve with buttered rice, mashed potatoes or fresh buttered noodles.

SERVES 6

1.8 kg (4 lb) veal stew meat (bone-in or boneless),
  cut into 2.5-cm (1-inch) chunks

3 carrots, cut into 1-cm (½-in) slices

3 stalks celery, cut into large chunks

1 medium onion, cut into 5-mm (¼-in) slices

1 garlic clove, coarsely chopped

3 leeks (white part only), cleaned well and cut into
  2.5-cm (1-in) pieces

3 g (¾ tsp) dried tarragon

2.5 g (½ tsp) dried thyme

2 bay leaves

4 cloves

10 g (2 tsp) coarse salt

2.5 g (½ tsp) white pepper

350 ml (12 fl oz) dry white vermouth

45 ml (3 tbsp) calvados

1.2 litres (2 pints) water

450 g (1 lb) pearl onions

115 g (4 oz) unsalted butter

5 g (1 tsp) sugar

450 g (1 lb) button mushrooms, wiped clean and
  quartered

50 g (2 oz) flour

2 large egg yolks

125 ml (4 fl oz) double cream

115 g (4 oz) finely chopped fresh flat-leaf parsley

lemon juice to taste (optional)

1. Line the bottom of a large, deep pot with half the veal cubes. Place half the carrots and celery over the veal and follow with half the onion slices, half the garlic and half the leeks. Sprinkle with 2.5 g (½ tsp) of the tarragon, 1.25 g (¼ tsp) of the thyme, 1 bay leaf, 2 cloves, 5 g (1 tsp) of the salt and 3 g (¼ tsp) of the white pepper. Repeat this process using the remainder of the above ingredients.

2. Pour vermouth, calvados and water into the pot and bring to a boil. Reduce the heat so that the liquid simmers gently and cook, uncovered, for 30 minutes, skimming the top frequently. After the 30 minutes are up, cover the pot and cook another 45 minutes to 1 hour, until the meat is very tender but not falling apart.

3. Remove the pot from the heat and strain the meat and vegetables, reserving the veal stock. Set the veal aside, discard the vegetables and return the veal stock to a clean saucepan. Boil the stock for about 30 minutes, until it has been reduced to about 1 litre (1¾ pints). *The blanquette can be made up to this point a day ahead. Store the veal in the stock.*

4. While stock is boiling, drop the pearl onions into a small saucepan of boiling water for 1 minute. Remove from water and when cool enough to handle, peel off the skins.

5. In a small frying pan, melt 25 g (1 oz) of butter over moderately high heat. Add pearl onions, sugar and water to just cover the onions. Cook until water has evaporated and onions are tender, about 20 minutes. (They should be coated with a light buttery glaze.) Set aside.

6. Melt 25 g (1 oz) butter over high heat in a large frying pan. When butter is hot, sauté mushrooms, turning once or twice, in batches until nice and golden, about 5 minutes total. (Do not overcrowd pan or mushrooms will steam and not brown properly.) Set aside.

7. Melt remaining butter in a large saucepan over moderate heat. Whisk in the flour slowly and when all is incorporated, stir well with a wooden spoon for 3 minutes. (The colour of the roux should not change.) Slowly add 700 ml (1¼ pints) of the hot veal stock, whisking constantly. Bring the liquid to a boil and boil it for 4 minutes, then reduce the heat and simmer, whisking occasionally, for about 8 minutes (It should be nice and thick).

8. Boil the rest of the stock until it has been reduced to about 125 ml (4 fl oz), about 10 minutes. Combine egg yolks and cream in a small bowl. Slowly pour about

30 ml (2 tbsp) of the boiling stock into the egg mixture, whisking the eggs constantly. (Do not stop whisking or the eggs will scramble.) Add another 30 ml (2 tbsp) of stock to the eggs and whisk well. Now pour the egg mixture back into the remaining stock, continuing to whisk well. (If any of the egg mixture has cooked, strain it to remove the lumps; then add this egg-bound sauce to the other veal sauce and stir well to combine.)

9. Bring the sauce to a simmer and cook gently, whisking constantly, for 5 to 8 minutes. (The sauce should be a nice, thick consistency, which coats the back of a wooden spoon). Add the veal, onions and mushrooms and heat through. Adjust seasoning and garnish with parsley. Add lemon juice if desired.

VEAL BREAST

One of our favourite cuts of veal is the cheapest cut of all. Veal breast is much prized for long, slow cooking in Europe and was a popular dish in this country among Jewish families of the last generation. Somewhere along the line, it lost its cachet; in the eighties, you would never have seen 'breast of veal' as the centrepiece of a power dinner party. In the nineties, however, along with a return to good sense, there's a return to this good cut of veal.

Most people prepare it by cutting a pocket between the main sheath of meat and the bone, then stuffing that pocket. Others like to discard the bones and roll up the remaining meat with a stuffing. We like it both ways.

Stuffings are usually called for because—despite the gargantuan proportions of a veal breast (a whole one weighs about 4.5 kg (10 lb))—only about one third of it is edible meat. Stuffings help to stretch.

BONE-IN VEAL BREAST STUFFED WITH SPINACH, CHEESE AND PINE NUTS

This delicious, Italianate recipe calls for half a veal breast; have your butcher cut a pocket into the breast

for you. When the veal is cooked, it's easiest to cut the breast into four portions; unless your diners are famished, you will certainly have veal left over. Serve with braised Italian greens, like broccoli, calabrese or curly kale.

SERVES 4 GENEROUSLY

50 ml (2 fl oz) olive oil
3 medium onions
125 g (4 oz) short-grain rice (like Arborio)
225 ml (8 fl oz) water
1 bay leaf
2.5 g (½ tsp) salt plus additional to taste
450 g (1 lb) fresh spinach
1 egg, beaten
125 g (4 oz) ricotta cheese
125 g (4 oz) freshly grated Parmigiano-Reggiano
  plus additional cheese for grating
50 g (2 oz) toasted pine nuts
freshly grated nutmeg to taste
freshly ground pepper to taste
half a veal breast (about 2.25 kg (5 lb)), with a
  pocket cut for stuffng
125 ml (4 fl oz) dry white wine
450ml (16 fl oz) veal or chicken stock
4 garlic cloves, smashed and peeled
4 carrots, quartered
40 g (1½ oz) unsalted butter
45 g (3 tbsp) all-purpose flour

1. Place 15 ml (1 tbsp) of the olive oil in a large omelette pan with a tight-fitting lid over moderate heat. Chop 1 of the onions finely and add to the hot oil. Cook 1 minute. Add the rice and stir to coat the rice with the oil. Add the 225 ml (8 fl oz) water, the bay leaf and the salt, stirring to blend. Cover and reduce heat to low. Cook 12 minutes, remove from heat and allow to stand, uncovered, for 5 minutes.

2. Remove the hard stems of the spinach and wash spinach in cold water until no grit remains (use several changes of water if necessary). Place 15 ml (1 tbsp) of olive oil in a large pot over moderate heat and add the spinach. Cook, stirring, until the spinach is completely wilted, about 2 minutes.

3. Place the wilted spinach in a large bowl. Remove the bay leaf from the cooked rice and add the rice to the spinach. Add the egg, ricotta, the Parmigiano-Reggiano and the toasted pine nuts. Mix well. Season liberally with nutmeg, salt and freshly ground pepper.

4. Stuff the pocket of the veal breast with the spinach mixture. Tie the open end shut, or close it with small skewers (like toothpicks). Season the breast with salt and pepper.

5. In a large, heavy roasting tin that's at least 13 cm (5 in) deep, add the remaining 30 ml (2 tbsp) of olive oil and place the pan over moderately high heat. When the oil is hot, place the breast in the pan, fleshy side down and brown it well, about 7 to 8 minutes. Turn the breast over and brown the other side. Remove the breast to a platter. Add the wine and stock to the pan, scraping with a wooden spoon to release any browned bits on the surface of the pan. Peel the 2 remaining onions, cut into coarse chunks and place in the roasting tin, along with the garlic and carrots. Bring liquid to a boil, then reduce heat and bring the liquid to a low simmer. Return the veal breast, fleshy side up, to the pan. Cover. Cook over very low heat (the liquid should be gently simmering), checking every 45 minutes or so to make sure the liquid is at the same level and adding more stock if necessary, for 2½ hours.

6. After 2½ hours, the meat should be moist and tender. Remove the breast to a carving board and let stand. While the veal breast is standing, pour the pan juices through a sieve into a saucepan over high heat. Press on the vegetables in the sieve with a wooden spoon to extract their juices. Discard vegetables. Boil the pan juices until they are reduced to about 450 ml (16 fl oz).

7. Place the butter and flour in another saucepan over moderate heat and cook, stirring, for 2 minutes. Add the reduced pan juices to the butter and flour and whisk in. You should have a medium-thick sauce. Season to taste with nutmeg, salt and pepper.

8. When ready to serve, cut the string or remove the skewers and slice the veal breast into 4 long, thick pieces, including 1 bone with each piece. Place the slices on 4 dinner plates and pour some of the sauce over and around each one. Grate Parmigiano-Reggiano over the veal at the table, if desired.

BONED, ROLLED AND BRAISED BREAST OF VEAL, SPANISH-STYLE

When a breast of veal is boned, stuffed and rolled, it's a little less messy, a little easier for everyone to handle. It can also be cut into thinner, more delicate portions, making it easier to serve more people from one breast of veal. This delicious, chorizo-stuffed breast is great with garlicky roast potatoes or rice flavoured with saffron.

SERVES 8

1 large piece of veal breast (about 2.7 kg (6 lb))
125 ml (4 fl oz) milk
50 g (2 oz) fresh breadcrumbs
225 g (8 oz) chorizo sausages (about 3)
2 large onions, quartered, plus 50 g (2 oz) chopped onion
15 g (½ oz) butter
1 egg, lightly beaten
salt and pepper to taste
flour for coating the veal
olive oil for brushing the roasting tin
2 carrots, cut into thin rounds
3 green peppers, seeded and cut into large chunks
dry white wine and beef stock for braising the veal

1. Ask your butcher to bone the veal breast, yielding a wide, flat piece of meat that weighs approximately

900 g (2 lb). Ask the butcher to give you the bones as well. Let the veal breast come to room temperature.

2. *Prepare the stuffing:* Place the milk and the fresh breadcrumbs in a saucepan. Bring to boil and boil for 2 to 3 minutes, until mixture is very thick. Place in mixing bowl. Remove chorizo casings and mince half the chorizo very finely. Cut the other half into medium dice. You should have about 1½ cups of sausage meat. Add to mixing bowl. Sauté the ¼ cup chopped onion in the butter over moderately high heat until the onion starts to turn soft, about 5 minutes. Add to mixing bowl along with the egg. Beat vigorously and season with salt and pepper.

3. Place the boned veal breast, cut side up, on a counter, making a rectangle with the long side directly in front of you. Season with salt and pepper. About one third of the way past the bottom edge of the rectangle, the edge that's nearer you, spread out the stuffing in a long mound, working from left to right. (Do not allow the stuffing to come to the left or right edges of the boned veal; the stuffing mound should start and end about 2.5 cm (1 in) from the left and right edges of the veal.) Grab the bottom edge, the one that's closest to you and roll it away from you, over the stuffing, rolling until you reach the top edge. You will now have a cylindrical, stuffed roast. Tie it well at the two ends to prevent stuffing from oozing out and tie it at 5-cm (2-in) intervals to make sure the flap stays closed during cooking. Season well with salt and pepper and coat lightly with flour.

4. You will need a very large pan to cook the breast; it's about a foot-and-a-half long and you will need a pan with high sides to accommodate the braising liquid. A deep, very heavy-gauge roasting tin is probably your best choice. Brush the pan with olive oil and place it over moderately high heat. Place 4 or 5 veal bones in the pan along with the quartered onions, carrots and green peppers. Sauté until the vegetables start to brown,

about 10 minutes. Make a space in the centre of the pan, increase the heat to high and place the rolled veal breast in the pan. Brown on all sides (this will take about 10 minutes). Then, add enough white wine and beef stock (using equal amounts of each) to the pan until the liquid comes halfway up the side of the veal breast. Bring to a boil, then reduce heat and bring to a bare simmer. Cover with a lid or with aluminium foil. Cook on top of the stove, or in a preheated 160°C (325°F) oven, checking the liquid to make sure it's gently simmering, for 3 hours.

5. When the breast is done, remove from the pan, place on a cutting board and cover with a tent of aluminium foil to keep warm. Taste the braising liquid; if it needs to be intensified, boil it until it is reduced to the desired consistency and season it. (We like to serve it as it is, with the remains of the braising vegetables strewn over slices of the veal breast.)

6. When ready to serve, remove the strings, then cut veal breast into 1-cm (½-in) slices. Serve immediately with sauce.

RED MEAT

Beef
Beef has certainly had its ups and downs on the American gastronomic scene.

For most of our history, beef production has been one of the most important activities in the American food industry. Cattle-herding was begun in California by the end of the eighteenth century, Texas followed suit by the 1820s and Chicago was a major beef centre by the 1850s. The rise of the cowboy—and the concomitant opening up of the West—was literally synonymous with the rise of the cattle industry.

The strength of this tradition led to great beef in America and great beef-eaters among Americans. For over a hundred years, American beef has been heralded as among the best in the world—getting serious competition, perhaps, only from Argentinian beef and from small pockets of French, Italian and Japanese beef production.

The situation remained unchanged for years. Then, in the last few decades, things started to go poorly for beef in America.

First of all, many Americans during the health frenzy of the seventies started to believe that eating a great deal of beef was not a good thing to do for fear of cholesterol. Beef consumption declined and cattle ranchers felt the pinch.

In the nineties, other health concerns followed. After an outbreak of deadly *e. coli* bacteria in fast-food hamburgers in Washington State, many Americans started feeling squeamish about eating rare beef. Startling as it seems, some states, like New Jersey and Utah, actually made it illegal for restaurants to serve beef that was not well-done. This was another blow to the beef industry, ever-hopeful of a better image.

Of course, the industry itself didn't help matters much. Many Americans growing wary of beef could have been seduced by the high quality of 'prime' beef—were it not that the industry presided over a dismal decline in the standards of 'prime' beef. What once passed as only 'choice' beef, by the eighties was being designated as 'prime'. The stuff that had been 'prime' shrunk to 1 per cent of all beef produced and the vast preponderance of that 1 percent was available only to restaurateurs.

Somehow, however, America is still beef country. The nineties have seen a significant shift back to beef, with consumption on the rise once again. Steak houses are booming in big cities across the country. Hamburgers—of the fast-food variety, the backyard variety and the Creative American Chef variety—are off the charts. New ethnic ideas for cooking beef—drawn from cuisines as disparate as Japanese, French and South American—have increased our repertoire greatly. Texas barbecue and the penchant for beef, has spread across the land. Moreover, Americans who once swore by steak only are

now paying attention to cheaper cuts of beef; short ribs, in particular, have become practically trendy at high-end restaurants.

And through it all, you can still get a great steak to cook at home—but only if you demand the best and only if you never let your butcher forget it.

RAW BEEF DISHES

The eighties saw a rise in the popularity of raw beef due, principally, to the trendiness of one specific raw beef dish from Italy. Soon, other ethnic dishes were discovered and some old favourites were revived. The movement was tempered, somewhat, by jitters over the safety of raw beef—but most raw-beef lovers, such as ourselves, realise that no one has fallen ill from top-quality beef that has been purchased from scrupulously clean, top-quality butchers. If you're making a raw beef dish, buy only the best.

STEAK TARTARE

Perhaps it was the new popularity of ethnic raw beef dishes like carpaccio that helped create a steak tartare renaissance. Once upon a time, steak tartare was a popular dish in American eating establishments—before health fears and general aversion to beef, pushed it into decline. But it kept thriving on Paris menus and it is now making a comeback in those American restaurants that model themselves on Parisian brasseries. We're delighted; it's a grand dish, which carefully plays the quiet flavours of raw beef against a slew of more vigorous flavours. It's important to keep the beef very cold and to use lean beef—the texture of cold fat is not particularly appealing. It is always served with a range of flavourings so diners can make individual adjustments and it is usually served with hearty bread, sometimes dark, upon which diners can spread the mixture. You may serve it as a first course (and halve the following quantities), but we like the Parisian brasserie idea: a first course of raw oysters, followed by a main course of steak tartare with pommes frites on the side.

SERVES 6

900 g (2 lb) lean topside steak

1 egg yolk

2 anchovy fillets, rinsed under cold water, dried and chopped

1 small sweet onion, finely chopped

10 miniature gherkins, finely chopped

30 g (2 tbsp) capers, chopped

5 g (1 tsp) sweet paprika

2.5 g (½ tsp) Dijon mustard

Worcestershire sauce to taste

Tabasco sauce to taste

salt and freshly ground black pepper to taste

For garnish

6 raw egg yolks

12 whole anchovy fillets, rinsed and dried

additional chopped onion

additional chopped miniature gherkins

additional capers

1. Make sure you buy your meat from a reputable butcher and explain that you will be eating it raw; therefore the knife and grinder must be clean. Have the butcher trim the fat and grind 2 times.

2. Place the steak in a bowl and add 1 egg yolk, the anchovies, onion, miniature gherkins, capers, paprika and mustard. Add Worcestershire sauce to taste (about 10 ml (2 tsp) and Tabasco to taste (10 to 12 drops). (Go slowly with the last two ingredients, because they can rob the beef of its subtle flavour; taste as you go.) Mix together well and season with salt and freshly ground black pepper. Chill meat well.

3. Divide the steak tartare among 6 dinner plates. Shape into long, thick ovals. Make a diamond pattern in the meat by drawing a crisscross on each oval with a blunt knife. Form a depression the size of an egg yolk in

the centre of each; fill depressions with yolks. Crisscross 2 anchovies on top of each yolk. Place the additional onion, miniature gherkins and capers, which individual diners can mix in to taste, around the tartare. Have Worcestershire sauce, Tabasco, mustard, salt and pepper available for further adjustments.

Note: If you want to make this dish in the really old-fashioned manner, do not purchase meat that has been minced in a meat mincer. Instead, buy impeccably fresh topside and shred the meat yourself by scraping it with a sharp knife into thin shreds. It's a lot mcre work, but the texture of the meat is noticeably more interesting.

CARPACCIO

Though there is a long tradition of raw beef dishes in Italian cuisine, Giuseppe Cipriani, the founder of Harry's Bar in Venice, claims to have invented 'carpaccio' in the fifties. What was different about his? The name, for one thing; he named his dish after the Renaissance artist Vittore Carpaccio, whose paintings with red and white tones were on exhibition in Venice. Cipriani also changed the traditional dressing for raw beef, which had been, simply, olive oil and Parmigiano-Reggiano; he came up with a creamy white sauce that is just homemade mayonnaise thinned out by the addition of a little Worcestershire sauce, lemon juice and milk. We find carpaccio to be a terrific starter for a dinner party and a miracle dish for wine; practically everything goes with it well. But when it comes to the sauce, we favour Italian tradition over Giuseppe's creation. We also deviate by using topside of beef, rather than the sirloin or filet mignon that Cipriani recommends; leaner beef is tastier than fatty beef when sliced thin and eaten raw, with a more resilient chew. You should have your butcher machine-slice it for you, as close as possible to serving time; we don't recommend freezing the beef to slice it thin or pounding it after slicing.

SERVES 6 AS A FIRST COURSE

450 g (1 lb) topside of beef

90 g (6 tbsp) shredded Parmigiano-Reggiano
(preferably young)

50 ml (2 fl oz) great extra-virgin olive oil

coarse salt and freshly ground pepper

1. Have your butcher slice the beef into the thinnest possible slices by machine, as close as possible to serving time. Keep them cold.

2. When ready to serve, arrange the slices in a single layer on 6 dinner plates. Scatter the Parmigiano-Reggiano over the beef and drizzle with the olive oil. Season with salt and pepper and serve immediately.

KOREAN RAW BEEF SALAD (YOOK HWE)

This wild dish, a favourite at the many Korean restaurants springing up across America, has one of the strangest textures imaginable: the beef is partially frozen, then thinly sliced, then served while still partially frozen! The chill certainly adds a bracing cleanness to raw beef.

SERVES 4 AS A FIRST COURSE

140 g (5 oz) very fresh lean flank steak

45 ml (2½ tbsp) thin soy sauce

40 g (1½ tbsp) sugar

15 g (1 tbsp) finely chopped spring onion

10 g (2 tsp) very finely chopped garlic

15 g (1 tbsp) toasted sesame seeds, ground to a powder

30 ml (2 tbsp) Asian sesame oil

1 medium Asian pear

1 very large egg yolk

4 leaves of red-leaf lettuce

15 g (1 tbsp) toasted pine nuts, finely chopped

1. Freeze the flank steak until just firm, about 1 hour. Using a sharp knife, slice beef across the grain into broad slices. Then, cut each slice into thin strips.

2. In a large bowl combine the soy sauce, sugar, spring onion, garlic, ground sesame seeds and sesame oil. Add meat and mix gently. Peel and core the pear and cut into strips the same size as the beef strips; toss strips with the beef. Toss beef with the egg yolk. Taste for seasoning.

3. Arrange the lettuce leaves on 4 plates, and top each leaf with one quarter of the beef mixture. Sprinkle with toasted pine nuts and serve immediately.

Note: An alternative way to serve this dish is to leave out the egg yolk, but top each plated portion with a raw quail's egg yolk; then, each individual diner stirs his or her small yolk into the beef salad.

STEAK

One of the restaurant surprises of the eighties and nineties was the booming business in steak houses, despite the ongoing national repudiation of beef. There's no denying this simple fact: steak-house steak is one of the glories of American cuisine and Americans will never lose their taste for it.

They might, however, lose their ability to pay for it, as steak-house steaks creep up to $30 apiece, before a single French fry is served. So then the question arises: can you make steak at home that's as good as steak in a steak house?

Admittedly, it's not easy. There are two reasons that steak-house steak is as good as it is: the quality of meat available to restaurateurs and the high heat available to restaurant chefs. But if you're determined to reproduce the steak-house experience at home, you can come pretty darned close.

First of all, the steak itself. We're proud of the steak we sell at our meat department. You must find a butcher who takes pride in his meat and who has access to the small quantity of top-flight steak in the marketplace. A 'prime' designation alone is no guarantee of the best; the butcher has to have sought out the very best of 'prime'. Then there's the question of aging. Many steaks today are aged in wet bags, which do the job more quickly. But the finest flavour comes from the more expensive 'dry-aging' process; check with your butcher to see which process his steak has undergone.

Next question: which cut of steak? Here are the leading possibilities for great steak house–style steak at home.

Skirt steak and hanger steak

Two less expensive cuts of steak grew in popularity in American restaurants in the last 2 decades.

Propelled by the fajita craze, skirt steak, taken from the steer's diaphragm—once an extremely inexpensive cut—has now zoomed up to $6 and $7 (£3.60 and £4.20) a pound. It was once chiefly seen on old-fashioned menus as 'Roumanian tenderloin', but is now seen in all kinds of ethnic menu contexts. It is an extremely long, fairly narrow steak, with deep grains, that takes very well to marinating and grilling.

The new 'hot' steak is hanger steak, called *onglet* on every bistro menu in France. It is also known as 'butcher's tenderloin', because butchers have traditionally kept this 'secret' cut for themselves. Hanger steak hangs off the kidney and its slight chewiness is usually overlooked because of its deep, robust, beefy flavour. So far, hanger steak hasn't gone far beyond American bistros wanting to be French—but this just means it is still available for a reasonable price at butcher shops.

Shell Steak These steaks have a plethora of names across the country; in addition to shell steaks, they are called strips, New York strips, New York steaks, Kansas City strips, sirloins and numerous other things. As with all of the great steaks, the meat comes from the hindquarter, between the primal sirloin (the animal's hip) and the small end of the rib. The shell steak itself comes from the top loin muscle. It is a fairly long steak,

usually served boneless, with a long strip of creamy white fat along one side. Its cachet is its flavour; it's chewier than filet mignon, but fattier—which means it has a deeper steak flavour.

Filet Mignon Near the portion of the steer that contains the shell steak, on the other side of a T-shaped bone, is a long strip of meat (it looks like a thin roast beef) known as the beef tenderloin. When this tenderloin is cut into individual steaks, you have individual 'filets'. The French are very precise about which types of filets come from which sections of the tenderloin: if the filets come from the thickest part of the tenderloin, they are called 'châteaubriand'; from a slightly thinner part they are called 'tournedos'; from the thinnest part they are called 'filet mignon'. Americans are much less precise about this; almost any cut from the tenderloin is likely to be identified as 'filet mignon'. This obfuscation doesn't bother us, because most of the tenderloin meat does have a similar quality: extremely tender (tending toward mushiness, in fact), fairly lean, not as flavourful as other cuts. The debate rages among cooks and diners: do you want the deeper flavour of the shell steak or the more velvety texture of the filet mignon?

Porterhouse Steak For those who can't make up their minds, there's always the porterhouse. This steak is a combination of the shell and the filet; they sit side-by-side, separated by a T-shaped bone. On the porterhouse, the filet portion is almost as large as the shell portion. It's a big steak, often served for two in steak houses.

T-Bone Steak This is another combination steak, very similar to the porterhouse, but cut from an area where the tenderloin is thinner. Therefore, the filet portion of the T-bone is smaller than the filet portion of the porterhouse and the whole steak is smaller—making it more manageable for one person.

For top-quality steak, you have no other options but these.

Now…once you've got your top-quality shell, or

filet mignon, or porterhouse, or T-bone home . . . how are you going to cook it?

The tremendous heat of restaurant grills and grills is capable of searing the steak on the outside, while leaving it deliciously juicy and rare on the inside. The interplay of that black, crusty exterior and the red, velvety interior is one of the joys of the genre. At home, with lower heat, steak exteriors tend to be more in the grey-brown range and interiors more in the medium-well stage. So the chief concern is getting the fire hot enough.

The following recipe includes every detail you need to make the best possible steak at home.

GRILLED PORTERHOUSE STEAK FOR TWO VERY HUNGRY PEOPLE

Okay, let's face it: the amount of steak in this recipe will feed 4 or even 6 people. But then you'd have to slice up the steak, depriving the diners of the lusty chance to consume a whole steak each, bone included. You could make smaller steaks—but these behemoth porterhouses, because they take longer to cook, are your best shot at replicating the taste of steak-house steak. So fast for a day or two, skip the appetisers, serve simple potatoes and salad on the side (like thick-cut tomatoes and onions with oil and vinegar)—and turn your house for a few magical hours into The Palm, a famous steak restaurant in New York City.

SERVES 2 VERY GENEROUSLY

2 porterhouse steaks (each cut 1½ to 5 cm (2 in) thick and weighing 1 kg (2 to 2½ lb))
melted butter to taste plus room temperature butter to taste
freshly cracked black pepper to taste
freshly ground coarse salt to taste

1. Let the steaks come to cold room temperature (remove them from the refrigerator about an hour before cooking).

2. Prepare the hottest fire you can in an outdoor grill. Gas grills, or fires made from charcoal briquettes, are minimally acceptable. It's much better to make a lump-charcoal fire, preferably from mesquite charcoal.

3. Just after the flames have died down and the coals have started turning grey, the grill is ready. Dry the steaks thoroughly with a cloth. Brush melted butter on both sides of the steaks and sprinkle both sides with freshly cracked black pepper. Place steaks on a grate over the fire, no more than 10 cm (4 in) from the fire. Cook, turning only once if possible, until steaks are crusty and dark on the outside, very rare on the inside (this will take about 15 minutes altogether). You can check them with an instant-read meat thermometer, if you wish; it should register about 46°C (115°F) for very rare meat.

4. Place knobs of unsalted butter on a large platter. Remove the steaks from the fire and place them on the butter on the platter. Top with more knobs of butter, which will melt over the steak. Sprinkle with freshly ground coarse salt. Serve. Enjoy. Count calories tomorrow.

Another way to cook steak at home

Grilling over high heat is by far the best way to cook steak at home. Don't even think about cooking under a regular home grill; it has nowhere near the heat of a restaurant grill and will turn your steak medium-well inside before it has begun to char it on the outside.

But there is a pan-frying technique that works reasonably well with thick steaks. Add equal quantities of butter and olive oil to a thick, heavy pan, preferably cast-iron, to a depth of about 3 mm (⅛ in). Place the pan over the highest heat. When the oil and butter are smoking, add the steak. Shift its position after 30 seconds or so. After it's well browned on one side, turn over and repeat. Cook until done. The butter in the pan will burn during the cooking and you'll get a smoky kitchen, but the steak should be crunchy-brown on the outside, rare on the inside.

BEEF TENDERLOIN

If the butcher chooses to remove and preserve the whole filet from the steer—rather than cutting it into individual filets mignons or tournedos—then you have a tenderloin of beef, or filet of beef. Looking like a long, narrow roast beef, a whole tenderloin of beef stands at least a foot-and-a-half long, is 7.5 cm (3 in) to 3½ inches in diameter and weighs approximately 5 pounds. It is a fabulous cut of meat for a fancy dinner party: easy to cook, easy to serve, very impressive and delicious.

Of course, you don't need to purchase an entire tenderloin to enjoy this cut. If you're just serving 4 diners, ask your butcher for a 2-pound hunk of tenderloin, of even thickness, preferably cut from the central 'chateaubriand' section of the tenderloin.

Simply roasted tenderloin is wonderful served all by itself, with no sauce to embellish it. But here are 2 recipes we love that add some wonderfully sympathetic flavours to the star performer:

ROASTED BEEF TENDERLOIN WITH HERBES DE PROVENCE AND MARROW

SERVES 4

45 g (3 tbsp) herbes de Provence
5 g (1 tsp) salt
3 g (¾ tsp) freshly cracked black pepper
900-g (2-lb) chunk of beef tenderloin of even thickness (preferably cut from the chateaubriand section)
7.5-cm (3-in) piece of beef marrow bone, split in half lengthways
25 g (1 oz) unsalted butter
50 g (2 oz) finely chopped shallots
50 ml (2 fl oz) dry red wine

300 ml (10 fl oz) beef demi-glace
50 g (2 oz) finely chopped fresh parsley

1. Preheat oven to 120°C (250°F).

2. In a small bowl blend the herbes de Provence, salt and pepper. Pat the beef tenderloin dry and coat the whole tenderloin with the herb mixture, pressing gently to make sure it adheres. Place the tenderloin in a roasting tin in the preheated oven and cook until rare, about 20 minutes. Let rest for 10 minutes before carving.

3. While tenderloin is roasting, cut the marrow out of the marrow bone with a sharp paring knife, keeping the marrow from each half in one piece if possible. Dip the paring knife into very hot water and slice the marrow into ¼-inch slices. Refrigerate the sliced marrow.

4. Meanwhile, place the butter in a heavy saucepan and melt over moderate heat. Add shallots and cook until softened, about 5 minutes. Increase heat to high and add red wine. Reduce until only 15 ml (1 tbsp) of the wine remains, about 5 minutes. Add demi-glace and simmer until thickened slightly, about 10 minutes. Taste for seasoning and keep warm.

5. Bring a small saucepan of salted water to a boil, reduce heat to bring to a simmer and drop sliced marrow into water for about 2 to 3 minutes to soften. Remove marrow with a spoon and set aside.

6. Carve tenderloin into thick slices (1-2 cm (½-¾ in)) and arrange on a serving platter. Dice marrow and add to warm sauce, heating gently for 30 seconds. Spoon sauce over tenderloin slices and garnish with chopped parsley. Serve immediately.

POACHED BEEF TENDERLOIN WITH WHITE PEPPERCORN SAUCE

Yes, we were amazed too when we came across this dish at a restaurant in Mainz, Germany. But poaching a tenderloin of beef is a marvellous way to emphasise its velvety texture—just as long as you don't poach it past rareness. Serve our version of this wonderful, surprising, Germanic dish on a cold winter night, with a garnish of poached root vegetables, such as carrots, turnips and celeriac.

SERVES 4

900-g (2-lb) chunk of beef tenderloin of even thickness (preferably cut from the chateaubriand section)

5 g (1 tsp) freshly ground white pepper plus more to taste

5 g (1 tsp) salt

2.25 litres (4 pints) dark beef stock

700 g (1½ lb) leeks, split, washed and cut into coarse chunks

225 g (8 oz) carrots, cut into coarse chunks

450 g (1 lb) onions, cut into coarse chunks

225 g (8 oz) white turnips, peeled and cut into coarse chunks

15 g (1 tbsp) whole black peppercorns

50 ml (2 fl oz) brandy

3 g (⅛ tsp) ground cloves

350 ml (12 fl oz) dry white wine

25 g (4 oz) coarsely chopped shallots

15 g (1 tbsp) plus ½ tsp whole white peppercorns

150 ml (5 fl oz) crème fraîche

1 egg yolk

pinch of freshly grated nutmeg

fresh chives for garnish

1. *Prepare the beef:* Trim the tenderloin of all fat and sinew, then tie it with a string at 2.5-cm (1-in) intervals to keep the round shape. Coat the meat with freshly ground white pepper and salt. Refrigerate for 3 to 4 hours.

2. *Prepare the poaching liquid:* Place the beef stock in an oval casserole, one that will hold the tenderloin snugly. Add the leeks, carrots, onions, turnips, black peppercorns, brandy and cloves. Bring to a boil, then simmer gently for 2 hours.

3. When ready to cook, make sure that the poaching liquid is at a very gentle simmer. Lower the tenderloin into it and picking up the poaching vegetables from the liquid with a slotted spoon, strew them over the beef. Cook until very rare, about 20 minutes. Remove tenderloin from the liquid, returning any vegetables to the pot.* Let stand for 5 minutes before carving.

4. *While the beef is poaching, prepare the sauce:* In a small, heavy saucepan cook the white wine, shallots and 15 g (1 tbsp) of whole white peppercorns over moderately high heat until the wine is reduced to about 20 ml (4 tsps). Place the crème fraîche and egg yolk in a bowl, whisk together and slowly strain in the white wine reduction. Pour crème fraîche mixture into the saucepan and cook over very gentle heat until the egg yolk thickens the sauce slightly. Add the grated nutmeg and season to taste with salt and ground white pepper.

5. When ready to serve, slice the beef and divide among 4 dinner plates. Pour the sauce over and around the beef. Crack coarsely the rest of the whole white peppercorns and strew them over the beef. Garnish with the chives. Serve immediately.

PRIME RIBS

Prime ribs, the apotheosis of roast beef, gets its name by being a 'primal' cut—that is, it is one, whole, natural section of the steer. In this case, the section is the 'primal rib'—seven of them, to be precise, which, if kept together and roasted together, is called a 'standing

*This very flavourful poaching liquid can now be used as the basis for other soups, stews, or sauces.

rib roast'. But a roast of any size from this section is colloquially referred to as 'prime ribs'.

Cooking prime ribs is at once simple and confusing. The meat is so intrinsically flavourful that it needs no seasoning other than salt and pepper and needs no fancy treatment other than a little time in the oven. This much is simple. But how long should it stay in that oven to produce the optimum roast? At what temperature?

Some books will tell you that 160°C (325°F) is the best roasting temperature for prime ribs and that 18 minutes per 450 g (1 lb) for rare meat, 22 minutes per 450 g (1 lb) for medium-rare meat, is a reliable guide. We find this workable—but only if the roast is medium size (say, 3 to 5 ribs). If it's smaller, it doesn't have enough time to develop a browned, crunchy exterior. If it's larger than that, it gets overcooked inside—because the amount of cooking time per 450 g (1 lb) *must decrease* as the prime rib roast gets larger.

We favour a lower roasting temperature, anyway, because this cooks the meat more evenly. Roasts cooked at higher temperatures, when sliced, always look grey on the outer edge of the slices and a different colour at the centre of the slice; roasts cooked at lower temperatures, when sliced, show an evenness of colour from edge to centre. The problem with low-temperature roasting, is that smaller roasts do not develop a crunchy-brown exterior by the time the meat is done.

So our solution is simple: we favour a medium-large prime rib (5 ribs altogether) cooked from beginning to end at 140°C (275°F). We try to time it per 450 g (1 lb), but lots of variables affect this estimate. Therefore, there is no substitute for a quick-read meat thermometer. If you're serious about roasting, you must have one of these in your *batterie de cuisine.* They are inexpensive and widely available. Whenever you want to test the doneness of a roast, you just insert your thermometer into the meat and within seconds you have an accurate reading of the internal temperature. Roasting goes from guesswork to science.

With our quick-read thermometer in hand, here's how we go about roasting prime ribs.

Some serving suggestions for prime ribs

Thin cut or thick cut? The English like to slice the meat thin, the Americans like a much thicker cut. You'll be amazed how different the chew is between the two cuts; the differently cut slices seem as if they came from different roasts. Well, we're Americans: when we have a great prime rib, we think that nothing compares with the lush, velvety chew of a thickly cut slice (about 3 cm (1½ in) thick).

Serving the bones? Yes! We always make sure to leave a little meat on the bones as we cut the 'eye' of the roast away from them—because we love gnawing on the bones and we like to make that as meaty an experience as possible. Unfortunately, a 5-rib roast will yield meat for 8 diners, but bones for only 5—so you'd better think in advance about the feelings of the 3 diners who get left out.

Accompaniments? Yorkshire pudding is overrated, in our opinion. We love potatoes with prime ribs—either mashed, roasted, or in a creamy potato gratin.

IDEAL PRIME RIBS

SERVES 8

5-rib prime rib roast
salt and pepper

1. Bring prime ribs to cool room temperature (about 1½ hours out of the refrigerator). Make sure you know the weight of the roast.

2. Preheat oven to 140°C (275°F).

3. Season roast extremely well with salt and pepper. Place in roasting tin, fatty side up and place in oven. Cook until desired degree of doneness is reached (resist the temptation to open the oven door a lot). For rare meat, the roast should take about 20 minutes per 450 g (1 lb). When you're within half an hour of your estimated finish time, remove the roast from the oven and plunge a quick-read thermometer into a fleshy part of the meat near the centre (don't go anywhere near a bone). We like to stop cooking the roast in the oven at 46°C (115°F); this is extremely rare, but the roast will continue to cook as it stands outside the oven (the temperature should go up 5 to 10 degrees). If you remove it at 48°C (120°F) it will be rare and at 52°C (125°F) it will be medium-rare; we wouldn't recommend going much higher than that.

4. Place the roast on a cutting board, uncovered and let it rest for 15 minutes.

5. When ready to serve, simply cut the meat away from the bone in one enormous chunk. Then, cut the 'filet' of meat into slices and serve immediately. Cut through the bones (you'll have 5) and serve them separately.

STEWED, BOILED AND BRAISED BEEF

Though 'beef stew' has always been popular in America, it has been only in the last 20 years that our fairly bland American version of this international specialty began to get some competition from the more decisively flavoured 'beef stews' of other cuisines. And the reawakened, nineties-style interest in slow cooking of cheaper cuts of meat has resulted in the growing popularity of boiled and braised meat as well, from a wide spectrum of ethnic sources.

Cuts of beef for stew

There are many possibilities for tough cuts of beef that, when long-cooked in stews, become tender and tasty. The most important thing is to use cuts of beef that have a relatively high fat content; this bastes the beef as it's cooking and keeps it tender. Following this strategy, our cut of choice is chuck.

BOEUF À LA BOURGUIGNONNE

Perhaps the first ethnic beef stew that made a big splash in America, along about the sixties, was this potful of wine-soaked beef from Burgundy. It's still an enormously satisfying stew, as it has been for hundreds of years. Our version, we think, tastes best if you make steps 1 to 6 a few days before serving.

SERVES 10

2.25 kg (5 lb) boneless beef chuck, cut into 4-cm (1½-in) cubes
4 carrots, cut into large chunks
2 stalks celery, cut into large chunks
1 large yellow onion, cut into large chunks
3 garlic cloves, quartered
1 bunch of fresh thyme, leaves bruised with dull end of a knife
2 bay leaves
4 cloves
1.4 litres (2½ pints) dry red wine
225 g (8 oz) thin bacon rashers, cut into 1-cm (½-in) strips
10 g (2 tsp) salt
2.5 g (½ tsp) ground black pepper
25 g (1 oz) flour
450 g (1 lb) pearl onions
50 g (2 oz) unsalted butter
5 g (1 tsp) sugar
450 g (1 lb) button mushrooms, wiped clean and quartered
50 g (2 oz) finely chopped fresh flat-leaf parsley

1. Put beef, carrots, celery, yellow onion, garlic, thyme, bay leaves and cloves in a large mixing bowl. Toss by hand to combine. Add red wine and cover tightly. Marinate, stirring once or twice, overnight in refrigerator.

2. Strain and dry off the meat and vegetables, reserving liquid separately. Allow meat to come to room temperature before proceeding (about 1/2 hour).

3. Preheat oven to 160°C (325°F).

4. In a deep, ovenproof casserole with a tight-fitting lid, fry bacon over moderately high heat until well browned and crispy, about 7 to 8 minutes. Remove bacon and set aside on paper towels to drain. Leave fat in pan. Sear meat in batches until deep brown, about 2 to 3 minutes per side. (Do not overcrowd pan or meat will not colour properly.) Remove meat with slotted spoon and set aside. Add vegetables from the marinade with the salt and the pepper and sauté, stirring several times so that vegetables do not burn, until nicely caramelised, about 7 to 8 minutes.

5. Add flour and stir it around, coating all the vegetables. Put meat back in the pot and slowly pour in the marinating liquid. Bring the liquid to a boil, scraping the bottom of the pot to deglaze it. Boil for 2 minutes, then cover pot with the lid and place in preheated oven. Cook, stirring only once, for about 2½ hours. (Meat should be fork tender but not falling apart.)

6. Strain off the liquid and separate the meat from the vegetables. Discard the vegetables and set the meat aside. Degrease the liquid and return to the pot. Boil the liquid over high heat for about 45 minutes, or until thickened to a saucelike consistency. Return meat to pot (include whatever bacon bits you can). *The stew can be made up to this point up to 2 days ahead. Cool, then refrigerate, tightly covered. Bring to room temperature and rewarm before adding the onions and mushrooms.*

7. Drop pearl onions into a small pan of boiling water for 1 minute. Remove from water and when cool enough to handle, peel off the skins.

8. Melt 25 g (1 oz) of the butter over moderately high heat. Add pearl onions, sugar and enough water to just cover the onions. Cook until water has evaporated and onions are tender, about 20 minutes. (They should be

coated with a light buttery glaze.) Add to the stew.

9. Melt remaining 25 g (1 oz) of butter over high heat in a large frying pan . When butter is hot, sauté mushrooms, turning once or twice, in batches until nice and golden, about 5 minutes total. (Do not overcrowd pan or mushrooms will steam and not brown properly.) Add to the stew.

10.. Heat the stew for 10 to 15 minutes over moderate heat. Before serving, adjust seasoning and sprinkle with the chopped parsley.

DAUBE À LA PROVENÇALE
With new interest in Mediterranean cuisine in the eighties, American chefs started looking toward Provence, not Burgundy, for their French beef stews. Happily, the stews of both regions are equally easy to make at home—and equally scrumptious.

SERVES 6

1 litre (1¾ pints) dry white wine
50 ml (2 fl oz) olive oil
50 ml (2 fl oz) pastis or Pernod
freshly squeezed juice of 1 orange
30 g (2 tbsp) herbes de Provence
2.5 g (½ tsp) freshly ground black pepper
4 juniper berries
45 g (3 tbsp) chopped garlic
1.8 kg (4 lb) boneless beef chuck, cut into 4-cm
  (1½-in) cubes
85 g (3 oz) dried cèpes (or porcini)
225 g (8 oz) salt pork, cut into 5-mm (¼-in)-thick
  slices that are 2.5 cm (1 in) long and 1 cm (½ in)
  wide
2 carrots, cut into ½-inch rounds
2 stalks celery, cut into 1-cm (½-in) slices
2 medium yellow onions, coarsely chopped
800-g (28-oz) can crushed tomatoes
225 g (8 oz) stoned black olives, coarsely chopped

450 ml (16 fl oz) beef stock

50 g (2 oz) finely chopped fresh flat-leaf parsley

1. In a large saucepan combine wine, olive oil, pastis, orange juice, herbes de Provence, pepper, juniper berries and chopped garlic. Bring to a boil, then turn off heat. Let cool to room temperature. When it's cool, pour the marinade over beef cubes in a large bowl. Stir meat well, cover and refrigerate overnight. One hour before proceeding with recipe, strain beef and bring it to room temperature, reserving marinade.

2. Put dried mushrooms in a small bowl and pour 225 ml (8 fl oz) of very hot water over them. Let sit until softened, about 30 minutes. Remove mushrooms and coarsely chop. Strain the liquid through a double layer of muslin and reserve.

3. Line the bottom of a large casserole with one third of the beef cubes. Sprinkle half the salt pork over the top, followed by one third of the carrots, one third of the celery, one third of the onions and one third of the mushrooms. Pour half the tomatoes over the vegetables, followed by half the olives. Repeat this once and then place remaining beef, carrots, celery, onions and mushrooms on top.

4. Pour reserved marinade into casserole and then the reserved mushroom liquid. Add just enough beef stock so that the daube is almost covered with liquid. Bring the mixture slowly to a boil and then reduce the heat so that the liquid barely bubbles. Cook for about 4 hours, skimming fat off the surface every half hour, until the meat is extremely tender. (The liquid will reduce by about two thirds and will have a nice, thick consistency.) Adjust seasoning, garnish with the chopped parsley and serve.

CARBONNADE OF BEEF WITH PRUNES

One of our secret gastronomic hopes is that after the

Mediterranean hubbub dies down, Americans will pay a little more attention to the superb cuisines of *northern* Europe. This fabulous stew, based on an idea from Belgian cuisine, is cooked with a delicious secret ingredient: beer. Make sure to pick a dark beer that's full-flavoured, but not too bitter; Brooklyn Brown Ale from the Brooklyn Brewing Company is an ideal choice.

SERVES 4

75 ml (5 tbsp) vegetable oil

1.3 kg (3 lb) boneless beef chuck for stew, cut into
  2.5 cm (1-in) cubes

10 g (2 tsp) coarse salt

5 g (1 tsp) freshly ground black pepper

2 large yellow onions,
  cut into 5-mm (¼-in) slices

225 ml (8 fl oz) beef stock

175 g (6 oz) stoned prunes, quartered

2.5 g (½ tsp) dried thyme

2 bay leaves

8 sprigs of fresh flat-leaf parsley, torn into pieces,
  plus 45 g (3 tbsp) finely chopped parsley for
  garnish

4 cloves

3 cups amber or dark beer (not porter or stout)

1. Preheat oven to 160°C (325°F).

2. In a deep, ovenproof casserole with a tight-fitting lid, heat 45 ml (3 tbsp) of the vegetable oil over moderately high heat. Dry meat thoroughly and sprinkle with 5 g (1 tsp) of the coarse salt and 2.5 g (½ tsp) of the black pepper. Sear meat in batches until deep brown, about 2 to 3 minutes per side. (Do not overcrowd pan or meat will not colour properly.) Remove meat with slotted spoon and set aside. Add the remaining vegetable oil and the onions and sauté onions, stirring frequently, until nicely caramelised, about 7 to 8 minutes. Set onions aside.

3. Increase heat to high and deglaze the pan with the beef stock, scraping the bottom of the pan with a wooden spoon. Boil for 5 minutes, until stock is slightly reduced. Turn off heat.

4. Put a layer of the browned meat on the bottom of the casserole, followed by a layer of cooked onions. Sprinkle with half the prunes, half the thyme and half the salt. Repeat this process and sprinkle the top with the rest of the black pepper. In a piece of muslin, tie up the bay leaves, parsley sprigs and cloves. Tuck this into the middle of the stew.

5. Pour beer over the stew and bring to a boil. Cover the casserole with the lid and place in the oven. Cook for 1 hour 45 minutes and check the meat for doneness. (Meat should be fork tender but not falling apart. The stew might take another 15 minutes.)

6. Remove muslin bag, adjust seasoning and sprinkle with chopped parsley just before serving. *Carbonnade can be made up to several days ahead. Cool and refrigerate, tightly covered. Bring to room temperature and rewarm gently. Garnish with parsley just before serving.*

STIFADO

The mention of Greek food conjures up images of lamb on the spit. But the Greeks are great stewers as well—particularly in the northern reaches of that spread-out country, particularly in winter. One classic Greek stew is called *stifado*, which can be made with any meat as the central player (sometimes it's even made with octopus); beef, however, is the most widely used meat in stifado. A proper stifado should contain wine, or vinegar, or both and pearl onions. Sometimes the stew is highly spiced and sometimes it has a sweet-and-sour character; we have pushed our stifado in those directions. This is, essentially, a very simple weeknight family dish that is interesting enough for guests. Great with orzo that has been tossed with butter and grated cheese (like kefalotyri, manouri or mizithra).

SERVES 4

450-g (1-lb) can peeled whole tomatoes, drained and chopped
125 ml (4 fl oz) red-wine vinegar
125 ml (4 fl oz) beef stock or water
90 ml (6 tbsp) olive oil
5 garlic cloves, halved
1 cinnamon stick
10-cm (4-in)-long strip orange zest removed with a vegetable peeler
15 ml (1 tbsp) dark honey
5 g (1 tsp) pickling spice (tied in muslin)
1 bay leaf
5 g (1 tsp) ground cumin seed
900 g (2 lb) boneless beef chuck, cut into 3-cm (1½-in) cubes
450 g (1 lb) fresh pearl onions
5 g (1 tsp) sugar
chopped fresh flat-leaf parsley for garnish

1. Stir together tomatoes, vinegar, stock, 50 ml (2 fl oz) of the olive oil, garlic, cinnamon stick, orange zest, honey, pickling spice, bay leaf and cumin in a large earthenware casserole or enamelled cast-iron casserole with a lid. Stir in the beef and marinate the mixture, covered and chilled, overnight.

2. Preheat oven to 160°C (325°F).

3. Place the beef, with its marinade, in the oven and cook, covered, for 1 hour.

4. While the stew is cooking, drop pearl onions into a small pan of boiling water for 1 minute. Remove from water and when cool enough to handle, peel off the skins. Place the remaining 30 ml (2 tbsp) of olive oil in a large saucepan over moderately high heat. Add pearl onions, sugar and enough water to just cover the onions. Cook until water has evaporated and onions are tender, about 20 minutes. (They should be coated with a light glaze.) After the stew has cooked for 1 hour, add onions to the stew.

5. Cook the stew, covered, for 2 hours more, or until the beef is very tender. (If the sauce has not thickened sufficiently, remove the cover for the latter portion of the cooking time.) Sprinkle with parsley and serve.

SAUERBRATEN

Sauerbraten is, quite simply, the best pot roast that we know of. Though we normally stay away from topside as a braising beef—because it's so relatively lean—we like to use it for sauerbraten, which requires intact slices of beef to be served at the table. Topside keeps its shape very well and, in this dish, comes to the table quite moist—due to the long marination and the long cooking time. To insure the moistness of the beef, have the butcher leave a thin outer covering of fat around the topside. Serve this deep, dark, sweet-and-sour treat with red cabbage and spaetzle.

SERVES 4

125 ml (4 fl oz) red-wine vinegar
400 ml (14 fl oz) red wine
450 g (1 lb) sliced yellow onions
6 parsley stems
6 black peppercorns
3 bay leaves
6 whole cloves
675-900-g (1½-2-lb) chunk of top sirloin
50 g (2 oz) flour
10 g (2 tsp) salt
5 g (1 tsp) freshly ground black pepper
30 ml (2 tbsp) vegetable oil
175 g (6 oz) chopped, seeded tomatoes
175 ml (6 fl oz) water (approximately)
30 ml (2 tbsp) cream sherry
15 g (1 tbsp) light brown sugar plus additional to taste
15 ml (1 tbsp) freshly squeezed lemon juice, or to taste
parsley sprigs for garnish

1. In a medium saucepan combine vinegar, 350 ml (12 fl oz) of the red wine and the onions. Wrap the parsley stems, peppercorns, bay leaves and cloves in a double layer of muslin and tie shut. Add this to the saucepan and bring mixture to a boil. Turn off the heat and cool to room temperature.

2. Prick the topside on all sides with a fork. Put it into a large resealable plastic bag and pour the marinade over it. Close bag and turn upside down a few times to cover meat well with marinade. Marinate, turning the bag once or twice a day, for 3 to 4 days in the refrigerator.

3. When ready to cook, bring marinated beef to room temperature, about 2 hours. Remove beef from marinade and pat dry. Strain marinade, reserving the liquid and onions; discard the muslin bag.

4. Preheat oven to 160°C (325°F).

5. Combine the flour, salt and black pepper on a large plate, mixing well.

6. Heat the vegetable oil in a heavy, ovenproof pan with a lid, large enough to hold the roast, over moderately high heat. When the oil is hot but not smoking, dredge meat in flour mixture, then sear well on each side, about 5 minutes per side. Pour extra fat out of pan.

7. Place 225 ml (8 fl oz) of the marinating liquid, the remaining ¼ cup red wine and tomatoes in the pan along with the reserved onions from the marinade. Add enough of the water so that the liquid comes about one third of the way up the side of the beef. Bring liquid to a boil and boil for 5 minutes. Cover beef pan with the lid and braise in the oven, turning sauerbraten every 30 minutes or so and spooning braising liquid over it, until meat is very tender, about 3 hours. Remove beef from pan and keep warm, covered with foil.

8. Strain and degrease the braising liquid and discard

the solids. Place the braising liquid in a small saucepan and add the remaining marinade along with the sherry and the 15 g (1 tbsp) brown sugar. Boil the liquid until it is reduced by half, about 10 minutes. Add the additional brown sugar, if desired and/or lemon juice to taste. Adjust seasoning.

9. Carve roast against the grain into slices that are about 8-mm (⅜-in) thick. Arrange slices on a serving platter, spoon sauce over them and garnish with parsley sprigs.

POT-AU-FEU

This fabulous French country dish did *not* make a grand comeback in the eighties and nineties—but we're hoping it will over the next decade. People are a little intimidated by it, perhaps, because it raises so many questions about cooking and serving; it's one of those French classics fraught with controversy. We say: relax! Boil up a hunk of beef with some vegetables, serve them together with the broth and you've got about as satisfying a January meal as you're going to find. Of course, we *are* particularly loyal to one cut of beef for this dish: the little-used beef shank, an enormous round of meat that simultaneously produces a delicious broth *and* provides fantastically tender fall-off-the-bone meat. When buying a beef shank, have your butcher cut the piece from the centre of the shank because the ends tend to be very fatty. It may cost more, but you'll end up with more meat.

SERVES 8

4 large onions
6 carrots
4 celery stalks
4 large leeks, washed
50 g (2 oz) unsalted butter
225 g (8 oz) slab bacon
2.7 kg (6 lb) piece of beef shank
10 garlic cloves, smashed

10 g (2 tsp) salt
4 yellow potatoes, peeled and cut in halves
4 medium turnips, peeled
1 large celeriac, peeled and cut in 8 chunks
As accompaniments
coarse salt in a small container
125 ml (4 fl oz) strong Dijon mustard
225 g (8 oz) miniature gherkins
125 ml (4 fl oz) grated horseradish in vinegar

1. Finely chop 2 of the onions, 2 of the carrots and 2 of the celery stalks. Cut off the green parts of the 4 leeks, reserving the white parts and chop the green parts finely. Put the butter in a large, heavy saucepan over low heat. Add the chopped onions and cook for 5 minutes. Add the chopped carrots and cook for 2 minutes longer. Add the chopped celery and the chopped green leeks and cook over low heat until the vegetables are softened, about 10 minutes. Then add enough water to cover vegetables by 2.5 cm (1 in) (this should take about 1.4 litres (2½ pints) water). Increase the heat to high and bring liquid to a boil; reduce the heat and simmer for 20 minutes. Let cool, then strain through a sieve. Reserve stock and discard the vegetables.

2. In a very large, heavy-bottomed pot put the bacon slab fat side down over low heat. Cook until a large amount of the fat has been rendered, about 10 minutes. Remove the bacon and reserve. Pour most of the bacon fat out of the pot. Put the beef shank in the pot and brown the beef on all sides over high heat.

3. When the beef shank is browned, return the reserved bacon to the pot and add the garlic, the 10 g (2 tsp) of salt and the reserved vegetable stock. Add enough water to cover the beef shank (about 1.8 litres (3¼ pints). Bring to a boil and cook for at least 2½ hours at a low simmer (the meat is ready when it easily falls from the bone).

4. Remove the meat from the pot and reserve it in a

bowl. Bring the broth back to a boil. Add the potatoes to the pot along with the turnips and the remaining 2 celery stalks. Cook for 5 minutes. Add the celeriac, the remaining 2 onions, quartered, the remaining 4 carrots, halved lengthways and the reserved white parts of the leeks, halved lengthways. Boil for 5 minutes. Return the reserved meat to the pot. (The liquid should cover the meat and vegetables; if it doesn't add more water.) Bring the broth back to a boil and reduce heat to a simmer. Cook 15 minutes more.

5. When ready to eat, place the beef on a very large dish. Arrange the onions, carrots, leeks, potatoes and celeriac around it. Make sure the broth is piping hot and pour some into 8 soup bowls. Serve immediately and pass around the meat and vegetable platter. Pass another plate containing coarse salt, mustard, gherkins and horseradish.

Serving Note: There are many ways to serve a pot-au-feu. Some like to serve the bowls of broth with pieces of meat and vegetables arranged in them. Some like to serve dinner plates with pieces of meat and vegetables arranged on them and serve the broth on the side. We like this arrangement; each guest is served a piping hot bowl of broth, which he or she can begin to savour as the communal platter of beef and vegetables is passed around. Then, each guest fills up his or her soup bowl with meat and vegetables from the platter. The garnishes may be put on the meat, or on a side plate. Serve with lots of crusty bread, butter and a very fruity, very young red wine (like Beaujolais or a simple Côtes-du-Rhone).

Bollito misto

One of the world's great boiled beef dishes, *bollito misto* means 'mixed boil' in Italian—and more than just beef is included. In Northern Italy, where the dish is a great favourite, it's likely to contain chicken, sausage (like cotechino and zampone), pork cheek, calf's head, calf's feet, veal shank and veal tongue in addition to beef. All of these meats are boiled together slowly in a flavourful broth, then piled up on a grand platter. Italian diners sometimes like to take the broth as a first course, often with some fresh pasta in it. For the main course, the meats are eaten with an herbal sauce (salsa verde) that has vinegar and capers in it, a flavourful tomato sauce and, most distinctively, a kind of relish of whole fruits called *mostarda di Cremona*. The mostarda is sweet from the syrup that coats the fruits, sharp from mustard and utterly delicious with the rich meats. We offer a fabulous version of mostarda di Cremona at our charcuterie counter.

Lamb

Lamb continues to be the one major meat that creates a gastronomic division among Americans.

Upscale diners in major cities, particularly on the coasts, have embraced lamb as never before. For those seeking a big, expensive restaurant portion of red meat, rack of lamb has become as exciting an option as shell steak, prime ribs, or veal chops. No less important has been the 'lamb shank revolution'; trendy restaurants across the country are selling enormous quantities of this inexpensive, long-cooked meat. High-end and low, lamb's presence in our top restaurants is stronger than ever.

But in the heartland, lamb continues to wallow. The average American, in fact, eats less than 900 g (2 lb) of lamb a year; considering all the lamb consumed by lamb-lovers, this amazing per capita statistic must add up to an awful lot of people who eat no lamb at all.

Why this division? Apparently, people love lamb and hate it for the exact same reason: its distinctive flavour. Interestingly, in Europe—where far more lamb is consumed—most of the sheep are slaughtered younger, which means that European lamb generally has a more delicate flavour than the older American lamb. If you're on the fence about lamb, keep this in mind: acquiring younger lamb from your butcher will mean less of that 'lamby' flavour. There's an official category called 'baby lamb', or 'hothouse lamb'; this is meat from sheep that were slaughtered under 6 weeks of age and is delicate in flavour. Much more widely available is 'spring lamb', from sheep slaughtered under 4 months of age; it's not the same as European spring lamb, which is much younger and more delicate than American spring lamb. Now if you have the opposite problem—that is, you can't get *enough* lamb flavour—you might want to consider mutton, which comes from sheep slaughtered after one year of age. Paradoxically, Europeans, who prize very young lamb, also prize very old lamb— sometimes waiting as much as 2 years to slaughter sheep for mutton. This strong-tasting lamb is practically impossible to find in the United States.

One great lamb development of the eighties and nineties—as with most other gastronomic products—is that so many more options are now open to Americans. Lamb at butcher shops was once just lamb; these days, butchers will discuss slaughter age and sheep sources with you. You can also specify domestic lamb or lamb; American lamb is very fine, but there's an enormous amount of terrific lamb coming into the country (about 18 million kg (40 million lb) per year, in fact) from New Zealand and Australia. Other countries may soon follow suit; look out for some of the most delicate lamb you've ever tasted that is trickling in from Iceland. Lastly, of course, there are boutique sheep farms—such as Jamison Farm in Pennsylvania and Whippoorwill Farms in Connecticut—that will send you high-quality lamb through the mail.

Alas, domestic lamb these days is bred to be a little leaner than it used to be, but the situation hasn't reached the disastrous gastronomic proportions of the low-fat pork situation; there's plenty of juicy tenderness left in this product. In fact, lamb is arguably still the most consistently delicious product offered by American butchers and one of the easiest meats to cook properly at home.

LAMB CHOPS

Lamb chops (along with roast leg of lamb) have always been one of America's favourite cuts of lamb. They are quick and easy to prepare and deliver a payload of flavour without any marination or saucing. They once had the additional virtue of being relatively inexpensive, but this is no longer the case.

If it's value you're after, you might want to consider the cheapest lamb chop: the shoulder chop. It is shot through with bone and fat and has no thick, luscious 'eye' as other chops do—but the bone and fat give it plenty of flavour. Unfortunately, the meat is sometimes tough, which is a problem if you're quick cooking the lamb to rare or medium-rare; happily, the meat is sometimes quite tender and is delicious after a quick grill. There's simply no way to tell which kind of meat you have. But keep in mind that thick-cut shoulder chops are wonderful meat for long, slow braising and will always be tender when they're done.

If you're planning to cook your chops quickly to rare or medium-rare (by grilling or frying), rib chops are much more reliable (and much more expensive, too). They feature a wonderful 'eye' of meat and lots of tasty peripheral meat along the bone. In Spain, thin-cut baby rib chops (chuletitas) are grilled over vine-wood fires until they're well-done; the meat is so delicate that this degree of doneness works very well. Rib chops available in America, however, taste better when cooked much less—just enough to sear the outside and bring the inside to about 54.5°C (130°F) on a quick-read meat thermometer (medium-rare). Rib chops are usually cut about 2 cm (¾ in) thick.

An even more lush, velvety lamb is to be had with loin chops, which—like T-bone and porterhouse steaks—offer a 'shell' side and a 'filet' side. For these expensive chops, we like a really thick cut—5 cm (2 in) or so—which allows the exterior to get good and crusty, without a risk of overcooking the interior.

PAN-FRIED DOUBLE THICK LAMB CHOPS WITH OLIVE-ANCHOVY-ORANGE BUTTER

Double-thick loin lamb chops from a great butcher (like ours) are so good that little extra flavour is required. But the pats of butter that go on the chops in this recipe are certainly worth the effort, because they support the flavour of the lamb—and have the additional virtue of transporting you immediately to the south of France. This is a really fast and easy recipe that will stand up perfectly at an elegant dinner party.

SERVES 4

For the olive-anchovy-orange butter
45 g (3 tbsp) shallots
10 ml (2 tsp) balsamic vinegar
10 ml (2 tsp) water
5 g (2 oz) unsalted butter, softened
13 g (1½ tbsp) finely chopped Mediterranean black
   olives
5 anchovy fillets, chopped
5 g (1 tsp) chopped fresh rosemary
3 g (¾ tsp) chopped orange zest
salt and pepper to taste
For the lamb chops
50 ml (2 fl oz) vegetable oil
25 g (1 oz) butter
4 double-thick loin lamb chops, trimmed and
   brought to room temperature (each about 5 cm
   (2 in) thick and 225 g (½ lb))
salt and pepper to taste
small rosemary sprigs for garnish

1. *Make the olive-anchovy-orange butter:* Cook together the shallots, balsamic vinegar and water in a small frying pan over moderate heat, stirring, until dry, about 3 minutes. Set aside to cool slightly. In a bowl stir together the shallot mixture with the butter, olives, anchovies, rosemary, orange zest and salt and pepper with a fork until well combined. In greaseproof paper or clingfilm, shape the butter mixture into a 2.5-cm (1-in) wide log and refrigerate until firm enough to slice.

2. *Make the lamb chops:* In a large, heavy frying pan heat the oil and butter over moderately high heat until hot but not smoking. Season the chops generously with salt and pepper and cook, turning occasionally with tongs, to desired doneness, about 15 minutes for medium-rare.

3. To serve, arrange each chop in the centre of a plate. Slice the olive-anchovy-orange butter into 8 rounds and arrange 2 rounds on each chop. Garnish with a small rosemary sprig.

RACK OF LAMB

Rack of lamb has zoomed to the top of the charts in restaurant lamb-eating popularity and rightly so: the eye of the rack, with its wonderful contiguous nugget of fat, is one of the silkiest, most succulent bites in all of meat-eating.

Happily, rack of lamb is very easy to make at home; we're hoping that this great treat will soon go from restaurant specialty to home staple. Moreover, though it's an expensive purchase, the quality of this item from butcher shops is consistently good; it's much more likely that you'll get stuck with a mediocre steak than a mediocre rack of lamb.

There are a few decisions to make about the butcher's work with your rack of lamb. The rack is the rib section of the lamb, at the beginning of the foresaddle, right next to the loin—all of the rib chops connected together in a single piece. Each side of the lamb contains one rack and each rack contains 7 ribs. How many racks should you buy to feed your guests? We normally figure one whole rack (7 ribs) for 2 people; if your guests don't have large appetites, 2 racks could feed 5 or 6 people.

Next comes the question of fat removal. After the butcher removes the backbone and chine bone and the long tips of the rib bones, he will slice off some of the sheath of fat that lies on top of the rack. If you want a more 'elegant' rack, encourage him to slice off most or all of it. He will then crack the rack between the bones to facilitate easy cutting once the rack is cooked. Now do you want your rack 'Frenched'? This means that the butcher cuts away all meat and fat between the ribs, leaving a rich eye of meat on each 'chop' with spindly, naked bones protruding from it. It looks more elegant, to be sure—but why would you want to deprive yourself of all that juicy interrib nibbling? Your call.

There are a few further decisions. Your overall goal in cooking rack of lamb is creating a crunchy, brown exterior, while keeping the inner meat rare. Grilling a rack of lamb over hot charcoal is a good solution, though perhaps not an everyday one. If you're cooking your rack indoors, it's best to do it in two stages. First, the outside gets browned in oil over high heat in a heavy frying pan; then, the rack is placed in a hot oven to finish. This combination gives the best results.

Do you want a crumb coating on the exterior of the rack? This is a traditional French frill for rack of lamb and though rack of lamb is still utterly delicious without it we do find that it adds an extra layer of excitement to the whole Rack of Lamb Event.

HERB-CRUSTED RACK OF LAMB

This is a delicious coating for rack of lamb, giving the already-succulent meat a subtle Provençal flavour. But if you'd rather not fuss with a crust, use the heat and timing directions in this recipe anyway—just eliminate the mustard and crumbs. Cooking time is the same for crumbed and uncrumbed racks of lamb.

SERVES 4 TO 6

25 g (1 oz) chopped fresh parsley
25 g (1 oz) chopped fresh tarragon
25 g (1 oz) chopped fresh rosemary
30 g (2 tbsp) chopped fresh thyme
225 g (8 oz) freshly made breadcrumbs (not too fine)
20 g (4 tsp) garlic, chopped
20 g (1½ tbsp) stoned oil-cured black olives,

chopped
125 ml (4 fl oz) olive oil
salt and pepper to taste
2 racks of lamb (each about 1 kg (2-2½ lb), Frenched if desired)
30 ml (2 tbsp) Dijon mustard

1. Preheat oven to 230°C (450°F).

2. Combine the fresh herbs, breadcrumbs, garlic, olives and 50 ml (5 tbsp) of olive oil. Season with salt and pepper and set aside.

3. In a large omelette pan heat rest of the olive oil until hot but not smoking. Season the racks with salt and pepper, place in the pan and cook until crispy brown on both sides, about 7 minutes. If the racks seem crowded, use two pans, or cook one rack at a time.

4. Remove the racks from the pan and carefully brush with mustard on the section right over the eyes of the chops and the section directly in front of the eyes of the chops; this will create one mass of mustard over the rounded top and front of the racks (do not spread mustard on skinny rib bones or on the undersides of racks). Gently pat the herb mixture on the mustard and place racks on an oiled roasted pan, crust side up. Cook in the preheated oven until rack reaches an internal temperature of 54°C (130°F), about 10 to 12 minutes, or 12 to 15 minutes for fattier racks. Allow racks to rest 10 minutes before carving.

LAMB ROAST

Many Americans know lamb best as a well cooked Sunday roast. Compared to the velvety-rare chops and racks described above, the roast is practically a different animal.

PROVENÇAL ROAST LEG OF LAMB WITH CARAMELISED AUBERGINE

This leg of lamb is infused with the old flavours of Provence. And a newfangled trick makes it even more delicious: by roasting aubergine along with the lamb, the pan juices get sweeter and darker, leading to a delicious made-in-the-pan gravy.

SERVES 8

4.5-kg (10-lb) leg of lamb, trimmed of excess fat
6 large garlic cloves, cut into slivers
30 ml (2 tbsp) olive oil
70 g (2½ oz) chopped fresh rosemary
50 g (2 oz) chopped fresh thyme
10 g (2 tsp) salt
5 g (1 tsp) ground black pepper
two 450-g (1-lb) aubergines, cut into 2.5-g (1-in) cubes
450 ml (16 fl oz) lamb or beef stock

1. Make 1-cm (½-in) slits all over the leg of lamb with the tip of a paring knife and insert slivers of garlic into each one.

2. Rub olive oil over the lamb, followed by the chopped rosemary and thyme. Sprinkle with the salt and pepper and place in a roasting tin large enough to hold both the lamb and the aubergine. Refrigerate, covered, for 4 hours.

3. Bring lamb to room temperature before proceeding. (Allow 2 hours for the lamb to come to room temperature.) Preheat oven to 190°C (375°F).

4. Place lamb, uncovered, in the middle of the oven and roast for 1 hour. Spread aubergine cubes around lamb and roast the lamb for 30 minutes more, basting aubergine and lamb with any accumulated pan juices or fat and stirring the aubergine so that it doesn't stick to the bottom. Continue roasting for another 45 minutes, or until the internal temperature is about 57°C (135°F) (for medium-rare). Remove roast to carving board and allow it to rest 15 minutes before carving.

5. While the roast is resting, degrease the pan juices. Then add stock to roasting tin and place pan over high heat. Boil until stock is reduced to about 1½ cups. Strain and taste for seasoning.

6. Carve the lamb and arrange the meat on a platter, spooning pan gravy over the meat.

ROAST SHOULDER OF LAMB, EASTERN MEDITERRANEAN STYLE

Shoulder of lamb, normally weighing 4 to 6 pounds, is a very flavourful cut; unfortunately, the meat is not particularly tender. The following marinade solves the problem: soaking the lamb in yogurt for two days breaks down the meat fibres, yielding a deliciously tender piece of meat. Some like to have the butcher bone and roll their shoulder of lamb—but we prefer to roast it bone-in, which adds even more flavour to an already flavourful dish. This preparation is delicious with a yogurt and cucumber salad on the side, a rice pilaf (see page 228) and good pitta bread.

SERVES 6

350 ml (12 fl oz) plain yogurt
15 g (1 tbsp) dried oregano
7.5 g (1½ tsp) ground marjoram
5 g (1 tsp) salt
2.5 g (¼ tsp) freshly ground black pepper
1.8 kg (4-lb) shoulder of lamb, bone-in

1. Combine the yogurt, oregano, marjoram, salt and pepper. Place the lamb in a pan just large enough to hold it and cover with the yogurt mixture. Marinate, covered and refrigerated, 2 days.

2. When ready to cook, preheat oven to 230°C (450°F). Wipe the marinade from the lamb (it should be dry).

Place lamb in roasting tin and place pan in oven. Roast for 15 minutes. Reduce the heat to 180°C (350°F) and continue to roast until lamb reaches an internal temperature of 63°C (145°F) (medium, about 45 minutes). Remove from oven, rest for 15 minutes, carve and serve.

LAMB STEWS

The long-cooked flavour of lamb is delicious in stews; it blends terrifically with well-chosen other flavours. Your biggest decision concerns the bones. Chunks of lamb without bone create a more elegant stew; bone-in chunks of lamb are less expensive and create a more rustic stew. We love lamb stew either way.

SPANISH LAMB STEW WITH WHITE BEANS AND CHORIZO

The boneless lamb in this delicious cassoulet-like stew makes for polite knife-and-fork eating. This dish tastes best when eaten right after cooking; it will not improve in the refrigerator, as many other stews do. Serve with a green salad and a good bottle of red Rioja.

SERVES 6

90 ml (6 tbsp) olive oil
350 g (12 oz) chorizo, cut into 1-cm (½-in) slices
2 medium onions, sliced thinly
6 garlic cloves, sliced thinly
1 kg (2½ lb) boneless leg of lamb, cut into 2.5-cm
  (1-in) cubes
125 ml (4 fl oz) red wine
30 ml (2 tbsp) sherry vinegar
225 ml (8 fl oz) rich beef stock
400 g (14-ounce) can plum tomatoes
3 bay leaves
2.5 g (½ tsp) Spanish paprika
50 g (2 oz) chopped fresh marjoram (optional)
salt and pepper to taste
550g (1¼ lb) cooked white beans

1. Heat 45 ml (3 tbsp) of the olive oil in a large casserole over moderately high heat. Add chorizo and sauté until browned, about 5 minutes. Add onions and garlic and sauté, stirring occasionally, until browned, about 5 minutes more. Remove contents of pan and set aside.

2. Add remaining 45 ml (3 tbsp) of olive oil to pan and heat until hot but not smoking. Add lamb cubes and cook until evenly browned, about 10 minutes. (Make sure the pan is not overcrowded; if it is, brown the lamb in batches.)

3. When all the lamb is browned, place chorizo-onion-garlic mixture back in pan. Increase heat to high and add red wine and sherry vinegar. Scrape the bottom of the pan with a wooden spoon to release any caramelised bits. Then, add beef stock and plum tomatoes with their juice. Stir, breaking up the tomatoes with the wooden spoon. Add bay leaves and paprika. If using marjoram, add half of it now. Season to taste with salt and pepper.

4. Bring the liquid slowly to a boil, then reduce the heat to low and partially cover. Simmer gently, stirring occasionally, for 1 hour. Remove the lid and simmer another 45 minutes, or until lamb is extremely tender. Remove bay leaves.

5. Add white beans to stew and stir to combine. Cook over low heat until beans are heated through, about 5 minutes. Adjust seasoning and serve. If using marjoram, stir in remaining 30 ml (2 tbsp) just before serving.

GREEK LAMB STEW WITH ARTICHOKES, ORZO, AND AVGOLEMONO SAUCE

Cooking this fabulous, subtle stew with bone-in lamb adds more flavour to the dish. Encourage your guests to pick up the bony lamb chunks with their fingers and to drink lots of retsina.

SERVES 6

1.8 kg (4 pounds) lamb shoulder, bone-in, cut into
  5-cm (2-inch) pieces
30 ml (2 tbsp) Greek olive oil
1 large onion, sliced
2 celery stalks with leaves, cut into coarse chunks
1 carrot, sliced
1½ quarts chicken stock
250 ml (1 pint) water
muslin bag containing 8 peppercorns, 8 sprigs
  parsley, 1 bay leaf, 15 g (1 tbsp) chopped fresh
  rosemary leaves or 5 g (1 tsp) dried
8 artichokes
100 ml (4 fl oz) orzo
5 large eggs
100 ml (4 fl oz) fresh lemon juice
100 ml (4 fl oz) double cream
50 g (2 oz) snipped fresh dill

1. Place the lamb in a casserole over high heat and cover with water. Bring to a boil, reduce heat and simmer, removing any froth that floats to the surface, for 5 minutes. Drain and reserve lamb.

2. Return the empty casserole to the stove over moderate heat. Add the olive oil, then add the onion, celery and carrot. Cook, stirring occasionally, until vegetables are softened, about 5 minutes. Add stock, water, muslin bag and reserved lamb chunks. Season to taste with salt. Increase heat to high, bring liquid to a boil and then reduce heat. Let stew simmer, partially covered, for 1½ hours.

3. Cut off part of the stem of each artichoke, leaving about 1 cm (½ in) of stem on each one. Remove the outer leaves from each artichoke until you can see the bulge of the artichoke bottom defined through the remaining leaves. Quarter each artichoke lengthwise (this will expose the hairy chokes). Working with a small, sharp knife, cut out as much of the chokes as possible. While working, rub all cut surfaces with lemon juice.

4. When lamb is done cooking, transfer it to a bowl and strain cooking liquid. Return lamb and strained cooking liquid to casserole, bring liquid to a boil and add artichokes. Reduce heat to low and simmer, partially covered, for 10 minutes. Add orzo and simmer, partially covered, for 15 minutes.

5. In a bowl whisk eggs well until light in colour. Whisk in lemon juice and 225 ml (8 fl oz) of hot cooking liquid, a little at a time. Remove casserole from heat and stir in double cream, then slowly stir in egg mixture. Return casserole to low heat and cook until stew is slightly thickened. (Do not allow stew to boil.) Just before serving, stir in fresh dill. Taste for seasoning and serve.

LAMB SHANKS

Lamb shanks—the last joint of the lamb leg—have become one of the trendiest meat items on restaurant menus. Touched off in the eighties by the success of Tom Valenti's lamb shanks at Allison's on Dominick, a restaurant not too far from our New York store, the lamb shank explosion in restaurants is even making it difficult for home cooks to find lamb shanks at butcher shops. Why are they so popular? With long, slow, moist cooking, they emerge from the pot tender and almost gelatinous, filled with a deep lamb flavour. And the bone with which they cook adds even more flavour to the braising liquid. Furthermore, diners seem to appreciate a whole one of something placed before them—in this case a shank, which looks something like a minileg.

LAMB SHANKS BRAISED IN RED WINE WITH ROOT VEGETABLES, SERVED WITH ROSEMARY GREMOLATA

This delicious, wintry dish is great with polenta.

SERVES 4

For the lamb shanks
45 ml (3 tbsp) olive oil

4 small meaty lamb shanks (about 2 kg
  (4½ pounds) total), trimmed of fat
salt and pepper to taste
1 large onion, chopped
4 carrots, finely diced
3 small sprigs of fresh rosemary
2 bay leaves
4 garlic cloves, chopped
560 ml (1½ pints) big-bodied young red wine
450 g (1 lb) of parsnips, peeled and cut into 5-mm
  (¼-in) rounds
For the rosemary gremolata
10 g (2 tsp) chopped fresh rosemary
10 g (2 tsp) finely grated fresh orange zest
1 small garlic clove, chopped

1. Preheat oven to 180°C (350°F). Heat the olive oil in a large, deep casserole with a tight-fitting lid over moderate heat until hot but not smoking. Season the lamb shanks with salt and pepper and cook, in batches if necessary, turning with tongs, until well browned, about 10 minutes each batch. Remove the lamb shanks with tongs to a plate and set aside.

2. Stir the onion, carrots, rosemary, bay leaves and garlic into the casserole and cook, stirring, until the onions are very soft, about 5 minutes. Add 650 ml (1 pint) of the wine and deglaze the pan. Bring the mixture to a boil, reduce the heat and simmer for 5 minutes. Taste for seasoning.

3. Return the lamb shanks to the casserole and braise the mixture, tightly covered, in the oven, turning the shanks once, for 1½ hours. Stir in the parsnips and the rest of the wine and continue to braise, covered, in the oven for 30 minutes. Discard the bay leaves. Season to taste with salt and pepper.

4. *While the lamb shanks are braising, make the gremolata:* Chop together the rosemary, orange zest and garlic. Place each lamb shank on a serving plate, top

with the vegetables, sprinkle with gremolata and serve immediately.

TURKISH-STYLE LAMB SHANKS BRAISED WITH VEGETABLES

Turkish lamb dishes are among the best in the world. This is so, in part, because Turkish sheep graze on wild thyme. Our American sheep don't—so we've added some thyme to the following to compensate. You could leave the meat on the bones if desired.

SERVES 4

6 tablespoons olive oil
2 large onions, chopped
4 trimmed lamb shanks (about 2 kg (4½ lb)
8 large ripe tomatoes, peeled, seeded, and chopped
1 to 4 hot chillies (like serranos or jalapeños),
  seeded if desired and chopped
12 garlic cloves, chopped
12 sprigs of fresh thyme
4 bay leaves
10 g (2 tsp) ground cumin
1.25 g (¼ tsp) ground cloves
1.25 g (¼ tsp) allspice
450 ml (16 fl oz) hot water
50 g (2 oz) chopped fresh flat-leaf parsley plus
  additional for garnish
4 red peppers, roasted, peeled, seeded and chopped
salt and pepper to taste

1. Heat the oil in a large, deep casserole over moderate heat until hot but not smoking. Add the onions and cook, stirring, until lightly browned, about 10 minutes. Remove the onions and set aside. Add the lamb shanks, in batches if necessary and brown all sides, about 15 minutes. Stir in the browned onions, tomatoes, chillies, garlic, thyme, bay leaves, cumin, cloves and allspice and cook, stirring, for 5 minutes.

2. Stir in the water, cover and cook at a bare simmer,

stirring occasionally, for 2 hours. Remove the lamb shanks with tongs and when cool enough to handle remove and shred the meat. Try to get some of the marrow from the bones and add the meat and marrow to the casserole with the parsley and roasted peppers. Season to taste with salt and pepper. Cook gently, uncovered, stirring occasionally, for 30 minutes longer, adding a bit more water, if necessary. Serve hot with rice.

SKEWERED LAMB

Lamb is the king of meat in Greek and Middle Eastern cooking; it's a staple of the diet as well as a symbol of religious sacrifice, of celebration and of hospitality. One of the favourite ways to cook lamb in this part of the world is on skewers, over a hot open fire—a practice that has become increasingly popular among American chefs. There are two traditional ways of cooking lamb on skewers: chunks of meat (called *kebabs*) and chopped meat (known as *kofta*).

SHISH KEBAB

This Greek version of skewered lamb chunks is a particularly mirthful summer barbecue item. Serve with a big Greek salad, lots of warmed pitta and chilled retsina.

MAKES 6 TO 8 SKEWERS, ENOUGH FOR 3 TO 4 DINERS

900 g (2 lb) boneless leg of lamb, cut in ¾-inch cubes
30 g (2 tbsp) dried oregano
15 g (1 tbsp) dried marjoram
5 g (1 tsp) salt
2.5 g (½ tsp) black pepper
125 ml (4 fl oz) retsina (or other white wine)
50 ml (2 fl oz) Greek olive oil
juice from ¼ lemon
3 garlic cloves, chopped
15 g (1 tbsp) sweet paprika

1. Coat the lamb cubes with 15 g (1 tbsp) of the dried oregano, the dried marjoram, the salt and the pepper.

2. In a large bowl mix together the retsina, olive oil, lemon juice and garlic. Add lambcubes to bowl and mix well. Marinate, covered and refrigerated, for 7 to 12 hours.

3. When ready to cook, prepare a hot charcoal fire. Remove lamb cubes from marinade and pat dry. Thread onto 6 to 8 skewers (depending on how many cubes you like on each skewer). Sprinkle the remaining tablespoon of dried oregano over each side of the skewered lamb along with the paprika. Sprinkle lightly with salt and pepper.

4. Place skewers on the hot fire. Cook, turning frequently and basting with marinade, until all sides are brown, about 7 minutes for medium-well meat. Serve immediately.

GRILLED LAMB KOFTA

This is a basic recipe for chopped lamb shaped on skewers. Very important in all koftas is the smooth texture that comes from mincing the lamb twice and from the thorough mixing like kneading bread dough, very unlike the coarse British and American mince where a quick and gentle mixing is the only way to keep the meat tender.

MAKES 8 SKEWERS

1 large onion, grated
15 g (1 tbsp) coarse salt
900 g (2 lb) lamb, ground twice
2 large eggs, lightly beaten
70 g (2½ oz) chopped fresh coriander
10 g (2 tsp) ground cumin
5 g (1 tsp) dried thyme
5 g (1 tsp) ground allspice

freshly ground black pepper to taste
olive oil for oiling skewers, lamb and grill

1. Stir together the onion and salt in a small bowl and let stand for 15 minutes.

2. Place the lamb in a large bowl. Squeeze onion juice out of the salted onion through a very fine strainer or muslin into the bowl with the lamb. Add the eggs, coriander, cumin, thyme, allspice and pepper and mix thoroughly, kneading with your hands and pounding the meat against the side of the bowl with a wooden spoon, for 2 minutes. Let the mixture stand at room temperature for 1 hour.

3. Prepare a charcoal fire.

4. With moist hands, shape the lamb into 8 sausages, about 2.5 cm (1 in) in diameter and 10 cm (4 in) long and taper the ends of the sausage shapes to keep the meat from slipping off the skewers during cooking. Oil 8 metal skewers and put the skewers through each sausage. Oil the surfaces of each sausage.

5. Grill the kofta on an oiled grill, preferably about 10 cm (4 in) above the hot coals, until evenly browned on the outside and pink on the inside. (Alternatively, the kofta may be cooked in the oven, about 5 minutes per side.) Serve hot with tzatziki (page 495) and pitta on the side. The kofta may be slipped off the skewers and served in pitta with the tzatziki, tomatoes and fresh parsley.

Venison
Though there has always been a small, dedicated band of deer hunters in the United States and though the object of their sport has appeared on American tables in game season (autumn), venison has hardly been popular in America. Beyond what has been described by foreigners as 'the Bambi problem' (our unwillingness to consume an animal we identify with in Disney movies), there is a gustatory problem as well: Americans have never taken to the gamey, traditional taste of venison, which is produced by 'hanging' the meat for a long time. The result of hanging was often tough, strong-flavoured meat, which required marinades and strong-flavoured sauces. It was all too strange and troublesome for most Americans.

Why, then, has venison become a hot, trendy menu item in the last decade?

Principally, we submit, because producers around the world have realised that fresh-tasting, unhung venison would be of greater appeal to the American consumer. Farms sprang up to raise deer that would come to the table consistently tender and with a very mild taste. The movement may have started in the U.S. South-west, where locally raised Axis venison became the rage. But even more important, on the national scene, has been the rise of Cervena.

Cervena is a newly coined word for farm-raised venison that's grown in New Zealand. Thousands of small producers there have banded together, under government supervision, to export a uniform product called 'Cervena'. It arrives in the United States both fresh and frozen. It is absolutely delicious: silky, velvety, tender, milder in flavour than beef. It is widely available today on restaurant menus across the country—but home cooks have yet to realise that it's one of the simplest meats of all to cook at home. The only imperative is cooking it a short time; once the meat goes past rare, its lack of fat makes it seem dry and unappealing.

When you find a source for Cervena, you will discover a somewhat bewildering array of cuts that you can use (such as boneless striploin, boneless tenderloin, boneless silverside, Denver topside and Denver rump). They are all cooked in the same way: high temperature (by shallow frying, roasting, or grilling) for a relatively short time (to assure a crusty outside and a rare inside). To make things as easy as possible, we always buy the same cut of Cervena. Our favourite one is the rack.

RACK OF CERVENA WITH TEXAS BARBECUE SAUCE

The rack of Cervena is very much like a rack of lamb in shape, though it's larger. It contains 8 ribs, but may be cut into two 4-rib racks. Remember—sharp or fruity sauces are not needed for Cervena, as they are for traditional venison, because the meat is mild-tasting to begin with. Nevertheless, we're very fond of rack of Cervena coated with a tangy Texas barbecue sauce. Serve with black beans and mashed potatoes that have been mixed with roasted poblano chillies.

SERVES 4

50 g (2 oz) lard or 50 ml (2 fl oz) vegetable oil
rack of Cervena
salt and pepper to taste
225 ml (8 fl oz) Texas barbecue sauce (see page 489)

1. Preheat oven to 220°C (425°F).

2. Place the lard or vegetable oil in a large, heavy frying pan over high heat. Season the rack of Cervena well with salt and pepper. When the oil is very hot, add the rack to the pan and cook, turning frequently, until the meat is seared on all sides, about 5 to 7 minutes. Remove from pan.

3. Place Cervena in a roasting tin and brush half the barbecue sauce all over it. Roast Cervena in oven for 7 minutes. Brush the remaining barbecue sauce over the meat. Roast until the meat registers 46°C (115°F) on a quick-read thermometer, about 12 to 15 minutes total cooking time. Remove from oven and let meat rest 15 minutes before carving.

OFFAL

Though eating practices in the United States over the last 2 decades have become more like those in Europe, the consumption of offal is still the great divider. Perhaps it's a long tradition of frugality that makes Europeans so happy eating the inexpensive organs of animals; perhaps it's New World conspicuous consumption that makes Americans abhor these very parts.

Whatever the explanation for the discontinuity, Americans have long missed out on some fabulous eating.

Happily, at least in American restaurants, the offal-eating scene has improved a great deal in the last decade. It has happened at both the high end and low end of the scale. The birth of an indigenous foie gras industry in the eighties has spawned a new generation of American diners crazed for the taste of duck liver. And the persistence of some American restaurant chefs in offering the less luxurious offal—like Lydia Shire at Biba in Boston—has led to much wider interest in such items as tripe, sweetbreads and brains.

Foie Gras

Foie gras means 'fat liver'—though 'fattened liver' would be a better description. For this product, which dates back at least to the Egyptians of 2500 B.C. or so, is made by forcing geese and ducks to eat more than they would normally eat. The livers of the birds become much larger and, at the same time, much more succulent. The result is a creamy, fatty, ultra-seductive chew that sends a shiver down the spine of most diners. Even people who hate other offal—heck, even people who hate liver!—are often won over by the extraordinary taste and texture of foie gras.

It is France that we most associate with this delicacy, particularly the regions of Perigord and Alsace—though significant amounts of foie gras consumed in France have been produced in Eastern Europe and in Israel. But no fresh foie gras produced abroad can be legally imported into the United States. Until a small company in New York State started producing fresh foie gras in the early eighties, not a speck of it was available there legally. No wonder Americans never took to foie gras: the only foie gras formerly available was cooked foie gras in little cans, which is to fresh foie gras what cooked peas in cans are to fresh peas.

With the arrival of Hudson Valley Foie Gras, in New York's Catskill Mountains, however, fresh, uncooked, fattened duck livers became available to chefs around the United States. Today, just a decade later, it's virtually impossible to find a menu from a top restaurant in America—even a high-end ethnic restaurant!—that doesn't include something made from fresh foie gras.

What's being made? American chefs are basically echoing the two main methods of foie gras cooking in France: terrines (called *terrine* or *pâté de foie gras*) and sautéed slices (usually called *foie gras chaud*). There has been much debate among foie gras lovers as to which of these is more delectable.

Good news for home cooks: both methods are really very simple. The terrine involves packing fresh pieces of liver in a loaf tin and cooking them in a very slow oven until the pieces have melted together into a loaf. The terrine de foie gras is then chilled and sliced. The resulting chew is unbelievably velvety, though the texture is firmer than the texture of sautéed foie gras slices.

Sautéed foie gras slices are even easier to do: you simply cut thick slices from a fresh liver and sauté them in butter, oil, or fat over high heat. Within moments, they're seared on the outside, fantastically creamy—almost runny—within. They are served hot, usually with a sauce.

Buying fresh foie gras

You can buy whole fattened duck livers at our store, or you can obtain them directly from the distributor, D'Artagnan, by calling directly 800-DAR-TAGN. A whole, fresh duck liver usually runs from 675-900 g (1½ to 2 lb). You must buy a whole liver; it is not possible to buy a smaller quantity. Because some of these recipes call for less than a whole liver, plan to use your leftover

foie gras in other ways. You may be given a choice of an 'A' foie gras or a 'B' foie gras. The 'A' is smoother, more expensive and essential for sautéed slices of foie gras. The 'B' is less expensive and more veiny—but after proper deveining, it works beautifully in a terrine.

Incidentally, only duck foie gras is produced in the United States today. If you want the richer fresh goose foie gras—the choice of many French chefs for a cold foie gras terrine—you'll still have to go to France. Happily, most chefs concur that duck foie gras is better for hot sautéed foie gras slices.

TERRINE OF FOIE GRAS

If you're making this deliriously delicious treat for a big dinner party, start it 5 to 6 days in advance. The reason: though a foie gras terrine tastes good enough 2 days after it's made, a 5-day sojourn in the refrigerator 'ripens' the terrine, makes it more velvety and deeper in flavour. The terrine mould to use for this dish, by the way, should just hold the pieces of duck liver, with very little extra room; a 1.2-litre (2-pint) terrine should be about right.

SERVES 18 AS A FIRST COURSE

2 fresh duck foie gras (each about 675 g (1½ lb), see box opposite)
7.5 g (¾ tbsp) sea salt
5 g (1 tsp) freshly ground white pepper
pinch of ground cinnamon
pinch of ground allspice
pinch of ground cloves
pinch of ground nutmeg
10 ml (1 tbsp) cognac

1. Separate the two lobes of the liver by gently pulling them apart. Scrape away any traces of green bile and allow the foie gras to warm up slightly so it is more manageable to clean. (Be careful not to let the liver get too warm or it will melt in your hands.)

2. To clean the foie gras, use a small knife and carefully dig into the middle of each lobe, slipping the vein under the knife tip and pulling it out. Gently pull out (with a knife or your fingers) any other veins you see throughout the liver. (Do not be concerned if in the deveining process you separate the foie gras into chunks; just make sure that the chunks are at least as large as golf balls.)

3. Fill a large bowl with ice water and let the foie gras chunks soak for 5 hours.

4. Preheat oven to 120°C (250°F).

5. In a small bowl, combine the sea salt and spices. Remove the livers from the ice bath, dry them and sprinkle them evenly with the spice mixture. Place half of the liver pieces, smooth side down, in a heavy terrine (they should almost completely fill the lower half of the terrine). Place the remaining pieces of liver on top, smooth side up (the terrine should be almost completely filled). Pour 15 ml (1 tbsp) of cognac over the top. Cover the top of terrine with greaseproof paper cut to fit and press down lightly.

6. Place the terrine in a deep roasting tin filled with warm water (just below simmering). Place the pan in the centre of the preheated oven and bake until internal temperature reaches 46°C (115°F), about 20 minutes per pound.

7. Pour the excess fat off the terrine and reserve. Allow the terrine to cool completely, about 2 hours, then pour the reserved fat back over the terrine until the terrine is full. Cover the top with foil and place a piece of cardboard cut out to fit the opening of the terrine. To compress the liver, place about 2.5 kg (5 pounds) of weight on top and refrigerate for at least 2 days.

8. When ready to serve, unmould the terrine and cut with a knife that has been dipped in hot water into slices about ½ inch thick with a coating of yellow fat. Cover slices with wax paper and let sit for a few moments so they may warm slightly. Serve with toasted slices of brioche.

FRESH SEARED FOIE GRAS STEAMED IN LEAVES OF SAVOY CABBAGE

This wonderful dish was inspired by one we tasted at Alain Senderens's L'Archestrate in Paris many years ago. It includes the basic searing process for fresh slices of foie gras . . . but most chefs, after searing the foie gras, serve it with some kind of sweet, fruity sauce. Senderens's innovation was to roll up the foie gras slices in cabbage, steam them lightly, then serve with only salt and pepper. It's wonderfully earthy and utterly simple. If you want to boost the flavour and the luxury quotient, slip a few thin slices of black truffle into each cabbage bundle.

SERVES 4 AS A FIRST COURSE

2 unblemished outer leaves of savoy cabbage (from a large head)
225 g (8 oz) fresh foie gras (see box)
potato flour or other thickener
25 g (1 oz) unsalted butter
coarse salt to taste
freshly ground black pepper to taste
freshly grated nutmeg to taste

1. Bring a large pot of salted water to a boil. Drop the cabbage leaves in the boiling water and cook for 3 minutes. Remove and spread them out on a counter. Cut away the central vein of each leaf, thereby bisecting each leaf. You will now have 4 half leaves of parboiled cabbage. Reserve.

2. Cut the foie gras into 4 pieces, each about 2 cm (¾ in) thick and weighing about 50 g (2 oz). Coat them lightly with the instant flour. Heat the butter in a large, heavy omelette pan over moderately high heat. When the foam subsides, add the foie gras slices and cook them until golden brown, about 1 minute on each side. Remove and drain on paper towels.

3. When ready to serve, spread a half leaf of reserved cabbage out on the counter. Place a slice of foie gras at one of the narrow ends. Season the foie gras and the cabbage with coarse salt and freshly ground pepper. Grate a little nutmeg over the cabbage. Roll up the foie gras snugly in the cabbage. Repeat until all foie gras slices are rolled.

4. Set a steamer tray over a pot of boiling water. Add the cabbage-foie gras rolls, cover and steam for 1 minute. Remove and place on paper towels to drain off excess moisture.

5. Place each cabbage-foie gras roll on an appetiser plate. At the top of the plate, make side-by-side mounds of coarse salt and coarsely ground black pepper. Serve immediately.

MELTED FOIE GRAS ON COUNTRY BREAD WITH ARMAGNAC

This fabulous recipe was inspired by an extraordinary restaurant near Baden-Baden, in Germany. The chef sautéed thick slices of country bread in duck fat, with garlic, then simply melted very thin slices of fresh foie gras over the bread. Though it's astoundingly simple to make, it's a mightily impressive starter for a lusty dinner party.

SERVES 4 AS A FIRST COURSE

115 g (4 oz) fresh foie gras (see box, page 448), chilled until very cold
coarse salt to taste
30 g (2 tbsp) duck fat
2 large garlic cloves, smashed into pieces
4 slices country bread (each about 10 x 7.5 x 2 cm

(4 x 3 x ½ in))
freshly ground black pepper to taste
15 ml (1 tbsp) armagnac

1. Run a long, sharp knife under hot water and shave the foie gras into paper-thin lengthwise slices. Lay the slices, in a single layer, on a platter and sprinkle them liberally with coarse salt. Reserve at room temperature.

2. Melt 15 g (1 tbsp) of the duck fat in a small, heavy omelette pan over low heat. Add half the garlic and cook it for 5 minutes. Push the garlic pieces to one side of the pan and increase the heat to high. Add 2 slices of the country bread and cook them until the undersides are golden brown, about 1 minute. Reduce the heat to low. Working quickly, turn the two slices of bread over and top them with half the shaved foie gras slices. (You will probably create a double layer of thin foie gras slices on top of the bread.) Immediately cover the pan and cook, checking after 30 seconds to make sure the bread is not burning, for about 1 minute, or until the undersides are golden brown. When the bread is done, remove it and top with black pepper and a splash of armagnac.

3. Spill out the fat in the pan and repeat step 2 with the remaining ingredients.

4. Serve immediately.

Calves' Liver

Many people *think* they don't like calves' liver, because they've been exposed only to overcooked, low-quality liver and onions. The fact of the matter is this, however: if you procure fresh, high-quality liver, free from veins and gristle and cook it just right, the sweetness, tenderness and lightness will make your prejudices simply fall away. Indeed, the palate sensation can be somewhat suggestive of foie gras—though there's more of a livery flavour in calves' liver.

SAUTÉED CALVES' LIVER WITH BALSAMIC VINEGAR

The key to sautéing calves' liver is this: start with a thick slice of it. Thin slices get grey and mushy on the inside by the time they're browned on the outside. But a thick slice—say, 4 cm (1½ in) thick—can develop a magnificent crust on the outside, while remaining pink and firm on the inside. Get your liver from a good butcher's and have the butcher custom-cut it for you. Top thick slices of the cooked liver with coarse salt and a drizzle of aged balsamic vinegar, serve it with creamy polenta and watch 'em swoon.

SERVES 4

2 slices of calves' liver (each about 4 cm (1½ in) thick and weighing 225 g (8 oz), as free of veins as possible
salt and pepper to taste
flour for coating
40 g (1½ oz) unsalted butter
coarse salt to taste
15 ml (1 tbsp) aged balsamic vinegar, or more to taste

1. Season the liver well with salt and pepper. Sift a little flour onto the liver, on all sides, to coat it lightly.

2. Place the butter in a heavy omelette pan over moderately high heat. When it's foaming, add the slices of liver. Sauté on one side until the liver is browned, then sauté on the other side (about 4 minutes per side). Reduce the heat to moderate and cook a little longer, turning, until the liver is crusty on the outside, medium-rare on the inside (total cooking time should be about 10 minutes). Remove liver from pan.

3. Cut liver into slices that are approximately 1 cm (½ in) thick. Place them decoratively on dinner plates, sprinkle with coarse salt, drizzle with balsamic vinegar and serve immediately.

Sweetbreads

Of all the offbeat offal, sweetbreads are probably the most acceptable to the largest number of Americans. Why? First of all, they come from an organ (the thymus gland) that people don't identify with, or have a strong image of; eating sweetbreads is not as brutal as eating a stomach or a heart. Secondly, they are extremely mild, positively unoffally in flavour. Lastly, they have a pleasant, mainstream texture—neither too firm nor too soft—a little like chicken or veal.

It is the treatment of that texture, however, that causes some debate among chefs. All chefs agree that sweetbreads should be soaked in water to facilitate removal of the thin membrane around the meat. But, after that removal, some chefs like to cook the sweetbreads just as they are—which yields a slightly puffy, spongy, soft texture. Other chefs like to weigh down the sweetbreads under refrigeration—which leads to a much denser texture, like veal. We prefer the second method.

By the way, when sweetbreads are discussed in America it is almost always the thymus glands of calves that are meant. You can have sweetbreads from other young animals, but they're rare over there. The glands disappear as animals age, so you can't have sweetbreads from older animals.

WARM SWEETBREAD SALAD WITH HARICOTS VERTS, WILD MUSHROOMS AND HAZELNUT VINAIGRETTE

Here is all the information you need for soaking, blanching and weighting down sweetbreads for any recipe. For this warm salad, use the best fresh wild mushrooms you can find—porcini, chanterelles or morels would all be suitable Serve as a first course at an important dinner party.

SERVES 4 AS A FIRST COURSE

450 g (1 lb) calves' sweetbreads
20 g (4 tsp) coarse salt

15 ml (1 tbsp) white-wine vinegar

450 g (1 lb) haricots verts, trimmed at ends

45 ml (3 tbsp) fresh lemon juice

10 ml (2 tsp) balsamic vinegar

45 g (3 tbsp) finely chopped shallots

50 ml (2 fl oz) hazelnut oil

salt to taste

2.5 g (½ tsp) freshly ground black pepper plus
additional to taste

75 ml (2½ fl oz) vegetable oil

450 g (1 lb) wild mushrooms (assorted), cleaned
and trimmed

50 g (2 oz) flour

fresh chervil for garnish

1. Soak the sweetbreads in a large bowl of cold water for 3 hours, changing the water several times. Then remove the sweetbreads from the water and gently pull away as much of the outer membrane as you can, being careful not to tear the flesh. Soak the sweetbreads again for 1 hour, this time in a large bowl of cold water with 5 g (1 tsp) of coarse salt. Remove from the water and peel away more of the membrane. Separate the sweetbreads into its 2 lobes.

2. Fill a medium saucepan with 1.2 litres (2 pints) cold water, 5 g (1 tsp) of coarse salt and the white-wine vinegar. Place the sweetbreads in the pan and slowly bring the water to a simmer over moderate heat (this should take about 10 minutes). Allow the water to simmer very gently for another 5 minutes. (The sweetbreads should be firm on the outside, but still give a little when squeezed.) Remove sweetbreads and place them in ice water for 10 minutes to stop the cooking.

3. Dry sweetbreads and place in a heavy loaf tin or a terrine lined with clingfilm. Cover with another layer of clingfilm. Place another heavy loaf tin or terrine on top to weigh down the sweetbreads and place in the refrigerator for at least 3 hours or overnight.

4. When ready to cook, bring a large saucepan of water to a boil and cook haricots verts until they are crisp but slightly tender, about 5 minutes. Remove and reserve at room temperature.

5. In a small bowl combine the lemon juice with the balsamic vinegar and 15 g (1 tbsp) of the shallots. Slowly whisk in the hazelnut oil. Season to taste with salt and the additional black pepper. Reserve.

6. Place 30 ml (2 tbsp) of the vegetable oil in a large frying pan over moderately high heat. When the oil is hot but not smoking, add remaining shallots and sauté, stirring constantly, for 3 minutes. Add mushrooms, making sure the pan is not overcrowded. (It may be necessary to sauté the mushrooms in 2 batches). Sauté with a big pinch of salt, shaking pan occasionally, until mushrooms are nicely browned, about 5 to 7 minutes. Remove mushrooms from frying pan and reserve. If there is liquid in the pan that the mushrooms have given off, boil it until it is reduced to 30 ml (2 tbsp) and pour over the mushrooms.

7. With a very sharp knife, cut the weighted sweetbreads into broad slices that are about 5 mm (¼ in) thick. Combine the flour, the remaining 10 g (2 tsp) of coarse salt and the black pepper on a plate and mix well. Add the rest of the vegetable oil to the frying pan in which the mushrooms cooked and place over high heat. Dredge sweetbread slices in the seasoned flour on both sides and add to hot oil. Sauté, turning, until sweetbreads are browned and crispy on the outside, about 3 minutes. Remove.

8. Toss reserved haricots verts and mushrooms together. Toss mixture with about half the hazelnut vinaigrette. Place one quarter of the mixture on each of 4 plates. Nestle pieces of the crispy sweetbread slices among the haricot vert/mushroom mixture and drizzle the remaining vinaigrette over the sweetbread slices. Garnish with chervil.

Brains

Many types of brains are eaten around the world, but it is almost universally acknowledged that the finest brains are the more delicate-tasting ones: calf's brains and lamb's brains. In the United States—where brains are nothing but an exotic ethnic specialty—the few places that sell them offer calf's brains only, usually in 'pairs', usually about 350 g (¾ lb) per pair. Though we at Dean & DeLuca are mad for offal, brains are not among our favourites. The mildly earthy taste is almost too subtle to be exciting and the extreme softness of the tissue leaves almost nothing to chew.

However, if you can crisp up the exterior of the brain slices and add just the right amount of sympathetic flavour , this seemingly odd specialty starts to make gastronomic sense.

CUBAN-STYLE DEEP-FRIED CALF'S BRAINS WITH CUMIN AND LIME (SESOS FRITOS)

This is the answer to the brain problem. Brains are much beloved in Cuba, where they are prepared in many different ways. Deep-frying them, however—and offering the crunchy morsels with a wedge of lime—is the most popular method. We've taken this great dish a step further, by giving it the light taste of cumin. Once you get the deep-fried bits to the table, you might also want to consider adding a few drops of your favourite Caribbean hot sauce—not a Cuban touch, but delicious nevertheless. This is an ideal pass-around starter for a night of Latin American dining adventure.

MAKES ENOUGH FOR 8 PEOPLE AS A PASS-AROUND
STARTER

1 pair calf's brains (about 350 g (¾ lb))
45 ml (3 tbsp) lime juice plus lime wedges for
  garnish
5 g (1 tsp) salt
10 g (2 tsp)ground cumin
50 g (2 oz) flour
175 ml (6 fl oz) cold water

225 g (8 oz) fine breadcrumbs or cracker meal
1 litre (1¾ pints) vegetable oil for deep-frying
coarse salt for sprinkling the brains

1. Soak the brains in cold water to cover for about 2 hours. Remove brains from water and pull off as much of the delicate filament that surrounds them as you can.

2. Place brains in a small saucepan and cover with water (about 225 ml (8 fl oz)). Add the 45 ml (3 tbsp) of lime juice and half the salt. Bring to a simmer, then simmer very gently for 15 minutes. Remove brains from water and let cool.

3. When brains are cool enough to handle, cut them into bite-size pieces. Toss them with the rest of the salt and the ground cumin.

4. Place the flour in a bowl and slowly add the cold water, making a medium-thick slurry. Dip the brains in the slurry, coating the pieces well, then roll the brains in the breadcrumbs. Let stand for 5 minutes.

5. Heat the oil in a wok, deep-fryer, or large pot until it reaches 185°C (365°F). Drop the brains into the oil in 2 batches. Cook each batch until the pieces are very crisp and golden brown, about 4 minutes. Drain on paper towels, sprinkle with coarse salt and serve immediately with the lime wedges. Pass hot sauce, if desired.

Tripe

There's nothing in the gastronomic world that divides people as much as tripe does: its devotees are mad for it, its detractors positively detest it.

For many people, the first problem is simply the physical reality of it: tripe is stomach. To be precise, it is the four stomachs of cattle, sheep or other ruminants—though, usually, when tripe is mentioned or sold, the tripe in question is beef tripe. Some diners make no moral distinctions between different animal parts; others find some parts (like stomach) too intimate to consider.

Then there's the texture: tripe, even after long-cooking, is spongy. If you like this texture, you can emphasise it by undercooking; if you dislike this texture, you can mitigate it somewhat by cooking the tripe in liquid for 4 to 5 hours. The best texture of all is in the type of tripe called *gras double (blanket tripe)* (from the large rumen, or first stomach), which is readily available in France and northern England but hard to find elsewhere.

SPANISH TRIPE STEW WITH CHICK PEAS, CHORIZO AND PAPRIKA

It's hard to select our favourite tripe dish of the world: French *gras double* Lyon-style with white wine and onions; Italian tripe with tomatoes and Parmigiano-Reggiano; Mexican tripe with posole; Turkish tripe soup with hot pepper oil (which is served all night in special Istanbul restaurants as a hangover cure). But the manifold tripe dishes of the Iberian peninsula may have the edge, for us—particularly because we're crazy about the pairing of tripe and red, paprika-scented sausage. Serve this stew to your tripe-ambivalent friends on a wintry night and watch their ambivalence disappear along with your stew. If you can, find a freshly packed, deep-tasting, spicy Spanish paprika (pimentón picante) for use in this dish. We sell a great one from the Alicante region called Carmencita, which is amazingly vivid in flavour, with a smoky dimension.

SERVES 4

50 g (2 oz) dried chick peas
900 g (2 lb) tripe, cleaned
350 g (¾ lb) fatty, boneless pork
salt and pepper to taste
30 ml (2 tbsp) flour
125 ml (4 fl oz) olive oil
225 g (½ lb) onions, chopped
8 garlic cloves, chopped
225 ml (8 fl oz) white wine

800-g (28-oz) can plum tomatoes
5 g (1 tsp) hot Spanish paprika
225 g (½ lb) whole chorizo sausages

1. Cover the chick peas with water and soak overnight.

2. Cut the tripe into strips approximately ¾ inch wide and 5 cm (2 in) long. Cut the pork into chunks a little smaller than dice. Salt and pepper well the tripe and pork, then toss them with the flour.

3. Place the olive oil over moderately high heat in a large, heavy stewpot. When it's hot, add the tripe and pork. Cook, stirring, until the meats are lightly browned on all sides, about 10 minutes. Add the onions and garlic and stir to blend. Add the white wine and scrape up the browned bits on the bottom of the pot. Crushing each tomato in your hand, add the canned tomatoes with their liquid. Add the paprika and stir to blend. Drain the soaked chick peas and add them to the stew.

4. Reduce heat to very low. Make sure the meats are covered with liquid. Cook at a low simmer, checking occasionally to make sure the meats are always just submerged in liquid, for 4½ hours (if the liquid level goes down, add a little water).

5. After the 4½ hours of cooking, add the chorizos, submerging them in the liquid. Cook for 30 minutes more. Remove the chorizos, cut diagonally into broad, thin slices and return chorizo slices to the stew. Season to taste and serve. (If you have a good Spanish paprika, you may want to sprinkle a little over each serving.)

FIVE INEXPENSIVE MEAT FAVOURITES

Meat Loaf
An important part of the American gastronomic revolution of the eighties and nineties was a return to the comfort foods that had nurtured baby boomers in the

fifties and sixties. Topping this list of foods, indubitably, was meat loaf—a dish that generated little excitement in its original time and place, but in its reincarnated form had foodies swooning.

What was that form? Lots of chefs got busy doing creative turns on the old classic, adding coriander here, pesto there and meats other than beef everywhere. But many chefs also played it straight—simply striving for the best traditional meat loaf that a loan tin could yield.

We like to break traditional meat loaves into three groups. The first—the meat loaf you see most often—is firm and dense; it derives its texture from a high proportion of fine breadcrumbs. The second meat loaf is meaty and crumbly; very little starch is used to bind it, which means it breaks into large, meaty morsels at the touch of your fork.

The last group is our favourite, soft and moist.

PERFECT SOFT-AND-MOIST MEAT LOAF

This style of meat loaf achieves its distinction by using cubes of white bread (not breadcrumbs) that have been soaked in eggs and milk; the finished texture is very tender and not particularly dense. The particular soft-and-moist loaf given here has a few other virtues. It is rather subtly seasoned, allowing the flavour of the beef to come through. It is not free-standing, but cooked in a loaf tin—which minimises the browning that occurs on the outside of the meat loaf, further emphasising the soft and moist textural qualities. And it is pale, without any tomato coating—which gives it a tremendous comfort-food rating and makes it a perfect partner for any pale gravy you'd like to pour over or around it.

SERVES 6

3 cups soft white bread cubes
1 egg
150 ml (5 fl oz) milk
15 ml (1 tbsp) Dijon mustard
8.5 g (1¾ tsp) salt
1.25 g (¼ tsp) black pepper

2.5 g (½ tsp) dried basil
1.25 g (¼ tsp) dried thyme
pinch of nutmeg
1 medium onion, finely chopped
115 g (4 oz) finely chopped celery with leaves
25 g (1 oz) finely chopped fresh parsley
12 rashers bacon, lightly browned and torn into
   small pieces
900 g (2 lb) minced beef

1. Preheat oven to 180°C (350°F).

2. Place bread cubes in large bowl. Beat egg and milk together in small bowl, then pour over bread cubes. Let stand until bread absorbs milk, about 15 minutes. Mash and stir mixture until bread is in very small chunks.

3. Add mustard, salt, pepper, basil, thyme, nutmeg, onion, celery, parsley and bacon. Mix well. Add minced beef and mix well. Refrigerate overnight.

4. Turn mixture into 20 x 13 cm (8 x 5 in) loaf tin. Bake in oven for 55 minutes. Let stand 5 minutes before slicing.

Pâté

Pâté is meat loaf with a difference. For one thing, though pâté, like meat loaf, is a loaf of minced and cooked meat, pâté is served cold or at room temperature—usually as a first course. More important, the textures and flavours of pâté are completely different from those of meat loaf. Pâté is more Gallic, deeper tasting, with a silky texture that is a function of the large amount of fat that goes into it. Don't let anyone fool you: if you're offered a low-fat pâté, the likelihood is that it will taste a lot more like meat loaf than like pâté. An authentic pâté should contain anywhere from 35 to 50 per cent fat.

Many Americans have erroneously assumed pâté to be a high-end, luxury product—undoubtedly because they associate its name with a very tiny subset of pâtés, pâté de foie gras. Most pâté, however, is made from the cheapest of ingredients and really is just meat loaf with a Gallic attitude. Unfortunately, the pâtés previously available in the United States tasted like meat loaf.

That changed over the last 10 years. Good charcutières started producing more authentic-tasting pâtés and many restaurant chefs followed suit. The next step, of course, is the exquisite joy of making pâté at home—a process that can take the better part of a week, but yields a tremendous sense of accomplishment along with a damned good bite.

COARSE COUNTRY PÂTÉ

Though we're fond of many different types of pâté, the coarse country pâté—usually made from minced pork, pork fat and seasonings—is our all-time favourite. This one has the unmistakable tang of rural France about it.

SERVES 12 AS A FIRST COURSE

900 g (2 lb) lean pork, cut in large cubes
225 g (½ oz) fresh, tender pork fat (jowl fat is best)
2.5 g (½ tsp) very finely chopped garlic
4 juniper berries, smashed with a heavy knife and finely chopped
2.5 g (½ tsp) dried thyme
pinch of ground cloves
pinch of ground allspice
10 g (2 tsp)salt
2.5 g (½ tsp) freshly ground black pepper
50 ml (2 fl oz) brandy
125 ml (4 fl oz) rich pork stock*
25 g (1 oz) lard or butter
115 g (4 oz) finely chopped shallots
225 g (½ lb) chicken livers
1.25 g (¼ tsp) saltpetre (optional, see box, page 457)
1 egg, lightly beaten
a few bay leaves

1. Start the pâté 3 days before cooking it and at least 4 days before eating it. Using a large, heavy knife, cut half of the pork cubes into a coarse paste that resembles minced pork. Cut the other half of the pork cubes into fine dice. (See box, page 457). Combine in a bowl. Cut the pork fat into very fine dice and add to the chopped pork. Blend in the garlic, juniper berries, thyme, cloves, allspice, salt, pepper, 30 ml (2 tbsp) of the brandy and the pork stock. Mix well. Marinate, covered and refrigerated, for 2 days.

2. One day before cooking, add the lard or butter to a heavy omelette pan over moderate heat. Add the shallots and cook for 3 minutes. Add the remaining 30 ml (2 tbsp) of brandy and cook until reduced by half. Add the shallot mixture to the work bowl of a food processor along with the chicken livers. Purée thoroughly.

3. Add the shallot-liver mixture to the marinated meat mixture. Add the saltpetre, if using and the beaten egg. Mix well. Sauté a small amount of the mixture in a frying pan over moderately high heat to make sure the seasoning is correct. (Remember: hot meat tastes saltier than cold meat, so if the mixture seems at all low in salt, add some more.)

4. Select a terrine that is practically filled up by the pâté mixture—a long, narrow French-style one (about 25 x 7.5 x 7.5 cm (10 x 3 x 3 in)) is especially elegant. Pack the pâté mixture into the terrine, place end-to-end bay leaves on top of the pâté (right down the centre) and cover the terrine tightly with aluminium foil. Refrigerate 24 hours.

5. When ready to cook, preheat oven to 110°C (225°F). Place the terrine in a large roasting tin and pour boiling

*The pork stock in this recipe helps give the pâté juiciness and a deep pork flavour. To make it, simply place a few pounds of pork bones in a saucepan, add a bay leaf and an onion stuck with a clove, cover with water, and simmer, skimming the foam, for several hours, or until liquid is reduced to ½ cup.

water all around the terrine, nearly up to the top. Place the roasting tin in the oven and bake until the terrine reaches 76.5°C (170°F) on a quick-read meat thermometer.

6. Remove terrine from oven and let it come to room temperature (about 3 hours). Then, place the terrine, still covered in aluminium foil, in the refrigerator. Wait at least 24 hours before eating it (it's even better after 'ripening' for 4 to 5 days).

7. When ready to serve, either cut 2-cm (¾-inch) slices right out of the terrine mould, or slice the terrine after unmoulding it onto a platter. To accomplish the latter, you must dip the terrine in warm water for half a minute or so and run a knife all along the interior sides of the terrine. Invert it on a platter. Once the pâté has come out of the mould, cut it into 2-cm (¾-in) slices.

Two important pâté issues

The way you cut or mince the meat for coarse country pâté is of prime importance. Many modern pâtémakers go for convenience, and use meat grinders, food processors, even shop-bought minced meat. We're on the side of the old-timers: we believe that machines that cut meat squeeze out too much of the precious juice, leading to a drier pâté. When we make coarse country pâté at home, we prefer to cut the meat by hand with knives. Actually, our preferred method is with cleavers—two Chinese cleavers, to be exact. Hold one in each hand and, working them in tandem, chop the meat as quickly as you can. You'll be amazed how efficient this primitive system is.

Another key pâté issue concerns saltpetre, which is another name for potassium nitrate. This is the chemical used to make ham, bologna, salami, hot dogs and other meats look pink. It is regularly used in France in pâtémaking for cosmetic purposes; without it, pâté looks brownish-grey, like meat loaf. You'll find it at pharmacies.

DUCK PÂTÉ WITH FOIE GRAS AND APRICOTS

Another type of pâté we favour is smoother but with a good, chewy texture due to large chunks of marinated meat embedded in it; sometimes pâtémakers add fruit and nuts as well. The following delicious pâté brims with duck flavour and gains a delicious, subtle sweetness from dried apricots. You can omit the nuggets of foie gras if you wish, but they add a silky excitement. Cut the foie gras and the strips of duck breast to meet the specifications of the terrine mould you're using.

SERVES 8 AS A FIRST COURSE

large duckling (about (2.25-2.7 kg (5 to 6 lb))
30 ml (2 tbsp) Armagnac
115 g (¼ lb) pork fat, cut in cubes, plus additional pork fat, sliced, for lining the terrine (have your butcher cut 350 g (¾ lb) fatback into thin slices)
1 egg, beaten
2.5 g (½ tsp) allspice
7.5 g (1½ tsp) fresh thyme
10 g (2 tsp) orange zest
1.25 g (¼ tsp) saltpetre (optional)
salt and pepper to taste
115 g (4 oz) dried apricots, halved and plumped in hot water
115 g (4 oz) good-quality canned foie gras, cut into 6 strips, about 1 cm (½ in) thick and 13 cm (5 in) long

1. Bone the duck completely, or have your butcher do so. Discard skin and bones. Keep duck meat and much of the fat clinging to it. You will need about 500 g (1¼ lb) of meat.

2. Take about 115 g (¼ lb) of breast meat and cut it into 6 strips, each one about 1 cm (½ in) wide by 13 cm (5 in) long. Place duck strips in armagnac and marinate for 3 hours.

3. Preheat oven to 180°C (350°F).

4. Pass the rest of the duck meat through a mincer twice. Mince the cubed pork fat once and mix with the duck meat in a large bowl. Add the beaten egg, allspice, thyme, orange zest, saltpetre (if using) and salt and pepper. Sauté a small portion over moderately high heat and test for seasoning.

5. Line a 1.2-litre (2-pint) rectangular terrine on the bottom and sides with thin slices of fatback. Place half the duck mixture in the terrine. Make a decorative pattern on top of the duck mixture with the marinated duck strips, the apricots and the foie gras strips. Top with the rest of the duck mixture. Cover with fatback slices. Place the terrine in a large roasting tin and pour boiling water all around the terrine, nearly up to the top. Place the roasting tin in the oven and bake until the terrine reaches 71°C (160°F) on a quick-read meat thermometer.

6. Allow to cool at room temperature for 1 hour. Then weight the terrine down with heavy cans or pie weights and refrigerate overnight. (The pâté will taste even better if you hold it in the refrigerator for several days.)

CHICKEN AND PORCINI PÂTÉ

Another type of pâté—and one that's very popular at the store—is ultra-smooth and made from light meat, like chicken. In some versions of this style of pâté, we find, the final texture is so light and mousse-like as to be practically insipid. Fear not. The following version has a real meaty texture and real chew. We especially like slices of it served as a first course on top of a tangle of salad greens, the whole dressed with a terrific homemade mayonnaise (like the three-lemon mayo on page 493) that has been thinned with a little water to the texture of a sauce.

SERVES 8 AS A FIRST COURSE

115 g (4 oz) dried porcini mushrooms
900 g (2 lb) skinless, boneless chicken breasts, fat and sinew removed, meat cubed
3 egg whites
1.25 g (¼ tsp) nutmeg
10 g (2 tsp) white peppercorns, finely ground
115 g (4 oz) mixed, coarsely chopped fresh herbs (preferably a combination of parsley, tarragon and thyme)
salt to taste
700 ml (1¼ pints) double cream

1. Cover the dried mushrooms with warm water and let stand for 1 hour. Then drain the mushrooms, straining and reserving 125 ml (4 fl oz) of the soaking liquid. Finely chop the porcini.

2. Mince the chicken cubes through the large blade of a mincer and transfer to a chilled food processor bowl.

3. Add the egg whites to the chicken and pulse until fully incorporated. Add mushrooms, reserved mushroom liquid, nutmeg, peppercorns, herbs and a generous amount of salt. Transfer to a chilled bowl (or place over ice) and fold in 450 ml (16 fl oz) of cream. Refrigerate for 2 hours.

4. Preheat oven to 180°C (350°F).

5. Remove mixture and add remaining cream, folding in until completely incorporated. (If cream does not completely incorporate, return the mixture to the refrigerator for 30 to 60 minutes.)

6. To check seasoning, make a test 'quenelle' by poaching a tablespoon of the mixture in simmering water. Make any necessary adjustments.

7. Line a 1.2-litre (2-pint) rectangular terrine dish with greaseproof paper that has been slightly moistened with a few drops of water. Pour the chicken mixture into the terrine and place in a large pan of hot water (the mixture should come almost to the top of the dish). Bake in the oven until pâté reaches an internal temperature of 65°C (150°F), about 45 minutes. Remove from the oven and allow pâté to cool to room temperature (about 2 hours) before unmoulding and slicing.

Sausages

Sausages have always been popular in the United States; the hot dog is practically our national food. In the eighties and nineties, however, the American sausage scene changed radically. Drawing on an expanded knowledge of ethnic cuisines and motivated by the contemporary lust for culinary creativity, restaurant chefs everywhere started turning out sausages that had never been seen before. In one case, one of American's most famous chefs, Wolfgang Puck, went so far as to create a whole restaurant based on creative, homemade sausages. The movement was helped along by innovative sausage-makers, principally in California, who sent their new creations into national distribution.

At home, American cooks, as ever, are happy to purchase sausage and boil it, or throw it on the grill, or slice it and add it to dishes with lots of other ingredients. But we suspect that if more Americans knew how much fun it is to make their own sausages at home, the price of sausage casings would go from next-to-nothing to at least next-to-something.

HOMEMADE SAUSAGES

It is a thrill to make your own sausages at home—and, especially if you're making *fresh* sausages (not cured or smoked), it's not very difficult, nor does it take a lot of equipment and ingredients.

Here's what you'll need.

Meat Mincer You'll have the most control and get the best results if you mince your own meat in a meat mincer. If you own a Kenwood Chef mixer, there is an inexpensive mincing attachment that you can buy for it. Other options are: chopping the meat by hand with

knives; pulsing the meat in a food processor; or asking your butcher to mince the meat for you.

Sausage Stuffer This is a device that passes the sausage meat through a long tube into your sausage casing; it can be hand-cranked or powered by electricity. Once again, there is an inexpensive Kenwood Chef sausage stuffer attachment. Our favourite option, however, is the 2.25-kg (5-lb) capacity Sausage Stuffer, made by The Sausage Maker, Inc. in Buffalo, New York. A hand crank forces a metal plate against the sausage meat, which squeezes the meat out of the long tube and into the casing. It gives you lots of control.

Casings Natural casings are best for sausages. These are the cleaned intestines of animals. Beef casings are the widest and make the biggest sausages. Sheep casings are the narrowest and make the thinnest sausages. For most sausages, pork casings are just right. Buy casings that are coated with salt and make sure to rinse them well before using. Leftover casing, still coated in salt, will keep in your refrigerator for years.

For all of the following fresh sausage recipes, the procedure is exactly the same: After you've minced the meat and made the sausage stuffing, keep it very cold. Make sure the stuffing machine (or attachment) is cold as well and very clean.

Cut off the amount of sausage casing that you need (for each of the following recipes you'll need about 90 cm (3 feet) of pork casing that's 32 to 35 millimetres wide) and soak the casing in cold water for ½ hour. Then, attach one end of the casing to the sink tap and let cold water run through the casing for a few minutes to clean the interior. Tie a double knot at one end of the casing, using the casing itself as a tie.

When ready to stuff, place the cold sausage mixture in the sausage stuffer. By cranking, or turning the machine on, pass a few grams of the meat through the machine and into a bowl; this will minimise the chances of a sausage-rupturing air hole exploding later.

Coat the casing and the sausage stuffing tube with cold water. Insert the stuffing tube into the open end of the casing, then, working quickly with your hands, push all of the casing onto the stuffing tube; when you come to the tied-off end of the casing, leave a few centimetres of casing dangling off the end of the stuffing tube.

Holding the casing slightly above the counter in one hand—so that the casing's at the same level as the stuffing tube—pass the meat stuffing through the machine in a continuous flow (either with the machine's motor or with a hand crank.) The stuffing will flow directly into the casing, creating sausage. When the casing is almost entirely filled, slip the open end of the casing off the stuffing tube and double-knot it (once again using the casing itself as a tie). Then, using strong kitchen string, tie off the long, stuffed casing into individual sausages at 13-cm (5-in) intervals. Tie tightly, don't worry that the casing will break.

All of the following sausages are made fresh at Dean & DeLuca. If you don't live nearby, you'll want to try out these delicious blends at home. If you do live nearby—you might want to try making them at home anyway, just for the thrill of it. They are all delicious fried, grilled or barbecued.

MILD ITALIAN SAUSAGES

MAKES 6 SAUSAGES, EACH ABOUT 13 CM (5 IN) LONG

2½ pounds pork (about 70 percent meat and 30 per cent fat), cut into 5-cm (2-inch) cubes
3 ounces cold water
30 ml (2 tbsp) fennel seeds
salt and freshly ground pepper to taste

Pass the pork twice through a meat grinder, using the plate with the widest holes. Mix in the water and fennel seeds and season with salt and pepper. Test a small amount of the mixture in a omelette pan for seasoning. Proceed with sausage stuffing (directions precede).

HOT ITALIAN SAUSAGES

MAKES 6 SAUSAGES, EACH ABOUT 13 CM (5 IN) LONG

2½ pounds pork (about 70 percent meat and 30 per cent fat), cut into 5-cm (2-inch) cubes
30 ml (2 tbsp) hot paprika
10 g (2 tsp) dried hot pepper flakes
75 ml (2½ fl oz) cold water
30 ml (2 tbsp) fennel seeds
salt and freshly ground pepper to taste

Pass the pork twice through a meat mincer, using the plate with the widest holes. Mix in remaining ingredients and season with salt and pepper. Test a small amount of the mixture in a frying pan for seasoning. Proceed with sausage stuffing (directions precede).

LUGANO SAUSAGES

This delicious, fine-textured sausage, with its slightly cheesy taste, is very popular in the shop.

MAKES 6 SAUSAGES, EACH ABOUT 13 CM (5 IN) LONG

1 kg (2½ lb) pork (about 70 per cent meat and 30 per cent fat), cut into 5-cm (2-in) cubes
225 g (8 oz) fresh spinach, chopped
225 g (8 oz) pine nuts, chopped
15 g (1 tbsp) chopped fresh garlic
115 g (4 oz) pecorino Romano, freshly grated
115 g (4 oz) ricotta
salt and freshly ground pepper to taste

Mince the pork 3 times using the plate with the widest holes. Mix in spinach, pine nuts, garlic, pecorino Romano and ricotta and season with salt and pepper. Test a small amount of the mixture in a frying pan for seasoning. Proceed with sausage stuffing (directions precede).

TOSCANO SAUSAGES

Tomato and basil give this fine-textured sausage an especially summery taste.

MAKES 6 SAUSAGES, EACH ABOUT 13 CM (5 IN) LONG

1 kg (2½ lb) pork (about 70 per cent meat and 30 per cent fat), cut into 5-cm (2-in) cubes
3 plum tomatoes, peeled, seeded and finely diced
10 large basil leaves cut into thin strips
salt and freshly ground pepper to taste

Mince the pork 3 times using the plate with the widest holes. Mix in tomatoes and basil and season with salt and pepper. Test a small amount of the mixture in a frying pan for seasoning. Proceed with sausage stuffing (directions precede).

LAMB AND ROSEMARY SAUSAGES

Lamb makes delicious sausage meat, more pronounced in flavour than sausage made from pork. If your butcher has it available, lamb breast trimmings make especially delicious lamb sausages.

MAKES 6 SAUSAGES, EACH ABOUT 13 CM (5 IN) LONG

1 kg (2½ lb) lamb (about 70 per cent meat and 30 per cent fat), cut into 5-cm (2-in) cubes
50 g (2 oz) chopped fresh rosemary leaves
125 ml (4 fl oz) red wine
salt and freshly ground pepper to taste

Pass the lamb 3 times through a meat grinder, using the plate with the widest holes. Mix in rosemary and red wine and season with salt and pepper. Test a small amount of the mixture in a omelette pan for seasoning. Proceed with sausage stuffing (directions precede).

CHICKEN, APPLE, AND SAGE SAUSAGES

This is our best-selling fresh sausage. Is it the lower fat content—or the intrinsic deliciousness? You decide.

MAKES 6 SAUSAGES, EACH ABOUT 13 CM (5 IN) LONG

1½ pounds skinless, boneless chicken thighs and breast
50 ml (2 fl oz) fresh orange juice
150 g (6 oz) slightly tart apples, peeled and cut into 1-cm (½-inch) chunks
1½ tbsp chopped fresh sage
15 ml (1 tbsp) calvados
salt and freshly ground pepper to taste

Mince the chicken twice using the plate with the widest holes. Mix in orange juice, apples, sage and calvados and season with salt and pepper. Test a small amount of the mixture in a omelette pan for seasoning. Proceed with sausage stuffing (directions precede).

DISHES MADE WITH SAUSAGES

Even if you're not about to purchase casings and a sausage stuffer, you can still make some terrific sausage-based meals at home. The range of sausages available in the market today is vast and many of them are delicious cooked in the simplest possible manner at home. But we also like incorporating shop-bought sausages into more complicated dishes, as in the following recipes.

CHOUCROUTE GARNI

One of our favourite dishes is this Alsatian specialty: a variety of sausages cooked in, then heaped on top of, a mound of wine-and-juniper flavoured sauerkraut. Finding sausages to use in this dish is easy enough; in France, they use a range of cured and lightly smoked sausages. If you can't find many different types, a combination of kielbasa and hot dogs will be delicious. What presents more difficulties, however, is the sauerkraut. In Alsace and in Alsatian restaurants around France, the very finely cut sauerkraut they use gives choucroûte garni an unlikely delicacy. Unfortunately, it's just not possible to find that kind of sauerkraut here. Never mind; the following version is lustier, browner, longer cooked and heavier than you'll find in France, but no less delicious. Serve with boiled potatoes, mustard and a good bottle of dry Alsatian Riesling.

SERVES 8

1.8 kg (4 lb) fresh uncooked sauerkraut
¼ cup lard, bacon fat, or vegetable oil
24 mixed sausages (a variety including bockwurst, bratwurst, knackwurst, frankfurters and French garlic sausage (about 115 g (4 oz) each)*
8 smoked pork chops
1 large onion, thinly sliced
1 Golden Delicious apple, peeled, cored, and thinly sliced
2 garlic cloves, smashed
2 bay leaves
15 juniper berries
15 g (1 tbsp) caraway seeds
1 bottle dry white wine (preferably Riesling)
225 ml (8 fl oz) water
boiled potatoes
chopped fresh parsley for garnish

1. Preheat oven to 150°C (300°F).

2. Rinse the sauerkraut in cold water for 10 minutes, remove and pat dry.

3. In a very large casserole, heat fat or oil over moderately high heat and sauté sausages and pork chops, in batches, until browned on all sides. Set meats aside and drain off half the fat. Add onion and apple and sauté until onion is translucent, about 4 minutes.

*If you can't find a variety of sausages as small as ¼ pound each, you could instead cut larger sausages into ¼ pound sections.

4. Add the sauerkraut to the casserole, blending it well with the onion and apple. Add garlic, bay leaves, juniper berries and caraway seeds and blend well. Add the bottle of wine and the water until the sauerkraut is barely covered. Bring to a boil, then reduce heat and bring to a simmer. Bury the pork chops in the sauerkraut. Cover and bake in the oven for 1½ hours.

5. After 1½ hours of cooking, bury the sausages in the sauerkraut. Bake for 45 more minutes. Remove the bay leaves.

6. To serve, place the sauerkraut in the middle of a large, warm serving platter. Place the meats over and around it, along with boiled potatoes. Sprinkle all with parsley.

KIELBASA STEW WITH ROOT VEGETABLES

It's cheap and it's accessible, but kielbasa (Polish boiling sausage) is nevertheless a delicious treat. If possible, buy your kielbasa from a shop like ours, or a central European butcher shop.

SERVES 2

4 medium carrots
4 garlic cloves, smashed
1 stalk celery, coarsely chopped
2 large parsnips, peeled
5 sprigs of dill plus additional for garnish
8 sprigs of parsley plus additional for garnish
1.3 litres (2¼ pints) water
225 g (8 oz) brussels sprouts, sliced thin
115 g (4 oz) celeriac, peeled and cut into matchsticks
1 large leek (white part only), cleaned and cut into thin rings
2.25 g (½ tsp) fennel seeds
450 g (1 lb) kielbasa, cut into broad 1-cm (⅓-in) slices

1. Cut 2 of the carrots into coarse chunks and place in a large saucepan. Add the garlic, celery, parsnips, dill and parsley and the water. Bring to a boil and boil over high heat until the liquid is reduced to about 850 ml (1½ pints), about 20 minutes.

2. Remove the parsnips and purée in a food mill, a food processor, or by mashing with a fork. Reserve. Pour the rest of the contents of the pan through a colander, reserving the broth and discarding the vegetables. Return broth to the pan. Cut the remaining 2 carrots into thin rounds, and add to the vegetable broth. Add the brussels sprouts, celeriac, leek, fennel seeds and kielbasa. Simmer over moderate heat for 15 minutes.

3. When ready to serve, thicken with the reserved parsnip purée. Garnish with the additional dill and parsley.

SAUSAGE IN BRIOCHE
This is one of the great traditional appetisers of France. The diner is presented with what looks like a slice of bread with a red circle in the middle. The 'bread', of course, is brioche and the 'red circle' is French garlic sausage, or saucisson à l'ail; the intensity of the sausage plays perfectly against the mildness and sweetness of the brioche. Now that wide sausages approximating the French garlic sausage are more widely available in the United States, there's no reason not to dazzle your guests with this great dish. Serve with warm French potato salad (dressed with vinaigrette only) and a tangle of greens for a wonderful first course.
SERVES 12 AS A FIRST COURSE

For the brioche dough
2 sachets dry yeast
175 ml (6 fl oz) lukewarm milk
375 g (13 oz) strong plain flour
140 g (5 oz) butter at room temperature
50 g (2 oz) sugar

2.5 g (½ tsp) salt
2 large eggs
1 cured and cooked French garlic sausage (about 5 cm (2 in) wide and 25 cm (10 in) long)
30 ml (2 tbsp) double cream

1. *Make the brioche dough:* Whisk the yeast into the lukewarm milk. Place 140 g (5 oz) flour in a large mixing bowl and stir in the milk mixture. Cover and let sit at room temperature for 30 minutes.

2. Combine the butter, sugar and salt in a mixing bowl and beat with a wooden spoon until mixture is blended well. Add the eggs, 1 at a time, blending well. Then add the remaining flour and blend well.

3. Add the yeast mixture and knead until smooth, about 15 minutes. (The dough should still be slightly sticky; if it's not, add a little more milk.)

4. Place dough in a lightly buttered bowl and cover with a damp towel. Allow the dough to rise in a warm place until it doubles, about 2 hours.

5. Punch the dough down and cover again. Keep refrigerated at least 2 hours.

6. Preheat oven to 190°C (375°F).

7. When ready to use, roll out dough on an oiled baking sheet into a rectangle 5 cm (2 in) longer than the sausage on each end and twice as wide. Cut the dough down the middle into 2 long halves. Centre the sausage on one piece of the dough. Place the other piece of dough on top and squeeze the edges to seal. Make a design with the extra dough if desired. Let sit for 15 minutes. Brush the top of the dough with cream and bake at 190°C (375°F) for 25 minutes, or until golden brown. Cut into crossways slices, approximately 2 cm (¾ in) thick and serve immediately.

Dishes with Minced Meat Stuffing

MOUSSAKA

Greek restaurants have grown in popularity in America—especially as Americans have realised that 'Mediterranean' means more than Italian and Provençal. And the dish that tops the charts in these Greek restaurants is moussaka, that great casserole of aubergine slices, minced lamb in tomato sauce and custard topping. It's a fabulous party dish; assemble it early in the day, bake and brown just before serving.

SERVES 8

1.3 kg (3 lb) aubergine
25 g (5 tsp) coarse salt
100 ml (3½ fl oz) Greek extra-virgin olive oil
700 g (1½ lb) chopped yellow onions
20 g (4 tsp) finely chopped garlic
450 g (1 lb) minced lamb
50 ml (2 fl oz) white wine
400-g (14-oz) can tomatoes in purée
1 bay leaf
1 cinnamon stick
5 g (1 tsp) dried thyme
5 g (1 tsp) dried oregano
pinch of freshly grated nutmeg
50 g (2 oz) finely chopped fresh flat-leaf parsley
150 g (5½ oz) butter
50 g (2 oz) flour
1.2 litres (2 pints) milk, heated almost to boiling
5 g (1 tsp) white pepper
280 g (10 oz) freshly made breadcrumbs
90 g (6 tbsp) freshly grated Parmigiano-Reggiano

1. Slice aubergines into 5-mm (¼-in) rounds and place on baking sheets. Using 15 g (1 tbsp) of coarse salt, sprinkle salt on each side of aubergine. Set aside to 'sweat' for 30 minutes.

2. In a large saucepan heat 50 ml (2 fl oz) of olive oil

over moderate heat and add onions, garlic and 5 g (1 tsp) of coarse salt. Cook, stirring occasionally, for 10 minutes.

3. Increase heat to high and add the minced lamb. Break up lamb with wooden spoon as it cooks. Cook until well browned, about 10 minutes. Remove as much fat from the pan as possible.

4. Add white wine and cook for 3 minutes, scraping bottom of pan to loosen brown bits. Reduce heat to low and add tomatoes, bay leaf, cinnamon stick, thyme, oregano, nutmeg and 5 g (1 tsp) salt. Stir well, breaking up tomatoes with wooden spoon. Simmer gently for 30 minutes, add chopped parsley, mix well and turn off heat.

5. Heat a large frying pan over moderately high heat and very lightly coat the bottom of the pan with olive oil. When oil is hot, dry aubergine slices well and sauté, in batches, until well browned, about 4 minutes per side. (If it is necessary to add more oil to the frying pan, add sparingly, as aubergine absorbs oil easily. Do not crowd the frying pan .) Set aside cooked aubergine.

6. In a medium saucepan melt 115 g (4 oz) butter over moderate heat. Add flour, 15 g (1 tbsp) at a time, whisking well after each addition. Cook roux gently, whisking constantly, for 2 to 3 minutes, without letting colour change. Add hot milk slowly, whisking constantly and cook over low heat, whisking frequently, for about 20 minutes, or until the sauce has the consistency of very thick cream. Season with 10 g (2 tsp) coarse salt and white pepper.

7. Preheat oven to 180°C (350°F). Sprinkle 50 g (2 oz) of the breadcrumbs on the bottom of a 28 x 23 x 4 cm (11 x 9 x 1½ in) roasting tin. Next, layer half the aubergine slices over the breadcrumbs. Spread lamb mixture evenly over the aubergine. Cover with 45 g (3 tbsp) of the Parmigiano-Reggiano and 115 g (4 oz) of the breadcrumbs. Add the remaining aubergine slices, then top with the béchamel sauce. Sprinkle with remaining cheese and breadcrumbs. Dot with remaining butter.

8. Bake in preheated 180°C (350°F) oven for 50 minutes. Before serving, brown moussaka under the grill for 3 to 4 minutes. Let sit for 10 minutes. Cut into squares and serve.

GREEK STUFFED PEPPERS WITH AVGOLEMONO SAUCE

This is a fabulous, deep-tasting dish; the flavour of green pepper works wonderfully with the more usual cast of Greek characters. Serve with rice, orzo, or olive oil-roasted potatoes.

SERVES 4

30 ml (2 tbsp) olive oil
450 g (1 lb) minced beef
2 medium onions, finely chopped
85 g (3 oz) butter
225 g (8 oz) cooked rice
7 canned tomatoes
5 ml (1 tsp) red-wine vinegar
5 g (1 tsp) cinnamon
50 g (2 oz) grated Parmigiano-Reggiano
6 small green peppers
225 ml (8 fl oz) chicken stock
30 ml (2 tbsp) flour
1 egg
30 ml (2 tbsp) lemon juice
salt and pepper to taste

1. Place the olive oil in a large, heavy frying pan over moderate heat. Add the minced beef and cook, stirring to prevent the beef from clumping, for 5 minutes.

2. Add the chopped onions and half the butter. Stir well to blend. Cook for 5 minutes.

3. Add the cooked rice and cook, stirring occasionally to prevent sticking, for 10 minutes.

4. Add the canned tomatoes, vinegar and cinnamon. Cook for 2 minutes more. Add the Parmigiano-Reggiano, blend well and season to taste with salt and pepper.

5. Preheat oven to 190°C (375°F).

6. Cut the tops off of the green peppers and reserve for another use. Cut the green peppers in half, discard seeds and ribs and stuff each half with some of the meat mixture. Place the peppers in a baking pan, add the chicken stock to the pan, cover pan with aluminium foil and bake in the oven, basting peppers occasionally with the chicken stock, for 1 hour.

7. When peppers are done, place the rest of the butter in a saucepan over moderate heat. Add the flour and blend well. Cook, stirring, for 2 minutes. Whisk in the pan juices from the peppers and stir until a smooth sauce is formed, about 1 minute. Break the egg into a bowl and beat it. Slowly add the sauce to the beaten egg, whisking vigorously. Return sauce to pan, add lemon juice and heat gently. Season to taste with salt and pepper.

8. Arrange 3 pepper halves on each of 4 dinner plates, then top with sauce. Serve immediately.

MANTI WITH YOGURT SAUCE (TURKISH RAVIOLI)

This quintessential Turkish combination features lamb-stuffed pillows of fresh pasta that are drizzled with two sauces: a garlicky one made from yogurt and a spicy one made with butter, paprika and hot pepper. The whole is topped with fresh mint and is unbelievably delicious. This type of Turkish ravioli originated in Mongolia. Manti was eaten at the Ottoman court and has been popular throughout Anatolia ever since; Kayseri is especially famous for them. Preceded by Middle Eastern salads and followed by grilled fish, manti could be the centrepiece of a dinner party.

SERVES 4 AS A FIRST COURSE

For the filling
30 ml (2 tbsp) olive oil
1 large onion, finely chopped
450 g (1 lb) minced lean lamb
50 g (2 oz) chopped fresh flat-leaf parsley
salt and pepper to taste
For the pasta
225 g (8 oz) strong plain flour plus additional for
   rolling
5 g (1 tsp) salt
1 large egg
125 ml (4 fl oz) water plus a little more if necessary
For the yogurt sauce
225 ml (8 fl oz) plain sheep's milk yogurt
4 garlic cloves, mashed to a paste with 5 g (1 tsp)
   salt
For the butter sauce
115 g (4 oz) unsalted butter
3 g ($\frac{3}{4}$ tsp) fine quality sweet paprika
coarse salt to taste
4 dashes of hot red pepper sauce, or more to taste
shredded fresh mint leaves for garnish

1. *Make the filling:* Heat the olive oil in a large, heavy frying pan over moderate heat until hot but not smoking. Stir in the onion and cook, stirring, until softened, about 5 minutes. Stir in the lamb and the parsley and cook, stirring and breaking up any lumps, until the lamb changes colour. Remove from heat and generously season with salt and pepper. Set aside.

2. *Make the pasta:* Sift the flour and salt together into a bowl. Make a well in the centre and a place the egg and water in the well. Work the dough with your hands or a wooden spoon into a smooth dough. (You might find that you will need more water if you are rolling the pasta by hand and less if you are using a hand-turned pasta

machine.) Knead the dough for at least 10 minutes until smooth and elastic. Cover the dough with a towel and let rest for 1 hour. Divide the dough into 4 pieces. Roll out each piece to 2 mm ($\frac{1}{16}$ in) thick with a rolling pin or a pasta machine and cut into 7.5-cm (3-in) squares, discarding the uneven edges. Place 10 g (2 tsp) filling into the centre of each square. Moisten the entire outer edge with water, bring the 4 corners together in the centre and pinch tightly to seal, then pinch together the 4 straight edges to seal completely (take care with this step, sealing the dumplings *thoroughly* will insure that they will not become unsealed in the water and lose the filling). Repeat with remaining pasta and filling. Place the manti on a lightly floured baking sheet in a single layer.

3. *Make the yogurt sauce:* Drain the yogurt at room temperature through a very fine mesh strainer over a bowl for 30 minutes and discard the whey. Stir together the yogurt and garlic in a bowl and let stand at warm room temperature until ready to use.

4. *Make the butter sauce:* In a small frying pan over moderate heat cook the butter until it is a very light brown, remove the frying pan from heat and stir in the paprika, coarse salt to taste and the hot red pepper sauce.

5. In a large casserole of boiling salted water cook the manti, in batches, stirring to keep them from sticking together, about 7 minutes, or until the pressed together edges are al dente (they will take the longest to cook). Remove them when done with a long-handled sieve or a large slotted spoon and keep warm with a little of the warm cooking liquid. Serve the manti very hot in individual bowls, spoon some of the yogurt sauce over, drizzle with the butter sauce and garnish with mint leaves. Pass the remaining yogurt sauce at the table.

Meat Pies

CHICKEN POT PIE WITH ROSEMARY

Admit it—you ate a lot of frozen pot pies when you were growing up. That's why, when pot pies got 'revived' in the eighties and nineties, they seemed so comforting and attractive. Of course, the fact that these freshly made ones were a hundred times better than the old freezer jobs also helped. This is a startlingly delicious version of pot pie, fragrant with fresh rosemary, made with a top crust only (which is wonderfully light, buttery, flaky), served family style from one communal dish. This one avoids the Big Pot Pie Problem: often, you put a pot pie in the oven with a perfectly textured filling, only to find the filling thin and runny when it comes out of the oven. That won't happen here.

SERVES 6

For the pie dough
350g (12 oz) plain flour
2.5g (½ tsp) salt
115g (4 oz) unsalted butter, chilled and cubed
50 ml (2 fl oz) ice water
For the filling
1-kg (2½-lb) skinless, boneless chicken breasts, cut into 2.5-g (1-in) pieces
salt and pepper to taste
45 ml (3 tbsp) olive oil
10 g (2 tsp) garlic, finely chopped
3 celery ribs, cut in 1-cm (¼-inch) dice
2 large carrots, cut in 1-cm (¼-inch) rounds
1 litre (1¾ pints) water
115 g (4 oz) haricot verts
225 g (8 oz) fresh tiny pearl onions
70 g (2½ oz) butter
50 g (2 oz) plain flour
850 ml (1½ pints) boiling chicken stock
225 ml (8 fl oz) milk
75 ml (2½ fl oz) single cream
2½ tablespoons finely chopped fresh rosemary
For the egg wash

1 egg
30 ml (2 tbsp) water

1. Preheat oven to 190°C (375°F).

2. *Make the pie dough in the food processor:* Place flour, salt and butter in a food processor and pulse repeatedly (about 6 or 7 pulses) until mixture resembles coarse crumbs. (Tiny chunks of butter in the flour ensure a flaky crust, so be careful not to overprocess.)

3. While the machine is running, add the ice water though the tube and process until the dough comes away from the side. (Do not let the dough form a ball.)

4. Working quickly and handling the dough as little as possible, put the dough on a lightly floured surface, shape into a ball and flatten slightly. Wrap in clingfilm and refrigerate 30 minutes to 1 hour.

5. *Make the filling:* Season the chicken well with salt and pepper. Heat 30 ml (2 tbsp) of the oil in a large omelette pan over moderate heat. Add chicken and cook, stirring occasionally, about 8 to 10 minutes, or until very lightly browned. Set chicken aside.

6. Add the remaining tablespoon of oil to the same pan along with the garlic, celery and carrots. Cook until vegetables are tender, about 6 minutes. Set aside.

7. Bring a quart of water to a boil in a saucepan and add the haricot verts. Cook until almost tender, about 5 to 6 minutes. Drain in strainer and immediately plunge beans into ice water. Remove beans and set aside.

8. Peel the pearl onions, but leave the root largely intact so the onions hold together. Add them to boiling water and cook for 10 minutes. Drain in a strainer, rinse and remove the root ends.

9. Melt the butter in a saucepan over moderate heat.

Add the flour and mix quickly with a whisk for about 1 minute. Add the stock, milk and cream. Bring to a boil, whisking, reduce the heat to moderately low and simmer for 5 minutes. Season with salt, pepper and rosemary.

10. Place the chicken and vegetables in a large baking dish (about 1½-quart capacity) and pour cream mixture over the filling, mixing thoroughly.

11. On a lightly floured surface, roll the dough into a round that is about 1 to 1½ inches wider than the baking dish. Place it over the pie and pinch the edge to form a decorative edge. Prick the top with a fork.

12. Make the egg wash by whisking the egg and water together and lightly brush the mixture on the dough. Bake in the oven until golden brown, about 45 minutes. Let rest for 5 minutes before serving.

SHEPHERD'S PIE

Making this dish is easier than pie: though it's called a 'pie', there's not a crumb of pastry involved. Shepherd's pie is simply minced meat and vegetables in a sauce, with a thick topping of mashed potatoes. The whole gets browned in the oven, for a delicious example of English comfort food. Great for cold winter nights. Serve with steamed brussels sprouts and hearty bread.

SERVES 4

2 large baking potatoes (about 450 g (1 lb)), peeled
125 ml (4 fl oz) milk
50 g (2 oz) butter
7.5 g (1½ tsp) salt
15 g (1 tbsp) chopped garlic
450 g (1 lb) minced lamb
5 g (1 tsp) finely chopped rosemary
40 ml (1½ tbsp) Worcestershire sauce
20 g (4 tsp) flour
115 ml (4 oz) chopped onion
115 ml (4 oz) diced carrot

50 ml (2 fl oz) white wine
125 ml (4 fl oz) beef stock
225 g (8 oz) sweetcorn kernels (optional)

1. Put potatoes in a large saucepan and cover them with water. Bring water to a boil and cook potatoes for about 40 minutes, until cooked through. Drain potatoes and place in a bowl. Mash them with the milk and 25 g (1 oz) of the butter. Season with 2.5 g (½ tsp) of the salt. Set aside.

2. Melt remaining butter in a large frying pan over moderate heat. Add the garlic and minced lamb and cook, stirring frequently, for 5 to 7 minutes, until lamb is well browned. Season with the remaining salt, rosemary and Worcestershire sauce. Stir well and then sprinkle mixture with 10 g (2 tsp) of the flour. Stir again and cook for an additional 5 minutes. Remove meat with a slotted spoon and set aside. Pour excess grease out of pan.

3. Preheat oven to 180°C (350°F).

4. Add the onion and carrot to pan and cook over moderate heat for 5 to 7 minutes, or until onion is translucent. Sprinkle with the remaining 10 g (2 tsp) of flour and stir. Increase heat slightly and add the white wine and beef stock, scraping the bottom of the pan with a wooden spoon to release any caramelised bits. Cook for another 5 to 7 minutes, or until the liquid is reduced by about half.

5. Add lamb mixture and corn. Stir well and cook another 3 to 4 minutes. (Enough of the liquid should have evaporated that the mixture is held together by a nice thick sauce.)

6. Butter a casserole dish well and spread lamb mixture over the bottom. Cover the lamb with the mashed potatoes and smooth the top. Bake casserole, uncovered, in the oven for 40 minutes, until heated through. Serve immediately.

GREAT ASIAN WAYS WITH MEAT

STIR-FRIES

Chinese cuisine has contributed many great ways with meat. The real genius of Chinese stir-frying is little known to Americans. For one thing, the meat is often coated with other ingredients that improve its texture. Secondly, Chinese chefs like to deep-fry the meat first, very quickly, because they feel this seals flavour in and gives the meat the best texture. After the deep-frying, the meat is then 'stir-fried' with the other ingredients.

CANTONESE VELVET CHICKEN WITH BROCCOLI AND HAM

In this lovely dish, the chicken gets an egg-white-and-cornflour coating, which creates a 'velvety' texture.

SERVES 4 AS PART OF CHINESE DINNER

1 skinless chicken breast fillet (about 175 g (6 oz))
1 egg white
1.25 g (¼ tsp) salt
12 g (2½ tsp) cornflour
1 litre (1¾ pints) peanut oil
75 ml (2½ fl oz) chicken broth
45 ml (3 tbsp) shao hsing (Chinese rice wine) or dry sherry
1.25 ml (½ tsp) white vinegar
1.25 g (½ tsp) sugar
pinch of monsodium glutamate (optional)
pinch of ground black pepper
280 g (10 oz) small broccoli florets
15 g (1 tbsp) paper-thin fresh ginger slices
15 g (1 tbsp) chopped garlic
8 pieces Smithfield ham (each about 1cm x 1 cm x 2 mm (½ x ½ x ⅟₁₆ in))*
6 baby corn
2.5 ml (½ tsp) Chinese sesame oil

1. Freeze the chicken breast slightly and cut on the bias into thin, broad slices. Mix with the egg white and the salt. Stir vigorously until the egg white foams. Add 5 g (1 tsp) of the cornflour and 5 ml (1 tsp) of the peanut oil. Blend well. Let sit, unrefrigerated and covered, for 1 hour.

2. *While the chicken is sitting, prepare the sauce:* mix together the chicken broth, shao hsing, vinegar, sugar, monosodium glutamate and black pepper. Mix the rest of the cornflour with enough cold water to make a milky cream; add to the sauce mixture.

3. When ready to cook, heat the rest of the peanut oil in a wok to 190°C (375°F). Add the chicken slices and deep-fry for 20 seconds. Remove to paper towels. Add the broccoli florets and deep-fry until just cooked, about 1 to 2 minutes. Remove to paper towels. Drain all but 15 ml (1 tbsp) of the oil. Over moderately high heat, stir-fry the ginger, garlic, ham and baby corn in the remaining oil for 1 minute. Increase heat to very high and add the sauce mixture. When it comes to a boil and thickens, add the chicken, broccoli and egg white chunks. Stir quickly, turn off heat, add the sesame oil and serve.

SZECHUAN SHREDDED PORK WITH GARLIC SAUCE

In this spicy stir-fry, the pork gets a baking soda marinade; this is a traditional Chinese technique for tenderising meat before it goes into the wok.

SERVES 4 AS PART OF A CHINESE DINNER

280 g (10 oz) boneless pork shoulder
5 g (1 tsp) baking soda
30 ml (2 tbsp) tomato purée
15 ml (1 tbsp) Chinese dark vinegar
15 ml (1 tbsp) chilli paste with garlic
15 g (1 tbsp) sugar
10 ml (2 tsp) shao hsing (Chinese rice wine) or dry

*Smithfield ham—cured in Virginia—is the closest we can come in the United States to authentic Chinese ham (which is not imported). Smithfield ham is sold at Chinese butcher shops.

sherry
10 ml (2 tsp) thin soy sauce
5 ml (1 tsp) Chinese sesame oil
pinch of monosodium glutamate (optional)
5 g (1 tsp) cornflour
50 g (2 oz) dried cloud ears
1 litre (1¾ pints) peanut oil
2 stalks celery, cut into julienne
30 ml (2 tbsp) chopped garlic
15 g (1 tbsp) grated fresh ginger
5 spring onions, finely chopped
7 fresh water chestnuts, peeled and diced

1. Freeze pork slightly, then cut into long, thin julienne strips. Mix well with baking soda and add just enough water to cover. Refrigerate, covered, for 5 hours.

2. When ready to cook, rinse pork and dry well.

3. *Make the sauce:* Mix together the tomato purée, vinegar, chilli paste, 15 ml (1 tbsp) water, sugar, shao hsing, soy sauce, sesame oil and monosodium glutamate. Blend the cornflour with a little water until it becomes a milky cream and stir into the sauce.

4. Soak the cloud ears in 225 ml (8 fl oz) of boiling water for 15 minutes, then remove and reserve cloud ears.

5. Heat the peanut oil in a wok to 190°C (375°F). Add pork and deep-fry for 30 seconds. Remove pork and place on paper towels. Let the oil return to 190°C (375°F), add the celery and deep-fry 30 seconds. Remove and place on paper towels.

6. Pour off all but 15 ml (1 tbsp) oil. Over high heat stir-fry garlic, ginger and spring onions for 1 minute. Add water chestnuts, stirring. Add pork, celery and reserved cloud ears, stirring. Add sauce mixture. Bring to boil quickly and serve immediately.

CURRIES

Meat tastes fabulous in Western-style stews, of course, that emphasise the meaty flavours—but it also tastes great in Asian curries, which bombard the meat with a slew of other flavours.

There are two main curry methods in Asia: the Indian method, which involves making a powder from dried spices and cooking the powder with the meat; and the South-east Asian method, wherein the spices are mixed with wet ingredients into a paste, which becomes the flavour base of the curry.

Incidentally, only the Southeast Asians refer to these dishes as 'curries'. The name was apparently created by British colonials to describe the manifold, variegated stews of India—and to this day, Indians prefer to name these stews by the various categories to which they belong, not by the imprecise generic name 'curry'.

LAMB VINDALOO

Often known in this country as 'the hottest curry', vindaloo is a hot and pungent curry originally from Goa (on the southwestern coast of India), a Portuguese Christian settlement. It was there that the Portuguese introduced hot peppers to India and they also brought along their red-wine vinegar. Both are used in the dish, along with mustard oil. Vindaloo (sometimes spelled *vindalho*) is still served in Goa, where it is most often prepared for festive occasions—weddings, birthdays and Christmas. Serve with steamed basmati rice.

SERVES 4

125 ml (4 fl oz) red-wine vinegar
50 ml (2 fl oz) mustard oil (or vegetable oil)
30 ml (2 tbsp) grated peeled fresh ginger
15 g (1 tbsp) fine-quality hot paprika
15 g (1 tbsp) chopped fresh garlic
10 ml (2 tsp) tamarind concentrate
2.5 g (½ tsp) ground turmeric
5 g (1 tsp) jaggery or brown sugar
5 to 10 dried hot red chillies, broken up

15 g (1 tbsp) whole coriander, toasted

5 g (1 tsp) whole cumin, toasted

5 g (1 tsp) black mustard seeds

2.5 g (½ tsp) fennel seeds

2.5 g (½ tsp) black peppercorns

900 g (2 lb) lean boneless lamb, trimmed and cut into 2.5-cm (1-in) pieces

1 large onion, finely chopped

pinch of asa fœtida

chopped fresh coriander for garnish

steamed rice as an accompaniment, if desired

1. *Make the marinade:* Whisk together the vinegar, 30 ml (2 tbsp) of the mustard oil, ginger, paprika, garlic, tamarind, turmeric and jaggery in a bowl large enough to hold the lamb until combined well. Grind the chillies, coriander, cumin, mustard seeds, fennel seeds and peppercorns in a coffee/spice grinder to a fine powder and stir into the vinegar mixture. Prick the meat all over with the tines of a fork and add it to the spice paste. Let the lamb marinate, covered, for at least 4 hours at room temperature and up to 24 hours, chilled.

2. Heat the remaining 30 ml (2 tbsp) of mustard oil in a casserole over moderate heat until hot but not smoking. Stir in the onion and cook, stirring occasionally, until the onion is a dark golden brown, about 10 to 15 minutes. Stir in the asa fœtida and cook, stirring, for 1 minute. Add the lamb and the marinade. Reduce the heat and cook, covered, stirring occasionally, at a bare simmer for 2 hours, or until the lamb is very tender. Remove the cover, taste and adjust seasonings (especially the salt), increase the heat and boil, stirring and watching carefully, until most of the liquid evaporates, about 5 minutes. (You will need to stir more often as the liquid evaporates. The dish should have a thick sauce clinging to the meat, but no excess sauce.) Garnish with the fresh coriander and serve with rice.

CHICKEN KORMA

A 'korma' is a good example of the kind of dish the British would have called a 'curry'. To the Indian chef, a korma is a type of stew in which the meat is braised, then mixed with something creamy (yogurt is the traditional addition, but modern chefs improvise beyond that). Kormas are never particularly chilli-hot.

SERVES 4

1 whole chicken (about 1.8 kg (4 lb)), cut into 8 pieces

1.25 g (¼ tsp) whole cumin

1.25 g (¼ tsp) yellow mustard seeds

1.25 g (¼ tsp) fenugreek

1.25 g (¼ tsp) whole coriander

2.5 g (½ tsp) ground cardamom

1.25 g (¼ tsp) cayenne pepper

pinch of ground cinnamon

pinch of ground allspice

pinch of ground nutmeg

12.5 g (2½ tsp) coarse salt

30 ml (2 tbsp) vegetable oil

20 g (4 tsp) chopped fresh ginger

15 g (1 tbsp) chopped garlic

175 g (6 oz) finely chopped onion

150 ml (5 fl oz) chicken stock

1 litre (1¾ pints) double cream

50 ml (2 tbsp) plain yogurt

1.25 g (¼ tsp) white pepper

50 g (2 tbsp) chopped fresh coriander for garnish

1. Split each breast, thigh and drumstick into 2 pieces.

2. Place cumin, mustard seeds, fenugreek and coriander in a small, heavy frying pan and toast over high heat for 1 minute. Place toasted seeds in a spice grinder and process until finely ground. Place 10 g (2 tsp) of spice mixture in a small bowl and mix with the ground cardamom, cayenne pepper, cinnamon, allspice, nutmeg and 5 g (1 tsp) of the salt.

3. Place oil in a frying pan or casserole large enough to hold the chicken and heat over moderately high heat. Sprinkle chicken with 5 g (1 tsp) of salt. Brown the chicken well on all sides, about 5 to 7 minutes. Remove chicken and set aside. Drain off excess fat.

4. Add ginger, garlic and onion and cook until soft, about 5 minutes. Stir in the spice mixture and cook for another 2 minutes, until spices are fragrant. Increase heat to high and deglaze the pan with the chicken stock, scraping the bottom of the pan with a wooden spoon. Cook until almost all the stock has evaporated and then add the cream. Bring the cream to a boil, reduce the heat so that the liquid bubbles gently and simmer for 10 minutes, until the cream has thickened.

5. Return the chicken to the pan and simmer gently, turning the pieces often, for 18 minutes. Remove the breast pieces and simmer the remaining chicken, turning often, for 12 more minutes.

6. Stir in yogurt and season with white pepper and remaining salt. Add breast pieces back in and gently heat through. Garnish with coriander and serve immediately.

THAI RED PORK CURRY

This is a perfect example of the Thai way with curries: the first step is making a wet paste in a mortar and pestle, or you could put modern technology to work and use a food processor instead. The finished dish is remarkably fragrant. Serve with steamed jasmine rice.

SERVES 4

For the red curry paste
15 g (1 tbsp) whole coriander
5 g (1 tsp) whole cumin
5 g (1 tsp) white or black peppercorns
2.5 g (½ tsp) caraway seeds
115 g (4 oz) shallots

10 to 20 dried hot red chillies
30 g (2 tbsp) chopped lemongrass (tender parts only)
30 g (2 tbsp) chopped garlic
15 g (1 tbsp) chopped peeled fresh galingale
7.5 g (1½ tsp) kaffir lime peel
15 g (1 tbsp) ground red chilli powder
15 g (1 tbsp) shrimp paste
coarse salt to taste
900 g (2 lb) pork shoulder, cut into thin, broad slices
850 ml (1½ pints) medium thick coconut milk (see page 60)
30 ml (2 tbsp) nam pla (Thai fish sauce)
15 g (1 tbsp) palm sugar (or brown sugar)
12 green beans, trimmed and cut diagonally into 5-cm (2-in) lengths
50 g (2 oz) fresh basil leaves, cut into julienne
50 g (2 oz) fresh mint leaves, coarsely chopped
6 kaffir lime leaves, cut into chiffonade (very thin strips)
steamed jasmine rice as an accompaniment, if desired

1. *Make the red curry paste:* Pound the coriander, cumin, peppercorns and caraway seeds to a powder in a large mortar with a pestle. Gradually add the shallots, chillies, lemongrass, garlic and galingale and pound to a paste. Add the kaffir lime peel and pound until smooth. (Alternatively, this may be done in a food processor with a bit of water.) Transfer the curry paste to a bowl and add the ground red chilli powder, shrimp paste and coarse salt, stirring until smooth. The curry paste may be stored, refrigerated, in an air-tight container for a few weeks. (Makes about 115 g (4 oz)).

2. In a heavy casserole over moderate heat add 50 g (2 oz) red curry paste and the pork and cook for 2 minutes, until pork is evenly coated.

3. Add the coconut milk, bring to a boil and cook at a

medium boil for 10 minutes. Bring to a simmer, add the nam pla and palm sugar and simmer, adding the green beans for the last 10 minutes of cooking, for 30 minutes.

4. Stir in half the basil, half the mint and all the lime leaves. Transfer the curry to a serving bowl. Top with remaining basil and mint and serve with the rice.

GREEN CURRY PASTE

Here's a great version of green curry paste, which is often the foundation for curries made with poultry.

MAKES 350 ML (12 FL OZ)

10 g (2 tsp) whole coriander
10 g (2 tsp) whole cumin
5 g (1 tsp) whole black and/or white peppercorns
30 g (2 tbsp) chopped shallots
5 to 15 fresh green kii noo chillies (tiny, incendiary ones), stemmed, seeded, and coarsely chopped
2 stalks fresh lemongrass (tender parts only), sliced thin
30 g (2 tbsp) chopped fresh galingale
15 g (1 tbsp) chopped garlic
30 g (2 tbsp) chopped fresh coriander roots
30 g (2 tbsp) chopped fresh coriander stems
30 g (2 tbsp) chopped fresh coriander leaves
6 kaffir lime leaves, chopped
10 g (2 tsp) chopped kaffir lime zest
5 g (1 tsp) shrimp paste
coarse salt to taste

1. Pound the coriander, cumin and peppercorns to a powder in a large (preferably south-east Asian) mortar and pestle. Gradually add the shallots, chillies, lemongrass, galingale and garlic and pound to a paste. Pound in the fresh coriander roots, stems and leaves until you have a smooth paste.

2. Add the kaffir lime leaves and zest and pound until

smooth. (Alternatively, the curry paste may be made in a food processor with a bit of water.) Transfer the curry paste to a bowl and add the shrimp paste and coarse salt, stirring until smooth. The curry paste may be stored, refrigerated, in an airtight container for a few weeks.

Thai curry pastes
There are several traditional Thai curry pastes (or krung gaeng) that serve as the bass lines for a number of traditional Thai curries. In any Thai kitchen, you're likely to find red curry paste, green curry paste, orange curry paste, yellow curry paste and Mussaman curry paste (which has more of an Indian character to it). These pastes are now available in stores and the Thai products we carry are first-rate. But, if you have the time, it's rewarding to make your own curry pastes at home.

SATAY
Satay is probably the world's first barbecue—and certainly one of its favourites. Though it began in Indonesia—there are satay stalls in villages and cities all over the country—its popularity spread up through Malaysia, to South-east Asia and ultimately to trendy restaurants in the United States. Satay is tremendously easy to make at home; it's basically skewers of meat (in Indonesia the skewers are always made of bamboo) that are grilled over hot coals and dipped into a sauce before eating. The sauces are usually based on peanuts and can be mild or incendiary, or anything in between. Sometimes the meat is marinated before grilling, but not always. Satay is very versatile: serve the skewers as an appetiser, a snack, as part of a large meal, or as a main dish with rice.

INDONESIAN CHICKEN SATAY
This delicious satay is great for a summertime grill party. Make it as spicy as you wish by adjusting the

amount of chillies and type of curry powder in the sauce. You can also make this recipe with duck, pork, lamb, or beef.

MAKES 12 SKEWERS

For the marinade
50 g (2 oz) dried unsweetened shaved or shredded coconut
45 ml (3 tbsp) vegetable oil
3 shallots, chopped
2 garlic cloves, crushed
50 g (2 tbsp) natural chunky roasted peanut butter
5 g (1 tsp) ground coriander
1.25 g (¼ tsp) Asian chilli powder
salt to taste
1 large, whole chicken breast, skinned, boned, split and cut crossways into 2.5-cm (1-in) strips (about 550 g (1¼ lb) of meat)
For the peanut sauce
15 ml (1 tbsp) vegetable oil
1 shallot, chopped
1 to 4 fresh or dried hot chillies, seeds discarded and the chillies finely chopped
5 g (1 tsp) hot or mild curry powder
1 garlic clove, chopped
225 ml (8 fl oz) water
115g (4 oz) natural chunky roasted peanut butter
10 g (2 tsp) brown sugar
20 g (1½ tsp) chopped fresh lemongrass (very tender parts only), if desired

1. *Make the marinade:* Toast the coconut in a small dry frying pan over moderate heat, shaking the pan often, until just golden, about 4 minutes (watch it carefully, because once it begins to turn golden it can burn quickly). Transfer to a plate and reserve.

2. Heat the oil in the same frying pan over moderately low heat until hot but not smoking. Add the shallots and garlic and cook, stirring, for 2 minutes, or until softened. Stir in the peanut butter, coriander and chilli powder and

cook, stirring, for 2 minutes longer. Remove from the heat and add the reserved coconut and salt to taste. Place the marinade in a deep dish just large enough to hold the chicken. Add the chicken to the marinade. Let stand at room temperature, turning occasionally, for 2 hours.

3. Soak twelve 30-cm (12-in) bamboo skewers in water to cover for at least 1 hour.

4. Prepare a hot charcoal fire.

5. *Make the peanut sauce:* Heat the oil in a small saucepan over moderate heat until hot but not smoking. Add the shallot, chillies, curry powder and garlic and cook, stirring, until the shallot is just lightly browned, about 4 minutes. Whisk in the water, peanut butter, brown sugar, lemongrass and salt and bring just to a boil. Reduce the heat and cook, stirring, just until the sauce is thick and smooth, about 2 minutes. Remove from heat. If the sauce thickens on standing, thin it with a bit of water.

6. Thread the chicken on bamboo skewers, evenly dividing it among the 12 skewers. Grill the satays over glowing charcoal, turning frequently, until nicely browned and just cooked through, about 5 minutes. (Alternatively, you can cook the satays under a preheated grill. Lightly oil a foil-covered baking sheet, place the satays on it and grill, turning once, for 5 minutes.) Serve hot with the peanut sauce for dipping.

CONDIMENTS AND SAUCES

AMERICANS HAVE ALWAYS BEEN FOND OF CONDIMENTS AND SAUCES.

UNFORTUNATELY, WE'VE ALWAYS BEEN SOMEWHAT LIMITED IN OUR CHOICES.

CONDIMENTS USUALLY MEANT THE UBIQUITOUS BOTTLES AND JARS OF

KETCHUP AND MUSTARD, AND SEVERAL MASS-MARKET RELISHES...WITH AN

OCCASIONAL HOMEMADE CHUTNEY IN AMBITIOUS HOME KITCHENS.

SAUCES USUALLY MEANT EITHER TOMATO SAUCES, BOTTLED BARBECUE

SAUCES, GRAVIES OUT OF CANS, OR THE OCCASIONAL FORAY INTO HOLLANDAISE

TERRITORY.

TWO FACTORS CONTRIBUTED TO THE RECENT WIDENING OF THESE

CATEGORIES IN AMERICA: WE BECAME MUCH MORE FAMILIAR WITH ETHNIC

TRADITIONS IN THESE CATEGORIES, AND, IN OUR QUEST TO PUT MORE

FLAVOURFUL FOOD ON THE TABLE IN LESS TIME, WE REALISED THAT A SIMPLE

DIPPING SAUCE, SALSA OR MEDITERRANEAN SPREAD CAN DO WONDERS FOR A

QUICKLY COOKED MAIN COURSE.

SO THE EXPANDED UNIVERSE OF CONDIMENTS AND SAUCES HAS BECOME AN

INTEGRAL PART OF THE NEW AMERICAN KITCHEN.

AND MANY OF THESE FLAVOURFUL PREPARATIONS ARE EXTREMELY SIMPLE

TO MAKE AT HOME.

VINAIGRETTES AND SALAD DRESSINGS

Along with the explosion in salads in America (see Chapter One), there has obviously been a concomitant explosion in ways to dress those salads. Preparations based on oil and vinegar—modern examples of the classic vinaigrette—have been the most popular; many of them, however, vary from the classic vinaigrette in that a higher proportion of vinegar to oil is used and many new flavourings have crept in.

In Chapter One, you'll find our favourite basic vinaigrettes for basic salads. Here are some of our favourite vinaigrettes and salad dressings with more creative elements.

SHALLOT VINAIGRETTE

MAKES ABOUT 350 ML (12 FL OZ)

115 g (4 oz) coarsely chopped shallots
75 ml (2½ fl oz) white-wine vinegar
25ml (5 tsp) balsamic vinegar
5 ml (1 tsp) Dijon mustard
350 ml (12 fl oz) extra-virgin olive oil
salt and pepper to taste

Put all the ingredients except the olive oil in a food processor. Turn the motor on and slowly add the oil through the feed tube until all of the oil is added and incorporated. Season to taste with salt and pepper. The dressing keeps, covered, in the refrigerator for 1 to 2 days.

Oil and Vinegar

For a discussion of specific oils and vinegars to use in salad dressings, see page 9.

ROASTED GARLIC VINAIGRETTE WITH LEMON ZEST

This extraordinary dressing packs a big flavour punch—both garlic and vinegar. Intriguingly, except for a little olive oil used to cook the garlic, it is oil-free. Avoid using it to dress delicate greens. We like it best in chunky salads—combos of tomatoes, olives, big croutons and cubes of cheese (like feta). It's also delicious as a dip for grilled bread.

MAKES ABOUT 100 ML (3 FL OZ)

1 head of garlic with about 16 cloves
10 ml (2 tsp) extra-virgin olive oil
50 ml (2fl oz) white-wine vinegar
30 ml (2 tbsp) water
2.5 g (½ tsp) grated lemon zest
salt and pepper to taste

1. Preheat oven to 200°C (400°F).

2. Place the garlic cloves in a small roasting tin and toss with the olive oil. Roast in oven for 15 minutes or until garlic cloves start to brown. Cover with foil and roast until garlic cloves are soft, about 10 minutes more. Remove garlic and let cool slightly.

3. Place garlic in the work bowl of food processor. Add the vinegar, water and lemon zest and purée thoroughly. If mixture seems too thick, add a little more water. Season to taste with salt and pepper. The dressing keeps, covered, in the refrigerator for 1 to 2 days.

GREEK SALAD VINAIGRETTE

We love this idea: not a vinaigrette for Greek salad, but a vinaigrette that *tastes* like a Greek salad. It adds terrific zip and substance to leafy greens.

MAKES ABOUT 225 ML (8 FL OZ)

50 g (2 oz) finely diced green pepper (about
½ small pepper)
50 g (2 oz) finely diced peeled and seeded

cucumber (about ½ small cucumber)

1 small onion, finely diced

4 kalamata olives, stoned and finely diced

45 g (1½ oz) Greek feta cheese, crumbled into fine pieces

7 anchovy fillets, finely chopped

30 ml (2 tbsp) lemon juice

90 ml (6 tbsp) Greek olive oil

salt and pepper to taste

Place all the solid ingredients in a bowl, and add the lemon juice. Add the olive oil in a stream, whisking and whisk the dressing until it is smooth. Season to taste with salt and pepper. The dressing keeps, covered, in the refrigerator for 2 days.

CREAMY LEMON AND TARRAGON DRESSING

One of the great treasures on our shelves is an extra-virgin olive oil that is pressed with fresh, untreated lemons. It emulsifies fabulously into this rich, fairly thick dressing, brimming with the flavour of fresh lemons.

MAKES ABOUT 125 ML (4 FL OZ)

30 ml (2 tbsp) crème fraîche (or sour cream)

30 g (2 tbsp) chopped shallot

10 ml (2 tsp) tarragon wine vinegar

5 g (1 tsp) chopped fresh tarragon leaves

7.5 g (1½ tsp) finely grated fresh lemon zest

1.25 g (½ tsp) Dijon mustard

pinch of granulated sugar

50 ml (2 fl oz) rapeseed oil

15 ml (1 tbsp) lemon-flavoured extra-virgin olive oil

salt and pepper to taste

In a small bowl whisk together the crème fraîche, shallot, vinegar, tarragon, lemon zest, mustard and sugar until smooth. Add the rapeseed oil in a stream, whisking and whisk the vinaigrette until it is emulsified. Whisk in lemon-flavoured olive oil. Season to taste with

salt and pepper. The dressing keeps, covered, in the refrigerator for 2 days.

SHERRY VINAIGRETTE WITH GREEN OLIVES

MAKES ABOUT 350 ML (12 FL OZ)

50 ml (2 fl oz) sherry vinegar

225 ml (8 fl oz) Spanish olive oil

90 g (6 tbsp) finely chopped brine-cured green olives (such as picholine)

salt and pepper to taste

Whisk together the vinegar and olive oil. Blend in olives. Season to taste with salt and pepper. The dressing keeps, covered, in the refrigerator for 2 days.

MUSTARD-BALSAMIC VINAIGRETTE

MAKES ABOUT 250 G (9 OZ)

45 ml (3 tbsp) Dijon mustard

50 ml (2 fl oz) balsamic vinegar

175 ml (6 fl oz) extra-virgin olive oil

salt and pepper to taste

Combine the mustard and balsamic vinegar in a bowl. Slowly whisk in the olive oil. Season to taste with salt and pepper. The vinaigrette keeps, covered, in the refrigerator up to 2 weeks.

Holding and storing vinaigrettes

As soon as you've blended your vinaigrette, it is ready to use—but you can keep vinaigrettes, too, for later use.

If you wish to use a vinaigrette within a few hours, you may keep it at room temperature. The oil and vinegar may separate, but a good whisking just before serving will bring them back together.

If you wish to hold a vinaigrette longer, keep it in the refrigerator. If the vinaigrette has only oil, vinegar and mustard in it, it should keep in the fridge for several weeks. If you've added dried herbs, it will keep for a week. If you've added anything fresh to it—like herbs, garlic or chopped vegetables—it probably won't taste fresh for more than a few days.

WHITE BALSAMIC VINAIGRETTE WITH FRESH MINT
MAKES ABOUT 225 ML (8 FL OZ)

50 ml (2 fl oz) white balsamic vinegar
350 ml (12 fl oz) extra-virgin olive oil
50 g (2oz) finely chopped fresh mint
salt and pepper to taste

Whisk together the vinegar and olive oil. Whisk in the mint. Season to taste with salt and pepper. The vinaigrette keeps, covered, in the refrigerator for 2 days.

HAZELNUT-RASPBERRY BALSAMIC VINAIGRETTE
MAKES ABOUT 225 ML (8 FL OZ)

25 ml (1½ tbsp) raspberry vinegar
25 ml (1½ tbsp) balsamic vinegar
50 ml (2 fl oz) hazelnut oil
125 ml (4 fl oz) neutral-tasting vegetable oil (such as rapeseed)

Blend the vinegars together. Whisk in the oils. Season to taste with salt and pepper. The vinaigrette keeps, covered, in the refrigerator for 2 weeks.

THE OLIVE OIL DRIZZLE

Americans used to have two uses for olive oil: in salad dressing and as a cooking medium. But that was in the era before really great olive oil was so widely available. Now that we've got it, we're learning to use it as the Europeans do: by merely drizzling great olive oil on the right food, you supply a 'sauce' or a 'condiment' that couldn't be simpler or more delicious.

But how do you find great olive oil? In almost every case, it will be marked 'extra-virgin', which, among other things, means that there's less than 1 percent oleic acid in the oil (which, in turn, means that the olives were pressed before they started to deteriorate). In most cases, great oil will cost at least $30 (£18) a litre, sometimes more. But be careful when you're spending this much: olive oil, to most palates, does not improve with age and an old $30 oil won't be worth the price. Make sure the oil you buy was made not more than two years ago (some labels carry harvest date) or that the 'use by' date on the label hasn't been reached.

And what foods do you anoint with your expensive olive oil? The possibilities are endless. Here's a short list of some of our favourite targets for great oil (most of them even better with a little coarse salt, as well):
grilled bread
warm white beans
baked potatoes
tomatoes
roasted red peppers
pasta with garlic
carpaccio
prosciutto
salami
thick soups
grilled vegetables
grilled fish
grilled meat
Parmigiano-Reggiano

It's fun to match the specific flavours of your drizzle targets with the specific flavour of your olive oil. Here's a quick guide to the general profiles of olive oils from the world's greatest producing regions:

Tuscany This is our favourite olive-oil region. At its most characteristic, Tuscan oil is green, intensely fruity-grassy (some say it suggests wheat grass, some say artichokes, some say watermelon rind) and quite peppery in the finish. We love it on starchy things—like bread, beans and potatoes.

Liguria Oils from the Italian Riviera are very different in character; made from riper olives, they are usually more viscous in texture, quieter in flavour, with buttery-nutty overtones. We love them with grilled fish.

Provence Olive oils from southern France are very much like the olive oils from Liguria.

Andalusia This is one of the world's great olive oil regions, producing rich oils with a very specific flavour—kind of grassy-minty, something like the flavours of wines made from Sauvignon Blanc. These oils lend a very specifically 'Spanish' flavour to a wide range of foods.

Greece There are many different styles of oil produced across this great olive-oil country (a country that offers the best bargains in high-quality olive oil). But one flavour seems to recur: the flavour of olives, which, surprisingly, is not a flavour that's found all that often in olive oil.

California Olive oil from California today is roughly analogous to wine from California 30 years ago. A lot of experimentation is going on and it's hard to generalise about the results. In some cases, odd flavours are cropping up that have no precedents in the styles of oil made in Europe. In other cases, however, astoundingly exciting oils are being produced that do taste 'Tuscan' or 'Andalusian', in roughly the same way that California Pinot Noir can taste 'Burgundian'. This is definitely an oil-producing region to watch carefully.

Vegetable oils and shellfish oils

Two other popular infused-oil categories are vegetable oils and shellfish oils.

Vegetable Oils The best of these are actually somewhere between an infused oil and a vegetable purée. To make a vegetable oil, start with the juice of a vegetable (say, fresh carrot juice). Then cook the juice over moderate heat until it is reduced to a near glaze and mix the glaze with an equal quantity of neutral oil. This is particularly spectacular with vegetables that are brightly coloured (like beetroot).

Shellfish Oils These intensely flavoured oils are great to have on hand; imagine drizzling a little coral-coloured lobster oil over a bowl of seafood risotto. To make a shellfish oil, sauté about 900 g (2 lb) of crustacean shells (shrimp, lobster or crab) in 30 ml (2 tbsp) oil over high heat, stirring, for 15 minutes. Reduce heat to extremely low, add 450 ml (16 fl oz) oil and heat for 20 minutes (use a thermometer to make sure the temperature doesn't rise above 105°C (220°F)). Let mixture stand in the refrigerator overnight. Bring to room temperature, then pour through a muslin-lined fine sieve.

INFUSED OIL

Starting in the mid-eighties—and particularly through the work of New York chef Jean-Georges Vongerichten—infused oil became one of the hottest new items in American restaurants. An infused oil is simply an oil that has been mixed with one or more other ingredients until it picks up new flavour. Chefs have been drizzling infused oils for over a decade now on whatever drizzle targets seem appropriate. Homemade ones are not often seen in home kitchens, but that's because many home cooks don't realise how simple they are to make.

Here are the main steps.

Choosing the Oil Make sure to use oil that is absolutely fresh and clean tasting (un-fresh oils may taste a little like stale nuts). For most infused oils, a neutral-tasting oil is the best backdrop. Many chefs like to use rapeseed oil; other neutral vegetable oils, like safflower, are also good. A little harder to find, but a trendy favourite, is grapeseed oil. If the flavours you're using in the infusion have a Mediterranean cast, you might want to use olive oil.

Choosing the Flavours A very wide range of ingredients can be used to make infused oils. But here are the two main categories that you see most frequently: oils made from fresh herbs (such as basil oil, coriander oil and rosemary oil) and oils made from dried spices (such as cardamom oil, cinnamon oil and curry oil).

Combining the Oil and the Flavours This can be very simple indeed; just mixing a flavour with oil begins the infusion process. You can let the flavour steep in the oil for a few minutes, a few hours or a few days (keep tasting to see if the oil has enough flavour). You can hasten the infusion by shaking the mixture frequently. You can really speed up the process by whirring the flavour and the oil together in a food processor.

A good rule of thumb for quantities is: 115 g (4 oz) firmly packed fresh herbs or 115 g (4 oz) for 450 ml (16 fl oz) oil.

In some cases, chefs like to intensify the flavouring agent by subjecting it to heat. If you're making an oil with, say, fresh basil, a 30-second sojourn in boiling water heightens the flavour of the herb. If you're making an oil with, say, cumin, toasting the seeds in a heavy pan for a few minutes brings out their flavour.

In some cases, chefs like to actually heat the oil together with the flavouring agent. This draws even more flavour into the oil and pasteurises any fresh ingredients, such as herbs, so that they won't spoil as the oil is stored. But there's a downside: too much heating can ruin the taste of the oil. A good guideline is 20 minutes of steady heat at 105°C (220°F).

Straining the Oil After the oil has been infused with enough flavour (remember: taste to determine this), it should be strained to remove the flavouring agent (this will improve the oil's longevity). To do this, pour the oil

through a cheesecloth-lined fine strainer.

Using the Oil There are a million great ways to use infused oil. Salad is only the beginning—though we feel that if you want an herbal taste in salad you might as well just toss in fresh herbs. The real glory of infused oil is as a drizzle on beautifully plated foods, when just a few drops can transform a dish into something magical. An infused oil, for example, drizzled over a raw fish appetiser (like tuna tartare, carpaccio of salmon or seviche of scallops) makes all the difference in the world. Sometimes chefs like to drizzle other liquids over the food as well (like vegetable purées) to produce a collage of colours on the plate (particularly with an infused oil that is brightly-coloured, like a green basil oil).

Storing the Oil There has been some concern about botulinum growing in the oxygen-free environment of a tightly stoppered infused oil. Therefore, many chefs like to make their infused oils every day. At home, we feel comfortable keeping the infused oil in a clean glass container for a week or so. If you do the same, keep it in the refrigerator; this will cloud the oil, of course, but let the oil return to room temperature before using it.

SHISO OIL

Here's a good, basic technique for making a fresh herb oil. Of course, the herb itself is a bit unusual; it's the shiso leaf, a piney-tasting herb that is often used at sushi bars. This oil is delicious drizzled over raw fish. But substitute any herb you like for the shiso.

MAKES ABOUT 450 ML (16 FL OZ)

115 g (4 oz) firmly packed shiso leaves
2 cups grapeseed oil

1. Blanch the shiso leaves for 30 seconds in boiling water. Dry the leaves thoroughly on towels.

2. Place the shiso and the oil in a food processor. Purée for 30 seconds. Pour through a cheesecloth-lined fine strainer. (If you wish a stronger shiso taste, let the oil sit for a few hours before straining).

CUMIN AND CHIPOTLE OIL

And here's a good technique for making infused oil from dried flavouring agents. This smoky, spicy oil is delicious when drizzled over almost anything in the American South-west/Mexican idiom; try a little on quesadillas, for example.

MAKES ABOUT 450 ML (16 FL OZ)

50 g (2 oz) cumin seeds
50 g (2 oz) dried chipotles
450 ml (16 fl oz) rapeseed oil

1. Place a heavy cast-iron skillet over moderately high heat. Add the cumin and the chipotles and toast them, stirring, for 5 minutes. Let the cumin and chipotles cool, then place them in a spice grinder or coffee mill; process to a fine powder.

2. Mix the powder in a glass container with the rapeseed oil. Let stand at room temperature for at least 1 day and up to 3 days. When ready to use, pour the oil through a muslin-lined fine strainer.

SALSAS

In the early nineties sales of salsa surpassed sales of ketchup in the United States. This was truly a historic moment in American food—a quantifiable, dollars-and-cents verification of the notion that the old American eating habits were really being changed forever by the advent of ethnic culinary ideas. However, salsa's a lot more confusing than ketchup; it can mean so many different things. The word comes from the Spanish word for 'sauce', but what we usually think of as salsa is much chunkier than a sauce and, unlike most sauces, is served at room temperature.

Then it really gets confusing. Salsa can be made from raw ingredients (salsa cruda) or from cooked ingredients. Sometimes salsa seems almost like a chopped salad, without any liquid, but sometimes it seems like chunks of things in a sauce. Sometimes that sauce is thick, sometimes it's watery. Salsa often has tomatoes in it, but it doesn't necessarily have them. Some salsas are very hot in flavour and some are mild. Some salsas are on the sweet side (salsa with tropical fruit in it has become extremely popular), but most salsas aren't sweet at all.

Here are a few of our favourite salsas.

PICO DE GALLO

Salsa doesn't get more basic than this: pico de gallo is a fresh, uncooked blend of tomatoes, chillies, coriander, onions and lime juice. Usually, in Tex-Mex restaurants, pico de gallo is the chunkiest of the salsa possibilities, with the least surrounding liquid. In Northern Mexico, it's called *salsa mexicana, salsa cruda orsalsa fresca. Pico de gallo* is the Texan name for it—though no one can figure out what a fresh relish has to do with a 'rooster's beak'. Is there a colour in it reminiscent of beaks? Do the chillies resemble beaks? Might the salsa resemble rooster feed? Who knows? The important thing is that pico de gallo is great with fajitas, tacos, tortilla chips, beans, grilled fish, grilled poultry and grilled meat. Easily doubled or tripled, this relish is best right after being made; it does not improve with standing.

MAKES ABOUT 225 ML (8 FL OZ)

1 large ripe tomato, seeded and chopped
50 g (2 oz) finely chopped sweet white onion
50 g (2 oz) chopped fresh coriander
1 to 3 serrano chillies, seeded, if desired, and finely chopped
1 garlic clove, chopped
5 ml (1 tsp) fresh lime juice or more to taste

Stir together all ingredients in a bowl, season with coarse salt and serve immediately.

PINEAPPLE AND HABANERO SALSA

Here's a good example of a sweet, tropical-fruit salsa. It also happens to be very spicy, because habaneros are the hottest chillies available. We like the sweetness and heat together. But if you can't stand the heat, get those habaneros out of the kitchen and substitute a milder chilli. This salsa's great with grilled chicken and pork.

MAKES 350 ML (12 FL OZ)

225 g (8 oz) diced fresh pineapple

15 g (1 tbsp) chopped shallot

45 g (3 tbsp) chopped spring onion (white and green parts)

30 g (2 tbsp) diced red pepper

10 ml (2 tsp) lime juice

5 ml (1 tsp) wine vinegar

5 g (1 tsp) light brown sugar

5 g (1 tsp) finely chopped habanero chilli, or to taste

15 g (1 tbsp) chopped fresh coriander

1. Combine all ingredients except coriander in a small bowl and stir well. Let sit for 15 minutes, taste and adjust seasoning. If it is too hot, add a little more brown sugar; if it is too sweet, add a little more vinegar or lime juice.

2. Just before serving, stir in coriander. The salsa can be made 1 day ahead through step 1 and stored in the refrigerator. Bring to room temperature before serving and stir well.

CHIPOTLE SALSA

In the language of the Aztecs, *chil* refers to chilli and *pochilli* to smoke; what we know as a chipotle is a smoked chilli, most often a jalapeño. It was the Aztecs who first began to smoke chillies; theirs was a humid climate and the skins of many of their chillies were thick and very difficult to dry without fire and smoke. How fortuitous for the rest of us! Chipotles have a complexity that goes beyond fire and smoke; they can have hints of spices, chocolate, caramel and even fruit. Chipotles always have a pronounced effect on other foods; they can really grab your attention in a salsa. This fabulous one is like a cold, chunky tomato sauce with a haunting difference. It is absolute magic on grilled meats and fish. If you'd like it thicker, simply strain out some of the liquid.

MAKES ABOUT 450 ML (16 FL OZ)

900 g (2 lb) (about 6 medium) ripe tomatoes, halved and seeded

225 g (8 oz) chopped sweet white onion

15 ml (1 tbsp) fresh lime juice or more to taste

15 ml (1 tbsp) olive oil

2 cloves garlic, chopped

1 chopped chipotle from canned chipotle chillies in adobo sauce or more to taste

50 g (2 oz) chopped fresh coriander (optional; see note)

1. Preheat a barbecue, grill or ridged grill pan. Place the tomatoes on an oiled grill rack over glowing coals, on a grill pan or on a ridged grill pan over high heat. Grill or broil (broil as close to the heat as possible), turning as necessary, until skins are blackened in spots and slightly softened, about 5 minutes on each side (slightly less time under the grill). Remove.

2. When tomatoes are cool enough to handle, coarsely chop them, place in a bowl and stir in remaining ingredients. Season to taste with salt and pepper.

Note: Using the coriander adds a familar Mexican note and not an unwelcome one. But it will lessen the impact of the smoked chilli flavour in the salsa. Your move.

TOMATILLO SALSA

This is a delicious salsa verde that's especially good with grilled fish and with corn tortillas. Make sure to keep it slightly chunky; otherwise it will become watery. For the same reason, don't hold this salsa more than a few hours.

MAKES ABOUT 225 G (8 OZ)

10 small tomatillos (about 225 g (8 oz))
5 g (1 tsp) finely chopped garlic
5 ml (1 tsp) honey
30 g (2 tbsp) finely chopped spring onion (white
    part only)
15 g (1 tbsp) diced red onion
15 g (1 tbsp) finely chopped jalapeño
45 g (3 tbsp) coarsely chopped fresh coriander
salt and pepper to taste
pinch of sugar to taste

1. Husk the tomatillos and rinse in cold water to remove any gummy resin on the outside. Cut into quarters and place in a food processor with the garlic and honey. Pulse until the tomatillos are broken down, but the mixture is still slightly chunky. Transfer to a small mixing bowl.

2. Add the spring onion, onion, jalapeño and coriander. Set aside for 10 minutes to allow the flavours to mingle. Season with the salt and pepper and add the sugar if you find the salsa too acidic. Serve immediately.

CHUTNEYS AND RELISHES

The great tradition of Indian chutneys—flavourful side dishes, sometimes sweet, always served at room temperature—is echoed in traditional American cookery by the use of relishes. Usually, 'chutney' refers to a mixture that has been cooked, and 'relish' refers to a mixture that has not been cooked. But there's much crossover as well as a raft of other, similar preparations called *chowchows* and *piccalillis*, not to mention

analogous side dishes in a number of other world cuisines.

Whatever they're called, they make for a particularly delicious group of preparations that will perk up any main course when served on the side.

MANGO CHUTNEY

MAKES ABOUT 450 ML (16 FL OZ)

1 large mango
50 ml (2 fl oz) apple vinegar with honey
115 g (4 oz) demerara sugar
225 ml (8 fl oz) water
2.5 g (½ tsp) shelled cardamom seeds
2.5 g (½ tsp) ground ginger
2.5 g (½ tsp) ground cloves
150 g (5½ oz) sultanas
2 cinnamon sticks

1. Peel the mango, remove the stone and cut flesh into large chunks.

2. Place mango chunks in a saucepan and add all the remaining ingredients. Stir well. Place over high heat and bring to a boil, then reduce heat and bring to a simmer. Simmer for 15 minutes. Let cool.

TOMATO CHUTNEY

MAKES ABOUT 350 ML (12 FL OZ)

500g (1¼ lb) tomatoes
50 g (2 oz) chopped onions
2.5 g (½ tsp) chopped garlic
115 g (4 oz) light brown sugar
50 ml (2 fl oz) apple vinegar with honey
5 g (1 tsp) ground ginger
2.5 g (¼ tsp) turmeric
115 g (4 oz) sultanas

1. Peel and seed the tomatoes. Cut into large chunks.

2. Add the tomato chunks to a saucepan and add all the remaining ingredients. Stir well. Place over high heat and bring to a boil, then reduce heat and bring to a simmer. Simmer for 30 minutes. Let cool.

PINEAPPLE AND MINT CHUTNEY
MAKES ABOUT 450 ML (16 FL OZ)

1 ripe pineapple
50 ml (2 fl oz) pineapple juice
225 g (8 oz) raisins
225 g (8 oz) demerara sugar
2 cinnamon sticks
2.5 g (½ tsp) ground cloves
115 g (4 oz) fresh mint

1. Peel and core the pineapple, then cut the flesh into coarse chunks. Place chunks in a saucepan and add all the remaining ingredients. Bring to a boil, reduce heat and simmer for 45 minutes. Remove from heat.

2. Strain out the solids and reserve in a bowl. Return the liquid to the pan. Boil the liquid over high heat until it is reduced to a sticky glaze, about 5 minutes. Add reduced liquid to pineapple solids and let cool.

TAMARIND CHUTNEY

'Chutney' conjures up images of a thick concoction, but it doesn't have to be that way. This rather thin chutney makes up in sweet-sour-spicy flavour what it lacks in body. It is a very popular dipping sauce in Indian restaurants in America today. To make it, you need to find tamarind, which is carried in specialty food shops and in Asian and Hispanic markets. Tamarind comes in several forms; the type we've used for this recipe is a compressed block of dried tamarind, with seeds. It's similar in flavour to prunes, but is much more sour.

Tamarind chutney is traditionally served in India with fried foods and with kebabs.

MAKES 300 ML (10 FL OZ)

115 g (4 oz) dried tamarind pulp (not tamarind concentrate)
15 g (1 tbsp) chopped fresh ginger
500 ml (18 fl oz) hot water
90 g (6 tbsp) sugar (preferably jaggery or demerara)
1 or 2 hot green chillies, seeded, if desired and chopped
5 g (1 tsp) whole cumin
5 g (1 tsp) garam masala
ground cayenne pepper to taste, if desired
salt to taste

1. Soak the tamarind and ginger in the hot water in a small saucepan for 30 minutes. Drain. Squeeze the pulp firmly between your fingers to extract and discard as much liquid as possible. Add the sugar and chillies to the pulp in the pan, bring the mixture to a boil and cook at a bare simmer, stirring, for 15 minutes. Transfer the mixture to a food processor and purée until smooth. Return tamarind chutney to the pan.

2. Toast the cumin in a small frying pan over moderately high heat until very aromatic, about 2 minutes. Transfer the cumin to a bowl and let cool completely. Grind to a fine powder in a coffee or spice grinder.

3. Stir the ground cumin and the garam masala into the tamarind chutney. Add the cayenne pepper and salt to taste. Cook over the lowest possible heat, stirring, for 5 minutes. Strain the mixture through a coarse sieve, pressing hard on the solids with a rubber spatula. Thin the sauce with water to reach the desired consistency (you may need 125 ml (4 fl oz)). Chill before serving.

ORANGE, FENNEL AND CAPER RELISH WITH FRESH MINT

This zippy relish is fantastic alongside or on top of, many things, especially pork. It's also good with duck, chicken and grilled fish.

MAKES ABOUT 450 ML (16 FL OZ)

50 g (2 oz) chopped red onion
225 g (8 oz) finely diced fresh fennel plus the
  leaves, chopped, for garnish
115 g (4 oz) finely diced peeled orange sections
10 picholine olives or other brine-cured green olives,
  stoned and chopped
30 g (2 tbsp) drained capers
15 g (1 tbsp) granulated sugar
30 ml (2 tbsp) fresh orange juice
10 g (2 tsp) chopped fresh mint
coarse salt and ground cayenne pepper to taste

Soak the red onion in a bowl with cold water to cover for 30 minutes, drain in a colander and dry on kitchen towels. Stir together the red onion, diced fennel, orange, olives, capers, sugar and orange juice in a bowl and let stand at room temperature for 15 minutes. Just before serving, toss in the mint. Sprinkle with salt and ground cayenne pepper. Garnish with chopped fennel leaves.

ROASTED ONION AND POMEGRANATE MOLASSES RELISH

Pomegranate molasses (also called grenadine molasses) is a wonderful thing to have in your pantry. It's *not* grenadine syrup (that very sweet stuff used to make bar drinks); this is a luscious, aromatic and deeply flavoured condiment. Once it's in your cupboard and you're familiar with the magic it can bestow on the simplest of foods and dishes, you'll find yourself adding it in all sorts of unexpected places. One especially creative cook we know glazed her Thanksgiving turkey with it! Pomegranate molasses is a staple in the countries of the Middle East and the Eastern

Mediterranean; you can order it through the mail order department at Dean & DeLuca, purchase it there or in a shop that carries Middle Eastern supplies. Serve the following delicious relish with grilled meats, poultry, or fish—especially when you're looking for an exotic accent.

MAKES ABOUT 225 ML (8 FL OZ)

4 small red onions, unpeeled
15 ml (1 tbsp) olive oil
coarse salt to taste
125 ml (4 fl oz) chicken stock
10 ml (2 tsp) pomegranate molasses
2.5 g (½ tsp) sugar
15 g (1 tbsp) chopped fresh coriander
1.25 g (¼ tsp) dried hot red pepper flakes, or more
  to taste
salt and black pepper to taste

1. Preheat oven to 200°C (400°F). Place the onions in an 20-cm (8-in) cast-iron frying pan, toss with olive oil and sprinkle lightly with coarse salt. Roast the onions, shaking the frying pan occasionally, for 30 minutes or until they are very soft to the touch. Remove the onions from the pan, let them cool slightly, cut in half through the root and cool further.

2. Add the stock, 5 ml (1 tsp) of the pomegranate molasses and sugar to the frying pan and place it over moderately high heat. Bring the liquid to a boil, scraping the bottom of the pan and boil, stirring, until the liquid is reduced to about 1 tablespoon, about 10 minutes.

3. Remove the papery outer skins from the onions, slice them as soon as they are cool enough to handle and transfer to a bowl. Add the reduced liquid, the rest of the pomegranate molasses, coriander and red pepper flakes. Stir until combined well and season to taste with salt and pepper. Serve at room temperature.

HOMEMADE HOT DOG RELISH

And why not make it yourself? It's fresher and less sweet than store-bought relish and it's delicious with many things other than hot dogs (try it with pork chops).

MAKES ABOUT 350 ML (12 FL OZ)

1 red pepper, finely diced
1 green pepper, finely diced
juice of 2 lemons
4 garlic cloves, finely chopped
2 small red onions, finely diced
50 ml (2 fl oz) red-wine vinegar
50 g (2 oz) light brown sugar
10 g (2 tsp) ground ginger
5 g (1 tsp) ground white pepper
125 ml (4 fl oz) water

Combine all ingredients in a saucepan. Bring to boil and simmer for 15 minutes. Let cool.

HOMEMADE BARBECUE SAUCES

Real Southern and Midwestern barbecue is not an easy thing to achieve; it takes patience (the meats may cook for more than 12 hours) and a smoking unit capable of holding a low, steady 105°C (215°F) of heat. Therefore, many barbecue-hungry but time-pressed Americans have discovered a wonderful trick: cooking the meat much more simply (like slapping it on a hot outdoor barbecue grill for a few minutes) and slathering them at the table with barbecue sauce. This method achieves at least some of the flavour that real barbecue delivers.

What is barbecue sauce? No two regions of the South or Mid-west would agree on a specific answer. But the general idea is the same: it's a sauce used at the table to moisten barbecued meat. Northerners sometimes are confused about its purpose, thinking it a sauce to be used in the preparation of the meat. But this ain't so. Dry rubs, marinades and wet mops flavour the meat before and during cooking. Barbecue sauce is a finishing sauce.

Of course, 'finishing' is loosely defined and many barbecue chefs paint the meat with barbecue sauce 10 to 15 minutes before it comes off the fire. But caution is recommended in using this approach; if the sauce has lots of sugar and if the fire is hot, charred barbecue may be the result.

The question of smokiness

The flavour of smoke is one of barbecue's most important features. It is achieved in meat by long, slow cooking over aromatic smoke. But modern mass-market geniuses have found a way to bypass the long cooking and get smoky flavour to meat anyway: they add smoke flavour to barbecue sauce (most of the supermarket sauces have it).

To barbecue connoisseurs, this seems like cheating. On the other hand, it's awfully nice to cook chicken for only 20 minutes and still get a smoky flavour by merely applying some sauce.

However, the typical means of smoke addition to the commercial sauces does give us pause: liquid smoke in the barbecue sauce. Now, this is not, as you might imagine, a health concern: liquid smoke is actually all natural, made from condensed hickory smoke and not full of unhealthful chemicals. Still, it seems somehow artificial as a sauce addition. If you want to try it anyway, add about 15 ml (1 tbsp) liquid smoke to every 450 ml (16 fl oz) barbecue sauce.

We prefer to actually smoke our barbecue sauce. We make an impromptu smoker by moistening hickory chips, then adding them to a very hot wok. We set some kind of cylinder in the chips (like a clean, empty can), then balance a wide, shallow bowl of barbecue sauce on top of the cylinder. Cover the wok tightly, keep the heat at a level that keeps the chips smokin' and smoke for about 60 minutes. Works like a charm!

KANSAS CITY–STYLE BARBECUE SAUCE

In most parts of the country, when we think about barbecue sauce—like the bottled ones we buy in the supermarket—it is Kansas City–style sauce that comes to mind. Thick, spicy, tomatoey, sweet and pungent, it is a great all-purpose sauce for a variety of meats. The following version is one of the most complex we've ever tasted.

MAKES ABOUT 450 ML (16 FL OZ)

45 ml (3 tbsp) vegetable oil
115 g (4 oz) chopped onion
115 g (4 oz) finely chopped celery
30 g (2 oz) chopped garlic
175 fl (6 fl oz) cider vinegar
125 ml (4 fl oz) tomato paste
125 ml (4 fl oz) water
30 ml (2 tbsp) molasses (mild flavour)
45 g (3 tbsp) light brown sugar
30 ml (2 tbsp) Worcestershire sauce
10 g (2 tsp) paprika
5 g (1 tsp) powdered mustard
5 g (1 tsp) celery seed
2.5 g (½ tsp) ground black pepper
2.5 g (½ tsp) ground cayenne pepper
20 g (4 tsp) coarse salt

1. Heat the vegetable oil in a heavy saucepan over moderate heat. Add onion, celery and garlic and cook for 5 minutes or until slightly soft.

2. Add all the remaining ingredients and simmer sauce, uncovered, for 30 minutes or until it is quite thick. Purée sauce in blender until smooth. (If you prefer an extra-smooth sauce, pass mixture through a fine sieve.)

How to use barbecue sauce

The thicker barbecue sauces (Kansas City, Texas, western Carolina, South Carolina) present multiple possibilities. You can slather them on pieces of grilled or barbecued meat or you can paint the meat with the sauces during the last few minutes of cooking. At the table, you can pour the sauce in your plate and dip meat in it or you can put your cooked meat on a sandwich and slather that with sauce.

The eastern Carolina–style and the Kentucky black barbecue sauces are another story. They are quite different from what most of us call barbecue sauce: thin and vinegary. Many Northerners wonder how to use them.

The procedure is simple. You take meat that has been cooked for a long time and is falling apart (typically, pork in Carolina, lamb around Owensboro, Kentucky), you pull the shreds apart, you moisten the meat with the barbecue sauce in a bowl (shreds from a 1.8-2.25 kg (4-5- lb) bone-in hunk of meat will need about 450 ml (16 fl oz) of sauce) and you serve the dressed meat shreds on cheap, innocuous white rolls or on supermarket white bread.

Connoisseurs may add coleslaw and hot sauce.

TEXAS-STYLE BARBECUE SAUCE

Texans also like a tomato-based barbecue sauce, though theirs is usually less tomatoey than the Kansas City sauce. It's also less sweet, less thick and filled with the flavours of the southwest.

MAKES ABOUT 850 ML (24 FL OZ)

50 ml (2 fl oz) vegetable oil
225 g (8 oz) chopped onion
50 g (2 oz) finely chopped celery
30 g (2 tbsp) chopped garlic
125 ml (4 fl oz) cider vinegar
50 ml (2 fl oz) distilled white vinegar
175 ml (6 fl oz) ketchup
125 ml (4 fl oz) tomato purée
125 ml (4 fl oz) water
30 ml (2 tbsp) Worcestershire sauce
15 g (1 tbsp) chilli powder
7.5 g (1½ tsp) ground cumin

5 g (1 tsp) hot paprika

20 g (4 tsp) coarse salt

1. Heat the vegetable oil in a heavy saucepan over moderate heat. Add the onion, celery and garlic and cook for 5 minutes or until slightly soft.

2. Add all the remaining ingredients and simmer sauce, uncovered, for 20 minutes or until it is quite thick. Purée in blender until smooth. (If you prefer an extra-smooth sauce, pass mixture through fine sieve.)

NORTH CAROLINA BARBECUE SAUCE, WESTERN-STYLE

The barbecue sauces of North Carolina are amazingly varied. West of Raleigh, tomato-based sauces rule, just as they do in Kansas City and Texas. The typical western Carolina sauce relies heavily on ketchup, is very sweet and features a heavy dose of vinegar. The following sauce is relatively simple . . . a good sauce if you like your barbecue to be unimpeded by lots of complex (distracting?) flavours.

MAKES ABOUT 2 CUPS

15 g (½ oz) butter

75 g (2¾ oz) chopped onion

125 ml (4 fl oz) ketchup

50 ml (2 fl oz) tomato paste

50 ml (2 fl oz) water

125 ml (4 fl oz) lemon juice

125 ml (4 fl oz) cider vinegar

175 g (6 oz) light brown sugar

15 ml (1 tbsp) Worcestershire sauce

10 ml (2 tsp) Tabasco sauce

10 g (2 tsp) coarse salt

1.25 g (¼ tsp) freshly ground black pepper

1. Melt the butter in a heavy saucepan over low heat and add the onion. Cook until slightly soft, about 5 minutes.

2. Add all the remaining ingredients and simmer sauce over moderate heat for 20 minutes. (The sauce will thicken slightly.)

NORTH CAROLINA BARBECUE SAUCE, EASTERN-STYLE

As you move east of Raleigh, North Carolina and toward the Carolina coast, everything changes: eastern Carolinians can't abide tomato-based barbecue sauce. Here, barbecue chefs like to moisten their pulled pork with a sauce that is thin and vinegary, with nary a speck of tomato. It's a far cry from what most of the country thinks of as barbecue sauce. This is one sauce that only makes sense at the table; it doesn't have enough texture to cling to meat on the grill.

MAKES ABOUT 225 ML (8 FL OZ)

175 ml (6 fl oz) cider vinegar

50 ml (2 fl oz) distilled white vinegar

15 g (1 tbsp) light brown sugar

10 g (2 tsp) coarse salt

1.25 g (¼ tsp) ground black pepper

2.50 g (½ tsp) dried hot red pepper flakes

Mix all ingredients together in small bowl and allow to sit for 15 minutes before using.

SOUTH CAROLINA-STYLE BARBECUE SAUCE

The Carolina story gets even more complicated when you consider South Carolina. There, as in Georgia, yellow barbecue sauce, made with lots of commercial mustard, is often the sauce of choice. The following medium-thick, yellow, authentic sauce adds delicious layers of flavours to the mustardy core. We find it especially delicious with something quite un-barbecue-like: grilled prawns.

MAKES ABOUT 225 ML (8 FL OZ)

15 ml (1 tbsp) vegetable oil

50 g (2 oz) chopped onion

15 g (1 tbsp) chopped garlic
75 ml (3 fl oz) American mustard
45 ml (3 tbsp) ketchup
30 g (2 tbsp) light brown sugar
125 ml (4 fl oz) distilled white vinegar
50 ml (2 fl oz) water
10 ml (2 tsp) lemon juice
pinch of ground black pepper
pinch of ground cayenne pepper
15 g (1 tbsp) coarse salt

1. Heat the vegetable oil over moderate heat. Add the onion and garlic and cook for 5 minutes or until slightly soft.

2. Add all the remaining ingredients and simmer sauce, uncovered, for 20 minutes. (The sauce will thicken slightly.)

KENTUCKY BLACK BARBECUE SAUCE

This is one of the least-known—but one of the most delicious—Southern barbecue sauces. It is customarily served around Owensboro, Kentucky, where the meat of choice is lamb. The following version is thin, vinegary, dark . . . and loaded with the flavour of sweet spices, though it's not particularly sweet. It is, however, lip-tinglingly hot.

MAKES ABOUT 225 ML (8 FL OZ)

10 ml (2 tsp) vegetable oil
115 g (4 oz) chopped onion
150 ml (5 fl oz) distilled white vinegar
150 ml (5 fl oz) Worcestershire sauce
35 g (1¼ oz) light brown sugar
10 ml (2 tsp) lemon juice
1.25 g (¼ tsp) ground black pepper
1.25 ml (¼ tsp) Tabasco sauce
pinch of ground cloves
pinch of ground nutmeg
2.5 g (½ tsp) coarse salt

1. Heat the vegetable oil over moderate heat. Add the onion and cook for 5 minutes or until onion is soft and light golden brown.

2. Add the remaining ingredients and simmer, uncovered, for 15 minutes. (The sauce will thicken slightly.)

SEASONED SALT

Salt, all by itself, is a great 'condiment'—particularly a wonderful salt, like the light, flaky, flavourful Maldon sea salt (which Dean & DeLuca carries). However, you can take any salt, add a few flavourings to it and come up with a miraculous sprinkle that's always on hand to lift the flavour level of any dish.

HERB-AND-SPICE SALT

Dean & DeLuca's spice section is stocked with the finest herbs and spices from all over the world. We have found the following spice-and-salt combination to be a fabulous seasoning for many foods.

MAKES ABOUT 20 G (¾OZ)

15 g (1 tbsp) coarse salt
2.5 g (½ tsp) celery seed
pinch of whole coriander
½ bay leaf

Grind the ingredients together in a clean spice or coffee grinder to a very fine grain. Store tightly covered.

CELERY SALT

We also like to isolate the flavour of celery seed in a seasoned salt; it gives many foods a mysterious extra dimension.

MAKES ABOUT 20 G (¾OZ)

15 g (1 tbsp) coarse salt

2.5 g (1/2 tsp) celery seed

Grind the ingredients together in a clean spice or coffee grinder to a very fine grain. Store tightly covered.

CHIPOTLE SALT

This terrific salt, flavoured with smoked chillies, taste great on tortilla chips or even potato chips; it's also delicious on grilled fish and grilled meat.

MAKES ABOUT 20 G (¾OZ)

1 dried chipotle chilli (or enough to yield 5 g (1 tsp) ground chipotle)

15 g (1 tbsp) coarse salt

1. Cut the chipotle open with scissors and remove stem and seeds. Cut the chipotle into small pieces and grind in a spice grinder until finely ground.

2. Combine the ground chipotle with the coarse salt in a small bowl.

LEMON SALT

Lemon salt is a great condiment to have near your stove to spice up a simple dish of almost any type— vegetables, poultry, sauces or whatever you're cooking that you think might need a little extra spunk. We especially like it on grilled fish (great with shrimp) and steamed leafy vegetables. To make this salt, you may grate your own zest and dry it on paper for a few days. Or you can use the fine version of dried lemon zest made by Frontier that Dean & DeLuca carries in the spice section; though most dried citrus zest packed in jars is of inferior quality, this one may be even better than your own. Another great product used in this recipe is Boyajian pure lemon oil, found with the sugar at Dean & DeLuca; again, it packs a lot of flavour.

MAKES ABOUT 40 G (1½ OZ)

15 g (1 tbsp) completely dried finely grated lemon zest

15 g (1 tbsp) coarse salt

5 g (1 tsp) whole white peppercorns, or more to taste

1.25 ml (¼ tsp) Boyajian pure lemon oil

Grind the lemon zest, coarse salt and peppercorns together in a clean spice or coffee grinder to a fine grain. Remove the mixture to a bowl and stir in the lemon oil, breaking up any lumps. (The salt will be slightly moist from the lemon oil.) The lemon salt keeps, tightly covered, for 1 week.

MAYONNAISE

Mayonnaise elicits very strong reactions from Americans. For years, it was one of our favourite condiments, ubiquitous on sandwiches, with nary a negative connotation. America's most famous commercial mayonnaise, Hellman's (called 'Best Foods' west of the Rockies), was even that rare mass-market product that foodies admitted liking.

Then the Fat Police emerged and millions of Americans started to disdain a product that is, after all, pure oil and eggs. Why, a whole new generation of fat-conscious Americans would no sooner slather mayonnaise on a sandwich than eat a few fried chips.

To some, however, this new view of mayonnaise's evils has only served to make them more selective when contemplating the consumption of all those fat grams. It really may be true that we were once too indiscriminate in our use of mayonnaise, spreading large amounts of inferior versions of it with impunity on our sandwiches or beating gobs of it into salads.

After the fall, some Americans returned mayonnaise to its original context: a sauce, made at home, to be used sparingly alongside fish and vegetables.

The following mayonnaise recipes are delicious; we urge you not to fear them. You can make them either

with the basic homemade mayonnaise at the beginning
of the section or with a good bottled mayonnaise, such
as the Walnut Acres All Natural Mayonnaise, made in
Penns Creek, Pennsylvania that we sell at the store.

BASIC HOMEMADE MAYONNAISE

This recipe yields a rich mayonnaise. If you desire a
thinner sauce, add a little bit of water to the finished
mayonnaise.

MAKES ABOUT 450 ML (16 FL OZ)

3 egg yolks
5 ml (1 tsp) Dijon mustard
2.5 g (½ tsp) salt
50 ml (2 fl oz) lemon juice
225 ml (8 fl oz) olive oil
225 ml (8 fl oz) rapeseed oil

1. Place the egg yolks, mustard, salt and lemon juice in
a food processor. Process for 10 seconds.

2. With motor running, add the oil, drop by drop at first.
After a few tablespoons have been added, start adding
oil in a thin stream. Continue until all the oil is added
and the mayonnaise has thickened. Taste for seasoning
and add a little additional salt or lemon juice if desired.

Rouille

For another great mayonnaise, take a look at the
reddish, spicy Provençal mayonnaise that appears on
page 78 in our recipe for bouillabaisse.

SAFFRON MAYONNAISE

If you like saffron, you'll love the taste of this intense
mayo. Terrific with chicken and fish.

MAKES ABOUT 1 CUP

20 ml (4 tsp) white-wine vinegar

10 g (2 tsp) saffron threads
225 ml (8 fl oz) mayonnaise
salt and pepper to taste

Warm vinegar over low heat in a small saucepan, then
remove from heat. Add the saffron threads and leave for
10 minutes. Add vinegar and saffron, blending well. Add
salt and pepper.

THREE-LEMON MAYO WITH DILL

The three types of lemon flavour used in this mayo—a
great accompaniment to fish—create a lemony wallop.

MAKES ABOUT 225 ML (8 FL OZ)

225 ml (8 fl oz) mayonnaise
20 ml (4 tsp) lemon juice
1.25 ml (¼ tsp) Boyajian pure lemon oil
10 g (2 tsp) very finely chopped lemongrass (tender
  inner core only)
45 g (3 tbsp) chopped fresh dill

Blend ingredients together. Season to taste.

ANCHOVY-CAPER MAYONNAISE

This delicious mayonnaise is good on bruschetta or as a
dip for crudités.

MAKES ABOUT 1¼ CUPS

225 ml (8 fl oz) mayonnaise
10g (2 tsp) garlic chopped to a paste with a little
  salt
10 ml (2 tsp) lemon juice
20 g (4 tsp) chopped capers
24 finely chopped anchovy fillets

Blend ingredients together. Season to taste.

GREEN OLIVE MAYONNAISE
MAKES ABOUT 350 ML (12 FL OZ) CUPS

225 ml (8 fl oz) mayonnaise (preferably made with
green Tuscan extra-virgin olive oil)
10 ml (2 tsp) lemon juice
about 48 brine-cured green olives, such as
picholine, stoned and chopped

Blend ingredients together. Season to taste.

Aïoli

Well, heck, mayonnaise works just fine in a food
processor, as our faith in all these mayonnaises
confirms. But there's nothing like making this ancient
Provençal garlic mayonnaise in a mortar with a pestle; it
feels better doing it and we think the finished product is
ineffably better. Make sure you have a marble mortar,
preferably with a wooden pestle. Make sure the garlic
you're using is very fresh, almost wet. And we find the
most delicious aïoli of all to be made not from Provençal
olive oil (which is mild-tasting) but from bright-green,
peppery, Tuscan-style olive oil, produced from unripe
olives. The following recipe produces a very thick
mayonnaise; if you like it thinner, add a little room-
temperature water to the aïoli as you're finishing it.
MAKES ABOUT 125 ML (4 FL OZ)

2 medium, very fresh garlic cloves, peeled
1.25 g (¼ tsp) salt
1 large egg yolk, at room temperature
75 ml (5 tbsp) green extra-virgin olive oil
a few teaspoons water (optional)

1. Fill a mortar with boiling water. After 1 minute, spill
out the water and dry the mortar. Add the garlic cloves
and the salt. Start pounding them with the pestle.

2. When a smooth paste is achieved, add the egg yolk.
Moving the pestle rapidly against the walls of the
mortar, blend the yolk together with the garlic.

3. When blended, begin adding the olive oil in a thin
stream, still moving the pestle rapidly against the walls
of the mortar. Continue until all the olive oil is added
and a thick mayonnaise is achieved. Add water if
necessary. Taste for seasoning and add more salt if
necessary. Refrigerate.

CORIANDER-JALAPEÑO MAYONNAISE
MAKES ABOUT 300 ML (10 FL OZ)

225 ml (8 fl oz) mayonnaise
510 g (2 tsp) chopped jalapeños
125 g (4½ oz) chopped fresh coriander
10 ml (2 tsp) cider vinegar

Blend ingredients together. Season to taste.

TARRAGON TARTAR SAUCE

This is really a sauce—it bears no relation to that
unnaturally thick and gloppy concoction usually brought
out under the name of tartar sauce. This sauce lightly
cloaks its object, rather than weighing it down. The key
to getting a tartar sauce that runs a little is using
mayonnaise that's not too thick. Either use a relatively
thin homemade one, buy a thin one (like Walnut Acres
All Natural Mayonnaise) or thin out a thicker bottled
mayonnaise with a little water.
MAKES ABOUT 400 ML (14 FL OZ) CUPS

225 ml (8 fl oz) mayonnaise
125 ml (4 fl oz) sour cream
2 shallots, finely chopped
4 miniature gherkins, finely chopped
18 brine-cured green olives (such as picholine),
stoned and chopped
20 g (1½ tbsp) chopped fresh tarragon leaves
15 ml (1 tbsp) white-wine vinegar or more to taste

hot red pepper sauce to taste

Whisk together all ingredients in a bowl until combined well. Cover and store in the refrigerator until ready to serve.

CLASSIC MEDITERRANEAN CONDIMENTS

TZATZIKI

Variations of this cucumber-and-yogurt dish are popular throughout the Middle East, Turkey (where it's called *cacik*), the Balkans and Greece. The Greek version, such as this recipe, often contains more garlic than the others; cut back a bit if you're garlic-shy. Tzatziki is terrific as part of a Greek spread of appetisers, along with warm pitta and olives or it can function as a great side dish/sauce with grilled meat and fish. Dean & DeLuca carries a fantastic Greek-style sheep's-milk yogurt from Hollow Road Farms in Stuyvesant, New York, that is perfect for this dish.

MAKES ABOUT 300 ML (10 FL OZ)

1 litre (1¾ pints) sheep's milk yogurt
1 long cucumber, unpeeled, seeded, and finely diced with a few very thin slices for garnish
5 g (1 tsp) salt plus additional to taste
30 ml (2 tbsp) olive oil (preferably kalamata)
30 g (2 tbsp) chopped fresh dill leaves plus dill sprigs for garnish
5 ml (1 tsp) red-wine vinegar or more to taste
4 garlic cloves, chopped and mashed to a paste with 1.25 g (¼ tsp) salt
pepper to taste

1. Drain the yogurt through a very-fine meshed sieve lined with muslin over a bowl for at least 2 hours at room temperature and up to 1 day, covered, in the refrigerator. Discard the liquid that drains off.

2. While the yogurt is draining, place the cucumber and 1 teaspoon salt in a colander over a bowl and let drain for at least 1 hour at room temperature and up to 1 day, covered, in the refrigerator. Squeeze batches of cucumber wrapped in kitchen towels to remove as much liquid as possible. Dry the cucumber on kitchen towels.

3. Stir together the drained yogurt and cucumber, the olive oil, chopped dill, red-wine vinegar and garlic. Season to taste with salt and pepper. Let stand for 1 hour before serving. Serve cool or at room temperature, garnished with the cucumber slices and dill sprigs.

ANCHOÏADE

Also called *la bagnaroto* in Provence, anchoïade—or anchovies pounded to a paste with olive oil and vinegar—may be used in two ways. You can spread it on bread and broil it, as this recipe indicates. Or, you can thin it (anywhere from 125-175 ml (4-6 fl oz) good olive oil will do the trick) and use it as a dip for vegetables. If you're making anchoïade, start with serious anchovies—that is, the ones packed in salt in big tins (you can buy these anchovies in small quantities at Dean & DeLuca). If you use the regular, oil-packed anchovies from the small tins, your anchoïade won't have the correct, meaty texture; it will be too soft. Remember that the salt-packed anchovies do need to be soaked before using.

MAKES ABOUT 125 ML (4 FL OZ)

12 large anchovy fillets packed in salt (about (5 oz))
1 garlic clove
45 ml (3 tbsp) extra-virgin olive oil
5 ml (1 tsp) red-wine vinegar or more to taste
leaves from 1 large sprig of fresh thyme
freshly ground black pepper to taste
8 x 2-cm (¾-in)-thick slices of rustic French bread, grilled or toasted on 1 side

1. Rinse the anchovy fillets under cold running water,

rub off the salt coating and soak in a bowl of cold water to cover for 30 minutes. Drain the anchovies, dry on paper towels and chop them coarsely.

2. Pound the garlic to a paste in a large mortar with a pestle. Add the anchovies, olive oil, vinegar and thyme leaves and pound to a smooth paste. Season to taste with freshly ground black pepper. Spread the mixture on the untoasted sides of the French bread and broil until hot. Serve immediately.

TAPENADE

The great Provençal paste tapenade is often thought of as an olive purée—and, indeed, it always does contain black olives. But the name derives from another key ingredient; in the Provençal dialect, capers are called *tapéno*. A third ingredient is also de rigueur: anchovies. Beyond this trio, increasingly, anything goes. Tuna, brandy, lemon, mustard and herbs are often added— which are all fine by us, as long as the essential flavours of olive and caper are not eclipsed. Since tapenade has become so popular among American chefs, we've even been seeing green-olive variations— but the taste is vastly different. The following version gets it just right, to our taste. Use black olives from the south of France, if you can find them; we also love to make tapenade with kalamata olives from Greece. Tapenade is wonderful as a spread on garlicky bread; as a little mound on a Provençal appetiser plate; as a flavour kick for a vinaigrette; as a component of egg salad or stuffed eggs; and as a condiment or stuffing for roasted or grilled meat or poultry.

MAKES ABOUT 275 ML (10 FL OZ)

225 g (8 oz) stoned black olives
10 g (2 tsp) chopped garlic
15 g (1 tbsp) chopped yellow onion
4 anchovy fillets (from a can)
15 g (1 tbsp) capers
pinch of dried thyme

pinch of cayenne pepper
50 ml (2 fl oz) olive oil
1.25 ml (¼ tsp) fresh lemon juice

1. Place the olives, garlic, onion, anchovies, capers, thyme and cayenne in the bowl of a food processor and pulse until the olives are broken down but the mixture is still chunky.

2. With machine running, pour the olive oil through the feed tube in a slow, steady stream. Process until the mixture is finely chopped and even in texture but not completely puréed. Add the lemon juice and stir. The tapenade keeps, covered, in the refrigerator for 1 week.

HARISSA

This spicy-hot condiment is very popular in the Maghreb, the strip of countries (including Algeria, Tunisia and Morocco) that runs along the Mediterranean Sea on the north coast of Africa. It always includes a base of hot, red chillies, but it can come in different forms: as a gritty purée of dried peppers, as a paste and as a thinned liquid or sauce. We prefer the latter variation. There are many different types of chillies and peppers that you can use as a base for harissa, but we find that a good, dark red powder made from chillies works best for the 'sauce-style' harissa. You can use a top-grade chilli powder or paprika (our preference is the wonderful, spicy Spanish paprika we sell called Carmencita). Harissa can be used in manifold ways: stirred into black olives, stews, soups, salads or vegetable dishes, rubbed on kebabs and grilled meat and served as a sauce for couscous.

MAKES ABOUT 225 ML (8 FL OZ)

25 g (1 oz) dark red chilli powder or Spanish
  paprika
7 g (1½ tsp) salt
3 g (¾ tsp) ground cumin
175 ml (6 fl oz) distilled white vinegar

15 ml (1 tbsp) olive oil
3 cloves garlic, peeled and lightly crushed

In a bowl combine all ingredients except garlic until a smooth sauce is formed. Add the garlic, stir and refrigerate for 24 hours. Remove garlic and serve. The sauce keeps, covered tightly, in the refrigerator for several months.

Note: This sauce picks up a lovely, subtle garlic flavour from its 24-hour marination. If you wish to make a quicker sauce with garlic flavour, eliminate the 3 cloves and substitute ¼ teaspoon very finely mashed garlic.

PESTO

Americans often think of pesto as a pasta sauce, but it can be a delicious condiment as well. Simply spread a little bit on tomatoes, grilled vegetables, grilled bread, grilled fish or grilled meat. To make the best pesto, use the freshest, most vivid basil you can find—without a trace of bitterness. In the summer, we like to use a small-leaf basil called 'bush basil'.

MAKES ABOUT 150 ML (5 FL OZ)

115 g (4 oz) fresh basil leaves
50g (2 oz) pine nuts
50g (2 oz) chopped garlic
90 ml (6 tbsp) Ligurian or Provençal olive oil
50g (2 oz) Parmigiano-Reggiano
10 g (2 tsp) firmly packed pecorino Romano
salt to taste

1. Wash and dry the basil well. Place in the work bowl of a food processor with the pine nuts and garlic. Process quickly to make a coarse, grainy paste. With the motor running, add the olive oil over the course of 5 seconds. Remove pesto from work bowl (it should still be fairly grainy).

2. Place pesto in a bowl and add the cheeses. Mix well.

(If the pesto is too thick, add additional olive oil to achieve the desired consistency. There should be some oil glistening around the edges.) Season to taste with salt.

Preserved lemons in charmoula
One fabulous way to use Moroccan preserved lemons is as an ingredient in the great Moroccan rub/marinade (often for fish) called charmoula, a blend of fresh herbs, spices and seasonings. Charmoula doesn't always include preserved lemons, but some of the best we've ever tasted have. We like to take the tradition a step further; sometimes, we add even more preserved lemon—giving the charmoula additional body—then we use the charmoula as a condiment alongside grilled fish or meats. Here's a recipe for charmoula as condiment.

MAKES ABOUT 225 ML (8 FL OZ)

75 g (2¾ oz) chopped Moroccan preserved lemons
3 garlic cloves, finely chopped
1 small onion, chopped
75 g (2¾ oz) chopped flat-leaf parsley
75 g (2¾ oz) chopped coriander
50 g (2 oz) chopped stoned Moroccan black olives
45 ml (3 tbsp) olive oil
5 g (1 tsp) paprika
2.5 g (½ tsp) ground cumin
2.5 g (½ tsp) ground coriander
2.5 g (½ tsp) ground ginger

Combine all ingredients well. Season to taste with salt, black pepper and cayenne.

MOROCCAN PRESERVED LEMONS
This great condiment from Morocco tastes something like lemon pickle, which is a great condiment from India. But the Indian version is very strong and not to the liking of most Americans who have tried it; the Moroccan

version is much milder and very versatile in its uses. We love a bowl of preserved lemon wedges as one dish among many in any type of Moroccan, African or Middle Eastern spread of foods; they are particularly delicious next to tagines, curries and grills. The following recipe, though it yields authentic flavour, is a slightly speeded-up version of the classic recipe; because the lemons are separated into eighths, they take less time to pickle. Once ready, the preserved lemons will keep in the refrigerator for 6 months.

2 lemons
75 g (2¾ oz) coarse salt
125 ml (4 fl oz) fresh lemon juice

1. Wash the lemons well. Cut them into 8 sections each and place them in a glass jar. Add the remaining ingredients. Cover tightly and shake the jar well to combine ingredients.

2. Leave lemons at room temperature, shaking the jar every day, for 2 weeks. Rinse lemons before using.

AJVAR

This absolutely delicious Eastern European specialty is also known as Serbian red pepper ketchup, but its actual, chunky consistency is more like a relish or a chutney. It can be made as hot as you like: just add more chillies. It is traditionally served like a ketchup— in small amounts alongside meats, cheeses, raw vegetables and fish.

MAKES 1½ CUPS

2 red peppers (or 1 red and 1 orange)
1 medium aubergine (about 225 g (½ lb), pricked with a fork 4 times
3 hot chillies or more to taste, seeded and chopped
3 cloves garlic, mashed to a paste with 2.5 g (½ tsp) salt
50 ml (2 fl oz) vegetable oil

50 ml (2 fl oz) red-wine vinegar or more to taste
coarse salt and ground cayenne pepper to taste

1. Preheat oven to 180°C (350°F). Roast the peppers and aubergine on a baking sheet in the oven for 1 hour or until soft. Transfer the vegetables to a plate to cool and save any juices that accumulate. Remove the stems, skins and seeds from the peppers and chop the flesh. Remove the stem and skin from the aubergine and chop the flesh.

2. Place the peppers and aubergine in a medium frying pan, add the chillies, garlic, oil, vinegar, coarse salt and cayenne pepper, adding any reserved juices and cook the mixture over very low heat, stirring, for 30 minutes or until very thick, like a chutney. Let the ajvar cool and store covered tightly in the refrigerator.

MODERN FRENCH SAUCES

Though French cooking in America used to be considered the ultimate and most desirable approach to food, the Gallic hegemony started to decline with the rise of American interest in 'healthy' eating. And many Americans cited the rich quality of French sauces as one of the great culprits in French cuisine. It has taken many of us on this side of the Atlantic some years to realise that in the seventies the French themselves started to evince the same health concerns that we did and they have lightened up their sauces considerably in the modern era.

BEURRE BLANC

This sauce had an incredible renaissance in French and American restaurants of the eighties. It's an old, classic concoction from France's Loire Valley, but it fell into disfavour during the Reign of Flour-Based French Sauces, which lasted through most of the twentieth century. Then, starting in the seventies, nouvelle cuisine chefs started calling for lighter food and flour-based sauces went out of fashion. Ironically, no one should call a sauce that's practically pure butter 'light', but it turned up in one 'lightened' kitchen after another. No matter what its degree of saturated fat, it's a delicious sauce that goes especially well on simply cooked fish. It's also lovely with vegetables.

MAKES ENOUGH TO SAUCE 8 ENTRÉES

900 g (2 lb) unsalted butter
2 shallots, peeled and finely diced
225 ml (8 fl oz) dry white wine
15 ml (1 tbsp) white-wine vinegar
1 lemon
salt and white pepper to taste
very finely chopped parsley or fresh tarragon
  (optional)

1. Cut the butter in small cubes and put in a bowl. Set the bowl in ice water. (The butter should be very cold; otherwise it might melt too quickly and the sauce might break.)

2. Place shallots in a medium stainless-steel saucepan. Add the white wine and wine vinegar. Boil the liquid over high heat until it is reduced to about 10 ml (1 tbsp).

3. Just before serving, add the pieces of butter to the pan, 1 at a time, whisking well after each addition, until it has all been used. (The sauce should be fairly thick.) Add a little lemon juice to the sauce. Season with salt and white pepper.

4. If you're a purist, you'll want to strain the shallots out of the sauce before serving. Some chefs prefer to leave the shallots in; if you're among them, you might also want to mix finely chopped parsley or tarragon into the sauce. And some chefs like to bolster the sauce with a little crème fraîche just before serving.

TOMATO COULIS

'Coulis' is an old French word with changing meanings. A long time ago, it referred to meat juices rendered by the cooking process. Then, it became a general word for sauce. Later, it described liquid purées made from meats and vegetables. In the eighties, the word was re-invented again, when it became very trendy on French restaurant menus in France and in the United States; this time, however, it was used to denote any thick purée. 'Tomato coulis' was perhaps the most frequently used coulis. It can be served warm or at room temperature as a lovely, light sauce for fish, meats and vegetables. Most typically, the tomato coulis is spread out on a plate, beneath the fish, meats or vegetables. Here's a delicious version.

MAKES ABOUT 350 ML (12 FL OZ)

50 ml (2 fl oz) extra-virgin olive oil
30 g (2 tbsp) chopped shallots
900 g (2 lb) ripe tomatoes, peeled, seeded, juiced
  and chopped
leaves from 1 thyme sprig
1 bay leaf
salt and pepper to taste

1. Place the olive oil in a heavy saucepan over moderate heat, add the garlic and shallots and cook for 5 minutes. (Do not brown.)

2. Add the tomatoes, thyme and bay leaf and cook, uncovered, stirring occasionally, for 15 minutes.

3. Remove the pan from heat and discard the bay leaf. Allow sauce to cool for 5 minutes or so. Purée thoroughly in food processor. Place coulis in a fine strainer and let excess liquid drip through. (What remains in the strainer is the coulis. If it is too thick, place it in a bowl and whisk enough of the drained liquid into it to reach the desired consistency.) Season to taste with salt and pepper.

BEETROOT SAUCE

One of the most interesting developments in modern French cooking has been the rise of the vegetable sauce: a light, flourless sauce based on fresh vegetable juice that brings intense vegetable flavour and vivid colour to the table. But there is no fat-free lunch; butter is often used to give the sauce a little texture. Additionally, modern chefs like to play with flavours that complement the central vegetable. In this beetroot sauce, star anise provides a lovely counterpoint.

MAKES ABOUT 350 ML (12 FL OZ)

150 ml (5 fl oz) beetroot juice from about 1.3 kg
  (3 lb) beetroot, see box)
1 whole star anise
50 g (2 oz) cold unsalted butter, cut into bits
1.25 g (¼ tsp) salt
white pepper to taste
juice of ½ lemon

1. Put beetroot juice in a small saucepan with the star anise. Boil the juice over high heat for about 3 to 4 minutes or until it is reduced to about 125 ml (4 fl oz). Turn off heat and let juice sit for 15 minutes.

2. Turn heat to moderate and whisk in butter, a few pieces at a time. When all butter is incorporated, continue to cook, whisking constantly, for another 3 to 4 minutes to thicken the sauce slightly. Season with the salt, white pepper and lemon juice. Serve immediately.

The vegetable juicer

Infomercials blare endless info about it, and modern snake-oil salesman hawk it as a panacea-maker: it's the vegetable juicer, which can quickly reduce a pile of veggies to a manageable glass of juice. But good chefs have also discovered its virtues—particularly when it comes to extracting vegetable juice as a base for light, vegetable sauces.

For150 ml (5 fl oz) of fresh beetroot juice, you'll

need about 1.3 kg (3 lb) of fresh beetroot. For 225 ml (8 fl oz) of fresh carrot juice, you'll need about 40 carrots. Follow manufacturer's instructions.

CARROT SAUCE

Here, the taste of the Indian spice blend garam masala does a delicious tango with the central vegetable.

MAKES ABOUT 170 ML (6 FL OZ)

225 ml (8 fl oz) carrot juice (from about 40 carrots,
  see box)
85 g (3 oz) cold unsalted butter, cut into bits
3 g (¾ tsp) salt or to taste
2.5 g (½ tsp) garam masala

1. In a small saucepan boil the carrot juice over high heat for about 15 minutes or until it is reduced to about 150 ml (5 fl oz).

2. Reduce heat to moderate and whisk in butter, a few pieces at a time. When all butter is incorporated, add the salt and garam masala. Whisk together and serve immediately.

ASIAN CONDIMENTS AND SAUCES

THAI SWEET AND SPICY DIPPING SAUCE

Thai food features a wide range of dipping sauces, each one a different combination of basic flavour elements: salty, sour, sweet and hot. This sweet-and-spicy one is great for deep-fried appetisers. It is also delicious on grilled chicken.

MAKES ABOUT 100 ML (4 FL OZ)

75 ml (2½ fl oz) rice-wine vinegar
30 g (2 tbsp) sugar
1.25 g (¼ tsp) salt

5 g (1 tsp) finely chopped garlic

4 small red chillies, stemmed and finely chopped

30 g (2 tbsp) chopped fresh coriander

1. Combine the vinegar, sugar and salt in a small saucepan and cook over moderate heat, stirring until sugar has dissolved. Turn off heat.

2. Stir in the garlic and chillies and let cool to room temperature. Just before serving, add chopped coriander.

THAI HOT AND SOUR DIPPING SAUCE
Many kinds of food are dipped into this classic Thai sauce; a little bit is also sprinkled over many Thai dishes, particularly noodle dishes.

MAKES ABOUT 115 G (4 OZ)

75 ml (3 fl oz) lime juice

30 ml (2 tbsp) nam pla (Thai fish sauce)

10 ml (2 tsp) vegetable oil

35 g (2½ tbsp) finely chopped shallot

30 g (2 tbsp) finely chopped garlic

2 small green chillies, stemmed and finely chopped

2 small red chillies, stemmed and finely chopped

1. Combine the lime juice and nam pla in a small bowl and set aside.

2. Heat the oil in a small frying pan over moderate heat. Add the shallot and garlic and cook, stirring, for about 2 minutes or until softened and fragrant. Add the chillies and cook an additional 30 seconds. Let cool.

3. Combine the shallot mixture with the lime juice mixture and stir well. The sauce keeps, covered, in the refrigerator for 1 day.

SPICY THAI 'DIP' WITH DRIED SHRIMP
A whole category of Thai food that we rarely see in the United States is 'the dip'—a thickish, highly seasoned paste that is often served as an appetiser with crispy wafers made from fried rice. You can buy rice wafers in Asian stores, or, if you prefer, you can use light and airy Thai shrimp crisps for dipping.

SERVES 4

30 g (2 tbsp) Thai shrimp paste

6 large garlic cloves, finely chopped

4 small green chillies, stemmed and finely chopped

50 g (2 oz) dried shrimp

30 g (2 tbsp) sugar

50 ml (2 fl oz) lemon juice

15 ml (1 tbsp) nam pla (Thai fish sauce)

2 small red chillies, stemmed and finely chopped

30 g (2 tbsp) chopped fresh coriander

1. Wrap the shrimp paste in aluminium foil. Place a small frying pan over moderate heat and 'dry-fry' the shrimp paste for 5 minutes, until aromatic.

2. In a mortar with a pestle mash the garlic and green chillies until the mixture starts to form a paste. Add the dried shrimp and mash them into the paste until they dissolve. Add the shrimp paste and sugar and mash well (by now a real paste should be forming). Stir in the lemon juice, nam pla and red chillies and mix carefully. Just before serving, add the coriander.

THAI COCONUT 'DIP'
This intriguing dip, based on a recipe from the Oriental Hotel in Bangkok, uses chicken as a thickener.

SERVES 4

300 ml (10 fl oz) coconut milk

45 g (3 tbsp) finely chopped shallots

30 g (2 tbsp) peanut butter

30 g (2 tbsp) chilli garlic paste

5 g (1 tsp) sugar

225 g (8 oz) shredded cooked chicken breast

2.5 g (½ tsp) salt plus additional to taste

30 g (2 tbsp) chopped fresh coriander

1. Bring the coconut milk to a boil and whisk in the shallots, peanut butter, garlic paste and sugar. Reduce heat and simmer for 15 to 18 minutes, until mixture has thickened slightly. Add the chicken and the salt and simmer for another 5 minutes. Remove from heat.

2. Put the mixture in the bowl of a food processor and process until the mixture is smooth. Cool to room temperature. Adjust seasoning, adding additional salt if desired. Stir in chopped coriander and serve.

THAI YELLOW CURRY CONDIMENT FOR SOUP

Another interesting Thai gastronomic habit is adding spicy pastes to Thai soups. This one is based on Thai yellow curry paste, which can be purchased in tins. Or, you can prepare your own paste by following steps 1 and 2 of the recipe for steamed singing scallops with Thai yellow curry broth on page 343.

MAKES ABOUT 50 ML (2 FL OZ)

50 g (2 oz) Thai yellow curry paste

10 g (2 tsp) very finely chopped shallots

30 g (2 tbsp) Thai dry coconut powder

water for making the paste

Mix the curry paste, shallots and coconut powder together. Beat in just enough water to make a medium-thick paste.

BASIC VIETNAMESE DIPPING SAUCE (NUOC CHAM)

Vietnamese dipping sauces are much like Thai dipping sauces. But though either may include fermented fish sauce, the Vietnamese versions will be stronger tasting, because their fish sauce (nuoc nam) is more pungent than Thai fish sauce (nam pla). Nuoc cham is a ubiquitous chilli-garlic-fish sauce dipping sauce, served

at every meal in Vietnam. Sometimes fresh herbs are added; the following version includes fresh mint.

MAKES ABOUT 50 ML (2 FL OZ)

1 fresh red chilli, seeds and membranes removed, if desired

1 garlic clove

50 g (2 tbsp) fresh mint

5 g (1 tsp) sugar

¼ fresh lime, peel and pith removed

30 ml (2 tbsp) Vietnamese fish sauce

1. Pound the chilli, garlic and mint in a mortar with a pestle until the mixture forms a paste. Add the sugar and lime and pound until smooth.

2. Place mixture in a bowl and mix in the fish sauce. (If mixture is too strong for your taste, add a little water.)

INDONESIAN SHRIMP AND TOMATO SAMBAL

The most basic meaning of *sambal* is something spicy and fried; more often than not, a sambal is a condiment that includes chillies and at least some fried ingredients. But there are condiment sambals that don't include fried ingredients. Condiment sambals can also be saladlike or slightly chunky or mostly smooth. There are also main dishes in Indonesian cuisine that are called sambals. The following sambal is a 'salad', sambal condiment, something like a Mexican salsa cruda. Serve it as an accompaniment to south-east Asian curries and rice.

MAKES ABOUT 115 G (4 OZ)

20 g (4 tsp) Indonesian shrimp paste*

10 g (2 tsp) finely chopped shallots

10 g (2 tsp) finely chopped lemongrass (the tender inner core only)

10 g (2 tsp) palm sugar (or brown sugar)

*Indonesian shrimp paste is called *trasi*. If you can't find it, you can substitute Thai shrimp paste (kapi) or Malaysian shrimp paste (belacan).

5 ml (1 tsp) lime juice
20 g (4 tsp) mango powder
water to make the sauce
1 plum tomato, chopped
1 fresh red chilli, seeded and chopped
30 g (2 tbsp) toasted and crushed peanuts

1. Place a heavy frying pan over moderately high heat and add the shrimp paste. Dry-fry on both sides for a total of 2 minutes. Add the shallots and lemongrass, stir briefly and place mixture in a mixing bowl.

2. Add the sugar, lime juice and mango powder to mixture, blending well. Add just enough water to make a medium-thick sauce. Add the tomato, chilli and peanuts and blend well. Serve immediately.

CHERIMOYA SAMBAL

Sambals sometimes include tropical fruits. Here's an interesting relishlike version, tangy and a little sweet, that absolutely preserves the flavour of this unusual fruit. Great with south-east Asian curries and rice.

MAKES ABOUT 300 ML (10 FL OZ)

1 cherimoya (anona, soursop or custard apple), flesh scooped out
(1½ tbsp) chopped fresh tamarind†
2 tablespoons coconut milk powder mixed with 2 tablespoons water
25 g (1 oz) finely chopped shallots
15 g (1 tbsp) finely shredded basil

Cut the cherimoya into small chunks. Mix with remaining ingredients. Serve immediately.

†You can find pods of fresh tamarind in Asian grocery stores. To use, simply snap open the pods, remove the seeds, and mince them finely until the desired quantity is obtained. If you're using tamarind concentrate instead for this recipe, dissolve ½ tablespoon of it in 1 tablespoon hot water, then add the mixture to the sambal.

KUMQUAT SAMBAL

This is especially good with pork that has been marinated in a Southeast Asian fashion and grilled.

MAKES ABOUT 125 ML (4 FL OZ)

15 g (1 tbsp) shrimp paste
2.5 g (½ tbsp) finely chopped garlic
24 kumquats, halved
45 ml (3 tbsp) lime juice

1. Place a heavy frying pan over moderately high heat and add the shrimp paste. Dry-fry on both sides for a total of 2 minutes. Add the garlic, stir briefly and place mixture in a food processor.

2. Add the kumquats and lime juice. Pulse until the mixture forms a coarse paste. Let rest for a few hours before serving.

JAPANESE PONZU SAUCE

Ponzu is a lovely, light, soy-based dipping sauce that is enlivened by the zippy citrus fruits of Japan. Juice of the yuzu, that wonderful Japanese citron, is available in bottles at Japanese grocery stores. Ponzu is used as a dipping sauce for many things: sashimi, nabemono (quick-cooked stews) and as a dressing for vinegared Japanese vegetables. You can also go beyond Japanese practice and use it as a dip for fried chicken, grilled fish and grilled vegetables.

MAKES ABOUT 300 ML (10 FL OZ)

150 ml (5 fl oz) fresh lemon juice
150 ml (5 fl oz) fresh lime juice (or, instead of lemon and lime juice, use ¾ cup yuzu juice)
75 ml (2½ fl oz) Japanese rice vinegar
225 ml (8 fl oz) dark Japanese soy sauce
45 ml (3 tbsp) mirin
7 g (½ oz) dried bonito flakes
a piece of kombu, about 7.5 cm (3 in) square

Blend all the ingredients in a bowl. Let stand, unrefrigerated, for 48 hours. Strain. The ponzu sauce may be used immediately, but it picks up complexity as it matures. The sauce keeps, covered, in a cool place for up to 1 year.

TERIYAKI SAUCE

Americans usually have the wrong idea about teriyaki sauce. In Japan, it is *not* used as a marinade; rather, it is brushed on grilled meat and fish near the end of the cooking time, lending a lovely glaze to the exterior of the food. The following recipe makes enough sauce for about 1.8 kg (4 lb) of meat or fish, cut into 2.5-cm (1-in)-thick pieces; apply it about two thirds of the way through the grilling. We especially love this subtle, delicate glaze on thick, firm-fleshed fish steaks (such as cod or halibut). It can also be used as a dipping sauce.

MAKES JUST OVER 225 ML (8 FL OZ)

50 ml (2 fl oz) mirin
160 ml (5½ fl oz) sake
160 ml (5½ fl oz) dark Japanese soy sauce
15 g (1 tbsp) sugar
1.25 g (¼ tsp) grated fresh ginger
1.25 g (¼ tsp) finely chopped fresh garlic

In a small saucepan combine the mirin, sake, soy sauce and sugar and boil, stirring, for 3 minutes. Remove from heat and add the ginger and garlic. Cool to room temperature. You may keep the sauce under refrigeration.

CABBAGE KIMCHI

One of the glories of Korean cuisine is the range of pickled vegetables (and sometimes fish) that are collectively known as kimchi. There are hundreds of kinds and at a good Korean restaurant a dozen different kimchis will turn up on your table. The one most often seen in America is cabbage kimchi, a spicy red condiment made from frilly heads of Chinese leaves. Eat it alongside Korean barbecues or any type of Asian-grilled meat—or just by itself as a great snack. You may add salted Korean prawns (saewoo jut) to this dish for a little extra flavour, though they are normally added to kimchis other than this one.

MAKES 350-650 G (1-1½ LB)

1 head of Chinese leaves (about 900 g (2 lb)), separated into leaves
50 g (2 oz) coarse salt
4 garlic cloves, finely chopped
5 g (1 tsp) grated fresh ginger
8 large spring onions, halved lengthways and cut into 5-cm (2-in) pieces
2 fresh red chillies, chopped
50 ml (2 tbsp) fish sauce
75 g (3 tbsp) Korean chilli powder or more to taste
75 ml (3 tbsp) hot water
50 ml (2 tbsp) Korean salted prawns, chopped (optional)

1. Place the cabbage leaves in a long pan or on a deep tray. Sprinkle the coarse salt over the cabbage leaves and let sit at room temperature for 8 hours.

2. Remove the cabbage from the pan and rinse it with running water. Squeeze the cabbage in your hands to press out the liquid.

3. Cut cabbage leaves into coarse chunks (coarser chunks at the frilly top, thinner slices near the root). Taste for seasoning; if all the salt flavour has been washed away, sprinkle cabbage with a little coarse salt.

4. Mix together the garlic, ginger, spring onions, chillies, fish sauce, chilli powder and hot water. Toss with cabbage. Add salted shrimp, if desired. Place kimchi in tightly covered jars.

5. Refrigerate kimchi for a few days for a crunchy, fresh

taste; refrigerate for 1 week or so for a soft, pickled
taste.

KOREAN DIPPING SAUCE FOR BULGOGI

Bulgogi is the classic Korean barbecue dish: strips of
marinated beef grilled over a smoky fire. Each diner gets
a small bowl filled with an extremely tasty dipping
sauce for the beef strips. There's moderate heat in the
following version but increase the amount of Korean
chilli paste (gochu jang) if you want it hotter. If you
can't find gochu jang, substitute the more widely
available Chinese chilli paste.

                    MAKES ABOUT 115 G (4 OZ)

    1 garlic clove, crushed
    5 g (1 tsp) grated fresh ginger
    15g (1 tbsp) finely chopped spring onion
    12 g (½ tbsp) Korean chilli paste (gochu jang)
    15g (1 tbsp) sugar
    5 ml (1 tsp) sesame oil
    1.25 g (¼ tsp) toasted sesame seeds
    15 ml (1 tbsp) rice wine
    50 ml (2 fl oz) soy sauce

Sprinkle the garlic with a little salt and mince to a
paste. Place the garlic paste in a mixing bowl, add all
the remaining ingredients and blend well. Serve
immediately or keep in the refrigerator for a few days.

ACKNOWLEDGEMENTS

The Dean & DeLuca Cookbook was four intense years in the making. Along the way, many, many talented people helped bring it to reality.

Thanks, logically enough, first go to the members of the Dean & DeLuca staff, present and past, who gave so much to the project. Phil Teverow contributed an enormous amount of information and many great ideas in the early stages of the effort. James Mellgren was also instrumental in getting the project off the ground. Most of the recipes in the book were developed by me and the Dean & DeLuca kitchen at the New York shop; thanks go to Frederic Coppernolle, chef of the New York kitchen; to Patrice Blenman, the sous-chef; and to Rashne Desai, the kitchen manager. The former New York store manager, Theodore Matern, played a major role in coordinating it all. Carmine Dellaporta, assistant manager of the New York store, was, as ever, a font of information.

Thanks also go to a pair of hired guns who contributed terrific Dean & DeLuca–style recipes to the book: Lori Longbotham and Whitney Clay. Every single recipe in the book was carefully tested by me and a great team of independent testers that included Linda Dann, Elizabeth Fassberg, Kelly McNab, Naidre Miller, Melinda Moutzouris, Susan O'Rourke, Marissa Perry and Jacques Williams. Two of the testers went beyond testing, contributing a few excellent recipes to the book: Janie Feinstein and Shelly Thomas. And food writer Rebecca Karpeles provided invaluable research for the book's sidebars and commentary. Along the way, many people—notably Maricel Presilla on the subject of Cuban and Caribbean food—contributed key bits of information.

At Random House, the project could never have been realised without the guidance of my editor, Jason Epstein—a legend in literary circles, but a man as talented with a whisk as he is with a pen. Jason's assistant, Joy de Menil, worked tirelessly in prodding along and hammering out this complicated project. Thanks to Joanne Barracca as well, who was in charge of the book's production at Random House and to Martha Schwartz, who performed the tremendously important but often thankless task of overseeing the copyediting. For the wonderful overall look of the book I owe a debt of gratitude to Tom Walker, the book's designer and to Jack Ceglic, creative director of Dean & DeLuca.

Thanks are also due to my creative team at the TV Food Network, with whom I unearthed so many nuggets of great food information over the last three years. Without the creative contributions of Georgia Downard, Julia Harrison, John Jenkins and Susan Stockton and a score of others, this book would not be what it is.

I would like to give a special thanks to my agent, Kathy Robbins of the Robbins Office, who, from the moment she joined the project, offered tremendous support that will always be deeply appreciated.

Lastly, some personal acknowledgments. My heartfelt thanks go to all members of the generous Childs family, who helped me in countless ways during the creation of this book. It simply couldn't have been written without them. And I simply couldn't have accomplished anything in this field without having had the enthusiasm and love of my father, Leonard Rosengarten.

—David Rosengarten

INDEX

pâté with foie gras and apricots, 457–458
rendered fat, 396
  with wine, 397
roast, 393
  old-fashioned crispy, 393–394
types of, 392–393
Dumplings, fish, Bergen fish soup with, 53–54

Eggs:
  fried, red pepper, garlic and herb topping for pasta,
    128
  and prosciutto sauce, creamy, 128–129
  scrambled, with salmon roe smørrebrød, 97
Endive, 3
  Belgian, 2
Escarole, 3
Esqueixada, 301

Falafel, 247
  serving suggestions for, 247
Farro (spelt grains), 262
  "risotto" with wild mushrooms and Parmigiano-
    Reggiano, 262
Fast country-style ribs with Kansas City barbecue sauce,
  408
Fast roast chicken, Tandoori-style, with spiced onion
  sauce, 374–375
Feijoada, 251–253
  what to drink with, 253
Fennel:
  Italian sausage sauce with fresh, 139
  minestrone with white beans and sausage (*minestrone
    finocchio*), 46–47
  penne with roasted tomatoes and, 28–29
  tomato sauce with olives, orange zest and, 135
Feta cheese. *See* Cheese
Firm polenta cut-outs, 267–268
Fish, 273–276
  batter, beer-milk-and-butter, 297
    light, 296–297
    tempura, 297–298
  black cod, 284
  bluefish, 284
    fillets with lemon and onions, baked, 305–306
  in bouillabaisse in three courses, 76–78
  catfish, 284
    sandwich with smoked salmon and rocket, roasted,
      84
  cod, 298

    fillets, cream-poached, 298–299
    in fish dumplings, 53–54
    steaks with green olives and sherry vinegar, roasted,
      299–300
  deep-fried, 292–293
    batter, 296–297
    crumb coating, 293–295
    flour coating, 292
    Panko crumb coating, 295–296
    tips for, 298
  Dover sole, 282
    whole sautéed, 278–279
  dumplings, Bergen fish soup with, 53–54
  fillets, 284–285
    with delicate vegetables, steamed, 286
    grilling, 287
    guide, 284–285
    in merluza à la Vasca, 285–286
  flounder, 282, 284
    Cantonese steamed, 280–281
    fillets with cracker meal coating, fried, 294
  fluke, 282
  freshness of, 277–278
  grilled, degree of doneness for, 289
    heat and fuel for, 289
    marinades and coatings for, 289
    sauces and condiments for, 289
  halibut, 284, 302
    seviche with grapefruit and chillies, quick, 353–354
    steaks with mustard coating, grilled, 302
  herring, smørrebrød with apples and beetroot, 98
  John Dory, 282
  lingcod, 284
  mahimahi, 303–303
    sandwich on grilled sourdough bread with saffron
      mayonnaise, 303
  monkfish, 284, 303–304
    fillets with buttery tomato and garlic sauce, sautéed,
      304–305
    in paella, 229–230
    tail with bacon, potatoes and fresh thyme, roasted,
      304
  opakapaka, 284
  orange roughy, 284
  petrale sole, 284
  poached, 291–292
    Greek, 292
    Indian, 292
    Malaysian, 292

in cassoulet, 248–250
chops, 438
   pan-fried double thick, with olive-anchovy-orange
      butter, 439
couscous with chicken, merguez, hearty vegetables,
   and, 260–261
grilling, 369
kofta, grilled, 445–446
leg of, with onion jam on brioche, roasted, 85–86
   Provençal roast, with caramelised aubergine, 441
   in shish kebab, 445
minced, in moussaka, 464–465
   in shepherd's pie, 468
rack of, 439–440
   herb-crusted, 440
and rosemary sausages, 461
sauce with peas, Sicilian, 141–142
shanks, 443
   braised in red wine with root vegetables, 443–444
   braised with vegetables, Turkish-style, 444–445
shoulder, roast, Eastern Mediterranean style, 441–442
stew, 442
   with artichokes, orzo and avgolemono sauce, Greek,
      442–443
vindaloo, 470–471
Lasagna. See Pasta
Lasagne al forno, 146–147
Lasagne verde Bolognese, 148
Lebanese rice and lentils with caramelised onions
   (mujadarah), 227
Leeks:
   in many-onion soup with ginger and goat cheese
      croûtes, 51
   in soupe au pistou, 47–48
   in vichyssoise, 66–67
Legumes, dried, 236–241
   choosing, 241–242
   cooking, 241–242
   storing, 241–242
   varieties, 236–341
fresh, 236
see also Beans; Lentils; Peas
Lemon(s):
   herb risotto with yellow pepper purée, 224–225
   mayo with dill, three, 493
   preserved, in charmoula, 497
      Moroccan, 497–498
   salt, 492
   and tarragon dressing, creamy, 479

Lentil(s), 238, 241, 258
   and ancho chilli soup, creamy, 72–73
   red, soup with yogurt and lemon, Middle Eastern, 73
   and smoked salmon salad with walnut oil vinaigrette,
      23
   and wild mushroom soup, Italian, 72
Lettuce:
   Belgian endive, 2
   chicory, 2
   endive, 3
   escarole, 3
   frisée, 3–4
   green-leaf, 4
   iceberg, 4
   ideal blend of, 7
   lollo rosso, 4
   mesclun mixes, 2
   radicchio, 5
   red oak, 5
   red-leaf, 5
   sorrel, 6
   types of, 2–6
   washing and preparing, 6–7
   see also Greens
Light fish batter, 296–297
Ligurian stuffed tomatoes with olives, anchovies and
   basil, 231–232
Linguine. See Pasta
Liver, calves', 450
   with balsamic vinegar, sautéed, 451
   chicken, in coarse country pâté, 456–457
      in sauce Bolognese, 138–139
      and sausage sauce, Tuscan, 142
Lobster, 327–328
   bisque, 51–53
      Thai, 53
   boiled, 328–329
   in bouillabaisse in three courses, 76–78
   grilled, New York restaurant style, 329
   medallions with herbed and truffled butter sauce,
      331–332
   rolls, New England, 330
   sausage, 331
   in shellfish with saffron-olive oil broth, 77–78
   sizes, 328
   stir-fried Szechuan, with chilli sauce, 329–330
   tips for buying, 327–328
Long-cooked tomato and basil sauce, 132–133
Lotus root, 212

lasagna with smoked mozzarella and fresh sage, 148–149

and lentil soup, Italian, 72

see also Truffles

Mussels, 332–333

with black bean sauce, Cantonese, 334

in bouillabaisse in three courses, 76–78

in Chinese hot and sour fish soup, 64–65

and chorizo in saffron-garlic broth, 333–334

with garlic and parsley à la Vaudeville, sizzled, 334–335

in merluza à la Vasca, 285–286

Mexican rice salad with corn, lime, coriander and, 234

in paella, 229–230

in shellfish risotto with saffron, 225

in shellfish with saffron-olive oil broth, 77–78

Mustard seeds, black, 201

Mustard-balsamic vinaigrette, 479

Nam prik pao, 58

Name, 215

Nantucket bay scallops with beurre blanc and caviar, 343–343

New England clam chowder, 38–39

New England lobster rolls, 330

Noodles. *See* Pasta

Nopales, 215

North Carolina barbecue sauce:

Eastern-style, 490

Western-style, 490

Norwegian cream of salmon soup, 54–55

Nuoc cham (basic Vietnamese dipping sauce), 502

Octopus, 335

with ouzo and fresh thyme, Greek-style grilled, 336–337

pulpo gallego, Galician-style, 335–336

Offal, 447

brains, 453

Cuban-style deep-fried, with cumin and lime, 453

foie gras, 447–448

buying, 448

on country bread with armagnac, melted, 450

steamed in leaves of savoy cabbage, fresh seared, 449–450

terrine of, 448–449

sweetbreads, 451

salad, warm, 451–452

tripe, 453–454

stew with chick peas, chorizo and paprika, Spanish, 454

see also Liver

Oils:

cumin and chipotle, 483

infused, 481–482

nut, 9

olive, 9, 480–481

sesame, 9

shellfish, 481

shiso, 482–483

vegetable, 9, 481

Okra, 43

Chinese, 212

thickened green gumbo with chicken, prawns and fresh herbs, mild, 40–41

Old-fashioned crispy roast duck, 393–394

Old-fashioned Italian-American lasagna with ricotta and tomato sauce, 147

Olives, 183–184

Alfonso, 185

Andalusian marinated, 187

arbequina, 185

Bella di Cerignola, 185

black, in tapenade, 496

cracked Provençal, 185

gaeta, 185

Greek, 185

Greek oil-cured, 185

green, mayonnaise, 494

sauce with fresh mint, 131

Italian San Remo, 185

Jordanian homestyle, 185

kalamata, 185

feta, fresh oregano and caper sauce, 140

tuna sauce with sun-dried tomatoes and, 131

Lebanese, 186

manzanilla, 186

Moroccan, 186

Moroccan black and citrus sauce, 187

Moroccan oil-cured, 186

naphlion, 186

niçoise, 186

in pissaladière, 109–110

Nyons, 186

picholine, 186

picholine, tomato sauce with fennel, orange zest, and, 135

radiatore salad with, 27